Cultural Anthropology

Cultural Anthropology: Global Forces, Local Lives helps students understand the application of anthropological concepts to the contemporary world. It offers an exceptionally clear and readable introduction to cultural anthropology, closely relating it to key topics such as colonialism and post-colonialism, ethnicity, the environment, cultural change, economic development, and globalization.

This second edition includes additional material on medical, urban and political anthropology, as well as increased coverage of religion and culture, with particular focus on Islamic societies. An updated and expanded range of case studies explores the diverse nature of anthropology through appealing subjects such as "Blue Jeans Going Global" and "Music and Nationalism in Trinidad." Students will especially welcome the additional focus on careers in anthropology and how it is used in everyday life.

The design of this second edition has various aids to facilitate student learning:

- A wealth of additional color images help bring concepts and theories to life.
- Explains difficult key terms with marginal glosses and promotes further reading with "key texts" feature.
- Assists study with boxed chapter summaries, an extensive bibliography and index.
- Exclusive to purchasers of this new edition is access to the Routledge Interactive version of your textbook, including audio introductions from the author, exclusive supplementary case studies and study guides, and quiz material to test your learning.

Jack David Eller is Associate Professor of Anthropology at the Community College of Denver, USA.

"Finally, an introductory textbook with real substance. Eller's thoughtful account takes his readers seriously, providing them with a no-nonsense rendition of cultural anthropology, both past and present. This book does true justice to our discipline."

John T. Friedman, *University College Roosevelt Academy/Utrecht University*

"This is the first textbook that I outright like from all aspects . . . Dr Eller's voice is clear and carries through what is exciting and fascinating about anthropology while also [being] critically rigorous and complex . . . In short, for me, this is the best textbook I have yet encountered."

Faidra Papavasiliou, *Georgia State University*

"I would definitely recommend this text to students . . . it is simply excellent."

Dr Peter Collins, *Durham University, UK*

"I think this is one of the strongest texts on the market, particularly [as it takes] globalization and change seriously throughout."

Julie Jenkins, *Ball State University, Indiana*

Cultural Anthropology

Global Forces, Local Lives

Second edition

JACK DAVID ELLER

Routledge
Taylor & Francis Group

LONDON AND NEW YORK

First edition published 2009
by Routledge

Second edition published 2013
by Routledge
2 Park Square, Milton Park, Abingdon, Oxon, OX14 4RN

Simultaneously published in the USA and Canada
by Routledge
711 Third Avenue, New York, NY 10017

Routledge is an imprint of the Taylor & Francis Group, an informa business

British Library Cataloguing in Publication Data
A catalogue record for this book is available from the British Library

Library of Congress Cataloging-in-Publication Data
Eller, Jack David, 1959-
    Cultural anthropology : global forces, local lives / Jack David Eller. --
    Second edition.
        pages cm
    1. Ethnology. I. Title.
    GN316.E445 2012
    306—dc23   2012030414

ISBN13: 978-0-415-50877-3 (pbk)

Typeset in Berkeley by
Keystroke, Station Road, Codsall, Wolverhampton

Printed in the United States of America by Courier, Kendallville, Indiana

Contents

CHAPTER 13   POLITICAL INTEGRATION AND POLITICAL IDENTITY IN THE
             POST-COLONIAL WORLD   260

CHAPTER 14   THE STRUGGLE FOR ECONOMIC INDEPENDENCE: DEVELOPMENT,
             MODERNIZATION, AND GLOBALIZATION   281

CHAPTER 15   CULTURAL SURVIVAL, REVIVAL, AND REVITALIZATION IN A
             GLOBALIZED WORLD   301

             SEEING CULTURE AS A WHOLE #3: AUSTRALIAN ABORIGINAL ISLAM   323

             Glossary   325
             Bibliography   340
             Index   352

Detailed chapter outline

Illustrations

We are indebted to the people and archives below for permission to reproduce photographs. Every effort has been made to trace copyright holders, but in a few cases this has not been possible. Any omissions brought to our attention will be remedied in future editions.

PLATES

Introduction

"The world has come to the conclusion – more defiantly than should have been needed – that culture matters. The world is obviously right – culture does matter" (Sen 2006: 103). Indeed, culture has entered public consciousness and political discourse, often, literally, with a vengeance. This fact demands examination.

Human beings have always had culture, that is, learned and shared ways of living; even some non-humans can and must learn essential skills and habits. And human cultures have always been diverse: humans in disparate groups in disparate places and times have inevitably developed different – sometimes strikingly, even shockingly, different – tendencies and codes of thought and behavior. Yet, people have not always, in fact until recently generally have not, appreciated the significance and value of these differences and certainly have not actively and systematically set out to study and explain these differences. Instead, "our kind" was deemed to be truly human, and other kinds were judged as less. This is clearly not a position that anyone can afford to hold.

Cultural anthropology is the modern science of human behavioral diversity. While it aimed initially to describe "primitive cultures," it always had the ambition and the potential to be a complete subject of human ways of life, including "modern," urban, technological life. In recent years, cultural anthropology has begun to realize that potential, at the same time narrowing the distance between "others" and "ourselves." For instance, there is no such thing

as a "primitive" culture. It is to introduce and celebrate the achievements of cultural anthropology, and to indicate the contributions that it can and will make to our understanding of contemporary and future cultural circumstances, that this book was written.

PHILOSOPHY AND HISTORY OF THE BOOK

I have taught cultural anthropology for over twenty years, yet I have been frustrated from the very start of my teaching career with the structure of most courses and texts on the topic. All of them naturally include a discussion of the concept of culture and its major components, like language and gender and personality. All of them present an analysis of the important areas of culture – economics, politics, kinship, and religion. However, virtually all offer at most a couple of concluding chapters on "culture change" and "the modern world" as if these matters are tangential to, almost anathema to, anthropology and barely within its purview. This is simply not true: change is an inherent part of culture, and the modern world is the most critical matter for all of us, since it is the world that we, modern nation-state populations and indigenous peoples alike, inhabit.

So, I found teaching a course with thirteen weeks dedicated to the basics of cultural anthropology and a couple of weeks devoted to "the modern world" to be akin to spending thirteen weeks learning the grammar and vocabulary of a foreign language and only two weeks actually speaking (that is, *applying* or *using*) the language. That is inadequate. If cultural anthropology cannot be applied usefully to contemporary life, then its utility is fatally limited. Happily, it can be. Of course, in the days before the internet, it was more difficult to provide students with information that was not already integrated into textbooks. It was possible, although costly, to photocopy materials for distribution; often, as a teacher I was compelled to talk about topics for which the students had no readings in hand.

In response, I created my own addendum to formally published books, covering crucial issues like colonialism, nationalism and ethnic conflict, economic development and "Third World" poverty, indigenous peoples, and cultural movements. That addendum evolved into the third section of this book, which was obviously composed first. Subsequently, after years of teaching, I realized that I had a worthwhile perspective on the entire discipline of cultural anthropology, one that would allow me to craft an entire textbook embodying the same principles throughout the presentation as I had established in the final section. The result is the book you are holding in your hands.

COVERAGE OF THE BOOK

There are many fine and venerable textbooks on cultural anthropology. The world does not need another one unless the new offering has something new to offer. The student and instructor, and anyone interested in the discipline, will find that this book covers more topics more deeply than rival texts, and in so doing immerses the reader in the worldview, the history, the literature, and the controversies of cultural anthropology like no other.

Certainly, the present book includes all of the standard and necessary subjects of a cultural anthropology text, as mentioned above. Even these are presented in novel and usefully organized ways. However, it also provides original and nuanced coverage of a number of topics which are customarily given insufficient attention or no attention at all, such as:

■ A sophisticated and subtle discussion of cultural relativism

■ An integrated analysis of the biological/evolutionary basis of culture
■ A meaningful description of the emergence of anthropology out of the intellectual traditions of the Western world
■ Details on culturally relevant genres of language behavior, such as political speech, jokes and riddles, and religious language, based on the notion that language is social action
■ A refined discussion and critique of the race concept
■ The presentation of gender not only in relation to women but also to the construction of maleness and of alternate genders across cultures
■ The inclusion of consumption as part of the anthropology of economics
■ The integration of kinship-based groups into a more general analysis of social group formation
■ A contribution to an anthropology of war
■ A cutting-edge description of the composite nature of religions, set within the question of social legitimation
■ Extended discussion of colonialism and post-colonialism
■ Serious presentations on nationalism, ethnicity, and other forms of identity politics
■ Major attention to development policies and practices and the role anthropology has played and can play in them
■ The recognition and inclusion of indigenous sources and voices
■ A balanced analysis of possible futures of culture based on integrative and disintegrative processes
■ Inclusion of state-of-the-art anthropological concepts including globalization and glocalization, multi-sited ethnography, world anthropologies, microfinancing, diaspora, cultural tourism, popular culture, and multiple modernities.

FEATURES OF THE BOOK

The present book also incorporates a number of features, within specific chapters and across the structure of the entire book, which enhance the readability and the utility of the text. Each chapter, for example, includes:

- An opening vignette introducing the topic, to help students engage immediately with the material
- At least two boxed case-studies or discussions to help students pursue issues in more depth
- A concluding box concerning a "Contemporary Cultural Controversy" to indicate the relevance of the topic and to spark analysis and debate
- A brief but meaningful summary to reinforce understanding and aid revision
- A list of key terms, supported by flashcards on the website, to help students understand and retain unfamiliar terms
- Notes in the margins of pages, providing definitions, intra-text references, resources (books, videos, etc.) for further research, and references to the companion website

In addition to chapter-specific features, the overall construction of the book includes:

- An appealing but graphically simple design, leaving more room for full treatment of each topic and for difficult concepts to be fully explained
- Organization into three sections of equal length, with one-third dedicated explicitly to contemporary cultural processes
- Extensive intra-textual references, so that readers may find links between subjects discussed in more than one chapter
- Three in-depth case-study/discussions, entitled "Seeing Culture as a Whole," distributed evenly through the text (one-third, two-thirds, and end point) to summarize and integrate the preceding chapters
- A glossary
- A thorough and up-to-date bibliography, supported on the website by links to further reading, key digital resources, and video material.

Purchasers of this new edition will also be able to access an interactive version of the text which includes a wealth of additional material including extended case studies, testing material and audio clips of the author introducing each chapter. Details of how to gain access to these resources can be found on the inside front cover of your book.

For instructors much of this bonus material as well as extra teaching resources will also be available to download on the Instructor Resources tab from

the following site: www.routledge.com/978041550 8773.

FEATURES OF THE SECOND EDITION

In addition to the features retained from the first edition, the new edition includes the following expanded or enhanced features:

- New opening vignettes for almost all of the chapters
- New closing "contemporary cultural controversy" cases for almost all of the chapters
- Two recurrent themes throughout the book – Islam and the corporation
- New boxed case-studies for all of the chapters, with state-of-the-art anthropological discussions of urban anthropology, corporate anthropology, blue jeans as a global commodity, anthropology of virtual/online societies, utopian societies, racially correct dolls, the global Islamic *halal* industry, audit culture in China, "traditioning," corporations and colonialism, transitional justice in Guatemala, and the indigenous corporation, among others
- New or extended discussion of careers in anthropology and anthropology in careers, cultural competence, semantic range, psychological anthropology and the study of dreams and mental illness, feminist anthropology, industrialism, governmentality, religion and the everyday, traditioning and inculturation, the diversity of colonial practices, neoliberalism and neocolonialism, and popular culture and politics (e.g. music and dance)
- Two new "Seeing Culture as a Whole" extended case-studies, on religion and postsocialist society in Mongolia and on Islam among Australian Aboriginals
- Nearly twice as many photographs, and more maps
- More supplemental material on the companion website (at least three supplemental readings per chapter) more tightly integrated with the textbook, with references in the chapter to the relevant readings.

My hope is that this textbook, the fruit of two decades of my teaching experience and more than a century of the experiences of cultural anthropologists, will convey the relevance, urgency, and excitement of cultural anthropology that I feel and that I try to communicate to my students. Culture *does* matter, and there is no more pressing task for professional anthropologists and for the educated public than to realize that most if not all of the present problems and challenges facing humanity are cultural problems and challenges – related to how we identify ourselves, how we organize ourselves, and how we interact as members of distinct human communities. Cultural anthropology has made significant contributions to these questions, and it is my heartfelt hope that this book will help future anthropologists and world citizens make even more significant contributions.

Visual tour of the Interactive eTextbook

Access your Interactive eTextbook at home, on campus or on the move*. Your eTextbook offers note-sharing and highlighting functionality, as well as exclusive interactive content to enhance your learning experience. The notes you make on your Interactive eTextbook will synchronise with all other versions, creating a personalized version that you can access wherever and whenever you need it.

Throughout the text you will see icons in the margin where further multimedia resources are available via your Interactive eTextbook. These include:

Key texts (available offline)

Study guides can be found at the beginning of each chapter and supplementary case studies are located through the text on a range of topics including Native American independence and Chinese industrialization

Audio visual material

At the beginning of each chapter is an annotated audio summary from the author analyzing the key topics at hand, enhanced by a slide show of images

Online resources curated by the author

A list of further resources is located at the end of the chapter to promote further research

Testing material for each chapter

Multiple choice and fill-in-the-blank questions are located at the end of each chapter to aid revision and learning

INSTRUCTOR RESOURCES

Many of these exciting interactive teaching and learning resources are also available for instructors to download from the following site: www.routledge.com/9780415508773

This site will also include the following additional teaching resources:

- An additional chapter on Art
- Essay questions
- PowerPoint presentations

*BookShelf will provide access to your eTextbook either online or as a download via your PC, Mac (OS X 10.6>), iPad, iPhone, iPod Touch (iOS 3.2>), Android app or Amazon Kindle Fire.

1. Ainu
2. Albanians
3. Anang
4. Angola
5. Anuta
6. Apache
7. Argentina
8. Bali
9. Barabaig
10. Basseri
11. Belize
12. Berti
13. Burmese
14. Burundi
15. Brazilians
16. Cameroon
17. Canada
18. Cherokee
19. Cheyenne
20. China
21. Dani
22. Dinka
23. Dusun
24. Egypt
25. Fiji
26. French
27. Gisu
28. Greece
29. Guatemala
30. Hawaii
31. Hidatsa

32. Hua
33. Huron
34. Igbo
35. Ilongot
36. Iroquois
37. India
38. Israel
39. Japan
40. Konyak Nagas
41. Kuna
42. !Kung or Ju/hoansi
43. Kurds
44. Lenca
45. Maasai
46. Malaysia
47. Maya
48. Menomini
49. Mongolia
50. Navajo
51. Ojibwe
52. Omaha
53. Qemant
54. Quebec
55. Rwanda
56. Sambia
57. Samoa
58. Semai
59. Seminole
60. Senegal
61. Sierra Leone
62. Sikhs

63. Sinhalese
64. South Africa
65. South Sudan
66. Tamils
67. Thai
68. Tikopia
69. Trinidad
70. Tiwi
71. Ulithi
72. United Kingdom
73. United States
74. Utka
75. Wana
76. Warlpiri
77. Yir Yiront
78. Yugoslavia (former)
79. Zuni

MAP Major societies mentioned in the text

Understanding anthropology

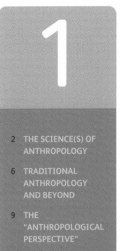

The English Defence League (EDL)

> believes that English Culture has the right to exist and prosper in England. We recognize that culture is not static, that over time changes take place naturally, and that other cultures make contributions that make our shared culture stronger and more vibrant. However, this does not give license to policy-makers to deliberately undermine our culture and impose non-English cultures on the English people in their own land.
>
> (www.englishdefenceleague.org)

Founded in 2009, its specific concern is the "Islamization" of English society – the imposition of Muslim *shari'a* law, the spread of allegedly oppressive customs like the veil for women, and of course the danger of radical Islam and terrorism. While claiming to be peaceful and non-racist, the EDL has held raucous marches in Muslim neighborhoods in Britain, often with name-calling and some violence. The group is organized into thirty-three regional "divisions" and uses the Cross of St. George, a medieval flag, rather than the current British Union Jack flag. Among its campaigns are opposition to *halal* or ritually slaughtered meat

(similar to Jewish kosher) and an attempt to prevent the construction of mosques. While the government of the United Kingdom does not condone the position of the EDL, Prime Minister David Cameron is on record saying that multiculturalism has led to a weakening of England's collective identity and therefore to a failure to assimilate young Muslims living in the country. Such exclusionary cultural nationalism can turn deadly, as the July 2011 killings in Norway illustrate: after he had exploded a car bomb in the capital city of Oslo, Anders Behring Breivik killed dozens of young Norwegians, apparently motivated by the same anti-Islamic sentiment as the EDL. In his manifesto titled *A European Declaration of Independence*, he raged against multiculturalism and a future "Eurabia" and called for the preservation of a Christian Europe.

Cultural differences are very real in the world today, perhaps more real than at any time in recent years. Most of the twentieth century was an era of ideologies (like communism and Nazism and capitalism), but the end of the century and the twenty-first century so far has been an era of culture – and often militant culture. Culture is more than just customs and traditions; it is often a marker of

See Chapter 15

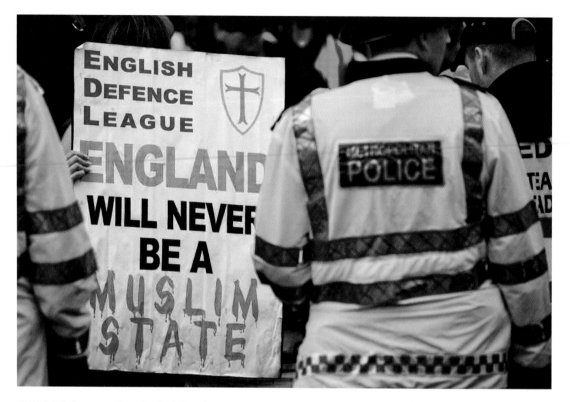

PLATE 1.1 Protesters from the English Defence League.

**CALENDARS AND
CULTURES**

identity, a point of pride, or a bone of contention. It has led to "culture wars" both virtual and literal.

The world of the twenty-first century (by Western time-reckoning; it is the fifteenth century by the Muslim calendar and the fifty-eighth century by the Hebrew calendar) is a complex world of difference and connectedness. The much-discussed processes of "globalization" have linked human communities without eliminating human diversity; in fact, in some ways they have created new kinds of diversity while injecting some elements of similarity. The local and particular still exists, in a system of global relationships, resulting in a combination that some have called "glocalization" (more on this below). But above all else, the conditions of the contemporary world virtually guarantee that individuals will encounter and deal with others unlike themselves in various and significant ways. This makes awareness and appreciation of human diversity – and one's own place in that field of diversity – a critical issue. It is for exploring and explaining this diversity that anthropology is made.

THE SCIENCE(S) OF ANTHROPOLOGY

Anthropology has been called the science of humanity. That is a vast and noble calling but a vague one and also not one that immediately distinguishes it from all the other human sciences. Psychology and sociology and history study humans, and even biology and physics can study humans. What makes anthropology different from, and a worthy addition to, these other disciplines?

Anthropology shares one factor with all of the other "social sciences": they all study human beings in action and interaction. However, all of the other social sciences only study *some kinds* of people and/ or *some kinds of things* that people do. Economics studies economic behavior, political science studies political behavior, etc. And above all, they tend to study the political, economic, or other behaviors of certain kinds of people – "modern," urban, industrialized, literate, usually "Western" people. But those are not all the people in the world. There are very many people today, and over the ages there has been a vast majority of people, who are not at all like Western people today. Yet they are people too. Why do they live the way they do? In fact, why do *we* live the way *we* do? In a word, why are there so many ways to be human? Those are the sorts of questions that anthropology asks.

Any science, from anthropology to zoology, is distinguished in three ways: its *questions*, its *perspective*, and its *method*. The questions of a science involve what it wants to know – why it was established in the first place and what part of reality it is intended to examine. The perspective is its particular and unique way of looking at reality, the "angle" from which it approaches its subject, or the attitude it adopts toward it. Its method is the specific data-gathering activities it practices in order to apply its perspective and to answer its questions.

As a unique science, anthropology has its own distinctive questions, ones that no other science of humanity is already asking or has already answered. Some sciences, like psychology, suggest in their very name what their questions will be: psychology, from the Greek *psyche* meaning "mind" and *logos* meaning "word/study," declares that it is interested in the individual, internal and "mental," aspect of humans and human behavior. Sociology, from the Latin *socius* for "companion/ally/associate," implies the study of humans in groups. The name anthropology does not speak as clearly, and many readers, and many members of the public, may have little notion of what anthropology is or what anthropologists do. Anthropology is a fairly new word for a fairly new science, asking some fairly new questions. Derived from two Greek roots, *anthropos* for "man/human" and *logos*, anthropology was named and conceived as the study of humanity in the widest and most inclusive possible sense.

Anthropology's uniqueness is thankfully not in its name but in the questions that it asks, which include:

- How many different ways are there to be human? That is, what is the "range" of human diversity?
- What are the commonalities across all of these different kinds of humans and human lifeways?
- Why are humans so diverse? What is the source or explanation of human diversity?
- How do the elements of a particular human lifeway fit together and influence each other?
- How does one way of being human transform into another way over time?

Given these questions, we can think of anthropology as not just the study of humans but *the study of human diversity*. Further, humans are diverse along two dimensions. The first dimension is the past versus present, while the second dimension is the physical versus the behavioral, our bodies as opposed to the ways we organize ourselves and act. Therefore, the definition of anthropology can be refined or expanded to *the study of the diversity of human bodies and behavior in the past and the present*. We can now see that there are several possible subfields of anthropology, depending on exactly what area of this diversity each focuses on – what specific anthropological questions it seeks to answer. These subdisciplines give anthropology its familiar "four-fields" character.

Physical or biological anthropology

Physical or biological anthropology is the area that specializes in *the diversity of human bodies in the past and present*. It is plain to see that humans differ in their physical appearance: there are different skin colors, different hair colors, different body shapes, different facial forms, etc. What can we hope to learn from it? First and foremost, we learn that *there is more than one way physically to be human*. All of the various human body shapes and facial features are human. Physical anthropologists can also relate those physical traits to the natural environment: is there a reason why people in some parts of the world, in some climates for instance, have this or that physical characteristic? This is the question of physical adaptation, and it is entirely possible that a group, if it has lived in a particular environment long enough, could develop traits that fit well in that environment. Finally, physical anthropologists can discover things about human migrations, intermarriages, and such phenomena from the distribution of traits like blood type, gene frequency, and so on. We will return to the question of "race and ethnicity" below.

In addition to the present diversity of human bodies, there is considerable historical diversity as well. The evidence indicates clearly that humans have not always had the bodies we have today. This evidence is fossils. Anthropologists have found no human bodies quite like ours that are older than a couple of hundred thousand years at most, and

Physical anthropology
the study of the diversity of human bodies in the past and present, including physical adaptation, group or "race" characteristics, and human evolution.

See Chapter 6

Artifacts
physical objects created by humans, often specifically the "portable" objects like tools, pottery, jewelry, etc. (as opposed to the non-portable ones like buildings and roads, etc.)

Primatology
the study of the physical and behavioral characteristics of the category of species called primates

Features
in archaeology, the large and non-portable objects or structures created and left by humans, including walls, buildings, roads, canals, and so on

See Chapter 2

Ecofacts
the environmental remains from past human social contexts, including wood, seeds, pollen, animal bones, shells, etc.

Archaeology
the study of the diversity of human behavior in the past, based on the traces left behind by past humans or societies

even during that time there have been other "humans" who looked remarkably different from us. If you saw a Neandertal (who lived between 130,000 and 40,000 years ago) on the street today, you would recognize him or her as human but not exactly "normally" human. As we look further back in time, human-like beings become progressively less human-like while still retaining certain critical human features, like upright walking, a relatively large brain, and a human-like face. How then did we humans come to have the bodies that we have today, and what other forms did our human ancestors take in the past on their way to becoming us? That too is a question for physical anthropology – the question of human evolution. Some scientists even specialize in the physical characteristics of other species that are similar and related to our own, the primates, for which their science is called **primatology**. We will examine the subject of human evolution later.

Archaeology

One common image of the anthropologist is a sort of Indiana Jones figure: the researcher who digs up pyramids in Egypt or ancient cities in Mexico. In fact, the researchers who conduct this kind of work are archaeologists. From the root *arche* for "beginning," **archaeology** is *the study of the diversity of human behavior in the past*. Archaeologists may do

their work in the company of physical anthropologists, who examine the actual anatomical remains of past humans. However, the archaeologists do not focus on the bodies but on the behaviors of those humans. How can they do that, when the people are all dead and their ways of life have vanished? The answer is that they examine the things those humans left behind – their tools, their homes, their art, their writing if they had it, and so on. Archaeologists divide this evidence roughly into two categories: artifacts and features. **Artifacts** are the more or less portable objects that people made and used; things like pottery, clothing, jewelry, tools and weapons, and the like are considered artifacts. **Features** are the larger, more or less immovable objects like buildings, walls, monuments, canals, roads, farms, and such. To understand more about the environmental setting of these societies and how the humans made use of them, archaeologists also consider **ecofacts** such as plant (wood, seeds, pits, pollen) and animal (bones, shells) remains.

Studying artifacts and features is fascinating, but archaeologists do not study them just to learn about them. They excavate and interpret this evidence to discover the thoughts, the ideas, the feelings, and the social patterns of the people who made them. How did those past people make these things? Why did they make them? How did they use them? What did the objects mean to the makers and users? Archaeologists try to go from the objects themselves to the minds and hearts of the people

PLATE 1.2 Archaeologists study the sites of past societies, such as Teotihuacan near Mexico City.

UNDERSTANDING ANTHROPOLOGY

BOX 1.1 TIME AND POWER IN MAYAN SOCIETY

If you are reading this, then the "prediction" of the end of the world in the Mayan calendar did not come true. However, it is true that the Mayans had an intense fascination with time; in fact, for many years the archaeological image of the Mayans was that of mystical timekeepers with little interest in the mundane world. One of the greatest mysteries has been the so-called 819-day count (see for instance http://www.pauahtun.org/Calendar/819.html). Gerardo Aldana y Villalobos (2011) recently attempted a new interpretation of this dating system, relating it to very practical matters of politics and religion. The city of Palenque, he tells, experienced a devastating military defeat, so when the future king Janaab' Pakal came to power, he needed not only to revive the city but to ensure and legitimate his authority. The sovereign and/or his priests and astronomers discovered "the significant overlap between. . .the computing year and the periods of Saturn, Jupiter, and Mars" (116), which was seen as a great truth. With the esoteric wisdom in this numerological practice he and his son "anchored [contemporary] events in the mythic past" (185). Not only was the dynasty of Janaab' Pakal "able to reconstruct their own sacred history" (201) – a history in which they literally reconstructed the sacred at Palenque – but they managed to do so in an astro-numerical language that was "held secret in order to restrict access to the leadership" (193). Indeed, Aldana y Villalobos speculates that under-standing the mysteries of the 819-day count may have been "considered an infallible test of royal or at least noble origins" (193).

who lived among those objects long ago. It is a creative, interpretive activity, but the artifacts and features are often the only traces that those people and their ways of lives have left behind.

Archaeologists do not look exclusively at the ancient past. They can also study the recent past, such as medieval Europe or colonial America. And since modern humans also make and leave remains behind them, archaeologists have found that their methods can be practiced on living societies to learn how contemporary humans exploit and affect their environments. One recent form of this work has been dubbed **garbalogy**, since it sifts through contemporary trash to discover what kinds of objects humans produce, consume, and discard today.

Linguistic anthropology

Linguistic anthropology focuses on *the diversity of human language in the past and present*. Linguistic anthropologists can study the similarities and differences between present-day languages, looking into their grammar, their vocabulary, and their everyday use. This will not only shed light on each language but also on the possible relationships between languages. Are there, for instance, lan-guage "families" that are related historically, by migration or intermixing or other processes? Linguistic anthropologists can also investigate changes within a language over time. Anyone who has read Shakespeare or even older English liter-ature knows that English has evolved fairly dramatically over the recent centuries. All languages undergo similar processes, and linguistic anthro-pologists can analyze the reasons for and the particular directions of this change. They can also attempt to reconstruct "ancestral" languages – ones that link, say, English to German and both to ancient Greek or Sanskrit – even to the point of reconstructing the very first language.

More essentially, linguistic anthropology attempts to understand language use in its relation to social life and social practices. How are values and concepts captured in and expressed by lan-guage? How is language employed to structure and communicate social differences, for example of status and rank or age or gender, etc.? Linguistic anthropology has increasingly emphasized the element of "performance" in language, discovering specialized forms for various purposes (for exam-ple, speech-making as opposed to story-telling) and the role of language in forming and maintaining social relationships, including power relationships.

Garbalogy
the study of contemporary trash to examine how humans make, consume, and discard material objects in the present

Linguistic anthropology
the study of the diversity of human language in the past and present, and its relationship to social groups, practices, and values

See Chapter 4

Language in anthropological perspective will be the subject of another chapter.

Cultural anthropology

Cultural anthropology
the study of the diversity of
human behavior in the
present

Cultural anthropology, also sometimes called social anthropology, is *the study of the diversity of human behavior in the present*. The large majority of anthropologists are cultural anthropologists, and they have one tremendous advantage over both physical anthropologists and archaeologists: they have living people to talk to. The goal of cultural anthropology is still to learn about the thoughts and feelings of people that lead to their behavior, but now we can ask them, "Why did you do that?" or "How did you make that?" or "What does that mean to you?" Cultural anthropology is the activity that many people associate with *National Geographic* magazine, the Discovery Channel, or similar media, where strange-looking (to us) people are portrayed doing exotic or unfamiliar or maybe even shocking (to us) things. Of course, observers can appreciate the sheer spectacle of such people and their behavior, but cultural anthropology is more than the observation and collection of behavioral curiosities. It is about making humans unlike oneself seem less "exotic" and more human – in fact, just as human as each of us is. It is about getting to the heart and mind of people very different from oneself in at least some ways. But it is also about getting to one's own heart and mind, since "we" are one of the diverse kinds of human as surely as "they" are. In so doing, cultural anthropology penetrates to the very nature of humanity. What separates one kind of human from another yet unites us all? What makes one group's hearts and their minds different from another group's and yet similar and related?

Please remember, as the first lesson in cultural anthropology, that others may appear strange and incomprehensible, even abnormal, to you but that you may appear just as strange, incomprehensible, and abnormal to them.

TRADITIONAL ANTHROPOLOGY AND BEYOND

See Chapters 3 and 11–15

We have now seen the traditional four subfields of anthropology. However, in important ways,

anthropology has outgrown this narrow categorization, if it was ever actually constrained by it. For instance, a number of well-developed subdisciplines have emerged under the general heading of cultural anthropology, including, among others:

- Urban anthropology, or the study of humans in urban settings, the effects of urbanization on previously non-urban societies, and the relationships between cities and their surrounding hinterlands (such as labor migration).
- Medical anthropology, or the study of knowledge systems and practices concerning health and medical treatment cross-culturally.
- Forensic anthropology, or the use of (mainly physical) anthropological knowledge and methods to solve crimes (e.g. identify murder victims, determine time and cause of death, etc.).
- Visual anthropology, or the study of the production, presentation, and use of material or "artistic" media such as painting, body art, clothing designs, and so on. It can include not only the arts that other societies make but the arts that anthropology employs to study them, such as film and photography.
- Ethnomusicology, or the study of musical forms and their relation to culture.
- Ethnobotany, or the study of knowledge and uses of plants in various cultures.
- Development anthropology, or the study of as well as the practical contribution to how "modern" forces affect and change societies. This can include attempting to minimize the negative impact of change on traditional societies and even in some cases advocating for the rights and wishes of those societies.
- Feminist anthropology, or the study of women's issues and roles across cultures. This is often expanded to include gender issues and roles more generally, particularly how gender is defined, practiced, and controlled through language, values, and power.

It is important to understand that anthropology is not and never has been a purely "academic" pursuit, disconnected from the real world. In its pre-modern form it was to be found in the early European colonial encounters with non-Western peoples, providing data and often service in the colonial

BOX 1.2 URBAN ANTHROPOLOGY

Most people associate anthropology with tribal societies in remote villages on some island or in some jungle, and much conventional anthropology has indeed been of the "village study" sort. As recently as 1980 Ulf Hannerz could claim that urban anthropology was little more than a decade old. But anthropology, as the study of human diversity, certainly *can* examine the city as a form of social behavior, and it *must* examine it, because cities have been part of human experience for thousands of years and because urbanization has finally brought the majority of humanity into cities. While sociology entered the city ahead of anthropology (and anthropologists duly acknowledge this), Alan and Josephine Smart found in their 2003 review of urban anthropology that the field had "made important contributions to our understanding of migration, housing, social and spatial organization, informal economies, and other topics" (Smart and Smart 2003: 267). Anthropology's explicit interest in urbanization began in colonial Africa, especially the "copperbelt" of Zambia where new cities arose and formerly non-urban people migrated. Anthropologists noticed new organizations and identities forming, such as mutual aid groups, trade unions, nationalist movements, and "supertribes" or what we would today call ethnic groups. However, critics often accused urban anthropologists of perpetuating anthropology's village focus by examining communities or enclaves within the city – that is, doing anthropology "in the city" but not "of the city." In more recent years, urban anthropologists have investigated the city as a social system, finding great diversity inside as well as between cities; not all cities are alike, nor are all inhabitants of any particular city alike. They have also studied the links between cities and their non-urban surroundings, as well as between specific cities and the wider and global economic and cultural system.

URBAN ANTHROPOLOGY

PLATE 1.3
Anthropologists study the city as a distinct social system and way of life.

Boas, Franz. 1928. *Anthropology and Modern Life*. New York: W. W. Norton & Company, Inc.

See Chapters 11–15

enterprise, for better or worse. Some of the first anthropologists, like Franz Boas (1858–1942) in his 1928 book *Anthropology and Modern Life*, were deeply concerned with practical social issues, like racism, nationalism, eugenics, criminology, and education.

And of course all anthropological findings can be used for real-world policy- and decision-making. But many anthropologists overtly practice a kind of "applied anthropology" intended to bring the concepts, perspectives, and methods of the science to non-academic initiatives (see discussion of anthropological careers below).

The continuing evolution of cultural anthropology

Who are the subjects of cultural anthropology's curiosity – what we sometimes call the "anthropological gaze"? The conventional impression, virtually the stereotype, of the science is that it is exclusively concerned with small, "traditional," even "primitive" groups. Actually, one of the great early anthropologists, A. R. Radcliffe-Brown, defined anthropology as "the study of what are called primitive or backward peoples" (1965: 2).

The equally esteemed E. E. Evans-Pritchard insisted that anthropology was the branch of social science "which chiefly devotes itself to primitive societies" (1962: 11). However, Evans-Pritchard situated the emphasis on remote exotic peoples within the context of anthropology's greater subject which "embraces all human cultures and societies, including our own" (4).

If you consider the questions posed by anthropology generally and cultural anthropology specifically, you will immediately realize that there is nothing about them that limits them to any particular kinds of peoples or cultures. Accordingly, as the human world has changed – especially becoming more interconnected, more fluid, more "modernized" – cultural anthropology has changed too, partly because it can and partly because it must. Cultural anthropology was never really exclusively the study of small, isolated, traditional societies, although it did occupy the "savage slot" (Trouillot 1991), for tactical reasons (because it is easier to analyze compact and unfamiliar cultures) and for the simple reason that no other science did. But

anthropology cannot and does not aspire to remain in that slot, if only because there are no more isolated and "primitive" societies and probably never were.

The three main phenomena that have forced a reconceptualization of cultural anthropology are colonialism, post-colonial independence and nationalist and indigenous movements, and modernization and globalization. Colonialism brought far-flung societies within a single political, economic, and cultural sphere, imposing changes and inequalities. Independence, nationalism, and indigenous movements have transformed the sometimes "passive" objects of anthropological scrutiny into active subjects, actors and producers of culture who speak for themselves. Finally, modernization and globalization have threatened and attempted to integrate cultures into a single world system which is, Thomas Friedman (2005) notwithstanding, anything but "flat," if only because they are driven from centers of wealth and power and generate uneven outcomes. In the contemporary world, globalization is the most heralded cultural force, regarded as "processes that take place within [groups] but also transcend them, such that attention limited to local processes, identities, and units of analysis yields incomplete understanding of the local" (Kearney 1995: 548). But the local does not disappear, nor is it bleached of all its distinctive characteristics; rather, in each location and occasion, a distinct combination or manifestation of the local and the global emerges, leading to a result that some observers have wryly called **glocalization**, linking local or small-scale changes to large-scale or global factors. The message is that even within a global context, cultural realities are local, and therefore cultural anthropology's questions, perspectives, and methods still apply.

In response to "glocal" realities, some anthropologists have taken "big picture" approaches to the world, as in Eric Wolf's (1982) *Europe and the People without History* and the various works of Ernest Gellner (e.g. 1988). Others have explored specialized aspects of human behavior, such as war and violence (e.g. Eller 1999, 2005; Fujii 2009; Scheper-Hughes and Bourgois 2004), globalization (e.g. Lewellen 2002), consumption and shopping (e.g. Howes 1996; Counihan and Van Esterick 2007; Miller 1998), environment and conservation (Guneratne 2010; Igoe 2004), homelessness (Finkelstein 2005),

Radcliffe-Brown, A. R. 1965 [1952]. *Structure and Function in Primitive Society*. New York: The Free Press.

Evans-Pritchard, E. E. 1962. *Social Anthropology and Other Essays*. New York: The Free Press.

Glocalization

a combination of the words "globalization" and "local," suggests the unique local and situated forms and effects of widespread and even global processes

Wolf, Eric. 1982. *Europe and the People without History*. Berkeley, CA: University of California Press.

BOX 1.3 ANTHROPOLOGY BEYOND ANTHROPOLOGY

Cultural anthropologists are certainly not the only scholars who study human social behavior. Sociologists ask similar questions and even sometimes employ similar methods. For instance, in the investigation of urban society, sociologists Robert and Helen Lynd (1929) did anthropological-style work on the early urbanization of the United States, while Carol Stack (1974) interacted with African American families and Herbert Gans (1962) studied the "urban villagers" of Italian-American Boston. Even journalists and talented amateurs have emulated anthropology, exploring their own society to bring back stories of little-known corners of life in the modern world. Ted Conover specializes in such work, living or working with undocumented Mexican laborers (1987) and New York State prison guards (2000). Barbara Ehrenreich reported "from the inside" on the working poor (2002), while Iain Levison (2002) described his adventures in challenging but low-paying jobs. Jimmy Lerner (2002) even recounts his time in prison.

natural disasters (Hoffman and Oliver-Smith 2002), material culture like denim (Miller and Woodward 2011) and lycra (O'Connor 2011), and even psychedelic trance dance (St. John 2010).

THE "ANTHROPOLOGICAL PERSPECTIVE"

Cultural anthropology is distinct among sciences for the questions it asks. However, it also stands out in its approach to or its way of thinking about its subject, that is, its perspective. The **anthropological perspective** has three components. The first is obvious, the second less obvious but fairly uncontroversial, and the third not at all obvious and quite controversial. They are:

1. Comparative or cross-cultural study
2. Holism
3. Cultural relativism

Comparative or cross-cultural study

Cultural anthropology does not look at just one kind of culture, certainly not just the anthropologist's own kind of culture. A cross-cultural perspective or emphasis means that anthropologists are curious about human behavior in a wide and inclusive sense, embracing many or potentially all human ways of being. Anthropologists are perhaps particularly interested in cultures that are *unlike*

their own. After all, people already know their own culture pretty well – or think they do. One premise of human sciences is that most people in fact are not as aware of the causes and consequences of their own behavior as they often or like to think that they are. This is a reason why sociologist C. Wright Mills (1959) referred to the "sociological imagination": researchers must learn to see meanings, rules, relationships, institutions and such phenomena that are "invisible" to or outside the attention of group members even as those phenomena influence human behavior, individually and collectively. Therefore, one reason why cultural anthropology has insisted on a comparative perspective is that it is often easier to see what is unfamiliar than what is familiar; familiar things tend to be taken for granted or overlooked, whereas the unfamiliar demands attention. Anthropology if anything serves to question assumptions and to expose the taken-for-granted.

However, even if anthropologists knew their own culture very well, that would not be sufficient. Anthropologists, like all scientists, cannot use a sample of one to draw conclusions about other cases. Whether it is plants, planets, or people, it is not acceptable to assume that they are all alike. In fact, it is wise to assume exactly the opposite. Anybody who is truly interested in knowing and understanding humans needs a bigger sample than one. We cannot know ourselves, no matter how thoroughly, and claim that now we "know humanity." Actually, in almost every way, Western culture in general or American culture in particular

Anthropological perspective
the unique "angle" or point of view of anthropology, consisting of cross-cultural or comparative study, holism, and cultural relativism

is quite atypical and non-representative. But then, there is no "typical" culture. Since no culture pertains to all humans, or even a majority or close to it, every culture is a minority. *Whatever you do or think or feel, in the human world you are in the minority.*

So it should be apparent why cross-cultural or comparative study is a valuable part of anthropology. The first reason is that the diversity is there. There simply *are* other cultures than one's own. But more, by exposing ourselves to the plethora of human cultures, we can make two important discoveries:

- The commonalities or "universals" that occur across cultures – that is, is there anything that most or all cultures do, that seems to be *necessary* for humans?
- The full range of variation between cultures – that is, just how different can humans be? How many different kinds of language, personality, economics, religion, etc. are there? Just how many ways are there to be human? In other words, what is *possible* for humans?

I like to think of anthropology, then, as the study of what is possible and what is necessary for humans.

Holism

Holism refers to "the whole," the entirety. Each particular culture is and must be approached as a whole, not just as a single trait (say, a political system or an economy) or as a disconnected list of traits. A whole, cultural or otherwise, is a system containing multiple parts in some kind of integrated relationship with each other. The first significance of this fact is that a culture *has parts*, and anthropologists discover these parts and the different forms they can take. If, for instance, kinship is a part of culture, then what different kinds of kinship are there? What are the possibilities of marriage, child-rearing, household residence, descent, and so forth? The second significance is that the parts are interconnected in some way. If an anthropologist wants to study, say, the religion of a particular society, s/he cannot study the religion in isolation; rather, s/he must consider the language, the politics,

the kinship, the gender roles, etc. Potentially – and actually – every part of a culture relates in some way to every other part. The parts might not be as tightly integrated as the parts of a car engine, but they are interrelated. The third significance is that each part has its unique function and each contributes to the function of the whole. Just like an organ in the body or a part in a car, each has its own "job to do" and each contributes to the overall job of the whole. So, wherever we enter a culture to begin to analyze it or whatever we care to focus on, we will find ourselves swept into considering all of its parts and the whole which they constitute.

The holistic perspective has helped lead cultural anthropology into a "case study" approach. In a traditional or classic anthropological description of a specific culture – known as **ethnography** – the writer typically would begin with a discussion of the environment in which the group lives (mountain, desert, jungle, island, etc.) and then proceed to provide details on each aspect of the culture. Sometimes these accounts would center on a particular part of the culture, depending on what was most noteworthy, but all of the parts required analysis. In some instances an entire book was written on one aspect of culture, as in the case of *Nuer Religion* (Evans-Pritchard 1956), but even then it was a contribution to a body of literature on including all facets of that particular society. In other words, any single ethnography prepared by a cultural anthropologist might not cover every single aspect of the culture, but collectively the research on the culture would.

PLATE 1.4 The author standing in front of the Basaki Temple in Bali 1988.

Ethnography
a written account or description of a particular culture, usually including its environment, economic system, kinship arrangements, political systems, and religious beliefs, and often including some discussion of culture change

See Chapter 2

Holism
the part of the "anthropological perspective" that involves consideration of every part of a culture in relation to every other part and to the whole

Cultural relativism

It is a fact that cultures are different; that is why anthropologists study them. Cultures are different in how they see, interpret, value, and respond to the world, including other human beings in their world. What is done in one culture may not be done in another. What is important or valuable in one culture may not be in another. What is good or right in one culture may not be in another. For example, in mainstream American culture, polygamy is deemed to be bad, immoral, and illegal (there are of course minority sections of America that practice and value polygamy, such as the sect of "fundamentalist" Mormons). However, in many cultures – in fact, in most cultures – polygamy has been not only acceptable but normal or even preferred. Who is right about this?

Actually, that is not the correct question to ask. In fact, it is not even a possible question to ask. But let us say this for now: *different cultures can and do have different notions of what is good, normal, moral, valuable, legal, etc.* An anthropologist investigating a headhunting society would find men with human heads in their possession, perhaps displayed on their walls or hung from their ceilings. The tendency might be to judge them with the anthropologist's own values and norms: "Those men are all immoral criminal killers!" An outsider might want to call the authorities and have the "deviants" and "murderers" arrested. The visitor might, then, be surprised when the authorities ask us why he or she is bothering them; in fact, the owners of heads may be the authorities – the chiefs, the priests, or other leaders. That might be hard to accept, but imagine this: a man from the same headhunting society comes to your society and sees that you do not have heads on display. What would he think? He might think you are weak or inconsequential, a person of no courage, fame, or prominence, or that you are just "deviant" from the ideal of headhunting. If the headhunter visited the White House or Ten Downing Street and observed no heads, he might assume that the resident has no political authority, since great men collect heads.

Notice that the headhunter got Western people wrong, just as Western people got him and his culture wrong. What do we learn by thinking this way? Not very much, at least not very much about them. We do learn about ourselves (that we

disapprove of headhunting), but we already knew that. Clearly, understanding – let alone judging – others by our standards is not helpful. We might call them bad or immoral or criminal, but that does not explain why they do what they do – and they could just as easily say the same thing about us from their point of view. If anthropologists therefore want to understand the behavior of members of another culture, we cannot apply *our* norms and morals and values and meanings to them, because they do not use ours. They use their own. That would be like trying to apply the rules of chess to poker. The rules of chess are neither bad nor good; they just don't pertain.

If anthropologists want to understand another culture, then *we must understand or judge them in terms of their own notions of good, normal, moral, valuable, meaningful, etc.* That is **cultural relativism**. Cultural relativism asserts that an observer cannot apply the standards of one culture to another culture, at least not in an informative way. Rather, a phenomenon in a culture must be understood and evaluated *in relation to, relative to,* that culture. Why? First, it is always tempting and easy to conclude that different is bad: they do not do it my way, so they are wrong. Scientific observers must avoid this arrogance and shortsightedness. Second, it is quite likely to breed misunderstanding. If you impose your own cultural outlook on a cross-cultural encounter, you may misjudge the whole situation. This happens, for instance, in international business. A meeting of Western and non-Western businesspeople might easily end with each side thinking it understands what happened in the meeting. Later, if one side does not respond as the other expected they would, there can be confusion, anger, even real financial loss. What went wrong? Each side interpreted the meeting from its own cultural point of view, not realizing that the other side had a different point of view – until it was too late.

Accordingly, any judgment about norms, morals, values, meanings, laws, and so on is a cultural judgment, made "in relation to" some standard of norms, morals, values, meanings, and laws. That is what cultural relativism means. Sticking out one's tongue is an insult here, a greeting there. If an anthropologist gets mad or offended when members of a society where tongue-sticking is a greeting stick their tongue out at him or her,

See Chapter 8

Cultural relativism
the reaction to the fact of cultural diversity in which one attempts to understand and judge the behavior of another culture in terms of its standards of good, normal, moral, legal, etc. rather than one's own

Culture shock
the surprise, confusion, and pain we feel when we encounter a way of life that is very foreign to our own

See Chapter 5

Ethnocentrism
the attitude or belief that one's own culture is the best or only one, and that one can understand or judge another culture in terms of one's own

ISLAM IN TEXAS

those members will be quite surprised and confused by our response. This experience is called **culture shock** – the surprise, confusion, and actual pain that one feels in the presence of the profoundly unfamiliar and unexpected. This is probably the most common experience in the world. So is the reaction: to judge people from other cultures by the standards of one's own culture. This is called **ethnocentrism** (from *ethno-* for a way of life or culture and *center* for putting it in the center or pride of place), the attitude or practice of assuming that one's own cultural point of view is the best, the right, or even the only point of view. Of course, ethnocentrism is possible – it is the easy, even the automatic, thing – but it is simply not helpful. One can be ethnocentric from one's own cultural perspective, but others can be ethnocentric from their cultural perspective. Nothing is gained by this except mutual (and probably negative) judgment.

Every judgment, then, of good/bad, moral/immoral, normal/abnormal, valuable/valueless, etc. is made from some cultural point of view – in relation to some standard of good, moral, normal, valuable. And a culture is precisely a set of standards for such judgments. Cultural relativism says that we need to take this fact into account when we confront and interact with other cultures; it must be part of our perspective on cultural difference. However, there are many fallacies and misconceptions that people, both relativists and non-relativists, have about cultural relativism.

1. Cultural relativism *does not mean* that "anything goes" or judgment is impossible. Some critics of relativism insist that it means, or leads to, a position of no standards at all, a "do what you want to do," "if it feels good, do it" ethic or anti-ethic. That is not at all what cultural relativism advocates. It does not say, "Anything goes" but rather "Here this goes, and there that goes." It is *descriptive*. It does not tell us what moral or value judgments to make, only that diverging moral or value judgments are made. And it certainly does not conclude that value judgments are impossible. Rather, it is a description of exactly how such judgments are made – in relation to some standard of judgment – and investigators should find out what that standard of judgment is. But there is no such thing as a "standardless" judgment, and there does not appear to be a single standard that all cultures share. Instead, there are multiple standards.

2. Cultural relativism *does not mean* that anything a culture does is good/moral/valuable/normal, etc. Some critics of relativism claim that taking a relativistic stance toward another culture is essentially condoning it. But to condone means to judge favorably, and relativism is not about judging but about understanding. If we encountered a culture that practiced polygamy or infanticide or "honor killing," cultural relativism would not require us to say, "Those attitudes and behaviors are good or acceptable." What it would require us to do is determine where those attitudes and behaviors come from and what they mean to the people who practice them. One certainly does not have to approve in order to understand. In fact, not only do anthropologists not have to but they cannot "condone" these or any other behaviors, because *condoning, like condemning, is a value judgment*. To say a behavior is good or bad is to judge it, and that means judging by some particular value standard. That would mean abandoning the relativistic perspective and referring to one's own community of values, one's own culture. As an anthropologist it is possible to understand a behavior without judging – in fact, it is *only* possible to understand without judging – while as a member of one's own culture one can say that s/he does not share or condone that behavior. But you must always remember that your judgment is a product of your culture and may not be shared by all cultures.

3. Cultural relativism *does not mean* that anything a culture believes is true. Some critics of relativism assert that relativism compels us to accept as valid any belief or "knowledge" that a culture asserts. If, for instance, a culture believes that the earth is flat, then it is flat *for them*, even while it is round for us. This is of course nonsense and has nothing whatsoever to do with cultural relativism. There is a philosophical position known as "epistemological relativism" that does actually hold that all knowledge and truth is relative, but that is not the claim made by cultural relativism and is quite beyond the ability or need of anthropology to address. Let us consider the problem of knowledge by contrasting two different kinds of statements:

Polygamy is good.   The Earth is round.

Both take the superficial form of *noun-is-adjective*. But the similarity ends there. The latter is a fact-statement, or rather a fact-claim. Is it true or false? More importantly, how do we decide? We make observations and measurements, that is, we check against reality. We find that the earth really is round, not flat, and verify the initial statement. How about the statement on polygamy? Is it true or false that polygamy is good? The answer is – neither. It is culturally relative. That is, in Warlpiri (Australian Aboriginal) or in fundamentalist Mormon culture, polygamy is good. In mainstream American society, polygamy is bad. So "polygamy is good" is not the same kind of statement as "earth is round." Again, the latter is a fact-claim (either true or false), but the former is a *value-claim*. It is neither true nor false.

Value claims are judgments and therefore must be made by reference to, relative to, some value standard. But what standard? Shall we use mainstream Western standards, or Warlpiri standards, or Japanese standards, or Yanomamo standards, ad infinitum? The answer is that any of those standards is equally usable – and equally used by somebody. Therefore, a value statement like "polygamy is good" is not, cannot be, true or false because *it is not even a complete statement yet*. Before we can evaluate the statement, we need to know more: good *for what*, good *according to whom*? If one says, "Polygamy is good among the Warlpiri," an anthropologist can respond, "That is true." If one says, "Polygamy is good," the anthropological response is not "True" or "False" but "Please finish your statement." It is not clear yet which cultural value-standard the speaker is applying, so the statement is unfinished and meaningless as formulated.

Since there are multiple potential and actual value standards that can be used to evaluate the claim, the final judgment will be *relative to* whichever standard one ultimately uses. In other words, value statements are culturally relative, whereas fact statements are not. Or, we might say that fact statements are relative to a single standard (reality) that is objective and universally shared. The acceleration of gravity on earth (thirty-two feet per second per second) is the same for all people in all cultures because they share a single common physical reality. If all people in all cultures shared a single common standard – a single common cultural reality – for evaluating polygamy, then they would all come to the same evaluation, but then there would not be many different cultures for it to be relative to.

4. Cultural relativism *does not mean* that cultures are different in every conceivable way, that there are no cultural universals. Cultural relativism does not rule out the possibility of any commonalities or universals among humans. Relativism does not say that commonalities cannot exist; it merely correctly asserts that we cannot *assume* that they exist. The question of cultural universals is an empirical question: that is, if we find them, then they exist. If we do not find them, then they do not exist. But the lack of *universal meanings or values* is not the same thing as the lack of *meanings or values*. Even if there are not universal ones, there are "local" ones geographically and historically – very many local ones, in fact – and if that is all there is, then that has to be enough.

5. Cultural relativism *does not mean* that "everything is relative," including cultural relativism itself (cultural relativism is not self-contradictory). Some things are culturally relative, and some things are not. Cultural relativism is simply an awareness and acknowledgment of differences in human judgment about norms, values, meanings, and so on. It amounts to saying, "Different cultures have different notions of good/normal/moral/valuable." But that statement is not a value statement itself; it is a fact-claim. It is not saying that culture is good, or cultural relativism is good, or multiple value standards are good. Perhaps from certain viewpoints, multiple value standards – multiple cultures – are not good at all. They definitely make the human world more complicated and contentious. Still, culture *is*; multiple value standards *exist*. That is a fact. How we respond to it, what sense we make of it, is the important question.

6. Cultural relativism *does not mean* that cultures cannot be compared. Cultural relativism does not mean that comparison is impossible, any more than it means that judgment is impossible. What it means is that when any comparison is being made, the terms or criteria of the comparison must be specified. One cannot say culture X is "better than" culture Y without specifying "better at what?" Some cultures certainly are larger than others, and some cultures certainly are better at hunting or making war than others. As long as the standards of comparison are stated (and perhaps it is also explained *why those particular standards* were

PLATE 1.5 Warlpiri (Australian Aboriginal) Women preparing ritual objects.

selected) comparisons can of course be made. In fact, recall that the first part of the anthropological perspective was "comparative" study. We can compare two or more cultures on any variable without making value judgments about them.

In short, cultural relativism is three things simultaneously. It is a fact: cultures are different in their standards, values, meanings, and judgments. It is a method: if we want to understand a culture accurately, we must understand it in its own terms. And it is a theory: the explanation of *how* individuals and groups make their determinations of judgment and action depends on the awareness of the role of cultural meanings and standards. That is, there is no way for humans to behave or evaluate *other than* relative to some standard of behavior and evaluation.

PRACTICING ANTHROPOLOGY

You may be wondering at this point what an anthropologist does and what you could do with a degree or a career in anthropology. Anthropology is a lively, diverse, and growing discipline. According to a survey undertaken by our primary professional organization in the United States, the American Anthropological Association, the number of Bachelor degrees earned in anthropology nearly doubled from 1992–93 to 2001–2, from 5,945 to 9,728; the number of Master degrees rose by around

50 percent (1,049 versus 1,519), while almost three times as many doctorates were awarded (367 versus 1,025) (Boites, Geller, and Patterson n.d.). Significantly, more than half (up to 60 percent) of anthropology graduate degrees are earned by women. Another study (Givens, Evans, and Jablonski 2000) happily discovered that the vast majority of anthropology graduates (85 percent) would choose anthropology again as their major and career if they had it to do over.

The U.S. Bureau of Labor Statistics also recently issued a prediction for the job market in anthropology: during the decade from 2008 to 2018, they projected a growth of 22 percent in all social science occupations but a growth rate of 28 percent in anthropology and archaeology.

Careers in anthropology

What exactly do anthropologists do for a living? Many are teachers and scholars (researchers and writers) of anthropology, but not all. Givens, Evans, and Jablonski calculated that only a little over half (59 percent) of all anthropology Ph.D.s worked in academia in 1990, with somewhat more (71 percent) holding academic jobs in 1997. The U.S. Bureau of Labor Statistics data mentioned earlier indicate that only a little more than a third (34.2 percent) of anthropologists and archaeologists in 2008 worked in the conventional area of research and advanced teaching, with almost as many (30 percent) employed by government. The remaining third performed many tasks, including management and consulting, museum and historical site work, and even architecture and engineering. Indeed, the Society for Applied Anthropology estimates that actually most anthropologists work outside of colleges and universities, if Master degree-holders are included, and no doubt the number would be greater still for Bachelor degree-holders. The authors conclude: "Presently, there is no discernible ceiling or cap. . .for Ph.D. anthropologists targeting the nonacademic realm of employment." An anthropology major or minor can in fact be a fine preparation for a non-anthropological career, in education, business, law, journalism, and medicine, especially if one expects to be working with diverse populations or in an international setting.

For anthropologists who want to practice anthropology but do not seek typical academic careers, many opportunities exist in business and government, and anthropologists have made important contributions in both areas. For instance, writing in the bulletin of the National Association for the Practice of Anthropology (NAPA), Shirley Fiske (2008) finds that the federal government is probably the single largest employer of anthropologists in the United States after colleges and universities, especially archaeologists but also cultural, physical, and linguistic anthropologists. The five main federal agencies that hire people with anthropological talents are the Census Bureau, the National Park Service, the National Marine Fisheries Service, the Centers for Disease Control (CDC), and the U.S. Agency for International Development (USAID). For instance, at the Census Bureau "anthropologists have played a critical role in identifying the causes of and recommendations for overcoming the traditional undercounts of nontraditional households and populations in U.S. decennial censuses"; the expertise of anthropologists has helped the Bureau "improve its methods and approach to enumerating the national population, develop reliable methodologies for identifying marginalized and difficult-to-enumerate populations. . .and to recruit community-knowledgeable people to help conduct the census" (111–14). There are even anthropologists in the employ of the Department of Defense.

Anthropologists have been equally if not more successful in the world of business and commerce. According to Ann Jordan (2003) in her book titled *Business Anthropology*, corporations can benefit in at least five ways from hiring anthropologists: they can better understand their own work processes as well as the processes of their users/customers, they can comprehend and manage group behavior in the company, they can navigate organizational change, they can facilitate diversity within the corporation, and they can cope with globalization and international business. As early as 1931, American anthropologist W. Lloyd Warner, who had done research on Australian Aboriginals, investigated how the workplace environment at the Western Electric Company affected worker productivity. The 1930s and 1940s were a busy period for industrial anthropology, and Warner subsequently became the chairman of the Committee on Human Relations in Industry. In 1941 the aforementioned Society for Applied Anthropology was formed, and in 1946 Warner joined some other experts in creating Social Research Incorporated, an anthropological consulting firm with such clients as Sears, Roebuck and Company.

www.sfaa.net

In the contemporary high-technology and information economy, knowledge about learning, change, and user/customer behavior is more important than ever. Anthropologists have been especially valuable in studying how employees and customers interact with technology, leading to better training methods and better design features. The most famous example is the Xerox Palo Alto Research Center (PARC), discussed in Box 1.4.

www.practicing
anthropology.org

Other companies, from huge corporations like Microsoft and Intel to smaller ones like the Minneapolis marketing agency Olson, do better business by hiring anthropologists. And anthropologists have founded their own businesses, like AnthroTECH, which provides corporate services and also "partners with other firms specializing in marketing, research, and technology to provide the best and cost-effective solutions for our customers" (www.anthrotech.net).

Beyond the university and the corporation, there are many important and even critical applications of the discipline. NAPA promotes the use of anthropology "to address social issues related to public health, organizational and community development, information technology systems,

BOX 1.4 ANTHROPOLOGISTS AT XEROX

In 1991, John Seely Brown, a corporate vice-president at Xerox, wrote glowingly in the *Harvard Business Review* about the contributions by anthropologists to product development in his company. He fully understood that a modern company must not only invent new products but must innovate knowledge, learning processes, user experiences, and the very nature of the corporation itself. For that purpose, the Palo Alto Research Center (PARC) was established in 1970, and "some of the most important research at PARC in the past decade has been done by anthropologists" (Brown 1991: 106). Two key hires for Xerox were anthropologists Lucy Suchman and Jeannette Blomberg, who "studied occupations and work practices throughout the company – clerks in an accounts-payable office who issue checks to suppliers, technical representatives who repair copying machines, designers who develop new products, even novice users of Xerox's copiers. This research has produced fundamental insights into the nature of innovation, organizational learning, and good product design," including making Xerox copiers easier to understand and use (106–8). One of Suchman's most important discoveries was that official procedures and knowledge often did not reflect how people actually did their jobs; rather, workers and customers possess informal knowledge and skill which they use to accomplish their tasks – and which managers and product designers can use to improve their processes and products. There may have been an anthropologist's hand in the copier or other product that you buy or use every day.

housing, social justice, law, the media, marketing, environmental management, and the arts." Ervin (2000) mentions a wide variety of ways for putting anthropology into practice, including policy-making in such areas as health, education, social-economic problems, environment and resource management, and technology. Anthropologists can perform functions in needs assessment (determining what problems need to be solved and what inputs will be required), program evaluation (determining the effectiveness of programs), and social impact analysis (determining the effects of programs on people). Some of the specific tasks that anthropologists can perform include training, supervision, administration, consultation, interviewing, grant-writing, and expert-witness testimony.

One particular arena where anthropologists can make and have made a contribution is in advocacy for indigenous peoples, bringing cultural considerations to the attention of governments and corporations. Organizations like Cultural Survival (which publishes a magazine by the same name) in the United States or Survival International in the U.K. promote awareness of indigenous issues. The American Anthropological Association maintains a Department of Government Relations which "works to increase public understanding of anthropology"

See Chapters 14 and 15

and to lend an anthropological voice to political discourse. Some of its activities include initiating and responding to governmental policies, working with federal agencies, preparing briefings from the anthropological perspective, serving in advisory positions, and developing testimony to support funding allocations. Participation and advocacy can take many other forms as well, such as working for indigenous groups like Native American communities and societies to help them advance their practical claims (e.g. water or land rights) and cultural interests. When I was doing my fieldwork in Australia, there were anthropologists assisting Aboriginal groups to collect and present their tradition-based land claims in Australian courts; they would conduct the research, brief the lawyers, and sometimes even testify themselves in court. Others were helping them produce and sell their art.

Anthropology in careers

Most students who take an anthropology course will not go on to a career in anthropology. However, virtually if not all workers and citizens of the future will find anthropology in their careers. Given the diversity and interconnectedness of the human world, even if you are not a professional anthropologist, *you will be an amateur anthropologist whether you know it or not.* Most jobs will require interacting with diverse coworkers, customers, or clients, and the skills and perspectives of anthropology will be increasingly valuable, whatever work you do.

In its "Future Work Skills 2020" report, the Institute for the Future (Davies, Fidler, and Gorbis 2011) has identified six factors that will shape the work and the world of tomorrow – extremely long lifespans, the rise of smart machines, the computational world, the new media, superstructured organizations, and a globally connected world. These circumstances, which are largely already here, demand a set of capabilities beyond merely knowing one's job. The "ten skills for the future workplace" include:

1. sense-making, "the ability to determine the deeper meaning or significance of what is being expressed" (8)
2. social intelligence, "ability to connect to others in a deep and direct way, to sense and stimulate reactions and desired interactions" (8)
3. novel and adaptive thinking
4. cross-cultural competency, "ability to operate in different cultural settings" (9)
5. computational thinking
6. new media literacy

7. transdisciplinarity, "literacy in and ability to understand concepts across multiple disciplines" (11)
8. design mindset, "ability to represent and develop tasks and work processes for desired outcomes"
9. cognitive load management, "ability to discriminate and filter information for importance, and to understand how to maximize cognitive functioning using a variety of tools and techniques"
10. virtual collaboration

Most of these are precisely the skills on which anthropologists depend and which are conferred through the anthropological perspective.

Many careers already urge a kind of "**cultural competence**" akin to the anthropological perspective. The Center for Effective Collaboration and Practice (http://cecp.air.org) defines cultural competence as "the integration and transformation of knowledge about individuals and groups of people into specific standards, policies, practices, and attitudes used in appropriate cultural settings to increase the quality of services; thereby producing better outcomes." More specifically, cultural competence entails valuing diversity, being able to assess one's own culture, being conscious of intercultural interaction, institutionalizing this cross-cultural knowledge, and developing procedures to deliver culturally appropriate services. A

Cultural competence the skills necessary in the workplace and in life to recognize and value diversity, see one's own cultural influences, understand the dynamics and challenges of intercultural interaction, institutionalize cultural knowledge, and develop practices and policies for delivering culturally appropriate services

BOX 1.5 CONTEMPORARY CULTURAL CONTROVERSIES: SHOULD ANTHROPOLOGISTS BE ENGAGED?

Like any science, anthropology tries to maintain a certain level of neutrality and objectivity in its work. More than most sciences, anthropology appreciates the relativity of meanings and judgments: what is important – or objectionable – to me might not be important or objectionable to someone else. However, anthropologists are human beings too, and the amount of injustice and suffering in the world has led some to call for an "engaged anthropology," even a "militant anthropology." One of the most outspoken is Nancy Scheper-Hughes (1995), who argued that ethics must trump scientific neutrality and indeed cultural relativism: she went so far as to declare that cultural relativism "is no longer appropriate to the world in which we live, and anthropology, if it is to be worth anything at all, must be ethically grounded" (409). She insisted that anthropologists should be activists, criticizing and condemning injustice when they find it. But it is also true that different individuals and groups have different ethical standards. And if anthropology becomes militant and non-relativistic, some counter that it will not be able to do its job – in fact, it may cease to be anthropology at all. What do you think?

number of professions have formally integrated cultural competence into their standards for job performance, including nursing, pharmacy, health-care of all kinds, social work, police and criminal justice, counseling, and education. The National Association of Social Workers has published guidelines for cultural competence in social work practice, and there is even an organization called the National Center for Cultural Competence (http://nccc.georgetown.edu).

SUMMARY

Humans are diverse. Anthropology did not create this diversity but emerged as a response to and an investigation of it. Anthropology is thus the science of human diversity; it takes as its "question" or subject matter the full spectrum of human forms and ways and the explanation of that spectrum. The diversity that anthropology observes takes the form of bodily and behavioral differences, for which specialties within the field have been established:

- Physical anthropology to study the diversity of the human body in the past and present
- Archaeology to study the diversity of human behavior in the past
- Linguistic anthropology to study the diversity of human language in the past and present
- Cultural anthropology to study the diversity of human behavior in the present.

In addition to its question, anthropology is distinguished by its perspective, or the approach or attitude it takes toward its subject. This "anthropological perspective" includes:

- Comparative or cross-cultural study, or the description and analysis of the complete range of variation of humans and our ways
- Holism, or the interrelatedness of all of the "parts" of culture and of the culture to its natural environment
- Cultural relativism, or the awareness that we can make (useful) judgments of a culture only in terms of its own standards of good and normal and moral and meaningful and legal.

There are many ways to practice anthropology, only one of which is as a teacher, researcher, and writer. Anthropologists outside the academy work in business and government, among other occupations. Even academic anthropologists may be involved in consulting, policymaking, and advocacy.

Most people in the modern world are not professional anthropologists (and none were until fairly recently). However, all of us today live "anthropological lives" in the sense that we will experience and deal with human physical and cultural diversity continuously, both locally and globally, both professionally and personally.

MCQS

FILL IN THE BLANKS

Key Terms

Anthropological perspective	Cultural relativism	Garbalogy
Archaeology	Culture shock	Glocalization
Artifacts	Ecofacts	Holism
Cross-cultural study	Ethnocentrism	Linguistic anthropology
Cultural anthropology	Ethnography	Physical anthropology
Cultural competence	Features	Primatology

Understanding and studying culture

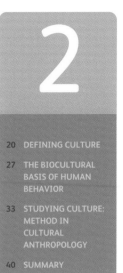

Like many people today, in the mid-nineteenth century Matthew Arnold felt that Western society was experiencing a crisis and a general decline. The point of his book *Culture and Anarchy* was "to recommend culture as the great help out of our present difficulties; culture being a pursuit of our total perfection by means of getting to know, on all the matters which most concern us, *the best which has been thought and said in the world*, and, through this knowledge, turning a stream of fresh and free thought upon our stock notions and habits, which we now follow staunchly but mechanically" (1869: viii, emphasis added). Note how he divided "culture" from mere "habit" or "tradition." However, if culture is the "good" tradition, indeed the *best* tradition, that raises some serious problems. First, who is to say what is the best? And what criteria should we use to decide? Second, what about those things that are less than best: if ballet and symphony are deemed culture, does that mean that bowling and *The Simpsons* are not culture? And are those people who do not care for the ballet – or those societies that do not have a tradition of ballet – to be labeled as lacking a culture? If this seems absurd, then consider some white men I met in Australia. When I told them that I had come to Australia

to study Aboriginal culture, one of them said, "Aboriginals do not have culture, and they never did." There are several possible explanations for this attitude. One is that he was simply uninformed about Aboriginal peoples. Another is that he was a racist. A third is that he was operating with a definition of culture like Matthew Arnold's, which is not and cannot be the definition in anthropology.

"Culture" is an old word, derived from the Latin root *cultura* for cultivation and agriculture and other usages such as a bacteria culture. The common thread among them involves raising something or growing it into a particular form. In human groups, culture refers to how people are raised and formed to become the kinds of individuals who can take their place within their group. Therefore, anthropology uses the term in a non-elitist and inclusive way, to refer to all of the things that humans must learn to know and do in order to be competent members of their society. Sometimes scholars have used it in an even more inclusive sense, as the total social heritage of the human species, capitalized as Culture. But no single human being, nor even any single human society, possesses the sum total of the heritage of humanity. Rather, each person and group holds a part or version of that heritage, a culture that is similar to yet different from every other. Cultural anthropology focuses on these cultural particulars, without losing site of the bigger question of the range and commonalities of particular cultures or of the forces and processes outside of a culture that enable and shape it.

DEFINING CULTURE

Part of the methodology of every science is its vocabulary, its set of core terms and concepts. In physics, these include mass, force, velocity, and momentum. Cultural anthropology too has its core terms and concepts, which, according to Evans-Pritchard (1962: 2), include "society," "custom," "structure," "function," and of course culture. Of these, culture is the most central. The problem is that there is no single official definition of culture. There are almost as many definitions of culture as there are cultural anthropologists; in fact, there are fundamentally different approaches to a definition. One approach understands culture as primarily ideas or beliefs, that is, as essentially "in people's heads." From this perspective, we cannot really "see" culture but we can infer it from the behaviors that people engage in. Another approach perceives culture as a set of real facts, albeit "social facts," regarding observable behavior and the products of that behavior, including the rules, groups, and institutions that shape people's lives. Culture can even refer to material objects like tools and houses. Ultimately, culture undoubtedly encompasses all three.

So there is no authoritative or universally shared definition of culture. But the most influential and widely quoted definition of culture in anthropology was given by E. B. Tylor, who helped to found modern anthropology in his 1871 book called *Primitive Culture*. It is quoted here not because it is perfect or final but because it captures most of the components of culture and of cultural anthropology.

Tylor, E. B. 1958 [1871]. *Primitive Culture*. New York: Harper Torchbooks.

> Culture or Civilization, taken in its wide ethnographic sense, is that complex whole which includes knowledge, belief, art, morals, law, custom, and any other capabilities and habits acquired by man as a member of society.
>
> (1958: 1)

Culture, then, can be understood as those ways of thinking, feeling, and behaving, and the social and material products of those ways, which are shared among a group of people not on the basis of innate or physical traits but rather on the basis of common experience and mutual learning. This and Tylor's characterization of culture include several key notions which we could consider the classic qualities of culture:

- Learned
- Shared
- Symbolic
- Integrated
- Adaptive

Contemporary encounters with culture in the modern globalized context suggest that these standard features do not quite capture its full richness. In particular, culture is and always has been characterized by its "mobility (geographical and social), complexity, fragmentation, contradiction, risk, and disembedding" (Coupland 2007: 29). Therefore, we could and should add that culture, at all times and places but especially and crucially in the present moment, is produced and practiced through situated human action and that it circulates across social and national borders. This means that "a culture" cannot be simply and unproblematically attributed to "a society" nor restricted to some clearly bounded territory.

Culture is learned

Culture is not something in our genes or brain or blood or any other aspect of our body. No one is born with a particular language or religion or gender role or political persuasion or economic skill. Neither is any particular language or religion determined in any way by human biology. The evidence for this is simple: any human baby, given the experience, can speak any language, believe any religion, or practice any skill (for example, throw a spear, play a guitar, use a computer). Culture is not "in" humans in the sense that skin color, eye color, blood type, or height is "in" humans.

So, if culture is not "inside" the individual at birth, where is it? The obvious answer is "outside" the individual. Culture, at the moment of birth, is what is going on around the individual, what the people in his/her social environment are doing. Think of culture as a great, ongoing conversation (which to a large extent it is). When a person is born, the conversation is already in progress all around him/her. The new member does not create it and does not initially understand it. Gradually, s/he begins to participate – haltingly and imperfectly. Eventually, the person becomes a competent member and joins the conversation. Maybe in small or large ways s/he affects the content or direction of the conversation, adding new words or ideas. Then, ultimately, each individual leaves the conversation for good. However, during his/her time, the person "kept it going." Moreover, each individual served as part of the social environment for members born afterward, who experienced what the individuals in the group did and said and who learned to be competent and full participants in their turn, they too keeping the conversation going – maybe in old channels, maybe in new ones.

Humans, then, are not born with a culture but acquire one. That is easy to say but not so simple to grasp. What does it mean to acquire a culture? What process takes place from the learner's point of view – and from the teachers'? Anthropologists most often call it **enculturation**, although it is also known as **socialization**. Basically, enculturation or socialization is the process by which a person masters his/her culture, ordinarily as a child.

While culture is not "in" humans at birth, it is "in" humans by the time they reach maturity. That is, culture "gets in" over time and by some means. Until recently, many scholars thought that the means was a straightforward process of observation, imitation, and reward and punishment. However, this account is insufficient. What humans appear to do is observe behavior, surely, but not simply imitate it but rather somehow actively extract meaning from it, derive the rules or principles by which good language or good behavior is produced. In other words, culture-learners are not passive recipients of cultural lessons but active constructors of their own cultural competence. Clearly, adults do not model every possible behavior for a child, nor do they directly and explicitly describe every rule and principle; the adults do not have the time, and often they themselves do not know the principles or "grammar" of their own culture. Instead, they provide an environment in which and from which

children actively "learn." In other words, to paraphrase Hans Freudenthal (1973), the acquisition of culture consists of a **guided reinvention of culture**. New humans must essentially reconstruct culture for themselves from their experiences, with of course the assistance and guidance of fully competent members of the group, who correct "mistakes."

What would happen if a human did not learn culture? What would a human without a culture be like? To conduct such an experiment would be unethical. However, a few "natural experiments" have occurred in which children were somehow separated or excluded from society and later discovered. Sometimes they were "lost in the woods" and grew up as "feral children"; sometimes they were deliberately abused, isolated and given minimal human contact (see e.g. Maclean 1979). Regardless of the source, such children grow not into "natural" humans and certainly not into any particular kind of human – i.e., you would not expect to leave a child in a French forest and have him/her emerge French – but rather as something "incomplete," not quite socially functional. They do not speak any language, profess any religion, or possess any social skills. And if they are discovered too late, they may never be able to fully acquire these human capabilities.

What this suggests is that culture is not an option, a superficial extra for a human like a coat

Guided reinvention of culture
the process by which individuals, ordinarily children, "acquire" ideas, concepts, and skills actively by observing the behavior of others, extracting meanings and rules, and testing those meanings and rules in social situations; fully competent members "guide" the learning by providing models of behavior and correction for inappropriate behaviors

Enculturation
the process by which a person learns or acquires his or her culture, usually as a child. Also known as socialization

Socialization
from an anthropological point of view, a synonym for enculturation

See Chapter 5

PLATE 2.1 Feral children.

BOX 2.1   LIVING WITHOUT CULTURE – THE "WILD BOY OF AVEYRON"

In 1797 a boy was seen running, naked and on all fours, alone through a French forest. In 1799 he was captured and brought to Paris for observation and training. The boy, eventually named Victor, was described by Pierre-Joseph Bonnaterre, who, like others at the time, knew that they had come across something unique and important. In his report (Lane 1977: 35–54), Bonnaterre claimed that, while Victor did not walk on all fours, he also did not walk normally and "steadily" but rather rocked "from one side to the other" and that he never seemed to tire, no matter how long he ran. The boy's senses were "more like an animal than a man"; his senses of smell and taste were the most developed, the observer reasoned, because Victor would sniff foods before deciding what to eat or refuse. He seemed indifferent to cold. He had no language at all, making only "cries and inarticulate sounds." "His expressive sounds, rarely emitted unless he is emotional, are rather noisy, especially those of anger and displeasure; when joyful, he laughs heartily; when content, he makes a murmuring sound, a kind of grunting. He does not utter raucous or frightening cries; almost all of them are guttural and depend only slightly on the movement of the tongue." He was an intelligent child: presented with a mirror "he looked immediately behind it, thinking to find there the child whose image he perceived." However, he lacked "conventional" knowledge or morality: "While not wicked, he is not good, for he is unaware of both." He showed no glimmer of a religious or spiritual nature. Emotionally, he displayed excitement and agitation and anger but not love: "he loves no one; he is attached to no one; and if he shows some preference for his caretaker, it is an expression of need and not the sentiment of gratitude: he follows the man because the latter is concerned with satisfying his needs and satiating his appetites."

Geertz, Clifford. 1973. *The Interpretation of Cultures.* New York: Basic Books.

that can be put on or off at will and without consequence. The American anthropologist Clifford Geertz stressed that culture is *necessary*: humans at birth are "incomplete or unfinished animals who complete or finish ourselves through culture – and not through culture in general but through highly particular forms of it" (1973: 49). Other beings come more or less ready-made with a set of instincts that suffice for them, although often not quite as completely as we think: predators like lions and birds of prey can and must learn how to hunt, and primates like monkeys and apes can and must learn how to parent. So humans are not the only species that depend on learning to complete their behavioral possibilities; humans just depend more totally and urgently on this learning.

See Chapter 15

Culture is shared

Since culture is learned, it obviously cannot be a trait or possession of only one individual. Culture is "outside" the individual before it is "inside," and so its location is within the community that "has" it or "does" it. Such a community we call a **society**,

that is, a group of humans who live in relative proximity to each other, are more likely to marry each other than members of different groups, and share a set of beliefs and behaviors. Culture, then, becomes the learned and shared ways of thinking, feeling, and behaving of the societal group.

It is not quite so simple, though. Surely, an individual can originate something – a new behavior, a new word, a new style, a new invention, a new religion – that becomes culture; an individual can also be the last person to use some word or style or religion. Surely too, any item of culture need not be *completely* shared within a society to qualify as culture. "Cultural" does not mean "shared by 100 percent of a society." But if not 100 percent, what is the quantitative cutoff? Perhaps we must accept that culture is not exactly a quantitative thing. The anthropologist Ralph Linton (1936: 272–74) suggested that culture consists of a variety of "modes" or "degrees" of sharedness. Or rather, culture may not be so much shared as *transmitted and distributed*. Some individuals and subgroups in a society know or do some parts, others know and do other parts. Yet it is still culture if it is acquired through social experience.

Society

a group of humans who live in relative proximity to each other, tend to marry each other more than people outside the group, and share a set of beliefs and behaviors

Universals ←→ Alternatives ←→ Specialties ←→ Individual Peculiarities

FIGURE 2.1 Ralph
Linton's modes of cultural
distribution.

Linton used the term "universals" to designate those things that all or the vast majority of a society do in generally the same way; a common language may be an example. "Alternatives" refer to things that some individuals or subgroups do in one way but other individuals or sections do in another way; different religions or cuisines within a society would qualify. Even less widely shared, "specialties" are things that some individuals or subgroups do while others do not do them (playing the guitar, for instance, which must be learned but is not learned by everyone). Finally, some capabilities and habits are very narrowly shared; such "individual peculiarities" may be practiced by one person or at most a small number of people. Some members of the group may even perceive such practices as "abnormal," but they are still cultural.

In this view, there are many ways to be cultural. Culture need not be and often is not uniformly shared within a society. For instance, priests probably know a lot more about religion than laypeople do. Professional chefs know a lot more about cooking than amateurs. Western societies are accustomed to the idea that cultural knowledge is "public" and available to all. However, not every society holds this view. Knowledge is often exclusive to a subgroup, a particular category of people, or even a single individual. In many religions there is the "popular" version of doctrines or rituals and the "esoteric" version for the worthy or the fully initiated. Among Australian Aboriginal societies, knowledge is systematically distributed. First of all, there is discrete male knowledge and female knowledge. Some aspects of religion are public and open to all, but some are highly closed, to the point of death for revealing them. The secrets of male ritual knowledge are not only limited to men but to adult circumcised men. The secrets of women are likewise limited to fully initiated women. Of course, such knowledge is also stratified by age: young people will not and cannot possess it all, and they will achieve greater and greater "sharing" as they mature and prove their ability and worthiness. Finally, even knowledge that one is qualified to "hear" one may not be qualified to "speak." Some knowledge is virtually private property, and no one but the rightful owner may perform it or transmit it. Certainly it must be transmitted if it is to endure, but only the owner may confer rights on others to perform it. Accordingly, no man or woman could ever possess all the knowledge of the society, even if s/he could potentially remember and master it all (see e.g. Morphy 1991; Keen 1994; Dussart 2000; Bell 1993).

Society then – especially a society of greater size and complexity – will consist of subgroups and

BOX 2.2   WHEN TWO CROWS DISAGREED

In 1938 Edward Sapir exploded the myth of cultural uniformity within a society (even a "primitive" society) when he found a moment of profound cultural disagreement in J. O. Dorsey's book *Omaha Society*. Dorsey was studying "Omaha culture," which presumably all Omaha knew and shared, but after reporting some aspect of that culture, he added, "Two Crows denies this." What Dorsey had discovered, and what all anthropologists discover, is that a society consists of a "number of human beings who [give] themselves the privilege of differing from each other" (2001: 3). More importantly still, an individual like Two Crows can influence or change culture: "if we get enough Two Crows to agree. . .we have what we call a new tradition, or a new dogma, or a new theory, or a new procedure" (4). Then, a variation that "starts as a thoroughly irresponsible and perhaps psychotic aberration seems to have the power. . .to lose its purely personal quality and to take on something of that very impersonality of custom." Ultimately, "The fact that this rebel, Two Crows, can in turn bend others to his own view of fact or theory or to his own preference in action shows that his divergence from custom had, from the very beginning, the essential possibility of culturalized behavior."

Subculture
a group or subset within a
society that is distinguished
by some unique aspects of
its behavior (such as
clothing styles, linguistic
usages, or beliefs and
values)

Counterculture
a group or subset within a
society that more or less
intentionally adopts
behaviors, beliefs, or
practices that are at odds
with or opposed to the
mainstream of society

Symbol
an object, gesture, sound,
or image that "stands for"
some other idea or concept
or object. Something that
has "meaning," particularly
when the meaning is
arbitrary and conventional
and thus culturally relative

sections with their own distinct knowledge, beliefs, values, norms, and so on. In traditional Plains Indians societies like the Cheyenne, various warrior associations had their own names and traditions and symbols and interests (Hoebel 1960). In modern Western society there are many **subcultures** and even **countercultures** that vary from – often deviate from – each other and the "mainstream" culture. Certainly, an anthropologist would not want to study only tattooed and pierced skateboarders to learn about American or Canadian culture, but neither would an anthropologist want to ignore them. They would represent one "tributary" or "rivulet" or "current" in the cultural stream – one that belongs to the culture as much as any and sheds light on it like all the others.

Culture is symbolic

Earlier we likened culture to a conversation. The analogy immediately suggests language; however, not all human communication is linguistic, and not all language is verbal (hearing-impaired people have a rich manual language in such forms as American Sign Language). What is really interesting and important about language in particular, and culture in general, is that it is a set of meanings based on the human capability and need to create and assign meaning.

Humans are beings who can and must "mean." No doubt, other beings also mean sometimes. When a cat snarls and hisses, it means something. However, a cat apparently does not have to learn to snarl and hiss, nor do different cats in different places snarl and hiss differently. The gesture is natural or instinctive. And when a fire gives off smoke, the smoke "means" that there is fire below, but the fire hardly has an intention to mean. The meaning is natural and objective, directly connected to the event that causes it.

Symbols are things with meaning too. However, unlike the smoke of a fire or the hiss of a cat, the meaning of a symbol is added on, "bestowed upon it by those who use it," and this meaning "is in no instance derived from or determined by properties intrinsic in its physical form" (White 1940: 453). That is, a symbol's meaning is *arbitrary and conventional*, not immediate, natural, or necessary. As a symbol, the sound "dog" represents or means the familiar domesticated animal. However, the symbol does not sound like a dog or look like a dog. There is no obvious or objective connection between the sound and the creature. The proof of this is that different societies use different verbal symbols for the same creature – *chien* in French, *Hund* in German, *perro* in Spanish, *maliki* in Warlpiri, and so on. Any of these symbols works equally well, as long as users know the symbol and know that others know it. Similarly, a shake of the

PLATE 2.2 Culture is composed of symbols, like these Australian Aboriginal artworks.

head can mean "yes" in one culture and "no" in another – and nothing at all in a third.

Certainly in many cases there is a contingent relationship between the symbol and its meaning. The cross as a symbol for Christianity is not utterly arbitrary, but it is not the necessary or only possible symbol, nor was it the first. Even more importantly, the cross *does not always* mean Christianity: other societies have used cross-like designs without "meaning" Christianity. Clifford Geertz called a symbol a "vehicle for a conception" (1973: 91), but what precise conception is loaded into what precise vehicle depends on the society and even the historical moment of that society. A dramatic example is the swastika, a symbol with a very distinct meaning for most modern Western people. However, this ancient symbol has not always had its association with Nazism and Hitler; long before National Socialism was imagined, South Asians and some Native Americans used a similar design to convey a radically different meaning.

Culture, thus, is a great meaning system – a "web of significances" in which we are suspended, as Geertz said. The symbols of a culture act like a lens, shaping the reality that is refracted through them. No human experiences the natural or social world except through the symbol-lens of culture, which no doubt affects how different peoples perceive and respond to their world.

Culture is integrated

Tylor opened his definition of culture by calling it a "complex whole." Any particular culture, that is to say, is not a single item or a homogeneous mass. Neither is it a jumble of loose parts. Rather, a culture is a system composed of many elements in some functional interrelation. Some of the early analogies for culture were highly "organismic," depicting culture as an organism with internal organs and organ-systems. Although the metaphor goes a bit too far, it may be useful. Each part or domain of a culture, like each organ in a body, has its own particular function to perform, its own "job to do," even as each part contributes to the functioning of the whole. This position is known as **functionalism**. As a model it provides a way to conceptualize culture – internally differentiated, multiply functional, and structured. The specific structure in any particular culture may differ from another, but a structure of some sort is always present. That is, culture is a (loose) system – or better yet, a set of systems, a system of systems. As a research method it gives anthropologists something to look at or look for. Researchers can aim to identify the various parts, examine their separate functions or contributions, and relate them to the functioning of the whole.

Cultural anthropology has analyzed cultural systems into four rough areas of functionality. This does not mean necessarily that all cultures have equally articulated and formalized institutions of all

Functionalism
the method, and eventually the theory, that a cultural trait can be investigated for the contribution it makes to the survival of individual humans, the operation of other cultural items, or the culture as a whole

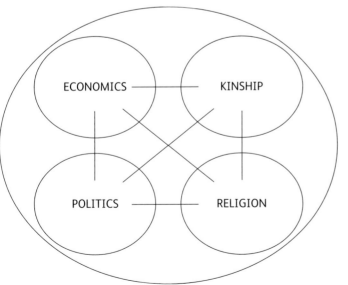

FIGURE 2.2 A model of cultural integration.

four kinds, but it does mean that all cultures have four kinds of functions that must and will be performed by some means in the system. These areas of functionality or "domains" of culture include economics, kinship, politics, and religion. One way to visualize them and their interconnections is as four circles within the larger circle of culture:

Each domain is analytically distinct, but each is integrated with every other just as the parts of a car or the organs of a body are interrelated. In fact, the domains probably actually overlap each other, such that sharp lines between them cannot be drawn. No matter where cultural anthropology starts its research and analysis, it will be unavoidably drawn into consideration of all of the other domains. Even more importantly, the addition, removal, or modification of a part can and often will have consequences for the functioning of the other parts and the whole – often unforeseen and undesired consequences.

Culture is an adaptation

Cultures and the societies that "have" them do not float in space. Every society and its culture exist in a specific physical context, an environment. That environment may be desert or jungle, volcanic island or arctic tundra, but each presents its unique practical challenges and opportunities. There may be too little water or too much, certain kinds of plants and animals, harsh and unpredictable or gentle and consistent climates, and so on. Most living species are highly specialized to live in a particular environment; even our primate cousins tend to need forest habitats to survive. Humans, on the other hand, are the most non-specialized, the most "generalized" of beings (see below). Because humans come with so little genetic or instinctive preprogramming (as Geertz stated), humans can be culturally programmed in nearly infinite ways. Where most living creatures adapt to their environments with their bodies, humans adapt with their behavior.

The adaptive power of behavior is a quantum leap above physical/genetic adaptation. Physical adaptation is slow; behavioral adaptation is fast. Physical adaptation is "chance" or random – that is, a species cannot will itself to have thicker fur or a bigger brain. Behavioral adaptation is intentional and "free" at least to an extent – that is, humans can innovate where they perceive a need. Anthropologists must not overestimate the creativity of humans: most people in most places and times have been much more imitative than inventive. Still, the overall creativity of humans makes it possible and inevitable that there will be many ways to be human. Finally, behavioral adaptations and inventions are simple to transmit across group boundaries and require nothing more than mutual observation.

So, the diagram of culture above should set the society that carries it within some environmental context. Perhaps we should draw another larger circle that encloses the circle of culture. Then, we can relate not only the domains of culture to each other but each of them and the cultural whole to its environmental setting. Again, without major inputs of energy and technology, the environment will be a limiting and shaping factor on how the society works, organizes itself, and even relates to the natural and supernatural world. In a word, culture is how humans get along in and with their external circumstances.

As with so many claims, anthropologists must be cautious about the adaptive quality of culture. For one thing, human societies are not always in harmony with their environments. It is something of a romantic fallacy to assert that pre-modern societies lived in perfect ecological balance, and it is clearly impossible to think that modern industrial ones do. Australian Aboriginal hunters burned the desert flora, and Easter Islanders stripped their island bare. For another, when societies migrate, as they often do, they bring with them practices and values that may have been adaptive in the former environment but are less adapted to the new one; over time, they may conform themselves more to the requirements of their new location, but not always or quickly enough. Finally, it cannot be said that culture is always advantageous for all of its members. Societies have engaged in activities from war to slavery to human sacrifice to the destruction of twins that were certainly not beneficial to the victims of such behaviors. The perpetrators of these actions may have felt that the actions were justified, even necessary (as in Aztec sacrifice, to keep the sun alive and strong), but that does not mean that the actions were good for all involved. In short, the "freedom" of humans enables them to engage in activities that are not always rational or healthful.

Culture is produced, practiced, and circulated

Too often social scientists and the public have labored under a static view of culture – static historically as in fixed and unchanging (i.e., "traditional"), and static geographically as tied and limited to one "local" group or society. Members of a society tended then to seem like passive recipients of a discrete and immutable culture, which we realize from our discussion above is untrue. Individuals and groups are active, in conjunction with larger-scale entities like corporations, organizations, and governments, in producing and reproducing – or altering or eliminating – aspects of culture.

The production of culture calls our attention to "how the symbolic elements of culture are shaped by the systems within which they are created, distributed, evaluated, taught, and preserved" (Peterson and Anand 2004: 311). This is easiest to see in the realm of arts, which are obviously produced, usually by a single person or small collection of people; however, it is equally relevant to science, technology, language, law, and religion – indeed, all areas of culture. These production processes also link our descriptions of culture to issues of media and culture-making and culture-disseminating technologies (like recording, publishing, broadcasting, etc.), of markets (for the sale and purchase of cultural products), and of power (in terms of who owns and/or dominates these media, machines, and markets). Anthropologists have examined, for example, the uses of cinema in Peru (Himpele 2008) and India (Velayutham 2008), radio among the Ojibwe of Canada (Valentine 1995), and television in Aboriginal Australia (Deger 2006; Michaels 1986), among many others.

The production and reproduction of culture has consequently shifted focus away from "traditions" and "rules" to the *practice* of culture; that is, culture is presently seen less as a fixed body of knowledge or as a set of coercive rules than as socially structured action. Geertz was one of the first to suggest that culture is best understood not as abstract ideas or as concrete behaviors but "as a set of control mechanisms – plans, recipes, rules, instructions (what

computer engineers call 'programs') – for the governing of behavior" (1973: 44). In this view, human activity and the groups and institutions that emerge from it are not simple enactments of cultural "rules," but neither are they random products of "free" individuals. Rather, according to Pierre Bourdieu (1977), who attempted to formulate a theory of practice, human behavior is an outcome of predispositions and strategies – acquired capabilities and habits, as Tylor put it – which are produced in the individual by culture and enculturation and then usually reproduced by the individual in culturally informed and culturally situated action.

Cultural anthropology has been strongly influenced by the practice and production perspectives, which are clearly intimately linked. Together they offer to transcend oppositions like individual/culture and action/structure. The other common dualism is local/global, which is transcended by the notions of cultural circulation and glocalization. Indisputably, an item of culture (a work of art, a piece of technology, a clothing style, a word, a song, a religion, etc.) is not trapped within the boundaries of a particular society. Culture circulates within a society – between regions, classes, generations, and so on – and between societies. Culture is mobile, along chains of migration and chains of exchange, and this is no recent fact: in pre-contact Australia, societies traded not only materials like stone and objects like axes but entire religious complexes (sets of rituals, myths, songs, and dances) and kinship systems. In the modern globalized world, the paths of exchange are only extended and accelerated, so that one finds blue jeans and rock 'n' roll music in non-Western societies, and sushi and Buddhism in the United States and Europe. Culture flows, blending with or beating against elements already in place, and cultural anthropology has discovered that it must go with the cultural flow.

THE BIOCULTURAL BASIS OF HUMAN BEHAVIOR

The diversity of human behavior proves that this behavior is not programmed in the human body in any precise way. However, the fact that all humans can and must learn culture, and that no other beings do or can learn culture fully, means that there is something about human beings that makes culture

Bourdieu, Pierre. 1977. Outline of a Theory of Practice. Cambridge: Cambridge University Press.

See Chapter 11

Biocultural

the mutual interaction between physical/biological and behavioral/cultural factors, in which physical traits make certain behaviors possible, and behavior feeds back to influence physical traits

Primate

the term for the classification of mammals, including prosimians, monkeys, apes, and humans, that share a collection of physical characteristics including a distinct tooth pattern, five-fingered hands, a tendency toward erectness of the spine, large eyes and good vision, and a relatively large brain in relation to body weight, among others

Prosimian

the category with the classification Primate that includes the least derived or "most primitive" species, such as lemurs, lorises, bush babies, galagas, and so on. Most have long tails and protruding snouts, but they exhibit other basic features of primates

THE NEURAL BASIS OF CULTURE

Erectness

the tendency to have an "upright" posture based on a spine that is vertical rather than parallel to the ground

Bipedalism

the ability and tendency to walk to two feet

BOX 2.3   BLUE JEANS GOING GLOBAL

In 2007, Daniel Miller and Sophie Woodward issued their manifesto calling for the anthropological study of denim. The blue jean "is clearly a global presence, it not only exists in every country in the world, but in many of these it has become the single most common form of everyday attire" (2007: 336). The existence and importance of denim around the world, they said, was "blindingly obvious," but it is the obvious and taken-for-granted that is too often overlooked by members of a society as well as by scholars; anthropologists instead "delight in exposing unexpected or unnoticed behaviors" that provide "a sign of a larger order" (337). They specifically offer three comparisons, between the United States, Brazil, and Britain. In the United States, where blue jeans originated, the pants were first associated with manual labor; however, through a combination of marketing, media, historical forces, and changes in values, jeans became the wear of first the cultural rebels (like James Dean and Marlon Brando), then of the middle class, and finally of the mainstream. In Brazil, denim has been stretched (literally) in "response to the degree of emphasis within Brazil on the female buttocks" (339), leading to the invention of a new local material that looks like denim but is much more elastic; consequently, these stretch-jeans "accentuate the shape of the body almost in the manner of a body stocking." Woodward herself did research among women in London, spending time "in women's bedrooms watching how they chose what they wear" (340). She found that blue jeans played a pivotal role in women's self-definition, in their struggle between conformity and individuality, and in their sense of comfort and habit. Their edited volume *Global Denim* (2011) extends the comparison to India and other parts of Europe, where blue jeans have diverse gender, class, and ethnic meanings.

---

possible and necessary. Culture, that is, is constructed on a foundation of physical characteristics which, while they do not determine behavior in detail, set the general outlines for the kinds of behavior that humans can and must perform. This feedback relationship between biology and culture makes humans **biocultural** beings – not merely biological, but not merely cultural either.

The distinctive human physical traits are not entirely uniquely human but are generally shared by a category of species known as **primates**, which includes apes like the chimpanzee and gorilla, monkeys of various kinds, and the most "primitive" of primates classified as **prosimians**. Primates are grouped together in the first place on the basis of these common characteristics, such as:

■ hands with five fingers and (usually) fingernails instead of claws, with an opposable thumb that makes grasping possible. The fingers have sensitive tactile pads on the tips, and the hands and feet (which are also "grasping" in orangutans) come at the end of very flexible limbs capable of a wide range of motion.

■ teeth that are varied and generalized, with cutting teeth in the front and grinding teeth in the back. There is even a regular pattern of teeth, consisting of two incisors, one canine, two premolars, and two or three molars on each side, top and bottom. The variety of teeth makes a varied and omnivorous diet possible.

■ large brains relative to body weight, with special development of the frontal and back areas. There is also an emphasis of eyes over noses on the face. Vision is acute, while the sense of smell is weaker. The result is a flattened face with large eyes.

■ a tendency toward spinal **erectness**, with the head "on top of" rather than "in front of" the spine. This gives primates a relatively upright posture and a tendency toward **bipedalism** or walking on two feet.

■ relatively long lifespan, with a long period of immaturity or "childhood," during which youths are highly dependent on and very interactive with parents as well as other members of the group.

The combined effect of this constellation of traits is a kind of "freedom" or "openness" of behavior, an

BOX 2.4 PRIMATE CULTURE

In 1949 Japanese scientists began observing a troupe of small monkeys called macaques on the Japanese island of Koshima and providing them with food. In 1953 one young female, whom the researchers called Imo, was seen carrying a sweet potato to a stream where she rubbed it in the fresh water. On subsequent trips to the stream, she waded deeper into the water and held the food with one hand while washing it with the other. Within three months, three other individuals began practicing the behavior, and by the end of five years 75 percent of the younger members of the group were habitual potato-washers. Only the old males did not adopt the behavior. But sweet potatoes are a big food that allowed them to eat fast and flee. So observers decided to give them small foods like wheat or rice which the macaques would have to laboriously pick out of the sand. Imo once again outsmarted the scientists, inventing a new behavior in which she scooped a handful of sand and grains and carried it to the water, tossed it all in, and quickly skimmed the food off of the surface. This new solution also spread among most members of the group (Kawai 1965). No other population of macaques had ever been observed engaging in this behavior. What appeared to be going on here was the innovation and then learning and sharing of a new behavior as an adaptation to a novel environmental circumstance – the key qualities of culture. Since that time scientists in the field have noted many other kinds of "cultural" behaviors, such as tool use and tool-making, and even some that appear to be "symbolic." For instance, in 1993 a young male chimpanzee dubbed Kakama was watched moving through the forest in Uganda with his mother and clutching a small log. At first he handled it the way a female handles a baby. He went to considerable trouble to bring the log along as they traveled, eventually stopping to build a nest in the branches, in which he placed it. Over the course of two hours, Kakama took the log everywhere he went, carrying it on his back or on his hip. At one point it fell to the forest floor, but he retrieved it. Wrangham and Peterson concluded that they "had just watched a young male chimpanzee invent and then play with a doll" (1996: 254–55).

adaptability which most other species lack; primates are not highly physically specialized for any single way of life, which means that they – and we – are capable of diverse ways of life. The biocultural approach, and the evidence discovered through this approach, suggest not only that human physical characteristics make human behavioral characteristics (culture) possible but that *culture is not an "all or nothing" thing.* Humans have a great deal of it, but other species may have some measure of it too, depending on how human-like their biology is.

Beings with bodies like primates are prone to engage in behaviors like primates. The most fundamental primate behavior is living in social groups. Other animals (and even plants) live in groups, but social groups are distinguished by their internal diversity of rules and roles – that is, different parts to play or "kinds of individuals" to be. One particularly clear and important expression of social behavior is **dominance** or **hierarchy**, in which some individuals have more status or social power than

others. This can of course be based on sheer strength, but it typically is not. Such factors as age, sex (males are often but not always dominant), family relations, and "alliances" with other individuals can all enhance status and the likelihood of achieving leadership and enjoying its benefits, such as more and better food and mates. Indeed, as Frans de Waal's chimp "ethnography" *Chimpanzee Politics* (1998) suggests, primates engage in distinctly "political" actions when they are seeking or exercising power. There are even data to support the notion that sex roles in some primate societies are learned. Hamadryas baboons, for instance, live in male-dominated harems, while savannah baboons do not. When Hans Kummer (1995) transplanted Hamadryas females into savannah troupes, the females initially acted submissive, only to discover that the males did not herd and bite them, and they quickly became as "free" as native female savannah baboons; on the other hand, freedom-loving savannah females placed in Hamadryas troops were

de Waal, Frans. 1998 [1982]. *Chimpanzee Politics: Power and Sex among Apes*, revised edition. Baltimore, MD: Johns Hopkins University Press.

Dominance

the social relationship in which certain individuals have higher prestige or power in the group, allowing them to enjoy more or better resources as well as the deference of lower-ranked members

Hierarchy

see dominance

bitten and herded by males and eventually "learned their place," although they still remained rebellious and hard to control.

There is reason to believe that primates not only enjoy being social but *need to be* social. The famous primatologist Robert Yerkes went so far as to claim that one primate is no primate at all (Lorenz 1963: 100). A series of experiments by Harry Harlow (1959) supports this position. He took baby rhesus monkeys and raised them in isolation. The result was often a "neurotic" monkey who cringed in the corner of his cage and even rocked back and forth the way some disturbed humans do. When introduced to other monkeys, the response tended to be either fear or aggression but hardly ever successful social interaction. And if an isolated female became a mother (difficult enough, since mating behavior itself appears to be learned), she usually had little or no idea what to do with the infant; she would either be neglectful or actually aggressive toward it, often ending in its death.

Non-human primates demonstrate a range of other behaviors that are familiar and similar to humans. Among these behaviors are:

Aggression and territoriality

Primates tend to defend a specific territory or "home range" within which they move about but generally remain. Essentially, each local group within the species has its "borders" which it patrols and polices. Other local groups of the same species that infiltrate these borders may encounter aggressive resistance. An important aspect of primate aggression is intergroup or intraspecies aggressive behavior (IAB), which is defined as aggressive or violent interactions between two or more spatially separate, distinct, and identifiable groups by individuals acting as members or representatives of such groups. Johan van der Dennen (2002) has identified sixty-four species practicing IAB, of which fifty-four are primates. Most such aggression is "ritualized" and not fatal. Individuals will "display" with threatening gestures or sounds and perhaps tussle for a few moments until one realizes he is the loser of the encounter and runs away or displays submissive behavior, which ends the face-off. However, not all aggression concludes so peacefully, and the more human-like the primate, the more human-like the aggression. Jane Goodall, the

pioneering primatologist who has observed chimps in the wild since the 1970s, reported what could only be called a war between two groups of chimps that had recently split apart. Over a period of years, the larger group hunted down the smaller splinter group and killed the males and killed or captured the females until the latter group was exterminated. She even calculated that approximately 30 percent of male chimp deaths were due to violence (Goodall 1986).

Communication and social interaction

While all animals communicate, primate communication is also unique in many aspects. For one, primates communicate visually much more than other species, given their evolved vision. When a primate encounters a novel situation, it explores the situation by *looking* rather than smelling. Primates also interact with each other and their world by touch more than most species, employing the sensitive pads on their fingers. One classic primate behavior is grooming or running their fingers through each other's hair. This is no doubt both hygienic and pleasurable, but it also has a social component: grooming shows and establishes affiliation, even affection. Friends groom each other, adults groom infants, and males groom females as part of courtship. Grooming behavior indicates or creates social ordering: lower-ranking individuals tend to groom more dominant ones, unless the dominant one is seeking allies, in which case dominant ones may groom subordinates to win their favor. Chimps in particular will put their arms around others or pat them on the back to comfort them. They even appear to hold or shake hands and kiss hands, especially as an introduction between strangers. Bonobo or pygmy chimps are famous for their much more sexual touching, which has little or nothing to do with reproduction; this touching even takes place within the same sex. Finally, primates communicate "orally" or with sound. Apes have even been shown experimentally to communicate "linguistically" (that is, to use "language symbols" like sign language or meaningful shapes and objects).

Eating and hunting meat

It was believed prior to the 1970s that chimpanzees were primarily vegetarian and that they might

Goodall, Jane. 1986. *The Chimpanzees of Gombe: Patterns of Behavior.* Cambridge, MA: Harvard University Press.

See Chapter 4

PRIMATE MORALITY?

PLATE 2.3 Chimpanzees learn to use twigs or grass stems to "fish" for termites, an example of non-human culture.

occasionally eat a small animal or bird but not deliberately and systematically kill larger animals for meat. However, as Goodall witnessed, they not only eat and relish meat but also hunt for meat. In particular, they hunt monkeys, which are not easy to catch for the larger and more terrestrial chimps. Hunting such prey requires cooperation and coordination, foresight and planning. The hunters usually divide the assignment between those who will give chase through the branches and those who will pursue along the ground below. Together they try to steer the prey to a congenial spot for capture. A successful hunt is often followed by sharing or "politicking" with the resultant meat. Hunters may bring meat back to share with females and young, and they may share it with (or steal it from) other males to form or secure alliances. Successful males may occasionally keep all their catch to themselves, but the dietary advantage of such behavior is set against the social disadvantage of the selfish and "unfriendly" aspect of it.

Tool use and production

For a long time, it was supposed that humans are the only primates that use tools; in fact, the accepted definition of human was based on tool use. A few

species here and there appeared to use tool-like objects as well, including otters that bash open mollusks with a stone, but these are not full tools. A tool is a natural object that is not only used but is made or modified for use to accomplish some task that the body cannot do or cannot do as effectively. So, when we smash a can of beans with a rock to open it, that is tool-like, but when we sharpen the rock to make a cutting edge for slicing open a dead zebra, we are making a true tool. Goodall was the first to document that chimps use and make simple tools. Chimps like to eat termites, but termites retreat inside their hard hills. Another animal would wait patiently or dig or try to insert a claw or tooth into the hole – that is, use its body – but chimps will search for a good-sized and -shaped branch or stem, trim and fashion it just so, and stick it into the hole, pulling it and the clinging termites out. This kind of "fishing" behavior requires not only mental skills like imagination and foresight but a dexterous and grasping hand. Since that time, primatologists have watched chimps and a few other primates using stones or sticks to hammer nuts, leaves to scoop water, and chewed leaves to soak up juices from their meat. Even more interestingly, they have noticed regional diversity within a given species of primate; that is, chimps in one location have been

Oldowan

the earliest known stone tool technology, associated with Homo habilis and named for the location of its discovery, Olduvai Gorge in East Africa

Homo erectus

an extinct human species that lived from approximately 1.8 million years ago until a few hundred thousand years ago or perhaps even more recently

Australopithecus

a genus of the category Hominid, closely related to and earlier than genus Homo

Acheulian

the stone tool technology associated with Homo erectus, which involves a more complex flaking of bifacial implements

Homo sapiens

the species name for modern humans

Homo habilis

an extinct human species that lived from over 2 million years ago until less than 2 million years ago. They are also known as the first stone tool makers

Homo

the genus that contains the modern human species (Homo sapiens) as well as several other extinct human species

Hominid

the category of primates that includes only modern humans and extinct human-like species that fall within the genera of Homo and Australopithecus (although other and even more ancient genera have been proposed)

seen learning and practicing one set of behaviors, while members of the same species in other locations have their own distinct local "cultures." In the laboratory, chimps have shown powerful cognitive abilities in using and combining objects to achieve goals (like stacking boxes to reach bananas hanging from the ceiling or using keys to unlock chests with food inside). There is little doubt that the more we give primates to think about and do, the more they will surprise us with their intelligence and ability.

Finally, just as culture as a general phenomenon or capability is apparently not all-or-nothing, neither is human culture in particular all-or-nothing. Rather, what we see in the fossil and archaeological record is that as humans developed into their present-day physical form, something like present-day culture gradually but inexorably emerged. For instance, the most ancient well-documented category of pre-human species is called **Australopithecus**, which includes the famous Australopithecus afarensis, known popularly as "Lucy." Living 3 or 4 million years ago, these pre-humans already had some key human traits like upright bipedal walking and smaller teeth but also some primitive traits like a small brain (no larger than an ape). There is no firm evidence that they made or used tools.

Around 2.5 million years ago, a new species, designated **Homo habilis**, commenced the category or genus called **Homo**, which would eventually include modern humans. This species, its descendants, and their key physical and behavioral characteristics are as follows:

Homo habilis

They possessed a larger brain than Australopithecus afarensis, up to half of modern size (600–700 cubic centimeters versus 1200–1400 for moderns). They showed the first firm evidence of stone tool use and manufacture, based on a simple stone chopper, called **Oldowan**, made by hammering one stone with another to produce a cutting edge.

Homo erectus

First appearing around 1.8 million years ago, **Homo erectus** marks another advance in brain size, reaching ⅔ or more of modern brain mass (1,000 cc). They were also the first species of fossil humans to migrate out of Africa, eventually reaching most of Eurasia (where they are popularly known as "Peking Man" and "Java man"). They developed a more sophisticated stone tool technology called **Acheulian** in which the entire surface of the stone was chipped to yield a symmetrical "bifacial" tool. They apparently used fire and may have also constructed rudimentary shelters.

Archaic Homo sapiens

By around 600,000 years ago, the first **Homo sapiens** appeared, although they were not quite the modern human species of today. Their brains were equal to or larger than modern, and their bodies were similar enough to be placed in the same species. They lived in many parts of Eurasia,

---

BOX 2.5   THE DISCOVERY OF ARDI

In 2009, a series of papers announced the oldest well-established **hominid** species (so far). Technically named Ardipithecus ramidus, but more affectionately known as "Ardi," this small female individual lived a million years before Lucy, approximately 4.4 million years ago. According to the principal investigator, Tim White (White et al. 2009), remains of Ardi were first found in 1994, but it took fully fifteen years to complete the analysis and publish the results. Inhabiting present-day Ethiopia, Ardi had a small brain, no larger than a chimp, but reduced incisors, a flatter face, and a less-prominent brow. Most significantly, the skeleton indicates bipedal walking: the pelvis is short and broad, like the human pelvis, and the spine is long and curved, like the human spine. White and his collaborators conclude that Ardipithecus shows a compelling blend of pre-human and human-like traits and supports the interpretation that humans diverged from a hominid ancestor sometime around 6 or 7 million years ago. Ardi became something of a media sensation, even getting its own PBS special.

where they had regionally diverse behavior and in some cases probably language. The best-known of the archaic Homo sapiens populations is the **Neandertals**, a local group that inhabited Europe and the Middle East starting about 130,000 years ago. They had large bodies and brains, and their behavior was remarkably sophisticated. They made new and better tools, named **Mousterian**, which included a variety of implements specialized for particular purposes, with more "finishing" of the tools. Most notably, there is evidence from various sites of intentional burials, suggesting some symbolic abilities and perhaps some "beliefs" about death and after death. Some anatomists conclude that they had the anatomy for speech.

Modern Homo sapiens (Anatomically Modern Humans)

As long ago as 200,000 years, the first fully modern Homo sapiens appeared, probably in Africa. They migrated to the rest of the world, displacing the Neandertals in Europe by 35,000–40,000 years ago. Their tools and culture were not more advanced than those of other species originally, but since 30,000 years ago or so, their – or our – cultural development has been rapid. Soon they were producing realistic paintings, often on cave walls, as well as carving and jewelry and other "arts." New

"composite tools" (made of multiple parts, like an arrow or a spear) distinguished their technology, as well as fast-changing and regionally diverse technologies and cultures. No doubt they had fully functional languages and belief- and meaning-systems comparable to those found in any society today. Students of early modern humans agree that, if one of them could be brought to the present day, he or she would look like and learn to act like a normal modern human.

STUDYING CULTURE: METHOD IN CULTURAL ANTHROPOLOGY

Our presentation of anthropology began by introducing its distinct questions, its distinct perspective, and its distinct set of terms and concepts. But in order to answer its questions, to put that perspective into action, and to employ those terms and concepts, cultural anthropology also needs a method. How exactly do cultural anthropologists go about answering their questions, in particular collecting the data that they require to solve the problems that they have put before themselves? The social sciences have a battery of tried-and-true data-collecting techniques. These include surveys, interviews, questionnaires, experiments, and of course analysis of the data that other social scientists

Neandertal
the species or subspecies of Homo that first appeared around 130,000 years ago and is associated with the cold climate of Europe. They go extinct in the last 35–40,000 years and are generally not regarded as direct human ancestors, although this interpretation is still somewhat controversial

Mousterian
the stone tool technology associated with Neandertals, first appearing less than 130,000 years ago

PLATE 2.4 Hominid fossil skulls (from left to right): Australopithecus afarensis, Homo erectus, Neandertal.

have already collected. Cultural anthropology would be remiss to ignore these techniques. However, none of them, nor all of them in concert, are adequate to accomplish what cultural anthropologists want to accomplish. Imagine, for example, that you wanted to learn about Nuer cattle-herding culture in Africa or the Japanese tea ceremony. What would you do? You would probably first read every available book, watch every available movie, talk to every available researcher and traveler, that/who might provide some information. One vast limitation of this procedure is that you would not learn anything new; there would be no opportunity for original discovery.

Seeking new knowledge, you might design a survey or a questionnaire to probe the issues you want to understand. So now what do you do with it? There being so few Nuer or Japanese nearby, you would have to send it to them by mail or email. You might find that very few receive mail or email, even fewer read it, and fewer still respond. Besides, they may not speak your language, and they definitely do not know who you are or why you are asking these strange and perhaps personal questions. Even if they did receive it and cared to respond, they might find the questions invasive, or they might be inclined to tell you what they think you want to hear or what makes them look good. It is possible you would not ask the right questions to begin with, and it is highly possible that you would not understand the information you received anyhow.

Or, to make the example even closer to home, imagine that a cultural anthropologist wanted to learn about the life of students at a college. The problems are roughly the same. Students at the college might not respond, or perhaps only the "good" ones will respond (giving a skewed sample). Knowing that the researcher plans to publish and share the results, and that the findings may come back to affect them, the students might lie or admit only the positive parts of their behavior. And the anthropologist still might not really understand the results that come back from the subjects. In order to overcome the limitations of these techniques – whether in remote or familiar contexts – a cultural anthropologist has only one real choice: go and live among the subjects.

Anthropology solves this problem with **fieldwork**. All sciences depend on some manner of fieldwork. Geologists go out and dig rocks. Paleontologists go out and excavate fossils. Marine biologists go out and observe ocean life. The thing they have in common is *going out*. Accordingly, anthropologists cannot complete their research in a library or classroom; a person can study *cultural anthropology* in the classroom (that is, what anthropologists have done and learned from it) but not *culture*. Culture is where the practitioners of that culture are.

So anthropologists go to the "field." They could take their surveys and questionnaires with them, recruit a sample of volunteers, and administer the tests to them. The researcher could get closer, perhaps get a house near the subjects and sit on the porch and watch them go by, perhaps even invite them to sit on the porch too. The researcher would see where the people are going and what they are doing, but would that necessarily provide any understanding of what is going on?

Cultural anthropologists have discovered that the only way to acquire a serious, deep understanding of the lives of other people is to place themselves as much as possible within those lives. This is known as **participant observation**. Participant observation is the truly unique and original aspect of cultural anthropology. Anthropologists go to live among the peoples they study, but more than that, they go to live *like* the peoples they study. No other social science does quite the same thing, although some have adopted the method on occasion. The first step in successful anthropological fieldwork is learning the local language. This is critical not only because most of the locals probably will not know the anthropologist's language but because even if they do, their ideas and concepts possibly cannot be properly conveyed in another language. A language, like the cultural whole of which it is part, is a lens for seeing the world. Forcing them to function in the anthropologist's language is forcing them to reshape, perhaps fatally distort, their thinking into something that is familiar to an outsider. For instance, it would be easier for an English-speaking anthropologist to force the local people to interact in English, but there would be something – maybe something critical – "lost in translation." It is much better to learn their words for things, their concepts, and their realities. There are often no exact equivalents for their words and ideas in English or other foreign languages.

Participant observation
the anthropological field method in which we travel to the society we want to study and spend long periods of time there, not only watching but joining in their culture as much as possible

Fieldwork
the anthropological method of traveling to the society one wants to study and living there for a prolonged period of time to collect data first-hand

Learning the language is not only a necessary step but it is a good way to earn one's way into the society and to spend time with them. An anthropologist will eventually want, and if lucky be able, to visit with them, travel with them, work with them, even live with them. They are not coming to the anthropologist's world; the anthropologist is going to theirs. The goal is to eat their food, perform their tasks, participate in their rituals. In this way, cultural anthropology is the most intense and personal of the sciences. No other research takes such a commitment of one's life. An astronomer may spend every night for weeks peering through a telescope, but at least he or she goes home, takes a shower, and sleeps in his or her own bed. Anthropologists may not even have showers or beds where they do their studies. Often there is no going home for a long time. A typical fieldwork experience may take a year or more. And usually, a professional anthropologist goes back to the field periodically to see what new things have transpired, what s/he missed before, or simply what one cannot learn in such a "short time." Some anthropologists take their families with them, but most travel alone. Depending on how far away the society is, the anthropologist may not see friends or family during the entire period. The work can also be physically challenging: climate extremes (most of the world's small-scale societies live today in the most inhospitable environments), natural dangers, strange food, exotic diseases, few amenities, few or no facilities in the event of injury. It can be lonely and isolating.

But if all goes well, the anthropologist slowly wins his/her way into the confidence and friendship of the people. S/he may even be "adopted" into a family, given a kinship name, and assigned local responsibilities. This is not easy to achieve or to perform. Generally the local people do not know the anthropologist when s/he first arrives. It would be like someone coming to your neighborhood, knocking on your door, and asking to live in your house for a year or two. New people are always strangers first, friends later (if they are lucky). And anthropologists depend on that friendship – sometimes to keep them fed, always to keep them informed. An anthropological fieldworker needs at least a few good informants or consultants, people who will take the time and effort to explain their culture. That sounds very scientific, but it is not.

Informants/consultants are the people who like and trust the fieldworker well enough to want to take time from their busy lives to talk to the stranger, answer silly questions, and teach their ways. In an essential way, the informant/consultant is a teacher. Likewise, anthropologists in the field are students, virtually children. Many local people consider anthropologists to be literally like children – petulant, demanding, prone to error (see e.g. Briggs 1970 for an unusually honest account of the foibles of fieldwork). The analogy is not bad: if anthropologists are like children, then anthropological fieldwork is like enculturation. The fieldworker is learning the culture "from the inside."

Once in the field, there is a variety of activities that the researcher can engage in. S/he may still administer his/her surveys and questionnaires. Interviews are a standard technique in the field, either in a **structured** (with the questions prepared in advance) or an **unstructured** (unplanned and free-flowing) format. It is always important to collect genealogical information, not only because anthropologists need to know who is related to whom and how, but because kinship and **genealogy** are so central to the organization of most societies. Commonly anthropologists will collect oral histories, either biographies of individuals or accounts of the history of the group; a well-told life story can shed light on a society far beyond the experiences of that single individual (see e.g. Shostak 1983 for a classic biography of a hunter-gatherer woman). And a few anthropologists, especially in the early twentieth century, carried formal tests (for instance, psychological and "projective" tests, like the Rorschach "ink blot" test) into the field to measure specific cognitive or perceptual tendencies and to compare these to other traditional societies and to their own.

Often enough, even the best-prepared anthropologist will encounter two surprises: (1) the things that s/he came to study are not the really important things and/or (2) s/he does not even know what the right questions are at first. By jumping into the society and its culture, by taking his/her place in its structure, the researcher gets a better idea "on the ground" of what should really be studied. Most fieldwork diverges from its initial plans when it confronts the reality of the new culture, and this is fine: one cannot know what one will find, or what will be important to consider, before arriving in the

Structured interview
a fieldwork method in which the anthropologist administers a prepared set of questions to an informant/consultant

Unstructured interview
a fieldwork method in which the anthropologist conducts a relatively free-flowing conversation with an informant/consultant, either without prepared questions or unconstrained by these questions

Genealogy
kinship or "blood" and "marriage" information about a society

Shostak, Marjorie. 1983 [1981]. *Nisa: The Life and Words of a !Kung Woman.* New York: Vintage Books.

PLATE 2.5 A virtual fieldwork site: doing anthropological research in Second Life.

From Tom Boellstorff, *Coming of Age in Second Life: An Anthropologist Explores the Virtually Human*, 2008, Princeton University Press

THE ETHNOGRAPHER'S MAGIC

field. But if there is one critical fact to remember, it is that anthropological fieldwork is a relationship, and the knowledge an anthropologist takes home is a product of those relationships. S/he will have talked to specific people at specific times in specific contexts, and each anthropologist as an individual brings a certain quality to the experience. Cultural anthropology is science, but it is also a personal encounter between human beings.

The ultimate goal for most anthropologists is what Geertz (1973), following the philosopher Gilbert Ryle, called "thick description." We do not

only want to report the facts from the field but to communicate the quality of life, the systems of meaning and structures of relationships, the "webs of significance," within which real-life people think, feel, and act. This offers one solution to the problem of urban anthropology met in the previous chapter, where it was complained that anthropologists tend to "study in cities" but not to "study cities." Geertz answered that the "locus of study is not the object of study. Anthropologists don't study villages (tribes, towns, neighborhoods. . .); they study *in* villages" (1973: 22). Or rather we might now say

---

BOX 2.6   DOING PARTICIPANT OBSERVATION IN VIRTUAL SOCIETIES

People are spending more of their time than ever before online, interacting with each other in cyberspace and even in virtual communities and "massively multiplayer worlds." Should anthropology study this? *Can* anthropology study this? In his very cleverly named *Coming of Age in Second Life* (playing on the title of a famous book by Margaret Mead, *Coming of Age in Samoa*), Tom Boellstorff proves not only that anthropology can investigate "cybersociality" but how we must investigate it – in fact, that "ethnography has always been a kind of virtual investigation of the human" (2008: 249). His goal is explicitly to "take the methods and theories of anthropology and apply them to a virtual world accessible only through a computer screen" (4). By creating a character or avatar and "living" and even interviewing people within the Second Life world, he does a brilliant job of illustrating how virtual communities are not mere copies of the real world, nor are they autonomous communities detached from the real world. Rather, they are specific if non-physical "places" or contexts within which people interact. They develop their own language (like "afk" for "away from keyboard"), their own conventions, their own relationships and intimacies, even their own political and economic practices and institutions. He concludes "that virtual worlds are distinct domains of human being, deserving of study in their own right" (238) and that anthropology is up to the challenge.

that anthropologists examine the thick lives of humans wherever and however they interact – even if they do not interact in a "place" at all.

Fieldwork in a globalized world: multi-sited ethnography

The classic image of anthropological fieldwork is the solitary researcher sitting in the forest or desert with an isolated "primitive" tribe. This approach may have been, and may still be, appropriate in certain times and places. However, increasingly this sort of "village anthropology" – or what we might call more technically "the intensively focused upon single site" style of observation (Marcus 1995: 96) – is inappropriate and inadequate in many contexts. Local cultures, or subcultures or classes or ethnic groups and so on, are affected by and implicated in wider networks of institutions and relations, including "media, markets, states, industries, universities" (97), from the regional to the national to the global level. In a real sense, not all of the culture that influences the people under investigation, and therefore not everything that the anthropologist wants or needs to know, is "in" the local society. Accordingly, "in response to empirical changes in the world and therefore to transformed locations of cultural production," fieldwork methods have also changed.

The most interesting and important shift is toward "multi-sited ethnography," which literally takes the fieldworker to multiple physical locations in order "to examine the circulation of cultural meanings, objects, and identities in diffuse time-space" (96). For instance, the anthropologist may move from the village to the city to the factory and beyond, even to the national and international levels.

Multi-sited research, Marcus writes, is premised not on enclosed societies and cultures but on "chains, paths, threads, conjunctions, or juxtapositions of locations in which the ethnographer establishes some form of literal, physical presence" (105). The fragmented and mobile quality of such work reflects the fragmented and mobile quality of modern global culture. Instead of becoming rooted in one place, the anthropologist travels through a discontinuous sequence of "positions" or "scapes," guided by a set of imperatives – to follow the people as they migrate and circulate,

the "things" (commodities, money, cultural products like art), the ideas and metaphors and narratives, the lives and life-stories, and the conflicts (106–10). In this practice, fieldwork itself, and the reporting on culture, becomes both local and global, truly glocal.

The ethics of fieldwork

Anthropological fieldwork is a "social" activity in a way that no other science's method is. The fieldworker has injected him/herself into the lives of other people – often people who do not know him/her, want him/her there, or particularly want to help him/her. In an earlier era an anthropologist could often rely on a colonial administrator to order the "natives" to accept and assist a stranger. Those days are for the most part long gone. In many parts of the world, local peoples have acquired at least some modicum of control over their lives, so outsiders cannot just barge in and expect the locals to do their duty as "anthropological subjects" and informants. At the very least, they may ask, "What's in it for us?" and at the very most they may say, "Go away!" I was personally told to get the Warlpiri's permission before entering their community or face the prospect of being marched straight out of town.

Participant observation by definition puts researchers skin to skin, life to life, with "subjects" who are living people. That fact demands a particularly self-conscious code of ethical behavior. At the minimum, this includes "Do no harm." Increasingly it includes "Ask first." At the highest level, it includes "Make a contribution" (perhaps an opportunity and call for more applied anthropology) and "Consider your own impact on them."

In the contemporary context, fieldwork usually commences with some form of permission from the local society; for such purposes, institutions like community governments or the regional associations, like the Aboriginal "Land Councils" in Australia, have been established. By now most well-known traditional societies have been studied repeatedly, and the locals know what anthropologists want and what the arrangement will be like. Some members are warm to the idea, some not. An anthropologist should never expect to make friends with every member of the society, any more than people expect to make friends with every member of their own society. A few friends are worth the world in the field.

In the field, it will be necessary, and desirable, to abide by the society's rules and norms as much as possible. The members of the society usually understand that the foreigner is not one of them; the anthropologist is an outsider, a stranger, a child. Sometimes a fieldworker will arrive with the reputation (often nothing to do with that individual personally) of an oppressor, colonizer, or at least of the last bad anthropologist who passed through. On the other hand, s/he may benefit from a previous positive experience with an anthropologist, as I did in one community: the famous Jane Goodall had been there long before, and they assumed that I knew and worked with her. Accordingly, one evening a man walked me around the settlement, introducing me as the "anthropology man" and friend of Ms. Goodall. At any rate, the local people frequently know that anthropologists come to learn their secrets and publish those secrets for the world to see. They may understand that anthropologists come for their own career advancement. They know that the fieldworker will stay for a while and leave, maybe never to return again. In ways, they know the outside world better than the outside world knows them.

Having obtained permission somehow (the "somehow" will depend on the circumstances of each field experience), it is obligatory to be as honest as possible about why the anthropologist is there. If s/he has come to study religion, the locals should not be told that s/he merely wants to "learn the language" or some other neutral excuse. Some anthropologists have shown their research notes to the local people before leaving or before publishing them, but that is not always possible or politic, especially in the case of sensitive or personal data. But one must always remember that some of them can read English or other world languages and will see what is written about them – in case the writer ever wants to come back again. Also, there is value in showing them these notes and analyses in advance, because they may be able to correct or interpret certain items that have been misunderstood or misinterpreted.

There is no ignoring the fact that much of the world today is a battleground and that many fieldwork settings are tense and dangerous. If an anthropologist wants to do fieldwork among refugees, for example, or in a war zone, or among a "terrorist" or insurrectionist population, life will be more complicated and research will be more sensitive. They may perceive the outsider – rightly or wrongly, intentionally or unintentionally – as a threat, a "security leak," even a spy. I was personally accused by one man of being a spy for the CIA on one occasion (falsely, as it turns out), but their concern is real enough. They never know who foreigners are really sent by, what foreigners will do with the information, or who else might see it.

One way that anthropologists have traditionally handled the problem of "cooperation" is by giving gifts, trading, or paying for information. All

PLATE 2.6 Bronislaw Malinowski conducting fieldwork with Trobriand Islanders.

of these practices have their issues. Giving gifts to some people and not others can create jealousy and hurt feelings, as well as inequalities in the society that may have never existed before. Trading is a good idea but can become expensive and saddle the researcher with lots of stuff that s/he doesn't really want; it can also upset the local economy, as they begin to produce goods for trade rather than consumption. And paying for information can undermine the friendship aspect of fieldwork, although it is sometimes necessary and desirable. Fieldworkers may even want to "hire" an informant, translator, or travel companion.

In the contemporary context, one of the best exchanges for information – while also being a great way to learn – is offering some useful service that the local people need. (Ironically, this can also foster dependence and resentment.) For example, many indigenous societies have been involved in land claims or "development" struggles (for example, over dam projects or mining or similar related issues) for decades, and many anthropologists have helped by researching culture (land tenure, political organization, kinship structure, etc.) and organizing this data for presentation to courts or governments. Along the way, scholars have learned many valuable things about these and other aspects of the culture by being so intimately involved with real-life practical matters. It has been good for the local people and for scholarship. At the same time, it is important that the fieldworker not "go native" and lose him/herself among the locals. This means, among

other things, that visitors should probably not get too intimately involved in their daily lives, especially sexually. Like any professional, one must maintain a certain distance from one's clients or subjects. Often this is hard: one may be inclined to intervene in domestic matters, to introduce one's values, medicines, or other practices. Each situation will be a judgment call, and each person must be his/her own judge. But there are lines that should not be crossed, and a trusty rule of thumb is this: after the anthropologist is gone, the local people still have to live there. We can walk away, but they cannot. Do not leave things worse for them and for the next anthropologist who may visit.

In the end, it is unavoidable that one will have some impact on the society one lives with. These days, the impact may be fairly light, as many major changes have already long since occurred. The introduction of new tools and technologies, new ideas and concepts, new diseases, even the mere awareness that there is a bigger world out there with strange-looking and strange-acting people in it irretrievably changes local peoples. Anthropologists can neither force them to alter their ways of life nor prevent them from doing so, but anthropologists and all other outsiders can never forget the fact that we ourselves are agents of change. The ethical guidelines that have been adopted by the American Anthropological Association are available on their website.

See Chapter 11 and beyond

See Chapters 14 and 15

www.aaanet.org/committees/ethics/ethics.htm

BOX 2.7 CONTEMPORARY CULTURAL CONTROVERSIES: STUDYING KENNEWICK MAN

"Kennewick Man" consists of a skull and a few bones discovered on the banks of the Columbia River in Washington State in 1996, but he touched off a scientific, political, and cultural firestorm. Some anthropologists (Chatters 2002) concluded that the remains were those of an ancient Caucasian – much more ancient than any known in North America. This announcement was met with concern by Native American activists, who saw it as an attempt to debunk their claim to original settlement of the continent. And the local Umatilla society filed a claim to take possession of the bones, since the Native American Graves Protection and Repatriation Act (NAGPRA 1990) allows Indian societies to demand return of their artifacts and physical remains. Scientists insisted it was their right and duty to study the materials and that NAGPRA did not apply since the skeleton was not Native American. The Umatilla and others countered that such treatment was desecration of their ancestors, that science was invasive and disrespectful, and that the political uses of Kennewick Man could be detrimental to their rights. What do you think?

SUMMARY

The questions and the perspectives of anthropology lead almost inevitably to its concepts and methods. Central to cultural anthropology is the idea of culture – that humans are not born knowing and doing all of the things that we see them do. Rather, from the experience of human diversity, anthropologists have determined that culture is

- Learned
- Shared and distributed
- Symbolic
- Integrated
- An adaptation

In the modern global context, it is increasingly clear and important that culture is also produced, practiced, and circulated.

While culture is not "in" the body in any particular way, human physical characteristics make cultural behavior possible – that is, human behavior has a two-part biocultural basis. Therefore, culture is potentially not exclusive to humans. Beings with physical traits similar to humans have behavioral traits similar to humans, and as humans gradually acquired their present traits, their behavior became more recognizably cultural.

Anthropology has developed special methods for collecting the information that it needs to answer its questions. The most fundamental method is participant observation, during which researchers may perform a variety of kinds of activities. Everything that anthropologists do includes some degree of interaction with "subjects" who are real human beings, and fieldworkers must conduct that interaction ethically, aware that they are humans too and that their actions will have impacts on the people in that society.

MCQS

FILL IN THE BLANKS

Key Terms

Acheulian	Genealogy	Oldowan
Australopithecus	Guided reinvention of culture	Participant observation
Biocultural	Hierarchy	Primate
Bipedalism	Hominid	Prosimian
Counterculture	Homo	Socialization
Dominance	Homo erectus	Society
Enculturation	Homo habilis	Structured interview
Erectness	Homo sapiens	Subculture
Fieldwork	Mousterian	Symbol
Functionalism	Neandertal	Unstructured interview

The origins of cultural anthropology

The Persian Empire under Darius encompassed a wide variety of different peoples and cultures, as did all ancient and modern empires. According to a story recounted by the Greek historian Herodotus, Darius once summoned some Greek and some Callatian (Indian) subjects to explain their burial practices. The Greeks said that they cremated their dead, whereas the Callatians reportedly ate theirs. Darius asked the Greeks if they would ever eat their dead, which mortified the Greeks. He then asked the Callatians if they would ever burn their dead, at which suggestion they "uttered a cry of horror and forbade him to mention such a dreadful thing." Herodotus concluded from this and similar experiences:

> if anyone, no matter who, were given the opportunity of choosing from amongst all the nations in the world the set of beliefs which he thought best, he would inevitably, after careful consideration of their relative merits, choose that of his own country. Everyone without exception believes his own native customs, and the religion he was brought up in, to be the best; and that being so, it is unlikely that any-one but a madman would mock at such things.

PLATE 3.1 Herodotus, an ancient Greek observer of human diversity.

. . .One can see by this what custom can do, and Pindar, in my opinion, was right when he called it "king of all."

(Herodotus 1972: 219–20)

No doubt Herodotus was not the first person to notice that humans differ in their beliefs, their behavior, and their bodies across space and time. However remote and "backward" they may seem, no society in the history of humanity has probably been so isolated that they did not have neighbors who varied from them in language, religion, and other customs. Even so, as abundantly obvious as human diversity is, and as attentive to such details as Herodotus was, neither he nor most societies went a step further to organize a systematic study, a science, of human diversity. Herodotus came very close, and his insights seem convincing to this day, but no such thing as anthropology was created in his day or for many days afterward. Finally, in passing, Herodotus was wrong about one thing: given a choice between one's own customs and the customs of some other society, there is usually no "careful consideration of their relative merits." If you were given the choice between burying and eating your dead, would it really require – or even allow – weighing the two options? Rather, our customs are often so deeply ingrained in us that the preference is automatic and strong – like "second nature."

WHAT MAKES CULTURAL ANTHROPOLOGY POSSIBLE – AND NECESSARY

There is a sort of professional joke in anthropology: anthropologists are people who approve of every culture except their own. Of course, that is not true, because approval is a kind of judgment, and our disciplinary relativism discourages both approval and disapproval. However, the joke does raise a question: *why* anthropology? What is anthropology *for*? As the discipline went through its own identity crisis a few decades ago (see below), George Marcus and Michael Fischer offered two answers. "One is the capturing of cultural diversity, mainly among tribal and non-Western peoples. . . . The other is a cultural critique of ourselves, often underplayed in the past, but having today a renewed potential for development" (1986: 20).

Let us begin by noting that anthropology is a very new science and that anthropology is a very unlikely science. The first of these claims is easy enough to understand and defend. Until about 150 years ago, there was nothing quite like modern cultural anthropology in the pantheon of human sciences. Some social and natural sciences, from history and philosophy to mathematics and physics, are ancient. Anthropology is easily the last of the major social sciences to emerge, and what we recognize as contemporary cultural anthropology assumed its form only about a century ago. Why was this discipline so late to appear on the horizon of human inquiry?

The answer relates to the second statement: something about anthropology must be very unlikely. That is, anthropology is an unlikely skill to practice, an unlikely way to think. Philosophy of a familiar kind was being done over 2,000 years ago. By observing the various cities and states and their political forms, something like political science was fairly obvious. By pondering the events occurring before and during one's lifetime, something like history was fairly obvious. By examining the sky and the stars, something like astronomy was fairly obvious, and by watching objects in motion, something like physics was fairly obvious. But despite encountering other human societies, something like anthropology was apparently not obvious at all.

Why did observation of human diversity not lead to a science of human diversity? The best way to think about this is to consider not the observations themselves but the responses to the observations. Human diversity has always been an acknowledged fact, but what humans do with – or about – that fact is another matter entirely. Clearly, anthropology is not the default response. Rather, the default or first response seems to be some combination of:

■ Indifference toward the Other
■ Fear and hostility toward the Other
■ Judgment and condemnation of the Other
■ Desire and/or effort to eradicate the Other, either through conquest or "conversion"
■ Rejection of the Other as less than one's own kind – and sometimes less than completely human

These attitudes are immanent in most of the surviving records we have from past societies, ancient and not so ancient. Other societies were typically regarded as "savages," "barbarians," "infidels," "primitives," "uncivilized," "evil," and so on. To be different was to be bad, to be wrong. This is definitely not a perspective from which cultural anthropology will grow.

As with Herodotus, there were some near-misses in the ancient world. The Greek philosopher Xenophanes observed the differences and the relativity of religion across cultures:

> Ethiopians have gods with snub noses and black hair, Thracians have gods with gray eyes and red hair. . . .If oxen or lions had hands which enabled them to draw and paint pictures as men do, they would portray their gods as having bodies like their own; horses would portray them as horses, and oxen as oxen.
>
> (quoted in Wheelwright 1966: 33)

Ultimately, neither the ancient Greeks nor the Romans ever developed an anthropological science, despite the fact that a school of Greek philosophers, the Sophists, explained social institutions like religion or politics as products of human convention rather than aspects of nature. Nevertheless, the reigning opinion was that of Socrates and Plato, that society was an outcome of absolute Ideals and divinely given virtues. And Roman imperial interests, while they led to a considerable curiosity about foreigners (Julius Caesar wrote a tract about the Gauls against whom he warred), did not really permit the sort of holism and relativism that characterize anthropology. Yet at moments the ancients demonstrated serious anthropological potential.

Medieval Europe, as well as most other religious and cultural traditions, did no better. In fact, during the "dark ages" dominated by Christianity, social life was once again seen as divinely given, and diversity was discouraged or condemned (e.g. as heresy): "For the Middle Ages only the 'Christian man' – an expression still familiar from Luther – was really a man in the full sense of the word" (Landmann 1974: 31). Our predecessors thus evince the two recurring obstacles to the very possibility of something like cultural anthropology:

■ Absolute certainty in the truth and goodness of one's own culture (ethnocentrism).

■ Lack of information about other societies, or poor or patently false information about them.

Certainty in one's own truth and goodness, a kind of "one-possibility thinking," is characteristic of most societies, traditional or modern. Cultural certainty is a barrier to relativism and thus to cultural anthropology, since only one kind of thought is permitted or at least valued highly; all others are by definition false or unacceptable. Why then would you want to know more about those barbarians, those infidels, those blasphemers?

Lack of information or possession of poor information poses its own challenge. If you do not know much about another society and culture, it will be difficult to say anything meaningful and useful about it, and you will naturally try to assimilate the Other into your own schemes of understanding. This led to some amusing if not depressing results. For example, even the most hard-headed medieval Europeans could not ignore the fact of anomalous archaeological features in their own territories. Saxo Grammaticus, writing in the twelfth century about the enormous stone edifices of Denmark, opined that "the country of Denmark was once cultivated and worked by giants. . . . Should any man question that this is accomplished by superhuman force, let him look up at the tops of certain mountains and say, if he knows how, what man hath carried such immense boulders up to their crests" (quoted in Slotkin 1965: 6). Into the sixteenth century men of good conscience still struggled with the signs of otherness in their midst; of the Paleolithic and Neolithic artifacts scattered around Europe, Ulisse Aldrovandi said that "they were natural accretions developed by geological processes," while Conrad Gesner guessed "that they were thunderbolts. Stone projectiles were usually called 'elf arrows' or 'thunderbolts' by laymen" (quoted in Slotkin 1965: 44). In yet other cases, unexplainable but obviously non-Christian phenomena were either ignored or dismissed as demonic. Much more recently, the devoutly Muslim Taliban destroyed the enormous Buddhist statues at Bamiyan rather than allow those idols to corrupt Afghanistan.

Now, attribution of stoneworks and artifacts to giants and elves might inspire a science of giants and elves, but it is not likely to launch a science of human diversity. In fact, it *cannot* do so, since no connection is drawn between those objects and humans; rather, such opinions led observers *away from* humanity and from a science like cultural anthropology. Humans do what we do; giants and

Slotkin, J. S., ed. 1965. *Readings in Early Anthropology*. London: Methuen & Co. Ltd.

THE EXPERIENCE OF DIVERSITY IN THE ANCIENT WORLD

BOX 3.1   THE "MONSTROUS RACES" OF THE PRE-MODERN WORLD

PLATE 3.2 A Blemmyae, one of the "monstrous races" of ancient and medieval literature.

From the Greeks through the Romans to the medieval Europeans, travelers and scholars spoke and wrote about various pseudo-human if not non-human races such as

- Amazons, warlike women who amputate their right breast so as to better draw a bow
- Amyctyrae, beings with such large lower lips that they can use them for umbrellas
- Androgini, who have the sex organs of both men and women
- Antipodes, beings who walk upside down
- Astomi, people who have no mouths and are covered with fur. They survive by smelling food.
- Blemmyae, creatures who have no heads but have faces in their chests
- Bragmanni, who stand all day in fire staring at the sun
- Cyclopes, beings with one large eye
- Cynocephali, people with dog-heads
- Panotii, beings with ears that dangle down to their feet
- Sciopods, people with a single huge leg and foot, who lie on their backs and shade themselves with their foot
- And the usual panoply of pygmies, giants, hairy men and women, and cannibals.

More amazing still, writers described them as if they were real, as if the reporters had seen them for themselves, even producing maps illustrating where each monstrous race dwelt – Astomi in east India, Blemmyae in Libya, Bragmanni in India, Cyclopes in Sicily and India, etc. A full accounting would show that these races tended to inhabit the East (India), the North (the Baltic and Arctic regions), and the South (Africa) – everywhere that was remote and exotic to Europeans except the West, where no people lived since the world was believed to end there (see e.g. Friedman 2000).

elves – non-humans – do those odd and remarkable (or terrible) things. And if that is not bad enough, the reports of "monstrous races" that persisted from ancient times right up to the late Middle Ages in Europe were the tombstones of a stillborn anthropology.

ENCOUNTERING THE OTHER

As colorful as such descriptions are, it should be apparent that such a state of knowledge is not conducive to a serious discipline like cultural anthropology. First, if these beings are as weird and unpleasant as they sound, no one will be inclined to study them. Second, if they are not human at all, there is little light they could shed on humanity. Third and most dramatically, fear and revulsion will tend to keep people far away from them.

At some point this all had to change if anthropology was ever to emerge. So the question for us is, what is it that makes a science like anthropology possible? And more than just possible but *necessary*? What kind of society can, and must, enter upon a line of inquiry that will end with the birth of anthropology – and not specifically professional anthropology so much as the anthropological perspective described previously? It must be a society that has lost or at least shaken its own cultural certainty as well as one that has accumulated a body of accurate and useful information about the Other. This will inevitably depend on and follow from a new and sustained kind of encounter with the Other. That is, someone does not say, "Let's invent anthropology" and then start to seek out different forms of humans. Instead, one first bumps into different forms of humans and then, gradually and grudgingly, comes to a point where s/he is doing anthropology.

The time and place where these conditions began to coalesce was Europe *c.* 1500, where and when a series of separate yet interrelated developments began to force on observers not just an awareness but a curiosity, even an appreciation, of otherness. Among these new experiences were the following.

The "voyages of discovery" and the rise of colonization

The most famous and prominent new factor in late medieval Europe was the "discovery" of new lands and new peoples in places where lands and people were not known or even imagined. Europeans had long ago met other societies – Muslim, African, Asian – but the encounter with Native Americans and the vastly greater number of African, Asian, and eventually Australian peoples encountered by European travelers opened their eyes to a diversity that was previously undreamed of. But, as exciting (and profitable) as all this discovery was, it presented a psychological and cultural challenge. Who were these people? How did they get all the way out there? In fact, were they people at all? As incomprehensible as that question sounds to us, to early explorers it made sense and required an answer, since the Christian Bible did not mention these natives. Were they descendants of Adam and Eve, like the Western Christians and supposedly all humans? If so, why did they look and act so differently? But if they were not descendants of Adam and Eve, then what were they? Animals? Degraded humans? Creations of Satan? Or just as bad, creations of some other god?

The question of the humanity of the "Indians" was quite a serious one. Within decades of Columbus' arrival in America, there was an actual debate within the Catholic Church about the identity of the natives. Were they human or not? What this meant was, did they have souls or not? The "conservative" position was that they did not have souls and therefore were not human; if this were the case, then they could be classified and treated as animals (also believed to have no souls) – chased off, carried away, enslaved, or killed as suited the conquerors. The "liberal" position, championed by Bartolomé de las Casas, was that they did have souls and therefore were human. If this were the case, then they deserved "humane" and "Christian" treatment – they could not be killed or enslaved wantonly. But neither could they be left alone; their human souls required "saving," and they deserved and needed the benefits of the "true" culture and the "true" religion. The Church finally decided in 1537 that the Indians were humans and ordered that they be dealt with in a humane way, but this did not stop the ravages and abuses to which they were

See Chapter 2

See Chapters 12 and beyond

subjected by administrators, missionaries, soldiers, traders, and settlers.

The explorations of the late 1400s and early 1500s, which continued into the late 1800s, brought new otherness to the attention of Europeans, who were well satisfied with the truth and goodness of their own society. This was the kind of otherness that is "out there," far away and intellectually manageable, but still an ideological and religious problem. And the sheer volume of it – hundreds and hundreds of new societies with their own languages, religions, and complete cultures – was daunting but thought-provoking.

Encounters with other Eurasian civilizations

"Primitive" societies were a problem of sorts but the kind of problem that visitors could ignore or excuse most of the time. Other "advanced" societies were a bigger problem. Since at least the 1300s, European adventurers had been traveling to and bringing back reports from distant civilizations like China,

the Islamic world, and India. Marco Polo is a well-known example, whose descriptions of splendor in China were at first taken as fiction. Even earlier, the Crusades (in the twelfth and thirteenth centuries) had gotten Europeans far from home and into exotic new places where they saw the wonders of Constantinople, Syria, and Mesopotamia. They could not help but notice that these societies were not only different but in some inescapable ways superior to their own. The Eastern civilizations were often more urban, more literate, richer, more "cultured," and more powerful than anything in Europe. This should not be: Europe supposedly had the "true" religion and culture. The foreigners were idolaters, infidels, devil-worshippers. Yet they had things that Europeans valued and desired and would acquire and utilize – not the least of which were block printing and gunpowder.

So, the experience of these travels and conflicts showed not only that other civilizations existed and were different but that they were "better" in some ways. Otherness could not be laughed away as inferiority; there were things the Other did better and things the newcomers needed to learn from them.

PLATE 3.3 The Renaissance introduced new interests in ancient culture, visual perspective, and humanism.

The "Renaissance"

The so-called Renaissance of the fifteenth and sixteenth centuries refers to a "rebirth." What was coming "back to life," and what had been dead or moribund for centuries in Europe was city life, literacy, long-distance trade, and the widespread exchange of ideas that marks the modern world and marked the ancient Mediterranean world. After the fall of Rome, cities had declined and disappeared, literacy had retreated to the monasteries (or at least books had – often monks could not read them but copied them by rote), and a subsistence level of agriculture tying serfs to the land and to the lords who owned the land ossified culture and stultified diversity. What little art and literature existed was made for and about the dominant class, culture, and religion.

The Renaissance was thus a rebirth of ancient Greece and Rome culture, as seen through the lens of late-medieval or early-modern Europe, which had always maintained a vague dream of Rome but knew little about it. Ancient texts had long been lost, and the ability to read what remained suffered as well. Meanwhile, the Islamic world had preserved the works of Plato and Aristotle and others, studied them, advanced them, and incorporated them into their civilization. With the Crusades and the subsequent (ambivalent) trade relations with Islam, Europe rediscovered its ancient texts and began to familiarize itself with its own ancestry. Of course, the assumption had always been that, while the Greeks and Romans could not possibly be Christians, they were in some way "pre-Christians" or "proto-Christians." They simply presumed that the ancients were a lot like them.

However, the reality was very different – and disturbing. Greeks and Romans had their own distinct and non-Christian religions. They had their own political systems, kinship systems, economies, and so on. Reading ancient texts was not like reading texts from one's own time; the ancients lived in a very different mental and cultural world. Many of the ideas and styles were very appealing, but they were most definitely foreign and other. But this meant that Europe's own ancestors, their own forebears, exhibited otherness. It was one thing to face the Other across the ocean; Europeans could disregard or belittle that difference. It was worse to face the Other in a rival civilization; they could not be ignored, but they could be resisted. But it was deeply troubling to face the Other in one's own ancestry, in one's own family tree. Early-modern Europeans found that own ancestors were Other to them.

The "Protestant Reformation"

Since the establishment of Christianity as the official religion of Rome and then of post-Roman Europe, there had been only one official truth about religion, which was the Roman Catholic truth. All other opinions about religion were "heresy," from the Greek word *hairesis* meaning "to choose." One did not choose one's own views and truths but received them from authority. Of course, there had always been disagreements about those truths, but those disagreements were always settled by and in favor of authority. So, reform had been repeatedly attempted and thwarted over the centuries, but Martin Luther's movement escaped that fate. It caught on, much to the consternation of authorities. Luther claimed (often in the most shocking language) that the Church was wrong about many of its beliefs and was actually anti-Christian. He called the Pope and all Catholics blasphemers and atheists. And he said he could prove it: just go back to the "source," to the Bible itself. To assist, he produced a German translation of the Bible.

The Protestant Reformation introduced a schism into Christian Europe that would not go away, no matter how hard anyone tried. And they tried hard. Religious wars tore Europe apart for years, until a peace was declared, allowing the two "religions" to coexist. Note that the peace did not allow all religions to exist, only Catholicism and Lutheranism. Other "protestant" sects like Unitarians, Shakers, Quakers, Anabaptists, as well as non-Christian religions like Judaism, were still out of bounds. But two religions are much more than twice as many as one: one is monopoly, two (or more) is diversity. When the compromise broke down, resulting in the Thirty Years War (1618–48) and millions of deaths, a new peace recognized *three* religions – Catholicism, Lutheranism, and Calvinism. Europe was never again to be a homogeneous, one-possibility place. Religious diversity was here to stay, despite everyone's best efforts. No one had wanted multiple religions; the Catholic Church wanted just one (Catholicism) while Luther wanted just one (Lutheranism). Instead, what they got was not two, not three, but hundreds and hundreds. Westerners were now, and would forever be, the Other to each other.

The scientific revolution

The so-called scientific revolution drew its inspiration from many of the same sources as the above and had many of the same consequences. Like Luther, people were taking it upon themselves to "go to the source" and verify the claims and beliefs of the time. In this case, the source is the natural world. Science did not say then, and does not say now, that all authorities are wrong. It merely says (a) that you must cross-examine authority or tradition, that you cannot accept a position simply because it comes from an authority or tradition (in other words, you must be skeptical, no matter what the source of the claim); and (b) that you must base your conclusions on careful and sustained observations of external reality. This can mean experimentation, or it can mean merely the collection of empirical data from the natural world.

While the intent was not and is not to challenge and undermine all received opinion and tradition, the consequence was and is to stop taking mere authority as an authority. They have been wrong before, and they could be wrong again. The ultimate authority is one's own experience and observation:

if traditions or rulers say one thing but experience suggests another, then a person should trust experience. So, if tradition says there are dog-headed people out there but observation reveals none, we should conclude that there are not dog-headed people.

RETHINKING SOCIETY: SEVENTEENTH- AND EIGHTEENTH-CENTURY SOCIAL THEORY

By the middle and end of the seventeenth century, European scholarship and society were in ferment. The old certainty, while not vanquished, had been shaken and cracked. It was no longer possible for Europeans to delude themselves that theirs was the only society in the world nor even the best society in the world. It was perfectly obvious that their own society was full of problems – crime, vice, inequality, injustice, hunger, poverty, war, and other undesirable conditions. Criticizing one's own society became an increasingly common thing to do, although often in indirect and fictional ways, like the so-called "utopian" literature (see Box 3.2 below). One necessary prerequisite of any social criticism, let alone any social change, is an alternative. If not this, then what? Is it possible for society to be better? Is it even possible for society to be different? And where would a model for another possibility come from?

BOX 3.2   UTOPIAS IN THE FOUNDING OF THE ANTHROPOLOGICAL IMAGINATION

While professional anthropologists travel to "other" places to observe diversity, humans have also traveled in their minds to "no place" – the literal meaning of *utopia* – to envision alternatives and to criticize their own culture and era. Sometimes, as when kinds or churches were very strong, veiled fictional criticism was the only acceptable kind. But as Lewis Mumford wrote, "Nowhere may be an imaginary country, but News from Nowhere is real news" (1962: 24). The first utopia in recorded history was Plato's Republic, with a well thought-out political system and culture, including what form of music and poetry citizens should be exposed to. But the early modern era was the great age of utopian literature, often presented as if reports of real voyages. Sir Thomas More's 1516 *Utopia* gave the genre its name; fully titled *On the Best State of a Republic and the New Island of Utopia*, it claimed to refer to an actual place called Utopia – and to describe a better society than More's own. Many other writers offered their images of an ideal society, including Johannes Valentinus Andreae's 1619 *Christianopolis*, Francis Bacon's 1624 *New Atlantis*, and Jonathan Swift's 1726 *Travels into Several Remote Nations of the World, in Four Parts, by Lemuel Gulliver.* Again, such writings were often a parody of the author's contemporary society, and they were clearly inspired by the real explorations of the time. The second great era of utopian writing was the nineteenth and twentieth centuries, which produced Samuel Butler's 1872 *Erewhon* (roughly a reversal of the word "nowhere"), Edward Bellamy's socialist (and futuristic) 1888 *Looking Backward*, and Jules Verne's 1863 *Paris in the Twentieth Century*. More recently, utopias have sometimes given way to dystopias – bad places – like Aldous Huxley's 1932 *Brave New World* or George Orwell's 1948 *1984*. Contemporary science fiction performs many of the same functions as this utopian literature, allowing writers to explore futures just beyond the present horizon and to play with alternatives to or extensions of present-day society.

PLATE 3.4 Utopian literature was an important precursor to modern anthropology.

A model appeared in the seventeenth and eighteenth centuries: all those "primitive societies" that had just been "discovered." Actually, two views or models of the primitives eventually emerged based on those same experiences – the "brutish savage" and the "**noble savage**." The former model is represented by the political philosopher Thomas Hobbes. A pivotal moment in European history arrived when one of those "Protestant" sects, the Puritans, staged a revolt against King Charles I that led to his 1649 execution. No contemporary European society had ever attempted such a radical social experiment, and many thought it could not succeed, including Hobbes, who argued for the need for a strong central government like the old monarchy. To prove his point, he employed primitive societies as his example of a world without government. In his famous 1651 *Leviathan* he characterized primitives as living "in a state of nature" without society or government, which might sound like a good thing: everyone was equal, but they were also solitary. Humans did not interact with other humans, not peacefully at any rate.

Because all were equal, and totally independent from each other, competition and conflict naturally followed.

Hobbes never set foot in a "primitive society," and his judgments of them are at best based on second-hand accounts if not pure fantasy. His opinion was clearly negative: probably the most quoted phrase in his entire work describes the quality of primitive life as "solitary, poor, nasty, brutish, and short." Whether it is true or false (and it is mostly false), it is important for taking non-Western societies seriously. Hobbes had established that those remote and exotic societies are not irrelevant, not mere objects of curiosity and derision, but important windows onto the human condition – perhaps into the past of our own condition. This was not anthropology just yet, but it was a real (if troubled) step in that direction.

The "noble savage" model is most closely associated with Jean Jacques Rousseau, author of *The Social Contract* in 1762. In certain ways, he compared "savages" favorably to his own countrymen and institutions, finding in them the very

Noble savage

the notion, often associated with Rousseau, that non-Western or "primitive" people are actually happier and more virtuous than Westerners. Based on the idea that humans are free and equal in "a state of nature" but that social institutions deprive them of that freedom and equality

BOX 3.3   BRUTISH SAVAGE VERSUS NOBLE SAVAGE

In *Leviathan* Hobbes wrote:

> From this equality of ability arises equality of hope of attaining of our ends. And therefore if any two people desire the same thing, which nevertheless they cannot both enjoy, they become enemies; and. . .endeavor to destroy or subdue one another.
>
> Hereby it is manifest, that during the time men live without a common power to keep them all in awe, they are in that condition which is called war; and such a war, as is for every man, against every man.
>
> In such a condition, there is no place for industry; because the fruit thereof is uncertain; and consequently no cultivating of the earth; no navigation, nor use of the comfortable buildings; no instruments of moving, and removing, such things as require much force; no knowledge of the face of the earth; no account of time; no arts; no literature; no society; and which is worst of all, continual fear, and danger of violent death; and the life of man solitary, poor, nasty, brutish, and short.

In *The Social Contract* Rousseau wrote:

> Although, in this state [civil society], he deprives himself of some advantages which he got from nature, he gains in return others so great, his faculties are so stimulated and developed, his ideas so extended, his feelings so ennobled, and his whole soul so uplifted, that, did not the abuses of this new condition often degrade him below that which he left, he would be bound to bless continually the happy moment which took him from it for ever, and, instead of a stupid and unimaginative animal, made him an intelligent being and a man.

archetype of free and natural humanity. He too saw them as living in a "state of nature," independent and equal, enjoying "the peacefulness of their passions, and their ignorance of vice." He contrasted their "natural existence," distinguished by instinct, amorality, appetite, natural liberty, and individual strength, to his own "civil society," with its formal justice, morality, reason, civil liberty, and public will.

Of course, Rousseau's image of primitive society is as simplistic and stereotyped as Hobbes'; there is no such thing as "natural man," since all humans are cultured and none live in a state of raw nature, and there is no such thing as "savage society" but a rather a staggering variety of traditional cultures – from the happy to the miserable, from the peaceful to the warlike. And also, he was by no means recommending a return to the primitive state but merely pointing out the two possible states of humanity and the costs of evolving from one to the other.

Rousseau was clearly not doing anthropology – we would never call our subjects "stupid and unimaginative" – but his perspective was different from anything we have seen before. Rousseau and Hobbes and others like them took the Other seriously, declaring them a worthy – even a necessary – subject of study and discussion. And Rousseau's view, while not much more realistic than Hobbes', was definitely more positive: not only were there things to learn about distant societies, there were actually things to learn *from* them. Contemporary Westerners could admire them and wish that Western culture was, in some ways, more like them.

TOWARD AN ETHNOLOGICAL SCIENCE IN THE NINETEENTH CENTURY

Approaching the nineteenth century, we do not find anything yet that is quite recognizable as modern anthropology. We do, however, begin to see the foundations on which such a science will rise. First, the cultural certainty of Europe has been challenged, though not destroyed. In fact, the nine-teenth century was a particularly ethnocentric period, partly a cause and partly an effect of the new phase of industrial colonialism and the relations between (white) Europe and the (non-white) colonies. But even that was a mixed blessing for what would become anthropology, since this prolonged contact between the two worlds pro-vided the second ground for the new science – more and higher-quality observational information about non-European societies. It is no coincidence that a discipline like anthropology – or "ethnology," the study of culture or ways of life – would develop at this moment, in relation to colonial administration, which provided the access to other societies and the practical utility of knowledge about them.

Out of the wealth of new information came a desire if not need to classify it and arrange it in some sensible order, and thus to "explain" it. Writing years later Evans-Pritchard defined ethnology as the project "to classify peoples on the basis of their social and cultural characteristics and then to explain their distribution at the present time, or in past times, by the movement and mixture of peo-ples and the diffusion of cultures" (1951: 4). The questions asked by early ethnologists, then, were largely *historical and geographical*: how are cultures related to each other (and to Western culture), where did these relations come from, and what was the ultimate source from which they all flowed? In other words, how did Culture as a whole or partic-ular cultures or specific institutions and practices within cultures originate, and how did those things change over time into their various manifestations, including the "modern" Western one?

Two similar but different answers emerged. One was **diffusionism**, the idea that Culture (with a capital "C") had originated once or at most a few times and then spread from that center or those centers of origin outward to other locations on the globe. This approach was expressed in the German *Kulturkreis* ("culture circle") school of thought that envisioned culture as one or more circles emanating out from their center(s) like ripples on a pond. The greater the proximity between societies in space, the greater the similarity in culture. The center was iden-tified sometimes as Egypt, sometimes elsewhere, but the idea of following the ripples "backward" in space suggested the possibility of following them back-ward in time as well – back to the first culture.

The other approach, especially after the middle of the nineteenth century, was **evolutionism**. In this view, the observed cultures descended from one or more "ancestral" cultures, passing through various stages or phases of cultural development along the way. Whether there was a single (unilinear) series of cultures or several independent (multilinear) series was an open question. Either way, cultures had a "history" which could and should be reconstructed. The goal was to arrive at a set of cultural types or stages that would describe the actual process by which cultures evolved from one state to another – something like a timeline with different cultural types attached to certain moments in time.

However, how would nineteenth-century ethnologists go about this research? It was impos-sible to board a time machine and return to selected moments to observe the culture. All that was available was the present. Fortunately for cultural researchers, they thought they saw all around themselves "survivals," traces, virtual living fossils of those earlier days still in existence – namely, "primitive societies." Since they could not study time, they could study space and project it onto time, that is, convert geography into chronology. By taking the various primitive peoples of the world today as representatives of, if not actual frozen specimens of, days gone by, they could rebuild the history of culture.

Different ethnologists arrived at different solu-tions to the problem at hand, but all of the solutions shared a few features. For one, they arranged the observable societies "in order" of evolutionary progress. The "simplest" or "most primitive" natu-rally filled the "lower" and earlier spots; Australian Aboriginals were a common candidate for that honor, as Emile Durkheim concluded in *The Elementary Forms of the Religious Life* (1915). What, he asked, was the first kind of religion, or what is the most minimal, elementary form? It is the Aboriginals, who have totems and rituals but no gods or institutionalized practices and offices like modern European/Christian ones. Ethnologists would disagree on the precise order of stages and the precise choice of representative for each stage, but the general idea was fairly standard. Thus, Lewis Henry Morgan (1877) boiled the stages of cultural evolution down to three – savagery, barbarism (each subdivided into lower, middle, and upper), and

Evolutionism
see cultural evolutionism

See Chapters 12 and 13

Diffusionism
the early ethnological or anthropological position or theory that Culture, or specific cultural practices, objects, or institutions had appeared once or at most a few times and spread out from their original center

VOLKERPSYCHOLOGIE: A PRECURSOR AND SOURCE OF MODERN ANTHROPOLOGY

Durkheim, Emile. 1965 [1915]. *The Elementary Forms of the Religious Life.* New York: The Free Press.

Morgan, Lewis Henry. 1877. *Ancient Society, or Researches in the Lines of Human Progress from Savagery, through Barbarism to Civilization.* New York: Henry Holt and Company.

BOX 3.4 THE INSTITUTIONALIZATION OF ANTHROPOLOGY IN THE NINETEENTH CENTURY

Present-day anthropologists tend to remember their science appearing in the early 1900s (see below), but of course no discipline or way of thinking forms out of nowhere. In the mid-1800s the word "anthropology" was already in use, and as far back as 1839 there was a *Société Ethnologique de Paris* operating in France. The horrors of colonialism led to the founding the Aborigines' Protection Society in 1837 as an early "human rights" organization, followed by the more scholarly Ethnological Society of London in 1843. The Anthropological Institute was established in England in 1871, the same year as Tylor's *Primitive Culture*, and Tylor went on to write the first textbook in anthropology, simply called *Anthropology*, in 1881. The journal *American Anthropologist* made its debut in 1888. However, there were two major differences between this first institutionalization of anthropology and what anthropologists do in the twenty-first century, both well illustrated by considering the "guidebook" for anthropology known as *Notes and Queries*, originally published in 1874. For one, nineteenth-century scholars were much more focused on physical/anatomical questions; indeed, the first section of *Notes and Queries* was dedicated to "anthropography" or the measurement of the body, which included such topics as measuring instruments, the skeleton, physiological factors like respiration and odor and the senses, and medical questions like diet, pathology, surgery, diseases, and insanity. "Ethnography" received secondary attention and was considered to be less easily accessible; Christopher Pinney (2011) goes so far as to argue that "culture" was not the main interest of early anthropology, which preferred to examine the body. Even in the case of "culture," scholars preferred "hard evidence" over the dubious verbal accounts that natives gave; hence, a favorite tool of research was the newly invented camera, which produced photographs, or what one author in *Notes and Queries* called "facts about which there can be no question." Second, the tradition of fieldwork and participant observation had not yet developed, so anthropological research still very much depended on what has been called "the man on the spot," who might have been an explorer, trader, missionary, soldier, or government official. Much valuable material was collected by such people: missionaries were especially valuable for studying language, and explorers like Mungo Park or Henry Morton Stanley traveled and published long before professional anthropologists did. Remarkably, *Notes and Queries* acknowledges this fact and actually tries to exploit it: as the preface to the first edition suggests, "those who are not anthropologists themselves" are able "to supply the information which is wanted for the scientific study of anthropology at home" (Garson and Read 1899: vii). *Notes and Queries* then constitutes a list of questions that "travelers" can ask to ensure that their information is complete and standardized.

See Chapter 6

PHOTOGRAPHY IN THE EARLY HISTORY OF ANTHROPOLOGY

civilization – characterized by certain diagnostic cultural features (e.g., bow and arrow, farming, writing). "Progress" was based on technological achievement (the threshold from savagery to barbarism was the invention of pottery, for instance), a standard which was important to Westerners and in which Westerners excelled. And of course, "civilization" was his own society – nineteenth-century Euro-American culture.

THE TWENTIETH CENTURY AND THE FOUNDING OF MODERN ANTHROPOLOGY

By the turn of the twentieth century, a few observers were despairing of the ethnological, diffusionist/evolutionist, and amateur approach to anthropology. Two men in particular would turn from it vehemently and put their stamps on the new science of cultural anthropology. They are Franz Boas and Bronislaw Malinowski.

Boas (1858–1942) is widely regarded as the father of modern cultural anthropology. Trained

PLATE 3.5 Franz Boas, one of the founders of modern anthropology, posing for a museum exhibit around 1895.

originally in Germany in the late 1800s as a physicist and geographer, he brought a keen observer's eye and a strict scientist's method to the new science he shaped. In the 1880s he came to the Arctic coast of North America to study the color of sea water. While working there, he inevitably became acquainted with the local Inuit (Eskimo) people; soon, he realized that they were even more interesting than sea water, and not at all "primitive." He soon turned his back on the nineteenth-century "comparative" model as inaccurate and ethnocentric; as a scientist, he knew that to judge or evaluate your subject is to not observe or understand it adequately. By this decision, he essentially invented cultural relativism.

One of Boas' first and most important statements about what would become anthropology was his 1896 paper "The Limitations of the Comparative Method of Anthropology," first published in the journal *Science*. In this classic essay, still read in anthropology, he proposed that there are no "higher" or "lower" cultures and that all such judgments are merely relative to one's own standards of culture. Thus, any "ranking" of cultures is suspect from the outset and probably says more about the student than about the cultures studied. He went on to state that the similarities or differences between cultures are not as significant as diffusionists and evolutionists think, because widely separated cultures can arrive at similar adaptations due to environmental factors. Rather than ordering cultures on the basis of supposed progress or similarity, he recommended actually observing each single culture in maximal detail and each single part of a culture within the context of the whole. Thus, he gave voice to holism. He emphasized that the goal of this science should not be the construction of elaborate and speculative cultural histories but rather the careful and accurate description of individual cultures through intense and objective observation. This observation would require personal, close-up experience with the culture for prolonged periods of time. When he settled into his academic position in America, he became the teacher and mentor of the first generation of American anthropologists. Thus, he essentially invented American anthropology.

Bronislaw Malinowski (1884–1942) did his work slightly later than Boas but has probably had an equally profound influence on the discipline, if only because Boas was so resistant to the idea of making any theories of culture. Boas in particular insisted that the data required to make good theories was still lacking, so any proposed theory would be premature. It would be better to collect data now – do the "science" now – and make theories later. But of course a science, even in its infancy, cannot proceed without theory. Theory helps to identify the question, suggest the method, and organize the evidence. Accordingly, Malinowski proposed a theory that would become extremely influential in the first half of the twentieth century.

Malinowski got his start in anthropology by accident like Boas. Originally trained in mathematics and physics in Poland, he turned to the science of humanity after reading James George Frazer's ethnological classic *The Golden Bough* in 1910. *The Golden Bough* has affected many readers since it appeared in 1890 and is perhaps the "gold standard" of the nineteenth-century comparative project. Frazer took examples of myth and religion from all around the world and juxtaposed them in a fascinating but decontextualized way; on any one page, he could alternate from Mexico to Madagascar to India to Greece and back again. However, the cultural setting or context of each of these references was not developed and could never be developed by this procedure and in the space allotted to it.

Malinowski's exposure to the comparative and evolutionary method came at a time when a few scholars had begun to call for more in-depth knowledge and description of particular societies. Boas had helped inspire this approach, and by the turn of the century expeditions were setting out intentionally to collect cultural data – a team from Cambridge to the Torres Straits in 1898–99, another to India in 1901–2, still another to Melanesia in 1907–8. The future anthropological star, A. R. Radcliffe-Brown, made such a trip to the Andaman Islands in 1906–8. However, most of these visits were extremely short (often only a few days), were conducted by people who were not specially trained in anthropological field methods (since such methods did not really exist yet), and necessarily involved working through interpreters and acculturated local people.

However, by this time some scholars like W. H. R. Rivers were beginning to recognize the need for and to call for more "intensive" research, which he defined as research

> in which the worker lives for a year or more among a community of perhaps four or five hundred people and studies every detail of their life and culture; in which he comes to know every member of the community personally; in which he is not content with generalized information, but studies every feature of life and custom in concrete detail and by means of the vernacular language. It is only by such work that one can realize the immense extent of the knowledge which is now awaiting the inquirer, even in places where the culture has already suffered much change. It is only by such work that it is possible to discover the incomplete and even misleading character of much of the vast mass of survey work which forms the existing material of anthropology.
> (quoted in Kuper 1983: 7)

Malinowski was one of the main figures to accept the challenge thrown down by the likes of Boas and Rivers. Malinowski started his fieldwork career at age thirty with six months in New Guinea. He

returned to the Trobriand Islands for two more years of work in 1915–16 and 1917–18. In so doing, he helped establish the modern fieldwork methods of cultural anthropology.

He determined that there were three general types of cultural data, each requiring its own collection technique. The first was the description and analysis of institutions, which were to be studied by thorough documentation of concrete evidence. More precisely, this meant the creation of charts of activities and customs associated with a particular institution, based on accounts given by the natives as well as on observations by the investigator. This method would yield a literal visible representation of the "mental chart" that members of the society possess. The second type of data, constituting another dimension of cultural reality, were the minutiae of everyday life, which filled out and deepened (if complicated) the analysis of general institutions. As he noted, the emphasis on rules and structures and institutions left an impression of more precision and consistency than is actually seen in real life. So, abstract or generalized presentations of social structures had to be complemented with particular and personal instantiations or uses of those rules and structures in the details of everyday life, anticipating the distinction between "structure" and "action" that anthropologists like Raymond Firth would elaborate. The third type of data included cultural content like narratives, utterances, folklore and other conventional sayings and activities. The immediate result of his methods was his epic ethnography *Argonauts of the Western Pacific* (1922), in which he modeled what a sensitive and informed fieldworker could do with the data he collected.

The other profound influence of Malinowski on the fledgling field of anthropology was his theoretical approach, which was significantly connected to his method. Like Boas, he rejected **cultural evolutionism** and speculative historical reconstructions. As he wrote: "I still believe in evolution, I am still interested in origins, in the process of development, only I see more and more clearly that answers to any evolutionary questions must lead directly to the empirical study of the facts and institutions, the past development of which we wish to reconstruct" (quoted in Kuper 1983: 9). Thus, anthropologists should study the present with all possible attention and clarity before they indulge in

---

Cultural evolutionism
the early ethnological or anthropological position or theory that Culture started at some moment in the past and evolved from its "primitive" beginnings through a series of stages to achieve its "higher" or more modern form

Malinowski, Bronislaw. 1984 [1922]. *Argonauts of the Western Pacific*. Long Grove, IL: Waveland Press, Inc.

Kuper, Adam. 1983. *Anthropology and Anthropologists: The Modern British School*, revised edition. London and New York: Routledge.

speculations about the past. What a fieldworker sees today is institutions, the individuals acting within them, and standard "narratives" or "scripts" which those individuals produce and reproduce in the process. These investigators can hunt for – and perhaps only for – the *function* of institutions and practices today, in the present. Hence, he recommended an approach known as functionalism. Rather than pursue its history (a potentially vain pursuit), the anthropologist can observe its function here and now. What is the function, for example, of marriage, or political systems, or religion?

For Malinowski, the essence of function was to be found in the needs of the individuals who compose a society. Society, he asserted, is ultimately a collection of individual human beings. So, culture "functions" according to the needs and nature of those individuals, who have two kinds of needs – physical and psychological. Each item of culture, or culture as a whole, must serve to fill one or more of these needs. It is the job of the ethnographer to determine what needs it fills and how.

Functionalism became a reigning idea during the early twentieth century and not only in anthropology (Durkheim had already elaborated it in sociology). However, others began to turn the idea in new directions, if not turn against it altogether. Radcliffe-Brown argued that culture does in fact function but not in the way that Malinowski imagined. Radcliffe-Brown maintained, rather, that individuals are relatively trivial; what is important – and enduring – is society itself, the community, the social whole. In opposition to Malinowski's functionalism, he advocated a "social" or "structural" functionalism, the social function of institutions defined by him as "the contribution that they make to the formation and maintenance of a social order" (1965: 154). Radcliffe-Brown's focus on institutions versus individuals and on order versus action was hugely influential on the British tradition of social anthropology, which came to emphasize law, kinship systems, and such. Social order or social structure was not a mere idea, an abstraction in the mind of the anthropologist, in this view but a real and concrete thing. He went so far as to assert that society can be studied, but culture cannot: "You cannot have a science of culture. You can study culture only as a characteristic of a social system. . . .If you study culture, you are always studying the acts of behavior of a specific set of

persons who are linked together in a social structure" (quoted in Kuper 1983: 55).

THE ANTHROPOLOGICAL CRISIS OF THE MID-TWENTIETH CENTURY AND BEYOND

Just as approaching maturity often entails a life crisis and a rebellion against convention in individuals, so cultural anthropology suffered a disciplinary crisis and rebellion in the mid-twentieth century that was perhaps a sign of maturation and a breakthrough to a deeper level of understanding – and self-understanding. The sources of this crisis and the call to "rethink" or "reinvent" anthropology probably included the aging and passing of the founding generation, as happens in all disciplines. However, even more important was the change in the subjects of cultural anthropology themselves, the "primitive peoples" and small traditional societies, which forced a change in the science that purported to study them. Not the least of these changes was the rush of independence movements that ended the centuries-old European project of colonialism and empire. Finally, perhaps a critical point had been reached which compelled anthropology to look at itself in new and sometimes uncomfortable ways – not only at what it was doing but even at the very tools and concepts it was using to do it.

One of the first and most important moves in this "new anthropology" was the announcement by Edmund Leach that societies are not always as discrete and traditional as we think they are. In his seminal *Political Systems of Highland Burma* (1954) he described a situation in which societies overlapped each other without clear and permanent boundaries and in which the very politics and culture of the multicultural system fluctuated over time. Given the realities of highland Burmese social relations, he concluded that "ordinary ethnographic conventions. . .are hopelessly inappropriate" (281). In fact, he went so far as to argue that the entire notion of discrete societies was an "academic fiction": "the ethnographer has often only managed to discern the existence of 'a tribe' because he took it as axiomatic that this kind of cultural entity must exist" (291). At almost the same moment J. S. Furnivall published his study of Burma and

See Chapter 13

Leach, Edmund R. 1954. *Political Systems of Highland Burma*. Boston, MA: Beacon Press.

Neo-evolutionism

the mid-twentieth-century
revival of focus on the
historical development of
cultures and societies, as in
the work of Leslie White
and Julian Steward, which
generally sought to repair
the failings of nineteenth-
century evolutionism by
proposing specific processes
and a "multi-linear" path of
change

Structuralism

the theory (associated most
closely with Claude Lévi-
Strauss) that the
significance of an item
(word, role, practice, belief)
is not so much in the
particular item but in its
relationship to others. In
other words, the "structure"
of multiple items and the
location of any one in
relation to others is most
important

Wagner, Roy. 1975. *The
Invention of Culture*.
Englewood Cliffs, NJ:
Prentice-Hall, Inc.
Hobsbawm, Eric and
Terence Ranger, eds.
1983. *The Invention of
Tradition*. Cambridge:
Cambridge University
Press.
Hymes, Dell, ed. 1972
[1969]. *Reinventing
Anthropology*. New York:
Random House, Inc.

Indonesia entitled *Colonial Policy and Practice* (1956) in which he introduced the concept of "plural society" to describe the mixed yet segregated social realities in those locations. Burma and Java were not homogeneous societies at all but a jumble of "separate racial sections" which "mix but do not combine" (304), linked (and stratified) by sheer economic interests.

One of the other conventions of early anthropology – the peacefulness and stability of traditional societies – was upset by ongoing researches in Africa. Meyer Fortes and E. E. Evans-Pritchard had already discovered that various supposed tribes "appear to be an amalgam of different peoples, each aware of its unique origin and history" (1940: 9) and not always on easy terms with each other. Max Gluckman even more decisively burst the fiction of simple integration of societies in his aptly named *Custom and Conflict in Africa*, which found that not only are societies not as integrated and harmonious as thought but that conflict could actually be the social structure of the society: by way of the contours and variations within a society, "men quarrel in terms of certain of their customary allegiances, but are restrained from violence through other conflicting allegiances which are also enjoined on them by custom" (1956: 2). The simple view of primitive order was forever dashed.

These reports from the field heralded an identity crisis within anthropology that was expressed in such subsequent titles as *The Invention of Culture* (Wagner 1975), *The Invention of Tradition* (Hobsbawm and Ranger 1983), *The Invention of Primitive Society* (Kuper 1988), and first and perhaps most dramatically *Reinventing Anthropology* (Hymes 1972). These books and others like them shone the spotlight directly on cultural anthropology itself, identifying clearly anthropology's own "culture" and how its methods, concepts, and assumptions had influenced its findings and conclusions. Anthropology would subsequently become more self-reflective as it discovered that it was at least in a sense not only science but also literature – that is, a tradition of writing – as in James Clifford and George Marcus (1986) *Writing Culture: The Poetics and Politics of Ethnography*.

Along the way, cultural anthropology split into more schools and theoretical camps than ever, as some practitioners returned to the roots of the discipline to reform them while others took

inspiration from fields and advances outside anthropology. Among these elaborations of anthropology are:

Neo-evolutionism

Leslie White (1949, 1959a, 1959b) and Julian Steward (1950, 1953) are considered the most prominent thinkers to reintroduce a more sophisticated version of cultural evolution. White suggested a principle behind the evolutionary progress of societies, namely the amount and kind of energy it could harness and exploit. As societies developed newer and greater sources of energy (from domesticated animals to electricity and nuclear power), not only their economic but also their other social characteristics would change in correspondence. Steward contributed the notion of "multilinear" evolution to combat the impression that all societies evolved in the same manner or that all societies were part of some grand Cultural evolution. In this view, each particular culture pursued its own developmental course, and societies at similar points in their evolution (perhaps due to their similar environments) would exhibit similar cultures.

Structuralism

Instead of looking back into the heritage of anthropology, Claude Lévi-Strauss looked across at the developing discipline of linguistics for a new approach to vexing problems like kinship and religion (e.g. the analysis of myth). Drawing on the work of Ferdinand de Saussure in particular, Lévi-Strauss took the notion of culture as a language seriously: language has "bits" or elements (sounds, words, and so on) in structural relationships with each other (that is, "grammar"). The grammatical relations between linguistic elements determine their meaning more than the individual elements themselves. Therefore, he proposed that we might approach anthropological problems in the same way. Rather than looking for the "meaning" of some cultural element – totemism, mother-in-law avoidance, a particular theme in a myth – in the thing itself, he proposed that we look for it in the relations between the elements. In other words, if a society has the crocodile for a totem animal, the meaning of that totem is not be found in the properties of the crocodile but in the system of relationships between the various totem-animals and, more importantly, the system of relationships between the social groupings associated with those species.

Ethnoscience

Combining two interests of American anthropology in particular – personality or cognition and classi-fication – **ethnoscience**, also known as cognitive anthropology, sought to examine and expose the mental classification systems that shaped local people's experiences and actions. As formulated by Goodenough (1956), Frake (1962), and Tyler (1969) among others, ethnoscience aimed to be more scientific while also pursuing the psycho-logical side of culture, which had always been a focus in American cultural anthropology. The point was to bring to light the intellectual models of reality that humans have in their heads (often if not usually implicitly) that organize their world in specific ways. Thus, the scientific anthropologist would reconstruct the "folk taxonomy" or the "knowledge structure" of a society, which was the

skeleton and structure of its entire meaning and action system.

Symbolic/interpretive anthropology

In some ways moving in the opposite direction and in other ways very comparable, **symbolic anthropology** also sought to get access to the deeper meanings of other societies, but it tended to do this through "symbols" rather than through taxonomies. Influenced heavily by the philosophies of Suzanne Langer (1942) and Ernst Cassirer (1954) who saw all human thought and action as mediated by symbols, the meanings of which could not always be described rationally, anthropologists like Victor Turner (1967, 1981), Clifford Geertz (1973) and Sherry Ortner (1973) attempted to identify the "key symbols" that functioned as lenses through which people perceived their worlds. This was at least in part a reaction against Lévi-Straussian structural-ism, which posited a single mental structure for all human beings and stripped away all of the par-ticulars and context from anthropological analysis. Geertz coined the phrase "thick description" for the practice of trying to penetrate to the deep meanings of people's realities and to present that meaning in

Symbolic anthropology
the school of thought (often associated with Clifford Geertz and Victor Turner) that the main goal of anthropology is to elucidate the meanings within which humans live and behave. Rather than focusing on institutions and rules, it focuses on symbols and how symbols shape our experience and are manipulated by people in social situations

Turner, Victor W. 1967. *The Forest of Symbols: Aspects of Ndembu Ritual.* Ithaca, NY and London: Cornell University Press.

Ethnoscience
the anthropological theory or approach that investigates the native classification systems of societies to discover the concepts, terms, and categories by which they understand their world

PLATE 3.6 Claude Lévi-Strauss integrated anthropology, psychology, and linguistics in his work.

Marxist/critical anthropology
the theory, based on the work of Karl Marx, that emphasizes the material and economic forces that underlie society, relying on notions of power and inequality, modes of production, and class relations and conflicts

Feminist anthropology
the anthropological theory or approach that focuses on how gender relations are constructed in society and how those relations subsequently shape the society. Also examines how gender concepts have affected the science of anthropology itself – the questions it asks and the issues it emphasizes

Rosaldo, Michelle and Louise Lamphere, eds. 1974. *Women, Culture, and Society*. Stanford, CA: Stanford University Press.

See Chapter 7

Reiter, Rayna, ed. 1975. *Toward an Anthropology of Women*. New York: Monthly Review Press.

World anthropologies
the perspective that anthropology as developed and practiced in the West is not the only form of anthropology, and that other societies may develop and practice other types of anthropology based on their specific experiences and interests

Harris, Marvin. 1974. *Cows, Pigs, Wars, and Witches: The Riddles of Culture*. New York: Random House.

Cultural materialism
the theory that practical/material/economic factors can explain some or all cultural phenomena

all of its richness and complexity. Anthropological analysis and description thus became an interpretive or "hermeneutic" exercise, aiming to "read" a culture and to render its symbols and meanings understandable to us without washing out all of the uniqueness and particularity of the society in question.

Marxist/critical anthropology

In the second half of the twentieth century especially, Marxist or "critical" theory exerted a strong pull on cultural anthropology. In the works of Maurice Bloch (1983), Maurice Godelier (1978), and many others, there was a new concern for issues of economics, class, power, and domination. Working from the Marxian claim that the culture of a society is the culture of the dominant class of that society, they looked for practical and material relationships that shaped the ideologies and institutions of any social group. A key concept was "mode of production," the means and relationships of the production of goods and wealth, which led to and shaped the "relations of production," that is, the actual social relationships between individuals and groups like ownership and property relations, kinship and gender relations, and so on. This perspective emphasized and actively looked for competitive or conflictual relations in society in a way that early anthropology did not and perhaps could not, with its perspective of integration and homogeneity. While it claimed to be scientific and practical, it also tended to be abstract and "theoretical" (even inventing a new word for practice – "praxis") and often openly partisan and critical of existing values and institutions.

Cultural materialism

Championed especially by Marvin Harris in popular writings like *Cows, Pigs, Wars, and Witches* (1974) and technical books like *The Rise of Anthropological Theory* (1968) and *Cultural Materialism: The Struggle for a Science of Culture* (1979), this perspective extended the ecological views of White and Steward as well as the Marxist view, basing cultural behaviors firmly on "the practical problems of earthly existence" posed by the encounter between "womb

and belly" on the one hand and the material world of food, climate, and competition for territory or offspring on the other (Harris 1979). Like ethnoscience it aimed at a more scientific anthropology, exposing the "causes" of human action.

Feminist anthropology

A feminist approach to anthropology also appeared in the 1970s as a reaction to male-centered perceptions of the field and its literature ("man the hunter" type approaches and so on). Happily, from early in its history women have played a prominent role in cultural anthropology (as evidenced by Margaret Mead, Ruth Benedict, and Cora Du Bois, to name a few), but a literature on women and their activities across cultures had been lacking, partly because many cultures have sex-segregated knowledge which male anthropologists could not access. Michelle Rosaldo and Louise Lamphere (1974) and Rayna Reiter (1975) were two of the early founders of the movement to explore gender relationships, gender inequalities, and the participation of women in cultures where that participation had been overlooked or minimized. **Feminist anthropology** does not focus exclusively on women but rather on gender diversity and gender issues broadly conceived.

Finally, one of the most exciting and promising new directions is the emergence of a **world anthropologies** perspective, the recognition that, just as there are many diverse cultures in the world, there are many diverse ways to do anthropology. The fact is, as the editors of the recent volume entitled *World Anthropologies* explain, the existence and practices of various local anthropologies, especially in the non-Western world, means that "the idea of a single or general anthropology is called into question" (Robeiro and Escobar 2006: 1). Indeed, anthropology as it has been traditionally known and done has, it turns out, been distinctly Western, and world anthropologies promises to expand anthropology while "provincializing Europe" – not denying or denigrating the Western perspective but showing conclusively that Western thought, and with it anthropological thought as it has so far existed, "are particular and historically located, not universal as is generally assumed" (3–4). Happily, organizations like the World Council of Anthropological

BOX 3.5 CONTEMPORARY CULTURAL CONTROVERSIES: THE FUTURE OF ANTHROPOLOGY

Anthropology has changed and will continue to change, as the world in which it lives and works changes. Some wonder and even worry about the future of the discipline: what is anthropology today, and what will it be tomorrow? Will it survive at all? Surely the intent of anthropology as Marcus and Fischer saw it is still valid, if not more urgent than ever: "to offer worthwhile and interesting critiques of our own society; to enlighten us about other human possibilities, engendering awareness that we are merely one pattern among many; to make accessible the normally unexamined assumptions by which we operate and through which we encounter members of other cultures" (1986: ix). But, perhaps reflecting the world around it, anthropology today is fragmented and fluid: "the current absence of paradigmatic authority is registered by the fact that there are presently many anthropologies" (16) with no single driving or unifying question or theory. Further, other disciplines have adopted or invaded some of anthropology's traditional field, including sociology, ethnic studies, and "cultural studies." The future of anthropology is uncertain but potentially very exciting. What do you think?

Associations, the World Anthropologies Network, and International Union of Anthropological and Ethnological Sciences represent anthropologists from Africa, Latin America, Europe, North America, and Asia, to embody and advance just such a global prospect.

www.wcaanet.org
www.ram-wan.net
www.glocol.osaka-u.ac.jp/iuaes

SUMMARY

Anthropology is a new science and an unlikely science, and it is new because it is unlikely. If people had thought to do anthropology – that is, the study of human diversity – as easily as they thought to do history or algebra, then they would have done it long before. The two main barriers to an "anthropological perspective" were always, and continue to be

- Certainty in one's own correctness and goodness
- No information or poor information about others

Western civilization like all others suffered from these two limitations, although there had always been a somewhat dissatisfied and self-critical tendency in it. However, a series of experiences around the early 1500s forever shattered that certainty while providing a new quantity and quality of experience of the Other. These included

- Voyages of discovery to new lands
- Encounters with other "advanced" civilizations
- The Renaissance
- The Protestant Reformation

While European societies first struggled with and tried to assimilate these new cultures, they also began to use them for purposes of their own imagination – in particular, to imagine alternatives (whether positive or negative) to their own contemporary social and cultural realities. Hobbes and Rousseau were two of the first to do so, with diametrically opposed results. Even so, the first steps toward taking other cultures seriously were taken.

MCQS

FILL IN THE BLANKS

Early "anthropological" thinkers typically came from a historical and "progressivist" direction, interested in the origins of culture (or Culture) and the stepwise "progress" of culture from "primitive" to "modern." However, the first modern anthropologists, like Franz Boas and Bronislaw Malinowski, rejected this approach and adopted a more empirical, relativistic, holistic, and humanistic stance. The main thing was to collect good data and use that data to understand cultures as we found them – not as they (allegedly) once were or as we would like them to be. Since those early days, anthropology has altered as its subjects have altered, referring back to its origins, looking for models from other fields, and studying itself with the same tools and the same intensity as it studies other cultures. Anthropology will continue to grow and change for these same reasons. What the anthropology of the future will look like is as hard to predict as – and will depend critically upon – the cultures of the future.

Key Terms

Cultural evolutionism

Cultural materialism

Diffusionism

Ethnoscience

Feminist anthropology

Marxist/critical anthropology

Neo-evolutionism

Noble savage

Structuralism

Symbolic anthropology

World anthropologies

Language and social relations

4

Among the Berti, as for most Islamic societies and probably all societies, words are important. Converted to Islam only since the mid-seventeenth century, the farming and animal-herding Berti have absorbed the Muslim emphasis on the written and spoken word, particularly the words inscribed in the Qur'an. The act of chanting the Qur'an "is seen as a worthy religious practice which protects the whole village" (Holy 1991: 23), and a special role, the *faki*, is charged with learning, preserving, and performing this verbal and literate knowledge. A *faki* is a person who can recite the Qur'an, even if he cannot "discuss or explain it" (25). For the Berti, the role of the *faki* is "knowing which verses have the power to cure certain diseases, which bring about rain, repel locusts, etc."; that is, religious speech is not so much knowledge as power. And other forms of language confer power too: a *faki* collects all kinds of information – "astrology, divination, dreams, and other 'secrets' as well as hand-written notes about anything he learns." Such words are of course powerful when spoken, but they are also powerful in written form. This is why a *faki* will make an amulet (*hijab*) containing a verse from the Qur'an or a list of divine qualities on a piece of paper, which can protect the wearer from

sorcery, illness, or injury and attract wealth, customers, or lovers. Most remarkably, a Berti *faki* will also write scriptural verses on a slate and then wash the words off with water and have a client drink the fluid (*mihai*). For Berti Muslims, the Qur'an "is considered to have an immense power which guarantees the well-being of those who have internalized it" (33) – through their ears (by listening), through their eyes (by reading), or through their mouth (by drinking).

One of the most conspicuous areas of difference between human groups is their language. Sometimes language difference has been taken as the defining feature of a distinct society, although not always: two or more societies can speak the same language (e.g. the U.K. and the United States), and one society can speak two or more languages (e.g. Flemish and Walloon in Belgium). The overt qualities of language – the specific sounds, words, and grammars of each – are easy to observe and clearly fall within the prerogative of anthropology. In fact, language is such a vast subject that anthropology has developed a specialized subdiscipline to investigate it, namely, linguistic anthropology. However, linguistic anthropology is interested in more than the sounds and grammar of

PLATE 4.1 Linguistic anthropologists began collecting language in the field in the late 1800s.

languages. It is also concerned with what kinds of variations and choices exist within a language, how people use those variations and choices to convey social information and to express and maintain social relations, and how the concepts and values in a language shape the experience of its speakers. That is, linguistic anthropology finds that language is not merely a communication system but a kind of social action with real (at least as perceived by the society) effects and consequences.

HUMAN LANGUAGE AS A COMMUNICATION SYSTEM

Humans are hardly the only species to communicate. All species, even plants, communicate in various ways, in the sense of transmitting and receiving "information," for example by exchanging chemical markers. Bees are famous for their "dance" that communicates the distance and direction to flowers. Humans are not even the only species that communicates "orally." Cats, dogs, and birds, and of course monkeys and apes, make sounds that carry meaning for others of their kind. In the laboratory we have discovered that the primates most closely related to us are the most like us linguistically; they cannot speak, but they can understand speech and can communicate through linguistic media like hand signals, shapes and objects, and buttons and

keyboards. That non-human primates have some linguistic ability is no surprise, given their physical and behavioral similarity to us.

Most of what we consider human language is performed in the medium of speech, but not all of it. People who are completely without speech ability can communicate linguistically, as with American Sign Language. Beyond that, all humans communicate non-verbally all the time, using hand gestures, facial expressions, body postures, and so on. Regardless of the medium, however, language has a set of distinct characteristics, referred to as "design features" (Hockett 1958; 1977). Among these features are

- rapid fading – the communication lasts only a brief time (except for writing)
- interchangeability – individuals can be both senders and receivers of messages
- feedback – language users can monitor their own messages and correct errors in them
- semanticity – the elements of language have "meaning" or reference to the world
- arbitrariness – the connection between a linguistic signal and its "meaning" is not "natural" or "given"
- discreteness – language is composed of small, separate, and reusable "bits"
- **displacement** – language can refer to things that are not "present" in time or space

Displacement

the linguistic feature that allows for communication about things that are "not here" in the sense of absent or out of view, past or future, conceptual or even imaginary

- productivity – language users can make and understand new messages using old familiar "bits"
- reflexiveness – language users can employ language to communicate about language
- prevarication – language use can be false, deceptive, or meaningless
- learnability – users of one language can learn another language
- cultural transmission – the rules or conventions of language are the property of a social group and are acquired or learned by interacting with that group.

Clearly then, language is profoundly connected to culture. The human abilities or skills or tendencies that make culture possible also make language possible. In fact, many of the features of language on Hockett's list are also features of culture in general.

Language first of all consists of symbols; it depends on the capacity to engage in symbolism, to think symbolically. Language is a set of acts or gestures – largely but not essentially verbal – that "mean something." Many things "mean something": when a dog barks, it means something to the dog, to other dogs, and to us. When dark clouds appear on the horizon, it means something (that it might rain, for example). But no one would call the dog barking, or the clouds appearing, symbolic. The difference between such signs and real symbols is that symbols are *conventional* and *arbitrary* vehicles for their meanings. There is no necessary or "natural" relationship between a symbol and its meaning. We could use any sound or hand gesture or facial expression or picture, etc. to represent any meaning, as long as we all agree to use it and understand its use. There are of course certain words in any language that sound like the thing they mean, such as the word "boom" for an explosion or the child's word "choo-choo" for a train, but these are a special class of words called onomatopoeia and are not typical of human language.

All languages contain a relatively small number of basic units (sounds) that can be combined in various ways to produce a theoretically unlimited number of meanings or utterances. This is what Hockett called the quality of **productivity**: sounds are arranged into words which are arranged into sentences which are arranged into statements or speech-acts. And while the sounds are finite and conventional, we can say infinite and original things with them. Still more remarkably, humans can talk about things that are "not here" in a variety of senses. For example, humans can talk about things that are not immediately in front of us – behind us or in another room or on the other side of the planet. We can also talk about things that do not exist in the present at all, that is, the past and the future. Humans can talk about things that are blocked from view, invisible, or even completely abstract or general – things like ideas or concepts or relationships, like "justice" or "same/different." We can even talk about things that are purely imaginary or fictional: we can talk about dragons and leprechauns and elves and Hamlet or Harry Potter just as easily and surely as about dogs and cats and clouds. In fact, in a certain important way, it does not really matter whether these things are real or not; if people think they are real and act as if they are real, then those things have real social consequences.

The point is that human language ultimately and crucially exploits some unique human cognitive or mental abilities. Humans could not produce symbols unless they were cognitively "free" to make meaning. Similarly, our kind of language would be impossible without the human talents of creativity, imagination, and even fantasy. In language, as in culture in general, humans invent their own worlds and live in them. Humans *can* create their own cognitive, "meaningful," world, and they *must* create it.

See Chapter 2

THE STRUCTURE OF LANGUAGE

Any particular language has a finite set of elements and a set of rules for combining those elements into larger and more complex units. The speaker of the language must learn and master these elements and rules, achieving linguistic **competence**, the ability to make intelligible utterances. To learn a language – and for anthropology to study the cultural phenomenon of language – we must start with the smallest bits and build up higher and more complex linguistic behavior out of these lower-order units. Language thus proceeds from sound to meaning to utterance and finally to practical use.

Competence
in language, the mastery of the elements (sounds, semantics, and grammar) of a language to be able to make intelligible utterances

Productivity
the capacity of language to combine meaningless sounds to create new words or to combine words to create new utterances

Phonology

Phonology
the study of how sounds are used in a language (specifically which sounds occur and the practices for how they combine and interact)

The most basic bits in any human language are its sounds, and **phonology** (from the root *phone* for sound) is the study of how those sounds are combined and used in language (*phonetics* is usually understood to refer to the processes of the physical production and sensory reception of sounds). More specifically, phonology is the study of which sounds are used in a language and how those sounds are used to generate words. We are not talking yet about meaning; we are still at the pre-meaningful stage of language.

Humans can make very many different sounds, but no language employs all of them. Any particular language contains some sounds and not others; it uses sounds that other languages do not and uses them in ways that other languages do not. Linguists call the smallest bit of conventionalized sound in a language a **phoneme**. English contains *th* and *f* and *sh* sounds or phonemes that do not occur universally, and some speakers of other languages have difficulty distinguishing or making such sounds. French for example does not contain the *th* sound, which is often replaced with a *z* sound, rendering the word "the" as "ze." Japanese speakers struggle with the *r* and *l* sounds in English. Other languages use sounds that are foreign to English. The !Kung or Ju/hoansi in Africa's Kalahari Desert use a set of click sounds in their words that English speakers can make but would never include as parts of English words. (Even the names for their society include sounds that are not part of any possible English word and for which English has no alphabetic symbol, which is why we use punctuation symbols to represent them.) The total number of sounds available in a language can vary widely: Warlpiri (Australian Aboriginal) has only three vowel sounds – "ah," "ee," and "oo" – while Nuer (African) reportedly has fourteen vowels, each with at least three "lengths," two degrees of "breathiness," and three "tones," producing over 200 possible combinations (Needham 1972: 18). When a person pronounces the words of one language with the phonology of another, it is known as "speaking with an accent."

The production of speech sounds is of course a physical skill or action, literally bodily movement. For instance, Tagalog, the predominant local language of the Philippines, requires speakers to manipulate their vocal tracts in ways unfamiliar to English speakers:

> The Tagalog /L/ differs from the English /L/ in that in the formation of the former the tongue is relatively straight and flat from the tip to the root, whereas in the corresponding English sound it forms a deep hollow in the middle with the air coming out of one or more sides of the hollow. When pronouncing any Tagalog word with /L/, with final /L/ particularly, the English speaker must be careful not to lower the middle part of the tongue. The English /L/ is very noticeable and its pronunciation in Tagalog words brands the speaker as definitely non-Tagalog.
>
> (Philippine Center for Language Study 1965: 175–76)

Phoneme
the smallest bit of contrastive sound in a language, that is, the minimal sound-unit that serves to distinguish between word-meanings in a language

This is one reason why speaking a foreign language often feels strange and difficult.

The second issue is how those sounds are used in combination. There are often rules, for instance, for which sounds may occur together or where in a word a sound may occur. English allows for clusters of consonants, as in the word "straight," with its initial string of three consonants, [s], [t], and [r]. Abbreviating "consonant" with C and "vowel" with V, linguists would represent the sound-structure of the word "straight" as CCCVC. Not every language can do this, and some do not do it at all. English also allows many other variations, such as CVC ("sat"), CV ("so"), VC ("is"), VCV ("away"), V ("a"), and even CCCVCCC ("squirts"), some of which are difficult or nearly impossible for other language-speakers to master. Languages like Tahitian and Hawaiian only allow CV or V syllables, that is, every consonant must be followed by a vowel, and a vowel can occur alone.

There are also linguistic norms governing where in a syllable or word a sound can occur. The sound /ng/ (as in "sing" and rendered by linguists as ŋ) exists in English but has specific (if implicit) rules for its use: it may come at the end of a word (like "sing") or in the middle of a word (like "singer") but never at the beginning of a word. Any word that started with the sound ŋ would be immediately recognizable as a non-English word. Warlpiri, on the other hand, uses the ŋ phoneme as an initial sound in many words, such as *ngapa* (water), *ngarni* (to eat), *ngaka* (after), and

THE INTERNATIONAL PHONETIC ALPHABET (revised to 2005)

CONSONANTS (PULMONIC)   © 2005 IPA

Where symbols appear in pairs, the one to the right represents a voiced consonant. Shaded areas denote articulations judged impossible.

PLATE 4.2 International phonetic chart.

Morphology

the area of language dealing with how meaningful bits (usually but not exclusively words) are created and manipulated by the combination of language sounds

Semantics

the study of meaning in language. See *morphology*

Morpheme

the smallest bit of meaningful sound in a language, usually a word but also a prefix or suffix or other meaning-conveying sound that can be used in conjunction with a word

Free morpheme

a morpheme that has meaning in its own right, that can stand alone as a meaningful sound (for the most part, a word)

Bound morpheme

a morpheme that has meaning but only when used in conjunction with a word (such as the suffix –s to indicate plural)

ngarlarrimi (to laugh). Most English-speakers, while they can make the sound, cannot pronounce these words easily; the initial ŋ is just too unfamiliar. Conversely, the Shoshone (Native American) language contains several consonant sounds (including but not limited to [ch], [f], [j], [k], [p], [sh], [t], and [z]) that cannot be used as initial sounds.

The appearance of a sound in a syllable or word may affect its surrounding sounds. Turkish contains eight vowels, classified as "front" or "back" depending on where the tongue is positioned to make them. Then, any particular word can include front vowels or back vowels but not both; of course, suffixes added to words must agree with the vowel-type and thus come in two different forms. In French, on the other hand, rules of *liaison* and *elision* link one syllable or word with another: *ils ont* ("they have") is pronounced "eel zon" ("on" being pronounced nasally, not as in English), somewhat similar to the English tendency to run sounds together ("the mall" sometimes sounds like "them all"). The French *je* ("I") and *ai* ("have") are spoken as *j'ai*, while *de* ("of") and *les* ("the"-plural) are combined as *des*.

Morphology or semantics

Upon the foundation of orderly sound, speakers build a set of meanings, depending on the structural relations between these sounds; the form or shape of the combination of (meaningless) sounds carries us to meaning. Therefore, linguists call the study of the "meaningful bits" of language **morphology** (from the root *morph* for form or shape) or **semantics**.

Just as phonemes are the smallest bits of useable sound in a language, **morphemes** are the smallest possible bits of meaning. Words constitute a class of morphemes called **free morphemes** – that is, morphemes that can stand on their own to convey meaning. "Dog" is a free morpheme, since it is independently meaningful. There is another class, however, called **bound morphemes** which convey meaning but only in combination with another morpheme. In English, these usually take the form of prefixes and suffixes. The morpheme -*s* "means" plural, just as the morpheme *un*-"means" not, when used in conjunction with a free morpheme and in the right orientation. For instance, if an English speaker simply said "-s," others would not know

what it meant. But if the speaker attached the sound to "dog" and said "dogs," other speakers would understand perfectly. In the wrong order ("sdog" or "happyun") they would find the words erroneous, unclear, or nonsensical.

Not all languages function the same way morphologically. In English there is only one semantic plural form, which means "two or more" (although there are two phonetic forms, [-s] and [-z], depending on what sound precedes it, e.g. [dog][-z] but [cat][-s]). However, Warlpiri has two plural forms, neither of which use -*s*. To say "two dogs" in Warlpiri the suffix -*jarra* is added to the word for dog, *maliki*; this means exactly two dogs. To say "three or more dogs" the suffix -*patu* is used. German tends to use -*en* as the suffix to indicate plural (*Frau* for "woman" becomes *Frauen* for "women"). Languages with "gender" like French and Spanish and German add another wrinkle: for instance, French words tend to attach an *e* at the end of feminine words, which is not pronounced but changes the pronunciation of the syllable before it. Thus, *chien* (male dog) becomes *chienne* (female dog), changing the nasal -*ien* of the first word into a more familiar n sound for English speakers.

Many languages apply stress or emphasis to certain parts of words, either typically or to alter their semantic form. English is a stress-language, with every word given its unique emphasis pattern, producing a kind of "rhythm" in speech which can be exploited in poetry (known technically as "meter"). There is no consistent rule on how English stress operates, but one frequent pattern is emphasizing the final vowel (by stressing or "lengthening") in verbs but other vowels in nouns or adjectives; thus "to elaborate" or "to articulate" stresses the final [a] sound, while "elaborate" or "articulate" as adjectives shorten it. Old Irish, by comparison, always stresses the first syllable of nouns and adjectives, with stress on the second syllable for some adverbs. In Tagalog, sound stress has more profound morphological consequences, changing the word's meaning completely: for instance, *gabi* with emphasis on the second syllable refers to a particular starchy root but with emphasis on the second syllable means "night."

Other languages do not use stress/emphasis but rather "tone" to convey meaning, that is, the meaning of the word depends on the pitch or change of pitch in which it is spoken. Instead of rhythm this

BOX 4.1 SEMANTIC RANGE

The semantic characteristics extend – and differ – far beyond the simple construction of words. If words were merely "names" for "things," then the morphology of language would be relatively trivial. However, words vary across languages in terms of their **semantic range**, that is, the "area" of meaning that they cover, the variety of "things" to which they refer, or the constellation of meanings that they embrace. For comparison, the English word "to be" covers a wide range of meanings, which are divided in Spanish between two words, *ser* and *estar*. While there is no easy way to distinguish the two Spanish words, roughly *ser* refers to intrinsic qualities (what something "really" is) and *estar* refers to conditional qualities (what something currently or situationally is). Old Irish provides three forms of "to be," depending on whether the state of being is inherent and intrinsic, a temporary condition, or a regular condition. Warlpiri, in contrast, has no word for "to be." Obviously, when you translate from English to Spanish or Old Irish, you must choose the *correct* "to be." Semantic range becomes an even more complex problem when we realize that words in one language often have no precise equivalent in another; this problem is especially acute when talking about religion, since many languages and cultures have no such word or concept as "god" or "sin" or "hell," etc.

Semantic range
the set of meanings conveyed by a particular word, that is, the "range" of its referents or the variety of phenomena or conceptions that it names

See Chapter 10

gives the language a melodic quality. While rare in Western languages, this practice is common in Eastern and Africa ones; in fact, more than half of the world's languages incorporate tone in some way (Crystal 1987: 172). Some like Zulu use only two tones (high and low), others like Yoruba use three (high, middle, and low), and Cantonese Chinese uses six (middle, low, high-then-falling, low-then-falling, high-then-rising, and low-then-rising). Thus a single "syllable" like *si* in Cantonese can mean "poem," "to try," "matter," "time," "to cause," and "city" depending on how it is intoned. The Tai-Kadai language family of Southeast Asia and southern China reportedly contains eleven different tones.

Grammar or syntax

Grammar or **syntax** refers to the rules by which a language combines words (and other morphemes) into meaningful and intelligible utterances, like sentences. Obviously, being able to say "dog" or "dogs" is necessary, but it would not be very useful if that was all a speaker could say. Hopefully speakers can use the words in more sophisticated and informative utterances to convey complete ideas or statements.

There are some basic grammatical rules in each language that organize the "structure" of normal "good" speech. In English, the most fundamental rule or variable in sentences is word order. That is, English speakers make and understand sentences based on the sequence of the words: in a regular declarative sentence, they know to put – and expect to hear – the "subject" word first, then the "verb" word, then the "object" word (notated as SVO). Of course, things can get much more complicated, with dependent clauses and participial phrases and such, but this is the skeleton of a basic sentence. So, the sentence "The man hit the dog" has a specific meaning. The sentence "The dog hit the man," with exactly the same words in a different sequence, has a specific but different meaning. And any other sequence – like "The the hit man dog" – yields no meaning at all.

Up to 75 percent of the world's languages follow a SVO or SOV pattern (Crystal 1987: 98). However, other orders exist. Standard Turkish sentences place the subject first and the verb last. Old Irish typically took the VSO order. Tagalog can give the predicate before the topic (according to the Philippine Center for Language Study [1965: 13], concepts of "subject," "verb," and "object" do not quite apply to Tagalog grammar, since a verb can be a subject) or in reverse order with the addition of the morpheme *ay*. Thus "The dress is beautiful" can be said as *Maganda ang damit* ("beautiful" + "is" + "dress") or as *Ang damit ay maganda* ("is" + "dress" + *ay* + "beautiful").

Grammar
see syntax

Syntax
the rules in a language for how words are combined to make intelligible utterances of speech acts (for example, sentences). Also known as grammar

Some languages do not depend on word order at all or do not have to provide every grammatical element for a sentence. The order of words in a Warlpiri sentence does not determine its meaning. For instance, to communicate that a man hit a dog, in Warlpiri one would use the words *wati* ("man"), *pakarnu* ("hit" – past tense), and *maliki* ("dog"), but to make the appropriate sentence one cannot simply say *wati pakarnu maliki*. The subject-word in a Warlpiri sentence is identified not by its location in the sentence but by a bound morpheme that indicates "subject," in this case the suffix *-ngki*. The correct utterance thus is *wati-ngki pakarnu maliki*. In any order the meaning is the same. To change the meaning so that the dog is doing the hitting, the suffix must go on *maliki*, the correct suffix being not *-ngki* but *-rli* (based on the number of syllables and the terminal syllable of the word). Now the sentence is *maliki-rli pakarnu wati*, which can be arranged in any order. Latin is similar in using suffixes to indicate a word's role in a sentence, rather than the order of words.

Spanish does not even require that all of the elements of a "good" English sentence be included. The Spanish equivalent of the English "I love you" can take the form OV, without a "subject": *Te amo* ("you"-object + "love"). If an English speaker said "You love," the meaning would be ambiguous, since "you" can be a subject pronoun or an object pronoun (unlike "I" and "me"). However, Spanish makes clear the reference through the verb and its conjugation (*amo* is "love" – first person, as opposed to *amas*, "love" – second person). While this might seem confusing to English speakers, English does

something similar in imperative sentences, like "Go to the store!" in which the subject is not spoken but understood ("you-understood"). Old Irish, finally, has no personal pronouns at all; while Spanish may include a personal pronoun or not, Old Irish cannot include one and conveys all "person" information (see below) through verb endings.

Syntax/grammar can of course be much more intricate than these simple matters, and grammatical principles found in English may be absent in other languages and vice versa. For instance, English contains articles ("a" and "the"), but Turkish and Warlpiri do not. At the same time, many languages, including French, Spanish, and German, contain the concept of "gender" in which every noun is assigned one of two (or in the case of German, three – masculine, feminine, and neuter) genders. So, *chat* ("cat") in French is masculine, and *télévision* is feminine. Then, articles and adjectives must agree with the noun in gender and in number: *le chat, la télévision, les chats, les télévisions, le grand chat, la grande télévision*.

In English, nouns and pronouns are distinguished by "case," that is, their role in a sentence (basically, subject and object). In other languages the situation is considerably elaborated. For instance, German has four cases ("nominative" or roughly subject, "accusative" or roughly direct object, "dative" or roughly indirect object, and "genitive" or roughly possessive), each of which requires a modification of articles; added to three genders and two numbers (singular and plural), many people find German declensions maddeningly difficult. In Russian, nouns have cases – six of them,

BOX 4.2　THE NOUN CLASSES OF SWAHILI

Noun case indicates the function of the noun in a sentence. However, many languages have noun "classes," that is, different types of nouns that are grammatically distinguished and that affect the grammar of words (articles, adjectives, numbers, etc.) around them. An interesting example is Swahili, which contains eighteen noun classes. One class, for people, is marked by the initial sound m-, mw-, or mu-, as in *mtu* (person) or *motto* (child). Another class, for abstract nouns and mass nouns as well as elongated objects, natural phenomena, and countries, is marked by u-, w-, or uw-, such as *unga* (flour), *umoja* (unity), *uzi* (thread), and *Uingereza* (England). Yet another class of verbal nouns like *kusoma* (reading) or *kupiga* (beating) contains a ku- or kw -prefix. Finally, two "locative" classes (for nouns of indefinite location or in directed motion or for nouns inside something) begin with ku- or m-/mu-, respectively.

depending on the noun's function in the sentence (as subject, direct object, possessive/quantity/negation, indirect object, location, or means [i.e., by/with]) – and must be conjugated with the proper suffix (also considering gender, of which there are three).

Last for our purposes are "person" and "tense." "Person" is the grammatical category that indicates who the speaker and the audience of an utterance are; in English this includes the first (I/we), second (you/you all), and third person (he/she/it/they), divided into singular and plural. Verbs are conjugated somewhat differently for each person (although not as differently as in Spanish). Warlpiri contains more person-forms than English, including a second- and third-person inclusive and exclusive (that is, "we-but-not-you" and "we-all," and "they-but-not-you" and "they-all"), each taking a different verb ending. "Tense" is, generally speaking, the time-element in speech – present, past, and future – although this can be joined with "aspect" – that is, the relation of the action to other facts or events (e.g. completed in the past, ongoing in the present, simultaneous with some other actions, etc.). Not all languages can be fit neatly into the tense and aspect categories of English. For example, Shoshone verbs can take progressive (ongoing over time), continuative (happening over and over), customary-habitual, resultative (resulting from some previous action), future, completive (finished in the past but having effects in the present), and expective (expected to occur) tenses and aspects, each with different suffixes and other rules of use (Gould and Loether 2002).

Pragmatics or sociolinguistics

Our speech choices have social meanings and social consequences. There might be grammatical ways to say things that are not *appropriate* ways to say things. This indicates something very important: language does much more than exchange factual information. It may actually be, in the end, that most of what language conveys is not facts but other kinds of "social" information.

Pragmatics (from the root *pragma* for practical or practice) or **sociolinguistics** (literally, society + language) refers to the rules or conventions for using language appropriately in social situations –

that is, for saying the right thing to the right person in the right circumstances. The point is that *a language is a "code" not only for factual information but for social information as well*. The kinds of social information encoded, and how, will depend upon the society and the distinctions it makes between "different kinds" of people and situations. There is no society in which all individuals are exactly equal in status or in which all situations are exactly the same in meaning and value. Minimally, some people are "higher" than others and some situations are "more important" than others. Different speech forms will be appropriate in regard to these different people and conditions.

One good example of the social use of language is the area of **honorifics** or language forms specialized to indicate the relative social status or relationship of the speakers. In French, there are two forms of the subject pronoun "you" – the singular or familiar *tu* form (for friends and equals) and the plural or formal *vous* form (for strangers and superiors). Employing the *tu* form in talking with your superiors would either indicate closeness, disrespect, or error, just as employing the *vous* form with your spouse or friends would seem overly formal or distant. English lacks such basic vocabulary distinctions, but there are ways to convey respect, from "polite" terms of address like "sir" and "ma'am" to more specialized ones like "your honor" and "your majesty," as well as semantic additions like "please" and "may." We might even use a respectful syntax, like a question rather than a command, and a deferential tone of voice.

Other languages can go much further. For instance, in Thai there are thirteen different forms of the first person pronoun ("I") depending on whom one is addressing. *Phom* would be an appropriate polite word to use between equals, while *kraphom* would sound better when talking to someone higher in rank (say, a monk or a government official), and the most formal *klaawkramom* would be correct for addressing a member of the royal family. Japanese also has an extensive set of linguistic choices, expressed most simply in the distinction between *tatemae* (polite forms for strangers or people outside your in-group) and *honne* (familiar forms for close friends and family). The idea "Sakai drew a map for Suzuki" can take the following forms for the following reasons (Foley 1997, 319–21):

Honorifics
specialized forms of speech (terms, titles, tones, grammar, etc.) that convey respect or deference

Pragmatics
the rules or practices regarding how language is used in particular social situations to convey particular social information, such as the relative status or power of the speakers

Sociolinguistics
see pragmatics

Foley, William A. 1997. *Anthropological Linguistics: An Introduction*. London: Blackwell Publishers.

1   *Sakai ga Suziki no tame ni chinzu o kai-ta* (used
    if the two people mentioned, Sakai and Suzuki,
    are familiar or inferior to the speaker)
2   *Sakai san ga Suzuki san ni chizu o kai-ta/kai-
    mash-ta* (used if Sakai and Suzuki are equal to
    the speaker)
3   *Sakai san ga Suzuki san ni chizu o o-kaki-ni nat-
    ta/nari-mashi-ta* (used if Sakai is considerably
    higher in status than the speaker)
4   *Sakai san ga Suzuki san ni chizu o o-kaki shi-
    ta/shi-mashi-ta* (used if Suzuki is considerably
    higher in status than Sakai)
5   *Sakai san ga Suzuki san ni chizu o kai-te kudasai-
    ta/kudasai-mashi-ta* (used if Suzuki is con-
    siderably lower in status than Sakai but the
    speaker wants to show his solidarity/familiarity
    with Suzuki)

And so on. Clearly, learning Japanese involves much more than simply learning the Japanese translations for English words. Indeed, it would be difficult to render the Japanese connotations of these sentences into everyday English at all.

Overall, the style variations in a language are codes for the important social distinctions made by the society. These can include such social factors as age, gender, power, office, education, interpersonal relationship, class, title, race, geographical region, and many others. No doubt if a non-native speaker said any of the five Japanese sentences above, all Japanese speakers would understand the factual content of the utterance: somebody drew a map for somebody. However, all but the correct form would "feel wrong" to the native speakers and perhaps evoke negative reactions.

As we noted, English has a set of possibilities for communicating relative status and prestige and the formality of the situation, albeit limited compared to those of Thai and Japanese. In the United States in particular, there are not many honorific forms because there is no use for them. Americans do not make the same distinctions, or attach the same importance to them, that, say, the Japanese do. If Americans made such distinctions, they would have to have a way to talk about them. At the same time, British English includes forms of address to nobility and royalty, because nobility and royalty exist in that society. The fact that Americans do not have regular linguistic forms for such social distinctions means that they do not make those

distinctions: there is no royalty in the United States. It is probably fair to say that America, as a society with an egalitarian ideology, deliberately and con-sciously avoids making many social distinctions in its speech. For example, the fact that students usually speak in a comparatively informal style to teachers indicates that the "social distance" between students and teachers is not great. Americans would even address their president with the informal "you" because they have no other semantic choice (although they might express respect in other ways, including polite forms, tone of voice, and body language).

Much of the remainder of the chapter will explore the forms and occasions for pragmatic language use. Language will be seen not only to describe social (and of course "objective") facts but also to create, sustain, and contest those facts as well.

MAKING SOCIETY THROUGH LANGUAGE: LANGUAGE AND THE CONSTRUCTION OF SOCIAL REALITY

The previous discussion of speech styles and social status barely scratches the surface of the complex and intimate relationship between language and society. Language is much more than a set of words for things. It also fundamentally expresses and constructs social relationships, including political and religious as well as gender and age and other status relations, not just in terms of what different individuals and groups talk about but how they talk. We should think of language and its skillful manipulation as a social resource that both is produced by and produces interpersonal and intergroup bonds and fractures.

Language as performance

One of the best ways to introduce the social efficacy of language is in terms of what J. L. Austin called **performatives.** In *How to Do Things with Words* (1962), Austin distinguished between speech acts that describe the world and ones that *change* the world in some way. For example, there is a big difference between a declarative sentence ("You are getting married") or an imperative sentence ("Get

Performatives
linguistic utterances that do not merely describe but actually accomplish a transformation in the social world

Austin, J. L. 1962. *How To Do Things with Words*. Oxford: Clarendon.

PLATE 4.3
The courtroom is a typical
site for the use of
linguistic performatives.

married!") and a performative sentence ("I now pronounce you man and wife"). In such utterances, the saying of it makes it so – the words are more than words but a real social act that accomplishes some social effect. Put another way, speaking in such cases is not just saying something but doing something.

There are many kinds of linguistic performatives in any society. When a judge says, "Case dismissed" or a king says, "I knight thee," a social change has been worked. Notice that only certain kinds of people can perform certain linguistic acts; issuing performative statements is part of the role they occupy. Ordinary citizens cannot dismiss court cases or bestow knighthoods (in fact, no one in the United States can bestow knighthoods). Furthermore, the social context must be correct: a priest cannot walk down the street marrying people by saying, "I pronounce you man and wife." In extreme situations, the proper people must be present, the proper rituals must be observed, perhaps even the proper clothing must be worn. The speech act is part of a much more comprehensive social setting or "ritual."

Austin distinguished a variety of kinds of performatives, including "verdictives" in which a "ruling" of some sort is made, "exercitives" in which

power is exercised such as to appoint or advise or warn, "commissives" in which a commitment is made, such as a promise or agreement (e.g., an oath), and "behabitives" that express a socially recognized behavior, like as an apology or a congratulation. Two other interesting aspects of performatives are interrelated. One is that the "sincerity" of the utterance does not determine its effectiveness: if I am still angry with you but I say, "I forgive you," the words can be just as socially "successful." However, as in other dimensions of language, performatives allow for the possibility of deception or failure; that is, I can say, "I promise to do so and so" and never intend to do it, and I can attempt to apologize and fail, either because the recipient sees through my false sentiment or because I do not execute the verbal behavior correctly. Then they might say, "No, give a *real* apology!" or "Apology not accepted."

Performatives have what Austin called "illocutionary force" in that they do not convey meaning so much as bring about a social outcome – actually making someone a knight or a married person. Other kinds of utterances can have "perlocutionary force" in that they can have an effect on the audience and lead them to have certain feelings or take certain actions. Persuading is a key perlocutionary effect; others include frightening and upsetting. Perlocutionary acts do not directly change the social world, but they change people's attitudes, who may put those changes into action.

Language and political power

One thing that gets a leader elected in a democracy is the ability to give a good speech; sometimes it is the main thing. Pericles in ancient Athens and Mark Antony in Shakespeare's *Julius Caesar* swayed the crowd with skillful oration. Language is central to obtaining, exercising, and challenging power in many societies.

PLATE 4.4 Masterful use of political speaking is a path to power in many societies, as for American President Barack Obama.

Michelle Rosaldo describes the Ilongot of the Philippines as a society that took linguistic abilities very seriously; for them, "true verbal art has social force" (Rosaldo 1984: 140). Oratory or *purung* was a highly prized and formally structured speech form in which "art and politics are combined" (138). It was contrasted to ordinary forms such as gossip or *berita*, myths or *tadek* or *tudtud*, and tales, where the content was more important than the style; in *purung* the most important thing was how things were said rather than what was said.

One of the characteristics of good Ilongot *purung*, as in many societies, was a certain amount of indirectness and wit (*beira* or elaboration, *'amba'an* or witty flourish, *'asasap* or "crooked" speaking). This was possible because the community already shared knowledge and memories of past actions and events, and it was important to prevent emotions from becoming too enflamed. In practice, *purung* was delivered in the form of verbal exchanges, in which the speakers claimed that they

were "giving" or even "feeding" each other words. The target of a speech would repeat the words of the speaker, insisting that they "will not 'hide' their hopes, that in their hearts are no ill thoughts, that in their breath they know that they are kinsmen" (143). The ultimate purpose of these performances was to restore the kin bonds of the two speakers or sides, but this was accomplished "through deception, pretense, wit, and the display of unity and strength by 'sides' that are, initially, opposed" (143). As in this and most such instances, a kind of verbal negotiation not only of interests but of statuses was taking place, and neither side could afford to totally dominate or humiliate the other.

From the holistic perspective of anthropology, it is clear that the style and substance of political speaking would be related to the general quality of politics and to the hierarchies or lack thereof in the society. The box below illustrates a clear contrast between the form and the intent of public oratory based on the political relations within the society.

BOX 4.3   SPEECH AND POWER – A CULTURAL COMPARISON

In the descriptions by Atkinson and Firth, the Wana of Sulawesi (Indonesia) and the Tikopia had very different manners of public speaking, reflecting their very different social and political systems. The Wana were an acephalous (i.e., without a head or leader) and mostly egalitarian society in which no enduring political roles or groups existed. Tikopia was a highly stratified society with a formal system of chiefs with coercive power.

When Wana men met for the purpose of public speaking, they practiced *kiyori*, an extremely stylized poetic form broken into stanzas with rigid principles about syllabification, emphasis, and rhyme.

They might also use specialized terminology, especially as part of religious or legal occasions. It was ordinarily addressed to one man by one man, and the listener might repeat the speech several times as if memorizing it. Sometimes the receiver of the *kiyori* would answer with his own, setting off an exchange of lines. The intentions of speaking *kiyori* varied from establishment of alliances to advice to strong criticism. One of the key features of *kiyori*, however, was the use of ambiguous or conventional references, like aphorisms and metaphors. In fact, it was "an expressive form well suited for speaking in oblique and clever ways" (Atkinson 1984: 57), and skillful speakers took full advantage of the potential for ambiguity.

In Tikopia, a public assembly or *fono* might have a very different quality. The occasion of a *fono* was usually an announcement by a chief or one of his functionaries; it was for proclamation, not discussion. As Firth (1975) describes it, the speaker addressed the crowd with restraint, possibly standing still or walking back and forth. He spoke in a forceful staccato voice, issuing direct commands and declarations, without personal opinion or ingenious proverbs and allusions. There was no attempt to avoid directness.

The difference between the two oratorical styles relates to the two political contexts in which they occurred. Wana speakers, without permanent status or followers, could not afford to be abrupt. They had to appear to be intelligent and wise even while they avoided conflict and open opposition, because they were actively and precariously recruiting their allies via the speech act. Tikopia speakers did not have any such reticence, because their political positions were already firm. Being the dominant members of officially stratified societies, they did not have to spare any feelings or circumvent any conflict: they had the social right and duty to issue orders and expected the compliance of the listeners.

MAGICAL WRITING IN ECUADOR

Oral literature and specialized language styles

There are many other areas where language and social relationships intersect, including gender, to which we will return in the next chapter. However, one more that calls for our attention at this point is "cultural knowledge" and the specialized language styles that communicate it. Anthropologists and others often refer to this body of knowledge and the genres in which it occurs as **folklore**, a society's primarily oral and traditional knowledge which is "told" or "performed" in specific appropriate ways. To get some idea of the range of linguistic activities that can be regarded as folklore, consider Alan Dundes' list:

> Folklore includes myths, legends, folktales, jokes, proverbs, riddles, chants, charms, blessings, curses, oaths, insults, retorts, taunts, teases, toasts, tongue-twisters, and greeting and leave-taking formulas. . . .It also includes folk costume, folk dance, folk drama, folk instrumental music. . ., folksongs. . ., folk speech. . ., folk similes. . ., folk metaphors. . ., and names. Folk poetry ranges from oral epics to

autograph-book verse, epitaphs, latrinalia (writings on the walls of public bathrooms), limericks, ball-bouncing rhymes, jump-rope rhymes, finger and toe rhymes, dandling rhymes (to bounce children on the knee), counting-out rhymes. . ., and nursery rhymes. The list of folklore forms also contains games; gestures; symbols; prayers (e.g., graces); practical jokes; folk etymologies; food recipes; quilt and embroidery designs; house, barn, and fence types; street vendor's cries; and even the traditional conventional sounds used to summon animals or to give them commands.

(1965: 3)

Myth will be discussed in more detail in the context of religion, and there are too many others to explore them all here, but a few of these oral literature styles will highlight the variety and social importance of specialized linguistic performances.

1. Proverbs

In many societies, much "conventional wisdom" is contained in proverbs and other such traditional sayings. They tend to be brief, pithy, and often

Folklore
the "traditional," usually oral, literature of a society, consisting of various genres such as myth, legend, folk tale, song, proverb, and many others

See Chapter 10

PLATE 4.5 Herbert Jim, a contemporary Seminole (Native American story teller).

metaphorical. American English is full of them – "A penny saved is a penny earned," "A leopard can't change its spots," and so on. Other societies have their own culturally specific sayings as well as socially appropriate occasions for using them. Ilongot *purung* or Wana *kiyori* may incorporate apt proverbs, as well as original metaphors. John Messenger notes that the Anang in Nigeria employed proverbs for a variety of purposes, including entertainment and education but also more serious ones like rituals and court hearings. Particularly in the traditional courts known as *esop*, Anang litigants "take every opportunity to display their eloquence and constantly employ adages" (Messenger 1965: 303–4). A well-met proverb could make the case and determine the outcome of the proceedings. Of course, many of these maxims do not make much sense outside of their cultural context, for example:

"If a dog plucks palm fruits from a cluster, he does not fear a porcupine."
"A single partridge flying through the bush leaves no path."
"If you visit the home of the toads, stoop."
"The crayfish is bent because it is sick."

To use and understand such utterances well requires an understanding of the society's world of meaning.

2. Riddles

Like a proverb, a riddle "seems to depend on *metaphor*, on a kind of poetic comparison drawn between the thing actually described and the referent to be guessed" (De Caro 1986: 178). In contemporary American society, riddles are mostly told for fun and most often by or to children. However, in other societies they can have other and more serious functions. De Caro notes six contexts in which riddling takes place across cultures, including leisure, education (for instance, the famous Buddhist *koan*), courting and mating, greeting, initiations and funerals, and folk narrative. In Dusun society, riddles could be combative as well as humiliating, and Turkish society used riddles in festivals such as weddings and actually had professional riddlers and neighborhood riddling teams.

Beuchat (1957) tells that the Bantu made riddles for fun and to demonstrate intelligence and wit. The riddles were characteristically short verbal analogies which required a "solution" or answer, like:

"I have built my house without any door." Answer: an egg.
"The little hole full of grass litter." Answer: the teeth.
"Two little holes that refuse to be filled; there enter people, oxen, goats, and other things." Answer: eyes.

3. Ritual languages

In many societies, one or more specialized linguistic genre(s) may exist for specific purposes. Sherzer (1983), for instance, identifies three quite distinct speaking styles in Kuna society in Panama, associated with a particular ritual activity and distinguished from everyday speech or *tule kaya*. Political or chiefly speech (*sakla kaya*), curing song or "stick doll language" (*suar miimi kaya*), and girl's puberty rite language (*kantule kaya*) each had different pace and tone qualities, as well as specialized vocabularies and other aspects of increasing formality. Latin served the same general purpose in medieval Europe, conveying a gravity that ordinary vernacular languages did not. The use of archaic forms like "thee" and "thou" in English still confers an artistic and even religious aura. Richard Bauman (2001) proposes eight characteristics or "devices" that set specialized or ritualized speech apart from everyday talk: unique "codes" including archaic or esoteric terms, formulas like conventional openings and closings (e.g. "Once upon a time"), figurative language like metaphors, stylistic alternatives like rhyme or repetition, patterns of tempo or stress or pitch, "paralinguistic" usages (see below), overt appeals to tradition, and "disclaimers of performance."

Paralanguage and non-verbal language

Not all of human communication, or even of language, is verbal, and verbal language is not limited to its "words" or morphemes. Nonverbal gestures of various kinds can have meaning independent of spoken language, and they can be added to alter the meaning of speech. At the same time, the ways that speakers modulate speech can also affect its meaning.

Paralanguage includes the vocal features that shape the delivery of spoken language, such as tone, pitch, speed, rhythm, and volume. Saying the same thing rapidly or slowly, or in a high or low pitched voice, can change its meaning. Some specialized forms of speech, like the Tikopia *fono* just mentioned, are associated with particular paralinguistic variations. We can also communicate emotion and sincerity through voice qualities, as well as advanced skills like irony and sarcasm. Other paralinguistic features include sounds that are not strictly linguistic but that convey meaning; called **vocalizations**, some examples are "um" and "shhh" and "tsk tsk."

The vocal apparatus is not the only part of humans involved in the construction of meaning, including linguistic meaning. The entire human body can be a meaning-conveying medium. **Kinesics** is the general name for the bodily movements or gestures that augment and modify verbal communication (sometimes called "body language"). Among kinesics issues are facial expressions, hand gestures, and the physical distance between speakers. For

Bauman, Richard. 2001. "Verbal Art in Performance." In Alessandro Duranti, ed. *Linguistic Anthropology: A Reader.* Malden, MA and Oxford: Blackwell Publishing, 165–88.

Paralanguage
the qualities which speakers can add to language to modify the factual or social meaning of speech, such as tone of voice, volume, pitch, speed and cadence, and "non-linguistic" sounds like grunts and snickers

PLATE 4.6 Body language and personal space: Arab men hold hands as a gesture of friendship.

Vocalizations
non-linguistic sounds that can accompany and affect the meaning of speech

Kinesics
the study of how body movements are used to communicate social information, sometimes referred to as "body language"

Proxemics
the study of how cultures use personal space (or "proximity")

example, a wink in America can suggest dishonesty or conspiracy between speakers. Raised eyebrows indicate surprise, and lowered ones can express doubt or displeasure. In some societies there is a more or less complete "language" of hand signs, as in the Warlpiri system known as *rdaka rdaka* (literally, "hand hand"). There are hand signs for many common words, used by hunters to maintain silence, by mourners when certain words are forbidden, and most widely by women. In many other societies, there are less complete but still important culturally relative gestures.

Finally, **proxemics** looks specifically at the use of personal space in interactions. Different societies maintain different degrees of physical distance between members, depending on their relationship. American casual speakers keep a 24-inch or so zone between them, while Japanese maintain more distance and Middle Easterners less (the latter may even hold hands, as we noted at the opening of the first chapter). Diverging from these standard distances can communicate intimacy, respect, avoidance, or invasiveness depending on the culture and the distance.

LIVING SPACE AS RITUAL COMMUNICATION

BOX 4.4   GESTURES ACROSS CULTURES

Like so much else, gestures are culturally relative; the same gesture can have a different and even opposite meaning in different cultures. For instance (based on Axtell 1991):

Sticking out your tongue is an insult in the United States but a greeting in Tibet.
In the United States, the thumb and forefinger circle means "OK," but in Russia, Germany, and Brazil it is an insult. In Japan it is the sign for money (a round coin).
In Holland, tapping your forefinger on your forehead means "You are stupid."
In Iran and Australia, the "thumbs up" signal is rude.
In Bulgaria, Greece, Turkey, Iran, and Bengal, nodding your head means "no" and shaking your head means "yes."
In England, the two-fingered "V" gesture is an insult if the back of the hand is facing the audience; in that case, it means "Up yours."

Pidgin

a simplified version of a language that is usually used for limited purposes, such as trade and economic interactions, by non-native speakers of the language (as in Melanesian pidgin versions of English). Usually an incomplete language that is not the "first" language of any group

Creole

a pidgin language that has become elaborated into a multi-functional language and distributed into a first language of the community

Diglossia

the use of two varieties of a language by members of a society for distinct functions or by distinct groups or classes of people

Anti-language

a speech style used by individuals or groups in the performance of roles opposing or inverting the society outside of their group

OJIBWE COMMUNICATIVE PRACTICES

Language change, loss, and competition

Like everything else in the cultural world, language is dynamic, constantly changing, and available for humans to manipulate and compete over and through. One important aspect of real-world language use is the multilingual situation in many societies. In places from Belgium to New Guinea, multiple languages coexist side by side, with various relationships, from cooperative to hostile. "Linguistic nationalism" can threaten to pull societies apart, as in Canada, where the French-speaking Quebecois have tried several times to pass a referendum separating Quebec from Canada to form their own officially French-speaking country. When two languages share a social space, the choice of language may be a "political" or "symbolic" statement, as Leach (1954) noted in Burma: which language you speak, at any given time or habitually, can indicate "whose side you are on." Even within a single language, there may be two or more forms treated as "high" and "low" or "prestigious" and "common." This phenomenon is known as **diglossia** and is found in distinctions of function (say, lower form for "popular" or casual uses and higher form for official or formal uses) as well as class and stratification.

In situations of sustained and, particularly, imbalanced culture contact, changes may occur to one or both of the contact languages. Often a simplified working version of the dominant language, showing certain features of the subordinated language, will emerge for basic purposes like trade. Such a hybrid language is called a **pidgin** and tends to have a significantly reduced vocabulary and grammar; one defining feature is that a pidgin is not the first or primary language of either party. However, over time a pidgin may become more sophisticated and multi-functional, even becoming the first language of a community. When a new or hybrid language has achieved this level of sophistication and use, it is called a **creole**. Another possible and common consequence of language contact is language loss, which can occur when the members of a speech community adopt a foreign language to the exclusion of their previous one, voluntarily or not. Young people may cease learning it, and elders may be the last to speak it. In the worst cases, the entire language-bearing society dies or is exterminated.

Finally, language may be a focus of struggle between two societies, communities, or subcultures, or it may be a medium for staking out distinct and competitive or resistant identities vis-à-vis the dominant society. Technical or subcultural jargons or argots can signal differentiation from or even rejection of other segments of society. Halliday (1976) coined the term "**anti-language**" to refer to the most dramatic form of this behavior, a speech style (specialized phonetics, vocabulary, grammar, and/or pragmatics) used by individuals or groups in the performance of roles opposing or inverting the society outside of their group.

LANGUAGE ACQUISITION AND THE LINGUISTIC RELATIVITY HYPOTHESIS

No one is born knowing and speaking any particular language, yet we all have one within a few years of birth. Language is learned and shared like the rest of culture. For some researchers, this has profound implications.

It seems evident that language is not "in the brain" at birth; if language were innate, all humans ought to speak the same language. It also seems evident that there is something in or about the human brain that extracts or constructs language from experienced speech, some neurological capacity to acquire and use language. There is nothing contradictory in accepting both of these realities. Whatever the biological substrate, different societies speak different languages; language is relative to a particular society. However, theorists like Edward Sapir and Benjamin Lee Whorf went much beyond that obvious truth. They suggested that not just the words and the sounds but the very minds that produce those words and sounds are quite different. As Whorf wrote:

> the background linguistic system (in other words, the grammar) of each language is not merely a reproducing instrument for voicing ideas but rather is itself the shaper of ideas, the program and guide for the individual's mental activity, for his analysis of impressions, for his synthesis of his mental stock in trade. Formulation of ideas is not an independent process, strictly rational in the old sense, but is part of a particular grammar, and differs, from slightly to greatly, between different grammars. We dissect nature along lines laid down by our native languages. The categories and types that we isolate from the world of phenomena we do not find there because they stare every observer in the face; on the contrary, the world is presented in a kaleidoscopic flux of impressions which has to be organized by our minds – and this means largely by the linguistic systems in our minds.
>
> (1940: 231)

Edward Sapir, one of the great early professional anthropologists, joined Whorf in this assessment of the role and power of language. As he said:

> Human beings do not live in the objective world alone nor alone in the world of social activity as ordinarily understood, but are very much at the mercy of the particular language which has become the medium of expression for their society. It is quite an illusion to imagine that one adjusts to reality essentially without the use of language and that language is merely an incidental means of solving specific problems of communication or reflection. The fact of the matter is that the "real world" is to a large extent unconsciously built up on the language habits of the group. No two languages are ever sufficiently similar to be considered as representing the same social reality. The worlds in which different societies live are distinct worlds, not merely the same world with different labels attached.
>
> (1949: 162)

This quotation explains what is known as the **linguistic relativity hypothesis** or the Sapir–Whorf hypothesis. The idea is that a language is not just a list of words for things, not just vocabulary. It is also a code for concepts, ideas, relationships (and not just social ones but "natural" ones like cause, similarity and difference, time, and such), and even values and meanings. Humans are not born with any vocabulary, nor are we born with any concepts, ideas, relationships, values, or meanings. Then, as we acquire the "linguistic code" of our society's language we acquire these concepts, ideas, relationships, etc. If so, speakers of different languages (especially radically different ones) acquire different concepts, ideas, relationships, values, meanings, and so on and come to experience the world through them. In the ultimate formulation of the hypothesis, speakers of different languages live in very different mental worlds. As Whorf defined it, then, the linguistic relativity hypothesis "means, in informal terms, that users of markedly different grammars are pointed by their grammars toward different types of observations and different evaluations of externally similar acts of observation, and hence are not equivalent as observers but must arrive at somewhat different views of the world" (1956: 221).

This is clearly a controversial suggestion and can probably be taken too far. Some concepts, like causality or space for instance, can at least partially arise from embodied experience in the physical

Linguistic relativity hypothesis
the claim that language is not only a medium for communication about experience but actually a more or less powerful constituent of that experience. Language consists of concepts, relations, and values, and speakers of different languages approach and interpret reality through different sets of concepts, relations, and values. Also known as the Sapir–Whorf hypothesis

Whorf, Benjamin Lee. 1956. *Language, Thought, and Reality: Selected Writings of Benjamin Lee Whorf.* Cambridge, MA: Massachusetts Institute of Technology Press.

world. Yet even in these "basic" concepts, some cultural variation can and does occur.

Attempts to test the linguistic relativity hypothesis empirically have yielded mixed results. One area of testing has been color perception and terminology. While some cultures have as few as two color terms (essentially "black" and "white"), many have no more than four. Does the presence or absence of color terms affect the actual perception of color? The comparative work of Berlin and Kay (1969) suggested not: they discovered what they regarded as a set of standard hues that societies (although not all societies) recognize and name, as well as a universal sequence of named hues, starting (and sometimes ending) with black and white, followed by red, then yellow or green, then blue. But the fact that not all societies get beyond black and white, and that many do not get beyond black and white and red and yellow, makes the research inconclusive.

A much more recent experiment, however, suggests the power of the linguistic effect on thought. Ross, Xun, and Wilson (2002) studied bilingual Chinese-Canadians on a series of psychological and personality items. Some individuals were given the test in Chinese, and others were given the same questions in English. An even more provocative version of this investigation was conducted by Ramirez-Esparza et al. (2006), in which they surveyed the same bilingual English-Spanish

See Chapter 10

individuals twice, once in each language. Both studies found that the language of response affected the responses. Chinese-born individuals writing in Chinese showed significantly more typically Chinese views and self-perceptions than the same population writing in English. Likewise, English-Spanish bilinguals evinced personality traits more consistent with Spanish-speakers when functioning in Spanish and more consistent with English-speakers when functioning in English. Ramirez-Esparza et al. attribute the results to "cultural frame switching," a phenomenon in which individuals "change their interpretations of the world, depending upon their internalized cultures, in response to cues in their environment. . .as subtle as language" (2006: 20). Ross et al. go so far as to propose that "East-Asian and Western identities are stored in separate knowledge structures. . .in bicultural individuals, with each structure activated by its associated language" (2002: 1048).

The place of language in experience is most immediate and obvious in the area of social and cultural concepts, which may have no correlate at all in other cultures. The concepts may be embedded in language, or they may be lexical items themselves. As an embedded case, one cannot speak Japanese well without learning to make and express major culturally specific social distinctions, like those mentioned above. Likewise, in Ilongot or Tikopian society, the use or understanding of different speech styles attunes a speaker to matters of egalitarianism and hierarchy, fixed and fluid roles.

On the other hand, there are some ideas and concepts captured by words in any given language and culture that are divergent, if not absent altogether, from others (see "semantic range" above). The Warlpiri religious concept of *jukurrpa* has no equivalent in English or any other non-Aboriginal language; it is not just another name for God or heaven nor even for dreams, although its literal translation is "dream" or "dreaming." The range of this key term includes dreams as well as the creation-time at the beginning of the world, sacred designs and objects, and rituals; no single English word does or can convey all these meanings. Even when a society has words that we might render as "god" or "spirit" or "soul," etc., we cannot assume that their meaning is identical to ours or each others'. Culturally specific words like *brahma* in Hinduism, *nirvana* in Buddhism, *diyi* ("luck") in Apache, even *jihad* in Arabic, as well as many others, cannot be simplistically translated into some supposed "equivalent" in another language; yet these terms and concepts are central and motivational in their societies. This presents a fascinating challenge to cross-cultural translation and understanding: the key terms and concepts of another culture, expressed in language and also in practice, may be constitutive of a very different social experience, a very different "cultural reality."

BOX 4.5   CONTEMPORARY CULTURAL CONTROVERSIES: THE POLITICS OF LANGUAGE IN THE UNITED STATES

In George Orwell's prophetic novel *1984*, the philosophy of the regime was "Who controls the past controls the future. Who controls the present controls the past." And the regime understood that control of the present rests in the language, which was why it devised "Newspeak," a form of language in which it was easy to say and think certain things and difficult or impossible to say or think others. Opinion-makers and politicians of all points on the spectrum have equally understood that language can be used not only to inform but to persuade, motivate, and even "disinform" – usually to propagate their power or policies (hence the term "propaganda"). Recently, a figure named Frank Luntz has been using this insight to reframe the political discourse in American society. Acting primarily as an advisor for the political "Right," he has conducted "market research" on different words and phrases to determine which will best influence public opinion. It was his idea to replace "estate tax" with "death tax" and "global warming" with "climate change." He has actually advocated dropping certain terms like "globalization," "drilling for oil," and even "government" completely. Some people see this as blatant and dangerous manipulation. What do you think?

SUMMARY

Language is both a medium of human communication and interaction and a shaping influence on that communication and interaction. Humans are not the only species that communicate, nor even communicate linguistically. However, humans have unique linguistic skills, which are also the same skills that make culture in general possible:

- Symbolism
- Productivity
- Displacement

Language takes the form of a set of basic items and combinatory rules, from sound units to meaning units to utterances to socially appropriate speech-acts. Each of these dimensions is studied by a specific area of linguistics:

- Phonology
- Morphology or semantics
- Syntax or grammar
- Pragmatics or sociolinguistics

Language in its social production and use is much more than a list of names for things. It is a code for social information and social relationships. Any language includes a variety of specialized speech forms for different individuals and groups, different occasions, and different relationships. Language as a social phenomenon can express or determine functions such as

- Changes of social status and role
- Politics and power relations

MCQS

FILL IN THE BLANKS

www

■ Performance of specific linguistic genres, such as ritual or story-telling
■ Blending, stratifying, or differentiating of social groups

Language, as a set of concepts or categories, may also influence the way that humans experience and interpret, and therefore respond to, their world – both physical and social. The linguistic relativity hypothesis suggests that language mediates human thought and experience such that members of different speech communities think and experience differently. This is an area of controversy and ongoing research.

Key Terms

Anti-language

Bound morpheme

Competence

Creole

Diglossia

Displacement

Folklore

Free morpheme

Grammar

Honorifics

Kinesics

Linguistic relativity hypothesis

Morpheme

Morphology

Paralanguage

Performatives

Phoneme

Phonology

Pidgin

Pragmatics

Productivity

Proxemics

Semantic range

Semantics

Sociolinguistics

Symbol

Syntax

Vocalizations

Cultural construction of persons

Personality and gender

According to Jeannette Mageo, the islanders of Samoa have a formal or rigid sense of **self** and social propriety: Samoan personality is less about individuality than about social role or persona; in fact, "the subjective elements of the self [should] be relegated to the background of personality," where they are regarded as "a quasi-organ" called the *loto* (1991: 353). The most important social quality of an enculturated Samoan person is *fa'aaloalo*, which means "respect of status," and the ideal person should show respect and deference to social superiors while restricting "private thoughts, feelings, and volitions," that is, *loto*. "The *loto* is looked upon as incorrigibly resistant to socialization and as a reservoir of unsocialized energy within the self" (354). Young women are particularly supposed to submit their private selves to the interests of their extended family and village; the one thing she should not be is *sa'oloto*, free or unbound, impudent and disrespectful, acting in an improper, proud, and self-important manner. Thus, a particular kind of behavioral or mental disorder afflicts Samoans, especially the young women, known as *mai'i aitu* or "spirit sickness" or what we might call "possession." Two spirits, Telesa and Sauma'iafe, are most likely to possess the girls, and these spirits flaunt their

independence and beauty by literally "letting down their hair" and showing off in other ways, including sexually. Good girls fear being attacked by a spirit, and bad girls are suspected of being possessed by a spirit. So, *mai'i aitu* is simultaneously a form of social control and "a debilitating and dangerous illness" (365). But at the same time, *mai'i aitu* is an explanation and legitimation of the bad girl's behavior, for it is not her own self that is being expressed but the self of a wanton spirit.

A society is a system of human individuals in some structured relationships with each other, relationships that are informed and shaped by beliefs and values and meanings. More than that, a society is a set of "kinds of persons to be": individuals occupy culturally defined roles and positions, and they act within a universe of concepts and categories that make their actions meaningful and appropriate. Gilbert Herdt has referred to this universe of categories and meanings as a **cultural ontology**. Ontology is the study of being, of what kinds of things exist. Herdt defines cultural ontology as "local theories of being and metaphysics of the world; of having a certain kind of body and being in a certain kind of social world, which creates a certain cultural reality; and of being and

Self
the more or less enduring, bounded, and discrete part of an individual's identity or personality, and the reflexive awareness of this aspect of oneself

Cultural ontology
a society's system of notions about what kind of things (including kinds of people) exist in the world and their characteristics and social value. A socially specific way of categorizing and valuing the physical and social world

Herdt, Gilbert, ed. 1994. *Third Sex, Third Gender: Beyond Sexual Dimorphism in Culture and History*. New York: Zone Books.

See Chapter 10

knowledge combined in the practice of living" (Herdt 1994: 61). Culture posits many different kinds of beings, a great number of which pertain to what we would call "religion." However, a culture also contains an ontology of human beings – what kinds of humans are there, what makes them different kinds of humans, and how does the society treat and value them? As Herdt adds, "For a collective ontology to emerge and be transmitted across time, there must be a social condition, eventually a stable social role, that can be inhabited – marking off a clear social status position, rights and duties, with indications for the transmission of corporeal and incorporeal property and status" (60).

Humans, even within a single society, are born diverse, but culture provides a combination of increased diversification through enculturation and of categorization of innate and acquired differences. We might say that humans *learn how to be individuals in the presence of culture* and that culture assigns meaning and value to different kinds of individuals. The study of the individual in cultural context raises fundamental questions about "human nature": to what extent is human behavior given by nature or shaped by culture? This is a debate that rages to this day. Two particularly important and interrelated aspects of the argument are the questions of personality and of gender. Here, as in all other areas that it surveys, anthropology finds that the answers – or least the facts – are more complicated but at the same time more interesting than mere dualities.

Personality

the distinctive ways of thinking, feeling, perceiving, and behaving of an individual, shaped by enculturation as individuals internalize aspects of their society's culture

CULTURES AND PERSONS, OR CULTURAL PERSONS

Each human individual exists in a complex and dynamic relation to his/her society and culture. Persons are not carbon copies of society, but they are not utterly free agents from it either. In the course of their interactions with each other and the social systems they have erected, individuals develop a personality. Let us define **personality**, rather casually, as the distinctive ways of thinking, feeling, and behaving of an individual. Two things are clear. First, humans are not born thinking or feeling or behaving in any specific way; so, by this definition, one's personality is not exactly or entirely innate. Second, humans within a group or society share certain tendencies of thinking or feeling or behaving. After all, my personal thought or emotion or behavior patterns are not completely unique to me; I share them with others around me, and I mostly got them from those others. I think and feel and act like most Americans, and Warlpiri or Kwakiutl or Japanese or Samoan individuals think and feel and act much like other Warlpiri or Kwakiutl or Japanese or Samoans around them.

We might express the relation between culture and personality as an analogy: *Personality is to the individual as culture is to the society.* Personality is a quality or disposition of the individual in the same way that culture is a quality or disposition of a society. If so, culture and personality are intimately,

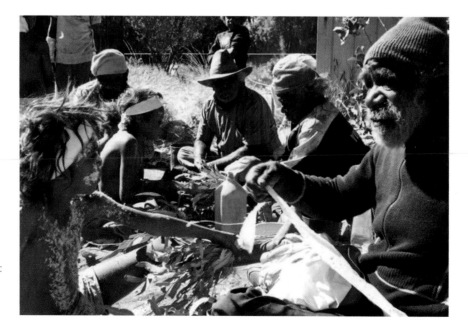

PLATE 5.1 Enculturation: Warlpiri elder men showing boys sacred knowledge and skills.

essentially, necessarily linked. If humans are not born with it, and if humans share important and major portions of it with others around them, then where does it come from? The answer is that very much, maybe the vast majority, of it comes from outside the individual – from what other people are doing and what they teach or influence the individual to do. And the process that links these external (to the individual) realities with the internal realities of personality is enculturation. Enculturation, as discussed earlier, is the process by which an individual learns his/her society's culture – that is, by which culture gets "in" the individual. During enculturation the ideas, beliefs, values, norms, meanings, etc. that exist before, apart from, and outside of the individual are *internalized* and become part of and "inside of" the individual. To say it once more, during enculturation, culture becomes part of the individual's personality. The fact that, as seen earlier, acquiring culture is an active and imperfect process guarantees that individuals will not be mere cookie-cutter versions of some cultural template.

Since different cultures have different categories and definitions of persons, the anthropologist must be careful to understand theirs and not impose his/her own. One fundamental area is the concept of "self." Self is a key concept in Western cultures. In a way it is taken for granted: self is real, everybody has one, and it is a good thing. Society keeps the self concept front and center by constantly invoking it and even "working on it." Self or person was characterized by Geertz as "a bounded, unique, more or less integrated motivational and cognitive universe, a dynamic center of awareness, emotion, judgment, and action organized into a distinctive whole and set contrastively both against other such wholes and against its social and natural background" (1976: 225). Particularly in American culture, people are encouraged to cultivate and develop the self, to become very "self-aware" and to improve the self, through physical exercise (equating the self with the body in some way) or more often through "psychological growth" or "self-actualization." Americans even talk about their "self-image" and "self-esteem" and how it can be askew from the "reality" of the self; that is, people can imagine or see themselves to be worse than they really are or occasionally better than they really are. But if one's self-concept can be so elusive and

problematic, then self is not quite as simple or self-evident as it may seem.

Two points have surfaced from the cross-cultural analysis of the self. First, self is not as certain as we like to think; it may not even be a universal human concept. Second, self may not be as exclusively human as we like to think. That is, not all humans may have the modern Western sense of self, and not only humans may have some sense of self. To take the first point, a fair amount of research has gone into the question of whether all societies conceive of and experience the self as Westerners do – as a bounded, enduring, private personal essence. There is at least some reason to conclude that they do not. Buddhism teaches explicitly, for instance, that there is no self. *Anatta* or selflessness (not in the sense of unselfishness but literally of having no self) is a central and formal concept in high Buddhism: there is no "you" that endures from moment to moment, let alone for a lifetime or an eternity. Instead, in each moment the person is remade, the previous moment lighting the candle that is the "self" for this moment. So, while there is some continuity for the individual, it is much less than and much different from the Western view.

In other cultures, the enduring, bounded, or personal self has been called into question, as in the case of Samoa just mentioned. Other anthropologists have described self concepts in other societies – Dorothy Lee among the Wintu (1959), A. Irving Hallowell among the Ojibwa (1967), and Catherine Lutz among the Ifaluk (1998), to name but a few. Lee made some intriguing claims: based on Wintu linguistic practices, she suggested that the Wintu did not share the Western sense of "an established separate self." Rather, "a Wintu self is identical with the parts of his body and is not related to them as 'other' so long as they are physically part of him" (135). Nor was the self concept nearly as crucial for the Wintu: "with the Wintu the universe is not centered in the self" (138). Likewise, Lutz's study of Ifaluk indicated for these Pacific islanders "the person is first and foremost a social creature and only secondarily, and in a limited way, an autonomous individual" or distinct self; the Ifaluk "are oriented toward each other rather than toward an inner world of individually constituted goals and thoughts" (1998: 81). Therefore, they think of themselves as "more public, social, and relational, and necessarily more dyadic than we do" (82).

See Chapter 2

Lee, Dorothy. 1959. *Freedom and Culture.* Englewood Cliffs, NJ: Prentice-Hall, Inc.
Lutz, Catherine A. 1998. *Unnatural Emotions: Everyday Sentiments on a Micronesian Atoll and their Challenge to Western Theory.* Chicago, IL and London: The University of Chicago Press.

OF MOUNTAINS AND MEN

Western society may overestimate the solidity of its own selves, as is shown by the ease with which that self is manipulated and even re-formed in cases of brainwashing and conversion. The well-known "Stockholm Syndrome" is a phenomenon in which kidnap victims or captives come – sometimes fairly quickly – to identify and empathize with their captors; by a few simple devices, a person's sense of self can be eroded and replaced with another more pliant one. Interrogators are all too familiar with the requirements for this pliability, and domestic abusers often count on it tacitly. The taken-for-granted sense of self appears to need constant reinforcement. Disrupt this process (with sleep deprivation, disturbances of natural rhythms, detachment from friends and family and everything familiar, and disinformation from "re-programmers") and the self quickly collapses and can be reshaped by the right techniques.

Finally, the self may not be uniquely human. Just as anthropologists find "a little culture" in closely related species, so we find "a little self" in these same beings. The question is whether a non-human animal can have an experience of "I" – an awareness of what is and is not its particular individuality. Chimpanzees seem to possess at least some sense of self, as discussed in Box 5.1.

Blank slates, elementary ideas, and human nature

The quintessential question of all social sciences and humanities is, what does it mean to be human? The two major competing perspectives in Western civilization have been the "idealist" one (that ideas are in us from birth) and the "empiricist" one (that experience shapes or fills our mind or personality over time). This dichotomy is popularly known as the "nature-versus-nurture" question. The empiricist or nurture position is associated with the analogy of the *tabula rasa*, the blank slate, which is inscribed by experience. The idealist or nature position would then be associated with a full slate of some sort, the "writing" already given by blood or genes or brains.

Psychology and anthropology were born at roughly the same time, attempting to answer roughly the same questions. Psychology quickly became the study of the "inner" life of individual humans, of that allegedly secret and invisible realm of "mind." Meanwhile, anthropology was coming at the question of human nature and the universal structures of mind from a different angle. One of the first important anthropological ideas was offered by Adolph Bastian (1826–1905), who used the term *elementargedanken* to designate the elementary

BOX 5.1　IS THERE A CHIMPANZEE SELF?

In 1970 the psychologist Gordon Gallup conducted experiments to determine if a chimp knows who s/he is. He set chimps in front of a mirror, and eventually they discovered that the image in the glass was "themselves." They related their motions to the motions in the mirror, and they even began to examine themselves for the first time, looking at parts of themselves that they had never seen before, like their ears and the inside of their mouths. Going a step further, once the animals had become familiar with themselves, Gallup made subtle changes in their appearance, like putting a spot of paint on their foreheads. Back in front of the mirror, they quickly realized that "they" were different and explored the spot, including touching it and sniffing their fingers to figure out what was going on. Chimps that had never seen a mirror before did not react to the spot at all – they had not yet acquired a sense of self. Other experiments have suggested that chimps may also have intersubjectivity – that is, an awareness that other beings have minds and even what may be in those minds. Chimps that are shown the secret hiding place of a key to locked-up food, and then shown humans who behave as if they do not know where the key is, will guide the humans to the key with facial and hand gestures, indicating that they know that they know what the humans do not know and what the humans need to know it.

thoughts or ideas that he believed were found in all humans in all places and times. The *elementargedanken*, few in number and completely universal, were expressed in various forms at various times and places as *volkergedanken* or folk ideas. Thus, the Aboriginals or the Samoans or the Japanese or the Americans would have local versions of religion or kinship, etc., but underneath these particular manifestations was a common shared humanity that merely "came out" in different ways due to local environmental or historical circumstances. One phrase to describe this notion was the "**psychic unity of humanity**," the claim that all humans share the same basic psychological processes. Lucien Lévy-Bruhl (1857–1939), on the other hand, argued that there were two radically different ways of being and thinking among humans – the modern or rational mentality as opposed to what he called the "primitive mentality" that was prelogical and mystical or mythical. How else, he wondered, could we explain the "odd" and ultimately "false" things that people did or thought in "primitive" societies? Lévy-Bruhl eventually withdrew his concept of **primitive mentality**, but ideas like it have persisted over the years to distinguish what appears (to the foreign observer) to be practical from impractical (symbolic? false?) beliefs and behaviors. Both Sigmund Freud and Carl Jung, for instance, posited that human minds operated on two different principles – for Freud, a primary or irrational "pleasure" principle (wish fulfillment) and a secondary or rational "reality" principle. For both, the irrational principle was associated with dreams, children, neurosis, and "primitive cultures."

The psychoanalytic influence on anthropology

Freud and Jung, just mentioned, exerted an important influence on early anthropology. Jung was particularly interested in non-Western and non-modern societies, and both thinkers placed great emphasis on symbols. Freud, the senior of the two psychologists, explicitly linked culture (including art and religion) to mental processes, roughly as a "symptom" of mental, including unconscious, forces. But he also made a number of claims that inspired early anthropologists to employ and/or test his theories. Two critical claims were the universality of certain phenomena (like the Oedipus complex) and the central role of childhood (both childhood experiences and childrearing practices).

A number of anthropologists took psychoanalytic concepts and tools into the field. Geza Roheim, for instance, explored the Oedipus complex among Australian Aboriginals, using myth and ritual to psychoanalyze entire societies. Bronislaw Malinowski (1927) himself tested Freud's claim of a universal (male) Oedipal complex in the Trobriand Islands, arguing that it was not universal but rather a product of particular social arrangements: patriarchal Austrian society might generate such anxiety, but in a matrilineal society like that of the Trobriand Islanders, fathers did not occupy such a central place in boys' mental lives.

Psychic unity of humanity
the position that all humans share a single set of mental processes, even if they think or believe different things; rejects the notion of primitive mentality

Malinowski, Bronislaw. 1927. *Sex and Repression in Savage Society*. Chicago, IL: University of Chicago Press.

Primitive mentality
according to Lévy-Bruhl, a way of thinking characteristic of "primitive societies" in which individuals cannot understand cause and effect and do not distinguish one object from another (e.g., they believe that an animal can be a person)

BOX 5.2   INKBLOTS IN THE FIELD: THE WORK OF A. IRVING HALLOWELL

One of the most confident users of psychoanalytic methods in anthropological research was A. Irving Hallowell, who took the Rorschach "inkblots" and other psychological tests with him on his studies of the Ojibwa. As he wrote, "Personality structure is a psychological dimension of human societies that is directly relevant to the functioning of a human social order" (1967: 33). More precisely, "The link between the psychological data and the cultural data lies in the processes by which, and the specific conditions under which, the human neonate is groomed for adult life and activity" (32). Thus, if personality structure "is never completely reducible to individuality" (36) but is rather "a product of training, experience, and psychological integration that is directly related to the cultural variables that constitute the individual's group-membership situation" (39), then he felt that psychological tests were

www.rorschachinkblottest
.com

appropriate and necessary for anthropology. Hallowell used the Rorschach images to measure the thoughts, emotions, and sense of self of the Ojibwa, as well as other "projective tests" like the Thematic Apperception Test (TAT) or the Draw-a-Person test, which are intended to get the subject to "fill in" or "project" his/her personality into the picture or story. The difference between the clinical use of such measures and the anthropological use was that therapists used them to diagnose single individuals, while Hallowell assumed that "a human being always thinks, feels, perceives, and acts as a socialized *person* who must inevitably share psychological characteristics with his fellows" (39)

American "culture and personality"

The United States is where the seed of psychological anthropology took firmest roots. Recall that modern anthropology emerged in the early 1900s, when social changes were occurring in Western societies, not the least of which were the first battles in the "sexual revolution." So, when Margaret Mead (1901–78) conducted the fieldwork that would culminate in her book *Coming of Age in Samoa: A Psychological Study of Primitive Youth for Western Civilization* (1928), it is clear not only that she was doing psychologically inspired research but that she intended it to have ramifications for Western society. She expected to find that the maturation process as we know it, in particular the turbulence of adolescence, was not a universal one but a culturally particular one. In Samoans (specifically Samoan adolescent girls), she claimed to find the happy, sexually free, well-adjusted youths that she believed Americans could and should be. The implication was not only that humans are psychologically quite malleable – that there are few if any real universals – but that Westerners could stand to learn a thing or two from other, in some ways "better," societies. (Mead's work has come under intense fire from Derek Freeman, who argues that her methods were inadequate, her conclusions wrong, and her agenda too overt.)

Closely behind Mead came another influential female anthropologist who wrote the most widely read book ever published in the field, *Patterns of*

Mead, Margaret. 1928.
*Coming of Age in Samoa:
A Psychological Study of
Primitive Youth for Western
Civilization.* New York: W.
W. Morrow.

PLATE 5.2 Margaret Mead studied enculturation and the acquisition of gender roles in Samoan children.

Culture (1934b). Ruth Benedict (1887–1948) was perhaps even more explicitly psychological in her approach and interests and became a leading force in the culture-and-personality school of thought. In *Patterns of Culture* she treated three different societies as each a unique and complete "configuration." A society, she concluded, has a culture with specific values and ideals, and it aims to construct – and generally succeeds at constructing – individuals who manifest those values and ideals. While the process of individual-construction is not perfect (a certain "range" of personalities emerges in the end), it is effective enough to produce a recognizable "type" of person or personality that is distinctly "Kwakiutl" or "Zuni" or "Dobuan" – or, by implication, American. Thus she could sum up a culture with a few key personality or temperament traits, such as "egocentric," "individualistic," and "ecstatic" for the Kwakiutl, "restrained" and "non-individualistic" for the Zuni, and "fearful" and "paranoid" for the Dobuans. It might be instructive to think of what the key personality traits of one's own culture would be.

Whatever human nature may be, it appears to be diverse and malleable; as Benedict framed it, human possibilities fall along a "great arc," and different societies select specific human qualities to groom and value. Thus, culture is not opposed to the individual or personality, and nurture is not opposed to nature. Both contribute to the shaping of human individuality.

On the assumption, then, that human personality is culturally but not infinitely variable, early and mid-twentieth-century anthropologists often sought to describe and explain the particular personality configuration(s) or type(s) in particular societies. One important concept was **basic personality**, used to refer to the "the effective adaptive tools of the individual which are common to every individual in the society" (Kardiner 1939: 237). This idea was pursued by a collaboration between anthropologists like Ralph Linton and psychologists like Abram Kardiner, resulting in Kardiner's *The Individual and His Society: The Psychodynamics of Primitive Social Organization* (1939) and *The Psychological Frontiers of Society* (1945), which included contributions from Linton, Cora Du Bois, and James West. The mechanisms unifying culture and personality in this approach were institutions (defined as "a fixed mode of thought or behavior which can be communicated, which enjoys common acceptance and the infringement of or deviation from which creates some disturbance in the individual or group" [Kardiner 1945: 24]) and childrearing.

A similar term was **national character**, which has tended to be applied to modern state-level societies, as in Benedict's World War II famous study of Japanese "national character" (1946). Again, the results of such work would be "The Japanese are X and Y," where X and Y are allegedly shared personality traits. Several important studies of national character were composed, including Benedict's report on the Japanese, *The Chrysanthemum and the Sword: Patterns of Japanese Culture* (1946) and Geoffrey Gorer and John Rickman's summary of *The People of Great Russia: A Psychological Study* (1950), often ridiculed for the so-called "swaddling hypothesis" that explained all of Russian personality in terms of wrapping babies too tightly and thereby teaching them to be passive.

Such interests led anthropologists to examine individuals more closely, to identify the connections between personal experience and personality. One outcome was a set of biographical studies, such as Leo Simmons' (1942) account of the life of the Hopi man Sun Chief. However, these more intimate studies, especially Cora Du Bois' 1944 portraits of *The People of Alor*, soon showed that all individuals in a society did not share a single personality, nor did their childhood experiences map one-to-one to their adult personalities. In reaction, Du Bois suggested the concept of **modal personality**, a statistical notion identifying "central tendencies in the personalities of a *group* of people" (1960: xix) – that is, the most commonly occurring personality

Benedict, Ruth. 1934. *Patterns of Culture*. New York: The New American Library.

National character
the purported personality traits shared by an entire society or country; the term was usually applied to modern societies/countries like the United States, China, Japan, or the Soviet Union

Basic personality
the psychological traits common to most or all of the members of a society (roughly synonymous with modal personality)

Modal personality
according to Du Bois, the statistically most common personality traits in a society

Kardiner, Abram. 1939. *The Individual and His Society: The Psychodynamics of Primitive Social Organization*. New York: Columbia University Press.

Primary Institutions ⟶ Basic Personality ⟶ Secondary Institutions
(family structures,   (culture, religion,
basic disciplines,   folklore, arts)
childrearingpractices)

FIGURE 5.1 The relation between culture and personality.

Ethnopsychology
the psychological "theory" or understanding used by any particularly society, including its ideas about and uses of emotions, dreams, mental illness, and personhood most generally

**SCIENTIFIC
ANTHROPOLOGY OF MIND**

traits, although not necessarily universally shared ones.

Contemporary psychological anthropology

Cultural anthropology has largely abandoned such grandiose projects; indeed, for a time psychological anthropology largely fell out of favor in the discipline. However, recent decades have opened new avenues of investigation in the relationship between individual thoughts and feelings and culture and society. Cognitive anthropology, also known as ethnoscience or componential analysis, attempted to get at what members of a society actually had "in their minds." Claude Lévi-Strauss revived psychoanalytic thinking and blended it with linguistic models, describing social phenomena from kinship systems to religious myths as products of a "deep grammar" of mental processes.

Additionally, anthropologists have discovered other person-oriented subjects to explore. One of these is emotions, which are usually viewed as *natural, physical, and subjective*. They are seen as "private" and therefore inaccessible to others (like anthropologists) and "factual," sometimes literal bodily states like a racing heart or a tearing eye. Catherine Lutz further suggests that Western society generally considers emotions irrational, uncontrollable (we are "carried away" by our feelings), dangerous, and frequently female. But not all societies share this conception of emotions nor, so it seems, precisely the same emotions. Indeed, Lutz insists that other societies have not only different emotional traits but different emotional or psychological "theories" or understandings, what she

calls **ethnopsychology**. She claims that the Ifaluk experience a number of emotions that are not quite translatable into Western categories. Among these are *fago*, which conveys compassion and love and sadness simultaneously, especially in reaction to the suffering or need of others; it cannot be translated as "love," for instance, since it has no romantic connotations, and it implies an inequality or dependence not always included in "love." *Song*, another Ifaluk emotional concept, refers to anger but to a particular form of anger, "justifiable anger" or "righteous indignation," and some people are more entitled to feel and express this emotion than others, notably chiefs and parents. *Metagu* or "fear/anxiety" is seen as a positive emotion and social force: "fear is what keeps people good" (Lutz 1998: 201).

Other observers have commented on the meaning and social use of emotions in other societies. According to Schieffelin (1983), anger, sadness, and shame play a special role, and form a special nexus of emotions, in Kaluli cultural life. Keeler (1983) re-examines the Javanese feeling of *lek*, which Geertz characterized as "stage fright" but which Keeler likens more to "respectful self-restraint" as a consequence of social-status differences. Perhaps most suggestively, Abu-Lughod (1985) reports that emotions such as *tahashshum* (embarrassment/modesty/shame) among Egyptian Bedouins not only have strategic functions – as they do in Kaluli, Javanese, and Western societies – but that the distinction between "real" and "conventional" or "private" and "public" emotions cannot be sustained. Some of the most intimate feelings in Bedouin life are communicated in conventional media like songs and poems; that is, even private emotions are conventionalized.

BOX 5.3 THE ETHNOPSYCHOLOGY OF VIOLENCE OR NONVIOLENCE

Are humans naturally violent or nonviolent? This is a question that has long interested humans, perhaps more urgently today than ever. The cross-cultural data suggests that the answer might not be a simple dualistic choice. Around the world we encounter many more societies that exhibit some form of violence than not; Bonta (1997) in his survey counts a mere twenty-five that deserve to be called generally nonviolent. But what makes one society violent and another nonviolent?

Dentan (1968) described the Semai of Malaysia as one of the least violent societies in the world. Part of the explanation was their large-scale social arrangements: as hunters and gatherers living in kinship-based communities without private property, they had little cause or opportunity to engage in aggression. Their gender relationships were also harmonious, and there was little competition of any kind. And at the heart of their culture was the concept of *punan*, the condition of being unhappy or frustrated, as well as the condition of making someone else unhappy or frustrated. It was bad to be *punan*, and individuals went to lengths to avoid it. *Punan* was uncomfortable and potentially dangerous: someone in a state of *punan* could have or cause accidents and misfortune. The Semai took the adage "It hurts me as much at it hurts you" quite seriously.

According to Heald (1986), the Gisu of Uganda had a well-earned reputation for violence. Even they bemoaned their level of aggression, condemning themselves as bad people. At the same time, they prized, and actively promoted, a quality they called *lirima*. *Lirima* was the manly aspect of powerful emotion, linked to anger, jealousy, and hatred. But when harnessed, it provided males with the strength, courage, and determination to overcome fear – and enemies. Men, it turns out, did not possess *lirima* by nature; it had to be inculcated. So they performed initiations in which youths were allowed and encouraged to acquire *lirima*, thus becoming exactly the kind of people they criticize themselves for.

The Ilongot illustrate an even more anomalous kind of personality and violence. Most of the time, they lived their lives in relative tranquility. At other times, they hunted human heads. Central to their sense of themselves and of the institution of headhunting was their concept of *liget* or passion. Men had much *liget*, more than women. They also had more *beya* or knowledge or experience. *Liget* and *beya* were not, though, opposed: "good" *liget* was focused and disciplined by knowledge, but unfocused passion was frightening and ugly. Accordingly, the Ilongot believed that as a man's knowledge grew, his passion subsided. There was a critical moment in early manhood when each was at its peak, and killing an enemy for his head was the "peak experience" of life, the moment of life lived to its fullest. After that event, which might occur only once in a man's life, he "settled down" and began his domestic life, with waning *liget* but expanding *beya*.

Anthropologists have also studied the diverse cultural meaning and importance of dreams and other altered states of consciousness. This includes, as we saw at the outset of the chapter, possession and trance states – which are sometimes seen as undesirable and sometimes, as in the case of shamans or other religious specialists, highly desirable. For many societies, dreams are important sources of cultural information and experience. Australian Aboriginal societies place a high premium on dreams as access to sacred material – songs, dances, symbols, and stories. Among the Mehinaku of Brazil, dreams were believed to be real experiences of the "eye soul" (one of many souls of a person, including the "shadow" and the "sweat soul," the latter of which transformed into a fox upon death). While asleep, the eye soul went "wandering" (*etanowakatapai*), and people explained that the "experiences of the soul in the course of a dream are the result of its contact with the souls of other villagers, who are also wandering about" (Gregor 1981: 711). From the point of view of the Mehinaku "theory of dreams," then, "a dream is as much the soul's experience as the dreamer's, who receives it only from afar" – in other words, Mehinaku understood their dreams to be "separate from" themselves, literally the experience of a detachable part of themselves.

Finally, anthropologists have documented cultural diversity in the prevalence and meaning of mental illness across cultures. First, as Ruth Benedict (1934a) asserted decades ago, what is abnormal or "mentally ill" in one society might not be so regarded in another; further, different societies explain abnormality or deviance in different ways. For example, Elialilia Okello and Solvig Ekblad, writing in the journal *Transcultural Psychiatry*, report that the Baganda of Uganda interpret what we would call depression as a problem of

See Chapter 10

thinking too much and [refer to it] as an *illness of thoughts*. This illness is seen as a nonchronic condition caused by psychosocial, economic and spiritual factors. When depression becomes recurrent or episodic and has psychotic features, as is the case with bipolar

PLATE 5.3 Cultures differ in their notions of, and treatment of, mental illness.

illness, the belief about its cause changes and is regarded to be a clan illness "*byekika*," usually caused by *Misambwa*/clan gods or *Mizimu*/ ancestral spirits.

(2006: 306)

Meanwhile, Mexicans and Mexican Americans are concerned with *susto*, a condition characterized by "restlessness during sleep, listlessness, loss of appetite, and depression," which is understood as the effect of "soul loss" or the departure of some non-material substance or essence or spirit as the result of fright. Clearly, these ethnopsychological concepts have profound implications for people doing counseling or therapy with members of diverse societies.

GENDERS AND PERSONS, OR GENDERED PERSONS

Wherever we find humans, we find them male and female. **Sexual dimorphism** (the occurrence of two discrete body forms based on sex) would seem to be a natural, biological, and universal feature of human existence. American culture in particular and Western culture in general tends to reinforce this impression: there are two kinds of humans – men and women – and two proper codes of behavior – male and female. A person is born a man or a woman, remains so for life, and acts accordingly. Even if things were as simple and universal as this, it would still be within the power of culture to "culturize" the physical differences, with relative values, meanings, and role assignments for the sexes. There is cross-cultural evidence to suggest that here too things are even more complicated.

Surveying the cultures of the world, anthropologists find exceptions to all of these notions. Not all societies believe that there are only two kinds, even two *physical* kinds, of humans. Not all believe that one's sex is set at birth and immutable. And not all assign the same names, tasks, or values along the same sex-line divisions. This is an even clearer case of cultural ontology, each specific society's understanding of what kinds of beings, including human beings, exist, why they exist, and what we

Sexual dimorphism
the occurrence of two physically distinct forms of a species, based on sexual characteristics as well as non-sexual ones such as body size

are supposed to do about it. As an introductory example, Will Roscoe (1994) told us that traditional Zuni culture held that a child's physical sex was a social achievement – that is, that it required social action (in the form of rituals and offerings) to ensure that a child had any sex at all, let alone a particular one, and that a child's sex was not firmly fixed until birth if not later; if a woman fell asleep during labor, the baby's sex might change. So the "settling" of a person's physical sex was the result of culture, not nature.

Further, a person's sex is not always determined in the same way (in particular, by what genitals they possess) or in a binary way. In fact, there are several related but independent variables in the arena of sex and gender, including sexual anatomy, sexual identity (what sex one "feels like" or "identifies with"), sexual preference (what sex one wants to have sex with, and how), and **gender**. By gender we typically mean the social or cultural characteristics – rules, roles, tasks, values, and meanings – that are assigned to people on the basis of (some or another) sexual characteristics. But if sex is not exactly a natural fact, then gender certainly is not. Indeed, Roscoe defines gender as "a multidimensional category of personhood encompassing a distinct pattern of social and cultural differences. Gender categories often draw on perceptions of anatomical and physiological differences between bodies, but these perceptions are always mediated by cultural categories and meanings" (341).

The rise of feminist anthropology

For most of its history, Rayna Reiter asserted in one of the key documents of feminist anthropology, *Toward an Anthropology of Women*, anthropology operated with a male bias – in fact, a "double male bias" adding "the bias we received if the society we study expresses male dominance" to "the bias we bring to our research" (1975b: 13). As Reiter stressed, the book was explicitly intended as a corrective to the male-centric nature of anthropology until the 1970s and firmly place "its roots in the women's movement" (11).

Although a number of important women contributed to the formation of anthropology, including Margaret Mead, Ruth Benedict, and Cora Du Bois (see the discussion of culture and personality above), still they were trained by, and the questions and problems of anthropology were perceived as largely driven by, men. The last straw for many women in the discipline was the volume titled *Man the Hunter* (1968), in which editors Richard Lee and Irven DeVore featured essays on the evolution of humanity and culture. As evaluated by Sally Slocum, also writing in *Toward an Anthropology of Women*, the thesis of *Man the Hunter* was that the "biology, psychology, and customs that separate us from the apes – all of these we owe to the hunters of time past" (1975: 38). But since this hunting behavior "is strictly male" (39), it follows that females contributed little to the development of the species or its cultures and at the extreme that "females are scarcely human" (38).

A series of responses were published, including Reiter's collection as well as *Woman, Culture, Society* (Rosaldo and Lamphere 1974) and *Woman the Gatherer* (Dahlberg 1981). Female anthropologists also conducted fieldwork to ask questions or to collect data ignored by men. For instance, Annette Weiner went back to one of the classic sites of anthropology, the Trobriand Islands where Malinowski did his work, where she explicitly took women's activities and objects "as seriously as any kind of male wealth" and concluded that women were "active participants in the exchange system, and thus I accord them equal place beside" the men (Weiner 1983: 11). Mary Douglas, in *Purity and Danger* (1966), voted one of the most important books of the twentieth century, added that concepts of "pollution" do not necessarily imply inferiority but rather mark social categories and boundaries: women do not pollute men because women are *bad* but rather because women and their activities/tools/bodies belong in one category and men and men's activities/tools/bodies belong in another. For many cultures, violations of categories are inherently dangerous and chaotic. The husband and wife team of Yolanda and Robert Murphy, in *Women of the Forest* (1974), argued that gender *segregation* does not mean gender *inequality/oppression* and that the women of Mundurucu society were actually relatively free and happy, despite the Mundurucu ideology of male superiority. (This conclusion has been questioned on the basis of physical threats to women, including beating and rape.)

Gender
the cultural categories and concepts relating to sexually distinct bodies, sexual preference, sexual identity, and sexual norms

Reiter, Rayna, ed. 1975. *Toward an Anthropology of Women*. New York and London: Monthly Review Press.

See Chapter 7

PLATE 5.4 Muslim women in "purdah" or veil.

Gender divisions and differences

Even in societies that simply and firmly assign human beings to one of two sex or gender categories, there is no absolute reason why those two categories should be segregated and/or valued unequally. Yet, Michelle Rosaldo asserts that "what is perhaps most striking and surprising is the fact that male, as opposed to female, activities are always recognized as predominantly important, and cultural systems give authority and value to the roles and activities of men" (1974: 19). This is not entirely universally true, but it is widespread enough to be noteworthy. Several students of Iroquois culture, for instance, have commented on the power and status of women in that society, but more often than not women and women's activities are held in lower esteem than men's – sometimes extremely so.

Rosaldo's explanation for this fact, which had great influence for a time, was to distinguish between the "domestic" and "public" spheres of a society. Women, she suggested, are typically consigned to a private/domestic space (the household, etc.), based partly on an essentialist view of their "nurturing" tendencies, which is closed off from the economically and politically important public space where men function. As appealing and intuitive as

this notion is, other observers have questioned it. Nelson (1974), for example, argued that women in the Middle East, one of the more patriarchal culture areas, still exercise more power in the public sphere than is usually appreciated. She names such prominent roles as marriage mediator, counselor to her sons, and sorceress/magician/healer as effective positions of power, not to mention their control over food, hospitality, and the family's reputation and honor, as well as over other women via informal friendships and formal women's organizations.

Rayna Reiter (1975a) took the case a step further. In the French village she examined, there was not a real public/private segregation at all. Rather, she referred to what she called a "sexual geography" of the village, such that men occupied and used certain spaces at certain times and women occupied and used some of those same spaces at other times. Women did indeed predominantly inhabit the home and a few other locations, such as the three shops in the village as well as the church (where no "self-respecting man" was willing to be seen), and most of their interests and activities centered on the family. Men, who did almost all of the outside-the-home labor, possessed the village square, the cafés, and the mayor's office in the evenings. However, Reiter noticed that when the men were working in the fields at midday, women

BOX 5.4 IS FEMALE "NATURE" WHILE MALE IS "CULTURE"?

"The secondary status of woman in society is one of the true universals, a pan-cultural fact" (1974: 67), Sherry Ortner concluded on the basis of three cross-cultural observations – "cultural ideology and informants' statements that *explicitly* devalue women," "symbolic devices, as the attribution of defilement," and "social-structural arrangements that exclude women from participation in or contact with" the power and prestige of society (69). But why this (near-) universal devaluation of women? She suggested that women are generally associated with or symbolic of "a lower order of existence" than culture, namely "nature." "It all begins of course with the body and the natural procreative functions specific to women alone" (73). First, women's bodies "seem to place her closer to nature," specifically in respect to childbirth, while the male body "frees him more completely to take up the projects of culture." Second, women's bodies put them "in social roles that in turn are considered to be at a lower order of the cultural process than man's," such as child care, housework, and death. Third, a woman's social roles produce in her "a different *psychic structure*, which, like her physiological nature and her social roles, is seen as being closer to nature" (74) – perhaps more emotional or more carnal. Thus, Ortner insisted, women in most societies are "seen to occupy an intermediate position between culture and nature" (84). Others have formulated it as the problem that women in most societies are not quite granted "social adult" status: they are forever perceived as immature or incomplete or incompetent. But this approach begs the questions (a) *why* women's bodies are seen as more "natural" than men's, and (b) *why* women's roles are valued less than men's.

took over the public village spaces: "The village is then in female hands" (257). Even more, women did not feel downtrodden or inferior at all. Rather, she depicted them as viewing men "as overgrown children strutting around and holding onto places and roles that are really quite silly; these have less value than their own homes and roles as family-cores. They even consider men's space to be inferior to their own" (258).

It might be useful to take the advice of these researchers and consider the relations between the sexes more in terms of a "gendered geography" than a simple and complete division or opposition. This geography can be and often is literally spatial. Herdt (1987) noted that the Sambia of New Guinea, a highly sex-segregated society, actually had separate buildings and even separate footpaths for men and women. However, this geographic exclusion can also be and probably more often is conceptual or cognitive, that is, in terms of knowledge and language than space. For instance, until a few decades ago it was widely believed that men in Australian Aboriginal societies had all of the ritual knowledge and responsibility; earlier studies described male rituals and statuses in detail. However, a new generation of anthropologists like Diane Bell (1993)

discovered a whole parallel world of religious knowledge and ritual activity among women, which led others to explore the relations to groups and to land which individuals can trace through fathers or mothers.

One of the better-studied domains of gender diversity is in language. Many attempts, both popular and scholarly, have been made to distinguish how men and women communicate, including whimsical associations between the sexes and different planets (Mars for men, Venus for women [Gray 1992]). Daniel Maltz and Ruth Borker (1996) summarized the state of the research into cross-gender communication, which determined that women ask more questions, encourage responses, interject more conversation-promoting utterances like "uh huh" and "yes," allow themselves to be interrupted, and use interactional pronouns like "you" and "we." Men are more likely to interrupt, to argue, to ignore the other's comments, to try to control the topic, and to offer opinions or declarations. Lakoff (1975) among others interpreted this as an effect of male domination and female subordination in society. Maltz and Borker proposed, instead, that men and women constitute "different sociolinguistic subcultures, having learned to do

THE OPPRESSION OF
WOMEN ACROSS
CULTURES

different things with words in a conversation" (1996: 84). Boys and girls, they argued, learn to speak differently "because of the very different social contexts in which they learn how to carry on friendly conversation" (87). Why there are divergent male and female conversational contexts, they do not explain.

While not universal by any means, there is evidence of linguistic segregation by sex/gender across cultures. In many societies, the "status" or "high" styles or genres of language are the exclusive province of males. The Wana *kiyori* form mentioned in the last chapter was used solely by men, as was the *kabary* style that comprises formal Malagasy; in fact, Ochs (1996) says that skilled speech and traditional speech types, distinguished by indirectness, relate to men, while plain speech, distinguished by directness, relates to women. Finally, in the Hindi Fijian village studied by Brenneis (1984), the "high" or "sweet" mode of speech called *parbacan*, used for religious occasions and characterized by indirectness, more traditional (Sanskrit) vocabulary, and a more complex grammar, was the unique province of men.

The construction of masculinity

Much of the attention in the discussion of gender focuses on women, which is an important corrective to the disregard of them in much of the past literature. However, in any gender system, men are a gender too, and their gender identity is just as culturally defined as women's. In fact, in some ways it appears to be more precarious. This is suggested by the fact that, in many societies, there is either an explicit belief or an implicit message that men are "made" whereas women are "born." To put this another way, there is a recurring cross-cultural theme that girls naturally mature into women but that boys must be "made" into men: femininity is seen as a "natural" fact but masculinity as a "social" fact. David Gilmore, in his cross-cultural study of masculinity, has claimed that there is a "deep structure of masculinity" in which "true manhood is a precious and elusive status beyond mere maleness, a hortatory image that men and boys aspire to and that their culture demands of them as a measure of belonging" (1990: 17). In this view, manhood (rather than mere physical maleness) is an

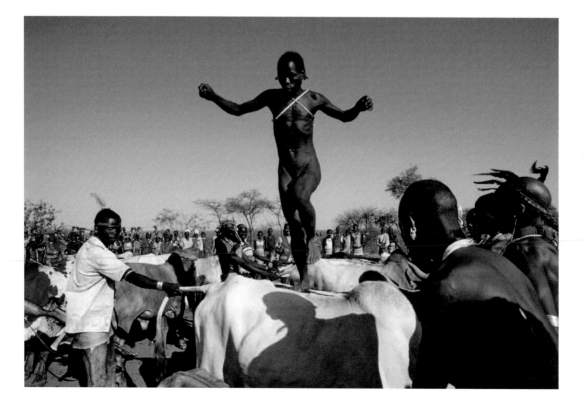

PLATE 5.5 In many societies, men must endure tests and ordeals to achieve adult masculinity.

embattled quality, a struggle against boyhood (and womanhood) that requires constant proving and testing in the form of fighting, competition, sexual prowess, economic success, and whatever a particular society values in its males.

One of the persistent manifestations of this struggle for manhood is male initiation rituals. In Aboriginal Australia, boys were "made into men" through physical operations – circumcision, subincision (cutting a slit in the underside of the penis), scarification, nose perforation, and/or tooth removal – which may take place over a series of ceremonies covering many years. As we saw above, the Gisu performed a ritual to instill the manly virtue of *lirima* in youths, and the headhunt was the culmination of the path to maleness for the Ilongot. This is not to say that female-oriented rituals never occur – of course they do – including scarification and **female circumcision**. Such practices seem to occur more widely in reference to men, but both sexes can be identified and even "created" by literal alterations of the body, which give individuals the culturally correct physical features for their sex. Harold Garfinkel (1967), the founder of ethnomethodology, has referred to modified sex organs as "cultural genitals," in which physical facts like the possession of genitalia become "cultural facts" either through interpretation or alteration of them. I, for instance, was told to keep it a secret from the Aboriginal men if I was uncircumcised, since only circumcised men were fully men and eligible to see the most secret of male rituals.

One practice that has been included in the ritual conception of men in some cultures is what the Western world would call "ritual homosex-

uality." (The very term suggests the problem with imposing foreign cultural categories – a foreign cultural ontology – on another society.) For example, in a variety of Melanesian societies, boys were occasionally or routinely exposed to the genitals and even semen of elders (but not always adults). The Etoro (Kelly 1977) and the Sambia (Herdt 1987) had young boys ingest semen by oral sex performed on adolescent males, while the Kaluli introduced semen by anal sex and the Onabasulu by manual stimulation of males onto the skin of boys. It is interesting that they sometimes found each other's practices offensive: the Kaluli disapproved of the Etoro behavior and vice versa (Kelly 1977: 16).

For the Sambia, as Box 5.5 below reports, ritualized and routine juvenile homosexuality was (it has since stopped) an acceptable and necessary part of their gender creation, based on their unique cultural ontology of maleness and femaleness. In other unrelated cultures, including ancient Sparta, male homosexuality served other functions, including the establishment of corporate spirit within armies. Men in Sparta, as in Sambia culture and elsewhere, were not "habitual" or exclusive homosexuals; in fact, Spartan men married and had children, and Sambians "graduated" from homosexuality to an adolescent bisexuality to adult heterosexuality. It is not the case in all cultures that "homosexuality" is a total and permanent identity or "lifestyle"; it may be a temporary situation or a cultural performance that does not define the man nor constitute an alternative or deviant gender role.

Female circumcision also known as female genital mutilation, the practice of cutting off some or all of a female's external genitalia, for purposes of "beauty" or the regulation of sexual sensations

Garfinkel, Harold. 1967. *Studies in Ethnomethodology.* Englewood Cliffs, NJ: Prentice-Hall.

BOX 5.5   THE CONSTRUCTION OF MALENESS IN SAMBIA CULTURE

The Sambia were a horticultural society in the eastern Highlands of New Guinea in which males were highly valued and a strict segregation, even tension, existed between the sexes. Their villages were divided into male and female spaces, and prior to marriage "all heterosexual relationships, intrigues, and even casual conversations among boys and girls are blocked and forbidden" (Herdt 1987: 3). Women were regarded as not only inferior but dangerous and polluting to men, and with marriage men claimed to own women. Masculinity was a prized quality among men, expressed most fully in the aggressive warrior or war leader, the *aamooluku*. No man wanted to be a *wusaatu* or rubbish man (literally, "soft person"). In the past, troops of men would raid neighboring villages, killing every man, woman, and child before burning it to the ground (53).

Masculine identity and power was based on the central concept of *jerungdu*, which was both a physical substance and the concept of male strength and prowess. One medium of this power was semen, which they believed was not naturally produced in a man's body but must be placed there. Male children also, obviously, had a female influence – physical and spiritual – on them by virtue of emergence from the womb, contact with the mother's skin, and the childhood diet of "soft" foods. It was of critical importance to remove this polluting and weakening female contamination from young males and convert them into real men.

One of the principal means for doing so, and for resolving the semen-shortage problem, was to inseminate the young boys orally, starting at their first initiation around age six. They would fellate older boys who were at a higher initiation status (boys passed through six initiations to achieve manhood). This might occur daily but in secret; adult men did not participate. It was believed that a boy would not grow, and would not become a man, without it. At about age fourteen, boys changed from the fellators to the fellated, and with marriage in late teens or early twenties, they discontinued the behavior altogether.

Oral insemination was hardly the only behavior intended to transform the youth's body from one that was mixed male/female to one that was all male. Boys were also rubbed with scratchy objects to "open" or "stretch" their skin, causing bleeding that washed out female pollutants. They were induced to vomit or defecate to "purge" their internal female contaminants, and they pierced their noses to draw blood (adult men continued to nose-bleed themselves, especially after their wives' periods). They observed food rules and taboos, avoiding "soft" foods that would reintroduce femaleness, and they performed other rituals involving the placement of saliva and hair in ritually selected trees.

In Sambia culture, maleness was a social accomplishment. Being born with male organs did not guarantee successful achievement of adult manhood. Only the ingestion of manly substances – symbolically and literally – and the removal of inherent womanly ones could build a proper man out of the natural raw materials of maleness.

The construction of "alternate" genders

Attitudes, practices, and beliefs regarding sex, sexuality, and gender – indeed the very categories on which these ideas and behaviors are based – vary across cultures. Readers might be prepared to learn, then, that not all cultures share the notion of two and only two sexes or genders at all. In fact, Thomas Laqueur (1990) has suggested that the idea of two sexes/genders is actually recent in Western cultures; until the eighteenth century, he asserts that there was only *one* sex – male – and that females were regarded as incomplete or damaged males (Freud's theories echo this sentiment, with his "penis envy" view). On the other hand, a story told in Plato's *Symposium* relates that in the beginning there were three sexes, each dual – one androgynous (male/female), one male/male, and one female/female – which were split in half by the gods, sending each person in search of his or "other half" (which might be the "opposite" sex or the "same" sex).

Be that as it may, in more than a few cultures there are categories of third or even fourth genders – and even sexes – based on beliefs and concepts that may not exist in other cultures. A few examples of such identities include:

Berdache

In many Native American societies there is or was a tradition of males who adopted certain female roles and traits. In fact, Roscoe (1994) indicates that nearly 150 societies had the third gender, and almost half of those had a fourth gender for women playing more masculine roles. Early Western observers deemed them "transvestites" or "homosexuals," partly judgmentally and partly because those were the only categories the observers possessed. However, within the societies, **berdaches** were members of a distinct and often highly regarded gender. Some were assigned to the category based on physical features, particularly hermaphrodite genitals. Others chose the role. One of

Laqueur, Thomas. 1990. *Making Sex: Body and Gender from the Greeks to Freud.* Cambridge, MA: Harvard University Press.

Berdache
a "third gender" found in many Native American societies, in which biological men adopt some of the norms usually associated with women

CULTURAL CONSTRUCTION OF PERSONS

PLATE 5.6 *Hijras* in India often sing and dance at weddings and childbirths.

the best cases of a berdache institution is the Navajo *nadleehe*, or "one who changes continuously." Like the Zuni, they believed that sex or gender was not entirely fixed, nor was it always related to external/bodily traits. The Navajo *nadleehe* was greatly respected, often given control of the family's wealth, and active as a religious specialist. They performed female economic roles and might dress as males, females, or neither. The Mohave *alyha* and the Lakota *winkte* are two of the better known examples (see Roscoe 1998: 213–47 for a more complete listing). Commonly, berdache status was not believed to be about bodies at all but about spirit – about have "two spirits," both male and female, in one body.

Eunuch

The common image of eunuchs is castrated males in ancient and medieval societies who were assigned specific roles and tasks, most famously guarding the harems of polygamist leaders. However, eunuchs were not always castrated; they might be sterile or celibate or simply lacking in sexual desire. The defining feature of the eunuch status was not absence of male parts but absence of "manliness," based on their non-generativity (i.e., they would or could not have children). Ringrose (1994) indicates that they were a legitimate third gender, neither male nor female, and that they performed functions that neither males nor females could do. Interestingly, these jobs often involved positions of

mediation and transaction across boundaries, such as doorkeepers, guards, messengers, servants, secretaries, and masters of ceremonies – suggesting that their own anomalous circumstances made them fit for dealing with anomalous boundary-crossing circumstances.

Hijra

In northern India, a virtual subsociety of individuals regarded as "neither man nor woman" – but also "man plus woman" – exists and participates in the greater society (Nanda 1999). *Hijras* may be born with male or hermaphroditic body parts; either way, they share the quality of impotence. The ultimate mark of a true *hijra*, though, is to have the male genitals removed completely (in a ritual called *nirvana*), so that the person truly is neither man nor woman but a third distinct type. *Hijras* typically live in their own communal groups under the leadership of a guru or teacher, forming a surrogate kinship system. Local groups are organized into "houses" (of which there are seven with names and histories and rules); each house has a regional leader or *naik*, and the regional leaders occasionally meet at the national level. *Hijras* are most known for their musical performances at weddings and births. Ironically to Westerners, *hijras* as nonsexual beings and ascetics are associated in Hindu tradition with fertility and procreation. They are sexually ambiguous, but in a culturally specific way: the god Shiva possesses androgynous traits and is ascetic, blurring

Hijra
a "third gender" in India, in which biological men renounce their sexuality (and often their sexual organs) and become socially neither male nor female

Nanda, Serena. 1999. *Neither Man nor Woman: The Hijras of India*, 2nd ed. Belmont, CA: Wadsworth Publishing Company.

Eunuch
a gender category involving non-sexual individuals (usually men), who may be castrated or merely celibate, sterile, or lacking sexual desire

the Western lines not only between male and female but between sexuality and asceticism.

Travesti

In Brazil, there is a type of effeminate male who actively attempts to achieve more female-like physical features and often works as a male prostitute. They are not transsexuals and do not claim to be women; rather, they say that they want to be "feminine" or "like women" (Kulick 1997). To that end, they take female hormones and get surgery to modify their bodies to a more culturally appropriate female shape. They are often appreciated for their beauty, by female standards. They do not, however, get sex-change operations, since they do not want to be women or to lose their male genitals. Sexually, they act as receivers of anal sex with men but never as penetrators. Kulick argues that **travesti** do not constitute a third gender but rather represent the Brazilian dualistic view of gender identity – two genders, "men" and "not-men" (including women and *travestis*) based not on bodies but on behavior. In this case, the behavior is partly the role in sexual intercourse (men penetrate, non-men are penetrated) and partly more general qualities of dress, manner, etc. A "real man" could have sex with a *travesti* and remain a real man, as long as he was the penetrator. In fact, *travestis* thought it would be offensive to have sex with each other, since they were the "same kind."

There are a few documented cases of "cross-gender" female institutions in various cultures. Schwimmer (1984) mentions female transvestism in four Melanesian societies. A number of Native American societies had female correlates of the male berdache status, including the Mohave *hwame* role. According to Gremaux (1994), there was a custom by which women could become "social males" in the Balkans. One process involved a biological female who renounced her femaleness in adulthood, often via a vow of abstention from sex and marriage. A

Travesti

an alternate gender role in Brazil, in which males take on certain physical traits and sexual behaviors typically associated with females

second process involved the decision of the parents to raise a baby girl as a son, giving her access to property and inheritance and even training her as a soldier (especially when the family had no sons). However, around the world, "alternate" or "third" genders tend to be institutions for what the West would consider "biological males," although not all societies, as we have seen, make the same assessment of that fact as Western societies do. Ultimately, the main difference between Western cultures and others that permit and value gender alternatives may be the latter's toleration for ambivalence, ambiguity, and even contradiction in sex, identity, and other factors.

Finally and not surprisingly, modernization and globalization have left impressions on cultural conceptions of sex and gender. In the "transcultural junctures created by science, modernization, and development programs" (Pigg and Adams 2005: 21), foreign, especially Western, notions of sex and gender have circulated around the globe. The media for these cultural notions and images have included of course movies and music but also political discourse about human rights and even scientific discourse about contraception, abortion, homosexuality, sexually transmitted diseases, and other "sexual health" issues. This supposedly neutral "medicalization" of sexuality has affected local concepts and practices in disparate ways. Readers might recall that the President of Iran recently denied that homosexuality even exists in Iran. Meanwhile, according to Cohen (2005), the Western or "cosmopolitan" category of "gay" has been introduced into India, vying with traditional categories like *hijra* or *kothi*. According to Nguyen the "new version of the 'facts of life'" is reorganizing male–female and male–male relationships in the Ivory Coast (2005: 245), and ideas of women's rights and practices like birth control are sparking reconstructions of the role of women, the nature of marriage, and the understanding of "morality" from Russia and India to China and Africa – and the West as well.

BOX 5.6 CONTEMPORARY CULTURAL CONTROVERSIES: DO MUSLIM WOMEN NEED SAVING?

Since the attacks on the United States on September 11, 2001 and the emergence of global Islamic terrorism, the custom in many (but not all) Islamic societies of "the veil" has become an icon of cultural difference. Well-meaning Americans and other Westerners often feel that we need to "save" Muslim women from the oppression of the veil and general gender segregation. And no doubt women have suffered under some Islamic regimes, like the Taliban of Afghanistan. But Lila Abu-Lughod notices that more than a few contemporary Muslim women have *chosen* to wear some version of the veil (sometimes a simple headscarf or *hijab*, sometimes a full covering or *burqa*), even if those women were raised or have lived in "modern" and "liberated" cultures. Also, the custom of the veil has different meanings for different women: some see it as an act of faith, even a religious duty, while for others it is modesty or privacy, or a marker of identity, or sheer tradition. Lughod insists that "we need to work against the reductive interpretation of veiling as the quintessential sign of women's unfreedom, even if we object to state imposition of this form" and that "we must take care not to reduce the diverse situations and attitudes of millions of Muslim women to a single item of clothing" (2002: 786). Rather than thinking in terms of "saving" them, she advises that we "use a more egalitarian language of alliances, coalitions, and solidarity," working together toward "making the world a more just place" (788). What do you think?

SUMMARY

Human beings are individuals, but they do and must learn to be particular kinds of individuals, and this occurs under the influence of culture. Psychological anthropology or culture and personality bridges the gap between the poles of "nature" and "nurture" – humans have an individual and a species nature which is nurtured in specific ways to achieve specific outcomes.

- Enculturation is the process that links the individual to his or her society and its expected and desired psychological and behavioral characteristics.
- Personality is the individual product or precipitate of a person's experience in a social context, based on more or less explicit and intentional practices aimed at raising the proper kind(s) of people
- Modal personality is the cumulative or statistical result, the most common personality traits in a society, where personality traits may or will be distributed according to factors like age, sex, class, etc.

Every society contains in the final analysis a unique cultural ontology or theory/system of what kinds of entities and beings – human and otherwise – exist, what their natures are, and how society should respond to them.

- Some societies, but not all necessarily, posit a "self" that distinguishes the individual.
- Humans may not be the only species capable of "self" awareness, any more than we are the only capable of "language" or "culture."

MCQS

FILL IN THE BLANKS

Part of a society's ontology includes its sex/gender system. A society may

■ Identify two sexes or genders based on physical traits
■ Identify two sexes or genders based on other than physical traits
■ Identify three or more sexes or genders based on physical or other than physical traits.

That is, human individuals come with particular physical/bodily configurations, but how society interprets and values – culturizes – those physical facts is relative.

Key Terms

Basic personality

Berdache

Cultural ontology

Ethnopsychology

Eunuch

Female circumcision (FGM or female genital mutilation)

Gender

Hijra

Modal personality

National character

Personality

Primitive mentality

Psychic unity of humanity

Self

Sexual dimorphism

Travesti

Individuals and identities
Race and ethnicity

When people travel, they often learn as much or more about themselves as about their destination society. This was certainly true for the American students, tourists, and workers whom Kathryn Mathers followed to South Africa. South Africa is famous – and infamous – for its race regime (see below), but this does not mean that "race" has the same meaning in South Africa as in the United States nor that the race categories are the same in the two countries. Indeed, American travelers were frustrated and confused "when they discovered that American race categories and their meanings did not apply in South Africa" (Mathers 2010: 112). For instance, individuals who would be called, and would call themselves, "black" in America often "were not recognized as black" – and certainly not as *Africans* – in Africa (149). One American fellow who regarded himself as "black to the core" was surprised and offended when South Africans told him he could pass for "colored" (mixed-race) and when he and his dark-skinned African American partner were called "an interracial couple" (103). And at the same time that their "racial" identity was being brought into question, their "American" identity was becoming clearer: inside America, race is often "visible" while "Americanness" is invisible

or taken for granted, but in another country like South Africa, race became much more complex or unfamiliar while American identity suddenly became much more obvious and consequential.

Human beings belong to a single species. However, it is an incredibly diverse species, behaviorally and physically – a "polytypic species," one that comes in a variety of different forms. Long before anthropology existed, people were trying to make sense of this diversity, and one enduring concept invented by Western societies to categorize and explain human diversity is race. More recently, observers suggested the concept of "ethnic group" to refer to the same, or sometimes quite different, human variables. Both terms, but especially race, have a troubled history, fraught with confusion and abuse. Both terms, like gender, are also ways to classify humans and, even more importantly, to assign value and tasks to humans. In other words, like gender, race and **ethnicity** are examples of an ontology or a taxonomy, a classification and evaluation system. As anthropologists, we are indeed interested in human difference – the characteristics of distinct human groups – but we are equally if not more interested in the systems by which those groups are conceived, the relations between those

Ethnicity
the phenomenon of organizing around some aspect of shared culture to integrate an identity group, differentiate it from other groups, and compete in a multi-ethnic context for resources

PLATE 6.1 Western tourists in Africa inevitably take their preconceptions with them.

groups, and the social practices by which, and the social purposes for which, those groups and relations are created, perpetuated, contested, or changed.

THE ANTHROPOLOGY OF RACE

Every English speaker has a general sense of what race means: physical differences (usually and especially surface differences, like skin color) between humans, or more often between major "types" or divisions, even "breeds," of the human species, generally geographically separated, and the groups characterized by those differences. Although race thus relates to physical or biological factors, there is a wide (though not quite universal) consensus that races are not "real" or "objective" entities but are rather social constructs. As Audrey Smedley asserts, the "reality of race" resides in "a set of beliefs and attitudes about human differences, not the differences themselves" (1999: xi). This is not to declare that there are no differences between human individuals or groups – there obviously are – but rather

to draw attention to the fact that the differences that matter and precisely how and why they matter are cultural and not natural issues. Smedley explains that biological variations between groups of human beings

> have no social meanings except what we humans give them. This is what is meant when we claim that races are culturally constructed. It is the social meanings imposed on the varying human populations that we must investigate to understand race.
>
> (xii)

It is not difficult to show that race is a slippery and problematic term: for instance, when a "black" person and a "white" person have a child, what race is the child? And does it matter if it is the father or the mother who is "black"? Does it matter exactly what the child looks like, that is, how "black" or "white" s/he appears? The talented "black" golfer Tiger Woods has publicly declared that he is not "black" since his ancestry includes Africa, Caucasian, Asian, and Native American; he even invented a new race-term for himself – Cablinasian

Smedley, Audrey. 1999. *Race in North America: Origin and Evolution of a Worldview*, 2nd ed. Boulder, CO: Westview Press.

– despite the fact that most Americans still consider him "black."

The truth is that different societies, or even the same society at different times in its history, have answered these questions differently. Part of the problem is that the term "race" has been chronically imprecisely defined, if it has been defined at all. Francis Collins, the head of the Human Genome Project, insists that

> it is essential to point out that "race" and "ethnicity" are terms without generally agreed-upon definitions. Both terms carry complex connotations that reflect culture, history, socioeconomic and political status, as well as a variably important connection to ancestral geographic origins.
>
> (2004: S 13)

Brazilian anthropologists Sergio Pena and Telma de Souza Birchal insist that race is not a scientific idea; rather, "The notion of race has been imported from the common sense to science since its appearance" (2005–6: 3).

Five obvious and fatal objections to the concept of race have been raised. First, no one has been able to specify exactly how many races there are. Common estimates range from three to five or as many as nine. Second, race classifications select certain physical characteristics (most often skin color) and not others on which to base the categories, and it is not explained how and why these particular traits were chosen as the relevant ones: why skin color instead of blood type or height or shoe size? Third and related to the first two, the classifications, evaluations, and applications of race change over time. For example, not so long ago English speakers used (and sometimes still use) the term race in reference to "the French race" or "the Scandinavian race" or "the Jewish race" or "the Arab race" or even "the human race." Groups that never regarded themselves as a single identity ("the Native American race") are subsumed under one category, as are people who are physically quite diverse, like the "Hispanic race," which includes "white" people, "black" people, "Indian" people, and every conceivable mixture of these and more. Fourth, some researchers have calculated that there is more physical and genetic variation *within* race groups than between them: according to Richard Lewontin (1972), for the eight race categories he considered,

85.4 percent of genetic diversity was found inside the categories and only 6.3 percent between the categories. Fifth and finally, race classifications have not always, if ever, been content to stop at physical characteristics but have attributed psychological, emotional, intellectual, and even moral qualities to the purported races as well. For instance, Madison Grant wrote in 1916 that "moral, intellectual, and spiritual attributes are as persistent as physical characters and are transmitted substantially unchanged from generation to generation" (226).

The evolution of the race concept

According to Dante Puzzo, a historian of Western ideas, race (and its evil concomitant racism) "is a modern conception, for prior to the sixteenth century there was virtually nothing in the life and thought of the West that can be described as racist" (1964: 579). Michael Banton (1987) finds that the word "race" did not appear in English until 1508. However, as Europeans acquired more experience with peoples from other parts of the world, and as they acquired power over those peoples, differences in body and behavior became more interesting to them – and frequently became intertwined for them.

See Chapter 3

The familiar system of race categories appeared in the work of Linnaeus (1707–78), the great classifier of natural species. In the first edition of his *Systema Naturae* published in 1740 he divided the human species into four subtypes based on color – white, black, red, and yellow. By the tenth edition in 1758–59, these types had evolved into *Homo europaeus*, *Homo afer*, *Homo americanus*, and *Homo asiaticus*, acquiring not only geographical but (often quite offensive) mental and behavioral features.

The elastic quality of race categories is seen again in the work of Johann Friedrich Blumenbach (1752–1840), who proposed the standard four races in his *On the Natural Variety of Mankind* in 1770 – European (for whom he introduced the term "Caucasian"), African, American, and Asian. Subsequently, he added a fifth race, Malayan, for southern Asian people. Interestingly, Blumenbach made several important qualifications to his race system, not the least of which was that each of the "five principal races" was actually composed of "one

BOX 6.1   LINNAEUS' FOUR RACES OF HUMANITY

While Carolus Linnaeus made the study of humans more scientific by including them in the animal kingdom, he made it less scientific by conflating physical and cultural traits in his four races of mankind. *Homo europaeus* he characterized as "white, sanguine, muscular. Hair flowing, long. Eyes blue. Gentle, acute, inventive. Covered with close vestments. Governed by laws," while *Homo afer* was "black, phlegmatic, relaxed. Hair black, frizzled. Skin silky. Nose flat. Lips tumid. Women without shame. Mammae lactate profusely. Crafty, indolent, negligent. Anoints himself with grease. Governed by caprice." Native Americans he termed *Homo americanus*, distinct for being "reddish, choleric, erect. Hair black, straight, thick; nostrils wide; face harsh; beard scanty. Obstinate, merry, free. Paints himself with fine red lines. Regulated by customs." Finally, Asians or *Homo asiaticus* were "sallow, melancholy, stiff. Hair black. Eyes dark. Severe, haughty, avaricious. Covered with loose garments. Ruled by opinions" (quoted in Slotkin 1965: 177–78). The pseudoscientific system was only worsened by the inclusion of other imaginary species of humanity such as *Homo ferus*, a hairy and mute quadruped, and *Homo monstrosus*, a monster-race of cavemen who roamed the world at night.

See Chapter 3

or more nations which are distinguished by their more or less striking structure from the rest of those of the same division. Thus the Hindoos [sic] might be separated as particular subvarieties from the Caucasian; the Chinese and Japanese from the Mongolian; the Hottentots from the Ethiopian" (Slotkin 1965: 191), and so on. In other words, he admitted considerable variation *within* "primary races." Also, he conceded that races were not entirely discrete: although the race-types were

> so many different species of man, yet when the matter is thoroughly considered, you see that all do so run into one another, and that one variety of mankind does so sensibly pass into the other, that you cannot mark out the limits between them.
>
> (ibid.: 189)

Finally and most consequentially, the races were not only distinguished but ranked in terms of antiquity and perfection, the first race in time and quality being the white/Caucasian one. As the original, "primeval" form of humanity, Caucasians were the most "beautiful," at the middle of a spectrum of races with Asians and Africans at the opposite extremes, Americans/Indians intermediate between Caucasians and Asians, and Malayans intermediate between Caucasians and Africans. The non-Caucasian races were deemed a product of *degeneration* from the first, ideal type and the admixture of the higher and lower types.

Race typologies multiplied and morphed over the centuries. George Cuvier (1769–1832) managed to condense them to three – Caucasian, Mongolian, and Negroid – with white Caucasians as the optimal form of humanity and black Negroids as "the most degraded race among men, whose forms approach nearest to those of the inferior animals, and whose intellect has not yet arrived at the establishment of any regular form of government, nor at anything which has the least appearance of systematic knowledge" (quoted in Green 1959: 235). Most whimsically of all, Carl Gustav Carus (1789–1869) created a four-race system consisting of Day People (Caucasian), Eastern Twilight People (Mongolians, Malayans, Hindus, Turks, and Slavs), Western Twilight People (American Indians), and Night People (Africans and Australians).

Measuring and managing mankind

The failure to achieve any accord on the number or nature of races, yet the persistence with which theorists have sought racial systems, alerts us to the urge toward race typing in Western societies: while thinkers have not settled on a uniform race classification, they have certainly believed that such classification was possible and important. None seemed to stop and ask the question that Sherwood Washburn posed only in the 1960s: what is a race classification for? What is its social origin and – still more significantly – its social function or effect?

The question of why people want and need to identify races and to build race classifications is indeed the central question of race. Several scholars have directed attention less toward race itself or any particular race system than toward what we could call "racial thinking,"

> the (erroneous) belief that humanity is divided into scientifically observable, homogeneous, and mutually distinct biological "types." Importantly, it assumes that these types exist transhistorically, that is, that these categories exist. . .as natural facts, and that these categories existed throughout time, whether people in a particular era realized it or not.
>
> (Eissenstat 2005: 239–40)

More crucial than the concept of race for describing physical differences between kinds of humans, then, is the use of those descriptions for *explaining and justifying* certain behaviors of and relationships between these kinds.

It cannot be overemphasized that Western societies developed their racial thinking in the context of political and cultural domination over non-Western societies. Far beyond the neutral or pure-scientific activity of cataloging and organizing human physical variety (a not illegitimate project), Western travelers and theorists were led to ask why the people they encountered acted and thought in unfamiliar and (often to Western eyes) nonsensical or reprehensible ways. And as this contact became increasingly exploitative, including conquest and slavery, Westerners were further led to ask why these other people were so "weak" or "backward" or "inferior." One possible and appealing answer was a sort of biological determinism – that humans with particular biological traits also had particular behavioral or mental traits that inhibited their "progress." The persistence of "backward/inferior" behavioral and psychological qualities after exposure to the "superior" ways of the West, and the failure of these other peoples to "improve" and "succeed" in the Western sense, gave rise to the notion that physical characteristics were a sign and a cause of mental and even moral deficiencies – most critically, that the physical and the mental/moral were inseparably connected and that both were innate and permanent.

Thus the conventional English-language, especially North American, concept of race arose, with its five key components (Smedley 1999: 28):

1 a race is an "exclusive and discrete biological" entity;
2 races are fundamentally unequal, and the relations between races are necessarily hierarchical (some are "better" than others);
3 "the outer physical characteristics" of races are "but surface manifestations of inner realities [such as] behavioral, intellectual, temperamental, moral, and other qualities";
4 all of the qualities of a race are "natural" and genetically inherited – and inherited as a single indivisible bundle;
5 therefore, the differences and hierarchies between races are immutable, "fixed and unalterable, [and] could never be bridged or transcended."

In the end, race was not simply a classification of human physical differences but a *bio-moral* judgment (Wolf 1994) on certain types of humans who were ranked inherently and eternally "higher" or "lower" than other types of humans. Race thinking accomplished the valuable task of "naturalizing" political, economic, and cultural status or class inequalities and ascribing them as intrinsic properties of the victims of these inequalities.

The obvious task then was to specify and quantify these natural differences. Accordingly, the nineteenth century became the great era of measuring mankind. In fact, in his study of the science of race, John Haller proposes that "The hallmark of anthropology in the nineteenth century was anthropometry" (1971: 7). **Anthropometry** was and is a practice of measuring the bodies of human beings for the purpose of describing individual and collective physical characteristics. In itself, recording people's height and weight and head size is neither unacceptable nor absurd; however, the generalizations and interpretations of this research could be problematic, distasteful, and patently false.

Certain traits emerged as central to Western race classification, including hair form and color, skin color, eye form and color, nose form, face form, overall height and body form, and especially head size and shape. One of the earliest measurable traits was **facial angle**, or roughly the amount that the

THE EVERYDAY LANGUAGE OF WHITE RACISM

See Chapter 12

Anthropometry

the measurement of human bodies to determine individual and group ("racial") physical characteristics

Facial angle

a concept in anthropometry that measures the shape of the face from the forehead to the bridge of the nose, on the assumption that sharper angles indicate "more primitive" kinds of humans

Miscegenation

a term for the undesirable effects of the mixing of different genetic types or populations, especially race groups. Often refers to the very notion of mixing the races

PLATE 6.2 Anthropometry – measuring racialized bodies.

Adoc-photos / Art Resource, NY

Cephalic index

a measurement of the skull/brain volume and shape, based on a ratio of the width of the head from ear to ear relative to the depth of the head from front to back

lower face and jaw protrudes, deviating from the ideal flat face of the ideal Caucasian. It was noticed that apes and even more so dogs and other animals had very acute facial angles, which was linked to their lower intelligence; by extension, humans with acute facial angles (resulting from sloping foreheads and/or large jaws or lips) were deemed more animalistic and less intelligent. Darker skin color was also taken as a lower and more primitive feature, as was short stature or especially long or short limbs.

However, the major factor then, as for many people today, was the head and brain: "scientific" measures like brain volume and cephalic index purported to quantify racial inequalities. **Cephalic index**, introduced by the great neurologist Paul Broca, was a ratio of the width of the head from ear to ear relative to the depth of the head from front to back; a higher index suggested a rounder head and a superior intelligence. Determining brain volume was fairly straightforward, on the assumption that larger brains meant greater intelligence. Happily for scientific racists, Caucasians scored well on both tests, with a cephalic index and a brain weight and volume higher than all other races. Samuel Morton ranked the brains of races in the descending order of Caucasian, Mongoloid, Malay, Native American, and African, further arguing that brains had not altered in four thousand years and thus could be deemed fixed and permanent. In the skull and in numerous other characteristics, Africans consistently ranked lowest, indicating to racial thinkers "a far closer relationship to the ape" than any other human species (Haller 1971: 34).

The implications of such racial thinking are obvious: if some races were naturally and permanently higher or lower than others, then it made little sense to preach the equality of races or to attempt to raise the lower races. It even seemed reasonable to subordinate and restrict the lower ones, and certainly interbreeding (**miscegenation**) was to be avoided as deleterious to the more perfect races – or, ironically, sometimes to be promoted as a means to "improve" the more degraded ones. Nineteenth- and early twentieth-century racial thinking was thus an ideal justification for slavery, segregation, colonialism, and genocide. Influential figures like Edward Drinker Cope insisted that the "inferior character of the Negro mind in the scale of evolution made him unfit for American citizenship" (Haller 1971: 198), while Nathaniel Southgate Shaler went so far as to excuse lynching as a legitimate form of race self-defense (ibid.: 184–85).

It should be noted, in conclusion, that biological-deterministic, bio-moral explanations and recommendations were not limited to race groups. In the nineteenth and even more so in the twentieth century, biological causes were often proposed for behavioral, temperamental, moral, or social circumstances. Measurements of brain size, cephalic index, and facial angle, or less "scientific" attributes like stature and skin color, were applied to the new immigrants arriving in the United States from eastern and southern Europe around 1900 – Caucasians all, by the standard typology. Various immigrant groups were regarded as congenitally prone to drunkenness or idleness or crime or violence. Predictably, all sorts of vices and social improprieties were explained in biological terms, including poverty: some people, it was held, were naturally unable to compete or succeed, and a few social engineers went so far as to recommend that the poor not be allowed to breed, since poverty was a transmissible condition. Criminals were subjected to bio-moral analyses, on the hope that a "criminal type" might be identified that would make capture and punishment of outlaws easier (a kind of biological "profiling"). Mental illness was often associated with physical imperfections and therefore with physical therapies: the "insane" were often thought to be animal-like in their insensitivity to heat, cold, pain, and exhaustion (which is not even true of animals), and somatic "cures" like bleeding, blistering, near-drowning, swinging and spinning,

BOX 6.2   THE POLITICS OF RACIALLY CORRECT DOLLS

Race is not only a cultural concept but, in more than one way, a cultural industry: society produces and circulates categories and judgments of race, as well as the material manifestations and representations of race. One example, explored by Elizabeth Chin, is "racially correct dolls," that is, toys that are intended, probably benignly, to be inclusive and positive: a little girl should be able, so the argument goes, to play with a doll that looks like her. In 1991, Mattel, the manufacturer of Barbie, introduced "minority" versions of their toy, with darker skin, African American facial features and hair, and names like Shani, Asha, and Nichelle. Ironically, while the dolls were no doubt meant to encourage racial awareness, they had the effect of "fixing racial boundaries more firmly" (Chin 1999: 305), that is, generalizations or stereotypes were not questioned but assumed, reproduced, and marketed. Other companies joined Mattel in offering ethnic dolls, including Shindana and Olmec, but Chin insisted that most such initiatives continue to take race as a given; they do not "significantly transform the understanding of race, or even racism" (310). They exemplify "an attempt to turn racism on its head but not an attempt to re-imagine race itself" (317). Interestingly, Chin argued that the little girls who owned dolls, including Barbies, were more "keenly aware of the complexity of race" (317), as indicated in a variety of ways. First, they did not find white Barbie as oppressive as toymakers might presume; further, they had ways of "ethnicizing" white Barbies, for instance by styling their hair in "ethnic" ways. Even more, the girls sometimes rejected the manufacturers' racial designations, like identifying Shani not as African American but as Native American. Thus, the children were actively refashioning race traits and categories, while the toymakers were simply repackaging the same old traits and categories.

or immobilization were practiced. This attitude extended to those with disabilities, like the deaf who were also regarded as lacking sense or intelligence, like wild animals, and were not allowed to vote in the United States until the early 1800s. Advocates of the **eugenics** movement like Victoria Woodhull echoed the sentiments of the racial miscegenists when she insisted that all such people, "imbeciles, criminals, paupers, and the otherwise unfit. . .must not be bred."

THE MODERN ANTHROPOLOGICAL CRITIQUE OF RACE

The confusions, abuses, and outright falsehoods surrounding racial thinking could not forever escape criticism, and cultural anthropology contributed significantly to this critique. The elaboration of the anthropological concept of "culture" combined with the growing body of observational data of non-Western peoples and the inclusive and relativistic attitude of anthropology provided it with a unique and authoritative perspective from which to judge the discourse of race.

One of the first and strongest voices to challenge racial thinking was Franz Boas. Much of his work was targeted specifically at the reigning ideas and practices of race, as in his 1928 *Anthropology and Modern Life*, as well as his 1940 *Race, Language, and Culture* and his 1945 *Race and Democratic Society*. Starting from the premise that there "is little clarity in regard to the term 'race'" (Boas 1928: 19), he took the key step of separating physical from psychological and cultural phenomena, concluding that "it is well-nigh impossible to determine with certainty the hereditary traits in mental behavior" (50). Rather, the variability of intelligence and personality within a group, and the rapidity and ease with which individuals change in new circumstances, convinced him that "cultural experience" was as important as if not more important than "racial descent."

Having placed learning above biology for explaining behavior, he went further to unpack the race concept itself. A race was not a closed, fixed physical type but something more akin to a family line, with its common but by no means immutable traits; mix in other family lines and the race-type dissolves. Still worse, a race is not a homogeneous

Eugenics
the scientific practice of "improving" a population or species by selective breeding or genetic engineering, to breed out "bad" traits and breed in "good" ones

PLATE 6.3 Children in central Australian Aboriginal societies have straight, often blond, hair, challenging the simple racial categories of the West.

Herskovits, Melville J. 1958 [1941]. *The Myth of the Negro Past*. Boston, MA: Beacon Press.
Montagu, M. F. Ashley. 1945. *Man's Most Dangerous Myth: The Fallacy of Race*, 2nd ed. New York: Columbia University Press.

BOAS ON PHYSICAL CHANGES IN THE DESCENDANTS OF IMMIGRANTS

unit but a vague division of humanity with much internal variety: obviously not all Caucasians or *Homo europaeus* have blond hair and blue eyes, and the alleged "race traits" of any race are a statistical abstraction from a diverse distribution of features. At best, the stereotype of a race is the *extreme or ideal* form, but these extreme forms "are not pure racial types. We do not know how much their descendants may vary from themselves and what their ancestry may have been" (22–23). Most devastating of all, Boas asserted that physical traits, as much as mental/behavioral ones, are plastic and subject to environmental pressures, not fixed permanent inheritances. Some of his most influential (and controversial) research argued that the children and grandchildren of immigrants differed measurably from their ancestors in head shape, cephalic index, and height and conformed more to the standards of their newly adopted land – indicating that "race traits" were highly changeable and only appeared stable as long as environmental conditions remained the same.

Under the tutelage of Boas, anthropology was academically and politically active on the question of race, even condemning Nazi racism in a 1938 resolution which stated that "Anthropology provides no scientific basis for discrimination against any people on the ground of racial inferiority, religious affiliation or linguistic heritage" (American Anthropological Association 1939: 30). Melville Herskovits attacked racism against African

Americans directly in *The Myth of the Negro Past*, which refuted five lies about the "Negro race": that they "are naturally of a child-like character"; that they are unintelligent since "only the poorer stock of Africa was enslaved"; that because slaves came from all parts of Africa, they had no common culture; that whatever culture they did have was "so savage and relatively so low in the scale of human civilization" that they would have quickly given it up; and that "the Negro is thus a man without a past" – and presumably therefore only a man (and woman) with a racial body (1958: 1–2).

But arguably the most vociferous critic of racial thinking was Ashley Montagu, calling it "man's most dangerous myth," not only as an error but as a tragedy (1945: 1). Races in the everyday sense do not exist, he explained, as it is a fact "that all human beings are so much mixed with regard to origin that between different groups of individuals intergradation and 'overlapping' of physical characters is the rule" (3). Worse still, as we have seen, the concept of race implies much more than physical similarity but "a compound of physical, mental, personality, and cultural traits which determine the behavior of individuals inheriting this alleged compound" (6). However, "Such a conception of 'race' has no basis in scientific fact or in any other kind of demonstrable fact. It is a pure myth, and it is the tragic myth of our tragic era" (8).

For Montagu, racial thinking was a way of translating cultural differences into physical differences; the real and crucial issues are status and caste issues, in which resources, opportunities, and social value are differentially assigned to groups and then these groups are "closed" to each other spatially (by segregation) and sexually (by rules of **endogamy**). Race is thus, he concluded,

> a term for a social problem which is created by special types of social condition and by such special conditions alone. In terms of social relations so-called "race problems" are, in the modern world, essentially of the nature of caste problems.
>
> (67)

In a racial system, physical characteristics "are merely the pegs upon which culturally generated hostilities are made to hang" (66). Accordingly, following a suggestion in the 1935 book *We Europeans* by Julian Huxley and A. C. Haddon, Montagu advocated the use of the term "ethnic group" (see below) to name these socially and culturally distinguished collections of humans – and rejection of the term "race" completely.

Like Montagu, Frank Livingstone insisted on the "non-existence" of races in the human species, claiming that "there are excellent arguments for abandoning the concept of race with reference to the living populations of *Homo sapiens*" (1962: 279). The physical anthropologist Sherwood Washburn, who raised the central question of the purpose of race classifications, seconded the analysis that race is a cultural construction and that there is "no possibility of studying human raciation, the process of race formation, without studying human culture" (1963: 522). The physical evidence tells us that there are "no three primary races, no three major groups. The idea of three primary races stems from nineteenth-century typology" (523). Rather, "Since races are open systems which are intergrading, the number of races will depend on the purpose of the

Endogamy
the marriage principle in which an individual marries someone who is in the same cultural category as himself or herself (e.g. marrying someone in your own race or religion)

PLATE 6.4 Human faces of many races.

classification" (524) – or, if no social purpose is served by it, no racial distinction might be made in the first place.

These and many other anthropologists have deflated the concept of race as a natural, objective, scientific tool and have redirected attention to the social phenomenon that Manning Nash calls the "ideology of race." Recognizing that the "non-existence" of races in the natural/objective sense does not mean the non-existence or irrelevance of race as a cultural force, Nash defines race ideology as

> a system of ideas which interprets and defines the meanings of racial differences, real or imagined, in terms of some system of cultural values. The ideology of race is always normative: it ranks differences as better or worse, superior or inferior, desirable or undesirable, and as modifiable or unmodifiable. Like all ideologies, the ideology of race implies a call to action; it embodies a political and social program; it is a demand that something be done.
>
> (1962: 285)

Perhaps we should add that it is also a justification for things that are already being done, such as discrimination, slavery, or genocide.

Nash goes beyond the identification of race ideology to theorizing about when such an ideology will appear, for not all societies in all times have possessed it. A race ideology, he hypothesizes, is likely to coalesce when there is a conflict between two or more groups distinguishable in physical terms; when there is a division of labor based on this distinction which results in the "subordination or systematic deprivation of one group"; when the subordinate group resists or refuses its subordination; and interestingly when there is dissent within the dominant group over the "prevailing facts of disprivilege" (288). In such conditions, the ideology of race serves not only to subjugate the "lower race" but to justify to the "dominant race" its own advantages and privileges. If he is correct, then the appearance and elaboration of a race system should come *after* the social inequalities which it explains, legitimates, and perpetuates rather than before.

The report was especially addressed to native and *métis* people who "have a long history of documented economic, social, and historical disadvantage in Canada" (54). Noting first that many Aboriginal people do not consider themselves "minorities" but rather members of a native nation, like the Cree, the report also acknowledges that such people in Canada experienced systematic mistreatment through such institutions as "the

BOX 6.3   POLICY ON RACE AND RACISM IN CANADA

While the United States is especially self-conscious of its race categories and race history, the United States is hardly the only society that struggles with race and racism. Canada is also a multiracial society, containing immigrants of many nations as well as linguistic minorities (particularly the French-speaking Quebecois), numerous native or Aboriginal groups, and people of mixed descent sometimes called *métis* in Canada. (There is even a Métis National Council in Canada, with its website at www.metisnation.ca/.) Like most other plural societies, Canada has suffered its share of racial injustice and violence; in fact, one alarming problem is the disappearance or murder of Aboriginal women along Canada's highways, as documented in the film *Finding Dawn*, Dawn being a missing native woman. In 2003, the provincial government of Ontario issued a statement condemning racial profiling, which the Ontario Human Rights Commission defined as

> any action undertaken for reasons of safety, security or public protection that relies on stereotypes about race, colour, ethnicity, ancestry, religion, or place of origin rather than on reasonable suspicion, to single out an individual for greater scrutiny or different treatment"
>
> (2003: 6)

residential school system and the wholesale apprehension and adoption of Aboriginal children into non-Aboriginal families" (55). In the present, many Aboriginal people testified to

> the intense humiliation they felt when dealt with negatively in plain view of others by storekeepers, security guards, transit employees, and police. Others talked about the frustration they felt when trying to obtain some kind of service or fair treatment from government services, health care, etc.

Individuals strongly believed "that they were being treated differently because of their race and/or appearance" (56). The Commission clearly condemns racism and racial profiling for being ineffective for its supposed goals and for having negative consequences such as loss of individual dignity or self-esteem and the erosion of trust in social institutions like government or police. The recommended solutions amount to an increase, and institutional practice, of cultural competence and sensitivity.

THE ANTHROPOLOGY OF ETHNICITY

Most English-speakers are not only familiar with the concept of ethnicity or ethnic group but commonly associate it with race, as in "race and ethnicity" or "racial and ethnic groups." Many may even consider the two terms synonymous, although they are not. Nevertheless, race and ethnicity are closely related in certain ways. Both are practices for categorizing people – by physical characteristics for "race" and by cultural or behavioral characteristics for "ethnicity." Often, a group that shares physical traits also shares behavioral ones; as just shown, racialist thinkers tended to link the behaviors of the group causally to its biology, while anthropologists realize today that behavior is learned and shared and, therefore, that groups of people who are genetically related will inevitably tend to interact more and to share more cultural characteristics as well. Furthermore, like races, ethnic groups are not objective or natural "things" but social concepts with social meaning and function. Accordingly, as with race, anthropological attention has shifted from the reputed qualities of particular ethnic groups to the relations between these groups

(frequently competitive and sometimes combative, including discrimination, oppression, and genocide) and to the processes by which the groups are formed and sustained.

When Huxley and Haddon proposed "ethnic group" as a replacement for "race," they were explicitly reviving a very old notion, one employed by the ancient historian and traveler Herodotus, who "found human beings divided into a number of groups, *ethnea*, and the *ethnos* forms his practical basis of classification" (Huxley and Haddon 1935: 30). However, the term *ethnos*, roughly translated as "a people," "a nation," or "a cultural group" (and incorporated into anthropology in terms like ethnology, ethnography, and various subdisciplines such as ethnobotany and ethnopsychology) was then as today a slippery and vague concept: "Thus, his *ethnos* is at times a tribe, at times a political unit, at times a larger grouping, and in using the word he guards himself against treating either type of unit as necessarily or even probably of common descent" (31).

So the root *ethnos* and the English words derived from it, including "ethnic group" and "ethnicity," entered the language with wide but various and uncertain meaning; they could refer to numerous kinds of groups with imprecise qualities and porous boundaries. Even so, or perhaps for exactly that reason, the concept of ethnic group has stuck and even grown in popular and scholarly usage. Max Weber wrote about it in the early twentieth century, defining the term as a human group

> that entertain[s] a subjective belief in their common descent because of similarities of physical type or of customs or both, or because of memories of colonization and migration; this belief must be important for the propagation of group formation; conversely, it does not matter whether or not an objective blood relationship exists.
>
> (1968: 389)

Notice in this definition that physical and cultural traits are still both included, yet neither is necessarily "real": membership in an ethnic group, he asserted, is distinct "precisely by being a presumed identity, not a group with concrete social action. . . .[Ethnicity] does not constitute a group; it merely facilitates group formation of any kind, particularly

AMERICAN ANTHROPOLOGICAL ASSOCIATION STATEMENT ON RACE

Weber, Max. 1968. *Economy and Society*, vol. 1. Guenther Roth and Claus Wittich, eds. New York: Bedminster Press.

in the political sphere." This led Weber to three crucial realizations about ethnic groups: first, that they need not be very culturally different from each other (that is, a small cultural difference is sufficient to construct an "ethnic" difference); second, that they need not be very internally culturally homogeneous (that is, there may be considerable diversity *within* the ethnic group); and third, that any cultural trait – language, religion, clothing, cuisine, and so on – can suffice to distinguish one ethnic group from another.

Since the reintroduction of "ethnic group" by Weber and by Huxley and Haddon (and the later invention of the noun "ethnicity"), the concept has become essential to discussions of and developments in human group relations. While there is no single authoritative definition for ethnic group or ethnicity, the definitions that have been offered share important common features and indicate important cultural processes. Thus, ethnicity has been defined as the "subjective symbolic or emblematic use of any aspect of culture [by members of a group], in order to differentiate themselves from other groups" (DeVos 1975: 16) or as the

> character, quality, or condition of ethnic group membership, based on an identity with and/or consciousness of group belonging that is differentiated from others by symbolic "markers" (including cultural, biological, or territorial), and is rooted in bonds to a shared past and perceived ethnic interests.
>
> (Burgess 1978: 270)

Rather than crafting definitions, another and more fruitful course is to identify the characteristics of the groups that are produced. Fredrik Barth suggests that an ethnic group has four key qualities: it is "largely biologically self-perpetuating" generally through endogamous marriage, "shares fundamental cultural values," "makes up a field of communication and interaction," and "has a membership which identifies itself, and is identified by others, as constituting a category distinguishable from other categories of the same order" (1969: 10–11). Andrew Greeley offers a list of six features of an ethnic group:

(1) A presumed consciousness of kind rooted in a sense of common origin.
(2) Sufficient territorial concentration to make

it possible for members of the group to interact with each other most of the time and to reduce to a minimum interaction with members of other ethnic groups.
(3) A sharing of ideals and values by members of the ethnic group.
(4) Strong moralistic fervor for such ideals and values, combined with a sense of being persecuted by those who do not share them and hence are not members of the ethnic group.
(5) Distrust of those who are outside the ethnic group, combined with massive ignorance of them.
(6) Finally, a strong tendency in members of an ethnic group to view themselves and their circle as the whole of reality, or at least the whole of reality that matters.
(1971: 120–21)

Ethnic culture, ethnic boundary, and ethnic mobilization

Whether or not all ethnic groups possess all the qualities highlighted by Greeley, such analyses raise two relevant points. First, ethnicity and ethnic groups bring together a set of powerful forces, summarized by Manning Nash (1989) as "blood, bed, and cult," to which we might add "soil" or "land" as well. In other words, there is, to some extent, a biological or genetic component: an ethnic group may be endogamous or in-marrying, so that the group is more or less genetically "closed." Some ethnic groups place a strong value on marrying within the group, and some practically or even legally prohibit marriage outside the group. When ethnic groups are thus sexually isolated, they necessarily come to share a biological bond with each other, like a family; some go so far as avowing an ineffable and almost mystical "essence" that sets them apart from – and often above – other groups. Pierre van den Berghe has likened ethnic groups to extended kin groups: an ethnic group, he argues, always contains at least a core "made up of people who know themselves to be related to each other by a double network of ties of descent and marriage. Ethnicity is thus defined in the last analysis by *common descent*" (1987: 24). Still, he admits that, "in many cases, the common descent ascribed to an

Nash, Manning. 1989. *The Cauldron of Ethnicity in the Modern World*. Chicago, IL: University of Chicago Press.

ethny [his term for ethnic group] is fictive. In fact, in *most* cases, it is at least *partly* fictive" (27). We should conclude that ethnicity is based not so much on ancestry as on "a myth of ancestry" (Horowitz 1985: 52) which may involve stories of the origin and struggles of the group.

The mention of myth brings us to Nash's "cult," which here means not just religious belief (although certainly religious belief too) but all of the cultural factors that unite the group and which serve more than instrumental functions for the group. Orlando Patterson has explicitly stated that certain aspects of its culture have "the functions of. . .rituals for the group – the ways in which they are used to maintain group cohesiveness, to sustain and enhance identity, and to establish social networks and communicative patterns" (1975: 305). Finally, "soil" or "land" is important literally and symbolically – literally as a place for the group to live and as a physical/territorial boundary around the group, and symbolically as a homeland where formative events occurred and/or where the forefathers lived and died.

The problem of ethnicity and ethnic groups can perhaps then be distilled to two issues – the *culture* of the group and the *boundaries* that enclose the group; both serve to distinguish and even segregate groups from each other. To begin, surely ethnicity is "about" culture, in the same way that race is "about" biology. However, in the same way that biological difference does not make straightforward or exclusive race classifications possible, cultural difference does not make straightforward or exclusive ethnic classifications possible. First, as DeVos noted earlier, an ethnic group does not use *all* of its culture in defining its ethnic identity; in fact, as Weber explained long ago, an ethnic group is not different in every cultural regard from neighboring ethnic groups. In Rwanda the Hutu and the Tutsi speak the same language, while in Northern Ireland the Protestants and the Catholics belong to the same major religion (Christianity). Any ethnic group is unlike other groups in some ways and like other groups in other ways.

Furthermore, there is potentially considerable cultural variation *within* an ethnic group. Anthropological studies of supposed African "tribes" in the 1940s illustrated conclusively that many such groups were highly internally heterogeneous and frequently appeared "to be an amalgam of different peoples, each aware of its unique origin and history" (Fortes and Evans-Pritchard 1940: 26). That is to say, not only were "societies" or "ethnic groups" often internally diverse, but many had only recently come into existence, through a process that anthropologists call **ethnogenesis**, the construction of ethnic identity out of the "raw material" of culture and history. On those grounds, it is accurate to conclude that "it would be misleading to state simply that ethnic groups are identical with cultural groups" (Eriksen 2002: 36).

For these reasons, anthropologists like Fredrik Barth have redirected the discussion away from the "contents" or traits of particular ethnic groups and toward the boundaries between them, which emphasizes the fact that ethnicity is a relationship and process. Criticizing the notion that there really are discrete "aggregates of people who essentially share a common culture" (1969: 9) – aggregates that can be identified by a trait-list of cultural characteristics (a specific language, religion, history, name, territory, and such) – Barth insists that the key to ethnicity and ethnic groups is "the ethnic *boundary* that defines the group, not the cultural stuff that it encloses" (15). This shift in focus allows us to see that ethnicity is a form of social organization, not merely a fact of timeless and immutable cultural difference. It therefore compels us to analyze the processes by which groups develop and preserve boundaries, even while individuals or culture-traits within the boundary change over time. Finally and critically, it answers a question implied by DeVos' definition above: if ethnicity is the use of aspects of a culture, why are *some* aspects used and not others, and what are they used for? In this new view, particular elements of culture function as "markers," "signs," "flags," or "badges" of membership and non-membership, of inclusion and exclusion. Even more, members who "wear" the markers signal their solidarity with other members – and their preparedness for common action.

For, in the ultimate analysis, ethnicity is a style of social action, specifically and commonly political and economic action. An ethnic group may be an identity group, but it is also, in most cases, an interest group and often a competitive group. Ethnic groups do not exist in isolation; a group by itself is not an ethnic group in the proper sense. Two or more ethnic groups share a social space, where

Ethnogenesis
the process by which ethnic groups come into being and/or attain their cultural characteristics

Barth, Fredrik, ed. 1969. *Ethnic Groups and Boundaries*. Boston, MA: Little, Brown & Co.

See Chapters 13 and 14

they are in some particular (if shifting) social, political, or economic relation to each other. Like races, they are regularly separated by territory or neighborhood, class or profession, and politics or power – and unequally at that. While ethnicity does not imply hierarchy as inherently as race, in practice it often has precisely that effect. So ethnicity can be a means to press the group into action, to mobilize it to strive for some goal, which can include or entail "closing ranks" and acting jointly *as* a group and *in the interests of* the group.

Types of ethnic organization and mobilization

Since ethnicity does not refer to any specific and universal kind of cultural difference or cultural goal, it follows that ethnic groups come in many diverse forms and relations to each other. In fact, not all cultural groups are fully and equally organized and "incorporated" *as* ethnic groups; in a word, not every cultural difference is the basis for an ethnic difference or an ethnic group. Eriksen (2002: 43) proposes that, at the lowest level of awareness and mobilization, an ethnic label might be no more than a "category," a name to call certain people or for a certain people to call themselves. When such people begin to interact in terms of their common identity, they constitute a "network." Once the group becomes not only organized but goal oriented, it transforms into an "association," and when that association develops a territorial base, it evolves into a "community." Not all (potential) ethnic groups, of course, achieve this complete evolution.

Among groups that attain ethnic awareness and organization, there is still great diversity. Eriksen (2002: 14–15) offers five different types of ethnic groups/relations:

1   urban ethnic minorities (usually as the result of migration)
2   indigenous peoples (usually as the result of colonialism and conquest)
3   proto-nations, that is, groups that "claim that they are entitled to their own nation-state"
4   ethnic groups in plural societies
5   post-slavery minorities.

Eriksen, Thomas Hylland. 2002 [1993]. *Ethnicity and Nationalism: Anthropological Perspectives.* London: Pluto Press.

Gurr and Harff (1994: 15–23) give a similar but somewhat different analysis, including four types which they call:

1   ethnonationalists, "relatively large and regionally concentrated ethnic groups that live within the boundaries of one state or of several adjacent states; their modern political movements are directed toward achieving greater autonomy or independent statehood";
2   indigenous peoples, "the descendants of the original inhabitants of conquered or colonized regions";
3   communal contenders, "ethnic groups whose main political aim is not to gain autonomy but is, rather, to share power in the central government of modern states"; and
4   ethnoclasses, "culturally distinct minorities who occupy distinct social strata and have specialized economic roles in the societies in which they now live. They are, in other words, ethnic groups who resemble classes."

RACIAL AND ETHNIC GROUPS AND RELATIONS IN CROSS-CULTURAL PERSPECTIVE

The characteristics of race and ethnic groups are less interesting or important than the relations between these groups. In fact, it is appropriate and useful to think of racial and ethnic relations as a subset of group relations more generally, whether those relations are based on race, ethnicity, gender, age, class, or any other criteria. It is never the differences between groups that matter as much as the social/cultural meanings of those differences and the relationships and inequalities between the bearers of the group "markers."

First and foremost, race and ethnic systems are not only methods for classifying and explaining human differences but for establishing (more or less) sharp and permanent separation between the groups distinguished by these differences. In a word, the concepts and practices of race and ethnicity create "distance" between socially defined and socially defended bounded groups. There are various ways to conceptualize and quantify this "social distance," such as the Social Distance Scale developed by Emory Bogardus (1933), a set of questions to test the willingness of people to enter into relationships (from superficial to intimate) with members of other groups. At the minimal level of acceptance, the scale asks whether the subject is willing to allow group X to inhabit or even visit his/her country; at increasingly intimate levels, questions assess whether the subject would accept members of group X in his/her town, neighborhood, workplace, circle of friends, or very family (through intermarriage). Obviously, the more exclusions raised against a group, the greater the "social distance" between the group in question and one's own.

But the relations between groups are not merely individualistic and subjective. There are large-scale, structural relationships as well, ones that persist despite the attitudes and actions of particular individuals. George Simpson and Milton Yinger (1972) constructed a useful typology of group relations, comprising six types arrayed from relatively benign to highly malignant:

Assimilation: the process by which a group loses some or all of its unique characteristics and adopts the characteristics of another or the dominant group. **Cultural assimilation** refers specifically to the loss of distinctive cultural traits, such as language or religion, while **racial assimilation** occurs when the physical traits of a group are lost through intermarriage. (Some analysts have also proposed a category of **social** or **structural assimilation** for groups that are integrated into the society

– say, sharing the same jobs or the same neighborhoods – whether or not they share the same culture. Significantly, a group may be culturally assimilated, that is, possess more or less the qualities of another or the dominant culture, but still not be socially assimilated.)

Pluralism: the coexistence in the same country or society of groups with distinct cultures. Rather than adopting a foreign or dominant culture, a group retains some distinct behaviors or values, possibly as a source of ethnic or racial pride, and may even maintain loyalty to their group (or, if migrants, to their former homeland) rather than to the wider society in which they live. (Other theorists have recommended distinguishing cultural from structural pluralism as well.)

Legal protection of minorities: since the personal interactions and attitudes between groups may be influenced by discrimination and hostility, a society may institute formal protections for the rights of subordinated groups. Examples would include the 1964 Civil Rights Act in the United States and the 1965 Race Relations Act in the United Kingdom, followed by many other measures to attempt to guarantee equality between groups and to reduce or eliminate the prejudice and animosity against disadvantaged groups.

Population transfer: a policy or practice of physically moving groups from one location to another, ostensibly to reduce tensions and hostilities. For instance, Native Americans were

Pluralism
the coexistence of multiple social/cultural groups in the same society or state

Assimilation
the social process by which individuals and groups are absorbed into another, usually dominant, cultural group

Cultural assimilation
a type of assimilation which refers specifically to the loss of distinctive cultural traits, such as language or religion

Racial assimilation
a form of assimilation in which the physical traits of a group are lost through intermarriage

Social assimilation
a form of assimilation in which groups are integrated into the society (for instance, sharing the same jobs or the same neighborhoods), whether or not they share the same culture

Structural assimilation
see social assimilation

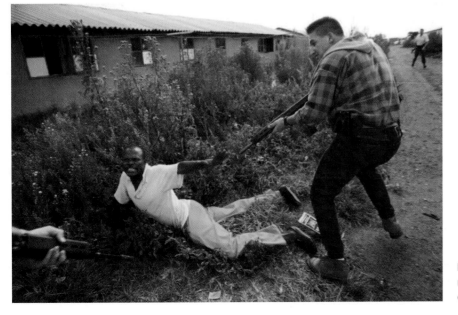

PLATE 6.5 Racial divisions, racial tensions, and racial violence were high during the apartheid era of South Africa.

See Chapter 11

Genocide
the destruction of a group
or society by harming,
killing, or preventing the
birth of its members

See Chapter 13

"removed" from parts of the Southeast in 1830 and resettled in "Indian country" (present-day Oklahoma) for their (and white Southerners') benefit; the surviving "reservation" system in the United States or "reserve" system in Australia is a product of such policies. At the partition of India in 1948, large populations were also transferred to the "correct" side of the India/Pakistan (i.e., Hindu/Muslim) border.

Continued subjugation: dominant groups may have no desire, and no awareness of a need, to change the subordinate position of other groups in the society or country. In such cases, the dominant group may institutionalize hierarchical relations (like slavery or ghetto neighborhoods), pass laws and adopt entire systems of exclusion (like segregation in the United States or *apartheid* in South Africa), or even use force to suppress groups and any resistance they might organize.

Extermination: the "final solution" to racial and ethnic "problems" may be the physical destruction of disfavored groups. Also known as **genocide**, the most familiar case is the killing of millions of Jews by Nazi Germany in the 1940s, but many other instances have been recorded in history (and no doubt many more unrecorded), including the eradication of Armenians by Turkey, of Hottentots by Dutch settlers in South Africa, of Aboriginals by Euro-Australians, and of Native Americans by Euro-Americans. Short of all-out extermination of ethnic groups is the outbreak of "ethnic conflict."

The race regime of South Africa

The most complete and rigid race system ever practiced by humanity probably reigned in South Africa in the second half of the twentieth century.

BOX 6.4   DEAFWORLD: THE CULTURE OF THE DEAF

Most people do not think of the disabled as a cultural group; however, many among the nearly 1 million deaf and nearly 8 million hearing-impaired Americans disagree. Indeed, as Owen Wrigley stresses in his *The Politics of Deafness*, at least some representatives of the deaf community "vigorously refuse the identity label 'disabled,' seeing themselves strictly as a linguistic minority" (1996: 7–8), even as "a distinct 'ethnic identity'" (13). They promulgate a conception of deafness not as a physical deficit but as a cultural difference. No doubt many a reader will find this use of "ethnic" and "cultural" to be a stretch of those terms: how is it that "a group of people who do not have any distinctive religion, clothing, or diet – or even inhabit a particular geographical space they call their own – could be called 'cultural'" (Padden and Humphries 2005: 1)? And while the use of these terms does at first appear to challenge or distort them, in reality the anthropological value of "ethnicity" and "culture" does not lie in any particular "distinctive" marker or location but rather in the creation and transmission of beliefs, practices, values, and relations. True, not all deaf (or, as some prefer, Deaf) are born deaf, nor is deafness passed from person to person in the deaf community. All the same, there is a Deaf community, sometimes named Deafworld or even "Deaf country," with its own traditions, most especially its (sign) language. American Sign Language (ASL) is more than a manual version of spoken English; it has its own style (characterized by candor and directness), its own practices for greetings, leave-takings, attention-getting, turn-taking, and so on, and even its own literature of stories, poems, plays, and jokes (Lane, Hoffmeister, and Bahan 1996). It has a social network with social institutions, from clubs to schools and colleges (most prominently Gallaudet University), and national and international organizations, like the National Association of the Deaf, the American Athletic Association of the Deaf, the National Theater of the Deaf, and the World Federation of the Deaf. More than a few members of Deafworld are protective of their unique identity, some going so far as to demand that members use ASL and not try to "pass" as Hearing by reading lips; the most militant citizens of Deafworld reject hearing aids and surgery on the basis that such efforts are genocidal – akin to forcing black people to change their bodies to conform to white biological standards.

A large region on the southern tip of the African continent, it was the home to diverse native people before the arrival of Europeans, first in 1652 but mainly in the 1800s. The original Dutch colonists established a racial division of labor, with themselves as the merchant and ruling class set over African manual and slave labor; against some native groups, like the hunting-and-gathering Ju/hoansi, the Dutch or "Boers" conducted a virtual genocide, while they fought hard wars with societies like the Zulu. When the British arrived in the early nineteenth century, conflicts followed between the two white groups and between them and the black peoples of the area, leading to the utter defeat and displacement of the native populations.

In 1931 South Africa became independent, with the white minority governing the large non-white majority. But racial differences and inequalities were formalized after 1948, when the newly elected Nationalist Party began to implement its *apartheid* program. Afrikaans for "apartness" or essentially segregation, *apartheid* structured life in South Africa for almost a half-century. With it came official registration of the "races" of South Africa, including "white," "Asian," "colored," and "African." Race labels were applied without regard to cultural assimilation: "coloreds," for instance, were generally fully Westernized and Christian like whites but were still legally and structurally set apart. Likewise, "westernized Indians and Africans [could] not lose their ascribed caste status. Membership in one of the four castes [was] by birth and for life" (van den Berghe 1967: 102).

Of course, the four race-castes were carefully separated and ranked in terms of wealth, power, and status, with the whites dominating in all three realms; each race had "a legally defined set of privileges or disabilities" (ibid.), with strong sanctions against race fraternization and intermarriage. Africans were at the bottom of the system, with coloreds second only to whites in most regards, and Asians (mostly Asian Indians) "subjected to a more hostile government policy and to more restrictions" than the coloreds although generally economically better off. The African majority (over two-thirds at the height of *apartheid*) was largely relegated to slums or to nominal "homeland" areas. In 1994, the long-jailed leader of the African National Congress, Nelson Mandela, became the first elected black president of South Africa, thus ending the utter political domination by whites but hardly solving all of the economic and structural problems caused by centuries of colonial and racial oppression.

Interestingly, Dunbar Moodie finds that the "tribal identity" of many South African black groups is a recent development, greatly shaped by colonialism. Before European intervention, he explains, lower-level collectivities like "homestead and lineage groupings, more or less structured into chiefdoms. . .were the standard forms of social organization" (Moodie 2005: 320). "Tribes" and "tribalism" were to a significant extent products of colonial administration, with Europeans introducing the notion of tribe (as some primordial, distinct, culturally bounded system) and even creating "tribal authorities" like "chiefs" for "tribes" that had never had chiefs before. Finally, the circulation of labor, especially the migration of men to cities, induced them to organize and to find native leaders in totally non-traditional ways, inventing "ethnicity" or "tribal identity" in the process. Predictably, then, some groups like the Xhosa are highly diverse, even amalgamations of numerous peoples such as Thembu, Bomvana, Mfengu, and Mpondo, to name just a few. In other words, not only the "races" but the "native tribes" of South Africa are at least partly constructions of modern forces.

See Chapter 7

Racial democracy in Brazil?

Clearly not all regions of the world suffer from the same level of race-consciousness and racism. Some, in fact, claim to be "race blind"; that is, to have no race problems and virtually no race consciousness at all. Among these, Brazil is sometimes held up – and sometimes holds itself up – as a "racial paradise," a "racial democracy" where the races are equal and where "race" in the English-language sense of the word does not even quite exist. It is true, as various observers have commented, that Brazilian society is not based on the rigid and highly binary (white/black) categories of European and American race thinking. Although colonial Brazil was characterized by the same "racial" composition as the United States (white colonists, African slaves, and Native indigenous people), interbreeding was more condoned and common, and "mixed-race" children more accepted and highly placed in the social structure.

van den Berghe, Pierre L. 1967. *Race and Racism: A Comparative Perspective.* New York: John Wiley & Sons, Inc.

Frequent blending of the "races" in Brazil "made the line between Black and White imprecise" (Daniel 2005: 89), and race categories "displayed fluid racial markers, such that Blackness and Whiteness represented merely polar extremes on a continuum" (91). Accordingly, Brazilian race thinking includes many more fine distinctions of color and other physical features: the Brazilian Institute of Geography and Statistics found that people used an incredible 134 different color terms to describe themselves and others, including *alva* (pure white), *alva-escura* (off-white or dark white), *esbranquecimento* (mostly white), *acastanhada* (cashew- or caramel-colored), *trigueira* (wheat-colored), *amarelo* (yellow), *verde* (greenish), *roxa* (purplish), *preta* (black), *queimada* (burnt), *quase-negra* (almost Negro), *pretinha* (light black), *meio-preta* (mid-Negro), *mulatinha* (lighter-skinned white-Negro), and of course *mulatta* (mixed white and black). The importance of this complicated and continuous terminology is that it has precluded the emergence of two or three closed and absolute race categories.

However, complexity is not necessarily equality. Contemporary researchers question the "myth of racial democracy" in Brazil, finding that physical appearances, while diverse, are not without social consequences. There may be more subtle distinctions in the Brazilian typology, but there nevertheless exist

> distinct aesthetic canons [that] lead one to regard certain types as more attractive than others. For example, light brown skin is valued over both pale and dark skin; straight hair is considered "better" than curly or kinky hair, and facial features approximating the Negroid type are generally regarded as ugly.
>
> (van den Berghe 1967: 71)

Additionally and more seriously, social opportunities are distributed in racially meaningful ways: individuals with more "African" characteristics disproportionately fill the lower rungs of income, jobs, and education. And, particularly in the interior of the country, many indigenous peoples live on the periphery of Brazilian society, their land and lives at risk from exploitation and latter-day colonialism.

Finally, while Brazil has traditionally avoided the simple dualistic race system of black-versus-white, there are some signs of change in that direction. Daniel refers to an ideology of "whitening" that encourages the increase of white physical traits in the population along with a purge of African and Native ones, through such means as expanded European immigration, restricted African immigration, and the promotion of marriage to partners "more culturally and phenotypically European" than oneself (2005: 91). At the same time, another movement operates in the opposite direction, to "raise black consciousness" and to unify darker-skinned Brazilians into a self-aware race group: the effect would be, and the goal is, to replace the spectrum of non-white color categories with a single one (*negro* or black), thus supplanting the loose Brazilian system with a more rigid, American-like system.

PLATE 6.6 Concepts and practices of beauty in Brazil relate to local notions of race and gender.

Mestizaje: the future of race in Mexico

The mixing of diverse populations has been a fact (although not always an equally welcome or statistically significant fact) whenever two groups come in contact for any appreciable length of time. However, in some times and places, "race mixing" has been positively encouraged, even praised. The part of the world in which this sort of mixing has perhaps been most common – and most lauded – is Latin America, especially Mexico. The local term for the fact of historical mixing and the positive value of such mixing is *mestizaje*, from the Spanish word *mestizo*, a person of dual (especially Caucasian and Native American) ancestry.

Mestizaje can be defined as "the claim – both scientific and ideological – that racial mixture throughout the [South American] continent has affected both genetic and cultural blending to the point where any racial distinction has become mean-ingless" (Tilley 2005: 54). For those who acknowl-edge the process, some bemoan it as a corruption of the "real" races, some accept it as a neutral fact, and others celebrate it as the undermining of the entire race concept – and even as the emergence of a single unified super-race. The most memorable spokesman for this position was Jose Vasconcelos, whose 1925 essay *The Cosmic Race* explicitly pits the English attitude of race exclusiveness against the race inclusiveness of the Spanish and Portuguese – and the future belongs to the inclusivists:

> The days of the pure white, the victors of today, are as numbered as were the days of their predecessors. Having fulfilled their destiny of mechanizing the world, they themselves have set, without knowing it, the basis of a new period: The period of the fusion and mixing of all peoples.
>
> (1979: 16)

Recognizing that the Spanish people themselves are "but a conglomeration of different types and races" (19) and therefore amenable to blending, he not only expects but desires the birth of a "fifth race" (after white, black, Asian, and Native American) which, created through "well-being, sympathy, and beauty," will be "a type infinitely superior to all that have previously existed" (31).

In some ways the *mestizaje* of Vasconcelos and others is accurate and tolerant, noting in a very modern manner that "No contemporary race can present itself alone as the finished model that all others should imitate" (32), or as a finished model at all; all "races" are a moment in the flux of human diversity. Still, there is covert and occasionally overt racism in the message as well. The white race, or more specifically yet the Latin race, is seen as the only one capable of civilization and of transcending current race limitations; the traits of the white race are also expected to predominate in the new cosmic race. Black traits will diminish and disappear, which is the only way that

> the Black could be redeemed, and step by step, by voluntary extinction, the uglier stocks will give way to the more handsome. Inferior races, upon being educated, would become less prolific, and the better specimens would go on ascending a scale of ethnic improvement, whose maximum type is not precisely the White, but that new race to which the White himself will have to aspire.
>
> (32)

And even the tolerant Latin must prevent "an unrestrained influx of Asians," since the Chinese, who "multiply like mice," would "come to degrade the human condition" by overwhelming the better races (19).

But if there is a real target of the cosmic race, it is the "Indian," the native peoples of the Americas. *Mestizaje* is a way of "undefining Indians" (Tilley 2005) by submerging them into a hybrid popu-lation in which Indianness or indigenous identity no longer exists or matters. Vasconcelos is blunt that the Indian race is a retarded race, a thing of the past, which, "by grafting onto the related race, would take the jump of millions of years" (1979: 32). Accordingly, the Indian race "has no other door to the future but the door of modern culture, nor any other road but the road already cleared by Latin civilization" (16). Nor was Vasconcelos the only person nor Mexico the only country to adopt such thinking: "in both El Salvador and Nicaragua, *mes-tizaje* facilitated the dominant claim that 'Indians' had vanished altogether" (Tilley 2005: 65), washed away by the tide of race mixing.

The Burakumin of Japan

Japan is widely regarded, by scholarly and popular opinion both inside and outside the country, as a homogeneous, mono-racial or mono-ethnic society: in 1986, then-Prime Minister Nakasone Yasuhiro asserted that, in contrast to such societies as the United States, "Japan has one ethnicity (*minzoku*), one state (*kokka*), and one language (*gengo*)" (quoted in Lie 2001: 1). Of course, other peoples and cultures reside within the territory of the Japanese state, including Koreans, Chinese, Ainu, Okinawans, Iranians (usually as guest-workers), even some Americans, and a group known as the Burakumin. However, the Japanese anthropologist Hasebe Kotondo nonetheless argued that the Japanese "race" was unique and that "the Ainu, Koreans, and others were completely different races from the Japanese" (Yonezawa 2005: 124).

The Burakumin are the most interesting case in Japan, because like many groups encountered already, as well as the Deaf, they challenge the conventional concepts of race and ethnicity. With a label derived from the word *buraku* meaning village (Burakumin thus meaning "people of the village"), they are also known as *eta* (extreme filth) or *hinin* (nonhuman), strongly indicating their separate and inferior status; they are also sometimes less prejudicially called *Hisabetsu*. The special problem of conceiving the Burakumin is that they are essentially physically indistinguishable from other Japanese, that is, they do not have the ordinary biological markers of a distinct "race." In fact, George DeVos and Hiroshi Wagatsumo (1966) have called them Japan's "invisible race," which seems like an oxymoron: how can a group be a race without racially specific physical features?

The origins of the Burakumin are unclear and controversial. While some Japanese think they are of Korean or indigenous ancestry, the dominant view is that they are descendants of workers in lower-class and "polluting" professions like leather-making and butchering. Their status was certainly recognized by the seventeenth century, when the three classes of warrior, peasant, and townsperson were established, leaving the Burakumin as outcastes at the bottom of society (like the outcastes or *pariah* of India, who incidentally did much the same work). Officially, the status of and discrimination against Burakumin were abolished in 1871 through the Eta Emancipation

See Chapters 12, 13, and 15

Act, but little changed in the short run and negative attitudes toward them linger today.

Many of the Burakumin lived and live in several thousand formal *buraku* villages in Japan, but many others do not; many are listed on the official registry of Burakumin, but many others are not. Most importantly, as Lie suggests, with their "emancipation" the Burakumin began a process of transition from a caste to an ethnicity: no longer (at least legally) required to perform certain economic tasks or to marry within the group, in a classic case of ethnogenesis they began to think of themselves – and to be thought of by others – as a "people" rather than as a class. An important development in their ethnic consciousness was the promulgation of government policies (like the *yuwa* or assimilation plan) that recognized and handled them as a distinct group. In addition, the twentieth century saw the formation of pro-Burakumin organizations, such as *Suiheisha* (Leveling Society) in 1922 and *Buraku Kaiho Domei* (Buraku Liberation League) in 1955, which attempted to unify and advance them as a group.

All the same, interpersonal and structural discrimination against the Burakumin continues. Negative stereotypes persist, such as that they are "rough in speech, crude or brutal in relations with each other, having a low boiling point, quarrelsome, highly sensitive to insult, born traders, and relatively much more cohesive than any other community" (quoted in Lie 2001: 88); they have even been accused of possessing unseen physical differences like one less rib or the bone of a dog, deformed sexual organs, or the inability to cast a shadow in moonlight (86). Many still live in segregated and substandard housing and work in limited low-paying jobs; they are sometimes explicitly excluded from higher-status work through name-lists and ancestry registries. Some even adopt noticeable behavioral markers, like a particular kind of sandal. The irony is that a Burakumin can be sitting next to a "regular" Japanese person on a bus without the latter even realizing the difference between them – which is why Burakumin sometimes exit the bus a stop or two before it reaches their segregated and lower-class neighborhood.

We will encounter other examples of racial and ethnic groups, relations, and problems in future chapters, particularly the Hutu and Tutsi, the Serbs and Bosnian Muslims, and various indigenous peoples.

BOX 6.5   CONTEMPORARY CULTURAL CONTROVERSIES: THE EXPULSION OF BLACK CHEROKEES

On August 22, 2011, the Supreme Court of the Cherokee nation, based in Oklahoma, ruled that it was legal to expel the African-descended members of tribe. But what is an "African-descended Cherokee" in the first place? Before the 1830s, the Cherokee occupied a southeastern area of the United States, from present-day Kentucky to Georgia. After Europeans settled and claimed the territory, the Cherokee were especially successful at adopting aspects of American life. They generated their own writing system and began printing their own newspaper. Some also owned their own plantations, complete with their own African slaves. In the 1830s, the Cherokee along with neighboring tribes were forced to evacuate, in what is widely known as the "Trail of Tears," bringing their black slaves with them. According to the 2000 census, there were more than 300,000 Cherokees in the United States, including 2,800 so-called "Freedmen," the descendants of those Africans, some of whom had intermarried with the Native Americans; there may be as many as 25,000 more Freedmen who could potentially qualify as tribal members. However, the Cherokee court's decision prevents their enrollment in the tribe and disqualifies existing members, making them ineligible for the benefits that pertain to Native Americans, like free health care, educational programs, and of course a share in tribal wealth. The tribe claims the right to regulate its membership, while black Cherokees call it racism and apartheid. What do you think?

See Chapter 11

SUMMARY

Like gender, race and ethnicity are cultural interpretations and utilizations of "facts," namely the facts of physical and behavioral difference, respectively. Racial and ethnic classifications are ways in which popular opinion – and scholarly analysis – in some cultures have made sense, and use, of human difference.

Race has been an especially salient concept in Western societies, imposing a purportedly scientific order on the human physical variation. However, efforts to make race more scientific only made it more problematic. Ultimately, the imprecision and disagreement in the practice of race categorization, together with the discovery of the role of learning independent of biological inheritance, leads anthropology to criticize the notion of race and to focus on the social creation and function of racial thinking and racial systems.

For some observers, ethnic categories take a place alongside, or take the place of, racial categories. Ostensibly based on cultural, historical, and actual kinship characteristics, ethnic groups have proved to be every bit as vague and socially constructed – and socially exploited – as race groups. Cultural differences are actually not always great between ethnic groups, and the relationships between groups emerge as more crucial than the cultural qualities within groups. Accordingly, a number of different kinds of ethnic groups, and of relations between such groups, have been identified, from segregation and violent conflict to peaceful coexistence and amalgamation. Still, race and ethnicity continue to be salient organizational concepts in the modern world.

MCQS

FILL IN THE BLANKS

(WWW)

Key Terms

Anthropometry	Ethnicity	Miscegenation
Assimilation	Ethnogenesis	Pluralism
Cephalic index	Eugenics	Racial assimilation
Cultural assimilation	Facial angle	Social assimilation
Endogamy	Genocide	Structural assimilation

Seeing culture as a whole #1

The relativism of motherhood, personhood, race, and health in a Brazilian community

Alto de Cruzeiro is a hillside shanty town hovering above the town of Bom Jesus da Mata in north-eastern Brazil, a sugarcane-producing region. The poor live at the higher altitudes, the opposite of arrangements in Western societies, where the rich tend to live on the hills. Most of the men of the Alto are seasonal cane-cutters, and some women work, though not all, most often as domestic servants and launderers. Many women live alone with their children in the *favela* after the men abandon their families, eking out a marginal existence in poverty.

Until the 1950s, laborers could supplement their incomes with food grown in family gardens; however, as the sugar industry expanded and modernized, that land too was converted into cane production, leaving the locals more impoverished and hungry than ever. One fallout of these changes has been rising infant mortality. In 1965, 44 percent of all deaths in the Alto were children under five; by 1989 49 percent of deaths were babies less than one year old (Scheper-Hughes 1992: 296). Since the cost of feeding a family of six was four times the minimum wage, many people were chronically undernourished.

Yet, the attitude of the upper classes in town is that there is no hunger problem locally or nationally.

One official said that "the people eat poorly. They have bad dietary habits. For instance, the rural workers don't have the custom of eating fresh vegetables, fresh meat. . .or even fresh fruits. Their diet is all carbohydrates" (63). Why are people struggling, then?

> There is not so much poverty in Brazil as there is poverty of spirit, which is worse. Poverty of spirit – which you find among the rural workers – means that one is unwilling to improve one's condition. It means that one does not hunger after the finer things in life, that one is content to live and let live. The *matuto* [peasant or "forest person"] is soft; he doesn't like to work hard. He is not ashamed to ask for things, to beg.
>
> (63)

Despite the fact that cane-cutting is a strenuous life, the workers have internalized this evaluation. They see themselves as weak and sickly, even in racial terms: they are an inferior race or type, who are physically smaller, always ill, always hungry. They even admit that they eat more than the rich because "their 'inferior' constitutions require it" (166). When they give birth to low birth-weight babies,

Scheper-Hughes, Nancy. 1992. *Death without Weeping: The Violence of Everyday Life in Brazil.* Berkeley, CA: University of California Press.

who do not often live very long, it just seems to prove the point.

The *matutos* cannot help but notice that they suffer from a variety of physical and psychological ailments. In their "folk medicine" terminology, they attribute this to a condition called *nervos*, the symptoms of which include headache, dizziness, muscle weakness, mental confusion, shaky hands, insomnia, and loss of appetite. Diagnosing this condition as a medical rather than a nutritional one, they visit doctors, who prescribe tranquilizers instead of food. Nancy Scheper-Hughes has called this concept of *nervos* a "social illness," in two senses; first, it is a social concept applied to a constellation of symptoms that can be (and perhaps should be) understood another way, and second, the syndrome is caused by the social situation in which the poor find themselves. The rich do not experience *nervos* – either because they are better bred or because they are better fed.

When the poor do eat, they indeed do not eat well. Partly this is a result of too little money to afford high-quality foods. Partly, it is a circular effect of seeking out "filling" foods with little nutritional value. Fruits and vegetables are categorized as "weak" or "light" foods that do not satisfy. Starchy foods like beans, rice, and pasta "kill hunger," but when people cannot even afford those, they eat substances that "fool hunger," such as flour and mere sugar-water. They also feed children and babies the same way, sometimes substituting *farinha* (manioc flour) for powdered milk in infant formula.

Babies born of starving mothers are born starving too. Mothers comment that babies often arrive small, shriveled, discolored, and feeble. Some infants are too weak even to eat, which is not blamed on hunger – after all, the hungry eat – but on *nervos*. Some babies are just born *nervos*, they believe. Worse yet, many such babies do not even want to live. "Our babies [are] born already *wanting to die*," one mother stated (315). "They come into the world with an aversion to life. . .food doesn't interest them; it doesn't hold their attention. You see, they are neither here nor there" (386). Scheper-Hughes calls this "Doomed Baby Syndrome," in which mothers allow babies to starve and die because that is what the mothers believe the babies want: "It is better to let the weak ones die," a mother claimed, because the babies are "little angels" who come into the world solely for the purpose of dying (368). So mothers may underfeed or completely neglect the weakest infants, allowing the self-fulfilling prophecy to come true.

How can a mother watch her child die? One way is to think that it is "natural" – the child's own wish and nature. The other way is by becoming accustomed to infant mortality: mothers there and elsewhere do not become too attached to newborns, since they know the little ones are so likely to perish. It is not an absence of "maternal instinct" but a social construction of it: children who live are the object of intense joy and affection. However, after a woman has five of her nine pregnancies end in mortality, she reserves that affection until the baby proves its "will to live." "Motherlove," Scheper-Hughes concludes, is not lacking but rather "grows slowly, tentatively, and fearfully" (359) as a reaction to brutal experience.

Economics

Humans, nature, and social organization

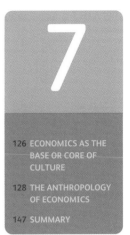

The *kibbutz* or communal farming settlement was a prominent feature of 1950s Israel, and the *kibbutz* studied by Melford Spiro was explicitly modeled after the Soviet Union. They were populated mostly by Polish émigrés, and a key principle was the collective ownership and use of property: neither land nor any other item – house, animal, vehicle, even clothing – was regarded as private property. The single highest value was labor: labor was a moral duty, and all members and only members of the community were called upon to support the community. The result was an ideology of equality, although not all work was equally valued: physical or "productive" labor was most prized, and agricultural labor was the most prized of physical labor. On the other hand, service or "intellectual" work (including teaching) was less honored. Even personal relations and parenting were collective rather than individual: the group discouraged marriage, people lived communally, and parents did not raise their own children. The family as we know it was essentially absent: "From the very beginning the terms 'marriage,' 'husband,' 'wife' were abandoned" (1963: 113). Overall then, "many of the social inequalities existing in a stratified society do not exist" in Spiro's *kibbutz* (24). Even so, power

differences did exist, and some amount of management was necessary. Much of the "politics" of the community was handled through town councils, in which every member of the group discussed and debated. There were some formal offices, including a general secretary and various committees, but office-holders "enjoy no special privileges and receive no material rewards" (26). Most social control, indeed, was informal, taking the form of gossip, criticism, quarreling and complaining, skits and plays, and ultimately expulsion. But such action was seldom necessary, as individuals tended to develop a collective conscience or *hakkara*, "a conscious awareness of one's moral responsibilities" to the group (88). Enculturation and formal education were intentionally aimed at producing what they called a "synthetic personality" (153) that combined or synthesized love of the soil and of manual labor with an appreciation of knowledge and art. One by-product of this experience, however, was a personality that was also characterized by "provincialism, naïveté, conservatism" (165).

All societies face a fundamental challenge – to feed, clothe, and otherwise provision their members using the available resources in their environment. Different societies have met this challenge in

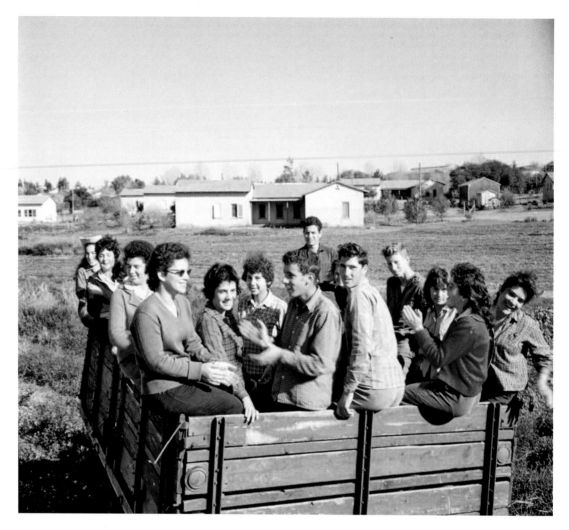

different ways, depending on their environment, but all shared one factor in common: they solved the problem of survival socially. It might be possible for humans to satisfy their needs totally individually, but it would be difficult and is essentially never done. So humans acquire, prepare, distribute, and consume goods and services in groups, and the means by which they do so will have ramifications for those groups. The economic practices of a society will be significantly influenced by the physical possibilities of their environment (the amount and quality of land, water, plants and animals, and other materials), and the economic practices that emerge will significantly influence other aspects of the culture – not in a deterministic, cause-and-effect way, but in specific and observable ways. Further, economic facts are seldom purely "practical"; they also have value and prestige and even "symbolic" and ritual significance that affect the social meaning of the products and of the relationships within which those products are made, distributed, and used.

ECONOMICS AS THE BASE OR CORE OF CULTURE

The mention of economics usually conjures up images of factories and money and markets and profit and many other familiar concepts. These are indeed all economic phenomena, but they are examples of one type of economy rather than a definition of economy. Some economies have factories, money, etc., but the vast majority across cultures and throughout history have done without them. In order to be anthropologically relevant, the study of economics must be cross-cultural and inclusive, as well as holistic and relativistic. This means that we cannot assume that *one* kind of economy is the *right* and certainly not the *only* kind of economy for humans.

Holism or cultural integration dictates that all of the aspects of a culture, including its environmental context, will be interrelated and interdependent. As we said previously, anthropologists envision a holistic cultural system as containing four domains of culture like networked spheres within the cultural whole. Understanding the relations between the domains of culture begins with the notion of adaptation. **Adaptation** is the process by which humans (or any species) fit themselves into and interact with their surroundings. Although humans adapt physically like all other beings, most of human adaptation takes the form of behavioral modification. Culture is the uniquely human adaptation. So human cultural adaptation starts with the environment which a human group or society inhabits. An environment is a particular combination of physical factors – climate, water and food supplies, natural resources, large-scale natural formations (rivers, mountains), etc. These factors will set constraints (technology notwithstanding) on what the society can and cannot, must and must not, do. In other words, the environment will set the fundamental terms of *what is possible and what is necessary* for the humans living in it. The environment is a challenge that must be met. Yet "nature" is not a completely independent or determinant variable: through culture, humans bring the world of nature within the world of culture, *culturizing* nature and integrating it into the cultural system. In the process, both culture and nature are mutually reshaped.

It is worth remarking that two quite different environments can pose quite similar adaptive challenges. For instance, few environmental settings seem less alike than a desert and the arctic, yet some of the conditions they present to humans or any life-forms located there are actually comparable. There is little liquid water as well as a relatively short supply and variety of potential foods and of potential tool-making and building materials. Plant life is scarce, so agriculture is virtually impossible. Thus, while they look superficially very dissimilar, the adaptations they will call for are actually surprisingly alike.

Therefore, the primary and overarching challenge that a human society will face is adapting –

behaviorally and, over the long run, physically – to its environment. In the extreme short term, this means getting sustenance from this environment. The first problem, then, for humans is and will always be how to transform their environment into the things that they need to support their life. In other words, the first problem for humans is and will always be *economic*.

If we think again now about how to model the relations between the domains of culture, we would want to start with an environment and then establish first a means of livelihood that is adapted to that environment. That is, if we were to "build" a culture from the "ground up," the environment would be the ground, and the "base" of the culture would be the part that "touches the ground." It is the economic system that not only metaphorically but literally makes contact with the earth and its resources and converts them into human-usable goods.

Imagine building any house or other structure. The first thing you need is a place. The nature of that place – its size, quality, climate, etc. – will (hopefully) suggest to you the kind of house to build. The "ground floor" of the house, shaped as it is by the environment, would subsequently shape the floors above it. Of course, this is not a purely "one-way" process. There is a kind of feedback relation between the upper and lower levels too: the upper floors exert pressure on the lower ones in particular ways, and once they have been formed, they will influence the levels "below" them, such that the politics or the religion can affect the economics and even the very environment. There is, in the final analysis, a reciprocal or mutual relationship but one in which the economic adaptation is still the base or core.

So, although our house analogy appears a bit static, it is necessary to understand that the relationship between the economy and the other aspects of a culture is quite dynamic. One other dynamic quality that the model does not convey is the inevitable presence of neighboring societies, which may have more or less impact on the society in question. In some cases, there may be neutral or friendly exchange relations between the two (or more), while in others there may be competitive or hostile relations. Societies may be completely surrounded or even engulfed by other larger and more dominant societies, and they may be highly

See Chapter 1

Adaptation
changes in a system, including a species, in response to changes in its context or environment so as to make that system or species more fit to survive in the context or environment

See Chapter 13

dependent on these external social structures. The society itself, finally, may be more internally complex than the model indicates, with multiple "layers" or subgroups/classes or even subcultures in various (and often unequal) relations with each other. All modern societies are and many pre-modern societies were actually composite systems of social groupings in diverse and problematic arrangements.

At any rate, a society's life begins with its practical, productive activities, which can be referred to as its **means of production**. The means of production consists of the tasks, the tools, and the knowledge and skills that humans use to get their daily bread (or kangaroo or whatever). It is labor and all that is required for labor. This may be as simple as picking a nut off a tree or as elaborate as working in an office or on an assembly line. Humans must engage in productive, practical, material activity in order to survive.

However, work cannot be done in social isolation – not in isolation from other humans, nor in isolation from other facets of society. Economic activity is always social – with and for other people too. Therefore, the means of production leads to and generates some **relations of production** – that is, ways that humans organize themselves to get the work done and the products distributed and used. The general factors involved in the relations of production include division of labor, ownership, "property," power, often class, and usually the family, as well as sharing and selling and the status or prestige that comes with having, consuming, displaying, giving, etc. the goods and services. These relations give shape and content to the rest of society. These two features – mode and relations of production – in tandem make up what we would call the economy of a society.

THE ANTHROPOLOGY OF ECONOMICS

An anthropological approach to economics, then, must be inclusive rather than exclusive – considering and encompassing all of the actual forms of economic behavior across cultures, not just one's own or others similar to one's own – as well as holistic and relativistic. Therefore, economics must mean for anthropologists not just capitalism or

industrialization and mass production but all of the processes and practices by which humans transform the natural environment into usable goods and services for humans and then put those goods and services to use. Additionally, any economic system has, from "start to finish," three phases:

1. Production – the phase of operation on the environment in which "raw" materials are transformed into human (and therefore "social" or "cultural") goods.
2. Distribution – the phase of moving goods and services from the people who produce them to the people who use them.
3. Consumption – the phase of actually using or "consuming" (eating, wearing, burning, etc.) products.

Anthropology has traditionally put very much emphasis on the production phase of the economy, considerable emphasis on the distribution phase, and less emphasis on the consumption phase. In the following sections I will discuss production and distribution but also show that anthropology has much to offer to the study of consumption. I will begin by offering the customary typology of the phases of economy, that is, the "types" of production or distribution that have been identified. However, in the real world, things are not as simple as that. Types are always abstractions or generalizations from reality; what we see in the field is often variation or even hybridization of these ideal types, as we will indicate below. Second, even within types, there is a fair amount of variation; the "pure" foraging or pastoralist society often took different shapes depending on the environment, the history of the group, or simply the indeterminacy of human beliefs and behaviors. Third, as we noted, groups with a particular economy were often in contact, if not integrated into a single system, with groups practicing very different economic forms, further complicating the picture. Finally, in the case of most of the "traditional" economic systems, either no society practices them anymore or no society practices them in a thoroughly "traditional" way anymore. We will return to examine the contemporary condition of many of these societies in the final several chapters of this book.

Means of production
the activities and tools that a society employs to satisfy its material needs. The form of "work" or "labor" that is performed in a society

ANTHROPOLOGY OF WORK

Relations of production
in Marxist theory, the social roles and relationships that are generated by the mode of production, including such things as class, ownership, "management," and in some lines of thinking "family"

Systems of production

If a culture is a system or formation with economics as the "base," then production is the "base of the base," the first level of the first layer. It precedes and sets the stage for subsequent economic activities, which in turn shape and influence non-economic activities, institutions, and values. Anthropology has identified five general systems or ideal types for the production of basic goods and services. These types are:

- Foraging
- Pastoralism
- Horticulture
- Intensive agriculture
- Industrialism

In characterizing any actual society's economic system, anthropologists want to accomplish two things. First, we want to understand their means of production and how it is anchored to the environment(s) they dwell in. Second and more importantly, we want to see what kind of culture and social order they produce – what specific relationships, values, beliefs, and so on flow from the economic base and how those things are related to and shaped by their economic activities. If what we have said already is true, then we should detect regular patterns of economics and culture – things that tend to go together and things that do not or cannot go together. That is, we should see patterns emerge that link particular types of economic factors with particular types of non-economic (kinship, political, and even religious) factors.

Foraging

Foraging was the first human production system. Also known as "hunting and gathering," it is the type of procurement that all humans practiced and depended on from the very first humans until some ten to twelve thousand years ago. Even since that time, when other production systems emerged and spread, foraging continued to be practiced in at least some places – and occasionally in contact with other later systems – until quite recently. Thus, for most of history foraging was practiced in all environments of the earth. During the past few millennia, it has tended to be relegated to the most "marginal" environments where other systems cannot be practiced or where societies that practice them cannot or have not chosen to penetrate. Examples of recent and well-known foraging societies include the !Kung or Ju/hoansi of the African Kalahari, all Australian Aboriginal societies, and the various Inuit or Eskimo peoples of the Arctic. While their environments could be quite different, the economic adaptations they made to them tended be quite similar.

Foraging
Also known as hunting and gathering, the production of food by collecting wild (undomesticated) animals and plants

PLATE 7.2 Koya hunter from central India.

FIGURE 7.1 A timeline of production systems.

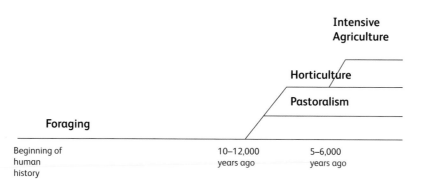

Turnbull, Colin. 1962. *The Forest People*. New York: Simon & Schuster.

Foraging is a mode of production involving minimal technologies to acquire food and other goods through a combination of hunting wild animals and collecting wild plants. Although it appears to entail the least transformation of the environment, still transformation it is, since humans did not simply walk up and take a bite out of a kangaroo or a tree. Foraging peoples had to apply technology, skill, knowledge, and capital to their natural environment in order to make the benefits of that environment usable or "edible" for them. In some cases, as in Australia, foragers routinely burned the landscape, undoubtedly affecting the local plant and animal life.

Therefore, at its most basic, foraging included the "work" of hunting and of gathering, two distinct skills or methods of food provision. This implies a potential and usually actual **division of labor** between the hunting/animal work and the gathering/plant work. The classic or stereotypical version of foraging involved a gender-based division of labor with male hunting and female gathering. This arrangement did indeed exist: the Warlpiri in the Central Desert of Australia tended to follow the pattern of male hunting and female gathering, although with two warnings. First, not all "animal work" was necessarily viewed as hunting; catching small lizards and insects might be done by women or children. Second, a man might "gather" materials of particular interest to him, such as bush tobacco. So even here the gender division was not absolute.

Ernestine Friedl (1975; 1978) identified three other foraging arrangements. In one, men hunted and both men and women gathered; the Hadza people of Tanzania (Woodburn 1968) and a few other societies were reputed to organize this way. In a second variation, men and women shared both hunting and gathering. Estioko-Griffin and Griffin (2002) described the Agta of the Philippines as

nearly undivided in economic activities by sex: women participated in the same productive behaviors as men, including hunting and fishing, and they gathered plants irregularly and only when more desirable food was not at hand. Turnbull (1962) also presented the Mbuti pygmies of the Congo forest as working together, male and female, to net game. In the third style, men hunted but women processed the catch of the men.

Because women's labor often produced a large proportion (if not the majority) of the group's food, there tended to be relative gender equality in foraging societies. In fact, they tended to be generally egalitarian, due to the inability of any individual to accumulate a surplus or to possess skills that other people did not. Concepts of "ownership" or "private property" were often limited if not lacking, particularly in regard to land. Foraging environments often prohibited economic surpluses, since there was not enough food available to accumulate it, and foraging values usually discouraged a person from trying to become superior to or richer than anyone else; values of sharing within the community provided no opportunity to hoard personal wealth. Some status differences existed, based on age, skill, ritual knowledge, and sometimes gender, but these statuses were often more interdependent than stratified. Without wealth and power differences, formal leadership and especially "government" were absent and unnecessary.

Other social features of foraging societies followed from their environmental and productive situation. For example, local groups, especially in marginal environments, tended to be small; in many instances, the residential group was only a dozen or less, or at most a few dozen, and ordinarily composed of kin. The entire society seldom if ever formed a single community. There was simply not enough food and water to support

Division of labor

the differentiation of the economy into a set of distinct production tasks, which are assigned to different individuals, groups, or classes, usually creating economic and political inequalities

Friedl, Ernestine. 1975. *Women and Men*. New York: Holt, Rinehart, and Winston.

large populations. The society was accordingly dispersed over a large territory and would only assemble as one in times of plenty or for special occasions like rituals. This means that groups also tended to be mobile, moving continuously in search of provisions. The groups may have lacked any permanent settlements or houses, but they migrated within an established "range" or territory. So, they could still have a sense of "home area," but one within which they circulated constantly. They might stop in one place as long as resources permitted, but the general ethos of society was a mobile one.

One common misconception about foragers is that they were poor and miserable, living on the edge of starvation. No doubt there were times of hardship in their history, as there have been in modern industrial societies. However, surprisingly, foraging peoples tended to have a very positive attitude toward their lives and their environments. The Warlpiri told me that their desert country was *ngurrju*, good. They enjoyed their way of life and had plenty of time for leisure. Traditional food-collecting took up a few hours a day, a few days a week; the rest of the time they spent visiting and socializing, doing ritual "business," or merely napping.

Since generosity and equality were the general rule, the occurrence of conflict and violence was limited. Therefore, foragers tended to be comparatively peaceful peoples. This is not to say that they never had conflicts and even violent outbursts, because they did and do, but these usually occurred over ritual concerns or marriage or other personal issues and were usually settled ritually, even if that ritual involved some symbolic or real violence.

Finally, because the life of foragers was so "close to the ground," they tended to have a major emotional and "spiritual" connection to their environment. For many foragers, the land itself was alive or was the handiwork of living beings – spiritual, mixed spiritual–human, mixed human–animal/plant, and so on. They may have had "totemic" or other social relations between human individuals or groups and other natural beings or forces. They often regarded themselves and their cultures as essentially autochthonous – that is, literally rising up out of the ground they inhabited.

Pastoralism

Somewhere around 10,000–12,000 years ago, one or more groups of humans in one or more locations

---

BOX 7.1   THE AINU FORAGERS OF NORTHERN JAPAN

The Ainu are an indigenous people of Japan who traditionally lived a life resembling Inuit or Eskimo societies. They were dependent on a harsh environment where small scattered habitations were demanded. At the time of Ohnuki-Tierney's research (1974), the Ainu of northwest Sakhalin Island were living mostly in settlements of twenty families containing around 150 people. Each house in the settlement consisted of a single room, although its internal space and overall orientation were organized by religion, for example, with the sacred side facing the mountains. In the winter, men hunted and trapped land and sea mammals and also fished, while women stayed mostly at home. Large animals, especially bears, had a distinctly spiritual quality, and hunting them was as much a religious as an economic activity; in fact, she writes that "there is no demarcation between activities relating to the obtaining of animal meat and those dealing with the deities" (20), since most animals were deities. Hares were not deities, so women were allowed to trap them but not to do any other type of hunting.

In the summer, men would turn their attention to fishing, spearing larger fish like trout and salmon and catching smaller fish in baskets. This was also the season in which women's economic contribution expanded. Plants would bloom, providing as much or more food than hunting, and women did most of the plant-gathering work. They knew about and collected bulbs of various plants, as well as leeks, berries, mushrooms, and a hundred other species for food or medicines.

Domestication

the process of modification of plants and/or animals to establish human control over them, leading to agriculture and pastoralism

Neolithic

the "New Stone" age, beginning around ten thousand to twelve thousand years ago with the first animal and plant domestication

Pastoralism

a productive system based on domesticated animals as the main source of food

See Chapter 8

discovered that they could control and **domesticate** certain species for human consumption. Thus, instead of having to roam in search of their food sources, they could bring the sources "home" to them. This is sometimes referred to as the **Neolithic** ("new stone" age) revolution, and it was revolutionary not only for how humans worked and provided food but for every aspect of their cultures and social relationships, as well as for the species they fed on. The revolution of domestication actually culminated in not one but two new economic systems. The first system I will describe is pastoralism. **Pastoralism**, from the word "pasture," is the production of food predominantly from the exploitation of domesticated animals. It is what might conventionally be called "herding" or "ranching." Thus, the primary "work" to be done was tending and exploiting – milking, bleeding, and slaughtering – such animals as cattle, sheep, goats, llamas, horses, pigs, and other smaller creatures, depending on the locally available species.

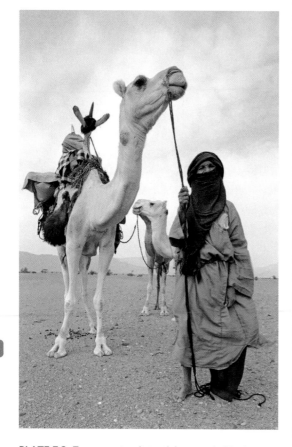

PLATE 7.3 Tuareg pastoralist with his camels, North Africa.

In the vast majority of these societies – and they were spread across the world, from the grasslands of East Africa to the mountains of Central Asia and the plains of North America – the ownership and control of herd animals was the prerogative of men. Women and children often performed the day-to-day work of tending the animals, but it was men who decided when one would be slaughtered or traded or sold. Thus, in terms of production and even more so control of production, pastoralism was a man's world, and the gender division of labor devolved into a gender inequality. Men's status was much higher than women's in typical pastoral societies. Men accordingly tended to be the heads of family and household; again, women might wield real "domestic" power in the home, but their political power was reduced compared to men.

Since a man's herd was his surplus and therefore his wealth, he usually tried to avoid killing his animals but rather consumed them in "sustainable" ways, such as drinking their milk or blood. Herds in some cases might be quite large; Klima (1970) reported that the average Barabaig (east Africa) cattle herd was around 70 head, and a very large herd could number more than 500. If one individual or household had a larger herd than another, he or it was wealthier, and wealth meant differential access to status and social opportunities. One such opportunity was marriage – the ability to marry well or to marry often. A wealthy Barabaig man would have four or more wives and many sons. And he would also actively seek to increase his animal holdings through a variety of social institutions. Barabaig society contained an assortment of rule-governed livestock transactions, such as the *gefuryed* in which a man would lend a bull to another man in exchange for rights to the future calf of his trading partner's cow; Klima also noted that men were not above deliberately manipulating and exploiting these arrangements for their benefit (30). Another way of adding to one's wealth was by marrying his daughters or sisters to men with mighty herds in exchange for a payment in cattle.

The differences in wealth and power and prestige in pastoral societies were not immense, because the wealth itself was not immense. Still, there could be men or families/households higher in rank or status than others. In Barabaig society, a man "who is successful in raising a large herd of cattle is socially recognized as being more knowledgeable and powerful than a person with a small herd" (Klima 1970: 32), and the man who was poor in cattle might have to work for a wealthier man. "Leaders" could emerge, with some power to command the efforts and allegiances of other men, at least members of their family, lineage, village, or "tribe." Formal government was still often lacking, but the rudiments or precursors of government were observable. Further, the existence of some surplus and a larger and more dependable food supply led to larger societies as a whole, sometimes with hundreds or even thousands of people (some of the large and important societies in history like the Mongols were pastoralists). On the other hand, not all pastoral societies were huge, and they often still had to disperse into smaller local communities. And migratory patterns, sometimes called transhumance, often had to continue, as herds required new sources of land, water, and pasturage. So pastoralists may or may not have achieved settlements in semi-permanent villages.

The presence of "wealth on the hoof," in tandem with the requirement for access to land and the dominance of males and maleness in society, almost inevitably led to a more aggressive stance than anything found in foraging societies. Foragers had little to fight over, but pastoralists had a lot. They could fight to control water and pasture resources. They could fight to raid other societies and steal their herds or to defend their own herds from theft; they could also steal women. They could fight over previous marriage exchanges and grievances about unsolved property disputes. And they could fight just to show they were men – tough, honorable, powerful. In fact, some of the most violent and warlike pre-modern peoples have been pastoralists, and it was pastoralists who were often most effective in fighting off the colonial advances of the Europeans. Foragers tended to succumb quickly and easily.

Pastoralists, being mobile, aggressive, and organized, also tended to encounter other, non-

BOX 7.2   LIMITS TO GROWTH IN BASSERI PASTORALISM

As described by Barth (1965), the Basseri lived in a mountainous region of southern Iran, where they raised sheep, goats, and donkeys; each household owned around 100 sheep and up to a dozen donkeys. Pasture rights were obtained through membership in an *oulad*, a kinship group consisting of roughly ninety families. There were no limits to how many animals a man or household could put on his *oulad*'s land. There were, however, other kinds of limitations that he faced. One was the size of the herds of his *oulad* mates. Another was the inverse relationship between the size of a herd and its productivity: that is, the larger a herd became, the harder it was to manage and protect it. A large herd may have to be trusted to hired or temporary help, who could cheat him or simply take less care of the animals than the owner would. The near-total lack of any kind of communal labor pitted each man against every other. Natural conditions like fluctuating weather and fertility introduced unpredictable variations in herd size. Finally, sons took a share of the father's herd as inheritance, while daughters could not provide the labor needed to expand the herd.

To protect themselves against these threats, men took a variety of steps. A father might attempt to postpone a son's marriage to delay the transfer of inheritance, sometimes until after age thirty or thirty-five. Men also saw the value of converting animals into "real" wealth like land; thus, large animal-holders became landowners and landlords to tenant farmers, who paid the owner with one-third to two-thirds of their crop. Such a landowner had special status and privilege. However, the wealth accumulation process could also run in reverse: a man with a small herd, many sons, heavy debt, and bad luck could watch his herd decline below the sustainable level (about sixty sheep), in which case he was forced to work for wealthier men and eventually settle as a property-less villager, becoming one of those tenant farmers hired by landowners. Barth refers to this process as "sedentarization by impoverishment."

pastoral peoples in their travels. In some instances, like the Bedouins of North Africa, they became the "traders" and entrepreneurs (literally, "between-carriers") of goods over long distances. In other instances, however, they engaged in conflict with and often conquest of their neighbors. Sometimes, they decimated these other societies, even pushing them to extinction; at other times, they ruled them from afar, extracted wealth from them in the form of tribute, or even settled among them as a dominant "class." This phenomenon is so common in human history that it deserves much more attention than it usually gets from anthropology and history. For instance, the impact of the Mongols on Eurasian society, especially China and Russia, cannot be overestimated. In Europe, it was pastoral tribes like the Germanic peoples who came to populate much of the continent, and it was pastoral tribes that finally toppled the Roman Empire. Similarly, pastoral peoples were on the move in India (the "Aryans"), the Middle East, and Africa, and many of today's "composite" societies like the ones in Rwanda and Burundi are products of this pervasive force. Even in the United States there was the classic confrontation between the "cattlemen" or pastoralists and the "sod busters" or farmers that played out and largely shaped the life of the western states.

Finally, understandably, pastoral attitudes and values reverberated through their religion as well. They tended to have male gods (often sky-gods) like the male god of the ancient pastoral Hebrews. Such pastoral gods often required sacrifices, particularly of male animals, killed and roasted for the gods' pleasure. The gods too were warlike and authorized the people to raid and fight, sometimes with a sense of tribal superiority or even an ideology that all cattle or other animals actually belonged to the tribe and were theirs to (re)capture. Males of course were the chief officiants of these religions, holding roles like priest or diviner or even "negative" ones like witch. Religion was still "decentralized," as was the economy and society as a whole, but that merely emphasized the point that what transpired in nature and society also transpired in the supernatural realm.

Interestingly, the dividing line between foraging and pastoralism was not perfectly clear or absolute. In his study of Melanesian societies, Paul Sillitoe discussed the production of pigs, a staple food. Some societies raised their pig herds as

essentially domesticated animals, while others left "their creatures more to forage and root for themselves"; the latter also did not so much breed animals as allow animals to breed in the wild. This "unsupervised" form of "pig herding" led Sillitoe to conclude that "it is sometimes difficult to decide whether a group preys on wild pigs or herds semi-domesticated ones" (1998: 47).

Horticulture

The other economic system to evolve out of domestication involved the production of domesticated plants and is known as horticulture. **Horticulture** can be defined as farming without the use of technologies like the plow, irrigation, fertilizer, or draft animals. The absence of these inputs also generally tended to limit outputs and to prevent the permanent use of farmlands, since the soil became exhausted of nutrients after a few years' tilling. Horticulture was once practiced in a wider variety of climate types but has recently been found most often in and is most suited for hilly inland areas and for tropical environments, like the rainforests of New Guinea or the Amazon, where soils are actually relatively thin, heavy rains can damage fragile soils, but growth rates are fairly high, such that displaced wild vegetation can quickly recover.

In fact, this is exactly the strategy in one of the more common forms of horticulture, known as "**slash-and-burn**" or **swidden** agriculture. In this technique, future fields were cleared of vegetation by cutting away brush and "slashing" trees to cause them to die and dry out; some time later, the horticulturists returned and set fire to all of the undergrowth, opening the fields for planting while restoring the nutrients in the native plants back to the soil in the form of ash. Sowing the fields could be as simple as tossing a few seeds into holes poked by digging sticks or could be more complex and labor intensive. Either way, stumps, rocks, and other debris were usually left in place; no attempt was made to plow the fields or to contour the land in any appreciable way. That is, the farmers basically "worked around" the obstacles in their fields. As you might imagine, a horticultural community would need to have a number of such territories in various states of readiness, from "in production" to recently burned to recently slashed to fallow. After two or three harvests, the fertility of the land was

Horticulture
A production system based on low-technology farming or gardening, without the use of plows, draft animals, irrigation, or fertilizers

Slash-and-burn
a horticultural practice in which trees and underbrush are cut, left to dry, and then burned as preparation for planting a garden. Also known as *swidden*

Swidden
see slash-and-burn

PLATE 7.4 Slash and burn is a common technique of horticulture.

often depleted, and it was necessary to allow it to "return to nature," only to be slashed and burned again in the future.

Horticultural labor, then, consisted of a sequence of stages that could be assigned to members in various ways; one common division of labor was for men do the heavy work of clearing the land while women did the planting and harvesting. The Dani of New Guinea were an example of this classic pattern (Heider 1979), but this labor arrangement was by no means universal. Among the Semai of Malaysia the women and children slashed the trees before the men chopped them down; then men and boys made the planting-holes, and women and children followed behind placing the seeds in the holes (Dentan 1968). The Yanomamo (South America) reserved both forest-clearing and planting for men (Chagnon 1992). And the Konyak Nagas of India had a very mixed system: older men and women would clear the undergrowth while younger men did the slashing. Then men sowed rice and millet, with women coming after to cover the grains with earth. Boys and girls weeded together, and men and women harvested together (Von Fuerer-Haimendorf 1969).

The diversity of productive relationships within horticultural societies guaranteed a diversity of cultural systems emerging from them. For instance, in some cases land was private property, in other cases not. The Konyak Nagas maintained very old links with ancestral lands, and almost all farm plots were individually owned; in fact, one person would own multiple scattered plots, as many as 250 in the extreme case. Among the Semai, there was no permanent ownership of land; the "owner" of a tract was simply the person or family who cleared and presently used it. If they abandoned or simply neglected it for too long, others would move in and occupy it (but still not acquire "title" to it); the same was true of houses.

The relationship with and productivity of the land also affected settlement or mobility. Some societies built fairly permanent villages and farmed the land in the vicinity on some kind of rotation. Other societies moved frequently to open new land and establish new temporary residences for a few months or years. Likewise, cultural values and practices like gender stratification and violence were diverse. The Iroquois (eastern North America) represented one of the most female-centered societies on record.

Iroquois women controlled the factors of agricultural production, for they had a right in

Chagnon, Napoleon. 1992. *Yanomamo*, 4th ed. Fort Worth, TX: Harcourt Brace College Publishers.

the land which they cultivated, and in the implements and the seeds. Iroquois agricultural activities, which yielded bountiful harvests, were highly organized under elected female leadership. Most important, Iroquois women maintained the right to distribute and dispense all foods, even that procured by men. This was especially significant, as stored food constituted one of the major forms of wealth for the tribe. Through their control of the economic organization of the tribe, Iroquois matrons were able to make available or withhold food for meetings of the Council and for war parties, for the observance of religious festivals and for the daily meals of the household. These economic realities were institutionalized in the matrons' power to nominate Council Elders and to influence Council decisions. They had a voice in the conduct of war and the establishment of treaties. They elected "keepers of the faith" and served in that capacity. They controlled life in the longhouse.
(Brown 1975: 250–51)

At the other end of the spectrum, some horticultural societies, like the Sambia mentioned in a previous chapter, maintained tense and profoundly unequal, even segregated, relations between the sexes. The Yanomamo were also highly male-dominated. Even so, overall horticulture was likely to provide prominent female status: according to one analysis, more than one-fourth of horticultural societies attached children primarily to their mother's kin group, compared to 10 percent of foraging groups and even less of pastoral and intensive agricultural societies (Lenski and Lenski 1982).

Violence varied as well but somewhat independently from other variables. The Yanomamo reportedly were male-dominated in their economics and their gender roles and also warlike, and the Semai were egalitarian in their economics and their gender roles and peaceful. However, the Iroquois and many other societies mixed these traits in many combinations: some were male-dominated but non-violent, while (more commonly) others were not male-dominated but violent.

Even such "low intensity" farming could produce a noticeable surplus, allowing for two effects. One was larger societies. Society could become so large that it included multiple local communities or

villages. These communities might or might not feel any significant affiliation with each other as members of the "same" society: for instance, the Yanomamo were infamous for conducting raids and warfare against other Yanomamo villages. The other effect was enhanced notions of, and competition for, wealth, power, and prestige. Horticultural societies sometimes developed more elaborate ranking and stratification systems and even "governments," up to chiefs and other political institutions. They certainly had more problems to solve and disputes to settle, with more people living in closer contact and potentially getting into squabbles about property. In some places, like Melanesia, complicated status contests like the kula eventually took shape, in which individuals or families strove to achieve and express status through trading and gift-giving and displays of wealth.

The weaknesses or vulnerabilities of horticulture were compensated by the new opportunities it offered. Among these opportunities was one of the prerequisites for further cultural elaboration – specialization. A small number of people could be "freed" from food production due to the surplus that others created. These people could practice other activities and develop new skills and techniques, including pottery and metalworking as well as more full-time religious and artistic roles. The "blacksmith" or iron-worker in particular often played an important not only economic but ritual role in society. In addition to these seminal technologies, other arts and crafts like weaving were possible with the economic surplus, not to mention the "intellectual" arts like teaching, priestcraft, and even "time-keeping" (the builders of Stonehenge were, after all, horticulturists).

Speaking of priestcraft, horticultural religion tended to reflect and reinforce the practical modes and relations of horticultural life. Religion often focused on fertility and the cycle of natural processes, from the "birth" (planting) to "death" of the plants. Gods or spirits of various species or natural forces (rain, sun, etc.) or moments in the planting cycle were important for organizing economic activity, as was an awareness of the timing of the seasons. Seasons did not make much difference to foragers, and little more difference to pastoralists, but for horticulturists there was "a time to plant" and "a time to reap." Doing things at the wrong time could leave the plants, and the planters, dead. So, for instance, knowledge of the solstices appeared, along with "calendrical" (annual) rituals to demarcate them and the key activities undertaken around those times. A "harvest" ritual (not unlike Thanksgiving in the United States) was common, or even a ritual recognizing the "season of death" (not unlike Halloween in the United States or the *Dia de los Muertos* in Mexico) at the end of the farming season. The winter solstice (late December), when the days started to get longer in the Northern Hemisphere, and the spring equinox (late March) were both commonly associated with birth or rebirth and moments for important rituals. Note that the two major Christian holidays fall at precisely those times.

Sillitoe also indicated that the distinction between foraging and horticulture was not always certain. The Gidra and Kiwai people of New Guinea engaged in "limited management of plant resources" (27), for instance claiming sago and coconut palm trees but only minimally tending them until harvest-time. Men might "dig them up and replant them elsewhere or leave them to self-propagate into dense stands." "There is not much difference between these activities and those of nearby Australian Aboriginals, customarily labeled hunter-gatherers," Sillitoe concluded (27).

Intensive agriculture

Approximately 5,000 or 6,000 years ago, a second revolution in human economics and culture occurred that eventually had even more profound and lasting effects on the species and the planet. **Intensive agriculture** is high-input, high-yield farming employing such technologies as the plow, irrigation, fertilizer, and draft animals (all the ones missing from horticulture), allowing for something else that horticulture cannot provide – permanent farmlands. Given this "base," intensive agriculture made possible not only more of what we have seen before but entirely new dimensions of culture not previously possible.

The most obvious difference between horticulture and intensive agriculture is the vast surpluses achievable with the latter; farmers were able to produce crops – sometimes two or three per year in extremely well-watered locations like Bali – sufficient to feed enormous populations, measuring into the tens of thousands even in ancient times and into the hundreds of millions today. The earliest environments for this new practice were frequently river valleys, which provided the requisite water and alluvial soils; however, not every early intensive agricultural society lived along a river (for instance,

Intensive agriculture high-input, high-yield farming on permanent farmlands through the use of technologies like irrigation, fertilizer, pesticide, and the plow

PLATE 7.5 Intensive agriculture societies use all available land, as in Nepal where hillsides are cut into terraces.

the Inca and Aztec). Rather, what intensive agricultural environments seemed to share was a restricted amount of productive land, such that the only possible response to increasing populations was intensification of production.

The work of early intensive agriculture was arduous and incessant and required the efforts of the entire farming family; men, women, and children alike were enlisted as farm labor. However, in contrast to horticulture, ownership and control of land, production, and surplus were usually concentrated in the hands of men, leading back to a male-centered and male-dominated society. Fathers tend to be heads of families, and membership, inheritance, and such issues were settled among and between males. This male pre-eminence, together with the accumulation of sometimes vast surpluses, made raiding, plunder, and inter-society aggression attractive. Accordingly, intensive agricultural societies tended and tend to be warlike, even promoting a social institution of professional soldiers on permanent military stand-by.

In fact, a key aspect of the form of society made possible – and probably necessary – by intensive agriculture was a high degree of social differentiation and social specialization. First of all, the enormous surpluses translated to enormous differences in wealth and power; while most people were still food-producers (which was true until very recently), a small but important class of wealth-

expropriators existed to "rule" and "manage" the economy and society. This class constituted and constitutes an elite or an actual government over the equally new political institution, the territorial state. There might be other classes intermediate between the elite and the agricultural **peasants**, the latter now not independent subsistence producers but providers of surplus to a "center" of society. As this suggests, the second possibility of intensive agriculture was an elaboration of the number of different kinds of jobs to do or literally different kinds of people to be. In addition to peasants and rulers, there could be professional priests, scribes, craftsmen, artisans, and naturally soldiers. All of this variation was financed by the surplus production of the laboring classes, often including slaves.

Where intensive agriculture first appeared – in the Middle East (so-called "Mesopotamia"), Egypt, India, and China – we find a new type of society and culture normally referred to as **civilization**. Civilization is a social formation centered on, although not exclusively consisting of, large, densely populated communities or "cities." Most of the population still lived in the hinterland, but the power and decision-making for the society emanated from the city; it was the "seat of power." Along with, or perhaps because of, cities came a constellation of new skills, technologies, and species of knowledge. Among these were the state, the first writing systems, mathematics, monumental

See Chapters 9 and 13

Peasant

an out-of-favor term for rural and agricultural peoples who live in but are peripheral to a centralized and often urbanized society. The peasants provide the food for the society but generally have the least power and wealth in the society

Civilization

a form of society based on cities as the centers of administration and the focus of social life, usually dependent on intensive agriculture in the surrounding countryside

---

BOX 7.3   ENSURING POWER IN AN INTENSIVE AGRICULTURAL SOCIETY

As described by Hilda Kuper (1963), the Swazi of South Africa stood on or just across the line of intensive agriculture. They cultivated maize and millet with a combination of old and new technologies: women used a simple hoe to sow small plots of maize and also reaped it, but men used ox-drawn plows to prepare land as well. There was no irrigation or crop rotation, however. Both men and women processed the harvest, shucking corn and threshing millet. Overall, farming was a low-status activity. Land was not owned or leased by individual farmers but was rather available to them through personal (what we might call "feudal") relationships with landowners. According to Kuper, "land, the basis of subsistence, is 'served' to the people by their political overlords" (42). This created a system of economic and political inequality, which was not only normal but desirable – but only when the advantages accrued to the overlords. Lower-ranking people, the "commoners," were not expected or allowed to accumulate wealth; a man with more – whether more animals or more wives – was open to accusations of witchcraft, for which the penalty was death. Then, the property that he had illicitly acquired "was legally 'eaten up' by chiefs" (49), adding to their already superior position.

architecture (e.g. pyramids and palaces), and representational art.

Another new institution created by intensive agriculture was the market (see below), a location and institution for exchanging goods based on their economic value. Eventually money was invented to symbolize that value and facilitate exchange. And to make the market function, a professional class of merchants evolved, who extracted a share of the value in order to mediate the exchange. This market, and the long-range trading that sustained it, introduced a circulation not only of goods but of ideas and cultures, as travelers from distant lands brought their produce and their languages, religions, and other cultural elements to the city. Cities thus, from the beginning, were sites for the mixing and transmitting of culture and thereby for the creation of new cultures and of new cultural awareness like "cosmopolitanism" (*cosmos* for world or universe, and *polis* for city) and "multiculturalism" – and ultimately globalization.

Religion predictably reflected social changes on the ground in these societies. Just as economics and politics were "centralized," so religion and the "spiritual realm" could become centralized too. There was often a single "high god" or a pantheon of gods (like the Greek "Olympian" gods) of the city or civilization that was believed to own and control the affairs of the society. The human rulers and the god or gods might be in close communication – or in the case of ancient Egypt, be one and the same. Professional priests ran the cult of the god(s) from the city center, collecting tribute (what we would call taxes) for the benefit of the god(s) which was used to fund all of the activities of the society. The god(s) was/were often judgmental and warlike, identical to the rulers themselves, who sat in judgment over the people and led the "defense" of society. Religion was so central to the function and identity of many of these ancient civilizations that they have been referred to as "temple communities."

Industrialism

In the last few centuries, changes in agricultural techniques together with technological advances have spawned a new kind of production based on *industry* or machines and machine-generated energy. Indeed, anthropology and sociology were born during and largely in response to the "industrial revolution" that was wreaking profound changes on Western societies and on the non-Western societies integrated into their empires to feed their industrial needs. It was nineteenth-century industrial capitalism that inspired Karl Marx to formulate his theory of societies or "social formations" as effects of material and economic forces; Émile Durkheim and Max Weber also discussed **industrialism** as a momentous change in human relations and organization.

The key new institution in industrialism is "the factory," which is a site of productive activity but also a set of social roles, attitudes, values, and symbols. As a concentration of workers occasioned by a concentration of machinery, the factory tends to create large dense population centers; of course, as we saw above, "the city" existed before industrialism, and some experts estimate that cities like imperial Rome reached a population of 1 million. Nevertheless, industrialism led to the growth of more cities and larger cities than previously seen, achieved through rural-to-urban migration and even international migration – that is, large-scale population transfers.

One effect of the factory system is a separation of productive functions from other social functions – in a word, the separation of "work" from "home." Within the factory, according to the historian E. P. Thompson (1967), new social habits of time (e.g. a preoccupation with clocks and schedules) and work-discipline have to be mastered and managed, many of which were resisted by rural people unaccustomed to the demands of the city and factory. Beyond the factory walls, the effects of industrialization on society are profound: Durkheim theorized that an entirely new kind of social organization, the "organic" society with its division of labor, interdependent classes, and fundamentally economic or practical motivations, emerged, while Weber believed that industry was one facet of a more general process of "modernization" that also included urbanization, bureaucracy, and even secularization (the reduction or disappearance of religion). Marx opined that industrial capitalism was necessarily destructive of traditional society: it depends on "creative destruction" and the continuous revolutionizing of the means of production, such that "all that is solid melts into air."

Much of the analysis of industrialism has focused on the Western experience, and, as just

See Chapter 11

Industrialism
an economic and social system based on the production of large quantities of inexpensive manufactured goods and the concentration of employment in urban factories

Thompson, E. P. 1967. "Time, Work-Discipline, and Industrial Capitalism." *Past & Present* 38: 56–97.

seen, much of it has been extremely negative about that experience. Anthropology joined the discussion of industrialism somewhat later than the classic sociologists, but anthropologists have noted the diversity and cultural relativity of the new production system. Some of the first works of urban anthropology arose from the impact of colonial industrialism in Africa, particularly in the so-called "Copper Belt" region. At the same time, some anthropologists were conducting participant observation inside factories, describing their processes and concepts. Our main discovery has been that there is more than one path or process of industrialism and that the relationship between industrial and "traditional" society is complex and variable.

For example, Morton Klass investigated the effects of a bicycle factory near a village in West Bengal in the 1970s. To be sure, Bengali industrial centers, like many others, were "overcrowded" with all the attendant problems of "disease, crowded slums, filth, poor sanitation and water, crime, and so on" (1978: 8). But the factory did not simply erode away traditional identities and organization, nor was it experienced as entirely negative. The factory managers were not even village people but already urbanized Indians. And while most of the laborers did come from the village, their pre-industrial social and religious identities and practices did not suddenly disappear. Rather, for example, the pre-industrial caste system not only continued but served as an important structural aspect of the factory, members of the same caste often "cluster[ing] together in particular factory departments or activities" (219). Pre-industrial religion also adapted, with a minor god named Bissokormo, the patron-spirit of men who work with tools, assuming more importance. And of course many workers regarded the factory as a distinct improvement over the labor, social conditions, and uncertainty of the farm.

Industrialism is often associated with smaller families, but the assumption that industrialism necessarily damages families is unjustified. David Kertzer found, for instance, that industrialization in the Italian community of Caselecchio di Reno actually *strengthened* the nuclear family. In the mid-1800s, 15 percent of children under the age of fifteen did not live with their parents but rather as "servants or apprentices in the homes of others"; by 1921, this number had fallen to 3 percent, largely as

a result of factory work for poor families (1987: 154). "Far from tearing children away from a nurturing parental family environment, industrialization often permitted children to grow up in their parental household to an extent that would not have otherwise been possible" (158), he concluded.

Finally, Aihwa Ong, like others, has explored the symbolic and religious effects of industrialism. Malaysian factories, as in many places, have tended to hire young women, who are often stereotypically valued for their dexterity and patience as well as their shyness, obedience, and deference (that is, they take orders well and do not complain) (1988: 33). However, "when young peasant women began to leave the kampung [village] and enter the unknown worlds of urban boarding schools and foreign factories, the incidence of spirit possession seems to have become more common among them" (32). Ong concluded that these outbreaks of spirit possession – in which women workers "explode into demonic screaming and rage on the shop floor" (28) –

> may be taken as expressions both of fear and of resistance against the multiple violations of moral boundaries in the modern factory. They are acts of rebellion, symbolizing what cannot be spoken directly, calling for a renegotiation of obligations between the management and workers.
>
> (38)

Systems of distribution

Once goods are produced, there is the task of providing them to the people who need them – or at least the people who will consume them, which is not necessarily the same thing. This second phase is distribution. Unlike the tendency for a society to have a single dominant system of production, it may have more than one distribution system or all three systems in operation simultaneously, sometimes in different realms of the culture. The three systems (Polanyi 1957) are:

- Reciprocity
- Redistribution
- Market exchange

Reciprocity

Reciprocity is an informal type of back-and-forth exchanging, of giving and taking. This does not particularly distinguish it from other distribution methods, where someone always gives and someone else takes. We might do better to think of it as a style of exchange in which individuals or groups of relatively equal power and status, and who know each other personally, mutually give and take goods as part of and as a commentary on their ongoing social relationship. Reciprocity really exists in three sub-forms, namely:

1. Generalized reciprocity. In this form, goods are given without any particular calculation of the value of the goods or any particular expectation for a "return" of equal value in any particular time frame. That is, if I have something to give, I give it, not worrying whether I will receive something in exchange any time soon but assuming that, if you have something to give, you will give it. In some societies, especially foraging ones, this may be the predominant or even sole distribution system; if one man had meat today as the result of a successful hunt, he shared the meat with everyone in his social group, and he did not expect compensation or praise for his behavior. Maybe tomorrow someone else would have meat, and he would

share likewise. The person who does not share, or who demands credit or acclaim for doing so, is simply impolite and socially inappropriate. Clearly, this type of sharing will only occur between people who know and trust each other and who have a long-term social relationship – during which "reciprocity" will eventually and "generally" be achieved.

2. Balanced reciprocity. In this form, goods are given with some calculation of their value and some expectation of an equal return within some reasonable time. It still entails a long-term and meaningful relationship between the exchangers but ordinarily transpires between individuals who are not quite as close as those who would do generalized reciprocity; after all, you would not give a friend or loved one a gift and then impatiently wait for an equal return.

3. Negative reciprocity. In this final form, goods are given with calculation of their value but also with an expectation or intention of receiving more value than one gives. This resembles most closely the modern "market" principle, except that it is characterized by the ongoing relationship found at the heart of all reciprocity, even if that relationship is more distant and tenuous than in other forms of reciprocity. Perhaps the most famous and well-researched example of negative reciprocity is the "kula" institution described by Malinowski in

Reciprocity
a form of exchange that involves giving and receiving between relative equals and as part of a larger ongoing social relationship

BOX 7.4   THE *HXARO* EXCHANGE

According to Richard Lee (1984), the !Kung or Ju/hoansi practiced a form of reciprocity called *hxaro*, a "delayed form of nonequivalent gift exchange" that had the effect of "circulating goods, lubricating social relations, and maintaining ecological balance" (97). All sorts of things were exchanged by *hxaro*, including tools and jewelry and weapons and utensils, and both men and women entered into such exchanges. Two things that were never traded in this manner were food and people. The range of *hxaro* trade relations could be quite extensive, and every visit between individuals and communities was an occasion for exchanging – starting new trades or completing old ones. In their self-effacing, egalitarian way, givers would downplay the quality of their gift with comments like "I couldn't find a really good thing, I just brought you this" (100). What was important, and explicitly so, was not the object itself but the social relationship between the participants: Ju/hoansi understood that a deficient reciprocation "could mean a *hxaro* partner was losing interest in maintaining the relationship and was allowing it to lapse" (101), and while such partnerships could end by agreement, they were also often the source of arguments and conflicts – although the lapse was usually a symptom of a changed relationship more than a cause of it.

Lee, Richard. 1984. *The Dobe !Kung.* New York: Holt, Rinehart, and Winston.

Melanesia. Men traveled great distances at considerable bother and risk in order to trade necklaces and armbands with their partners, each man hoping to receive the "best" necklace for his armband or vice versa. However, the point was not to get and hold a piece but to get it, display it, and eventually trade it for an even more prized piece. This way, a man achieved and expressed his status in society, his skill as a trader, and ultimately, if all went well, his elevation to "kula master." Still, in the end, his success depended not only on his tough bargaining and skillful manipulation of the game but on his relationships with other traders who could just as easily pass their prestigious objects to other partners.

Redistribution

One of the key characteristics of reciprocity is that it has no "center." No one person or group controls or oversees the exchange. In **redistribution**, on the other hand, a center is implicit and necessary, and the social implications of this fact are serious. Redistribution can be defined as exchange in which wealth is collected by a central person, group, or institution who/which then hands it out to the people who need it and/or "spends" it for purposes that are (ideally) beneficial to all in the exchange arrangement but which also reflect the power and interests of the distributor.

A classic example of redistribution also comes from Melanesia, where a "big man" might erect a redistribution system around himself. A man was not born a big man, even if his father was one. Rather, this was a status that each man had to gain individually. The point was to develop a coterie of followers or contributors who would turn their surplus over to you, which you could redistribute according to the needs and interests of the system. So, a potential big man first had to generate his own surplus, which he displayed and gave away in a very public gesture resembling a party. If his hard work and generosity were seen and appreciated, others might opt to associate themselves with him; like finding a good "patron," it was always desirable to attach oneself to a powerful and generous man. The more people who joined his "team" and contributed their surplus, the more the big man could display and redistribute. Eventually, he might become the

center of an important and powerful exchange network. Like a feudal lord (another center of redistribution), his favor was valuable and his support good or even necessary, and a follower was likely to return deference for various kinds of benefits.

In intensive agricultural and industrial societies, the "government" is effectively the center of redistribution. Whether this takes the form of king or priest or state, the center can compel and even coerce participation in the form of taxes or tithes or other expropriation of private wealth. This wealth goes to "social services" (like unemployment or retirement benefits) but also to large-scale projects which individuals could not afford alone (like roads), to "security" systems like the police or military, and to finance the government itself, which often enough meant and means the luxurious lifestyle of the leaders.

Market exchange

Market exchange was the last of the three distribution systems to appear historically and is still not the only existing system even in "modern" societies. However, it is increasingly defining the modern world and penetrating and displacing other systems. In Western society, even when people practice reciprocity or redistribution, it is usually in terms of goods and services acquired by market practices: people give gifts bought at the store and paid for by money.

We can think of market exchange as distribution which involves a specialized location or institution – the "market" – where people bring their goods or their symbols of wealth (like money) for the purpose of exchange based on self-interest and maximization of value ("profit") determined by "supply and demand" and where ongoing social relationships are reduced, not significant, or an actual impediment to exchange. Modernity or capitalism hardly invented the market principle; ancient intensive agricultural societies generally had markets, and many traditional African horticulturists, for instance, held markets but on a more limited scale and schedule. Villages might organize a "market day" once every several days, at which time people gathered to exchange foods or handicrafts or whatever they produced. After market day, people would not do market exchange until the

Redistribution
a form of exchange that involves collection of surplus or wealth by a "central" individual, group, or institution that controls how the wealth is redistributed and used

Market exchange
a form of distribution based on the use of a specialized location (the "market place") and relatively impersonal principles of supply and demand and the pursuit of profit

PLATE 7.6 Modern markets, like this one in downtown Tokyo, can generate great wealth.

next market day, leaving lots of occasion for reciprocity or redistribution.

In pre-modern marketing arrangements, it was of course the case that people usually knew each other over long periods of time. It is possible in modern Western market practices that participants know the people they "buy from" or "sell to" or even that they develop a personal relationship with them. Humans are humans and tend to make social bonds over time. This can facilitate the market "deal," as trust can grow between traders. However, in capitalist society, friendship is not enough and can be positively detrimental; that is why contracts and courts exist. And it is entirely possible and even preferable sometimes to have a minimal social relationship with one's market partner: most modern shoppers do not seek or particularly want to know and befriend their car salesman or grocery check-out clerk, and the system certainly does not depend on it. In fact, as many people have discovered, "doing business" with friends or family can be a vexing undertaking.

BOX 7.5 A PRE-MODERN MARKET

Like many traditional societies, the Igbo of Nigeria held rural markets in which not only local people but traveling merchants and traders gathered to exchange goods. Actually, Igbo society (Uchendu 1965) contained two parallel market systems. Village markets were owned and operated by sets of villagers and were dominated, as buyers and sellers, by women; long-distance markets in exotic goods like salt, slaves, cattle, and manufactured goods were the province of men. The village market was not only a place of business but a place to hear or tell news and gossip, to observe or participate in ceremonies and parades, and to meet friends, pay or collect debts, and make marriages and divorces. Inside the marketplace, sellers were "zoned" into areas of like commodities (all the sellers of corn were grouped together, etc.), and prices were arrived at by bargaining and supply/demand. Between markets a "market ring" system existed, such that nearby markets staggered their days or times, allowing traders to circulate between them. And the "market peace," essential to any large public gathering, was assured by three devices: a weather magician who "drove away the rain," a market court with police and judges to punish offenders who disturbed the peace, and a market god who punished those who escaped the arm of the human authorities.

Again, the market principle does not depend on money nor certainly on capitalism. Capitalism is one way of doing markets (even communists "went to the market" to buy bread), and money is a convenient "medium" or symbol of wealth and value: it is easier to carry some money to the market than some corn, and of course "service" workers like teachers do not produce material goods to take to market anyhow. Nevertheless, money and capitalist modes of production and exchange are increasingly pervading the economic and social world – not just in the United States or the West but globally – and they appear to be the future (at least the short-to-mid-range future) of economics and culture. Either way – with or without money (or credit cards, symbols of symbols of wealth) and with or without capitalism – market exchange, intensive agriculture, and industrialization/urbanization will continue to transform not only economies and politics but the social relations within which all humans live their lives.

Consumption

The third and most neglected phase of any economic system is consumption, the actual use of goods and services. It has received less attention in anthropology at least partly because it has received less attention in Western economic thinking in general: as Gregory expressed, "The consumption sphere is very much a subordinate sphere under capitalism, and as such was not subjected to any systematic analysis by the classical economists. . . . The methods of consumption under capitalism are disorganized relative to the methods of production" (1982: 75–76). Many cultural anthropology textbooks make little or no mention of it, which is regrettable, not only because it too is a cultural activity but because it is the "end" of the system, where goods meet real persons and social circumstances.

Anthropologists in the field have not ignored consumption, and a few prominent economic theorists have given it some thought. Marx, who was most concerned with the "mode of production," did also identify a "mode of consumption," but it was a secondary issue for him that received little elaboration beyond the distinction between subsistence consumption and luxury consumption,

associated with the working class and the owning class respectively. The first scholar to take consumption seriously was perhaps Thorstein Veblen, whose *Theory of the Leisure Class: An Economic Study of Institutions* (published in 1899) introduced the concept of "conspicuous consumption." Veblen's idea was that the drive to consume certain kinds of goods was based on the desire to create and display differences between people and on the capacity of goods to do so. In other words, products do not just have "uses" but they also have "values," and the people who possess – and can display – certain items have *their* social value enhanced as well. He imagined that the "upper classes" set the tone in a society, which the lower classes tried to emulate in order to acquire some of the status and prestige of their betters. One of the marks of high status in the past, he argued, was leisure itself (free time and freedom from labor), but now it was material objects.

While the study of consumption has progressed since then, a theory of consumption really has not appeared. To my knowledge, there is no system or typology of consumption available, comparable to those of production and distribution discussed above; there is certainly no standard and established typology. Still, we can begin to lay out some of the issues that would be part of any systematic anthropological study of consumption. First, consumption entails a variety of sub-processes, from acquisition to preparation to presentation to use. This leads to a series of research questions:

- Who acquires goods and services for consumption by the group, and how/where (i.e. the cultural phenomenon of "shopping")?
- Who prepares items for consumption, and how?
- How and why are products presented or displayed to potential consumers – and to potential audiences?
- When (for instance, at what time of day or on what occasions) and by whom are particular goods consumed?
- How are goods consumed in ritual contexts?
- Are different products consumed by different types of people, and are they consumed in different ways?
- Who can consume together, and who cannot?

How does consumption perform, perpetuate, and comment on social relationships and institutions? How can consumption be used to challenge and change social relationships and institutions?

The essence of an anthropology of consumption is that consumables are not neutral things, even when they are minimally processed natural commodities (like kangaroo meat). Food itself, as Roland Barthes asserts, "is not only a collection of products that can be used for statistical or nutritional studies. It is also, and at the same time, a system of communication, a body of images, a protocol of usages, situations, and behaviors" (1997: 21). That is, like all other parts of culture, consumable goods are *symbols* with meanings and effects. Any object – food, clothing, a house, a car – "sums up and transmits a situation; it constitutes information; it signifies" (ibid.).

Mary Douglas was one of the first anthropologists to think about consumption systematically. In her famous essay "Deciphering a Meal" from her book *Implicit Meanings* (1975), she discussed the social construction of various kinds of food-sharing. Central to her analysis was the distinction between the categories of "meal" and "drinks." Anyone in

Western society knows that "having drinks" is a more casual social matter than "having dinner." The social dynamic involved is "intimacy and distance": "The meal expresses close friendship. Those we only know at drinks we know less intimately."

Since food is such a ready medium for observing consumption, let us remain with it. The Barabaig, pastoralists from earlier in the chapter, consumed milk, but the preferences of the sexes differed: men liked raw milk, whereas women preferred churned or curdled milk. More significantly, a husband lived and ate in his own room in his homestead, apart from wives and children. A wife cooked in her room (*ged*) and delivered the food to his room (*huland*); if he had multiple wives, each woman cooked for him in turn, and he had to eat the same amount from each or cause dissension in his family (Klima 1970: 37).

As Douglas opined, consumption speaks to basic cultural notions of categorization – what is food, and what kinds of foods are there? The Hua of Papua New Guinea had rules for what foods could and could not be eaten by different kinds of people. For instance, a pregnant woman could not, according to Meigs (1997), eat cat or dog or possum because those animals speak in babble, which would negatively affect the child; likewise, a warrior

Barthes, Roland. 1997. "Toward a Psychosociology of Contemporary Food Consumption." In Carole Counihan and Penny van Esterick, eds. *Food and Culture: A Reader*. New York and London: Routledge, 20–27.

Douglas, Mary. 1975. *Implicit Meanings: Essays in Anthropology*. London and Boston, MA: Routledge & Kegan Paul.

ADVENTURES IN EATING

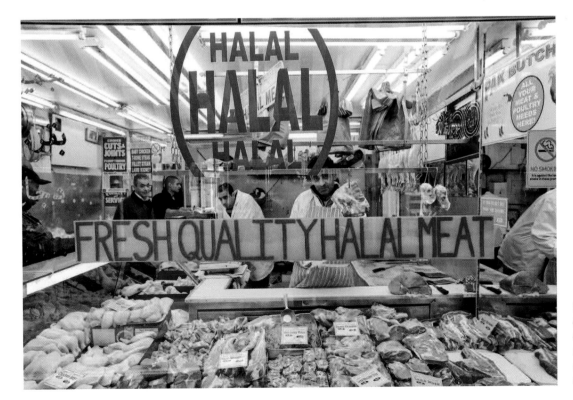

PLATE 7.7 Meat and other goods produced in conformity to Islamic religious norms of consumption are classified and sold as *halal*.

BOX 7.6   ISLAM, FOOD, AND NATIONALITY IN A GLOBAL CONTEXT

Like the more familiar concept of kosher, Muslims have a dietary code known as *halal*, which means "lawful" according to religious conventions. Certain foods are *halal* or not: pork and any pig-derived products are *haram* or forbidden, as is dog and alcohol. Acceptability also depends on how the food was produced: the proper slaughter of meat involves cutting the throat and draining the blood (the common Western practice of "stunning" is inadequate). In Muslim-majority countries *halal* food is relatively easy to acquire, but outside those places it is comparatively hard to find as well as hard to guarantee: is it really *halal?* Various Muslim countries or organizations have taken an interest in the sale and the certification of *halal* goods, partly because there is an emerging global market for them and partly as a way of guaranteeing religious piety and national identity. The Central Islamic Committee of Thailand as well as the Islamic Food and Nutrition Council of America set standards for items that claim to be *halal*, but Malaysians living outside their country mostly turn to *Jabatan Kemajuan Islam Malaysia* (JAKIM), or the Islamic Development Department of Malaysia. This service of course aims to aid expatriate Malaysians in observing Islamic law. But more significantly, it strives to make Malaysia an authority in international *halal* certification as well as to maintain the national and religious identity of Malaysian emigrants. The identity as well as legal citizenship status of Malays depends on their commitment to Islam, and the Malaysian government has been very interested to preserve the Malaysian/Islamic identity of overseas Malays, as well as to regulate and standardize Islam for those citizens. *Halal* is thus more than food but a way of "bridging the religious and the secular, as an example of the compatibility of the ethnicized state, modern Islam, business, and proper Islamic consumption" (Fischer 2011: 36). This is a particular problem not only for Malays living in the United Kingdom (the site of Fischer's research) but elsewhere – including in Malaysia – where other dietary options are available, where the *halal* status of foods is often uncertain, and where a rising middle class tends to seek more freedom from traditional standards while also engaging in new consumption habits like dining at restaurants or shopping at supermarkets.

should not eat sharp or scratchy food because such foods could draw blood. More profoundly, people could not eat food prepared by a "stranger," where strangeness was defined by not sharing the person's *nu* or spiritual substance. *Nu* was passed between people directly by physical contact as well as indirectly through food exchanges. "Food in Hua thinking contains the self and the feelings of its producer" (103); thus, "To eat a food. . .is not only an economic, social, and nutritive event but also an emotional and mystical one" (104).

The idea that food is more than food, and that goods are more than goods, is a common one, and it is closely tied to individual and group identity and status. In the village of Gopalpur, as in many parts of India, humans were classified according to social and spiritual qualities. One of the manifestations of this "caste system" was restrictions on who could sit with and eat with whom. The various castes or *jatis* did not "eat together," although this had a

culturally specific meaning: it applied to certain kinds of foods more than others (especially rice) and to certain acts more than others (especially eating off the same plate or bowl and sitting in a line to do so). Thus, different castes could eat together if they used separate plates and either faced each other or at a slant, but then by their cultural definition, they were not "eating together" (Beals 1980).

Let us quickly mention one other arena, which is the ritual and status aspect of food consumption. Obviously many societies have food taboos, such as the Hua rules about what kinds of food men and women should eat. Rituals and culturally significant occasions not only tend to call for different food behaviors (such as feasts and sacrifices) but for different foods; Americans eat more turkey at Thanksgiving than any other time of year. It is the "right food" for the occasion. One of the best-known food regulations in Western civilization is

See Chapter 8

BOX 7.7 CONTEMPORARY CULTURAL CONTROVERSIES: STUDYING CONSUMPTION OR MANIPULATING CONSUMPTION?

Modern market practices have not only come to dominate economic activity in industrialized Western societies but have become worldwide forces, shaping a national and global "buyosphere" (Hine 2003). The power of market concepts and behaviors to reconfigure social relations has been noted, from Max Weber's seminal study of the relation between capitalism and Protestantism to anthropologist Daniel Miller's *A Theory of Shopping* (1998). In fact, according to George Ritzer consumption not only "plays an ever-expanding role in the lives of individuals around the world" (2005: 1) but permeates activities and institutions from obviously economic (stores, restaurants, casinos, and cruise ships) to less obviously economic or superficially non-economic (education, medicine/health care, museum and charity organizations, and religion). Consuming, Ritzer claims, has become a form of entertainment in its own right. The explosive popularity and cultural importance of consumption has made it a worthwhile subject for anthropological investigation, including into what has been called "consumer behavior." Consumer behavior has actually been a topic of analysis for many decades, at least since the 1950s, and represents a sort of applied anthropology. It is certainly a valid endeavor to study the behaviors, meanings, and consequences of consumer action; however, in more than a few cases this kind of knowledge can be and has been employed to manipulate such action – to produce more effective marketing strategies, to perfect advertising campaigns, and ultimately induce people to consume *more* of *certain kinds* of goods. Anthropologists could participate in these investigations, and/or our research could be used by others for their own purposes. What do you think?

the Torah/Old Testament proscription against shell-fish and various other potential foods. Douglas (1966) analyzed this too as related to categories (e.g. animals that chew their cud and split the hoof versus those that do not), some of which are fit to eat and some of which are not. Thus, "purity" and cultural or religious "fitness" enter the calculation as to what people may eat and how and when (for instance, no calves boiled in their mother's milk). Finally, Allison (1997) has investigated the high-stakes game of packing nursery school *bento* lunch boxes for Japanese children, in which a mother's social status and aesthetic sense are on trial. She goes so far as to insist that making and eating *bentos* (since children are under pressure to eat them in particular ways) are ideological systems that enculturate both children and mothers into socially appropriate roles and principles of proper order, appearance, style, and "naturalness" – but, like all of culture, a kind of "naturalness made artificial" and perfected by humans, that is, a kind of culturized nature (299).

SUMMARY

Every society has an economic system as part of its culture, even if it does not have factories and money and supermarkets. Those are specific ways of doing an economy, not the definition of economy. An economy is the practices and institutions, and the associated beliefs and values and roles, involved in transforming the environment into usable products for humans. As such, the economic behaviors of a society will dramatically influence other aspects of the society, including how humans organize themselves and assign tasks and values and meanings to work, objects, and humans themselves.

An economic system has three phases:

- Production
- Distribution
- Consumption

Within each of these is a variety of possible arrangements or systems for accomplishing the functions of the economy. There are five major production systems, although a specific society's economy may combine or modify them in various ways:

- Foraging
- Pastoralism
- Horticulture
- Intensive agriculture
- Industrialism

There are three major distribution systems, which may co-exist in a society:

- Reciprocity
- Redistribution
- Market exchange

Finally, although it is has not been studied and systematized like the other phases, consumption is the final and important stage in which the roles, values, statuses, and meanings of goods and people converge in the actual use of cultural products.

MCQS

FILL IN THE BLANKS

WWW

Key Terms

Adaptation

Civilization

Division of labor

Domestication

Foraging

Horticulture

Industrialism

Intensive agriculture

Market exchange

Means of production

Neolithic

Pastoralism

Peasant

Reciprocity

Redistribution

Relations of production

Slash-and-burn

Swidden

Kinship and non-kin organization

Creating corporate groups

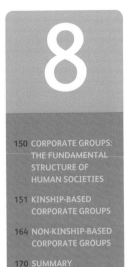

In February 2004, a French woman named Christelle Demichel married her fiancé Eric. The only thing unusual about the wedding is that the groom was absent, since he was dead, having been killed in a motorcycle accident in 2002. Ms. Demichel was able to marry him anyhow because of a 1959 French law legalizing wedding ceremonies between a person and his or her deceased partner. Prior to 1959, a flood resulting from the failure of Malpasset Dam had taken the life of Irene Jodard's fiancé, and she had asked the government to allow her to proceed with the wedding. From this request came the new law, giving the French President the power to authorize a marriage if the wedding had already been planned and the parents of the deceased approved. The legal marriage date would be backdated to before the death, and while no inheritance rights or other financial advantages could come from such a marriage, any child born from the couple would be regarded as legitimate.

There is no society on earth in which humans live, work, and fill all of their needs in isolation from each other. In fact, such would be the very opposite of a society. Rather, humans form relationships and groups to accomplish their ends and enjoy their lives. The kinds of relationships and groups they

can form, as in the case above, are incredibly diverse, but they form them for various and particular reasons, love and companionship being just two. Humans also cooperatively produce and distribute and consume wealth, establish residences, solve problems and exercise power, and create and perpetuate identities. The lone individual could not make or perpetuate these social arrangements and institutions. It is groups of people who share in tasks, results, and interests.

There are many types of human groups, including crowds and classrooms. Each has its own dynamics and its own "culture." However, the most socially significant groups are what we can call **corporate groups**, collectivities of humans that act and to an extent think as a single "body" (*corps*) in regard to such practical activities as production, distribution, consumption, ownership, decision-making, **residence**, inheritance, and ultimately "identity" or "destiny." They are the ones who see themselves as "in this together," who "look out for each other," who "keep it in the family." Accordingly, family or kinship is one way to provide this structure but clearly not the only way. In this chapter, then, we will consider the cross-cultural possibilities and necessities of kinship – the diverse ways

Corporate group
a social group that shares some degree of practical interest, identity, residence, and destiny

Residence
the kinship principle concerning where people live, especially after marriage, and therefore what kinds of residential and corporate groups are found in the society and what tasks and values they are assigned

in which people can arrange themselves into "family" groups and assign those groups not only tasks but meaning. Additionally, we will investigate other principles by which virtually all societies at least supplement if not replace kinship by other, either cross-cutting or more-inclusive, kinds of corporate identities.

CORPORATE GROUPS: THE FUNDAMENTAL STRUCTURE OF HUMAN SOCIETIES

A society is not only a group of humans but a group of groups, a structured constellation of collectivities. The most important and enduring of these are corporate groups. Corporate groups are the basic organizational and functional units of a society. The kinds of functions they provide vary by the society and by the specific corporate group, but they can include such things as:

ANTHROPOLOGY OF THE CORPORATION

1. Regulating behavior or establishing rights for members, as well as between members of disparate groups. Like a business corporation, each group is a system of interrelated roles, with rules for their interaction.
2. Owning property. A corporate group is often if not ordinarily an ownership entity, collectively possessing rights or title to land, buildings, wealth, and other resources.
3. Producing and distributing wealth. A corporate group is frequently a "work" group, which accomplishes productive tasks together and shares the fruits of that labor among the members.
4. Inheriting property. A corporate group often aims to keep its wealth and resources within the group when members pass away. Thus, it may establish a sequence of ownership and rights for the transference of property from current to future members.
5. Consuming and residing. A corporate group, since it may produce and distribute together, may also consume together. It may give members a place to eat and in most cases a place to sleep (although it is not necessary that all of the functions of the members are conducted together). It may be their "home" in figurative or literal ways.

6. Providing for the social and emotional needs of members. As human beings, the individuals in corporate groups have needs other than physical and material ones. The group may satisfy those needs through meaningful social interactions, camaraderie, and even affection.
7. Creating a sense of identity. A corporate group regularly shapes the sense of self of the members, giving them a common "name" and a feeling of belonging to something greater and more enduring than themselves. This identity can translate into a sense of destiny as well – that they have a future *as* a collectivity and will collectively face that future.
8. Perpetuating the group over time. Any group has a future only if it can persist beyond the lifetime of current members. A corporate group has some mechanism for obtaining new members (reproduction, adoption, capture, hiring, etc.) and inculcating them with the skills or values of the group. Perpetuating groups often equates to perpetuating social statuses – and differences in social status – in the society: in other words, poor or subordinate groups tend to reproduce poverty or subordination, and rich or powerful groups tend to reproduce wealth and power.
9. Establishing alliances between groups. No group exists in isolation, so there must be some system or standard for making (and breaking) relationships between groups with different members, interests, and identities. Corporate groups can enter or find themselves in diverse connections with each other, over the short or long term. These relations can be mutually beneficial, mutually exploitative, or beneficial for one and exploitative for the other.

No particular corporate group must fulfill all of these conditions. Some are very important and meaningful to members, while others are more trivial. Such groups can consequently be constructed on the basis of any number of natural or cultural characteristics of their members. Of the wide array of possible corporate foundations, we can distinguish two general types: groups that are based on kinship ties or relations and those that are based on other, non-kinship qualities or characteristics. In any society, both of these types of groups will exist simultaneously, such that any single

PLATE 8.1 Two mothers and their children from the Samantha tribe, India.

individual is a member of one (or more than one) kinship group as well as multiple non-kinship groups. This creates bonds with kin and non-kin alike, often of different types and functions and sometimes competing or conflicting with each other.

KINSHIP-BASED CORPORATE GROUPS

Kinship is a virtually universal way of organizing people into corporate groups, although it is by no means the only way. We can think of kinship as roughly what English speakers mean when they talk about "family," although, like everything else in culture, "family" is a culturally relative term. The physical or "blood" relations between individuals are of course exactly the same from one society to another, for instance, the man who is your father's brother's son or the woman who is your mother's sister's husband's sister is exactly the same person in every society. However, what is important is not the "objective" fact but its relevance for society. This is another case of how society culturizes physical facts to give them cultural meaning, value, and use.

Any kinship system is a product of three distinct but interconnected principles or concepts, namely:

- Marriage
- Residence
- Descent

Marriage might be thought of as the "horizontal" principle, which links individuals (and groups) together and establishes new groups. Residence is literally the geographic or spatial principle, the site where people actually live or perform their corporate activities. Descent constitutes the "vertical" or temporal principle, linking individuals and groups through time and "down" between the generations. Each of these principles or concepts comes in diverse forms and in various combinations, giving the society's kinship system its unique contours.

Marriage

Marriage is the first step in constructing kinship-based corporate groups. Marriage brings together individuals from different kin and corporate groups and binds them into one, or the other, or a new group. In considering the nature of marriage, as always anthropologists must build a definition that is inclusive, not simply impose their own cultural notion of marriage on all societies and assume that how their culture does marriage *really* is marriage and that if another culture does it differently, theirs is not "really marriage." Even in Western societies, marriage is a contentious issue. Is marriage only between a man and a woman? That is, can members of the same sex marry? Is marriage between only one man and only one woman? Is marriage only between two *living* people?

Marriage across cultures has certain core characterics but a great degree of flexibility. Wherever

Marriage
a socially recognized relationship between two (or more) people that establishes a kin-based group and that provides norms and roles for residence, property ownership and inheritance, labor, sexual relations, and/or childrearing

it is found, it is a socially recognized relationship between (two or more) individuals and often between their families as well. It has enduring if not permanent qualities (it is expected to last for more than a few days, although not necessarily forever), and it establishes various kinds of rights and obligations. Marriage can and usually does include economic functions (shared labor or other productive activities, distribution and consumption, ownership, inheritance, and so on), political functions (establishment and enforcement of rules, decision-making, and problem-solving for members), and of course sexual and reproductive functions. Societies universally culturize the physical act of sex by elaborating rules and norms for who, how, when, where, and so on. In some societies, this is more critical than others: some have fairly lax norms about sex and "fidelity" (including "premarital" sex) and some have harsh restrictions, down to premarital virginity sanctioned with the death penalty. The most common "rule" across human societies is the famous **incest taboo**, that members of the same "family" do not ordinarily have sexual access to each other, although again "family" is a highly diverse term.

One of the key aspects of marriage relates to children. Children are of course required in order to expand and perpetuate a kinship group. Child-bearing is an important function of marriage in virtually all societies, although not of all marriages, since many married people choose not to have children. It goes without saying that marriage is not necessary for making babies – it is again a way that society culturizes the biological function of reproduction. Many societies do deem that marriage is a prerequisite to produce "socially acceptable" or "legitimate" children. But birth is hardly the end of the member-making process. Children must be cared for and instructed, that is, *enculturated*, which is a typical though never exclusive function of family. Children must learn the social and practical skills they need to participate in society – from language and "manners" to gender roles and economic skills. Some societies feature full-time professional institutions to contribute to this process (like schools), but the family is always a place where it occurs first if not most. We can think, more broadly, of the care and teaching of children as one crucial part of the general concern of **social reproduction**, that is, keeping society going over time, including over generations.

Another major and often overlooked element of social reproduction is the reproduction of labor. In the short term, laborers must be prepared for the

Incest taboo
the nearly universal rule against marrying or having sex with "kin"

Social reproduction
the maintenance and perpetuation of society beyond mere childbearing, including enculturation and teaching of members to take their place in society and day-to-day activities to allow members of society to perform their specified tasks (including what is sometimes called "housework")

PLATE 8.2 A traditional wedding ceremony on the island of Vanatu.

next day's labor. The marriage relationship and resultant family is where much of this work occurs, including feeding the laborers, cleaning their clothes, providing them a place to sleep, and so on. In the "anthropology of housework," researchers in recent decades have investigated the various activities that are required to insure that the group and the society can continue from day to day – activities that are overwhelmingly associated with women but have become more problematic in societies where women are also wage laborers.

Finally, marriage can be effective in establishing alliances between families. Practices like arranged marriage and marriage exchanges suggest that marriage is often more than a relationship between the individuals entering into the bond. Often, and explicitly in many cases, the marriage is actually a relationship or alliance between families. Royal marriages in European history were frequently quite self-conscious in their intentions to unify powerful or rich "houses" or noble families, and entire countries have been created through such marriages. On a more mundane level, families may seek to marry their children to other specific families for economic, political, or status reasons. The alliance between families may be more important to both sides than the particular marriage at hand, as indicated by ways in which they may strive to sustain the alliance even if the marriage fails in some way, as we will see below.

We should not ignore the pleasant emotional potential of marriage for partners. Neither should we overestimate it. In Western societies, love is regarded as the best reason and reward for marriage, but this opinion is not universally shared. Many marriages cross-culturally are arranged, often between individuals who may not even know each other, let alone love each other. If the marriage grows into love, that is wonderful, but the marriage does not depend on it. Westerners tend to privilege the emotional aspect of marriage, even thinking of the "practical" aspects as "unromantic." However, marriage is also if not mostly a lot of daily minutiae – paying the bills, washing the dishes, etc. – that cannot be ignored or neglected. And many people realize they are in, and even choose to remain in, "loveless" marriages for various reasons – "for the children," out of fear or dependence, or out of mere convenience or inertia.

The first question that a society's marriage system must address is whom one can or should marry (that is, who is an eligible partner), which leads to a basic distinction between **exogamy** and **endogamy**. These terms are elusive, because they do

Exogamy
the marriage principle in which an individual marries someone who is not in the same cultural category as himself or herself (e.g. marrying someone of a different sex/gender)

Endogamy
the marriage principle in which an individual marries someone who is in the same cultural category as himself or herself (e.g. marrying someone in your own race or religion)

BOX 8.1   LOVE AND MARRIAGE IN ANCIENT GREECE AND ROME

While people and politicians argue about "traditional marriage," it is interesting to consider some of the actual traditions of marriage in the West. John Boswell in his study of relationships in pre-modern Europe writes that "nothing in the ancient world quite corresponds to the idea of a permanent, exclusive union of social equals, freely chosen by them to fulfill both their emotional needs and imposing equal obligations of fidelity on both partners" (1994: 38). This is partly due to the rigid gender inequalities of those societies as well as to their economic and emotional expectations. In fact, Boswell finds that there were four types of heterosexual relationships (with their homosexual counterparts). Marriage was one, in its monogamous and polygamous forms. Its function was largely to provide children and to establish property rights, which were often the same thing, since children (and wives) were the property of men. Love and sex were not essential features of marriage: "Spouses who were actually 'in love' with each other were thought extraordinary and odd" until late antiquity (39). Love and sex were often sought in other partners, specifically concubines, lovers, and sex-objects. Concubines were typically women of lower social standing who were "kept" by men, sometimes for years, as non-marital or extramarital partners, sometimes in the family household. A lover was a person chosen for love or sex but without the long-term and economic implications of concubinage. A sex-object tended to be a servant or slave (regarded as the man's property) who was used for sex. All three of the latter relationships could be and frequently were in addition to, not instead of, marriage.

Boswell, John. 1994. *Same-Sex Union in Premodern Europe*. New York: Villard Books.

not apply to a society as a whole but to groups or categories within society: any particular marriage will be exogamous in regard to some groups/categories and endogamous in regard to others. Most simply, exogamy (*exo-* for outside and *gamy* for marriage) means marriage to someone who is "outside" of (not a member of) one's own group or category, while endogamy (*endo-* for inside) means marriage to someone who is "inside" or a member of one's group or category. For instance, most societies have an exogamous rule or preference – even a quite strong one, sometimes a formal or "legal" one – in regard to sex or gender: you should marry someone who is not a member of your own gender. Almost all societies observe basic kin-group exogamy – that is, you should marry someone who is not a member of your kin group, although how "kin group" is defined differs by culture. Some may practice exogamy in regard to the village: you should marry someone from another village than your own.

Similarly, there may be a tendency (more or less explicit or formal) toward endogamy in terms of age group or social class or race/ethnicity or religion or locality. It is certainly possible for a very old person to marry a very young person in a modern Western society, but it is not the norm and draws some degree of social judgment. Members of the same social class or religion or region not only have a greater chance of meeting but also of having things in common, and some religions quite strenuously urge that members marry "within the faith." And, while the United States does not have a "race endogamy" law, in times and places in the past it did, and most American marriages today are still racially endogamous, even if most Americans do not disapprove of "inter-racial" marriages.

Exogamy and endogamy set the most general limitations on who is an eligible or acceptable candidate for marriage. However, societies typically provide much more structure for the practice than this. A second basic question then is how many people an individual can marry. There are really only two choices: one or more than one. Anthropologists refine this distinction, identifying three systems:

1. **Monogamy** (*mono-* for one) – the individual can only marry one person. The most common form is heterosexual monogamy, one man married to one woman; homosexual marriage

of course could also be monogamous. We should further distinguish between what we might call "absolute" or "lifetime" monogamy and **"serial" monogamy**, the distinction being whether a person can have only one spouse in an entire lifetime or merely one spouse at a time. In strict traditional Christian doctrine, marriage was a once-in-a-lifetime thing; remarriage was forbidden. Most modern Americans will probably marry more than once in their lives; monogamy then prohibits multiple *simultaneous* marriages, not multiple *consecutive* marriages. As "natural" as monogamy seems to modern readers, it is actually not the most common marriage rule cross-culturally, although it may be the most common form in practice; even when societies allow or prefer multiple marriages, individuals may not desire them or have the resources to accomplish them. And, since there is a rough balance of population between the sexes globally, there cannot be enough members of the opposite sex for each person to have multiple spouses.

2. **Polygyny** (*poly-* for many and *gyny* for woman) – a man may or should marry two or more women. While this seems undesirable, even perverse, to many Westerners, it is in fact the most common marriage rule or preference cross-culturally. Somewhere between 70 and 80 percent of the world's known societies have condoned multiple wives for men. This can be seen as, and often is, a means of male domination or at least a manifestation of male status and power. However, women are not always the helpless victims of polygyny; women in many societies welcome co-wives into the home (or sometimes a homestead consisting of multiple households, one for each woman and her children) for purposes of shared housework, female companionship, and division among them of the man's sexual demands. Women often feel that it is bad for a woman to sit alone in the household, and "first wives" may go so far as to play a role in selecting subsequent co-wives for their husbands. Men may marry sisters, termed **sororal polygyny**, which promises (but does not guarantee) to provide more domestic tranquility. Finally, in many polygynous societies, one or a few dominant males may monopolize the women,

THE WARLPIRI SUBSECTION SYSTEM

leaving other men with one wife or none. The Tiwi of Melville and Bathurst Islands north of Australia, a foraging society in which a few old men monopolized the young women, found an ingenious solution: a man was not allowed to marry at all until he reached the age of thirty or more, and his first wife would usually be an older woman, widowed from her own previous marriage to a much older man. Thus, every man and every woman married several times at various stages of life to spouses at various stages of their own lives (Hart and Pilling 1960).

3. **Polyandry** (*andro* for man) – a woman may or should marry two or more men. This marriage form is particularly rare, practiced in less than 1 percent of known societies. Among the few cases are the Toda of southern India, the Pacific island Marquesans, and the Tibetans. Often, a woman will marry a set of brothers, bearing children for all of them. The children may be assigned "social fatherhood" to the senior brother, since physical fatherhood cannot be known and is culturally irrelevant, or social fatherhood may be assigned to various husbands for various children. The "problem" of paternity might be one reason why polyandry is so rare.

A third question in marriage is how precisely individuals enter into the relationship. In some societies, the procedure was as informal as a man leaving gifts of food or other goods at the household of a woman; if she accepted the gifts and welcomed him in, they took up residence and were regarded as married. Among the Cheyenne, a man announced to his kin his desire to marry. If they approved, they would gather wealth and deliver it to the woman's parents. If her kin accepted the pairing, the wealth was distributed among her family, and the following day her kin would return gifts of equal value (Hoebel 1960).

However, in many societies marriage is a much more elaborate business that occupies the interest of entire families if not entire communities. Many societies traditionally practiced – and many still practice today – **arranged marriage**, in which the families of prospective marriage partners make the selection and plan the event. The partners may not know each other at all, may never have even seen

each other, and typically do not "date" before the marriage; unchaperoned dating is a unique characteristic of Western courtship and a relatively modern one at that. Arranged marriages are often handled by the men of the respective families, who make strategic alliances between themselves by exchanging sons and daughters for marriage. This practice illustrates quite clearly not only that marriage is an alliance-building institution in many cases but also that it is a device and field for male social dominance. Especially in situations of **hypergamy** (*hyper* for up or high), families may be seeking to raise their overall social status by marrying their daughter to a richer or more prestigious family, which may expose their women to potential abuse and even death.

Marriages, whether arranged or not, often are accompanied or even accomplished by property exchanges. This signals both the economic/contractual and the alliance aspects of marriage. Of course, while in American society there are minor wealth exchanges at weddings (e.g. guests bring gifts), some societies hand over substantial amounts of wealth in planning or consummating a marriage. The main forms this can take are:

1. **Bridewealth** or **brideprice** – In this practice, a man gives wealth to the bride's family, usually her male kin, in order to make the marriage. Nearly half of all recorded societies have done this, and it correlates to male social power and prestige, since men are not only giving and receiving wealth, but women are often not included in the negotiations nor are they recipients of the wealth themselves. This can sometimes be construed as "buying a wife," virtually treating women like property. However, more often it is viewed as compensation to the woman's family for the loss that her departure will mean – particularly, loss of her production (household work) and of her reproduction (the children she will bear). The woman's status in her marital family is often quite low, at least until she bears a child, preferably a son. However, in some cases today even a child does not enhance her status much. Bridewealth is especially closely associated with pastoral societies, where men dominate and have transferable wealth to offer, namely their herds. Thus, a man will typically offer a woman's male

Hypergamy
the marriage practice of marrying "up" with a spouse in a higher status, class, or caste than oneself

Polyandry
the marriage rule in which a woman can or should marry two or more men

Bridewealth
the marriage wealth-exchange practice in which a man or his family must pay an amount of property to his wife's kin before he may assume rights over his wife

Brideprice
see bridewealth

Hoebel, E. Adamson. 1960. *The Cheyennes Indians of the Great Plains.* New York: Holt, Rinehart, and Winston, Inc.

Arranged marriage
a practice in which family members (often parents) choose the partner for marriageable youths, sometimes with little or no input from or option for the partners themselves

PLATE 8.3 Great
amounts of wealth may
be displayed and
transferred in dowry or
bridewealth.

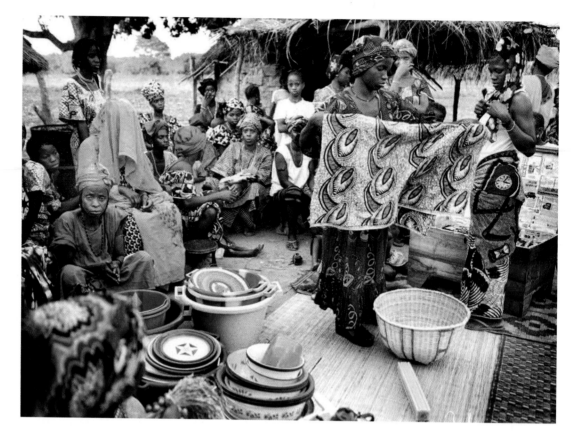

Bride service

the marriage wealth-
exchange practice in which
a man must labor for his
wife's kin for some period
of time before he may
assume rights over his wife

Dowry

the marriage wealth-
exchange practice in which
the woman's family is
required to provide the
husband with property
(money, land, household
goods, etc.) in order to
make the marriage

Sen, Mala. 2001. *Death by
Fire: Sati, Dowry Death,
and Female Infanticide in
Modern India*. New
Brunswick, NJ: Rutgers
University Press.

relatives a certain number of animals in exchange for her hand in marriage, and a father may search for the best bridewealth offer for his daughter, meaning that men with much wealth will be able to arrange more and "better" marriages for themselves and their sons than less wealthy men can.

2. **Bride service** – In societies where men are expected to give something in exchange but real "wealth" does not exist, they may be required to provide service instead. For example, in foraging societies a man may be obligated to bring meat from his hunts to the woman's family for a period of years before the marriage is considered fully made or before he can remove her to his family. The Torah/Old Testament story of Jacob and his efforts to marry Rachel is an example of the institution of bride service, wherein he was asked to labor for her father (Laban, his own mother's brother, making Rachel his first cousin; see Genesis 29) before he could marry her.

3. **Dowry** – In a minority of societies that practice substantial property exchange, the woman or her family give wealth to the man (occasionally

to the married couple) in order to make the marriage. In some societies this is interpreted as an "early inheritance" of her parents' property; however, when the wealth is transferred to her husband or his parents, it is hard to see how this constitutes an inheritance to her. In fact, the system of dowry can be a real disadvantage to the woman or her family and can be yet another path of male domination; not surprisingly, it is found in societies, like pre-revolutionary China, parts of India, and even the traditional United States, where men were or are dominant. The heavy burden of providing a dowry can lead parents to disdain having female children; as one advertisement for an Indian abortion clinic starkly framed it, "Pay 500 rupees now [for an abortion] or 50,000 in 18 years [for a dowry]" (Sen 2001). China's government recently outlawed extravagant dowries (although they still occur), and not long ago an American girl might be expected to bring a trousseau or "hope chest" of goods, money, and even land to her marriage; the last vestige of this practice is the "tradition" that the bride's family pays for the wedding.

These basic forms of exchange are not entirely mutually exclusive. The Barabaig pastoralists practiced a sort of combination of bridewealth and dowry, each with exceptional qualities. Bridewealth was important but more symbolic than economic: in fact, only one cow was paid to the woman's family, but it had to be a heifer (young female) and all one color. In addition, the married couple received "marriage cattle" to start their own herd. The woman would bring a dowry of two to forty cattle which remained hers until she had a son (when they were transferred to him), and the man received donations of animals from his kinsmen as well (Klima 1970).

It is worth mentioning a few other notable marriage practices that put the institution in perspective. For example, one practice – or pair of practices – found across cultures is the levirate/sororate. The **levirate** specifically entails that another man from the groom's family, ideally a brother, should marry the widow if her husband dies. From the woman's point of view, she is expected to marry her dead husband's brother or other kinsmen after she is widowed. This practice tends to be associated with male-dominated societies and families and with the high value of male children; in fact, in many cases any children issuing from the "second marriage" may still be attributed to the first (dead) husband. The practice also says something about the contractual and alliance nature of marriage, where the alliance outlives its human members. The **sororate** is the mirror-image, in which a widower is provided with a sister or other female relative of his dead wife. In another form of marriage known among the Nuer of East Africa and sometimes called "ghost marriage," a woman could be married to a man who had already died, particularly if he died young without children. As her ghost-husband, any children she later had (not by him, obviously) were looked upon as his children, who would continue his male line and perform rituals and ceremonies for him (Evans-Pritchard 1951). Perhaps most anomalously of all, the Na or Moso people of western China did not traditionally practice marriage at all: males and females engaged in a series of "furtive visits" or "secret romantic encounter[s]. . .without any consanguineal relatives knowing about it" (Hua 2001: 185), and the roles of "husband" and "father" were conspicuously absent.

English speakers tend to think of the "first cousin" relationship as "too close" for marriage. However, not all societies share this sentiment, since not all societies define "kin" and "cousin" in the customary English way (see the discussions of lineage and kinship terminology below). In fact, in many societies, cousins are the preferred marriage partners, resulting in **preferential cousin marriage**. Some cousins are more preferred than others, and it is important to make a distinction between "cross cousins" and "parallel cousins." Cross cousins are children of one's own parents' opposite-sex siblings – that is, father's sister's children or mother's brother's children. Parallel cousins are children of a parent's same-sex sibling – that is, father's brother's children or mother's sister's children. To English speakers, there is no significant social difference between these various cousins, but to other societies there may be a crucial difference. It is relatively common for societies to designate cross cousins as good marriage selections, since, in certain descent systems, cross cousins are not in the same kin group at all. Much less often, parallel cousins – who *are* regarded as kin – will be the preferred marriage partners, with the overt intention of keeping property, name, and honor in the family.

Residence

The second principle of kinship systems involves who actually lives together in local domestic groups. Residence is not essential for corporate behavior, but it definitely is a convenience; furthermore, people who form a residential unit will almost necessarily act corporately. We can thus think of residence as the spatial or geographic element of kinship.

Anthropologists make a distinction between a family or kindred and a household. A family or **kindred** is roughly all the people to whom a person considers him/herself "related" by blood or marriage. It is not probably or even possibly a residential group, since it is too large and dispersed to live in one house, or even one compound or neighborhood. A **household** is all the people who live together "under one roof" and act corporately within that residence. Obviously just as not all of a family or kindred shares one household, not all of the people who share a household need be family or

Preferential cousin marriage
the marriage principle that a person ought to marry a "cousin," that is, a child of mother's sibling or father's sibling

Levirate
a marriage practice in which the brother of a deceased man is expected to marry his brother's widow

Sororate
a marriage practice in which a woman is expected to marry the husband of her sister in the event of the married sister's death

Kindred
an ego-centered (that is, reckoned from the perspective of some particular individual) category of persons related by kinship, especially in bilateral societies, including members from "both sides" of the family in older and younger generations

Household
all of the people who live in the same house or compound of houses and act for some or all purposes as a corporate group

Evans-Pritchard, E. E. 1951. *Kinship and Marriage among the Nuer*. New York: Oxford University Press.

A SOCIETY WITHOUT MARRIAGE

Patrilocal

the residence practice of living with or near the husband's family after marriage

kindred; people can and do live in non-kin residential groups, as when a set of roommates shares a house or apartment. They may still be corporate in the sense of preparing and consuming food, owning property, and sharing responsibility for expenses, though they are not related by kinship.

Nevertheless, kinship and residence tend to overlap, and most residential groups or households are also kin groups. Anthropologists, therefore, regard residence as one of the building blocks not only of kinship but of corporateness in general. The kinds of corporate residential groups formed by residence practices will significantly shape society. There is a finite set of possibilities, although they can be mixed and modified in various ways.

Patrilocality or virilocality (patri- *for father* or viri- *for man*)

The vast majority of societies (approaching 70 percent) normally settled married couples in or near the residence of the husband and his family. Men brought their wives into the household, and women left their childhood homes to reside in their husband's household. The resulting household under such a system consisted of related men (fathers and sons, brothers, uncles and nephews, and so on) and their in-married wives as well as the children they produced together. They might literally all live in one big house, perhaps with separate corners or cooking areas for marital groups, or more often in separate houses in a family "compound." Either way, though, it should be no surprise that patrilocality tended to enhance male status and power, since daughters left their own household to move

BOX 8.2   MIGRATING BRIDES IN NORTHERN INDIA

The villagers of the central Himalayas practice a variety of kinds of marriage, including both dowry (*dan ka* or "gift") and brideprice (*dam ka* or "price") weddings – although according to William Sax brideprice arrangements are increasingly perceived as backward and uncivilized. The ideal of a civilized form of marriage is *kanyadana* or "gift of a virgin." After a *kanyadana* wedding, the woman is expected to leave her *mait* or place/village of birth and move to her *saurya* or place/village of marriage, that is, her husband's village. Henceforth, "she must bear children for, worship the lineage gods of, and observe birth and death pollution restrictions for her new family. . . . And her death or childbirth will result in impurity for her husband's family, not her father's" (Sax 1991: 78). Indeed, locals believe that the bride is completely and irreversibly transformed by her relocation from *mait* to *saurya*s, her very substance altered "as part of the process of uniting her with her husband and his lineage" (109). This transformation is naturally fairly traumatic for women. "No one who has lived in rural India can forget those pathetic scenes when the bride is dragged, sobbing and wailing, into the groom's bus or car, to be whisked away to the husband's place"; thus, marriage and relocation is "a situation that many young women dread" (117). And at worst, an unhappy marriage "can lead to divorce and even suicide. The latter solution is usually associated with a situation in which a woman is imperfectly incorporated into her *saurya*s and denied refuge in her *mait*" (113). Most women, of course, make the gradual transition into the home and life of the husband's family, although they may slowly or never entirely break their ties to their birthplace. "Even happily married women anxiously await their periodic visits to their *mait*s. Afterward, when they leave to return to their *saurya*s women wail loudly in a ritual display of sorrow" (118). Speaking of ritual, Sax also describes a major religious pilgrimage in which the goddess Nandadevi is carried through the countryside, ultimately to be delivered to the icy mountain abode of her husband Shiva. The regular pilgrimage rituals can therefore be understood as "the stylized journeys of a married female to the home of her husband, and as public, reflexive events that define the accepted mode of residence and exemplify proper marital relations. . . .[M]en are even prepared to force a recalcitrant goddess to return to her 'proper place' should she resist going" (206).

into their husband's. Thus, men remained to own and control the property, and women lived in places where they did not own and control much of anything. Worse yet, women were sometimes distantly separated from their male kinsmen who could protect and defend them; alone in their husband's household, surrounded by his male kin, women were at a distinct disadvantage.

Matrilocality or uxorilocality (matri- *for mother or* uxori- *for wife*)

A much smaller percentage (less than 50 percent) of societies advocated that people live in or near the residence of the woman and her family. Women brought their husbands into the home, and men left for their wives' homes. Here, the resulting household contained related women (mothers and daughters, sisters, etc.) and their "in-married" husbands and their joint children. This practice tended to enhance female status, since, being the consistent factor in the household, women tended to own and control the property, land, and wealth. Men were separated from their own families and allies and cast among related females, and their access to wealth and property might depend on their wife's family. Such an arrangement would be conducive to horticultural economies, where women often formed important land-holding and farm-laboring corporate groups.

Avunculocality (avuncu- *for uncle*)

In a distinctly small number of societies (perhaps 4 percent), married people preferentially lived with or near the man's mother's brother. This was essentially an adaptation to male property rights in a society that traced group membership through women (see below). In such a system, a man's maternal uncle was a kinsman in a way that his paternal uncle was not; the effect was to live with the most important male relative in the kinship universe.

Ambilocality (ambi- *for both or either*)

Somewhat more often (9 percent), married people were either free to choose which household to live with or elected to divide their time between the two households. This was a useful adaptation for societies that lived in difficult environments or

low-yield economies, which gave them maximal flexibility in their living arrangements. One place we might expect to find it, then, was in foraging societies, where nuclear families may need to travel and camp with the man's family at certain times and the woman's family at others.

Neolocality (neo- *for new*)

In a surprisingly small minority of societies (5 percent), married people preferred or were expected to start a new household on their own, apart from either family. While this is the norm in most Western societies, that fact simply reinforces the fact that those ways, although they are familiar and comfortable to Westerners, are often quite exceptional among the cultures of the world. **Neolocal** residence tends to produce small households, since families "fission" into nuclear units, and it also requires or breeds a unique mentality that values privacy, individuality, and mobility. It further requires a fair amount of wealth, since it is not cheap to own and furnish a home for each marital couple. Accordingly, neolocal residence is suited to intensive agriculture and perhaps even more to industrial and post-industrial societies. Not only are individuals and nuclear families fairly rich and independent, but labor needs to be mobile, since the family may be called upon to relocate in search of work. Neolocal households also maximize consumption, since each household requires a complete set of furnishings.

Within these ideal types, considerable variation and complication exist. According to their ethnographers, neither the Ulithi (Pacific Islands) nor the Dani (New Guinea) had residential nuclear families. The Ulithi nuclear family was not a "commensal" group, that is, they did not eat together; eating arrangements and living arrangements did not overlap in any serious way (Lessa 1966). Heider asserts that the Dani lived in multi-family compounds and that it was

> hopeless even to try to generalize about the composition's population. One can find unrelated nuclear families, polygynous families, families extended vertically into three or even four generations or laterally with siblings and cousins, as well as the odd singleton unrelated to anyone.
>
> (1979: 76)

Neolocal
the residence practice in which married people start their own household apart from their parents' or families' households

Avunculocal
a residence practice in which a married couple lives with or near an uncle, often a mother's brother

Matrilocal

the residence practice of living with or near the wife's family after marriage

Cheyenne nuclear or conjugal families were organized into what Hoebel called kindreds, which were **matrilocal** groups that camped together; these kindreds were further aggregated into "bands," of which there were ten, each of which would set up camp in its own area when the whole society gathered.

Descent

Descent

the kinship principle of tracing membership in a kin-based corporate group through a sequence of ancestors

Descent is the third principle in the system of kinship, the vertical or chronological relationship between the generations, "coming down" from parents to children and beyond. In this sense, descent is an absolutely physical thing; children really are related to their parents and their ancestors. However, what societies choose to do with it – how they employ it to create corporate groups – is cultural and therefore culturally relative.

Societies can create all kinds of different kinship arrangements, but anthropologists have found that they can represent the entire spectrum of such relationships with a kit of only a few symbols and abbreviations. In fact, only six are required to represent most kinship relationships (see Figure 8.1).

So, in order to diagram a simple nuclear family, we can draw a triangle linked to a circle by two parallel lines, with a descent line down to one or more children, which can "branch" as often as

necessary. In order to show siblings for the parents, we can draw branches above them; and in order to show multiple generations (say, the grandparents or grandchildren) we can add descent lines above or below the nuclear generations depicted. To represent a deceased kinsperson, anthropologists place a slash mark through that person's symbol.

It is also useful to have short-hand abbreviations for the "absolute" relationships between people, rather than invoking ethnocentric and loaded kinship terms like "uncle" or "cousin." For more complex and inclusive kinship diagrams, we can describe literal relationships with a limited set of letters (see Figure 8.2).

With this vocabulary, it is possible to specify relationships like "father's brother" (FB) or "mother's brother" (MB) instead of "uncle" – which might be an important difference in a society. Likewise, it is possible to distinguish precisely between "cousins" – "father's brother's son" (FBS) versus "mother's sister's daughter" (MZD) – or any other combination of relationships.

All societies use descent in at least some way to assign children to parents and to assign children and their parents to corporate groups. However, not all societies formalize descent into exclusive groups such that an individual belongs to one such group and not another. When such exclusive groups are created and used, anthropologists call them descent groups. The easiest and most common way for a

Δ	a male
○	a female
□	a person of nonspecific gender
=	a marriage
≠	a divorce
|	descent or connection between parents and children (can be "branched" to additional children)

FIGURE 8.1 Kinship notation.

M	for mother	Z	for sister	FZS	for father's sister's son
F	for father	H	for husband	MBW	for mother's brother's wife
S	for son	W	for wife	FF	for father's father
D	for daughter	MBD	for mother's brother's daughter	and so on	
B	for brother				

FIGURE 8.2 Kinship abbreviations.

society to do this is through **unilineal descent**, that is, tracing a single "line" of related ancestors based on a shared characteristic, particularly sex. Not all, but a majority (around 60 percent), of societies utilize the concept of unilineal descent to create corporate groups that include some people and exclude others. The disadvantage of such systems is that they do exclude some kin; the advantage is that they draw incredibly sharp lines of distinction between who is and who is not a "member" of the group. The two obvious alternatives in unilineal descent are patrilineal and matrilineal:

1. **Patrilineal** descent – Membership in the kin corporate group is reckoned through a line of male ancestors. That is to say, children belong to their father's corporate group, not their mother's. They of course know who their mother is, and they recognize her as a close relative, but she is not a member of "their group" in the same sense as their father. All siblings will belong to the same group – called a **lineage** – since they all have the same father. All other relatives who can trace their relationships through the same line of related men are also members of the lineage, in this case the patrilineage. So, all of the father's brothers (FB) are lineage members, as are all of their children (FBS and FBD alike). Females belong to the lineage too, but they do not perpetuate it: a woman's children belong to *their* father's

(her husband's) lineage, not her own. Anglo-Americans do not have a formal lineage system, but they do inherit their surname "patrilineally," at least traditionally. Thus, males continue the "family name" but females do not. Of unilineal descent systems, this is by far the most common (85 percent).

2. **Matrilineal** descent – Membership in the kin corporate group is traced through a line of female ancestors. In a reverse image of the patrilineal system, children belong to their mother's group or matrilineage but not their father's. Siblings belong to the same lineage, but only females will continue it; a man's children belong to *their* mother's lineage. Since the father is not part of his children's lineage, the most important male relative may be their mother's brother (MB), their maternal uncle, who is a member of their matrilineage. However, MB's own children will not be part of the lineage, since they will belong to his wife's lineage. This is a much less common way of reckoning descent (15 percent) but makes sense in societies where female-centered families make sense. Ulithi practiced a matrilineal descent system, in which lineages owned land and houses, maintained cooking hearths, and attended to their own ghosts at their own shrines; however, they also practiced patrilocal residence.

Unilineal descent
a principle in which individuals trace their ancestry through a "line" of related kin (typically a male or a female line) such that some "blood" relatives are included in the descent group or lineage and other relatives are excluded from it

Matrilineal
a descent system in which lineage relations are traced through a line of related females. Children belong to their mother's corporate group

Patrilineal
a descent system in which lineage relations are traced through a line of related males. Children belong to their father's corporate group

Lineage
a kinship-based corporate group composed of members related by descent from a known ancestor

PLATE 8.4 Individuals belong to their mother's kinship group in matrilineal societies.

Double descent

the kinship practice of reckoning one's membership in kinship-based corporate groups through two lines of descent, ordinarily the mother's and the father's

Moiety

one of the "halves" of a society, when kin groups are combined in such a way as to create a binary division within society

Ambilineal

a descent system in which individuals trace their membership through both "sides" or "lines" of the family, or optionally through one or the other

Ambilocal

a residence practice in which individuals may live after marriage with both "sides" of the family (perhaps alternating between them), or optionally with one or the other

Bilateral

relating to both "sides," as in a kinship system, in which individuals regard kin related to the mother and to the father as socially equivalent

Clan

a kinship group, sometimes an assortment of lineages, that can trace its descent back to a common ancestor

Phratry

a kinship-based corporate group composed of two or more clans that recognize common ancestry

In a few rare instances, societies may use the descent relationship to create corporate groups but not in a unilineal manner. We refer to such systems as **double descent**, where an individual belongs to both mother's and father's group, sometimes for different purposes. For example, among the Yako of Nigeria, people obtained access to land and forest goods through their father's group but access to other kinds of resources (such as animals and money) through their mother's. About 5 percent of societies did this.

Two other possibilities include **ambilineal** descent, in which, like **ambilocal** residence, children may be assigned to either group by their parents or may move freely between groups during their lifetimes, and **bilateral** descent, in which children are considered to belong to both "sides" of their family equally. Ambilineal descent, also like ambilocal residence, provides the most flexibility for individuals and families, while bilateral descent is not "descent" at all in an important sense. That is, this kinship system – which most resembles the American form – does not create "lines" of kin at all but rather "sides" of families and makes the least distinction between them. Some individuals might like their mother's or father's people more than the other, but there is no institutionalized preference. So, no "lineage" results at all, but rather the outcome is a kindred – a group of relatives reckoned from the individual's point of view. Like neolocal residence, this form of kinship provides the most independence and mobility.

It is possible for societies to extend the descent principle for creating even larger and more inclusive kinship groupings. The term **clan** is sometimes used to name a corporate group of related lineages, often one which cannot actually specify all of the lineal links between the members; the "founding" member may also not be remembered or may be "mythical" (a spirit or animal, for instance). When two or more clans are conjoined, we have a **phratry**.

And in a few cases, the various kin groups of a society may be agglomerated into two halves such that the entire society is bifurcated for at least some (perhaps ritual) purposes. We refer to such a "half of a society," the highest possible level of corporateness short of an entire society, as a **moiety**, which is often exogamous.

These institutions can also be surprisingly diverse. Dani society contained fifty clan-like entities, which were not territorial but did share corporate interests in marriage and ritual. These clans were combined into two named patrimoieties, called *Wida* and *Waija*. The moieties were exogamous, but strangely all children were born into the *Wida* side; around puberty, children of the other moiety were transferred to it (Heider 1979: 64). Barabaig patrilineages were organized into clans called *dosht* that Klima describes as territorial "mutual aid societies" that looked after their members (39). The sixty or so named clans were mostly autonomous, sharing few interests or institutions, and were divided into two types (not moieties), the five priestly *Daremgadyeg* clans and the fifty-five secular or "commoner" *Homat'k* clans.

Kinship terminologies

Since societies vary so widely in how they understand and use kinship relations, it figures that they would vary in how they talk about kin. Every society has a set of kinship terms or names, like the English "father," "mother," "uncle," "cousin," etc. Of course, what one society calls a "cousin" might not be called, or treated like, a cousin in another. The physical relationships that underlie any set of terms are the same; however, how those "blood" or physical relationship are valued and used diverges greatly by culture.

There is an almost infinite variety of permutations on kinship terminology, but there is a basic

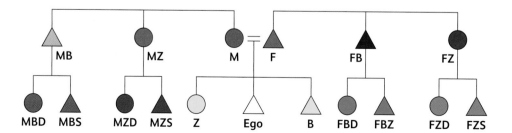

FIGURE 8.3 A generic kinship chart.

set of six systems that societies then modify or customize according to their local needs and interests. Use the kinship chart (Figure 8.3) to make sense of these systems described below.

1. **Hawaiian**. This common (about one-third of societies) terminology is nearly the simplest possible one, in which a very limited set of terms is used to make a very limited set of distinctions. There are only four main terms – two for the parent's generation (one male, one female, approximately equivalent to "father" and "mother") and two for one's own generation (again, one male, one female, roughly "brother" and "sister"). So, what English speakers would call "uncle" (both MB and FB) would be called by the same term as father, "aunt" (MZ and FZ) would be called by the same term as mother, and all "cousins" would be called by the terms for brother and sister.

2. **Omaha**. This system represents a patrilineal naming convention. Parallel-cousins are called by the same term as brothers and sisters, but cross-cousins are called by different terms. Even more, cross-cousins on the mother's side (MBS and MBD) are called by different terms – the same as for M and MB, respectively – than ones on the father's side (FBS and FBD). Finally, FB is called the same term as F, and MZ is called by the same term as M, but FZ and MB are called by different terms, roughly equivalent to "aunt" and "uncle."

3. **Crow**. The Crow system is the prototype of a matrilineal naming convention. The same basic logic applies as in the Omaha, but in mirror reversal. Mother and MZ are termed the same, father and FB are termed the same, and FZ and MB each get a unique term. Parallel cousins are all called "brother" or "sister," and FZ's children are referred to by the same term as FB and FZ.

4. **Iroquois**. This system is similar to the two unilineal systems above, with one major exception. Cross-cousins on both sides (MB's children and FZ's children) are called by the same two terms – essentially, what we might translate as "male cousin" and "female cousin." Parallel cousins are still designated as "brother" and "sister."

5. **Sudanese**. This "descriptive" system is the hardest to commit to memory but the easiest

to understand. It makes the most possible distinctions, using a different term for each relationship and collapsing no relationships into others; MB is not the same as FB, etc., and every possible variation of "cousin" is given a different name (that is, FBS and FZS are termed differently, ad infinitum).

6. **Eskimo**. Fairly uncommon, at about 10 percent of societies, is the system that most resembles the Anglo-American one. Here, no distinctions are made between cross- and parallel-cousins (that is, between "sides" of the family) nor between their parents. FB and MB are called by the same term (like "uncle"), as are FZ and MZ (like "aunt"). All cousins are distinguished by only one feature, sex (and in English, not even by that – there are no English words that distinguish "male cousin" from "female cousin," like the French *cousin* and *cousine* or the Spanish *primo* and *prima*). The key kinship unit based on the terminology is the nuclear family.

These diverse systems may seem odd and impenetrable, yet each is a "language" for talking about the society's kinship reality. The key is to appreciate that different societies have reasons to make the terminological distinctions that they do. That is, the kinship terminology of a society is a way of expressing things that are important (or not expressing things that are unimportant or not even "there") for them.

We can think, therefore, of a kinship terminology as a kind of language or code for important cultural aspects of family and kinship. Rather than naming people, they are naming relationships: the "cousin" relationship or the "uncle" relationship indicates a certain kind of role, feeling, and even social duty. A person would expect to feel generally the same and behave generally the same toward two different "cousins." However, s/he might feel and behave differently toward an "uncle" than a cousin, and definitely toward a "father" or "mother" than a cousin. So, ultimately we can think of a kinship terminology system as naming the different socially recognized and socially important kinship roles in society. If an individual calls two different people by the same term, then that individual's role towards them should be the same and their role towards him/her should be the same. On the other hand, if an individual calls two different people by two different terms, then his/her and their roles should be different. This is what we meant by "collapsing" different kin into the same term: if I call MB and FB by the same term, then they are culturally equivalent for me. I know that they are not the same person, but what is important is how I am supposed to act towards them and they towards me. And if I call MB and FB by different terms, that indicates a culturally relevant distinction between those two kinsmen.

Some of the things that are "coded" into a system of terms – or more significantly, the statuses they name – are:

- Generation – are they in my own, my parents', my children's generation, etc.?
- Sex or gender – are they male or female? Or, in some cases, are they the same sex as me or the opposite sex than me (relative gender)? For instance, Ulithi did not have terms that mean "brother" or "sister" but rather "sibling of my sex" or "sibling not of my sex."
- Blood vs. marriage – are they kin by descent or by marriage? In the American system, members do not even distinguish between, say, MB and MZH.
- "Side of the family" – are they on the mother's side or the father's side? That is not a terribly important distinction in American society. However, when laterality becomes lineality, it is important in a society to know which side the kinsman falls on. This is seen in the Omaha and Crow systems, where who is "in my lineage" and who is not is a serious concern.
- Age or relative age – are they older or younger? Or are they older or younger than me? Warlpiri, for example, has distinct terms for older brother (*papardi*) and younger brother (*kukurnu*).
- Marital status – are they married, single, widowed, etc.?

In other words, the "logic" of a kinship system can be decoded – the kinship terminology can be "read" – if we realize what social and kinship distinctions are made and are central in a society. Or, by reading the system, we can decipher what distinctions are made and central. In the United States, for instance, the same terms are applied identically to both

"sides." Americans do not care about age in particular, so they do not encode that distinction. In this, the American kinship system reflects the same social order that American language and honorifics do: social distinctions are not very extensive and not very important. If a society does make big distinctions (like lineage-mates and nonlineage-mates), it must and will have a way to talk about them.

NON-KINSHIP-BASED CORPORATE GROUPS

The "facts" and principles of marriage, residence, and descent exist in (nearly) all societies, and those societies use them – in unique and creative ways – to assign people to groups and to give those groups common tasks, common interests, and common identity. An observer might think that this would be enough structure for a society, but even in the smallest societies, other groupings are used too. Why would a society go on to elaborate non-kinship kinds of corporate groups too? There are probably at least three reasons:

1. Kinship-based corporate groups might not be large enough or dispersed enough to handle all the tasks and "corporate duties" desired in a society.
2. Kinship-based corporate groups alone might tend to fragment society into identity and interest groups with little common identity or interest, turning them into competitive or even conflictual groups. Of course, this can happen anyhow, but a society may benefit from "cross-cutting" groups that bring together members of divergent kinship groups in various kinds of non-kinship collectivities. Such cross-cutting or "vertical" groups provide more social "glue" or integration.
3. Other non-kinship kinds of traits and identities exist, so individuals tend to gravitate toward them and societies tend to exploit them. In other words, all humans have characteristics besides kinship that they share with other humans and by which they can be classified and organized.

There are many such traits or categories available in any society and many ways to exploit them where they are found. The following are some of these traits and some of the kinds of corporate groups that are constructed around them. In addition to those groups and traits discussed below, race and ethnicity are also vital organizing factors.

Sex or gender

The most universal and fundamental social distinction across cultures is sex or gender: the "gender division of labor" for example creates productive groups out of the sexes. Men or women widely comprise sex-specific work details, as when foraging men ventured together to hunt or foraging women formed parties to gather. Among the Abkhasians of Georgia, a territory in the Caucasus and formerly part of the Soviet Union, local men assembled into voluntary work cooperatives or *kiaraz* (literally "self-help") to tend each other's fields in order of need (ripeness of crop, weediness of land, etc.). According to Benet (1974), each task that the *kiaraz* performed had a name and a song, and the group would divide into teams to compete in races and contests during work breaks; also, if it passed a widow's land, it would tend her fields for her. Finally, the group also functioned as a militia and as a law court, with powers to confiscate property or even assign the death penalty.

In other societies, men and women would each have their particular spaces and prerogatives. We saw how the Sambia kept a men's house in the village. The Konyak Nagas in India, like many others around the world, also had a men's house institution, or *ban*, which functioned as a dormitory for older boys and unmarried men. Actually, each village might have several of these, associated with a neighborhood or ward of the village; some were large and ornate, with fancy carvings and a large drum or gong. Women were not totally forbidden from entering and in fact did enter on ceremonial occasions. Otherwise, the *ban* was corporate in many ways, including social, economic, legal, and ritual. It held joint ownership of land as well as of "symbolic property" like songs, dances, and decorations; it cultivated land together, defended and avenged its interests, and collected wealth for tribute. It also made up the core of the political system, sending officials (*niengba*) from each *ban* to sit with the chief as a village council, while other officers (*benba*) conducted rituals and sacrifices. Women also had a site, the *yo*, that served as a dormitory for young unmarried girls (Von Fuerer-Haimendorf 1969).

The Cheyenne offered an assortment of military associations for men. In the early nineteenth century there were five named associations (Fox, Elk, Shield, Dog, and Bow-String or "Contrary"), with two more added later (Wolf and Crazy Dogs). Young males were free to join any of the groups, which were not formally stratified (although they might rise and fall in prestige based on their

See Chapter 5

See Chapter 6

PLATE 8.5 At age fifteen, a Mexican girl would traditionally celebrate her *quinceanera*, at which she was introduced to adult society.

achievements). Each group was essentially a private army, with its own symbols, dances, songs, history, and internal organization; they could in fact conduct private raids and wars or act together as a tribal police force and army (Hoebel 1960).

Not all societies have demonstrated the same degree of segregation and stratification between the sexes, but some degree of "camaraderie" between sex-mates is common if not universal. From the National Organization of Women or the League of Women Voters to sex-specific sports teams to the modern "women's spirituality" movement, women in modern societies often meet and act corporately, as do men, who have done so for a very long time in their "old boy's networks" and "smoke-filled rooms."

Age

The second natural characteristic on which to build groups or to develop affiliation is age, and all societies employ it to some extent: every society has "adult" roles and rights and "child" ones. Americans consider child labor, child alcohol consumption, child sexuality, and child driving inappropriate or even illegal. There is a virtual "youth subculture" in the West (and increasingly around the world) that is very influential in cultural trends and tastes. And of course young people are assembled into age-based groups or "grades" or "classes" in school, which may affect their entire lives. Many graduates of educational institutions feel an attachment to their classmates long after school is over. And many societies mark the transition from one stage of life to another with ceremonies and rituals, or "rites of passage". From the Jewish tradition of *bar mitzvah* for boys to the Australian Aboriginal (and other) ceremony of circumcision, rituals especially relate to the attainment of adulthood; recall that some societies, like the Sambia, believed that a boy could not become a man "naturally" but only through cultural and ritual intervention.

Other societies have elaborated and formalized the idea of age-based corporateness, as in the so-called **age grade system**. Particularly common in pastoral societies, boys might be assigned in their early childhood to an **age set** along with their peers. At a certain age, depending on the society, they moved together as a group into the next stage or grade of life, sometimes given new labors to perform, new tools to use, and even new names. The transition between grades might be ritualized, especially the transition to the grade of adult, which was often the grade of warriors. The Maasai (east Africa) possessed a basic system with three grades, roughly equivalent to "youth," "warrior" (*moran*), and "elder." Males in the *moran* grade lived apart in a *manyatta* where they acted as the standing army of the society (Leakey 1930).

See Chapter 10

Age grade system
a non-kinship-based corporate system in which members, usually of one sex, are organized into groups or "grades" according to age and assigned roles and values as a group

Age set
a division or subset of a society based on shared age characteristics, as determined by the age grade system of that society

PLATE 8.6 Members of the *moran* or warrior age-set among the Samburu of Kenya.

BOX 8.3   FEMALE AGE GRADES IN HIDATSA CULTURE

The Hidatsa, a people of the Northern Plains of North America, had formal age grades for both men and women in which the latter were at least as important as the former. As a horticultural, matrilocal, and matrilineal society, they put more emphasis on women than many other societies. Accordingly, there were four named grades for women (each with a male counterpart), starting with the "Skunk Society" at age twelve and extending to about twenty, whose main role was to dance after successful wars. Young married women (age twenty to thirty) moved into the "Enemy Society," which also had responsibilities following wars. From age thirty to forty women joined the "Goose Society," a prestigious level concerned with fertility, farming success, and the annual return of migratory birds. Women who attained seniority were eligible for the "White Buffalo Society," charged with caring for certain sacred objects (medicine bundles) and with bringing the buffalo to the people. Altogether, this system not only conferred status on women but served as a social network through which they enjoyed guidance while youths and comradeship and support while adults.

The Dinka (east Africa) held an initiation ceremony for males around age sixteen, at which time they were assigned to an age set with a designated "father" for the group who named it, thus bringing it into existence. During the initiation, boys received deep cuts across their foreheads and moved into a separate village for several months. They received new rights, including the right to dance and flirt with girls, as well as new responsibilities, including adult expectations of courage and aggressiveness tempered with dignity and self-control. Most importantly, they became warriors. As they matured they remained forever connected to their age set, although its corporateness faded over time; marriage weakened it, as corporateness was transferred to the kin unit, and by old age it had almost disappeared. Women also had age sets, but they ceased to act corporately at marriage (Deng 1972).

Common interest

Any number of other shared traits or interests might form the basis for grouping of a more or less corporate nature. In modern societies these are frequently fairly trivial and short term; a person might belong to a service organization, fraternity/sorority, professional association, labor union, activist group, political party, church congregation, and so on. Some of these might have deep and abiding meaning for members, some might not. They are for the most part voluntary groupings, which one is not compelled to join (although there may be real social pressure to join a particular group or at least some group). And of course individuals can belong to more than one common interest group simultaneously – this church, that club, the other professional association. This situates each individual at a unique intersection of group identities and interests.

In a certain sense, all human groups are interest groups, since, among other things, they all have shared interests too. Although it is controversial among scholars and activists, it is at least partly appropriate to regard ethnic and racial and nationalist groups as interest groups, since they may definitely feel and/or be treated like "one people" and act accordingly to advance the corporate interests. Often if not usually, the discourse of such groups is that of "family," of a large, natural kinship group linked by "blood" and history – a kind of super-clan – but this is not always the factual situation; instead, like other mega-groups such as nations or ethnic groups, these collectivities are often what Anderson (1983) called "imagined communities." That is, while the group identities are founded on some shared "real" physical or historical characteristics, the meanings and values of those characteristics are culturally defined and deployed, and almost certainly the group is too large to ever meet or interact as one. Nevertheless, membership in or assignment to such a group, or to a category on which such a group is based, can significantly affect the quality of one's life.

See Chapters 6 and 13

Anderson, Benedict. 1983. *Imagined Communities: Reflections of the Origin and Spread of Nationalism.* London: Verso.

Socio-economic status or class

Class
an (at least ideally) open
socio-economic status,
which members can change
through their own
achievements

One last major social characteristic that individuals may share and orient themselves around is **class** or socio-economic status. Class is different from the other traits and groupings we have discussed in that it tends to be, if not is by definition, "vertical" or socially hierarchical. Again, not all societies exhibit this quality, but most did and do, from the moment of the appearance of the first economic surplus and the social and political distinctions that arise from it. This economic, social, and political inequality results in a system of **social stratification**, in which society is divided into discrete and unequal groups in terms of their access to wealth, power, and prestige. Each "position" or level within a stratified society is identifiable as a class, with its social and economic characteristics and opportunities and burdens. Societies that evidence this stratification are called stratified societies, and those that do not are called egalitarian societies.

Social stratification
the division of society into
different and unequal
groups or "layers" on the
basis of wealth, power, and
prestige

Social mobility
the possibility or ease with
which one may change
position in the social
stratification system

Exactly how many classes exist in a society and their respective rules and roles vary and are subject to dispute. The United States is commonly regarded as much less class-conscious than the U.K., and only the U.K. has a "royal" class. Some analysts in the United States, when they even acknowledge a class division, break it down into lower, middle, and upper classes, sometimes with a lower, middle, and upper substratum within each class (hence, "lower middle class" or "upper lower class"). The details depend on the definitions of each. The greater point is that individuals do face different life chances based on their position in the socio-economic system and that their position is in turn determined by other social and cultural factors, such as education, age, race, gender, and so on. In fact, we can speak of two general ways in which one's position or status is determined in a stratified society:

Caste
a closed socio-economic
status, often ascribed by
birth

1. **Ascribed status** – The status is determined by "birth" or by "nature" – literally "written on" the individual (although it is of course still given cultural significance). An ascribed status cannot be changed much, if at all, through the efforts of the individual.
2. **Achieved status** – The status is the result of some effort or action of the individual. It can, therefore, at least in principle be changed in a

Ascribed status
a social characteristic that
is attributed to a person
without any effort on their
part, either innate (like sex
or race) or acquired in the
normal course of
development (like age)

Achieved status
a social position or role
that a person acquires
through some effort or
accomplishment of his or
her own

person's lifetime, although this possibility may be difficult to realize.

Any individual will occupy at one time a combination of ascribed and achieved statuses: for example, one may be female, white, and a certain age (ascribed) while simultaneously being married, college-educated, and an anthropologist (achieved). The sum or product of these statuses and their relative weight in a given society will place her in a particular socio-economic status.

The important question is which status(es) most powerfully determine one's place in society, i.e. whether the ascribed statuses outweigh or trump the achieved statuses or vice versa. The answer to this question will define the **social mobility** in the society, that is, the extent to which one can change one's position in the stratification system. If there are few, or few meaningful, statuses that one can achieve, then one is socially immobile and one's position is settled once and for all. We refer to societies organized this way as "closed societies," and the positions within them are "closed classes" or even **castes**. If there are many and meaningful achieved statuses, then people can be quite socially mobile and one's socio-economic position is a momentary result of those achievements. We call such societies "open societies" and the positions within them "open classes" or simply classes. Of course, one's ideal mobility is up, but social mobility includes the possibility of negative mobility – moving down in the stratification system.

In their individualistic and achievement-oriented society, Americans like to think that everyone can "make it" and that all it takes is hard work, but that if a person does not succeed then this is somehow his/her own fault. Their "rugged individualism" suggests to them that each person can and does rise and fall on his/her own merits. This attitude has been diluted somewhat by the creation of a "welfare" system in which those who "have" contribute to the maintenance of those who "have not" – a kind of formal and obligatory "mutual support system" based, at least in part, on a notion of common "kinship" as Americans, of being "a family" that takes care of its own.

The real controversy in the United States over social mobility is whether or not some real persistent social factors prevent some individuals as members of groups from achieving the "American

BOX 8.4   THE INDIAN CASTE SYSTEM

The best-known closed or caste system is that of India, in which caste membership is ascribed at birth. It would not be quite correct to say that membership is ascribed "by" birth, although usually one belongs to the caste of one's parents. However, you are not in your caste because you are born to certain parents; rather, you are born to certain parents because you are in your caste. Castes, or *jatis*, represent a combination of economic, kinship, political, and religious elements. You do share your caste with your kin and most immediately inherit it from them. Your occupation or economic contribution is also defined by caste: castes are, in fact, occupational groups. Beals (1980) reported that Gopalpur had fifty different *jatis* resident in or passing through the village, each with its own role, including priest, farmer, blacksmith, saltmaker, barber, butcher, stoneworker, leatherworker, etc. While these were clearly economic roles, he noted that there was no direct correlation between the wealth of an individual or group and his/her/its caste: any person in any *jati* might be rich or poor, and there were as many rich shepherds and farmers as rich priests in the village. Rather, the defining feature of a *jati* was its spiritual condition – its ritual purity and spiritual cleanliness. Humans who were "purer" as a result of behaviors in their past lives were born into higher *jatis*, and those who were more "impure" were born into lower ones. The lowest castes did the dirtiest work, including handling dead (animals and human) bodies and other unclean substances. Castes might live in separate neighborhoods and observe different social rules and restrictions (like the eating rules in the prior chapter), and members of the same *jati* might consider themselves to be – and often were – kin.

BOX 8.5   CONTEMPORARY CULTURAL CONTROVERSIES: LOVE IN A TIME OF RECESSION

Marriage and kinship are very important institutions in the United States, other Western societies, and indeed all societies, but this does not mean that they are independent variables. Over the past few decades, the structure of marriage and family has changed dramatically, in response to economic, political, and even technological (e.g. contraceptive pills and devices) alterations. For instance, Americans marry later – and marry less – divorce more, have fewer children, and enter into non-traditional arrangements like cohabitation and second marriages more than in the past. It is no surprise that the global economic recession, beginning in 2008 and persisting through 2011, would have consequences for families. Research indicates that marriage rates for Americans aged 25–34 are lower than ever, and the year 2009 saw the lowest birth rate in a century. Women who might have stayed at home to raise children have been compelled to join the workforce, and many families have been made homeless. One noteworthy development is the "recession widow," resulting from the necessity for married couples to live in different cities in order to find jobs. Even before the recession, some observers thought that marriage was dead or in decline, in America and other Western societies, but the recession has certainly hastened or exacerbated the process, at least in the short term. What do you think?

dream." The most overt of these factors is race or ethnicity, leading to calls for "affirmative action" to correct the "closed" nature of racial/ethnic stratification and counter-calls of "reverse discrimination." This is not an easy problem to settle.

There seems to be little doubt that there are still differences of opportunity that lead to differences of outcome, based on ascribed characteristics not only of race and ethnicity but of gender and age and even physical appearance (so-called "lookism") as well. But the question is much broader than that. The "ideology" of social mobility may not match the reality, and this is a general and important cultural fact. Societies do not always entirely see or understand themselves clearly and may take ideals for actualities. A study of American incomes from 1967 to 1991 (Gittleman and Joyce 1995) came to two conclusions – that the income gap between rich and poor had actually widened during those years, and that mobility was actually less common than one would think. While it is possible to change one's position in the social stratification system (at least as indicated by wealth), it was not easy to improve one's situation and it did not happen all that often. Unhappily but not surprisingly, those who were most likely to be and to stay in the lower ranks of the system were the young, the uneducated, and the nonwhite. So, while the class structure of the United States is not "closed," it is "stiff" – and more so for some than for others.

SUMMARY

A society must assign individuals names, identities, roles, interests, and statuses. This entails establishing and perpetuating corporate groups. Kinship is one universal of making and maintaining such groups but not the only way. A kinship system is a confluence of three principles:

- Marriage
- Residence
- Descent

Within each of these principles are numerous sub-issues with considerable area for diversity in each, and the forms they take and the interconnections they make significantly shape the experience of the society, in particular gender, domestic, and property relations.

In addition to kinship principles, non-kinship characteristics and commonalities can be and widely are used to create corporate groups and allot tasks, roles, and social meaning and values. Some of the traits that humans share and that can be used to build groups and categories include

- Sex or gender
- Age
- Race
- Common interest
- Class or socio-economic status

Any individual in a society will occupy a complex and sometimes contradictory constellation of positions in regard to all of these kin and non-kin categories, which will affect their opportunities and often their outcomes in social life.

MCQS

Q

FILL IN THE BLANKS

www

Key Terms

Achieved status	Ascribed status	Clan
Age grade system	Avunculocal	Class
Age set	Bilateral	Corporate group
Ambilineal	Bride service	Descent
Ambilocal	Bridewealth/bride price	Double descent
Arranged marriage	Caste	Dowry

Endogamy

Exogamy

Household

Hypergamy

Incest taboo

Kindred

Levirate

Lineage

Marriage

Matrilineal

Matrilocal

Moiety

Monogamy

Neolocal

Patrilineal

Patrilocal

Phratry

Polyandry

Polygyny

Preferential cousin marriage

Residence

Serial monogamy

Social mobility

Social reproduction

Social stratification

Sororal polygyny

Sororate

Unilineal descent

9 Politics

Social order and social control

When cattle ranchers in Belize approached the government for permission to shoot jaguars that were encroaching on their land, the Secretary of the Ministry of Natural Resources took the question to the Belize Audubon Society (BAS), a non-governmental organization (NGO) dedicated to conservation (Medina 2010). Meanwhile, an officer of the Wildlife Conservation Society in New York read about the jaguars and conducted a study on the big cats' population in Belize. Together, these two organizations not only influenced the government of Belize but actually made proposals and wrote legislation that was enacted by the government: BAS helped create the Wildlife Protection and National Parks Systems Act, as well as convincing the government to add two new offices – a conservation officer in the Forestry Department and a liaison officer in the Ministry of Trade and Industry. Eventually BAS arranged for itself to have "day-to-day management of the protected areas, tourism, and public environment education" (253). This case, like many others around the world, illustrates the fact that official government (the "state": see below) does not have a monopoly of political power in contemporary politics but that there are multiple kinds and sites of power and that a network of local,

national, and international institutions "overlays and coexists with" the state in Belize and elsewhere (248). Indeed, there is no "neat divide between state and nonstate" political actors (250): in Belize, many members of BAS had relationships with elected officials and civil servants, some BAS members were former government representatives or civil servants themselves, and two members were sisters of a former prime minister.

When Westerners think of politics they usually think of governments and laws and police and courts – all of the formal institutions of power and authority in modern societies. These, like the factories and markets and money of economics, are one type or manifestation of politics but not the essence or definition of it. That is, governments and courts are one way but not the only or universal way of doing politics. In fact, as we will discover below, they may not be the predominant form of politics even in complex modern "political" societies.

The word "politics" derives from the ancient Greek *polis* or city, referring to the proper organization of the city or city-state and the proper behavior of its citizens. Not all societies, of course, have lived in cities, but they have all lived in organized and orderly social groups. The city in ancient

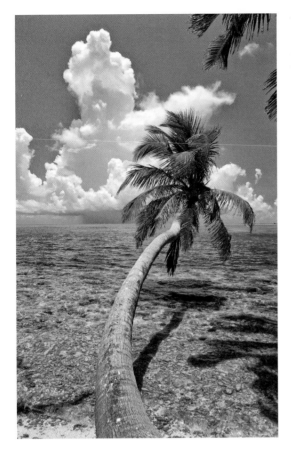

PLATE 9.1 The Belize Audubon Society acts to protect land and ecology in Belize.

Greece was the total society, and politics was the total way of life in the society. This is why Aristotle called humans a "political" species – because humans live in societies and must order ourselves to be able to coexist and cooperate in social groups.

Politics broadly conceived, then, refers to the cultural ideas, norms, values, and practices that regulate how people interact in an orderly and (more or less) mutually beneficial manner. This may involve formal, specialized, and large-scale institutions, like a congress or parliament, where the rules and laws of the society are formulated and propagated; it may involve informal, generalized, and nearly socially invisible norms and relationships that do not appear "political" at first glance. In most – or all – cases, it will involve both, and often the latter more than the former.

It might be more profitable to think of "political functions" than of the "politics" proper, since in many societies politics may not be distinguished from other social and cultural rules and roles, and

in no society is it *totally* distinguished from them. Other aspects of culture, including kinship and economics – and certainly religion – and even language and gender, have political functions and implications as well, if by that we mean informing people of the expected ways to behave and enforcing those ways. Thus, while we identify politics as a distinct domain of culture, we must remember that its functions can be and by and large are distributed throughout the social system – and that politics probably works better for being so distributed. Therefore, our task in this chapter is to consider the political functions that any society must accomplish, the various ways in which a society may accomplish them, and the relations between the "political" aspects of the culture and all of its other components.

SOCIAL CONTROL: THE FUNCTIONS OF POLITICS

Culture is by definition learned and shared ways of thinking, feeling, and behaving. Without these shared ways, members of society could not interact effectively, since they would not be able to anticipate what others are going to do, to interpret what they actually do, or to respond appropriately. Culture is a shared communicative and behavioral environment – a kind of all-embracing language of social life and social reality. In the normal course of social living, various kinds of problems and challenges arise that demand attention and resolution, if the society is to continue to living harmoniously, if at all. These issues include:

- Decision-making
- Norm/rule/law creation
- Dispute resolution
- Norm/rule/law enforcement
- Deviance punishment
- Social integration
- Defense of community and society
- Aggression/offense against other communities and societies.

We might think of all of these issues in tandem as the problem of "**social control**" – directing members of the group to perform their duties, to follow the established norms, and to do "the right thing" as

Social control
the political and general social function of getting members of a group to conform to expectations and rules and to obey authorities. Includes inculcating of social values as well as punishment of deviance from expectations

MAINTAINING SOCIAL ORDER AND HARMONY

defined by the society. Of course, who does the defining is a prime concern for anthropology as well as for the members of the society.

Social control then consists of the various types and sources of social pressures that can be brought to bear on individuals to get them to do, as individuals or as members of specific groups and categories, what the society demands and expects them to do. In its more sinister guise, which often enough actually exists in the human world, social control is the imposition of one person's or group's will on others: inducing members of society (the ones under the "political control" of the dominant person or group) to do what the "leadership" wants them to do. In other more benign versions, it is simply what is necessary for successful communal coexistence.

Social control can take two very different though related forms. The logically and chronologically prior form involves the actions of others upon the individual. Before any particular individual is born, the rules and norms and institutions of society already exist, and humans, for the most part, conform to them. Therefore, the other people who came before us and who introduced us and enculturated us into social expectations are the "authorities" of the society. They control – or perhaps it would be more accurate to say, they represent – the terms of the society, and they, like all of culture, are "before" and "outside" of us. Anthropologists refer to this factor as **externalized control**, the creation and enforcement of socially appropriate behavior by persons, groups, or institutions outside of the individual. Such persons, groups, or institutions are **agents of social control**, and every society abounds with them. They consist of such roles or positions as parents, peers, priests, professors, police, prison guards, parole officers, and presidents and prime ministers. When a person does "right," these agents can provide positive responses, but when a person does "wrong," the agents can administer negative feedback, from instruction to punishment. Hopefully and usually, the individual gets the idea and begins to voluntarily conform to expectations, even to accept and believe in them. However, in every society in some way or another, agents of social control stand over society to make sure that compliance occurs.

The second source of control, one that is related to and dependent on the first, is **internalized control**, the process by which the individual controls his/her own behavior in conformity with rules or norms or standards. This is by far the most efficient form of social control, since no society can have a policeman or a guard monitoring every member every moment of the day. Fortunately, most people most of the time do not require monitoring to ensure their compliance. They conform quite voluntarily – because they come to think it is the right thing to do. The key to internalized control is enculturation. The whole point of enculturation is the learning or acquisition of one's culture. What this "acquisition" means is that society's rules, norms, values, beliefs, and so on get "inside" the individual; they become part of the individual's personality.

As a result of enculturation and the internalization of culture, the individual "has" or "is" (some expression of) the society's culture – not a carbon copy to be sure, but a culturally informed product. S/he shares the sense that what the society deems as right really is right, that what the society deems as reprehensible really is reprehensible. Ideally, no further control would be necessary, since members of the group would not allow themselves to do, perhaps could not imagine themselves doing, those things that they have learned are wrong or evil or shameful, etc. A "conscience," in other words some part of the personality or self, monitors the individual and makes each one of us feel good when we do (socially) right and bad when we do (socially) wrong. Thus, internalized social control is a dimension of the cultural construction of persons.

However, internalized social control often is not total or totally effective. There are many reasons for this. For instance, given the "guided reinvention" quality of culture, it is possible that the individual may be exposed to all the normal rules and pressures and still not learn or internalize the preferred things; s/he might learn or construct an idiosyncratic lesson from cultural experience. In another case, the individual may be exposed to "abnormal" experiences, like violence or abuse in home life, internalizing a lesson that society would prefer s/he not. Individuals may even be enculturated into what some researchers call a "culture of deviance" (for instance, a gang or a criminal environment), in which they acquire "alternate norms" that are deviant by society's standard but "normal" by the subculture's standard. Finally, an

See Chapter 2

See Chapter 5

Externalized control
the source of social control that lies outside of the individual, in the form of individuals, groups, and institutions with the power to sanction behavior, such as parents, teachers, police, governments, etc.

Agents of social control
individuals, groups, or institutions that play a part in instilling social norms in members and protecting and perpetuating those norms through the use of their powers and sanctions

See Chapter 2

Internalized control
a form or source of social control in which individuals make themselves conform to social expectations through the internalization of rules and norms; by enculturation, social rules and norms become part of the personalities of members

individual may internalize all the right norms and values but find that social circumstances do not allow him/her to conduct normal, socially appropriate behavior. As an example, one may possess the "good" values of hard work and frugality and such but find oneself in a class or race or ethnic or gender, etc. situation where these values do not apply or "work" – where, for example, opportunities for employment or education are absent or blocked.

When individuals, through their own choices or through social constraints, violate the norms and rules of the group, the agents of social control can utilize specific social tools, depending on the particular agent, the particular society, and the particular deviance. These tools are called **sanctions**. English-speakers tend to think of sanctions as negative things: when the United States imposes sanctions on a country like Cuba or North Korea, a punishment is intended, which is meant to impel the belligerent countries to change their behavior in more favorable (from the sanctioning agent's point of view) directions. In reality, there are both positive and negative sanctions. Sanctions are merely reactions or responses by others that are intended to affect the sanctioned individual's or group's behavior. Positive sanctions are intended to encourage the individual to repeat "good" behavior,

while negative sanctions are intended to discourage them from "bad" behavior.

Sanctions can also be more or less formal. A **formal sanction** is one that is explicit, even "official," and perhaps written down; normally it applies to more serious social infractions, and usually members know exactly what behaviors will unleash it, exactly what the sanction will be, and exactly which agents of social control have the right to administer it. An **informal sanction** is more vague, implicit, and usually not written down. Individuals may have some general sense of what behaviors produce what sanctions, but there may be no specialized agents to impose them. In fact, the right to impose informal sanctions might exist for every member of society.

There are then four possible varieties of sanctions, not all of which are always recognized as "political":

- formal positive – for example, rewards and prizes and promotions
- formal negative – for example, jail and fines and, at the extreme, capital punishment
- informal positive – for example, praise and smiles and thanks and inclusion in the group
- informal negative – for example, insults and dirty looks and gossip/ridicule and ostracism

Formal sanction
a method of social control employing rewards and punishments that are explicit and well-known, often written down, and administered by special agents of control who possess the authority to administer them (such as police or courts)

Informal sanction
a "reward" or "punishment" that is widely understood in a society but not precisely defined, usually not written down, and for which no specialized role exists to administer the sanction

Sanction
any type of social pressure in the form of "reward" or "punishment" that can be imposed on people to influence and control their behavior

PLATE 9.2 Power is not only situated in governments but in many informal sites in society.

In trying to think of other examples, the reader might be inclined to conclude that there are more negative sanctions than positive ones; after all, the police seldom stop a driver to congratulate him/her for driving exactly the speed limit. It may be the case that there are more negative sanctions, depending on the society. It may also be that good behavior, being the ideal and the norm, draws less attention and intervention than bad behavior. Another important point is that members of a society tend to overlook all of the little ways in which they all sanction each other, positively and negatively, every moment of every day. All humans are continuously administering, and having administered to them, sanctions intended to shape the flow of behavior. The classic study of this phenomenon is the "elevator experiment," in which subjects intentionally break some minor norm like standing in an elevator facing the wrong direction; it becomes immediately apparent how many norms there are in society, how much people assume that everyone knows and follows them, and the ways in which they can show their disapproval or discomfort when those norms are broken.

The point is that politics is not just something that governments do, as noted at the outset of the chapter. Politics in any society is mostly informal and interpersonal and only secondarily formal and institutional. As humans we live perpetually in a "political" environment in which we press others – and they press us – to do the normal, expected, and valued things. We are all agents of social control to the other people in our society, and they are all agents of social control to us. Only when these pervasive political pressures fail, or when some person, group, or institution appears wanting to change and control the course of society, do we experience clearly and directly the formal side of politics.

POWER

Every kind and instance of sanction is an expression of power. Power is one person's or group's or institution's ability to influence and affect the behavior of others, as well as to influence and affect the disposition of the resources (material and symbolic) of society; power then becomes the capacity to influence the course and outcome of social interactions. When most people think of power, they tend to think of force, but not all exercise of power involves force. In fact, anthropologists have identified three quite different types or sources of power, which are independent but which may simultaneously exist in any society or in any specific role or agent of power. All of these variations of power are social phenomena which depend at least in part on the complicity of those under power, as the political scientist Hannah Arendt reminded us.

Arendt, Hannah. 1969. *On Violence*. New York: Harcourt, Brace, & World, Inc.

Authority
legitimate power or power that an individual, group, or institution is felt to rightly possess and exercise on the grounds of age, knowledge, office, and such

BOX 9.1 HANNAH ARENDT ON POWER AND AUTHORITY

In her book *On Violence* (1969) Arendt used the word "power" to mean what we mean by **authority** in the present discussion, arguing that authority/power is always a relationship between those "in" power and those "under" the power.

Power corresponds to the human ability not just to act but to act in concert. Power is never the property of an individual; it belongs to a group and remains in existence only so long as the group keeps together. When we say of somebody that he is "in power" we actually refer to his being empowered by a certain number of people to act in their name. The moment the group, from which the power originated to begin with. . .disappears, "his power" also vanishes. In current usage, when we speak of a "powerful man" or a "powerful personality," we already use the word "power" metaphorically; what we refer to without metaphor is "strength."

Authority, relating to the most elusive of these phenomena and therefore, as a term, most frequently abused, can be vested in persons – there is such a thing as personal authority, as, for instance, in the relation between parent and child, between teacher and pupil – or it can be vested in offices, as, for instance, in the Roman senate. . .or in the hierarchical offices of the Church. . . .Its hallmark is unquestioning recognition by those who are asked to obey; neither coercion nor persuasion is needed. (A father can lose his authority either by beating his child or by starting to argue with him, that is, either by behaving to him like a tyrant or by treating him as an equal.) To remain in authority requires respect for the person or the office, and the surest way to undermine it is laughter.

(44–45)

Authority

Authority can be thought of, and is experienced as, "legitimate" power, power that a person or group or institution possesses and uses "rightfully"; Morton Fried defined it precisely as "the ability to channel the behavior of others in the absence of the threat or use of sanctions" (1967: 13). Followers recognize the authority's right to this power and respect and obey it. Such authority derives from a variety of sources, including physical strength, skill or knowledge, age, education, charisma, or formal office. Most of these qualities belong to the individual; s/he is strong or knowledgeable or has "charisma" or charm. Some individuals seem to possess "charisma" and some do not: President John F. Kennedy was said to be charismatic, as was President Ronald Reagan. The twentieth century was distinguished by the large number of world leaders who effectively and often intentionally promoted "personality" as a foundation or manifestation of their power, fostering what has been named the "cult of personality." Enormous posters of and constant references to Josef Stalin or Kim Jong-Il or Saddam Hussein created and maintained an aura of the leader as all-wise or fatherly, etc. (which was backed up with other forms of power as well).

Office, on the other hand, is not a characteristic of an individual but bestows authority on the individual. An **office** is a defined position or role of power in a society. "Police officer" is an office, as is "teacher" or "boss" or "president." The power belongs to the role, not the individual; any person who occupies the office has the authority. As long as the individual occupies the role or position, he or she exercises the authority of the office; however, when the office is lost or vacated, the power is lost too.

Often the authority of leaders has a supernatural base as well. In his study of the Madagascar kingdom of Merina, Maurice Bloch (1989) discussed the central concept of *hasina* that energizes the entire system. *Hasina* is a mystical power associated with nature and reproduction; it is supposedly inherent in some people and not others. In the Merina worldview, it is inherent in the kings and not the commoners; commoners need kings to guarantee the continued fertility of the earth, and the subjects repay the kings with respect, obedience, and wealth.

One important characteristic of authority as a type of power is its limitation. It is limited in both scope and duration. A person of authority in one area of society may have no authority in another; you might recognize a stockbroker's authority in investing but not in medicine. And the stockbroker usually cannot compel you to invest the way s/he recommends; if you respect his or her opinion, you will follow the advice, but if you do not you will not. In terms of duration, an authority figure loses his/her power when his/her strength, skill, charisma, office, or whatever justification for that original authority disappears or terminates. Authority is not permanent but only lasts as long as the grounds for it.

Persuasion

Persuasion is an intermediate type of power, based on one's ability to influence or manipulate people into obedience or compliance, typically through skillful use of language or control of resources. One of the most familiar forms of persuasion is "talking people into" doing what the persuader wants them to do. In all societies, there are specific linguistic

Fried, Morton H. 1967. *The Evolution of Political Society: An Essay in Political Anthropology*. New York: Random House.

Office
a more or less formal social position with specific rights and responsibilities. One source of "political" authority and social control

Persuasion
a source of social and political power, based on the ability to move people to agree with or obey the persuader. Often exercised through linguistic skill (e.g. the ability to "give a good speech") and the manipulation of resources and social relationships

See Chapter 4

skills of oratory or "speech-making" that give certain individuals more persuasive power than others. In the United States, "political speaking" or speech-making is a special and highly elaborated and valued style of language, and leaders who can speak "well" are more effective – ultimately "more powerful" – than those who cannot.

The other foundation of persuasion is control or manipulation of cultural resources. These resources can obviously include money or property; if someone is rich – or, say, the boss – then people may tend to find his/her opinions and directions more compelling than other people's. The "big man" discussed below has persuasive power by virtue of his central position in the redistribution system. A teacher has a certain persuasive power by virtue of his/her control over grades. However, the control may not necessarily involve "economic" resources but may rest on what Pierre Bourdieu (1977) called cultural or symbolic capital. **Symbolic capital** can include things like flags and other markers or symbols such as white coats and robes and impressive titles, key words and concepts (in the United States, "freedom" or "rights"), specific bits of cultural knowledge, myths, rituals, and so on. Like the Madagascar *hasina* concept, as in most royal circumstances, kings and queens demonstrated and reproduced their power through ritual performances like coronations, state marriages, and state funerals. Clifford Geertz claimed that precolonial Bali took this principle to an extreme, establishing a "theater state" in which the rituals and demonstrations were the very basis and expression of power. Politics itself was display and acting:

> the kings and princes were the impresarios, the priests the directors, and the peasants the supporting cast, stage crew, and audience. The stupendous cremations, tooth filings, temple dedications, pilgrimages, and blood sacrifices, mobilizing hundreds and even thousands of people and great quantities of wealth, were not means to particular ends: they were the ends themselves, they were what the state was for. Court ceremonialism was the driving force of court politics; and mass ritual was not a device to shore up the state, but rather the state, even in its final gasp, was a device for the enactment of mass ritual. Power served pomp, not pomp power.
>
> (1980: 13)

Coercion
power based on the threat or use of force

Symbolic capital
"resources" that humans can use to influence situations and affect other people's behavior that are not "material" or "economic." These can include knowledge, social relationships/debts, prestige, etc.

Geertz, Clifford. 1980. *Negara: The Theatre State in Nineteenth-Century Bali.* Princeton, NJ: Princeton University Press.

Contemporary politicians often criticize their opponents for engaging in "political theater" without realizing (or at least acknowledging) that all politics is theater, or at least cultural performance, to an extent.

Coercion

When all else fails – or often in conjunction with other sources of power – a would-be leader can resort to **coercion**, the threat or use of force or violence. Arendt argued that coercion or violence is the very opposite or absence of authority: individuals only use force when authority is questioned or lost. There is no doubt that coercion can escalate as the legitimacy of the political leader declines, but it is probably not correct to see them as antithetical and foreign principles. A police officer combines authority, persuasion, and coercion in his/her power, and most members of a society recognize some form of "legitimate force," whether in the criminal justice system, in the military, or in personal self-defense.

As the sole basis of power, coercion can be very effective in the short term: if a police officer needs to subdue a suspect, physical force – up to and including deadly force – can achieve the goal. However, if Arendt is correct, coercion alone cannot control a society over the long term, and even coercive leaders attempt to project an aura of legitimacy on their actions. They may suggest that they are eliminating a threat to the society, preserving "law and order," or actually improving the society in some way. The leaders of the French Revolution, particularly in the period known as the Terror, explicitly employed violence and terror (the term "terror" or "terrorism" was invented at that moment) as a political device. In attempting to create a perfect society, deadly violence was a method or tool, as Maximilien Robespierre stated:

> We desire an order of things in which all base and cruel feelings are suppressed by the laws, and all beneficent and generous feelings evoked; in which ambition means the desire to merit glory and to serve one's country. In which distinctions arise only from equality itself. . .; in which all minds are enlarged by the continued conviction of republican sentiments and

by the endeavor to win the respect of a great people. . . .

> We must crush both the internal and foreign enemies of the Republic, or perish with it. And in this situation, the first maxim of your policy should be to guide the people by reason and repress the enemies of the people by terror.
> (quoted in Gershoy 1957: 159–60)

Coercion can and often does include guillotines and clubs and dogs, but there is also "soft coercion," as anthropologists, political scientists, and interrogators and advertisers have discovered. People do not have to be beaten or threatened to have their behavior largely determined for them. There are ways to bend them to another's will, from "strong" soft coercion like sleep deprivation, starvation, cold-water dousings, and emotional and informational manipulation to "weak" soft coercion like invasive advertising, product placement, and a host of marketing tricks that opinion-shapers have learned from decades of close observation of consumer habits and tendencies. Human voting behavior, buying behavior, and most other forms of behavior can be shaped quite effectively – and without the victim's knowledge – through much more subtle devices than torture. In fact, often such devices only work, or at least work best, when they are not seen or felt at all. Some of these techniques might perhaps belong in the persuasion category, but when options are denied or hidden, they begin to cross over into coercion, albeit "soft" coercion.

In a word, hegemony is "naturalized" power – or at least power that followers experience as natural. One of the most important processes for the construction and inculcation of this social consciousness, Gramsci insisted, was education, which was intended "to raise the great mass of the population to a particular cultural and moral level, a level (or type) which corresponds to the needs of the productive forces for development, and hence to the interests of the ruling class" (258). Steven Lukes (1974) also stressed the need to attend to the invisible or inaccessible aspects of power. Specifically, Lukes regarded the familiar overt kind of power, relating to conspicuous behavior, decision-making, and of course actual conflict, as merely the first dimension of power. The second and more subtle dimension relates to control over the political agenda, what questions are asked and how issues are defined. The third and most covert dimension of power consists of influence over people's very thoughts and wishes, their values and preferences, leading them to misunderstand their own interests – to want what is not in their interest and to oppose what is. In so doing, power can prevent dissent or even the expression of differences and grievances by producing thoughts and perceptions that are fundamental distortions of social reality.

THE ANTHROPOLOGY OF POLITICAL SYSTEMS

As in the domains of economics and kinship, anthropologists have identified a variety of political

---

BOX 9.2 INVISIBLE POWER

Not all power is visible to those under its effects; in fact, power may be more effective when it is invisible. Antonio Gramsci used the term "hegemony" to refer to this pervasive but largely unseen influence. For Gramsci, government is the official apparatus of political power and enforcement, while hegemony is the

> "spontaneous" consent given by the great masses of the population to the general direction imposed on social life by the dominant fundamental group [i.e. the dominant class]; this consent is "historically" caused by the prestige (and consequent confidence) which the dominant group enjoys because of its position and function in the world of production.
>
> (1971: 12)

Level of political integration
the extent to which political institutions unite a group of people into a single political entity, as measured by the size of the society, the complexity of the society, the formality and centralization of political rules and roles, and the amount of coercive force available to political leaders

systems, which can be organized along a rough continuum in terms of their **level of political integration**. By this phrase, we mean the extent to which politics "integrates" or literally "makes one out of" a society. This can be expressed as a combination of at least five variables:

1. Size of society. A small society is less integrated than a large one, since more people, groups, and institutions are "made one" and incorporated into a single polity or political community in a large one than a small one. Size of society may be measured in terms of population and/or in terms of the number of local groups (families, villages, towns, etc.) encompassed by the political system.
2. Complexity of society. A society that contains internal differentiations, such as class distinctions, is more integrated or requires more integration than one that does not. This internal complexity can also include multiple linguistic or religious or racial or ethnic communities.
3. Centralization of power. If there is no "center" of power – that is, if power is dispersed widely or evenly through society – then there is little political integration. The more that power is collected into a few hands (maybe as few as one), the more integrated the system. If power is distributed absolutely evenly in a society, then there is no real power at all, since no one has more power than anyone else and cannot really make anyone else do anything.
4. Amount of coercion. The more force that is available to the political system and its agents, the more integrated the society. Again, coercion by itself has a finite life span, but without coercion no leader or would-be leader can guarantee or compel obedience and integration; followers or would-be followers could detach themselves from the leader and disregard his/her mandates (which amounts to a "revolution").

5. Formality of power. The more explicit and specialized the agents and institutions of power and politics are, the more integrated the system. Societies in which rules, sanctions, and roles of enforcement are implicit or embedded in other non-political relationships and institutions are less integrated.

On a spectrum of political integration, different anthropologists have proposed different typologies. Fried, for instance, suggested four types including egalitarian, rank, stratified, and state societies. An egalitarian society is "one in which there are as many positions of prestige in any given age-sex grade as there are persons capable of filling them" (1967: 33); that is, political power is not limited to a few individuals in an exclusive way. A rank society emerges "when there are fewer positions of valued status than persons capable of filling them. A rank society has means of limiting the access of its members to status positions that they would otherwise hold on the basis of sex, age, or personal attributes" (52); individuals must then compete for rank. A stratified society "is one in which members of the same sex and equivalent age status do not have equal access to the basic resources that sustain life" and this unequal access is formalized into hierarchical (and often hereditary) strata or classes (186). Finally, a state is "the complex of institutions by means of which the power of the society is organized on a basis superior to kinship" (229). Put another way, a state is "a collection of specialized institutions and agencies, some formal and others informal, that maintains an order of stratification" (235) and thus strives for and defends its "sovereignty" or "monopoly of permanent control over a population and an area" (237).

Despite the utility of this typology, the one advanced by Elman Service in his 1962 book *Primitive Social Organization* has achieved the widest adoption. No typology is, of course, true or perfect, but since Service's is the best known, it is the one we will discuss in more detail.

Service, Elman R. 1962. *Primitive Social Organization: An Evolutionary Perspective*. New York: Random House.

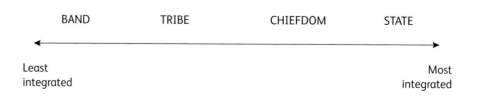

FIGURE 9.1 Political systems by level of political integration (following Service 1962).

Band

The **band** is the lowest level of political integration; anything less would consist of solitary individuals, which never happens and would be the very antithesis of society. A band tended to comprise a remarkably small number of people over a very local area, sometimes no more than a handful and seldom more than a hundred or so, typically averaging between thirty and fifty. This number was clearly too small to constitute an entire society; instead, bands tended to be local subunits of societies, dispersed over the territorial range of the society. Essentially a residential subset of a society, it was often simply an extended family that moved and camped on its own.

The decentralization of power was manifested in two ways. First, within the band, there was no single individual with a great amount of power compared to other members. Since the "political" and residential group was essentially a kinship group, kinship organization and power were synonymous with political organization and power. Elders, often both male and female, exercised nominally more power than youngsters, but this power was limited to authority and persuasion (with occasional coercion) and was not very extensive. It was basically "head of the household" power, like

any parent or elder would enjoy. Actually, it may have been less than most parents and elders enjoy: many band-level societies, like the Australian Aboriginals, the Ju/hoansi, or Inuit/Eskimo societies, did little in the way of disciplining or controlling the behavior of children, often explicitly believing that young humans lacked the "reason" or "maturity" to take instruction and discipline. Some, like the Semai, found it positively offensive to be told what to do.

The highest position of "leadership" in bands was sometimes referred to as the "headman," but even this man had little formal power. His authority came from age, kinship relationships, experience and knowledge, and perhaps spiritual/ritual prowess. Members of the band deferred to him in decision-making, but they were not bound to follow him and could follow other members whose authority exceeded the headman in specific arenas like hunting. And the headman's power was overtly circumscribed. The general and often self-conscious ethic was to maintain equality between individuals; any man who tried to get too "big" was reminded in no uncertain terms that he was out of line. This phenomenon, known as a **leveling mechanism**, intentionally prevents anyone from becoming more important, dominant, or prestigious than anyone else.

Band
a political system or "level of political integration" where small, autonomous, and typically leaderless groups constitute local segments of a decentralized society

Leveling mechanism
a practice to establish or re-establish social equality or parity, usually by "bringing down" individuals or groups that threaten to get "above" or "better than" others

BOX 9.3 TO BE OR NOT TO BE A HEADMAN

The term "headman" may be inappropriately attributed to societies where they themselves do not really recognize the role. Among the Ju/hoansi, Lee (1984) found the term *//kaiha* which translates as headman (or even worse, chief), but many members denied that such a person actually existed. When asked about it, one informant said, "In fact, we are all headmen. Each one of us is headman over himself!" (89). Dentan (1968) also found a headman concept among the Semai, but he reported that only around 1900 did the external political authority, the Sultan of Perak, invent the office and start to invest elders with it through "letters of authority." Even so, some Semai during his research had begun to obey these "headmen" and even attribute magical powers to the official letters. Among the Tiwi of Northern Australia, a few (but not all) old men achieved a status above others, based on their marriages and children and the successful personal alliances they formed throughout their lives. Hart and Pilling (1960) referred to this as a "primitive oligarchy" because it was very much an achievement of the few, not the elderly as a class or category, based on a "game" of "trying to win friends and increase prestige and influence over others" (52), by marrying "well" and arranging "good" marriages for their sons and daughters. In the economically more marginal desert area, the Warlpiri lacked anything recognizable as a headman; in fact, they consciously downplayed individual status and power.

See Chapter 12

The general absence of coercion made bands fluid and transient. People moved and resided together while it was desirable to do so. If a man did attempt to accumulate power, his alleged followers would either knock him on the head with a club or just leave and join another band or start their own band. The environment also played a prominent part in the life of bands. Bands lived dispersed mostly because it was necessary, their environments being difficult and relatively unproductive. In times of plenty, multiple bands might gather and reside together for a while, often conducting their ritual affairs. However, these larger aggregations were always short-lived, either through environmental constraints or through the social frictions they caused, and soon bands disbanded and headed their separate ways.

This exemplifies the second manifestation of decentralization, which was the lack of any enduring coordination or integration above the band level. Just as a headman did not have much power even within his band, there was no one with power over multiple bands. That is, there was no "pan-band" or "super-band" leadership. Diverse bands usually shared kinship or non-kin organization (for example, members of the same family or ritual-group might cross bands), and of course they shared a common language and religion and culture, but that was as far as inter-band cooperation went. This lack of higher level integration, which served them

well enough in their traditional circumstances, was often a severe handicap upon contact with Western societies; band societies were unable to mount an organized resistance to colonial invaders and were often swept aside like wildlife – which is often how the invaders regarded them – in the path of settlement and development.

Not surprisingly, the fluid, egalitarian, unspecialized, unintegrated ways of the band fit most closely with the foraging mode of production. Foraging peoples typically organized themselves into band systems, or rather, foraging organization *was* band organization. Especially in less productive environments, groups had to be small and dispersed, each band hunting and gathering within a specific "country" inside the society's territory. The band was typically a family unit, among whom distribution of food and other goods was accomplished mainly through reciprocity, although some long-distance trading might be conducted. Kinship expectations, economic exigencies, and religious beliefs and values tended to shape and integrate the society and accomplish the political functions.

Actually, in Service's original formulation, he distinguished (following Julian Steward's earlier ecological analysis) between the patrilocal band (the smallest type, basically a male-centered exogamous kin group), the composite band (lacking band exogamy or definite residence rules, therefore "more of an expedient agglomeration than a

BOX 9.4 THE TIWI BAND

According to Hart and Pilling (1960), the Tiwi – whom I briefly visited myself in 1982 – were organized into nine named bands or "hordes" across the two islands (Bathurst and Melville) that they inhabited. In a subtropical and relatively productive environment, the bands ranged between 100 and 300 members, and each was connected to a particular territory. Hart and Pilling describe the bands as "small tribelets or semisovereign groups," since the various bands almost never gathered together and each conducted its own foraging and marrying and warring independent of the others. Band membership was not fixed and static; members, especially women, would often shift band residence. Thus, they concluded that the homeland of the band was permanent, but the people who actually occupied that homeland and made up the band changed continuously. As we saw above, no real headman of a band existed, and certainly no "central authority" over all the bands existed. The closest thing to an authority was the handful of old men who happened to achieve some prominence and influence through the accidents of living a long time, marrying into the "right" families, and marrying their sons and daughters into the right families as well. Thus, no person is assured power as a function of old age, and no inheritable or transferable power exists at all.

structured society" [60]), and the anomalous band (a fragmented system that did not fit into either category).

Tribe

Non-anthropologists often use the word "tribe" to designate any small-scale, traditional society (such as the "Warlpiri tribe" or the "Ju/hoansi tribe"), but this is technically incorrect. A tribe is a very particular kind of society or polity; some pre-modern peoples lived in tribe-level societies and some did not. The word derives from ancient Roman politics, which divided the population into *tribus* or political/economic units (which paid taxes or "tribute" as a group). In contemporary anthropology, we use **tribe** to refer to a small-scale – but larger than band – political system, often encompassing multiple local residential groups that lose some of their local autonomy in a larger polity, with some at least incipient overarching political institutions. The organization of tribes may not be very extensive or very recognizably "political," but we witness what can justifiably be called "pan-tribal" politics.

Tribe-level politics is associated most closely with pastoralism and horticulture, which, as we know, yielded larger economic surpluses, more populous and settled social units, and more specialization of labor and other roles than foraging economies. They also produced more social inequalities and disputes (over property and the uses of property, such as bridewealth). The net result was more interpersonal friction in the society together with comparatively ranked or stratified individuals or groups who began to add other kinds of power than authority to their means of social control.

These new means of social control were what we meant above by "incipient overarching political institutions." There was usually nothing in tribe-level integration that equates to the Western conception of "government," but individuals or groups or institutions were able to exert various kinds of power on various grounds across one or more communities within a tribe, up to and including the entire tribal population. Some of the possible forms that tribal political institutions could take were:

- Age grade system and age sets. In some tribal settings, especially East African pastoralism, the male age grade system constituted a political arrangement. Men in the warrior set provided the defensive and "law enforcement" arm of politics, while the elder set provided the decision-making and/or problem-settling branch.
- Council of elders. Even in the absence of a formal age grade system, elder members of the tribe, sometimes as representatives of families, lineages, clans, or villages, met as an ad hoc decision-making or problem-settling body. This council was not a full-time government but only assembled when there was a specific pan-tribal issue to address. At other times, disparate families, lineages, clans, or villages handled their own affairs.
- Descent groups. As just mentioned, kinship corporate groups could serve a political function, perhaps by providing representatives to some political body. Another way that descent groups, like lineages and clans, could contribute to political integration was by having members resident in diverse local communities or villages. In this way, the group could preside over issues that concerned more than one local community and give some structure to the

Tribe
a political system or level of integration in which multiple local communities may be organized into a single system but in which political power is still relatively informal and usually flows from institutions that are not specifically political (such as elders, lineages, age sets, religious specialists, and so on)

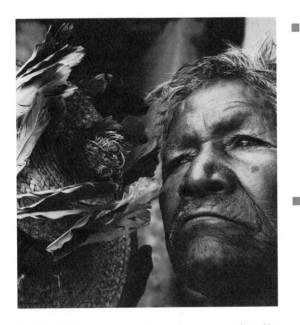

PLATE 9.3 In many societies, religious specialists like this *mara'acame* of the Huichol Indians provide political leadership.

wider social life of the tribe. Specific families or lineages might function as "segments" of a larger kinship corporate group, making for what we call a segmentary lineage system. As with the council of elders, for the most part each lineage segment functioned autonomously, but when an inter-segment problem arose, or an external threat challenged multiple segments, they could pull together at least temporarily, although they tended to fall apart again when the problem was solved or the threat was past.

See Chapter 7

See Chapter 10

■ The "big man." The big man was a type of tribal leader whose power flowed from his central position in the redistribution system. Redistribution was only possible in economic settings of greater surplus and greater control of that surplus. The big man did not in most cases have formal, permanent, or coercive power, but he did have both authority and persuasion. He was in a constant status competition with other rivals who may have their own entourage and their own power within the tribe – the very essence of a rank system. Collectively, the various big men in a village or tribe provided an amount of political structure to the society.

■ Common interest groups. These non-kinship corporate groups could also add political structure to a society. Like the Cheyenne warrior clubs, they were often law enforcers and agents of social control, although not quite a "government." Still, their existence and the sanctions they could impose – including physical force – made them potent intra-society and inter-society political forces. Cheyenne warrior clubs, for example, were "police" of the buffalo hunts as well as private armies for defense of their own interests as well as the whole tribe (when they acted in unison).

■ Religious specialists. In many tribal societies, men or women of distinguished religious or spiritual power and skill had a substantial political role to play. These specialists, who were usually "part-time," could act as mediators, "consultants" (like oracles and diviners, whom individuals might consult before making important decisions), problem-solvers, and sanctuaries to whom disputants and defendants could turn to get temporary protection from violence until a more pro-social solution could be found to arguments or "crimes" (crimes sometimes including murder).

What these and similar roles, institutions, and mechanisms have in common is (1) that they were "political" even while they also arose and drew power from other aspects of culture (economics,

BOX 9.5 CHEYENNE TRIBAL POLITICS

See Chapter 8

The Cheyenne warrior clubs constituted a "backbone" of political and military organization that, while ordinarily not unified, could be unified for pan-tribal purposes. However, the real "government" of the tribe was the Council of Forty-Four, the committee of representatives from the various subunits or "bands" of the tribe. The Council consisted of forty-four "peace chiefs," elder men who were proven warriors in their younger days. Each was selected for a formal, ten-year term, and they possessed a sacred character. Hoebel (1960) writes that they were expected to resign their positions in any warrior clubs and demonstrate other qualities, in particular "an even-tempered nature, energy, wisdom, kindliness, concern for the well-being of others, courage, generosity, and altruism" (37). They were addressed as "father" and "protector of the people." The head of the Council was the Sweet Medicine Chief, a religiously significant office referred to as *heum* or center of the universe, and he was joined by five other medicine chiefs and four sacred assistants, representing four supernatural beings. The political prerogatives of the Council were limited but specific: they deliberated on issues of concern to the entire tribe, such as camp moves, alliances or wars with other tribes, and criminal affairs, particularly murders (which were rare) and violations of protocol for buffalo hunts.

kinship, non-kin corporateness, and religion); (2) that they were part-time or ad hoc (that is, they only assembled or served when needed, unlike a permanent full-time sitting government); and (3) that their ability to dictate decisions and solutions to the society and its members was fairly circumscribed. Such was the nature of "politics" in societies of only limited size, surplus, wealth, and socio-economic and power distinctions.

Chiefdom

In larger and higher-surplus pastoral and horticultural societies, a more formal, full-time, and recognizably "political" system could develop, which anthropologists refer to as a **chiefdom**. A chiefdom is a polity usually consisting of multiple local communities over which an individual or a hierarchy of individuals exercises authority, persuasion, and at least some coercion. Since the chief and his "court" are full-time political specialists, they will be exempted from economic/productive activity, so obviously the economic system of the society must be productive enough to support this new "ruling class." Sometimes the role of chief is a ritual or ceremonial one; in other situations, it is a distinctly political one.

Besides – and based on – the economic aspect of chiefdom-level integration, the system depends on a clear, consistent, and often hereditary conception of rank, in which individuals, families, lineages, even entire villages or sets of villages are more or less literally and explicitly "ordered" from first to last in a prestige and power ladder (a kind of "pecking order"). Chiefs of course come from the "premier" families or lineages of society and/or control the premier resources of the society. This phenomenon should be familiar to Westerners in the case of European royal families: the next king or queen of England will, for example, come from the current ruling family (the Windsors), who are regarded as "higher" in some way than even other royal families (the dukes and earls and princes, etc.), let alone the "commoners." This is why royalty is often addressed as "your highness." Pre-modern and feudal European society was an elaborate set of ranked individuals and families, with middle-level office-holders in the system both a "lord" to somebody below them and a "serf" or "client" to somebody above them (a higher lord and ultimately the king).

The African countries of Rwanda and Burundi before colonialism were traditional chiefdoms, with a multi-layered hierarchy of small chiefs leading up to the paramount chief, who approximated a king.

Chiefdom
a political system or "level of integration" in which a central office, often hereditary, possesses formal political power and social prestige through some degree of redistributive control over surplus and the ability to organize and manage labor

PLATE 9.4 The king or Asantehene of the Ashanti Kingdom (present-day Ghana).

BOX 9.6   INTERNAL AND EXTERNAL POLITICS IN THE ULITHI CHIEFDOM

Lessa, William A. 1966. *Ulithi: A Micronesian Design for Living.* New York: Holt, Rinehart, and Winston.

Ulithi, a group of islands in the northwest Pacific (today part of Micronesia), was at the time of Lessa's research (1966) a thoroughly ranked society with a paramount chief over the entire island complex. Not only were lineages and villages ranked, but particular parcels of land and the resources on them were ranked as well. Each habitable island (some were too small for permanent settlement but might still be owned and used as farmland) contained one or more villages, and each village was headed by a council of elders, and the village council was headed by a *metang* or village chief. The villages were organized into eight districts, each of which contained a village and one or more outlying islands and was overseen by a district chief. Over all of the districts sat a top or paramount chief, who always came from the Lamathakh lineage. The chief of all Ulithi had some general powers in areas of justice and intra-Ulithi affairs, although his was not a role of command over the island chain. His main responsibility was in "external" political relations, particularly with the dominant island of Yap. Not only was Ulithi ranked internally, but it was part of a much larger ranking system that spanned many island chains and culminated in Yap, where "regional" power sat. In a kind of feudal relation, Yap was the lord of Ulithi, and Ulithi was the lord of even smaller islands to its east (Yap being the western-most end point of the "empire"). Yap itself was a caste society, with an exogamous upper caste that owned the land. Apparently the caste concept had spread from Yap to shape the relations between entire islands and island systems, in which Ulithi became the subordinate and paid respect and tribute to its overlord and in turn received respect and tribute from its own subordinates. Lessa suggested that these were not always happy relationships and that struggle and even war may have marked their pre-contact form.

State

a political system or level of integration in which a formal centralized government has power over a delimited territory to make and enforce laws, to establish currency and collect taxes, and to maintain an army and declare war

There were chiefs of villages, chiefs of particular hills, chiefs of districts, and chiefs of other chiefs, in interlocking allegiance and competition with each other. Individuals and families "below" a particular chief would pay gifts to their chief, who used that wealth both to "take care of his people" and to pay his own gifts to his higher chief. The paramount chief accepted gifts from the chiefs immediately below him, who accepted gifts from the chiefs below them, and so on, so that ultimately everyone was contributing indirectly to the paramount chief. When Europeans encountered this system, they found it quite convenient to exploit and manipulate for their own purposes, actually in some ways *increasing* chiefly power rather than dismantling it.

Chiefdoms are thus definitely more formal and explicit political relationships than anything we have seen before. Chiefs are not always such overt political and economic masters of their societies – in some societies, the chief is a symbolic or even ritual figure, perhaps even one who did not venture out of his "royal" compound and whose existence and health supposedly symbolized and determined the fate of the society – but most of the time their concrete effect on society is unquestionable. Chiefs obviously live off of the surplus of the economy, and they can in many cases compel (although this compulsion often takes the form of personal or religious obligation) contribution to it. A chief often "holds court," where important decisions are made and important problems are settled: "subjects" will "come to court" to get a hearing and a decision. The chief frequently even maintains a fighting force loyal to him, which he uses for external aggression as well as "control" of his own people. Some large and advanced chiefdoms, like the one on traditional Hawaii, have shaded into the next and final level of integration, the state.

State

The highest level of political integration achieved by humans (so far) is the **state**, which is the system with which Westerners are most familiar and under which they – and essentially all people of the world ultimately – live. By state, anthropologists do not mean the entities such as New York or Texas or California that Americans ordinarily call "states." These are not states in the anthropological use of the term but rather administrative units or sub-polities of the state (although, because of unique American history, "states" like New York retain some of the qualities of anthropological states). Rather, the United States is a state, the United Kingdom is a state, Mexico, Canada, Australia, Japan, France, Russia, Nigeria, India, and the other "countries" that one finds on political maps are states.

A state for the purposes of anthropology is a centralized political system with a formal government that has monopolistic power or "sovereignty" over a specific territory, including the power to make and enforce laws, to print money and collect taxes, and to maintain an army and declare war. A state is sovereign, that is, it is self-ruling or autonomous; there is no higher political power to which it must answer, certainly not the United Nations. (In fact, the United Nations might be better named the "United States," since all of its members are states, not nations.) If someday a trans-state or ultra-state polity arises – as some observers think the European Union is or might come to be – then there will be an even higher level of integration,

perhaps even to the level of a "world government," but no such thing exists today, and there are those who are opposed to such a development on both nationalistic and religious grounds.

States, which can achieve great size (up to hundreds of millions of people), depend on the most productive economic practices, namely intensive agriculture and industrialism. In fact, the first states (albeit small ones, merely independent cities or "city-states") appeared with the emergence of intensive agriculture in places like Mesopotamia, Egypt, India, and China, and later in Central America and Peru. What all of these societies had in common was a highly productive economy controlled by a powerful central government, often integrating military and religious power for the purpose of controlling territory and wealth. The size and density of society, especially the new social phenomenon called the "city" plus the elaborate stratification and specialization of society, was possible only because the new food-production methods were incredibly productive, yielding more than enough food for the farmers themselves. There was subsequently enough for a significant number of non-productive "specialists," including political leaders, religion authorities, and soldiers. Not

See Chapter 13

PLATE 9.5 State-level political systems, like the German one headed by Prime Minister Angela Merkel (pictured here) combine power and pageantry to control large, complex, and wealthy societies.

surprisingly, with the stockpiles of surplus in these societies and the male-dominated and hierarchical organization of politics, war was an inevitable and regular outcome.

State leaders still depend on their position as the center of a redistribution system, in which they can command not only production and labor but the contribution of that production and labor in the form of taxes or tribute or work on "public" projects like palaces, pyramids, roads, and city walls. In addition, the market plays a key role in state societies, and the state may exercise power over the market as well; the earliest cities and states were characterized by a marketplace. Certainly modern Western and Western-style governments manage their market economies (despite the ideology of "free markets") with centrally controlled monetary and banking institutions, like the Federal Reserve and the Federal Deposit Insurance Corporation, as well as domestic subsidies and international trade policies. States make rules and regulations for market players, tax those players, and protect them from players from other states.

Not all states have seen their primary business as business. In fact, the first states were probably more religious than economic institutions. The early Mesopotamian cities were "temple communities" where the priests and kings lived and which not only served as the religious and ritual center of society but lived off of the religious contributions of outlying rural inhabitants. This raises a critical point, which concerns the "legitimation" of this new social arrangement. Why would laborers, who work hard out in the countryside, participate in a system in which their labor and wealth is expropriated from them – in fact, in which they often constitute a poor and lower or "peasant" class? One answer to this question is religion. As the political power was centralized in the city and its ruler(s), so the religious power was centralized as well, and the two were closely identified. The king was often the chief priest (the ancient Roman ruler was also the *pontifex maximus*, from which the term "pontiff," a title for the Pope, is derived) or, in the case of ancient Egypt, an actual god himself. The diffuse and spiritualized religion of earlier societies became a centralized and ritualized religion of state power and prestige. Subjects participated in the political system because that was what the god(s) ordained; religion became a source of authority for the (new) political institutions.

Since state political integration is comparatively new to the human world, we need to see it as a specifically social and relative phenomenon. No states existed before 5,000 or 6,000 years ago, and many states have come and gone since then. States tend to emerge from social practices like war and political/cultural expansion; the early modern European states coalesced when local or regional rulers began to exercise their power and authority over larger areas and integrate them into a single political, economic, and cultural system, including things like a common currency, language, and set of weights and measures. Local communities and polities often resisted – and continue to resist – this "unification" and centralization. Even today, there are some disputes (some of international proportions) over what is or is not a state. Tibet is one example: many Tibetans consider their land a sovereign state, but China regards it as an historical part of China. Probably the most ominous debate is over the status of Taiwan, which was settled by refugees from Nationalist China when the Communists took control of the mainland in 1949. Today, Taiwan is less than a state but more than a territory of a larger state, with mutual defense treaties with the United States. However, China sees Taiwan as a rogue and separatist province of China (much as the United States saw the southern Confederacy during the Civil War) and intends to reintegrate it some day. When that day comes, there will be serious international ramifications. But the general point is that states are social concepts and social accomplishments, not "natural" or "real" entities.

State politics can take many forms, from monarchy and totalitarianism to democracy, with many economic arrangements from capitalist to socialist and communist. These are all merely ways of organizing state power and function. All of them – Mesopotamian and Greek city-states, empires, kingdoms, constitutional monarchies, capitalist democracies, socialist democracies, communist "people's republics," brutal autocracies, and even theocracies (like Khomeini's Iran or the Taliban's Afghanistan) – actually have much more in common with each other than with bands and tribes and chiefdoms. None of them contemplates doing away with borders, laws, capitals, taxes, or armies. Rather, they merely value different ways of arranging those social and political realities. Whether the state is one person (France's King Louis XIV famously

SOCIAL MEMORY AND THE STATE

BOX 9.7   THE QEMANT IN THE ETHIOPIAN STATE

While the term "peasant" is a problematic one in anthropology and economics, there are local communities and peoples who live within but at the margins of larger political systems in which they have little status or power. This reminds us that states are often composites of various societies or strata in complex and unequal relations. The Qemant were described by Gamst (1969) as a "peasantry" in modern Ethiopia, socially and politically distinct from the Amhara and Tegre, to whom they had been politically subordinate for 600 years. They were farmers who produced for their own subsistence and for selling at market as well as for paying taxes to the central government. Within their communities, they had their own three-level political system, including a council of elders at the bottom that ruled on most day-to-day matters of law and administration. There were both formal regular councils and informal ad hoc ones. Above that was a body of higher and lower priests, who mostly advised and assisted the highest level, the *wambar*, a religious/political leader who not only assessed political penalties like fines and even death but also spiritual ones like curses. The *wambar*, however, was subservient to the officials of the central government, and the entire local system enjoyed its autonomy at the indulgence of the Ethiopian state; in fact, Gamst noted that at any moment in history the freedom of the Qemant political institutions had depended inversely on the strength of central power, making the relationship an unstable and constantly moving one.

uttering, "I am the state") or "the people" (the U.S. Constitution starting with the words, "We the People"), states are the dominant ideas and forces in the modern world – at least until multinational corporations and ideologically based "civilizations" surfaced.

GOVERNMENTALITY: POWER BEYOND THE STATE

For the past few centuries, states have been the primary, if not the only legitimate, actors on the world stage. However, as noted above, the state is not a natural or necessary political arrangement, and historians and political scientists have described how modern states came to be formed, initially in Europe sometime after the year 1600 (and in the case of Italy or Germany, much later, well into the 1800s). The anthropological analysis of the state as a social form has recently added two crucial insights – first, that the state is not a single "thing" but a bundle of concepts, institutions, and practices, and second, that the state is not the sole site of these concepts, institutions, and practices. As Carole Nagengast (1994) put it, the state shares the political field with "sub-state" actors (class, race, ethnic, religious, etc. groups) and with "superstates"

or trans-state actors (e.g. global Islam, communism, or regional "families" of related societies or states often called "civilizations").

One of the key sources for thinking about the practices of the state – and the distribution or diffusion of those practices – is Michel Foucault, who advanced the notion of **governmentality**. Governmentality is not synonymous with government; rather, Foucault argued that modern "state" government was one recent variation of governmentality. Governmentality refers more generally to the forms of *power* that political actors of all sorts can marshal and manipulate, including not only the obvious tools of laws, police, courts, and armies but more subtle and widely diffused

methods of examination and evaluation; techniques of notation, numeration, and calculation; accounting procedures; routines for the timing and spacing of activities in specific locations; presentational forms such as tables and graphs; formulas for the organization of work; standardized tactics for the training and implantation of habits; pedagogic, therapeutic, and punitive techniques of reformulation and cure; architectural forms in which interventions take place (i.e. classrooms and prisons); and professional vocabularies.

(Lemke 2007: 50)

See Chapter 15

See Chapter 15

Governmentality
as formulated by Michel Foucault, the assorted practices, institutions, instruments, and discourses of power by means of which a "government" (state) or any other political entity can manage a population – and manage to get that population to manage itself

**Non-governmental
organization (NGO)**

any non-profit, voluntary
citizens' group which is
organized on a local,
national or international
level. Task-oriented and
driven by people with a
common interest, NGOs
perform a variety of service
and humanitarian functions,
bring citizen concerns to
governments, advocate and
monitor policies and
encourage political
participation through
provision of information

Council on Foreign
Relations http://www.
cfr.org/israel/hamas/p8968

World Association of
Non-Governmental
Organizations worldwide
NGO directory http://www.
wango.org/resources.aspx?
section=ngodir

Audit culture

a system of power between
scrutinizer and observed
which depends on cultural
concepts and norms –
an audit "repertoire"
– including "public
inspection," "submission
to scrutiny," "rendering
visible," and "measures of
performance"

See Chapter 14

States clearly do not enjoy a monopoly on the means of governmentality. First, all cultural institutions possess certain amounts and methods of governmentality, including corporations and colleges. Second, non-state and especially sub-state groups or categories may claim certain aspects of governmentality for themselves: ethnic or racial or class groups may contest the power of the state or even seize some of the functions commonly associated with the state. For instance, the "terrorist" organization Hamas also provides social services for the Palestinians of Gaza and operates schools, orphanages, healthcare facilities, soup kitchens, and sports leagues. Third and most remarkably, non-state institutions have been specifically created to assume some of the roles customarily associated with states.

One important expression of non-state governmentality is the **non-governmental organization** (NGO), defined by the NGO Global Network (www.ngo.org) as

> any non-profit, voluntary citizens' group which is organized on a local, national or international level. Task-oriented and driven by people with a common interest, NGOs perform a variety of service and humanitarian functions, bring citizen concerns to governments, advocate and

PLATE 9.6 A complex web of nongovernmental organizations provides much of the governmental structure of the modern world.

monitor policies and encourage political participation through provision of information. Some are organized around specific issues, such as human rights, environment, or health. They provide analysis and expertise, serve as early warning mechanisms and help monitor and implement international agreements.

Some examples of NGOs already encountered in this chapter include the World Wildlife Fund and the Belize Audubon Society (indeed, the international Audubon Society); there are many, many other special-interest NGOs, working in areas such as child protection, hunger and poverty, human rights, women's rights, peace, and so forth. The result is a thick web of national, regional, and international governmentality.

The relations of governmentality between states and non-state institutions are complex but critical. Non-state institutions can influence state policy through public opinion, political action, and even violence. As in the case of BAS in Belize above, such institutions can actually assume some of the functions of government, at which point "it becomes only too clear that NGOs are not as 'NG' as they might wish us to believe. Indeed, the World Bank baldly refers to what they call BONGOS (bank-organized NGOs) and even GONGOs (government-organized NGOs)" (Ferguson and Gupta 2002: 993). Indeed, the World Bank itself is an example of an intergovernmental organization (IGO) established *by states* to provide certain services of governmentality for states around the globe.

In short, then, the concept of governmentality redirects our focus from the "thing" called the state to the techniques of power that states *and other entities* can administer – that is, "practices instead of object, strategies instead of function, and technologies instead of institution" (Lemke 2007: 58). This takes the anthropology of power and politics to new places, for instance to what James Scott (1990) has called the "hidden transcripts" of power, a notion akin to Gramsci's "hegemony." Recently, though, attention has turned to a specific technique of governmentality, the audit. In 2000, Marilyn Strathern edited a volume examining **audit culture** in a discussion centering on academic institutions but equally applicable beyond them. Derived from the root for "hearing," an audit is a practice of monitoring, of checking results, of accountability. Cris Shore and Susan Wright, writing in Strathern's anthology, explicitly link auditing and audit culture to governmentality as "a relationship of power between scrutinizer and observed" which depends on cultural concepts and norms – an audit "repertoire" – including "'public inspection,' 'submission to scrutiny,' 'rendering visible,' and 'measures of performance'" (Shore and Wright 2000: 59). Associated with the rise of the audit culture is the view of the audited person or group "as a depersonalized unit of economic resource whose productivity and performance must constantly be measured and enhanced" (62), a change in the subjective experience of the audited person toward *self-monitoring*, and "the creation of new categories of experts including 'educational development consultants,' 'quality assurance officers,' 'staff development trainers,' and 'teaching quality assessors'" (62). All of these can be seen quite justifiably as micro-governmentality processes.

AN ANTHROPOLOGY OF WAR

Politics refers to both internal or domestic (intra-society or intra-state) social control and external or inter-society/inter-state social control, and one of the most important external or "foreign" political relations is war. It is by no means the only relationship between any two societies (many live in peace, or in tense mutual coexistence, or in occasional brief outbreaks of conflict, like raids and border skirmishes), nor is war the only form of political violence, which includes feuds, persecution, genocide, ethnic conflict, and others. There are those who might assert that an anthropology of war is unnecessary (war being simply a natural and instinctive trait of humans) or impossible (war being not a social phenomenon but the *breakdown* of society). But of course, whatever the status of the first claim, it is untrue that war is the absence or failure of social life or politics; after all, according to Clausewitz's classic study, war is the continuation of politics by other (deadly) means.

Anthropologists have, not surprisingly, devoted some attention to war. Malinowski himself wrote an essay entitled "An Anthropological Analysis of War" in which he defined it as "an armed contest between two independent political units, by means of organized military force, in the pursuit of a tribal or national policy" (1964: 247). Such an activity clearly requires at least two societies or states, with political interests and goals ("policies") and with sufficient social and political organization to field an army and prosecute an extended struggle.

Harry Turney-High therefore distinguished between what he called "modern" or "true" war and

Turney-High, Harry H. 1971. *Primitive War: Its Practice and Concepts.* Columbia, SC: University of South Carolina Press.

BOX 9.8 AUDIT CULTURE IN CONTEMPORARY CHINA

The concept of audit culture, and indeed of governmentality, is most often applied to "neoliberal" governments and economies, but there is no reason in principle why it should be so restricted. Yan Hairong finds that contemporary China is undergoing its own audit culture revolution in regard to *suzhi* or "quality," a term that "facilitates exploitation" of Chinese workers "*and* makes it invisible" (2003: 494). As Yan portrays it, there is a veritable crisis of *suzhi* in China today, with newspapers complaining of "the low *suzhi* of peasants [which] has become an excuse for many things not getting done or not getting done well" (495); President Jiang Zeming himself stressed the need for "cultivating millions of high-*suzhi* laborers and skilled technicians." Yan finds that "what *suzhi* is eludes precise definition" but that it seems to concern both "'hardware,' or embodied physical quality, and 'software,' which referred to a wide range of cultural qualities (*wenhua suzhi*), including psychological quality (*xinli suzhi*) and quality of consciousness (*sixiang suzhi*)" (496). Of course, before *suzhi* can be "improved" it must be quantified and measured, and "the most quantifiable index of *suzhi* is. . .wages" but other measures "include various kinds of psychological and practical ability tests and IQ tests offered by popular magazines" (497). Thus, as in all other instances of audit-culture governmentality, individuals are monitored and evaluated by authorities *and are encouraged to monitor and evaluate themselves.*

See Chapter 14

"primitive" or pre-modern or tribal war. True war, he insisted, includes tactical operations, command and control processes, "the ability to conduct a campaign for the reduction of enemy resistance if the first battle fails" (in other words, the ability to support a protracted military conflict, which involves a military institution like an army), a collective motive rather than a personal one, and "an adequate supply" which involves the organization of the entire society for the purpose and provisioning of war (Turney-High 1971: 30). By these standards, most pre-modern inter-society violence did not rise to the level of war. Combat practices of the Plains Indians of North America, who were more interested in "counting coup" by striking an enemy and retreating or stealing an enemy's horse than conquering or exterminating the enemy, would disqualify them. Raids or attacks out of personal interests like vengeance, jealousy, theft, or suspected witchcraft would also not constitute war; a classic example would be the Ok of highlands New Guinea, for whom "war" consisted of

> small-scale ambushes and raids, which probably produce the majority of casualties, as well as the rarer large-scale confrontations. . .and battles that are circumscribed by rules and conventions, such as the use of traditional fighting grounds. Confrontations or "nothing fights" escalate to all-out fighting with heavy casualties only infrequently. The proximate cause of particular incidents is the perceived need to retaliate for past wrongs summarized in the phrase *blood revenge*, often the murder or putative murder (by sorcery) of a group member by members of a neighboring group.
> (Morren 1984: 173)

Such are the reasons that Turney-High regarded the pre-modern fighter to be more of a "warrior" than a "soldier," the latter being a disciplined member of an extended military enterprise.

That war is a social institution or phenomenon is also evidenced in the amount of "social support" that it requires. This includes not only the logistics of war – the recruitment of large numbers of soldiers, the contributions of the non-combatants to the "war effort," the military and political decision-making systems, and the supply procedures to keep the armies fed and fueled in the field. As Turney-High rightly acknowledged, war depends on the social acceptance of war, constructed and maintained through warrior values, attitudes, norms, and rules. Among the martial values are high-minded principles like honor, bravery, patriotism, and self-defense and lower-minded ones like vengeance and the acquisition of war profits and trophies. Until very recently, war was typically seen as a glorious and manly undertaking; war preparedness is still a virtue, and participation in war is still widely regarded as "service to one's country." And, contrary to the image of war as anti-social chaos, there are indeed "rules of war" (codified in institutions like the Geneva Conventions) and standards for a "just war," such as not harming non-combatants and treating war prisoners humanely.

Not only is war orderly, but war can be constitutive of social order. Malinowski actually concluded – and he was by no means alone in this conclusion – that war produced the very state itself. The demands of centralization, of administration and decision-making, of recruitment and morale, required an institution like the state. And we can go far beyond Malinowski's view: war creates or sustains many other institutions, not the least of which are armies, war colleges, defense contractors, research institutes, hospitals, veterans' affairs offices, not to mention holidays (from Bastille Day to Veterans Day), parades, monuments, and many more.

Finally, we cannot overlook the cultural, even mythical, quality of war. War itself is a cultural or mythical condition, one that plays upon and activates the deepest meanings of a society. Chris Hedges has gone so far as to stress, as his book is titled, that war is a force that gives us meaning: "It can give us purpose, meaning, a reason for living. Only when we are in the midst of conflict does the shallowness and vapidness of much of our lives become apparent" (2002: 3). At such times, individuals transcend the individual existence and truly become part of a grander, sometimes even cosmic, endeavor.

**ANTHROPOLOGISTS
AT WAR**

BOX 9.9 CONTEMPORARY CULTURE CONTROVERSIES: IS WAR INEVITABLE?

Anthropologists, like the general public, have wondered whether war is an unavoidable, even instinctive, fact of human life. The discovery that some species of chimpanzee engage in "patrols" and deadly attacks against their own kind (but of "other groups") has led some to the depressing conclusion that humans have evolved to be warlike and aggressive. Steven Le Blanc for instance has claimed to find war at the very roots of human society; he writes that "We need to recognize and accept the idea of a nonpeaceful past for the entire time of human existence. . . . People in the past were in conflict and competition most of the time" (2003: 8). Others, like Douglas Fry, use the cross-cultural variation in violence – and the apparent absence of violence in some societies – to argue against the inevitability of war and even to show that a belief in war's inevitability is itself a dreadful thing: "The assumption that all societies are necessarily aggressive not only is incorrect but also poses a danger to world peace" (2006: xi), since, if war is "seen as natural, then there is little point in trying to prevent, reduce, or abolish it" (2). Here, perhaps more than almost anywhere else, the final conclusion from the anthropological evidence has profound consequences. What do you think?

SUMMARY

Every society has political functions that must be fulfilled, but not all have distinct and formal political institutions, separate from the economic and kinship and non-kin and religious roles and institutions of the society. The various functions can be encapsulated into social order and social control. Social control is achieved by a combination of

- Externalized controls
- Internalized controls

The agents of social control who make up the external controls have a variety of sanctions at their disposal, and, while formal agents can and do impose heavy pressures for proper behavior, most sanctions are informal and personal. In fact, all members of a society are informal agents of social control on each other.

Politics is the exercise of power, with different sources and different qualities:

- Authority
- Persuasion
- Coercion

Therefore, based on their level of political integration, including the types and roles of power, political systems can be distinguished into

- Band
- Tribe
- Chiefdom
- State

MCQS

FILL IN THE BLANKS

In the twenty-first-century world, states are not the only actors on the world stage. Many of the powers and functions of the state have been shared by, transferred to, or usurped by non-state groups or organizations, showing that governmentality is a set of practices that can be diffused through and layered in a society or in the entire international community. Governmentality directs attention away from "state" or "government" to power and the distribution and practices of power.

Finally, war is an endemic, if not entirely inevitable, aspect of modern politics. Contrary to the sense that war is anti-social, anthropologists have discovered that war tends to be, even needs to be, socially organized and that war can even produce elements of culture and society.

Key Terms

Agents of social control

Audit culture

Authority

Band

Chiefdom

Coercion

Externalized control

Formal sanction

Governmentality

Informal sanction

Internalized control

Level of political integration

Leveling mechanism

Non-governmental organization

Office

Peasant

Persuasion

Sanction

Social control

State

Symbolic capital

Tribe

Religion

Interacting with the non-human world

The indigenous Lenca people of Western Honduras are renowned for their pottery, but the materials necessary to make clay pots – namely, the claybeds, sand deposits, and colored soils – are scarce. Therefore, the society practices a form of group ownership of and communal access to these valuable resources. No member of the society can be prevented from using the resources, and no one may bar access to the sites or the paths that lead to the sites. However, worldly rules are not the only guarantees of good behavior. The Lenca claim that every place has a protector spirit or angel; the crucial claybed is owned and protected by Benigna, "a powerful earth spirit who punishes any potter who uses clay without respect" (Tucker 2010: 47). In addition, humans must make a periodic offering, *pago a la tierra* or "payment to the earth," to the spirit for use rights. Benigna and the spirits of other sites and resources "could wreak vengeance on a potter who fails to honor them," including "preventing potters from finding good clay and fine sand, breaking pots during tempering, or causing lengthy illnesses for the potter or her family" (48). Catherine Tucker concludes that the "intersection of socioeconomic, institutional, and spiritual factors facilitates the maintenance of

PLATE 10.1 A Lenca (Honduras) woman and her pottery.

common-property regimes" for these important cultural assets (49).

Religion has received extraordinary attention from anthropologists and the general public alike. One reason for this fascination among Western observers is religion's drama and color, if not its "strangeness." If anything, religion cross-culturally takes an even more dazzling array of shapes than the other areas of culture, which might be expected since it is the least constrained by practical or material concerns. This is not to say that religion is totally unrelated to the practical or the material, as the Lenca case above illustrates. Rather, it is to say that, at its more abstract level, religion is less determined – although still powerfully influenced and shaped – than other levels of culture.

Another reason why religion has attracted observers, while simultaneously repelling them, is the way in which it challenges one's own most basic conceptions of what is true and real, one's "ontology." Geertz (1973) even characterized religion as the realm of the "really real," those beliefs and behaviors and imperatives and institutions that are most important, most permanent, most "given" (literally, often given or ordained by the religious beings themselves), and most compulsory. However, scholars studying religion cross-culturally cannot help but notice that different societies have different notions of what is religiously real and that one's familiar ways of talking about religion and the real often do not apply.

The anthropology of religion, then, more than any other area of culture, not only has the task of describing and explaining the diversity of its forms and manifestations but also of reflecting back on our own practices and concepts. Just as the analysis of kinship forces us to ponder the definition and diversity of marriage, or the analysis of politics forces us to ponder the definition and diversity of power, so the analysis of religion forces us to ponder the definition and diversity of concepts like "god" and "spirit" and "supernatural" and the very notion of "belief" itself.

THE PROBLEM OF STUDYING RELIGION ANTHROPOLOGICALLY

The anthropological approach to religion, as to all other facets of culture, requires a cross-cultural,

holistic, and relativistic perspective. That is, we must consider all the variations of religion found among humans, search for the interconnections between religion and the rest of culture (not the least of which are language, politics, and gender), and understand and judge religion only in the terms of the society in which we find it and never merely our own. This is more difficult for religion than for other facets of culture, precisely because religion *does* seem to deal with the "real" in ways that the rest of culture does not. That is, it is hard to imagine someone (at least someone having reached any level of anthropological awareness) saying that their language is "true" or that their economic practices or political systems are "true." Language is easily recognized as culturally relative; it makes no sense to claim that English is "truer" or "better" than Spanish or Japanese or Warlpiri. However, people are much more comfortable asserting that their religion is "true"; in fact, it may be hard not to assert so.

Early (and not so early) researchers were attracted to but at the same time distanced themselves from the religious beliefs and practices they viewed and reported, in a way that is unusual if not unthinkable for most cultural behaviors. For example, James Frazer, the author of the massive comparative mythology *The Golden Bough*, testified that "I look upon [the myths] not merely as false but as preposterous and absurd" (1958: vii). Of magic he concluded that "every single profession and claim put forward by the magician as such is false" (53). E. E. Evans-Pritchard, writing on witchcraft among the Azande of Africa, asserted: "Witches, as the Azande conceive them, cannot exist" (1937: 63). They follow a long tradition, back to the historian Herodotus, who wrote: "My duty is to report all that is said, but I am not obliged to believe it all" (1942: 556).

It is obviously not an anthropological attitude to refute, let alone to disparage as "absurd," another culture's ideas and behaviors. Religion, then, has proven to be a place where relativism and objectivity are most challenged. Unlike other parts of culture, religion makes truth-claims about the world: this or that god or spirit or force or being, such as a witch, "really exists." For those who do not share the truth-claim – who think, as Evans-Pritchard did, that witches do not exist – the beliefs they investigate are false. So the "contents" of

Evans-Pritchard. E. E. 1937. *Witchcraft, Oracles, and Magic Among the Azande*. New York: Oxford University Press.

BOX 10.1 THE JINN "SPIRITS" OF ISLAM

According to Amira El-Zein, the jinn were an important part of classical Islam. While we might be inclined to call them "spirits" – more specifically, "angels" or "demons" or "dead souls" – El-Zein insists that none of these words describes them. Jinn "are intelligent and subtle beings" (2009: xv), like humans in many ways, including their free will and ultimately answerability to God. Also like humans, they lived in tribes and nations; they interacted with and occasionally fell in love with humans. They were not completely immaterial: scholars speculated over whether the jinn had bodies of light or fire, although they were able to become invisible or to change their form, sometimes assuming the shape of animals. They could carry information to humans, but they could also cause disease, misfortune, and possession. Ultimately, they were seen as another kind of being in the great scale of beings but actually spiritually inferior to humans, who were the sole inheritors of God's power and truth.

religion, as mutually incompatible truth-claims, clash in ways that differing languages or economic systems do not; *your* language or economic system does not render *mine* false.

From their experience with jinn as well as other religious notions, anthropologists have come to realize that many religious terms are loaded with highly cultural-bound meaning: a word like "spirit" tends to imply immaterial, disembodied existence, but not all religions attribute such traits to their "spiritual beings." Worse yet, not all religions include concepts like "god" or "heaven" or "sin," nor "karma" or "nirvana," etc. Therefore we cannot assume that all religions speak and think alike, nor may we use one religion's terms and concepts like neutral analytical tools to describe other religions. Rodney Needham has suggested that the very notion of "belief" itself is culturally relative and that not all cultures use it with the same meaning – or use it at all. "We have discovered grounds to conclude that the concept of belief is not expressed in all languages," therefore "we are not sharing their apprehension and are not understanding their thought if we foist this typically Western distinction on to them" when they do not possess it themselves (1972: 175).

Defining religion

The first problem in the anthropological study of religion is determining what religion is, that is, defining religion. E. B. Tylor offered what he considered to be the "minimal" definition that could apply to all observed cases of religion: *belief in spiritual beings*. But as simple and compact as it is, it faces at least one problem: it introduces another term, "spiritual being," that requires a definition. If by this we mean "beings without a physical body," then jinn would not count as spirits and believing in jinn would not count as religion.

Since Tylor's day, anthropologists have suggested a plethora of definitions for religion, sometimes emphasizing belief, sometimes behavior, sometimes **myth** or **ritual**, and so on. They are too numerous to count or recount here, but three influential ones include the following:

> a unified system of beliefs and practices relative to sacred things, that is to say, things set aside and forbidden – beliefs and practices which unite into one single moral community called a Church, all those who adhere to them.
>
> (Durkheim 1965 [1915]: 62)

> a set of rituals, rationalized by myth, which mobilizes supernatural powers for the purpose of achieving or preventing transformations of state in man and nature.
>
> (Wallace 1966: 107)

> a system of symbols which act to establish powerful, pervasive, and long-lasting moods and motivations in men by formulating conceptions of a general order of existence and clothing these conceptions with such an aura of factuality that the moods and motivations seem uniquely realistic.
>
> (Geertz 1973: 90)

Myth
a narrative, usually of the activities of supernatural beings, often telling of how some or all of the natural or social world was established. In addition to an "explanation" of origins, it also provides a "charter" or model for how humans should live today

Ritual
any type of formal, repetitive behavior that is felt to have significance beyond the actions themselves. In particular, religious ritual is often composed of symbols, re-enacts supernatural/mythical events, and is believed to have efficacy if performed correctly

Needham, Rodney. 1972. *Belief, Language, and Experience*. Chicago, IL: University of Chicago Press.
Durkheim, Emile. 1965 [1915]. *The Elementary Forms of the Religious Life*. New York: The Free Press.
Wallace, Anthony F. C. 1966. *Religion: An Anthropological View*. New York: Random House.

PLATE 10.2 Religions convey belief and meaning in symbols, like this golden Buddha in Thailand.

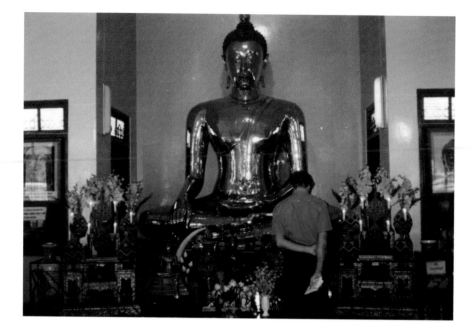

Even more, Anthony Wallace proposed that religion is not a "thing" or distinct and unitary phenomenon at all but a composite of lower-level building blocks, built upon the "supernatural premise" that supernatural beings or forces exist. Then, thirteen "categories of religious behavior" (such as prayer, music, myth, sacrifice, physical "exercises," etc. – many or all of which have their non-religious counterparts) are combined in particular ways in any given religion. These are further combined into religious or "cult" institutions which are finally combined into "a religion." Thus religion is

> essentially a summative notion and cannot be taken uncritically to imply that one single unifying, internally coherent, carefully programmed set of rituals and beliefs characterizes the religious behavior or the society or is equally followed by all its members.
>
> (78)

Contemporary scholars like Pascal Boyer (2001) and Scott Atran (2002) have expanded on this approach, Boyer for instance asserting that religion is a "by-product" of "mental systems and capacities that are there anyway, religious concepts or not" (311). If this is the case, then like belief for Needham, the "notion of religion as a special domain is not just unfounded but in fact rather ethnocentric" (311).

We cannot settle these questions here. What we need to do is to place religion in its proper cultural and adaptive context – not so much to see what it *is* as what it does and the various ways that it manages to do what it does. Therefore, let us offer the following not as a definition of religion but as an orienting statement for further study and discussion: *Religion is the parts of culture that involve ideas, and the associated actions and objects and institutions, about non-human and often "super"-human being(s) and/or force(s) that enter into "social" relationships with humans.* This statement is intentionally vague about the types of ideas, actions, objects, and institutions as well as their causal connection (i.e. which comes first). It also avoids slippery qualities like "spiritual" or "divine" and allows for the maximum flexibility and inclusiveness. Perhaps most importantly, it emphasizes that there is some reciprocal relationship between humans and the entities of religious interest. Humans must be able to interact with them, and them with us, in some ways, for good or ill. Humans must be able to communicate their desires, understandings, and problems to those entities and they to us.

In this sense, the relationship between humans and their religious entities is a *social relationship*. It is a relationship of agency, communication, intention, reciprocity, respect, avoidance, control, etc. The being(s) and/or force(s) *are like us* in some ways, despite the fact that they are greatly unlike us in others. They may have a language (usually ours), personality or will, desires and interests, and likes and dislikes. They can be approached and influenced. This takes us to the significance of religion as a cultural factor and its critical distinction from the other domains of culture. Economics, kinship, and politics are comprised of humans. People produce, distribute, and consume food. Kin are people. Political leaders are people, and the powers they have and the rules they make are human ones. But the entities that inhabit the religious world are not humans. They are non-humans: plants or animals or natural objects (the sun and the moon) or natural forces (the wind and the rain), or the dead ancestors, or non-human spirits or gods. Yet *they are social, they are part of society*. As Robin Horton phrased it, "In short, Religion can be looked upon as an extension of the field of people's social relationships beyond the confines of purely human society" (1960: 211).

In other words, religion is the system or the discourse through which human society and culture is expanded to include the non-human. Or, ultimately, it projects humanness on the non-human world, so that humans are not the only persons in the universe. Irving Hallowell told a story of an Ojibwa informant who, when asked if all rocks and trees are people, answered, "No, but some are" (1967: 28). A friend of mine, a senior Osage Indian, told another story of accompanying a spiritual leader to gather stones for a ceremony; asking how the leader would know which stones to gather, he responded, "The stones will tell me."

Throughout this book we have talked about how human actions and symbols and meanings "culturize" nature (e.g. sex and gender). Now we can conclude that religion takes this process further, perhaps as far as it can go, in "culturizing" supernature and simultaneously "supernaturalizing" culture. Human behavior and culture are seen in some ways to apply to the supernatural realm, while human behavior and culture are seen to depend on or come from the supernatural realm as well. The two – human and non/superhuman – become interdependent and mutually defining and sustaining.

Functions of religion

Why do humans have such a thing as religion, and what does it do for them? We can identify a diverse set of potential functions, each of which spawns a particular theoretical angle on religion. Malinowski emphasized religion's role in filling individual needs, especially psychological or emotional needs, such as comfort, hope, perhaps love, definitely a sense of control, and relief from fear and despair. A. R. Radcliffe-Brown, in a theory known as structural functionalism, insisted that society has its own needs, particularly the need for cohesion, solidarity, integration, and perpetuation. So, in times of crisis, or just in the ordinary course of events, people might drift apart or even blow apart, ending "society" altogether. Religion's shared beliefs, shared values, and shared activities (prayers, rituals, sacrifices, etc.) not only provide things to do together to get through the hard times but make them more alike, give them a sense of shared identity and shared destiny. Partly this position is derived from Durkheim, who focused on the social force which results from ritual behavior, creating almost a "group mind," a collective conscience, or at least a common experience.

Assessing these and other functions of religion, we can condense them into three main categories:

1 Explanation, especially of origins or causes. Humans wonder why things are as they are. How did the world start? How did humans start? How did society start? Most religions not only include cosmogony (the creation of the world) but the origin of specific cultural institutions, like marriage, language, technology, politics, and the like. Religions also explain why things happen in the present: why do we get sick? Why do bad things happen to us? Why do we die? In some societies, much if not all of sickness and misfortune is attributed to religious causes, as was true in Western society not so very long ago and still is for some people.

2 Control, both of culture and of nature. Religion has, in all societies, an inherently "political" function, to guide human behavior in certain directions; which directions in particular depends on the society and religion. So, religion provides rules and standards, sometimes quite explicit and formal ones (like the Judeo-Christian "Ten Commandments") as well as implicit and informal ones. It also provides models or paradigms of behavior: Christians are taught to imitate Christ (many literally

See Chapter 5

Hallowell, A. Irving. 1967 [1955]. *Culture and Experience*. New York: Schocken Books.

See Chapters 11 and 15

determine their behavior based on WWJD – what would Jesus do?), and Muslims hold up Muhammad as the paragon of human virtue. Finally, it provides sanctions and agents and institutions (human and non-human) to impose those sanctions, from sickness or misfortune to excommunication and eternal damnation. Religion also asserts itself as a means to control the physical world, including the human body. Religion may offer processes to control the wind and the rain, the fertility of land or animals, and the health of humans: curing rituals really are intended to drive out illness, and "black magic" really is intended to harm one's enemies.

3 Legitimation, of cultural and natural realities. Humans appear to need to legitimate or justify the arrangements of society and nature to themselves, that is, not merely to explain why some fact exists (like death or kingship) but *why it should exist, why it is right and good.* Why is it not only true but proper that women suffer in childbirth? Why is it not only true but desirable to have a king? Christianity has answered these questions with doctrines like the sin of Eve and the divine right of kings. In each case, either a spirit or ancestor set the precedent, or a supernatural figure made the choice. All religions meet the challenge of legitimating the reigning order by containing some element of "order-establishment" or "culture-establishment." This is the charter function of religion as identified by Malinowski (see below): it acts as the guideline or authority or "charter" by which humans organize themselves in particular ways and follow particular standards. Of course, there are many types of legitimation, such as popular opinion or majority vote. But religious legitimation is superior to any human legitimation, since the supernatural beings or forces – the "authors" of the religiously given order – have the "authority" to create order and are not subject to the imperfections and indecisions of humans.

In terms of these three functions, religion can be seen as a generally conservative force. Yet, with its rules, authorities, and institutions all in place, it can also be a powerful medium for change and protest – for adjusting to, challenging, resisting, and creating social relations. As we will see below, often the first change or resistance movements in a society take a religious form, and many of the most important movements for cultural change in the world today are religious in character.

THE ELEMENTS OF RELIGION: SUPERHUMAN ENTITIES AND HUMAN SPECIALISTS

Compared to economics and kinship and politics, typologies of religion are even less useful, since actual religions tend to defy or mix types in ways that make the typology fruitless; the conventional "types" of religion are not mutually exclusive and in fact can and often do coexist. Following the suggestion of Wallace, Boyer, and Atran, it may be more productive to consider the building blocks out of which any particular religion is constructed, rather than to attempt to find essences of different religious types. Therefore, this section presents two broad and interlinked categories of components of religion – religious entities and human specialists – within which vast diversity is possible and between which complex relationships are common.

Religious entities: beings and forces

The qualities of a religion will depend largely on what kinds of entities it posits as real and important. This area is often referred to as the "beliefs" of the religion, but that term is misleading and potentially ethnocentric, as we noted above. There are two general subcategories of religious entities – beings and forces – which can and often do appear together in any actual religion.

Beings

Tylor's minimal definition of religion depended on spiritual beings. Now, all of the beings that humans ordinarily meet and interact with are physical or material – that is, they have corporeal bodies, they occupy space, they are constrained by laws of motion, they age and die, etc. Spiritual beings are different in some (but not necessarily all) ways. In some versions they do not have physical bodies, or

CONSTRUCTION OF RELIGIOUS EXPERIENCE

they might not occupy space or might be able to share the same space as physical bodies, or they can move and act in ways that defy natural law, or they may not age or die (i.e., are "immortal" or at least "less mortal"). That leaves much room for elaboration across religions. But the one thing that spiritual beings have in common is that they are *beings*, that is, that they are individuals with some degree of will and mind and personality of their own. One possible distinction among spiritual beings is whether they are or once were human or whether they are fundamentally non-human – although the human/non-human boundary is a permeable one too.

One of the most persistent ideas across cultures is that humans themselves have a spiritual part or parts, which cohabits with the body to some extent and which survives the body after death. In the Christian tradition, the **soul** is an eternal, immaterial, indivisible, personal (that is, it preserves the individual's personality) entity. Not all religions have such a concept, and those that have it often have very different notions about it. According to the Buddhist teaching of *anatta* or "no soul," the human spiritual part is not a permanent unchanging essence but rather is in constant flux. Other religions speak of multiple souls or a soul with multiple parts. The Tausug of the Philippines said that humans were composed of four parts: the body, the mind, the "liver" or emotion, and the "soul." The soul also had four parts: the transcendent soul, which was all-good and always in the spiritual realm, even while one was alive; the life-soul, which was related to the blood and attached to the body but which wandered from the body in dreams; the breath, which was the essence of life and always attached to the body; and the spirit-soul, the person's "shadow" (Kiefer 1972).

The Huron of North America talked of two souls or *atisken*. Both were the same size and shape as the body, and one remained with the body after death while the other departed (Trigger 1969). The Konyak Nagas of India identified several different soul-parts that separated at death: the *yaha* contained the individual's personality and went off to the land of the dead, while the *mia* stayed attached to the skull (which explains their practice of head-hunting), and the *hiba* became a ghost if the person died a violent death (Von Fuerer-Haimendorf 1969). Finally, the Dusun of Borneo mentioned

seven soul-parts, one inside the other, the smallest the width of the little finger and the largest the thickness of the thumb. They were not born full-sized but grew as the body grew. The six "outside" souls or *magalugulu* were visible in human form, but the innermost soul or *gadagada* was formless and invisible (Williams 1965).

The spiritual fate of deceased humans also varies from society to society. Even in technologically advanced societies, many people believe that the dead can become ghosts. **Ghosts** are spiritual parts of dead humans that continue to exist and participate in the human world, usually to our detriment. Downs (1972) said that among the Navajo a ghost was the evil part of a dead person, so there were no good ghosts by definition. In Spiro's renowned study of Burmese religion (1978), he found that the dead could become *leikpya* if they did not receive a proper funeral or if they were powerful and ambitious people in their lifetime (like government officials), in which case they haunted their former house or village. Among the Anuta of the Solomon Islands, ghosts were one type of *atua* or "common spirits" that were recently deceased humans and looked like humans only bigger and stronger (Feinberg 1996). In other cases, humans may be dead but still "active" in the physical world, as in the case of the vampire or the zombie, both of whom are dead individuals who have somehow been reanimated but without a soul.

Ghosts and similar manifestations are therefore one possible destination for deceased humans. In other cases, dead people may carry on as **ancestor spirits**, although there is no clear dividing line between the two. Ancestor spirits may be benevolent or malevolent; it is not always correct to speak of "ancestor worship," since not all societies worshipped their dead ancestors, or even particularly liked them. The Swazi of South Africa regarded their ancestors as possessing "greater wisdom, foresight, and power" than the living but not divine or omnipotent; they were still "practical beings" (Kuper 1963: 60). Kuper also noted that ancestors were not as important to the Swazi as nature spirits. For the Dinka as for many peoples with strong lineage systems, the clan spirits or *yieth* were their prime concern, even more so than their god and their "independent spirits" or *jak*. *Yieth* spirits tended to be "partial [to humans] and protective," but they could also be punitive, in which case they

Ghost
a religious or spiritual being, generally regarded to be the disembodied spiritual part of a deceased human

Spiro, Melford. 1978 [1967]. *Burmese Supernaturalism*, expanded edition. Philadelphia, PA: Institute for the Study of Human Issues.

Soul
a religious concept of a non-material component or components of a living human. It is widely believed that a soul survives the death of the body, at least temporarily, and continues in another form of existence

Ancestor spirits
the spirits of dead family members who are believed to continue to reside near and interact with their living kin

BOX 10.2   THE AMBIGUOUS ANCESTORS OF THE JU/HOANSI

Ju/hoansi religion was a complicated mixture of virtually all of the entity-types discussed in this chapter. At the center of their focus were the *//gangwasi* or *//gauwasi* spirits of their dead kin. According to Lee (1984) and Katz (1982), the Ju/hoansi came close to dreading their ancestors, for two reasons. First, the gods tended to work through the ancestors as intermediaries, so that much divine punishment or misfortune came by way of the ancestors. Second, they thought that the *//gangwasi* caused a great deal of misfortune directly. Some Ju/hoansi reported that there were good and bad spirits, but others said that it was the position of the dead vis-à-vis the living that was the problem. As one woman expressed it,

> Longing of the living is what drives the dead to make people sick. When they go on the road that leads to the village of the *//gangwasi* they are very, very sad. Even though they will have food and company and everything they need there, they are not content. They miss their people on earth. And so they come back to get us. They hover near the villages and put sickness into people, saying, "Come, come here to me."

(Lee 1984: 109)

Hence much of Ju/hoansi curing activity was aimed at the ancestors, who may be fought off in curing ceremonies with words like "What business do you have here tonight? This man is not ready to go. He wants to remain with those who love him" (Katz 1982: 41).

---

recruited the *jak* to do their dirty work. In other words, "there is much crisscrossing in which spirits protect or injure people with justification, or as their whims may dictate" (Deng 1972: 123). On the other hand, the Huron of North America, who did not keep detailed genealogies, did not appear to have any ancestor-spirit concepts at all (Trigger 1969).

Finally, in other cases, not all individuals necessarily reached the ancestral realm. For the Anuta, only dead chiefs and other prominent people continued to be powerful after death. Such beings were named and venerated through prayer, song, and story, the greatest among them being Tearakura, an ancient chief turned culture hero and virtual deity (thus closing the gap between human spirits and "gods") (Feinberg 1996).

If humans had or could become spiritual beings, it stands to reason that other things might also have/be spirits. Perhaps the most common of these are the "nature spirits," the spirits that are or are in plants and/or animals and/or natural objects and/or natural forces. **Animism**, derived from the Latin *anima* for "breath" or "spirit" (the non-material part of a living thing that gives it life or motion), is the general conception that non-human beings can

and do have spiritual parts too. It is not always the case that every non-human thing is "animated." For the Warlpiri, some trees and rocks have spirit and some do not; they can point at one tree and say that it is "just a tree," while another of the same species is a spirit, just as the Ojibwa man told Hallowell that some rocks are persons. Also, in any society some animal and plant species were spiritual, while others were merely natural beings. A relationship between humans and non-human beings, sometimes called **totemism**, established a spiritual association between an individual or social group (family, clan, village, etc.) and a particular species, such that the person or group recognized the species as their "totem." ("Totem" is another case of applying a concept from one society – in this case, Ojibwe society – to other religions.) Humans and their totems were sometimes believed to share the same spirit or substance, and societies might observe taboos against harming or eating the totem.

The animistic spirits of plants and animals, etc., could be individual or collective – that is, each individual being may have a spirit, or there may be a spirit of all of them (say, a generic "bear spirit"). Ainu religion contained a vast number of spirits; in

---

Totemism

a religious conception that human individuals or groups have a symbolic or spiritual connection with particular natural species, objects, or phenomena

Animism

a type of religious belief in which natural objects (animals, plants, hills, lakes, moon, etc.) and forces (wind, rain, etc.) have spiritual components that interact socially with humans fact, they regarded all species (and practically all objects) as "soul-owning." Even artifacts like tools and utensils had souls. Accordingly, those beings and objects had to be treated with respect, like the "people" that they were. Hunting thus was never a purely material activity, since it involved interacting with spirits that could anger and withdraw cooperation; in other words, hunting was seen as a kind of "reciprocity" between human and animals/spirits. Also, at the end of its "life" a soul-owning being – human or otherwise – deserved a decent burial. For animals, a proper location, a bone pile or *keyohniusi*, was maintained for each species, and even household objects had a "final resting place." Rituals had to be performed as part of the disposal, "since their negligence brings forth much suffering, mostly in the form of illness" (Ohnuki-Tierney 1974: 87).

Sometimes the spirits had personal names; sometimes they were only vaguely and collectively known. Sometimes they were associated with specific locations or physical objects; sometimes they were diffuse and amorphous. They may be good, bad, or indifferent from a human point of view; they may be helpful, harmful, mischievous, or even unaware of their effect on humans. The Burmese villagers in Spiro's research told him about the *nat* spirits, which included three categories. The first were native spirits that resided in trees and hills and fields and bodies of water. The basic idea was that they guarded their domains, were "petty and irascible," and overall made the world a more dangerous place (1978: 47). The second category were the *devas* or Buddhist spirits, who were good and moral; the higher *devas* were too distant to be matters of ritual or speculation, but the lower ones took a positive interest in humans. (Spiro states that some of these lower *devas* were "gods" in the Western sense and that they were the spirits of former especially pious humans, bridging all four types of beings – humans, ancestors, spirits, and gods.) Finally, the "thirty-seven *nats*" were regarded as evil. Each was known by its name and myth, and each had to be appeased with offerings of food.

The volume and diversity of spirit-concepts are too great to discuss here in detail. Such beings included demons, devils, and any of a wide array of culturally local characters such as ogres (*bilus* in Spiro's Burmese village, which might be the spirits of deformed babies), fairies, elves, sprites, muses, furies, *jinns* or genies, and many others.

A final type of religious being is a god. There is no universal definition for a god, but they tend to be extremely powerful, usually creative, and comparatively remote spiritual beings. Many societies that recognized gods (and not all did) did not attempt to communicate or relate directly to those gods because they were so distant but rather approached them through lower-level spiritual intermediaries. The Ju/hoansi, for instance, included two gods in their religious system, a high god *Gao Na* and a lower god *Kauha*; however, most attention was directed to the ancestors. Across religions, some gods were highly personal and moral, while others were not. The sky god of the Konyak Nagas intervened in the moral affairs of humans; the god of the Azande, named *Mboli* or *Mbori*, was morally neutral and uninvolved in human moral business.

A religion that focuses primarily on god(s) is called a **theism** (from the Greek *theo-* or *deo-* for god, which also gives English the word "deity"). In any particular theism there may be one or more than one god, and gods are seldom if ever the only spiritual beings in the system, i.e. gods typically coexist in a religion with human spirits, nature spirits, ancestor spirits, and other supernatural entities (like angels or devils or jinn). A theistic religion that contains multiple gods is a **polytheism**, and a theistic religion that contains one god is a **monotheism**. Ancient Greek religion is a familiar example of polytheism, with its "pantheon" (from *pan-* for all) of gods residing on Mount Olympus. The Greek gods were not always good or "moral" (some of them did very reprehensible things, even in Greek eyes), nor were they always eternal or immortal (many Greek gods were born, often from other Greek gods, and many died). Judaism, Christianity, and Islam constitute the dominant monotheisms in the world, although there are other smaller and newer religions that hold the notion of a single god (like Baha'i).

Theism can take a few other forms. For instance, many of the colonial American leaders practiced **deism**, the position that there is or was a god who created the world and put it in motion but then withdrew from it; this god is more or less "impersonal" and may take no active part in the daily affairs of humans at all (thus Azande theism resembles deism). Finally, some thinkers have come to the conclusion that god is everything and everything is god, a belief known as **pantheism**. Some

Theism
the religious belief in one or more gods

Polytheism
the religious belief in two or more gods

Monotheism
the form of theism that includes belief in only one god/goddess

Deism
the form of theism or belief in god(s) that posits a creator god that does not take an active role or moral interest in human affairs

Pantheism
a form of theism in which it is believed that "everything" is god, that the universe and all of the material world is the same thing as god, that god is "immanent" in and coextensive with the physical world

BOX 10.3   THE GODS OF ULITHI

On the Pacific atoll of Ulithi, people knew many different gods, none of which, however, were active in the creation of the universe. In fact, Lessa (1966) proclaimed that there was not even a creation story in Ulithi religion. The highest god was *Ialulep*, who was seen as a very large white-haired person, old and feeble; he controlled the lives of humans by holding their "thread of life" and determined their death by breaking the thread. His son *Lugeilang* was not a paragon of virtue: he lusted after human women and sired the trickster god *Iolofath* who had many misadventures. A pantheon of other gods – earth gods – existed in a kind of supernatural division of labor. For instance, *Palulap* was the Great Navigator, the god of ocean navigation. His son *Ialulwe* (a being with four or more eyes) was the patron of sailors. *Solang* was the god or patron of canoe-building. *Ligafas*, a goddess and daughter of *Palulap*, ruined the canoe in which her divine family was riding, leading to the human restriction that menstruating women should not sail the sea. Finally, there was *Solal*, the god of the underworld as well as patron of certain magicians. On other islands in the Carolines he was held to be equal to the great god *Ialulep*, although Ulithians did not grant him such high status.

mystical traditions within larger religious systems, and to an extent the entire system of Hinduism, maintain that the whole universe is really god or the "mind of god" or one great cosmic soul (the *brahman* in Hinduism), of which the human soul (*atman*) is a small alienated piece.

Forces

Not all religions include beings, and many of those that do include beings include other entities as well. There are also recurring conceptions of impersonal spiritual forces – ones that do not necessarily have an individual "mind" or "will." Often these forces are more like "spiritual water" or "spiritual electricity" – a (super)naturally occurring power that exists in and flows through nature, giving it the qualities that we find there. The usual name given to this religious conception is **animatism**.

The classic example of a spiritual force is *mana* as understood in numerous Pacific Island cultures. Mana was an energy or power that presented itself in material objects, including people, but was not inherent in them; that is, it was a separate "thing" from them and could come and go. It was in the interest of a person, then, to know, use, and accumulate mana if possible, since luck, strength, virtue, and many good results came from having or controlling it. Likewise, a person without mana was destined to be unlucky, weak, and unsuccessful. Most English-speakers also have heard of the

Chinese animatistic principle of *chi*. It is probably a very ancient idea but is most clearly and poetically described in the *Tao Te Ching*, a book attributed to a sage named Lao Tze about the *tao* or the "way" or "path" of nature and the *chi* that informs it. The *tao* flows like water (water is the most often-used analogy for it), taking the path of least resistance. Thus, the person who would live well should go with the *tao*, leading to such insights as "Do nothing and leave nothing undone" or "The best ruler is he who rules least." The general idea is that human will, when it goes against the *tao* (as it usually does), ends in struggle, difficulty, and wasted effort; it is like trying to swim upstream. The wise person "goes with the flow," letting the force of (super)nature take him or her where it will.

Spiritual forces can take many other shapes. The Dusun worried about "luck," which was a finite spiritual resource of each individual that, if spent in one area of life, could endanger other areas (e.g., acquisition of property, success in disputes, etc.). Luck was also finite in society, making one person's gain in it another person's loss; this naturally led to arguments about surreptitious efforts to steal or damage each other's luck. In Apache religion the power was known as *diyi*, which was in infinite supply. Many forms of this power were recognized, related to different animals or natural phenomena. And unlike many such forces, *diyi* did in fact have some "personal" attributes, including the ability to seek out people to attach to (individuals could also

Animatism

a type of religious belief in which impersonal spiritual forces exist in the world and affect human life and behavior seek *diyi*) and to experience anger, which could of course harm humans (Basso 1970). The Menomini of North America spoke of a power called *tatahkesewen* ("that which has energy"), *meskowesan* ("that which has strength"), or *ahpehtesewesen* ("that which is valuable"). They described it as non-material and invisible but like a bright light that could be sought and mastered through dreams, vision quests, and the guidance of guardian spirits.

As one of the most religiously eclectic societies, the Ju/hoansi also had a concept of spiritual energy called *n/um*. Richard Lee defines it as a

> substance that lies in the pit of the stomach of men and women. . .and becomes active during a healing dance. The !Kung believe that the movements of the dancers heat the *n/um* up and when it boils it rises up the spinal cord and explodes in the brain.
>
> (1984: 109)

The Ju/hoansi shaman (see below) mastered this force and called upon it in healing rituals to transfer power and wellness to patients.

Religious specialists

As in all other walks of human life, there are some individuals who have more ability or power in religion than others. This facility may come from knowledge, skill, practice, training, personal experience, office, or other such factors. Hence, when the layman had a problem or an interest to which religion applies, s/he would turn to a specialist for assistance or intervention with the spiritual. Predictably, there is a variety of religious specialists across cultures, who vary in what they do, how they do it, and for what purposes they do it. Indeed, it might be better to think about religious specialists in terms of the tasks they perform rather than as discrete types.

Shaman

One of the most celebrated of all religious characters is the **shaman**, sometimes popularly known as the witch doctor or medicine man because the primary task of the shaman (yet another case of borrowing a concept from one society – this time, the Tungus

Shaman
a religious specialist, often part-time, who has personal power, based on unique life experiences or apprenticeship to a senior shaman, to communicate, interact, and sometimes struggle, with supernatural beings or forces. Often a healer

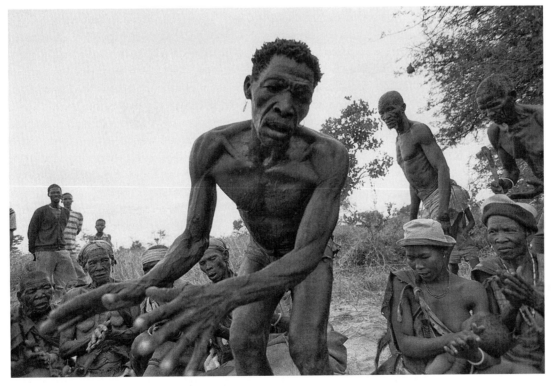

PLATE 10.3 Ganakwe bushman dancing into a trance.

of Siberia – to apply to other religions) was to help people who were suffering from physical, emotional, or social misfortune. The unique and important thing about shamans is that they were typically spiritually powerful individuals, that is to say, their specialist talents came from some quality of their own individual personality or biography. With this personal power, shamans could do spiritual things that other "normal" people could not.

A potential shaman did not go to "shaman school" or take a test to get a "shaman license." The process was both more informal and more profound than that. A person usually showed a propensity or tendency toward shamanic abilities early in life, such as talent for singing or ability to enter into trances or have visions. One very common element of the life-story of a shaman was a serious illness in youth, from which the person dramatically or miraculously recovered. This was evidence that s/he "had the power," and it was also often the first significant contact with the spirit world, since to be sick – and especially to die – was to interact with (and overcome) spirits.

The aspiring shaman often then became a student or apprentice to a senior shaman, who "taught" the novice. The master would seldom lecture to the trainee about how to be a shaman; rather, the apprentice received "hands-on" training. The teacher might subject the student to ordeals, like sleep deprivation, long hours of chanting, drug ingestion, seclusion, quests of various kinds, and other difficult and even painful experiences. One common factor in becoming a full-fledged shaman was acquiring a helper-spirit, sometimes called a "spirit familiar," which would show the trainee things that cannot be known any other way. It would teach him/her about the spirits and give him/her a personalized set of songs, dances, symbols, and other spiritual tools. That is why a shaman could not simply copy the knowledge of past shamans; each must have his/her own "kit." Paramount in many of these kits was the skill to enter into a trance-like state, during which the most "spiritual" of shamanic work was done.

Ju/hoansi shamans, for example, were called upon when a member of the band was sick or troubled. The shaman began his work (most were male) by singing and chanting until he fell, literally, into a trance; his body collapsed on the ground,

because his "soul" had left it and was sojourning in the spiritual dimension. The entranced shaman regained his senses and conducted "operations" that included rubbing his own sweat on the patient, which was thought to contain "boiling energy" or n/um. The shaman eventually literally "swam" back to consciousness, having performed the cure that the patient sought.

In Australian Aboriginal societies, shamans would often accomplish their cures by removing objects – like stones or feathers – from the body of the victim. (In many cultures, shamans themselves were thought to have supernatural objects in their bodies, which may be implanted as part of their training.) Elsewhere, shamans purportedly visited spirits while in trance and either questioned them or on occasion engaged them in combat; a shaman really could be a spiritual warrior. Shamans also might incorporate more "mundane" items into their cures, like potions, charms, sacrifices, and such. What Spiro translates as shaman in his Burmese study was nat kadow or "nat wife" and was a role almost entirely occupied by women. He argues that they did not journey to the spirit world or cure sickness at all but functioned through spirit possession by their nat husband who told them the nature of the spiritual offense that plagued the patient.

One of the last key features of shamanism is that the role was typically a "part-time" vocation. The shaman might take some form of compensation for his/her efforts, but this never amounted to an income. Furthermore, shamanism was not a formal position, certainly not an "office." One was a shaman if one had spiritual power; if one lost that power, one was no longer regarded as a shaman. There might be multiple shamans in a community or society, depending on how many people wanted to and were able to master shamanic techniques. Shamans were often a little feared and distrusted for their power and their personal oddity; being a shaman could be a lonely and uncomfortable existence. Finally, shamanism could not be truly or dependably inherited; sometimes the children of shamans became shamans too, but that was because they also "had the power," not because of who their parents were. Each would-be shaman had to prove his/her ability and gather his/her own spiritual resources.

PLATE 10.4 Shamanism is a common religious idea and practice across cultures.

Priest

For most English-speakers, the term "priest" conjures up an image of a man (usually a man) in a black robe leading a church service. That is definitely one variety of priestly activity but not the definition of priesthood. The **priest** is, in a word, all of the things that a shaman is not. S/he is often a full-time specialist occupying a formal office achieved by study, testing, and "ordination" by a religious institution or structure which has the power and authority to invest priests. Priests may or may not be powerful individuals – some are quite ordinary people – but they hold a powerful office.

One becomes a priest by very different means than one becomes a shaman. Commonly, acquiring a priesthood means mastering a body of knowledge and dogma, becoming an "expert" in some ortho-doxy (from the roots *ortho-* and *doxa* for "correct/straight" and "opinion"). Individuals with deviant or "heretical" ideas do not tend to receive priestly offices; thus, priests tend to be agents of conservatism. In fact, they represent the institution in which they belong, rather than being "free agents" like shamans. The activities of priests tend to differ as well. The occasional priest may engage in curing practices, but more often priests are ritual leaders, functionaries who organize, conduct, and preside over ritual situations with more or less formulaic words and gestures. Priests are not gen-erally encouraged to "improvise" or to receive their own private spiritual instructions or resources. Ideally, every time a priest performs or leads a ritual, it should be exactly the same, down to the finest detail. The efficacy of the ritual may depend on each bit of it being correctly done.

The priesthood, while not always hereditary, may have a hereditary component. In various societies there are priestly lineages or classes, most explicitly the Brahman caste in Hinduism. In traditional Judaism the Levite line provided the priests of the group. And as we commented, in Barabaig society five of the clans were priestly (the *Daremgadyeg*) and fifty-five of the clans were purely secular. So, priesthood tends to be associated with social stratification as well as "institution-alization" or "formalization" of religion and the conflation of religious with political power. The high officers of the Cheyenne Council of Forty-Four were religious personages too. Priests, especially in larger, richer, and more centralized societies, tend to be full-time employees of the religious

Priest

a religious specialist, often full-time, who is trained in a religious tradition and acts as a functionary of a religious institution to lead ritual and perpetuate the religious institution

See Chapter 8

establishment (depending on a considerable sur-plus to support them), and they often exercise "secular" or political power as well as religious. Many top political offices, like the kingship under Henry VIII, have had religious power or significance, and many religious offices, like the Pope of the Catholic Church, have had political power or significance. Often, it is impossible to separate the two functions.

Sorcerer

Sorcerers were generally people believed to exercise spiritual power, typically for the worse, through specific "technical" means. That is, sorcery might be classed as a subset of magic, which is normally understood as an instrumental action in which certain gestures or behaviors "automatically" lead to certain results. The line between magic and religion is thin and controversial, and we will not explore it here; there is no doubt that there is much magic in any religion and some religion in all magic, but we can perhaps distinguish them usefully, as anthropologists from Frazer and Malinowski have attempted to do. Frazer in particular made a further distinction, between what he called contagious magic and sympathetic or imitative magic. **Contagious magic** is the spiritual consequence of bringing two things together, sometimes literally touching. For example, if I do some kind of cere-monial act on or store up some kind of spiritual power in a wand or other object and touch you with it, that power will be transferred to you. Australian Aboriginal sorcerers would focus their power through a magical bone, which they would point at a victim to "shoot" the magic at them. The use of a piece of a person's hair or fingernail on a "voodoo doll" follows the same logic: the body-part was in contact with the person, so there is still a magical connection. **Sympathetic or imitative magic** relies on some similarity between the action or the object and its target; so, if I want to make rain, I might pour water onto the ground, simulating rain. Or, if I want to guarantee fertility, I might incorporate a particularly fertile animal (perhaps a rabbit, or a symbol of fertility, like an egg) into my technique. In all of these behaviors, the idea is that the behavior is sufficient to achieve the result. One does not have to pray or ask for results; the magical ritual has an almost "technological" relation to its outcome – do

this action or say these words and get that result. The sorcerer, then, can be regarded as a person who performed such activities ordinarily for the purpose of evil or harm.

According to Basso, an Apache sorcerer had to learn the techniques of negative magic, and most sorcerers were men, since men were thought to feel more *kedn* or hatred than women. Potential sorcerers would have to pay a senior expert, usually a maternal kinsman, for the knowledge and skills, which took three main forms – making and admin-istering poisons, casting spells, and shooting objects "into" the victim's body. The result of successful sorcery was a specific set of symptoms that appeared suddenly and without warning; further, the corpses of victims were distinguished by "swollen tongues and bluish markings around the face and neck. They are also reported to decompose at an unusually rapid rate" (Basso 1970: 76). On the African island of Mayotte, sorcerers worked through evil spirits, literally "hiring" them to do harm; the greatest sorcerers met spirits in person and used the souls of the recently deceased. Michael Lambek explained that the cure for sorcery was to find and remove

> a small, rotting cloth packet filled with dirt, nail clippings, hair, broken glass, and the like from either the body of the patient, his house floor, or the ground of his compound or fields. This packet of dirt is the physical representation of the harm caused by the spirit itself.
>
> (1981: 44)

Witch

Many societies were quite sure that **witches** were at work in the community. As a cultural concept, witchcraft is very diverse, but the common thread across cultures is that witches were responsible for bad things that happened to people – often all bad things. In one of the classic studies of witchcraft, Evans-Pritchard argued that the Azande of the Sudan saw the action of witches everywhere:

> If blight seizes the ground-nut crop it is witchcraft; if the bush is vaingloriously scoured for game it is witchcraft; if women laboriously bale water out of a pool and are rewarded by but a few small fish it is witchcraft; if termites do not rise when their swarming is due and a

Sorcerer

a religious specialist who uses techniques, including spells and potions, etc. to achieve supernatural effects

Contagious magic

the belief and practice that objects that come in contact with each other have some supernatural connection with each other

Witch

a religious specialist, often conceived as a human with a supernatural ability to harm others, sometimes through possession of an unnatural bodily organ or an unnatural personality. Sometimes viewed as an anti-social and even anti-human type who causes misfortune out of excessive greed or anger or jealousy

Sympathetic magic

also called imitative magic, the belief and practice that objects that have something in common with each other (e.g. same shape or texture) have some supernatural connection with each other

Imitative magic

see sympathetic magic

cold useless night is spent in waiting for their flight it is witchcraft; if a wife is sulky and unresponsive to her husband it is witchcraft; if a prince is cold and distant with his subjects it is witchcraft; if a magical rite fails to achieve its purpose it is witchcraft; if, in fact, any failure or misfortune falls upon anyone at any time and in relation to any of the manifold activities of his life it may be due to witchcraft.

(1937: 18–19)

Some societies held that a witch was a person with an innate, even anatomical, power to do harm; the witch may have an extra organ in his/her chest containing negative spiritual power, or the witch's emotions simply radiated some malevolent force. Witch power may actually be involuntary to the witch, at least initially; they may simply exude negativity in ways that even they did not understand or control. The Kaguru also said that witches (*wahai*) were congenitally evil people, the ontological opposite of normal human beings (Beidelman 1971). Or they may practice, sharpen, and intentionally employ their power for their benefit, especially against rivals, including rival witches.

Anthropological discussions of witches and witchcraft, and of sorcery, turn on the particular concepts and how they function in a particular society. One function of witch-concepts, as of sorcery-concepts, is explanatory: they explained why unfortunate things occurred. Additionally, fear of witches or of being branded as a witch had a strong means of social control. If one behaved to make other people angry or unhappy, the witch among them might afflict the perpetrator. Or, if one was accused of witchcraft, the social (and mortal) consequences could be severe, including ostracism, condemnation, or even death. The Swazi recognized witches as well as sorcerers, which they categorized together as *batsakatsi* or "evil-doers." On the other hand, the Menomini said that witches were not antisocial deviants but the group in society with the most power and prestige, namely the elders. Spindler and Spindler wrote that "social control is achieved. . .by the threat of witchcraft by power figures rather than through accusation of the witch by the community" (1971: 73). All elders were potential witches which, in a society of relative equals, was one of the few "power relations" available.

According to Spiro, some informants in Burma claimed that witches were not even human but evil spirits in a human guise; also they did not make a sharp distinction between sorcery and witchcraft. A witch might have innate evil powers or the learned and acquired power more usually associated with a sorcerer. The two main types were the witch (*soun*) and the master witch (*aulan hsaya*). A *soun* was almost always female, recognizable by her dimly colored eyes; her power could be inherent or learned, although the learned witches were less powerful but more deliberately evil (since they sought out the ability actively). They were believed to cause various illnesses and to eat feces by detaching their heads and rolling along the ground. They might also work in conjunction with bad spirits. The master witch was much more powerful and always male. He did his dirty work by controlling evil spirits, feeding them raw meat until they became dependent on him. Interestingly, though, there were also good master witches (*ahtelan hsaya*) who could counteract the malice of *aulan hsaya*.

Diviner/oracle

Non-human beings frequently if not ordinarily communicate with humans, but not all humans are able to receive or interpret these messages. The **diviner** or **oracle** had the ability to read or interpret the will of spirits, sometimes by asking direction questions and examining some material manifestation of an answer. Astrology has traditionally been a divining activity, looking for traces of "divine" communication in the stars. Any number of other kinds of signs have been read for spiritual meaning, from tea leaves and coins to the bones or entrails of animals; a diviner may put a question or request to the spirits, then kill and study the body of an animal for indications of an answer. The Barabaig diviner or *sitetehid* manipulated a pile of stones and examined the patterns for messages, usually involving witches or angry ancestor spirits, although he did not actually perform the cure, which was turned over to another specialist. Probably the most famous oracle in Western history was the Greek oracle at Delphi, where citizens – including kings, generals, and philosophers – would ask advice from young priestesses who gave cryptic responses while in a trance. Decisions to go

Diviner
a religious specialist who uses one of many techniques to "read" information from the supernatural world

Oracle
a religious specialist (or any religious object or process) with the power to forecast the future or answer questions through communication with or manipulation of supernatural forces

to war and other epoch-making decisions were sometimes made in this way.

Prophet

Prophet
a human who speaks for or receives messages from spirits

Another intermediary of religious communication is the **prophet**, an individual who receives direct communication from the spirits, often quite involuntarily (recall how Moses and other Hebrew prophets were reluctant to take on the role), and is then charged to pass that knowledge along to other humans. "Prophecy," which is often confused with telling the future, is a bulwark in the Judeo-Christian tradition, and Muhammad is revered among Muslims for being not only a prophet but "the seal of prophets" – the final and authoritative one. His prophecy, received as a recitation or *Qur'an* from Allah and his angels themselves, was intended to complete and correct all previous prophecies. Obviously, though, there are those who think that new prophets continue to appear, both inside and outside the Judeo-Christian-Muslim world.

RELIGIOUS SPECIALISTS IN THAI BUDDHISM

THE ELEMENTS OF RELIGION: SYMBOL, RITUAL, AND LANGUAGE

Religion is located or "stored" in many locations other than beliefs and specialists. Many of these locations can rightfully be called symbols because they "stand for" the spirits or forces or convey meaning in some way, although members of the religion would often disagree that they are merely symbolic. In fact, from the member's point of view, some "symbols" are symbolic and some are not. For a Warlpiri, a *churinga* stone or board is not a symbol of an ancestral spirit but a *manifestation* of that spirit – what the eminent scholar of comparative religion Mircea Eliade called a "hierophany" or eruption of the sacred in the material world.

Various significant objects, places, and behaviors exist in the religious domain. Every religion, for instance, has sacred spaces, either sacralized by humans or by the spirits who inhabit(ed) them. A ceremonial ground, a mountain, a building, or an entire city may be a sacred space. Religions contain sacred objects as well, such as the medicine arrows of the Cheyenne and carvings, paintings, masks and many other examples across cultures. Relics (pieces of the bodies of important human figures) have

religious value in some societies. Finally, symbolic or sacred behaviors are key to religion, in particular behaviors that are intended as interaction between humans and their non/superhuman partners. Because the religious beings and forces are powerful and real, it is of central importance for humans to get information from or give information to these entities, to show them respect, and to discover and follow their bidding – or to influence and change their minds. In this and other ways, the relationships between humans and non/superhumans are analogous to the relationships between humans themselves; they are social and (hopefully) reciprocal relations, predictable and controllable (to some extent) and shaped by the same roles, values, practices, and institutions as human interactions.

These religious behaviors can take diverse forms or be expressed in diverse media. Two obvious and not entirely separable media are language and "action" or bodily motion, although language ultimately *is* action and most religious behaviors feature both. Under these two major headings are a variety of types of behaviors, which, as Wallace and Boyer and Atran have noted, often also have their non-religious counterparts.

Religious behavior: ritual

Ritual is not an exclusively religious phenomenon; people can be ritualistic about anything, and even animals have rituals (mating rituals, fighting rituals, etc.). A ritual is a highly stylized and formalized behavior pattern that is thought to be effective if performed properly. Humans engage in all kinds of rituals that are not religious in any manner of speaking, from ritual greetings (some much more extensive and formalized than the English, "How are you? Fine, how are you?") to obsessive-compulsive rituals like hand-washing and "good luck" routines. Anything that an individual – and even more so, a society – does repeatedly in the same way is a ritual. In this sense, most or all of culture is ritual or ritualistic, because it depends on people knowing and doing the "right things" in particular social situations, from saying "Good morning" when you see someone for the first time of the day to saying "I do" when you officially marry someone. Rituals, then, have been characterized by the philosopher John Skorupski in his study of

Skorupski, John. 1976. *Symbol and Theory: A Philosophical Study of Theories of Religion in Social Anthropology.* Cambridge: Cambridge University Press.

anthropology as part of the *interaction code*, which he defines as behavior intended "to establish or maintain (or destroy) an equilibrium, or mutual agreement, among the people involved in an interaction as to their relative standing or roles, and their reciprocal commitments and obligations" (1976: 77). Interaction between humans is routinized and culturized by the elaboration of an interaction code that contains such elements as honor and politeness. Accordingly, with non/superhumans also now sharing the interactional universe of humans, the interaction code extends to them – and they tend to receive the "highest," most formal, and most "ritualized" behavior of all.

Religious rituals can take many forms, and Wallace (1966) suggested a typology, including

- Technical rituals – rituals that are intended to achieve certain specific ends, like divination or rites of intensification (see below)
- Therapeutic or anti-therapeutic rituals – rituals that are intended to cure illness and misfortune such as shamanic healing or to cause it such as sorcery and witchcraft
- Ideological rituals – rituals that are intended to express or achieve social goals, including rites of passage (see below), taboos, and rituals of rebellion or transgression (e.g. carnival)
- Salvation rituals – rituals that are intended to work changes in individuals, particularly at

moments of personal crisis, such as spirit possession or mystical experiences
- Revitalization rituals – rituals that are intended to work changes in society, particularly at moments of social crisis.

See Chapter 15

Within these types, a few specific ritual actions or "ritual processes" demand more attention. One of these is **rites of intensification** which are activated to "intensify" nature or society at specific times or on a regular schedule. A reason for intensifying nature is, for instance, to guarantee or increase the fertility of plants, animals, and even humans (leading to what are sometimes called "increase rituals"). Thus, a society may perform a ritual to increase the number or health or reproductive capacity of wild species or domesticated herds. A reason for intensifying society might be a crisis or shock that threatens to disorient or even disintegrate society, such as a natural disaster, a death, or a defeat in war. A ritual at such times could bring people back together as a society and strengthen the bonds that unite them. Some rites of intensification are ad hoc, while others are "calendrical," that is, are part of a society's ritual calendar. For farmers, a harvest will occur every year around the same time, so a harvest ritual can occur every year around the same time. Americans find remnants of this in the observance of Halloween, a version of a harvest (and death, which is often associated with the harvest and

Rite of intensification
a form of ritual in which members of the society are brought into greater communion, in which social bonds are intensified

PLATE 10.5
Warlpiri women lead girls in a dance ritual.

the approach of winter) festival. Some American rituals combine natural and historical occurrences (Thanksgiving), while some are purely historical (Fourth of July).

Sacrifice is not a specific kind of ritual so much as a recurring ingredient in rituals. A sacrifice is the voluntary surrender of something valuable, usually through destruction, usually as a way of communicating with spirits in the sense of offering a gift or "payment" to them. It is essentially religious reciprocity. In some systems, it is told that the spirits demand such sacrifices or else they will withhold their providence; in others, it is thought to be a good and generous gesture, as when various societies set a small portion of their meal aside in honor of the gods. Sometimes it is a matter of giving thanks. In other cases, as in Aztec religion, the sacrifice (including of humans) was believed to be necessary for the continued functioning of the universe (i.e. the hungry sun-god required sacrifices of human hearts and blood to make it return each day).

Finally, the anthropologist Victor Turner (1969; 1981) had identified a "ritual process" which follows a common pattern or progression. Turner noticed that many rituals have a recurrent structure, in which individuals undergoing the ritual are transformed – socially or even physically – from one condition or status to another. Following Van Gennup's suggestion, he called these **rites of passage**, indicating that the subjects "pass" from one social state to another. Familiar examples of rites of passage include weddings and graduations and (at least in some interpretations) funerals. Before a wedding ceremony, each party is a "single person," but after – and *because of* – the ceremony, each party is a "married person." They are moved from one social position or status to another, with different social roles and expectations.

Societies and religions are replete with rites of passage. Initiation rituals are one prominent example; ordination rituals of priests or training rituals of shamans are others. The key to the process of ritual passage is the removal of the subject-person from his or her previous role or status and re-placement into a new role or status; however, "in between" there is a period of "rolelessness," or non-identity, or undifferentiated status, which Turner called **liminality**. In the liminal phase, the person is neither this nor that but is between statuses and therefore without status. For most Western/Christian rituals

this moment is usually fleeting, but some religions or rituals sustain it for a long period. In Australian Aboriginal initiations, boys or young men would literally be isolated from society for weeks or months, following a ritual "capture" that was treated and mourned like a death. During the isolation they might undergo deprivations like silence and nakedness, as well as physical operations like circumcision and also some learning about or at least exposure to sacred knowledge and objects. Upon their return to society, they were "new people"; symbolically, the boy had died and a man had been made in his place, with an altered body to mark his transformation.

Religious language: myth

When most English-speakers use the word "myth," they imply a disbelief in or disdain for some story or claim (e.g. the "myths" of stock-market investment or the "myths" of ancient Greek religion). People do not usually apply the word myth to their own cherished and accepted beliefs, since the word feels pejorative: Christians do not call the story of Adam and Eve a myth. Anthropologically, myth does not indicate falsity; rather, we think of a myth as simply a form of religious narrative, a story of sacred events that has some explanatory function or contemporary effect. That is, a myth tends to be an account of how some aspect of the known world – the universe as a whole, the earth or the society's particular environment, human beings, or social institutions, for example – came into existence. The "creation" may be an act of god(s), animal or plant spirits, or human ancestors ("culture heroes") and can be as diverse across cultures as can possibly be imagined.

Socially, then, myths are a way in which members of a society communicate their ideas about the sacred and about their own "holy history"; as such, myths are a manifestation of the general human tendency to turn our lives and worlds into stories. Humans are storytelling beings, that is, we aim to "make sense" of the flow of events and facts by organizing the details into a continuous and meaningful narrative, one that usually has a message or "moral" of some sort. Myths then are "instructional" in the strongest possible sense of the word – they put "structure in" human thought and

---

Sacrifice
a ritual behavior in which something is destroyed or killed, as a form of offering to or communication with supernatural beings, which is usually believed to affect the social or spiritual condition of the sacrificer

Turner, Victor W. 1969. *The Ritual Process: Structure and Anti-Structure.* Chicago, IL: Aldine Publishing.

Rite of passage
a form of ritual intended to accompany or accomplish a change of status or role of the participants, such as initiation (change from youth to adult) or marriage

Liminality
the condition of being "in between" or "on the margins" of social roles, in particular of being in transition (as during ritual) between one social role and another

human social life. They have been described as "charters" or "models" for how humans should live their lives today, and of course for how they should think about their lives and their world. As Bronislaw Malinowski wrote in one of the most oft-quoted passages in anthropology:

> Studied alive, myth. . .is not symbolic, but a direct expression of its subject matter; it is not an explanation in satisfaction of a scientific interest, but a narrative resurrection of a primeval reality, told in satisfaction of deep religious wants, moral cravings, social submissions, assertions, even practical requirements. Myth fulfills in primitive culture an indispensable function; it expresses, enhances, and codifies belief; it safeguards and enforces morality; it vouches for the efficiency of ritual and contains practical rules for the guidance of man. Myth is thus a vital ingredient of human civilization; it is not an idle tale, but a hard-worked active force; it is not an intellectual explanation or an artistic imagery, but a pragmatic charter of primitive faith and moral wisdom.
>
> (1948: 101)

Religious language: prayer

Prayer is a type of religious speech directed specifically to supernatural beings. The form and intent of prayer depends intimately on the nature of the spirit being prayed to. Sam Gill (1981) conducted a major analysis of Navajo prayer, which cannot be understood apart from the concepts and myths of the society. He writes that "prayers are considered to be complex ritual acts whose performances engage and are informed by elements of mythology and the cultural contexts in which they are performed" (xxii). In fact, this context is critical, since any particular prayer can be used in different ways with different meanings, for instance "in one context to request and effect a smooth and healthy birth and in another to request and effect rainfall in a period of drought" (xxiii).

Reviewing 300 different accounts of Navajo prayers, Gill arrives at eight general types: blessings, prayers of restoration/recovery by reidentification/reassociation with the means of health, prayers of

restoration by expulsion of foreign malevolence, prayers of restoration by expulsion of the malevolent influence of native ghosts or witches, prayers of restoration by the removal of the malevolent influence of Holy People, prayers of restoration by the recovery, return, and reassociation with the means of health, prayers of procurement of protection against potential attack, and prayers of restoration by remaking/redressing the Holy Person's means of health and life. Even more, each prayer type has a standard structure of elements in a particular order. For example, an Enemyway prayer, which is part of a ritual to expel a foreign evil, opens with a place reference, which is followed by naming one or more sacred beings called Holy People, then a section asking for the removal of the evil force, and finally one or more references to an eventual state of blessing.

Religious language: specialized ritual speech

In many societies and religions, one way of indicating the special and "set-apart" nature of the religious occasion is through the use of forms of speech not used at any other time. For instance, until the Second Vatican Council (1962–65), the Catholic mass was performed exclusively in Latin, the language of religion and "high culture," and reformers like Martin Luther met with great resistance in efforts to translate the Bible into vernacular languages. (Many Catholics continue to reject the changes enacted at the Second Vatican Council, perhaps most famously Mel Gibson.) Likewise, Islamic tradition insists that the Qur'an can only be presented in Arabic and that all translations are misinterpretations at best and betrayals at worst.

As we mentioned already, special speech styles and formats are distinguishable by unique properties, including vocabularies that are not employed in any other type of speech, voice qualities (like chanting or singing), the use of metaphor, and specific formulas such as standard openings or endings. For example, Parks (1996) in his study of myths and narratives of the Arikara of South Dakota, proposes six areas in which their religious language differs from other more mundane language forms:

Malinowski, Bronislaw. 1948. *Magic, Science, and Religion and Other Essays.* Garden City, NY: Doubleday Anchor Books.

Prayer
a form of linguistic religious ritual in which humans are believed to speak and interact with supernatural beings

Gill, Sam D. 1981. *Sacred Words: A Study of Navajo Religion and Prayer.* Westport, CT: Greenwood Press.

See Chapter 4

1 Characters. Myths and tales often employ a cast of well known characters like Lucky Man, Stays in the Lodge Dressed in Finery, Bloody Hands, Scalped Man, and so on.

2 "Style." Myths and stories are often told in the third person, using quotation and a verb form that indicates that the teller did not witness the events himself or herself. Actions are frequently described after the results of the actions, with the actor identified last. Tellings use repetition, indeterminacy (e.g., words like *niikohna-* meaning "whoever/whichever"), and introductions like "This is what he said."

3 Morphology and syntax. Narratives contain many special words, phrases, and constructions, such as "introducers" and "connectors" like *nawah* and *wah* (for "now" or "well"), demonstratives and exclamatives, and "decedents" that refer to deceased characters (like *nuuxU* for "the one who was"). Also, sentences alternate between long and short.

4 Narrative structure. Stories often open with formulaic phrases like *kuwiteetuunu'a'* or *nuuneesawatuuNU*, for "the village was coming in a long procession" or "there over the hill," respectively (akin to the English "Once upon a time"). Specific stock episodes may be added or subtracted, or more or less elaborated. Explanations or "morals" may be given, and stories that are regarded as "factual" may end with a credit for the source, such as "Now this is what I used to hear when my grandmother told the story."

See Chapter 11

5 Context. Myths and tales also must be told and received properly in social terms. The teller must be shown respect and offered a gift of food or tobacco. References to directions and colors are part of the telling, and themes of power acquisition and sympathy for the unfortunate – orphans, the poor, the sick, etc. – are common.

6 Performance. Religious language, like all other forms of language and of social behavior, is a *performance* with its own rules and norms. There are proper ways and times to do it, and circumstances that distinguish it as one kind of behavior or narrative rather than another. Myths and tales, for example, were traditionally only told in the winter, preferably during the evening and mostly by men. The audience would interject with words like *hini* or "go on," and speakers might take turns adding an episode or telling a new version. When one was finished speaking, he would say something like *wetAhneesi'it* or "Now I am letting go of the gut."

RELIGION AND THE EVERYDAY

In his analysis of Australian Aboriginal religion, Émile Durkheim proposed that ritual was the primary site for the construction and perpetuation of religion, precisely because rituals (he believed) were especially dramatic and persuasive. However, anyone who has attended a ritual knows that it is not necessarily so exciting; in fact, it can be quite tedious. More importantly, most people are not in ritual situations all that often, and – most crucially of all – people would not understand and respond to rituals unless they had been prepared in some way for the events and meanings embedded in those occasions.

Anthropologists have come increasingly to appreciate how religion pervades and shapes the small, mundane, everyday aspects of social life. Indeed, religion can be and often is so pervasive and taken-for-granted that members of a society have religious "moods and motivations" without realizing that those ideas and feelings are specifically religious. It is also essential to remember that, while religions like Christianity emphasize the formal "belief" or dogmatic aspects of religion, most religions do not share that fixation, and all religions "live" in the everyday practices of society.

A short list of the social sites in which individuals may encounter and experience religion includes:

■ Bodily habits – religions often influence how we inhabit our bodies, including how we wear our hair or facial hair (e.g. Muslim beards and Jewish earlocks), how we dress, and even how we stand or bow.
■ Eating habits – most if not all religions have regulations on what may be eaten by whom, as well as rules for feasting or fasting (e.g. Muslim Ramadan) and ritual occasions of consumption.
■ Sexual behavior – most if not all religions add

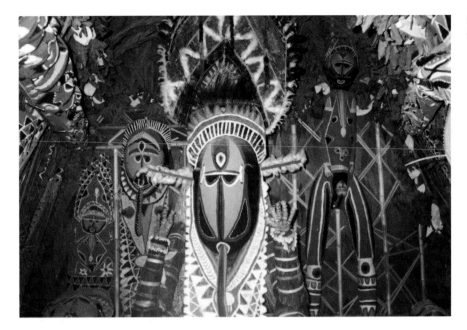

PLATE 10.6 A sacred site: the inside of a spirit-house in Papua New Guinea.

regulations on sex, such as with whom, in what positions, within what institutions (e.g. marriage), etc.

■ Timekeeping – many religions organize time in religion-specific ways, from calendar systems originating at key moments (e.g. the birth of Christ, Muhammad's flight to Medina) to weekly cycles and "sabbath" days to specific annual holidays ("holy-days").

■ Personal names – religions tend to reproduce the names of figures in their history in the naming practices of living members (e.g. Matthew, Mark, John, Daniel, Mary, Rebecca, etc. in Christianity and Judaism; Muhammad, Ali, Hussein, etc. in Islam, and so forth).

■ Place names – religions tend to reproduce the names of significant places, so that members literally inhabit the sacred landscape wherever they may live (e.g. Bethlehem, Pennsylvania; New Canaan, Connecticut; Corpus Christi, Texas).

In these and many other ways, religion provides less a belief system for members to accept than an experience for members to absorb. In a word, a religion is a lifeway more than a creed.

SECULAR AND SECULARIZATION

BOX 10.4 CONTEMPORARY CULTURAL CONTROVERSIES: CAN ISLAM BE FRENCH?

As noted at the opening of this book, the presence of Muslims in Europe and the United States has been the occasion for some curiosity and concern among the locals. France is another site where Muslims – both immigrants and converts – are in a complex relationship to the host society and state, especially because of the more aggressive secularism of that country (known as *laïcité*). The coexistence of Muslims and secular (and Christian) French folk provides an opportunity and a challenge for cultural adaptation, and John Bowen recently asked the question, "what forms of Islamic ideas and institutions enable those Muslims wishing to practice their religion to do so fully and freely in France?" (2009: 5). One answer is to carve out specific Muslim spaces within and even in resistance to French society, like the "cathedral mosques" in Lyon and Marseille as well as Islamic schools and other public forums for lectures, discussions, and so on. However, at these sites, the effect of government is felt "seeking to organize religious life for Muslims" (32) in order, as a French minister stated in 2007, "to build and control a French Islam" (27). Another answer is to tailor Islam to the French context, as in schools that seek to preserve a "Muslim ambience" while offering a state-approved curriculum with lessons on French civics, sexual diversity, and even science and evolution. In this approach, Muslims must ask themselves how to modify Islamic practices to fit with French practices (such as banking and marriage) – and which practices may be modified and which are non-negotiable. A third answer, of course, would be to change French society – either to make it more inclusive and plural or to make it, ultimately, more Islamic. So, while it is possible to ask, Can Islam be French, it is also possible to ask, Can France be Islamic? What do you think?

SUMMARY

Religion is part of human culture, but it presents unique problems for anthropology, not only because both members of societies and anthropologists themselves often take it more seriously and literally than other parts but because it poses profound challenges to the terms and concepts that we use to understand and analyze cross-cultural belief and behavior. A firm and authoritative definition is difficult to determine, but an essential feature is that it includes conceptions of non-human and superhuman beings and forces that are in social and cultural relationships with humans. Society and its prerogatives and meanings are thus expanded to include humans and other kinds of "persons." We can also identify social functions that religion fulfills, from explanation to individual emotional needs to social integration and social control.

A religion is a loose system of different kinds of concepts, roles, and behaviors. Every religion appears to include

- "Spiritual" being(s) and/or force(s), including a "spiritual" part of humans
- Roles for human specialists
- Behavioral or "ritual" activity
- Language or religious speech, usually as part of – or itself being – ritual activity

Within the category of beings and forces is a wide variety of overlapping conceptions, with permeable boundaries, such that humans can become spirits or demons or even gods and vice versa. Some beings and forces are intimately known, while others are vague and amorphous.

Religious ideas and practices help to explain, control, and legitimize the social and natural world. They also, like myths, linguistic "performatives," and rites of passage, are meant to affect the human and non-human world and to bring about actual changes in individuals, society, and the universe.

MCQS

FILL IN THE BLANKS

WWW

Key Terms

Ancestor spirits	Ghost	Pantheism
Animatism	Imitative magic	Polytheism
Animism	Liminality	Prayer
Contagious magic	Monotheism	Priest
Deism	Myth	Prophet
Diviner	Oracle	Rite of intensification

Rite of passage

Ritual

Sacrifice

Shaman

Sorcerer

Soul

Sympathetic magic

Theism

Totemism

Witch

Seeing culture as a whole #2

The spirits of postsocialist Mongolia

During his fieldwork in northern Mongolia, Morten Pedersen noticed an epidemic of *agsan*, a kind of "drunken rage" in which a person "loses control over himself. . .and screams, cries, and aims punches in all directions" (2011: 1). The most obvious reason for these attacks was the political and economic trauma experienced by the end of communism and the chaos and poverty brought about by entry into the postsocialist era of less state regulation, higher unemployment, and generally more uncertainty. However, this is not how the local Darhad people understood the problem: for them, there were too many shamanic spirits afoot and too few people who were able to control those spirits. Thus, many people were exposed to and troubled by spirits – they were like shamans – but were not sufficiently shaman-like to manage the situation.

Darhad country has had a complex social history. The environment is some of the harshest in central Asia, with frigid winters and short hot summers. In the past, Darhad people were pastoralists, but they shared the area with other groups such as Tuvinians, Hahls, Kazaks, and Chinese; Pedersen claims that Darhad society is actually "a heterogenous mix of cultural, linguistic, and political groups" (14), Mongolian and non-Mongolian.

The region has also been a site of political confrontation, invaded by Genghis Khan, then ruled by imperial China, and finally influenced by the Soviet Union, which helped make Mongolia the world's second communist state in 1925. In a word, "the ethnic group known as 'the Darhad people'" was "shaped by complex political processes on the fringes of the Qing [Chinese] Empire from the late seventeenth to the early twentieth century" (13).

The Darhad remember the socialist decades as a time of hard work but relative stability, even oppressive sameness. Oppression was especially cruel to religion: Buddhism was essentially wiped out, and shamanism was suppressed. The end of communism around 1990 ushered in a new era, one of "freedom" but also of "a growing sense of confusion and uncertainty" (21), resulting in a "seemingly irreversible slide toward poverty" (23) as the government provided fewer services while no longer guaranteeing jobs. As a result, many Darhad reverted to older pastoral forms – and the old spirits also reappeared. The problem for contemporary Darhad, though, was that those specialists who knew how to handle the spirits had been eliminated, and much of the knowledge and paraphernalia of shamanism had been lost.

All around the world, societies faced with the hardship and insecurity of modernization have experienced religious revivals – of spirit possession, of witchcraft, of fundamentalism. Many anthropologists have interpreted these religious expressions as symbolic attempts to grapple with unfamiliar social forces or to blame someone or something for the negative effects of those forces. Pedersen argues instead that there is nothing symbolic about the restless spirits in Mongolia; the end of communism really had unleashed the spirits, which were responsible for all sorts of misfortune and confusion.

We could say that the Darhad were understanding the postsocialist transition through the lens of traditional shamanism, but Petersen makes a much stronger and more fascinating claim: that modern global society and the postsocialist state are more similar to shamanism than we ordinarily appreciate. The central experience of the modern age seems to be uncertainty: social conditions change so rapidly, and the state provides so much less stability, and the world's societies are becoming so much more interdependent, that people are not sure what is happening and must continuously adjust to new (and often unpleasant) circumstances. Jobs are less stable, and the government feels like it is everywhere and yet nowhere; social life has a ghostly quality, with forces materializing in surprising ways out of what seems like thin air.

But Petersen claims that this is precisely the shamanic reality. Shamanism is not exactly a religion in the sense of a belief system; rather, it is a worldview or ontology based on *transition*. The power of the shaman, at least in Darhad society but possibly across cultures, is to adopt and move between perspectives – worldly and spiritual – that is, to inhabit "fluid and multiple" positions (67), to perform transformations. The shamanic ontology is "perpetual metamorphosis, malleability, and fluidity

expressed in the unpredictable movements of wild animals and the inchoate trajectories of the shamanic spirits" (164). Indeed, Petersen suggests that we think of shamanic spirits less as "beings" and more as pure movement or transition – "processes" more than "persons." The shaman, then, is the human who is most like the spirits, able to change and transform; s/he is also "the knot of knots in the community" (165), able to integrate in his/her person the multiple and shifting processes of spiritual/social life.

The key is that postsocialist society is like shamanism: "the spirits and the market were both variations on one immanent state of transition" (65). Unseen and incomprehensible forces seem to reach out from the void to affect the individual, the family, and the society. The "market" and the "state" have no face yet many faces, and they are as unpredictable as any spirit. Especially compared to the almost suffocating stability of communism, capitalism and democracy exhibit a "lability and capriciousness of forms" that resemble shamanistic reality. For the Darhad exposed to the modern global system, "the restless spirits simply *were* uncertainty as such; they were materializations, actualizations, instantiations, and condensations of the all-pervasive state of cosmological turmoil variously called 'democracy,' 'transition,' or 'the age of the market'" (39).

Again, this would all be potentially manageable if there were competent shamans among the people, able to absorb, embody, and control the agitated spirits. In their absence, instead the Darhad have individuals who are surrounded by and invaded by spirits – individuals who are *like* shamans in that they encounter spirits, but insufficiently like shamans in that they cannot handle the encounter. They are "not quite shamans" in a world defined by invisible and unstable supra-individual movement.

Cultural dynamics
Continuity and change

Tradition

some practice or idea or object that is (at least believed to be) continuous or associated with "the past." A tradition may be very ancient or very recent, but as an ideological element it is often assumed to be important, authentic, and even "superior" to non-traditional (especially foreign) practices, ideas, and objects

The tango is the national dance of Argentina, truly a national **tradition**. But just how "traditional" is it? Argentina could not have had a national dance at all before 1516, since there was no such thing as "Argentina" until the Spanish arrived that year in search of silver (the very name derives from the Latin word *argentum* for "silver"), and the independent state of Argentina was not founded until 300 years later (in 1816). Even then, no one in Argentina was doing the tango; rather, according to Christine Denniston, an expert on the history of the tango, the first piece of music calling itself tango was written in 1857, and the oldest tune that is still part of the "tango canon" did not appear until the 1890s. However, not only is the "traditional dance" of Argentina relatively recent, but it was a hybrid invention of the many different cultures and ethnicities that shared the country – Spanish and African, German, Italian, and Polish to name but a few. Even more, when it first emerged, it was regarded as not only new but scandalous: it was not invented and taught the "old fashioned way," by established experts in dance, but by the poor people of the streets, and it used the new dance-hold in which a man and a woman put their arms around each other – a shocking development at the time.

Further, the dance was largely a way for lower-class immigrant men to attract women, but the man first had to master the dance, which involved learning it at men-only practices where men danced in the arms of other men. It was also not entirely traditional in that it did not have a fixed form; instead, it was an improvisational dance. And the new dance needed not only new music but new sounds and instruments, and the iconic instrument of the tango, the large accordion-like *bandonéon*, was not native to Argentina but was introduced from Germany around 1910. Finally, it was not until the tango produced its first "star," Juan Maglio, and then became a sensation in Paris – both in the year 1912 – that the tango became an established, respected, and "traditional" dance.

Cultural anthropology is the study of the diversity of human behavior in the present. This is true enough, but it hardly conveys the depth or the urgency of the discipline. Even worse, anthropology has long had, and often helped perpetuate, the reputation that it is exclusively concerned with small, remote, or traditional societies. The influential A. R. Radcliffe-Brown actually described anthropology not so many years ago as "the study of what are called primitive or backward people"

PLATE 11.1 The Argentine Tango began as a dance of the streets.

1945 (the end of World War II), books like *The Science of Man in the World Crisis* (Linton 1945) and Malinowski's own *The Dynamics of Culture Change* (1945) illustrated that the discipline had become aware of the changes that were occurring in their chosen subject-societies, in the world around them, and in the discipline itself. Stanley Diamond, in anthropology's soul-searching phase in the late 1960s and early 1970s, finally recast it as "the study of man in crisis by man in crisis" (1972: 401). This is profoundly true and profoundly important but not profoundly new. In a certain sense, the human world has probably always been in crisis in some way or another, whether it was the Native Americans confronting the first European settlers, the ancient Israelites confronting the first Roman conquerors, or Neandertals confronting the first Homo sapiens.

So, anthropology has changed, and *had* to change, because the groups that it aims to study have changed. It has also come to see change as not "corruption" or "de-traditionalization" but as an inherent part of the cultural process, of the dynamic nature of culture and human ways of living. And it has, as a result of these realizations, taken a look at itself in new ways and come away from the experience better for it.

Linton, Ralph, ed. 1945. *The Science of Man in the World Crisis*. New York: Columbia University Press.
Malinowski, Bronislaw. 1945. *The Dynamics of Culture Change: An Inquiry into Race Relations in Africa*. New Haven, CT and London: Yale University Press.

(1965: 2). Aside from the fact that "primitive" and "backward" are harsh and judgmental terms which we avoid today, the statement itself is false in the twenty-first century and has been for decades – if it was ever true. If anthropology were seriously to consider itself, or to be considered, the science of the primitive and the traditional, then it would be finished, since there are no primitive or purely traditional people in the world to study. On the other hand, new "traditions" (like tango) are emerging all the time, and diversity remains and thrives, giving anthropology an endless supply of cultural phenomena to investigate, along with the basic processes of culture and tradition themselves.

If modern professional anthropology, marked by the innovations of Boas and Malinowski, could maintain an innocent and naïve attitude toward culture and tradition through the first half of the twentieth century (and on close inspection, it did not always), it certainly had shed that attitude by the second half of the twentieth century. As early as

THE TRADITION OF TRADITION

Many people (and perhaps a few anthropologists) still think of anthropology as the study of traditional cultures. Outside of anthropology, the word "tradition" has taken on major cultural and political significance, as American citizens, for instance, debate issues of "traditional marriage" or "traditional values," etc. "Tradition" is not just a term or concept of interest to anthropologists but to the general public as well, and in fact it is an anthropological concept because it is a general concept, not unlike "belief" or even "culture," as we have seen in past chapters. Anthropology is, or at least has been, a product of its own culture too.

The discussion of traditional culture – or the discussion of culture *in terms of tradition* – is not so much false as vacuous. What precisely is tradition? It implies something that exists and continues "from way back" or "following old ways." "Traditional," therefore, suggests continuity with the past, something that is rooted in and even identical to the past. But of course, no societies today are carrying on the past exactly as it was. First, no society is a living fossil, and no person resides in the past. All existing societies live in the present. Second, no society is or ever has been in such complete isolation from the "outside world" that it did not have some exposure to other societies and incorporate some elements of those other cultures in its own. Certainly many if not all of these societies have absorbed influences from the "modern" world, like cars and cell phones and blue jeans. But they have also absorbed influences from neighboring "traditional peoples" that were "changing" them long before the "modern world" arrived.

There is a third issue that makes the term and idea of tradition even more problematic: if "tradition" refers to the past, then which particular moment of the past and which particular parts of that moment? When you think for instance, of the "traditional cuisine" of Italy, you probably think of pasta and tomato sauce. And indeed, for the last few hundred years, pasta and tomato sauce have been staples of the Italian kitchen – but only for the last few hundred years. Further back in the past, 500 or 600 or 1,000 years ago, these dishes were not and could not have been Italian traditions. Tomatoes were not native to Europe; rather, they were domesticated by ancient Native American societies and introduced to Europe only after contact following 1492. Even pasta was not a local creation of Europe but was developed in China and brought to the attention of Europeans through the voyages of Marco Polo and others in the 1300s and 1400s. Travelers carried the practice of noodle-making back to Europe, modified it using local ingredients (wheat instead of rice), and came up with pasta. Later, tomato sauces were added to create a "traditional" cuisine that had never existed before.

We could multiply examples infinitely. When, say, Protestant Christians talk about their "religious traditions," those traditions cannot extend back more than 500 years (and often much less), since Protestantism only originated in the early 1500s. And "Christian tradition" as such cannot reach back more than two thousand years, since there was no Christianity at all before that time. Every tradition has its starting point, before which it could not be "traditional," and when it was first introduced it was not traditional but innovative, even radical.

The upshot of this discussion is that, like so much else in the cultural world, *tradition is relative*. It is relative to the particular society or cultural question at hand (that is, there are Christian

PLATE 11.2 Halloween in the United States is an invented tradition combining very old and general harvest and spirit practices with newer and uniquely American elements.

traditions and Jewish traditions and Muslim traditions and Warlpiri traditions, etc.). It is relative to the particular time-period to which "traditionalists" point (50 years ago, 500 years ago, 5,000 years ago?). And it is relative to the particular elements of that time-period which the "traditionalists" want to emphasize, remember, or revive. In other words, when Americans talk about preserving or returning to "traditional values," they usually mean not only a particular moment – usually the 1950s, certainly not the 1850s or 1750s – but only certain aspects of that moment. Presumably, they are not talking about returning to racial segregation or black-and-white television. And presumably, they are not talking about living without cell phones and computers and modern medicine. They are, in other words, picking and choosing from among the shards of the past to imagine a "traditional culture."

There is no such thing as a "traditional" culture – not today and probably not ever – because the very meaning of the term is so vague and relative. If by "traditional" we mean "living in some primordial unchanged condition," then the idea is not just wrong but nonsensical: no society lives the way it did "in the beginning." More importantly still for us, anthropology too has its "traditions." Doing fieldwork and writing ethnographies are anthropological traditions. Focusing on small-scale and remote societies is an anthropological tradition. And treating these societies as if they were "traditional" is an anthropological tradition. It has even been argued that the very notions of "society" and

BOX 11.1 "TRADITIONING": THE PROCESS OF TRADITION IN FOLKLORE AND RELIGION

As attuned to the problem of "tradition" as anthropology is, two related fields have struggled with it equally or more – folklore and religion. Since both of these disciplines purport to study traditional, even authoritative or canonical, materials, the concept is particularly critical. However, as Dan Ben-Amos commented in 1984, people tend to take "tradition" for granted, to think *with* or *through* the concept rather than to think *about* it and to analyze it. Accordingly, "tradition" comes to mean a particular body of material – a set of stories, a book of scriptures – that has existed, unchanged, from time immemorial. Ben-Amos responded that "tradition" can also designate a process, "the dynamics of transmission of cultural heritage from generation to generation" (1984: 116), which includes the ways and contexts in which it is performed and reproduced. The great folklorist Ruth Finnegan went further, appreciating that since people must practice a "tradition" in order for it to exist, then "this actual *usage* may be as liable to exploit, to modify, or to play with tradition as to follow it blindly. Traditions, it has become clear, are constantly open to change" (1991: 112). This opens such anthropological questions as "'traditional' in what sense? is it necessarily old? or collectively composed? or passed on passively without individual manipulation? *who* created it in whole or in part? how has its editing and interpretation affected the evidence, and with what assumptions or for what purpose?" (113) – not to mention for whose benefit and at whose cost? Within Christian theology, the matter is equally serious. Richard Heitzenrater explains that the "truth" of a tradition might depend less on the facts and documents than on "the willing reception and critical practice of the tradition in the present in a fashion that is. . .meaningful and relevant. . .to those who continue to hold and practice the tradition" (2002: 637). The persistence, even authority, of the tradition "depends upon the regularity of its repetition," and "'Good' traditions are those that give continuing special meaning to self-conscious identity. They have built-in biases, developed, practiced, passed on, and accepted down through the years" (637). Finally, the eminent Biblical scholar Walter Brueggemann literally made tradition a verb – traditioning – in describing "the work of tradition," the process or action of formulating, transmitting, interpreting, and employing tradition that always and necessarily involves "imaginative remembering" (2003: 7). "The traditioning process is endless and open-ended" (11), so tradition – even, by his own account, a tradition like the Old Testament – is never fixed or finished.

"culture" are anthropological traditions (Kuper 1988; Wagner 1975). It is well to recall that anthropology emerged at a specific place and time with specific interests. Anthropology's initial interests were in origins and history: how did culture start, what was the first kind of culture, what was the first religion or kinship system or other parts of culture, and how has culture "progressed" to its present state? These were the questions that informed the early approach of cultural evolutionism, looking for the "stages" of cultural evolution from "primitive" to "civilized." This perspective was roundly and thoroughly rejected by later anthropologists like Bronislaw Malinowski and Franz Boas as both speculative and ethnocentric.

Because the project of Culture history (with a capital C) required "survivals" from past cultural eras in order to fill in the line of progression, and

See Chapter 3

BOX 11.2   MALINOWSKI ON THE "CHANGING NATIVE"

The following passages from *The Dynamics of Culture Change* (1961 [1945]) demonstrate Malinowski's awareness of the changing nature of "traditional culture" and its importance to anthropology.

The figment of the "uncontaminated" Native has to be dropped from research in field and study. The cogent reason for this is that the "uncontaminated" Native does not exist anywhere. The man of science has to study what is, and not what might have been.

(2–3)

The scientific anthropologist must be the anthropologist of the changing Native. Why? Because what exists nowadays is not a primitive culture in isolation but one in contact and process of change.

(6)

The nature of culture change is determined by factors and circumstances which cannot be assessed by the study of either [European or traditional] culture alone, or of both of them as lumber rooms of elements. The clash and interplay of the two cultures produce new things.

(25)

To the student of culture change, what really matters is not the objectively true past, scientifically reconstructed and all-important to the antiquarian, but the psychological reality of today.

(29)

[T]he retrospective vision, however erroneous, is more important than the myth unknown or forgotten by old informants.

(31)

What the "old men of the tribe" tell us about the past can never be scientific or historical truth, since it is always affected by sentiment, by retrospective regrets and longings.

(154)

[E]lements of the old culture. . .are being revived with a secondary, almost ethnographic interest in racial history, customary law, and the artistic and intellectual achievements of their race. . . . This sophisticated nationalism or tribalism can still draw full strength from the enormous residues of old tradition.

(158)

because the researchers who arrived to study the "primitive societies" necessarily had no data on the prior state of those societies, it was easy and natural to conclude or assume that they had no history, that they were living "in some primordial unchanged condition." More, it was useful: only if those remote societies were preserved fossils of a lost cultural past could they play their role as exemplars of former and lower cultural formations. Eric Wolf, in his epic treatise on the contact between Europeans and non-European peoples, made light of this notion in the title of his book, *Europe and the People without History* (1982). As a result of the apparent dearth of historical information and of the obvious excesses of the Culture history approach, Malinowski and Boas advised on avoiding historical questions at all, probably perpetuating the impression that non-European societies really were ahistorical and static.

Interestingly, Malinowski, the father of ahistorical "functionalism," is wrongly accused of being unaware of or unconcerned with history and change. In fact, he was one of the first major scholars to draw attention to both, in his 1945 book mentioned above and excerpted in Box 11.2.

Later anthropologists took this insight much further, pondering whether the very concepts of "culture" and "society" might be impositions on social reality. Edmund Leach was perhaps the first to question the objectivity of terms like "society," calling clearly bounded and distinguishable societies an "academic fiction": the anthropologist, he wrote, "has often only managed to discern the existence of [a society] because he took it as axiomatic that this kind of cultural entity must exist" (1954: 291). This awareness led to a flood of publications with titles like *Reinventing Anthropology* (Hymes 1972), *The Invention of Culture* (Wagner 1975), *The Invention of Primitive Society* (Kuper 1988), and ultimately *The Invention of Tradition* (Hobsbawm and Ranger 1983). Roy Wagner, for instance, argued that we assume that culture is "a concrete entity, a 'thing' that has rules, 'works' in a certain way, and can be learned" and then go out and find what we expected to find (1975: 8). Kuper added the observation that the concept of society, especially primitive society, supported certain preconceptions and prejudices of Europeans of their day in regard to their own origins and to the relation of cultural "essentials" to identity. In other words, he said that

the idea of primitive society fed the common belief that societies were based either on blood or on soil, and that these principles of descent and territoriality may be equated with race and citizenship, the contrasting components of every imperialism and every nationalism.

(1988: 9)

Since those days of the "crisis in anthropology," brought about partly by the crisis in the subject peoples of anthropology, the discipline has become even more self-reflective. In a way, anthropology itself is not as "traditional" as it once was, just as the societies we examine are not as "traditional" either. Clifford and Marcus (1986) *Writing Culture: The Poetics and Politics of Ethnography*, Marcus and Fischer (1986) *Anthropology as Cultural Critique*, Crapanzano (1992) *Hermes' Dilemma and Hamlet's Desire: On the Epistemology of Interpretation*, and most scathingly Sandall (2001) *The Culture Cult* have questioned the objectivity, the scientific-ness, and even the motivations of anthropologists and others who use "traditional culture" for various purposes. Clifford and Marcus in particular point to the "literary" and even poetic quality of anthropological works, that they are "fictions" or "narratives" instead of or in addition to "factual accounts," and Sandall savagely criticizes the romantic and destructive "designer tribalism" that he sees in much professional and popular thinking about culture. What all of these authors, and the entire history of anthropology and the encounter with cultural difference, show is that the description of, analysis of, and participation in culture and culture change are much more problematic and subjective – in the end, more human – than once thought.

CULTURAL DYNAMICS: THE PROCESSES OF CULTURAL CHANGE

As a consequence of what we have discussed above, anthropologists have become

less likely to think of "culture" in terms of bounded, fully integrated, and static systems, and they are more inclined to ponder cultural processes, dynamics, and conflicts grounded in uneven fields of power that cross the contested boundaries of nation-states and peoples.

(Harrison 2008: 7)

Clifford, James and George Marcus, eds. 1986. *Writing Culture: The Poetics and Politics of Ethnography*. Berkeley, CA: University of California Press.

Hymes, Dell, ed. 1972 [1969]. *Reinventing Anthropology*. New York: Random House, Inc.
Wagner, Roy. 1975. *The Invention of Culture*. Englewood Cliffs, NJ: Prentice-Hall, Inc.
Kuper, Adam. 1988. *The Invention of Primitive Society: Transformations of an Illusion*. London: Routledge.
Hobsbawm, Eric and Terence Ranger, eds. 1983. *The Invention of Tradition*. Cambridge: Cambridge University Press.

See Chapter 13

This is why it is unprofitable to speak of "culture change" as if it is foreign, almost unnatural or hostile, to "traditional culture." In fact, cultural change is a constant and natural quality of culture, not something that only appeared in recent years or centuries with colonialism and globalization to disrupt tradition. Just as a living body does not stay the same throughout its lifetime, neither does a society or culture. This is why we will talk about the "processes of culture change" under the more general heading of cultural dynamics – dynamics meaning action, movement, growth, and generation. Culture never stands still but continuously moves and develops. Any actual culture is a complicated and sometimes contradictory fusion of continuity and change.

Innovation and diffusion

What the "original" form of culture was, or where it came from, we will probably never know. Primate studies suggest some indication of what pre-cultural or proto-cultural but highly social and imitative beings can be like, but non-human primates are just that – not human. So their study can answer some questions but not the most fundamental question: what is human culture and how did humans get it? Therefore, a better question to ask is, what are the means by which cultural novelty enters a society? Arguably, cultures do tend to be "conservative" in the sense that they try to preserve and repeat what they have done in the past. However, new elements do enter cultures, or else we would all still be sitting in caves making stone tools – which were themselves cultural novelties at first.

There are two main sources of novelty in any particular society, **innovation** and **diffusion**. Innovation is the ultimate source of all cultural novelty: at some point in time, somebody has to think of or start doing something different. An innovation (literally, "to make/do new") can take the form of an invention or a discovery, as well as the form of a **primary innovation** (the development of a completely new principle or object) or a **secondary innovation** (a novel application or combination of already-existing principles or objects, i.e. using old components in new arrangements, such as attaching wires and vacuum tubes to invent a television). In whatever form, the key

characteristic of innovation is that it is internal to the society: a member of the society introduces it into the society.

Innovation is not only the ultimate source of cultural novelty but tends to be an initially small-scale source. In other words, most if not all innovations (perhaps less so today, in the age of research teams) tend to be the work or inspiration of a single person or at most a small group of people. When fire was first made and controlled, or plants and animals were first domesticated, or the wheel was first invented, it was quite probably discovered by one person or a few people. We know that when a new religion like Christianity or Islam is introduced, it tends to be the idea of one or at most a few individuals – a prophetic figure like Jesus or Muhammad. Others of course helped shape and promote it (like Paul in the case of Christianity), but the original innovators were most often single individuals or at most small numbers of individuals.

Innovation may be the ultimate source of culture change, but it is not the most common source. For example, every modern Westerner knows how to write, but none of them created writing. Humans are very inventive, to be sure, but humans are above all else imitative. And thank goodness for it: if every person invented his/her own writing system, or language, or clothing style, or religion, there would be precious little communication possible between people. Most Americans, then, speak English not because Americans invented English but because the English language was carried to America by English-speakers. This process is diffusion, the spread of some cultural practice – an idea, an object or technology, a word or symbol or meaning, etc. – from one society to another.

Diffusion is orders of magnitude more common than innovation. There is good reason to believe that humans, for instance, invented writing at most three or four times in human history, and almost all of them quite long ago. But virtually all societies write today. That is because not only the notion of writing but a specific notation for writing diffused from another society to theirs; that is why there are so few major scripts or writing systems in the world today.

Whether the specific process of novelty is innovation or diffusion, the introduction of the new cultural element is not the end of the story but just the beginning. For, if Sequoyah or anyone else

ANTHROPOLOGY
AND THE "GREAT
TRANSFORMATION"

See Chapter 2

Innovation

the invention or discovery of a new cultural concept, idea, behavior, or object

Diffusion

the spread of a cultural trait (object, idea, practice, institution) from one society to another

Primary innovation

the invention or discovery of a totally original cultural item, as opposed to *secondary innovation*

Secondary innovation

an invention or discovery that uses or combines existing ideas, objects, or techniques in novel arrangements

BOX 11.3   THE INVENTION OF CHEROKEE WRITING

One of the only, if not the only, case of the invention of a writing system in recorded history (since recorded history could not start until writing existed) occurred in the 1800s among the Cherokee. According to the Manataka American Indian Council, a man named Sequoyah single-handedly developed a system for writing the Cherokee language where no such system had ever existed (although an ancient legend tells of a lost script). Sequoyah was born between two cultures himself, with a Cherokee mother named Wu-the and a white father named Nathaniel Gist or Guest. He was raised in Cherokee society, married a Cherokee woman, and learned to craft iron and silver. He also was exposed to the American practice of writing, although he supposedly never learned to read and write in English; however, he did witness the phenomenon of making marks on paper to represent sounds. Between 1809 and 1821 he worked on a set of language symbols for Cherokee and finally introduced it in 1821. It was not an alphabet but a syllabary, with "letters" for syllables rather than for individual sounds or phonemes. The Cherokee elders accepted the system after a demonstration by Sequoyah, and by 1825 the Bible and several other documents including religious and legal writings had been rendered into the new script. In 1828, after acquiring their own printing press, the Cherokee Nation began to produce their own newspaper, *Tsa la gi Tsu lehisanunhi* or "Cherokee Phoenix," with parallel columns of Cherokee and English. Whether this case constitutes an innovation or a diffusion, or something in between, is open to interpretation.

www.manataka.org

FIGURE 11.1 The Cherokee syllabary.

"invents" a new word or language or religion or clothing style or cuisine, is it culture now? What makes something "culture"? The simple criterion is learned and shared behavior. So, if someone starts a new language or religion, it is not "cultural" unless and until other people observe it, adopt it, practice it, and ideally pass it along to still others, especially their children. If no one ever learns and shares the innovation or diffusion, it never achieves "cultural" status. When the innovator dies, the innovation dies with him/her, since culture only exists so long as it is known and practiced. But as soon as it is learned and shared, it is cultural.

See Chapter 2

There is, as we said elsewhere, no precise quantifiable dimension to culture; that is, it is not necessary that all or even most or any specific percentage of society adopts the new behavior. Every innovation or diffusion originally starts as "individual peculiarities" on Linton's spectrum of the distribution of culture. If it never catches on or spreads any further, then it will remain a peculiarity and ultimately disappear from the culture. If it spreads a little further it can become a cultural specialty; a little further and it could achieve the rank of an alternative. If it becomes widely held and used, it may eventually become a "universal" within that society. Of course, any particular cultural item can get "lodged" at one of these stages and remain there, or even begin to decline again. Similarly, a cultural practice of age and prestige, even a universal one, can over time fade until it becomes a peculiarity of a few people or vanishes completely.

THE INVENTION OF AN AMERICAN TRADITION

So the question is what makes a cultural novelty "catch on" or not. Or, to put it in more technical terms, after an innovation or diffusion is introduced to a society, a process begins, which can end in any of three outcomes: acceptance, rejection, or acceptance-with-modification. Probably most cultural innovations fail, and virtually all alter from their original form before they are widely distributed. What kinds of factors lead a society to accept, modify, or ultimately reject some new cultural offering? Some of the criteria that affect the future of new phenomena are:

- How well it fits with already-existing preferences and tastes
- What local materials or ingredients are available
- How difficult or expensive it will be to implement

- What symbolic or social meaning or value exists in society
- How well it performs relative to competing items already in the culture
- How much it enhances or threatens other aspects of the culture
- How much power those who resist the change can muster
- How important it is that the phenomenon is "new" or "foreign"
- How much status the innovator or diffuser himself or herself possesses.

The basic issue in any case of adoption of cultural novelty is whether it fits with the culture that already exists. For example, if Americans already like to eat meat but not insects, then there is small chance that a new dish based on grasshoppers or cockroaches will gain very wide acceptance. If a society prefers that men wear pants and women wear dresses, then a dress for men will probably not catch on; this could also be a matter of symbolic or social meaning – of a behavior "appropriate for" one type of person but not another. One common factor is local tastes and ingredients; when I cook international foods, I often substitute exotic ingredients with local ones that I already have in my kitchen. When I was in Japan some years ago I found a pizza restaurant in my neighborhood that served not only pepperoni pizza and sausage pizza but seaweed pizza and shrimp pizza. My Japanese restaurateurs had simply adapted pizza to local tastes, using local ingredients, to make a "Japanese pizza."

The issue of expense or difficulty is illustrated well in the American resistance to the metric system. As useful and precise as it is, the changes involved in trying to convert the entire society and economy to another system of measure make it prohibitively difficult. Every machine, every tool, every cup and container, every thermometer would have to be replaced, at great cost both for the technology and for the training. It is easier just to leave things as they are. The English typewriter keyboard is another prime example. The familiar "QWERTY" keyboard (so named for the row of keys across the upper left) was in fact originally laid out to be as inconvenient as possible. In the days of mechanical typewriters, fast typists could jam the keys since they could type faster than the machine could respond. It was necessary to slow down these speed

BOX 11.4   STONE VERSUS STEEL AXES IN AN ABORIGINAL SOCIETY

The Yir Yoront of Cape York Peninsula, northeast Australia, used stone axes long before contact with Europeans. The tools were relatively easy to make, and men (but not women or children) could produce them for themselves. Women in fact were the primary users of the tools, for chopping firewood; however, men owned and kept them, and women or youths had to ask a man's permission to use one and return it promptly. Lauriston Sharp (1952) writes that access to axes was part of a general status system in which people were ranked by age, sex, and clan membership. The ax was a symbol of masculine power, an important trade good for establishing interpersonal relations, and a ritual object. When European Australians arrived and introduced steel axes, one might think that the impact would be minimal – perhaps cutting down more trees with less effort. However, the effects rippled through the society, from gender and political relations to religion. Aboriginals could not make their own steel axes, so they were dependent for them on whites, especially administrators and missionaries. Aboriginals who interacted with whites – and were perceived as "good" Aboriginals by the whites – had better access to the technology. This meant that older and more "traditional" men were more often excluded.

   Further, whites often gave the tools directly to women or children, unaware of, unconcerned about, or actively opposed to the gender segregation in the culture. Women and youths were freed from dependence on men for the property, depriving men of a practical and symbolic expression of power. Exchange relations between the Yir Yoront and other tribes broke down, as the Yir Yoront could not acquire steel axes from them and did not desire to trade steel axes to them. Sharp argues that the greatest effects were in the arena of "ideas, sentiments, and values," which radiated rapidly and contributed to the "collapse" of their society. Concepts of ownership, status, and even religion, myth, and ritual underwent stresses and transformations, "hacking," as he concludes, "at the supports of the entire cultural system" (22).

typists to compensate for the limitations of the devices. Today, electronic keyboards have no such mechanical limitations, so more "natural" keyboards, including the proposed Dvorak style, could be effectively used. However, again, the cost of replacement and of retraining would be so exorbitant that nobody seriously considers a change. The lesson from this discussion is that cultural elements are not always chosen or preserved because they are the best but because they are the most familiar or the "easiest" in the sense of requiring the least bother.

   One other issue to consider is the impact on a society and culture of the adoption of a new item, whether by innovation or diffusion. It can and often does happen that a modification in one area of culture, even a small one, can have ramifications, frequently unexpected and sometimes serious, in other areas of culture. The simple reason for this effect is that culture is an integrated entity; by the fact of holism, the consequences of change in one realm may be felt in other and seemingly "unrelated" realms – except that nothing in culture is unrelated. The effects can, in the end, be widespread and disastrous.

Cultural loss

Ideally, innovation or diffusion would result in at worst a substitution of one cultural practice for another and at most an addition to the cultural repertoire – a new specialty or alternative. However, culture does not proceed by addition and substitution alone but also by subtraction. In some cases, cultural elements are lost and not replaced by anything. The net result is an impoverishment of culture. It is important to remember that culture only exists so long as somebody is learning it, doing it, and transmitting it. When that process stops, culture ceases to be. This is why **cultural loss** is sometimes also referred to as **deculturation**.

Cultural loss
the process by which elements of a culture disappear over time, through natural/environmental changes, social pressures, or individual choices

Deculturation
see cultural loss

PLATE 11.3 Foragers are often forced to settle down, as in these concrete houses built for the formerly nomadic Warlpiri.

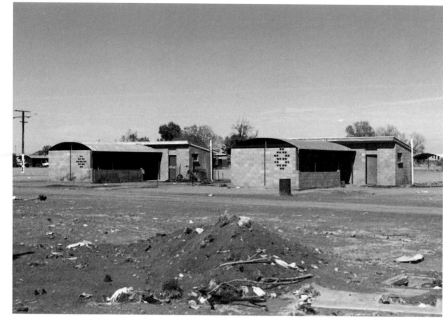

See Chapter 13

See Chapter 15

This is a major problem in the world today, especially in the context of the passing of culture between the generations. In many societies, young people often have little interest in the ways of the elders. Among the Gaguju people of Australia, as told in a recent National Geographic program entitled "Australia's Twilight of the Dreamtime," there are no longer enough men who know the traditional dances to conduct them in the old way; the Gaguju must invite men from other tribes to fill the required roles. The cause is a combination of the interests of the young and the decisions of the old. The young often do not care much about the old ways, and frequently they are not even available much of the time due to new demands of work and new opportunities for travel and play (not to mention plagues like alcohol and drugs). At the same time, the elders assess the readiness of the next generation before they share their secret-sacred knowledge. In Australia, religious knowledge is not for just anyone, and only men who are properly initiated and committed to and advanced in the traditions can receive it. If the elders never consider the youngsters qualified to get the knowledge, then the elders will keep it to themselves, and when they die it will die with them.

From the perspective of the young, there is sometimes a voluntary or involuntary detachment from their culture. In a changing and modernizing world, the young may see little use for or value in "traditional" knowledge or skills, from hunting or horticulture to music or language or religion. On the other hand, outside agents may intentionally or unintentionally interrupt the culture-transfer process, as with boarding schools, forced separation of families, and even involuntary adoptions. In some cases, other groups or classes, including the state government under which a society lives, have explicitly forbidden the use of some or all parts of a culture; for example, in the second half of the twentieth century, Turkish authorities literally outlawed the use of Kurdish language and symbols in an effort to eliminate not only Kurdish culture but even Kurdish identity as a distinct culture-bearing group.

All of these things have already happened in many parts of the world to many parts of culture – and in some cases, to entire cultures. By some counts there are hundreds of traditional languages, for instance, that are endangered today, and we can never know how many have already become extinct. An alarming number of languages are on the verge of disappearance, some with less than 100 surviving speakers. The Ainu language, spoken by natives of northern Japan, is one of the worst cases: with the youngest remaining speaker already sixty-five years old in the 1990s, such a language has little future.

It is of course not just language that is in the process of being lost. Religions, music, and other kinds of irreplaceable knowledge, including potentially important botanical and medicinal knowledge, are in danger. When these cultural things are dead, some will "live on" in the ethnographies of anthropologists, but some will be lost to humanity forever.

Acculturation

Enculturation is the name for the process of acquiring one's culture, ordinarily as a child, from the other members of one's society. It is the learning and teaching process by which Americans get their American culture, Warlpiri get their Warlpiri culture, and so on. Acculturation as a word sounds very similar, and conceptually it is very similar, but with a profound twist.

Acculturation can be thought of as the exposure to a second culture other than one's own, although this is too simple to be completely accurate: in the case of Sequoyah, which culture was "his own" culture? In a way, having two cultures might sound like a good thing, a kind of "multiculturalism" or cultural "bilingualism." And no doubt in some cases and in some ways it is a good thing. However, it can also be disruptive and it can also be coercive. In essence, acculturation is the process of culture change that occurs as a result of intense and sustained contact between two societies. Whenever there is such contact, there is going to be a circulation or flow of culture (and sometimes genes too) between the two societies; after all, that is how Europe got noodles and gunpowder and the compass and the zero and tomatoes and potatoes. Cultural exchange can bring benefits for both sides.

However, one crucial issue in acculturation is that there is usually a power differential between the two societies. In such cases, the smaller or weaker society is changed much more extensively than the larger or more powerful society, although both are changed some. When the first English settlers arrived at Massachusetts Bay, there is no doubt that they learned some critically important things from the Native Americans, and there are many elements of Indian culture in American culture today. Even so, no one can dispute that the changes for Native American societies were immeasurably greater and more negative than for the European immigrants.

One of the fascinating aspects of acculturation is that it is often extremely personal. That is, it is less true to say that a society is acculturated than that individual people are acculturated. Usually the first to feel the pressure are those in the most intimate and prolonged contact with the foreigners, including those engaged in trade or in political relationships. Others who feel the clutch of acculturation earliest are the children of mixed couples, like Sequoyah, who find themselves physically and culturally "in between." Sometimes referred to in the early anthropological literature as "marginal people," they often experience the personal sting of acculturation by being partly in each culture but not completely in either. They are the harbingers of the future.

As members of the dominated society (which may actually be larger demographically, as in the case of India under British rule) succumb to the pressures and lures of the new society, they may become in some ways more like this new society – that is, assimilate to it. They may learn its language, adopt some of its practices (clothing, firearms, and alcohol are three familiar ones), and in various ways emulate the new models. This process is partly natural and spontaneous, but it is also sometimes artificial and compulsory. In such cases, we can rightly speak of repressive acculturation or forced acculturation.

There are many known (and probably even more unknown) instances of forced acculturation. They are basically implementations of ethnocentric beliefs and attitudes. The activity of missionaries is one of the prime examples. Missionaries often did good work, bringing food and even peace to conflicting societies. However, the "mission" behind these works was always to change the society, most obviously (but not exclusively) its religion. Missionaries naturally would attempt to introduce foreign beliefs into the society, but they would often do so by ridiculing, condemning, or even punishing the "traditionalists" or at least by favoring the "converts." They were not above using the influence of their resources, including food and water, as weapons in this conversion effort, nor did they refrain from using corporal punishment or destroying native religious artifacts and buildings. In some places, missions became virtual prisons, from which natives were not permitted to leave once they arrived and where the missionary's will was law (see

Acculturation

the process of acquiring a "second culture," usually as an effect of sustained and imbalanced contact between two societies. Members of the "weaker" society are compelled to adopt aspects of the dominant society

See Chapter 6

PLATE 11.4 Native American children were often acculturated through the use of boarding schools, like the Carlisle School.

Tinker 1993). Obviously, too, the missionary's interests were not limited to religion as such, seeing as how all the domains of culture are integrated and that religion provides the rules and the sanctions for conduct in other regards. So, missionaries often imposed their (that is, Western or European) values and practices in the areas of kinship, gender roles, language, and economics on the local people too, forbidding, for instance, polygyny or child marriages or nakedness or gender equality or nomadism, etc.

In addition to (and often connected to) the missionaries were the institutions of education, most notably boarding schools. In America and Australia as elsewhere, native – and especially mixed-race – children were rounded up into these schools, sometimes by force, where they were compelled to change their appearance, their language, and their religion and where they were expected to receive "civilization and Christianity" including a new name, a "modern" education, and a trade. (The feature film *Rabbit-Proof Fence* is a splendid portrayal of this process in early twentieth-century Australia.) Boys were taught conventional white male roles and girls conventional white female ones. No matter what, they were subjected to acculturation pressures which neither they nor their parents could resist and which the dominant society thoroughly approved. Often, at the end of their stay, the children were turned back out into the bigger world, where they did not have the skills and knowledge to be Indians or Aboriginals nor the acceptance to be whites. They were literally marginalized.

These more overt methods to acculturate American Indian and Australian Aboriginal children were not the only ones employed. Children were sometimes actually seized from their parents and placed in white foster homes, to give them the benefits of white culture. And other more indirect means were used too, some of which were ostensibly in the natives' "best interests." For example, in 1887, after most Native American societies had been decimated and the survivors confined on reservations, some white Americans thought they were doing the Indians a favor (while others had different motivations) by breaking up communal tribal land and assigning it as private property to individual people or families. Known as "allotment," the intention was not only to turn Native Americans into private landowners and farmers like other Americans but also to tear down any communal identity and to destroy any vestiges of traditional economies and politics. After all, people could not practice foraging or pastoralism on sixteen acres of land. Individual Indians on their little

plots would cease thinking of themselves as "Indians" and assimilate to the white "individual land-holder" model (and "excess" land could be sold to or seized by non-Indians).

Genocide and ethnocide

Acculturation can be forceful and repressive, but it tends to leave people alive, more or less. However, when one society desires and seeks the complete eradication of another society, this is known as genocide (from the Greek *gens* for a people or group and *cide* for kill). Genocide as a practice has been formally identified and defined by the United Nations, which described it in Article II of the 1948 UN Genocide Convention as "acts committed with intent to destroy, in whole or in part, a national, ethnical, racial, or religious group, as such:

(a) Killing members of the group;
(b) Causing serious bodily or mental harm to members of the group;

(c) Deliberately inflicting on the group conditions of life calculated to bring about its physical destruction in whole or in part;
(d) Imposing measures intended to prevent births within the group;
(e) Forcibly transferring children of the group to another group.

By this definition, there have been many genocides over human history, most occurring in ancient times but plenty in contemporary history. It is indisputable that many societies and their cultures have vanished from the earth or had their remnants absorbed into other larger societies, without a trace or a memory. In recent historical times, the Nazi "final solution" against European Jews is the very face of genocide for most people, but it is by no means the only one. Around the turn of the twentieth century, the Turks committed genocide against the Armenians, while in the 1990s the Serbs conducted "ethnic cleansing" against Bosnian Muslims in Yugoslavia and the Hutus killed vast numbers of Tutsis in Rwanda.

THE *REQUERIMIENTO*

PLATE 11.5 A newspaper image protesting political oppression in Mongolia: main text reads: "Don't forget. . .This repression shouldn't be repeated."

BOX 11.5 GENOCIDE IN RWANDA 1994

Genocide takes many forms and has many motivations. While "weapons of mass destruction" like poison gas and concentration camps can kill thousands or millions, hand-held weapons like machetes can kill masses if enough of them are placed in enough hands. Through such face-to-face means, some 800,000 Tutsis and their supporters were exterminated in 100 days in the spring of 1994 by Hutu vigilantes and militias. The violence was not unexpected or unprecedented – or uncoordinated. As recounted previously, at the time of European invasion (late 1800s), Rwanda was a composite society, containing a dominant Tutsi minority (approximately 15 percent) and a subordinated Hutu majority (roughly 85 percent), plus a minuscule number of Twa bushmen. German and then Belgian colonial administration had perpetuated the power of the Tutsi nobility, even expanding their powers of taxation and labor recruitment; the Tutsis were inevitably favored in education and religion as well. As independence approached in the 1950s, the Hutus (formerly arguably more a class or caste than a "race" or "ethnic group" or "tribe") – in a classic case of ethnogenesis – began to organize and identify as a unified identity- and interest-group. After the proclamation of the "Manifesto of the Bahutu" in 1957, which declared the Tutsi and the Hutu to be distinct races and the Tutsi to be responsible for Hutu poverty and oppression, a Hutu political party, PARMEHUTU or Parti du Mouvement de l'Emancipation Hutu, was formed. In response, Tutsi leaders started their own party, UNAR or Union Nationale Rwandaise. Riots in 1959 led PARMEHUTU to become more militant and seize political power in 1961, establishing what one observer called "a racial dictatorship of one party" in which the Tutsi minority "may find itself defenseless in the face of abuses" (quoted in Lemarchand 1970: 194–95). Indeed, physical attacks on Tutsi drove some 120,000 (up to or more than half their population) into refuge outside the country. From those locations, they and their descendants organized paramilitary bands (known as *inyenzi* or cockroaches) to raid across the border in anticipation of their eventual return – and return to power. By 1993 the Rwandan government of Juvenal Habyarimana was in peace negotiations with Tutsi insurgents; however, hardline Hutus in units called *interahamwe* ("those who attack as one") opposed such initiatives. In April 1994, when Habyarimana's airplane was shot down, the Tutsi were instantly blamed for the assassination, and the bloodbath began. The violence was not, though, totally spontaneous. Government radio urged Hutus to destroy Tutsis and even broadcast the locations of Tutsis in hiding. Weapons and pre-prepared death-lists were distributed, and prominent Hutu citizens joined or promoted the killing. Some Tutsis were targeted as ethnic leaders, some for their wealth and property, some out of vengeance for past actions; Hutus who sympathized with or protected Tutsis were likely to be annihilated with them. Victims were often slashed along the neck or ankle and left alive, to be killed when the attackers returned, sometimes a day or more later, prowling for more prey.

See Chapter 12

See Chapter 6

The first or familiar impression of genocide is violence against "them," outsiders to a society or members of other societies. However, "them" is a relative term too, and some societies, or at least contingents within societies, have committed what we could call "auto-genocide" against what we would normally think of as "their own people." Cambodia under the Khmer Rouge party and then government is perhaps the most familiar instance. Pol Pot, the head of the Communist Khmer Rouge (as told in the popular media, like the movie *The Killing Fields*) was responsible for the death of up to a third of the population of his own country under various programs aimed at forced culture change. That is, in order to realize the desired communist workers' utopia, "enemies of the revolution" and counter-revolutionaries had to die, and this tended to include the intelligentsia, the urban population, and anyone who disagreed with official policy.

Genocide can be effective, but it is horribly expensive, messy, and unpopular; while the world does not always rush to stop it, it does usually rise up to condemn it. Genocide leaves evidence, literally in the form of corpses. However, it is not necessary to kill people in order to achieve the same basic result – the elimination of a social group. A much "cleaner" method that has proven just as effective is ethnocide. **Ethnocide** (from the Greek *ethnos* for a culture or way of life) means destroying the culture or institutions of a group rather than the people. It often masquerades as any other "educational" endeavor. The missions and boarding schools described above could and perhaps should be understood as ethnocidal projects and are often viewed as such by the indigenous people. The goal was, and was sometimes even stated as, the eradication of one kind of person and their replacement with another kind. This sentiment was expressed directly in the late nineteenth-century American slogan, "Kill the Indian to save the man." This meant rooting out the Indian-ness from Indian people, so that they would become "regular Americans." And many white Americans thought they were doing the Indians a favor – giving them a "modern" culture by means of which they could participate in broader American society and life.

Unlike genocide, ethnocide leaves living victims. The aftermath is people who "look like" Indians or Aboriginals, etc. but who do not act, think, or live like them. They are, culturally, indistinguishable from the dominant society. They have in effect been deculturated and then re-enculturated as members of the dominant society. The consequences can be and have been so abrupt, however, that some people refer to ethnocide as "cultural genocide."

Directed change

As we have acknowledged, culture change is inevitable in situations of culture contact, which has been the normal condition of human societies as long as there have been human societies. Even without that contact, individuals or groups continuously modify their cultures. Environmental changes may call for new behavioral adaptations, over the short or long term. Innovations introduce new material, and reinterpretations shift the meaning of previous material. The mere passing of generations brings new individuals with new perspectives on their "traditions." In all of these ways, culture change

is normal and natural. Cultures are always "in process."

Even in situations of culture contact, the changes induced are often unplanned, spontaneous, and uncoordinated. People observe this or that, transfer this or that, accept or modify or reject this or that in the normal course of cultural development without any specific goals in mind and without anybody dominating or driving the process. However, sometimes this change is not spontaneous and voluntary at all, and more and more in the modern world, such change is highly planned and even highly coercive.

Let us define **directed change**, then, as planned, coordinated, and sustained efforts to make changes to a part or all of a culture. There are two directions from which this initiative may come. In one case, changes are imposed "from the outside," by a foreign society that is aiming to change the culture of another society for the benefit of the former (and occasionally, at least the perception of the benefit of the latter). In the other case, changes are imposed "from the inside," by one element (class, religion, race, ethnic group, etc.) or region (e.g. urban versus rural, north versus south) of a society on another element or region of the same society. This distinction can be a little blurred, however, since in practice, "on the ground," it might not be quite clear when a group or society is "inside" or "outside." This too can be relative. When the United States wanted to encourage settlers into the Oklahoma territory in the nineteenth century, this could be regarded as promoting changes *inside American society and territory* or as imposing changes *on non-American, namely, Indian societies.* Or, in actuality, it can and should be regarded as both simultaneously, depending on the point of view. The same would be the situation in discussions of "developing" the Amazon rainforest, which is inside and under the control of the Brazilian state but also inhabited by societies that do not identify themselves as "Brazilian," as well as in many other parts of the world.

For our purposes, directed change will come in four major, world-historical manifestations, which will comprise the remainder of this book. The first is colonialism, a prime example of directed change from the outside; although modern European colonialism began as a piecemeal and even accidental project, it eventually coalesced into

Ethnocide
the destruction of a group's culture, without necessarily killing any of the members of the culture

Directed change
a cultural process in which internal or external agents make more or less intentional, coordinated, and sustained modifications or reforms to a society and culture

See Chapter 14

See Chapter 12

See Chapter 13

See Chapter 15

a very intentional and organized enterprise, with profound international repercussions that are still felt today. The second is nationalism, a type of cultural and political movement to unify and empower a social group, often with the ultimate goal of achieving sovereign political power and an independent state for the group. Closely associated with nationalism is ethnicity, a different but related form of cultural movement that may have political and/or other goals. The third is development, usually conceived as coordinated changes to the economy of a (most often poor) society, often along with or for the purpose of changes in the standard and quality of life as well. Development is an example of directed change that can come from the outside or the inside, and often both simultaneously, since states frequently propose and direct

development efforts within their territory with the assistance (financial and technical) of foreign states, corporations, or organizations. The fourth and final is what we will call generally "revitalization movements," including efforts to "reform" elements or institutions of a society as well as initiatives (particularly in the case of small, indigenous groups) to protect and preserve and in some instances revive cultural practices. These revitalization movements often, but not always, emphasize "tradition" but in a modern and "nontraditional" way and are not above using nontraditional media (like the internet) to achieve their objectives. All in all, they and the other types of directed change illustrate the power and pervasiveness of cultural innovation and diffusion and of the "invention of tradition" – which can become a "real tradition" tomorrow.

PLATE 11.6 Inculturation is a common way for religions to find a place in a new society.

BOX 11.6 CONTEMPORARY CULTURAL CONTROVERSIES: INCULTURATION AND RELIGIOUS CHANGE

Anthropology does not have a monopoly on the culture concept, nor can we control how it is used. For individuals and institutions that seek to impose cultural change, the concept of culture is indeed very useful, and Christian missionaries are among the most ardent agents of religious change. Missionaries and scholars of missiology (the study of missionary practices) have produced books like Paul Hiebert's 1986 *Anthropological Insights for Missionaries*, 1994 *Anthropological Reflections on Missiological Issues*, and 2008 *Transforming Worldviews: An Anthropological Understanding of How People Change*, as well as Charles Kraft's 1997 *Anthropology for Christian Witness*, to name but a few. The Catholic Church has been particularly thoughtful about culture and religion, overtly promoting the notion of "inculturation" or "the recognition that faith must become culture, if it is to be fully received and lived" (Shorter 1988: xi). Alwyn Shorter, a prominent theorist of inculturation, directly discussed culture and acculturation, but he rejected acculturation as "cultural domination." He also dismissed syncretism – mixing Christianity with local religion – as a compromise on Catholic truth. The beginning of real inculturation is translating Catholic doctrines and practices into local languages and cultures, as well as the reciprocal process of absorbing some local elements into Catholicism – not, to be sure, to change Catholicism but to produce locally meaningful Catholicisms and a more inclusive world Catholicism. The ultimate goal, of course, is "that the Christian message transforms a culture. It is also the case that Christianity is transformed by culture, not in a way that falsifies the message, but in a way in which the message is formulated and interpreted anew" (14). Many anthropologists are understandably apprehensive about this application of anthropological concepts; meanwhile, many Christians are apprehensive about this modification to Christianity, even while non-Western Christians are modifying Christianity on their own. What do you think?

SUMMARY

Anthropology has often been thought of, and thought of itself, as the study of "traditional societies," but no society today is perfectly "traditional," and "tradition" is a relative concept in itself. Anthropology has grown and changed, as the societies that interest it have grown and changed, into the study of cultural processes by which human groups adjust to changing internal and external realities, including contact with societies that are very different from and in very unequal power relationships with them. As it has done so, anthropology has become more self-aware of its own practices and of the entire project of conceptualizing and describing cultures.

Cultures are never static and unchanging. Even when they appear "continuous," this is an achievement of ongoing active cultural processes. In fact, every culture at every moment of its existence is a complicated alloy of continuity and change, and that is normal. Some of the processes that function in the dynamics of culture are:

- Innovation
- Diffusion
- Cultural loss or deculturation
- Acculturation
- Genocide and ethnocide
- Directed change

Whatever the original source of the cultural novelty, a process of circulation and distribution within the society is begun, which can end in three general outcomes:

MCQS

FILL IN THE BLANKS

■ Acceptance
■ Rejection
■ Acceptance with modification

It is also possible that the new cultural element may achieve a certain limited distribution and "stall" there. Culture, thus, emerges as a living system of elements that are differentially distributed throughout the society and moving (growing or shrinking) within that society. This process is often spontaneous and unintentional, or even unnoticed, but it can be – and in the modern world, increasingly is – very intentional as well as very contentious.

Key Terms

Acculturation	Directed change	Primary innovation
Cultural loss	Ethnocide	Secondary innovation
Deculturation	Genocide	Tradition
Diffusion	Innovation	

Colonialism and the origin of globalization

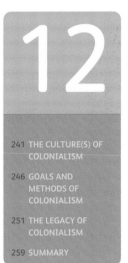

When Captain James Cook arrived at the Hawaiian Islands in 1778, a complex society already existed there. Humans had probably inhabited the islands for almost 1,500 years, bringing a cultural and physical mixture from various already occupied Pacific islands. Within a decade of Cook's "discovery" of Hawaii, American ships stopped there on route to Asia. Meanwhile, by 1810 King Kamehameha I successfully unified the island chain into a single kingdom while holding off the encroaching Westerners who sought to harvest Hawaii's rich sandalwood resources. However, after his death in 1819, American and European traders were able to penetrate the islands, and a year later Christian missionaries from the United States arrived as well. But the colonial era for Hawaii really began with the development of sugar plantations, the first established by American William Hopper in 1835. Interestingly, missionaries like Amos Starr Cooke often switched their work from Christianity to sugar. But sugar production was labor intensive, so as early as 1868 Japanese contract laborers were imported to the islands (Koreans were eventually hired after 1903 and Filipinos after 1907). Politically, a British citizen, George Paulet, had tried to seize the islands from Kamehameha III in 1843,

but it was a group of American businessmen, in conjunction with the American government and military, who finally overthrew the Hawaiian authorities in 1893. Despite the fact that an 1876 treaty had recognized Hawaii's sovereignty, with sugar production increasing tenfold over twenty years, the islands had become too valuable to resist. In 1898, the same year that the United States conquered the Philippines and Cuba from Spain, it annexed Hawaii as a U.S. territory. Hawaii's value also included an excellent harbor, Pearl Harbor, and soon a thriving new industry – pineapples. James Dole came to Honolulu in 1899, where his cousin Sanford Dole happened to be the governor since the 1893 coup. By 1907 Dole was canning pineapples for the American market, and in 1922 he managed to buy the entire island of Lana'i, which became a 200,000-acre pineapple plantation. With such profound economic and military interests in the islands, it was a small step to Hawaii's admission as the fiftieth state of the United States in 1959, only shortly after Alaska, another recently colonized territory.

The nearly 500-year-long enterprise of European colonialism profoundly changed the course of the world. Societies that had never been

PLATE 12.1

The proclamation of the independent "Republic of Hawaii," with American missionary Sanford Dole as president, after the overthrow of the Hawaiian monarchy.

See Chapter 9

in contact with another group so vastly different and so extremely remote were more or less suddenly drawn into a social system of global proportions and interconnections. However, the phenomena of culture contact, culture change, and unequal cultural relationships were not entirely new things invented by Europeans or modern colonialism. Muslim traders had long since reached Southeast Asia, and entrepreneurs from India worked in Africa. Even the Aboriginals on the northern shore of Australia had been in contact with Makassan or Malay fishermen who came annually to trawl the waters off the continent, and groups like the Qemant in Ethiopia had been surrounded by and integrated into foreign social and political systems for centuries. Complex, hierarchical, and multicultural societies and empires had risen and fallen throughout history, and no area of the earth was exempt from culture contact and the effects of long-distance trade and unequal power relations. In fact, societies that are associated with one "traditional" area or way of life, such as the Cheyenne of the plains of North America, have frequently been shown by historical,

archaeological, and ethnographic evidence to have reached these places and social patterns only recently in time (obviously, there was no horse-riding culture in the American Plains before the European introduction of horses).

Modern colonialism in a certain sense represented long-standing and familiar cultural processes of innovation, diffusion, acculturation, etc. In ways it merely escalated and intensified these processes, while in other ways it introduced a radically new moment in world cultural history. For the first time, cultural contacts and political and economic relationships were not merely local or regional but truly global. And the impact on the local societies was complex and contradictory: sometimes it appeared to freeze their "traditional" cultures at a particular moment in time, while it also altered those traditions or even destroyed them and generated entirely novel ones. Even before modern colonialism, it would be false to insist that indigenous societies had no history – were stable and homeostatic – or that such societies could be meaningfully described and understood in isolation. However, by 500 years ago we see the seeds of contemporary globalization, in which distant societies would become connected economically, politically, technologically, and "culturally." Societies were increasingly integrated into national, regional, and ultimately global systems that preserved, challenged, and changed them simultaneously. The events, decisions, and policies of any one society, state, or region could now affect other and perhaps all societies. In fact, that wider social context *becomes part of their contemporary culture.*

THE CULTURE(S) OF COLONIALISM

In 1492, when Christopher Columbus and his expedition made landfall in the "New World," an unprecedented expansion and alteration of cultural forces was already underway that would come to be known as **colonialism**; decades before, Portugal had taken the port of Ceuta, at the Straits of Gibraltar, from its Muslim occupants. Colonialism, as a world-system of occupation and exploitation of foreign territories within a European market economy, and eventually as a world-system of territorial empire, was to have unprecedented effects. Yet, the practice of establishing and controlling colonies was not new at all. In fact, colonies are not even unique to humans. The word "colony" comes from the Latin *colonia*, which derives from *colonus* or farmer, which further derives from *colere* or to cultivate (also related to the root of the term "culture"). A **colony** is a segment of a population that moves into and occupies a new territory; as such, there can be not only colonies of humans but of animals, trees, or bacteria. To "colonize" is merely to expand into areas previously unoccupied by the population, and the offshoot of the original population that pioneers this new occupation is the colony.

So fifteenth- and sixteenth-century Europeans did not invent colonization. Societies were colonizing new lands in the ancient and prehistoric past. Greek cities colonized the Mediterranean coast, "planting" colonies of Greeks as far afield as present-day Turkey and Spain. When Alexander the Great swept through the Middle East and Central Asia, he intentionally left behind colonies, often named Alexandria, with the full complement of Greek social, intellectual, and artistic institutions. Polynesian peoples colonized Hawaii after colo-

nizing other Pacific Islands, and modern-day European societies themselves are the product of multiple waves of colonization of the continent, from the first Homo sapiens who displaced the Neandertals to Greek and Roman and Germanic, Slavic, Celtic, Nordic, and other peoples (again refuting the "pure race" illusion of Europeans). Later, these products of ancient colonizations reached out to colonize a world that had itself been shaped by successive waves of occupation.

As James Clifford reminded us, "Everyone's on the move, and has been for centuries" (1997: 2). Therefore, the anthropological "study of colonialism erases the boundaries between anthropology and history or literary studies" (Pels 1997: 163), even as it erases boundaries between different societies – and sometimes creates new boundaries. The worldwide phenomenon that was sparked by the explorations of early-modern wanderers was to evolve into something quite extraordinary. In scale and impact, it was unmatched, since no society had ever flung its colonies so broadly nor wrought such grand changes on the colonized regions. And gradually it was to shift from mere colonization to a deliberate and sustained policy of colonialism. Colonialism eventually became a form of directed change, a deliberate and concerted attempt to place settlements in new territories for the purpose of economic and political domination of those territories and of the peoples who already lived there. This domination was, of course, primarily for the benefit of the transplanted foreigners (the colonists) or ultimately of the "mother country" from which the colonists were sent, rather than of the local indigenous people. In fact, the interests of the colonists and the locals or "indigenous peoples" usually if not invariably conflicted, leading to serious and often violent conflict.

The diversity of colonialism

Various attempts have been made to diversify colonial practices and forms. In 1972 Ronald Horvath proposed to define colonialism as a type of "intergroup domination in which settlers in significant number migrate permanently to the colony from the colonizing power," distinguishing it from "imperialism" which involved few if any settlers (1972: 50). While that is probably not the salient difference, he

See Chapter 6

Colonialism
the more or less organized system of occupation and exploitation of foreign territories through settlement and conquest, especially as practiced by Western states since 1492

Colony
a segment of a population (not exclusively a human population) that moves into and occupies territory not previously occupied by the population, often displacing or subduing the previous occupants

See Chapter 15

did make the valid observation that some colonies included many settlers while others included few. He added that in either case, the relation between local inhabitants and colonial invaders could take the shape of extermination of the locals, assimilation of the locals to the colonial culture, or "relative equilibrium" in an integrated or segregated society (see Furnivall on "plural society" below).

A more fruitful approach has been to identify as many as four different styles or experiences of colonialism, depending on precisely who or what did the colonizing and on how the power of colonialism was organized.

Colonies of settlement
colonies to which many foreigners immigrate, sometimes such that they and their descendants become the majority population of the territory

1. The most familiar and stereotypical form of colonialism was *direct rule*, in which a Western government directly intervened in local society, conquering the territory with state armies and administering the territory with state bureaucrats (governors, tax collectors, officers of the law, and even missionaries acting on behalf of the state). Direct rule was not the only or most common practice, though, especially in the early stages of colonialism: often direct governmental intervention came later, after the area had been occupied by settlers or merchants,

whose lives and property had then to be defended by the state.

2. Even when Western states could project power directly into foreign regions, they frequently chose to practice *indirect rule*, in which case they would co-opt native authorities to participate in the governance of the colony. Indirect rule was cheaper and often more effective, since the ordinary people in the colony still took orders from "traditional" leaders, who in turn took orders from Western states. In a word, "traditional" leaders became partners in the colonial enterprise, although they were not equal partners nor were they necessarily entirely traditional.

3. In most colonies, actually relatively few Westerners came to settle. However, in **colonies of settlement**, large numbers of foreign colonists flocked into the colonies, sometimes to the point where they outnumbered the native population. The United States is a classic case of a colony of settlement (actually several colonies of settlement that eventually united into a single polity); other colonies of settlement included Canada, Australia, New Zealand, South Africa, and Southern Rhodesia

PLATE 12.2 Indirect rule involved creating partnerships between European colonizers and local people, including recruitment of native soldiers into colonial armies, as depicted here in Rwanda.

BOX 12.1   INDIRECT RULE IN COLONIAL RWANDA

Rwanda at the time of European invasion was a kingdom with an elaborate hierarchy of chiefs and subchiefs who were essentially clients to the royal patron or *mwami*. When Belgium took control from Germany after World War I, rather than eliminating the local political system, Belgium joined the system, establishing itself as a kind of super-patron over native chiefs. At first, this relationship actually enhanced the power of king and chief, as they now had the financial and military support of a Western state, but it also added to the burdens of the masses: colonial administrators wanted labor and profit from the colony, and the chiefs were required to place new demands on their people as well as to collect taxes for their new master. But Belgian authorities also reshaped the Rwandan aristocracy, "streamlining" it in 1926 by eliminating some chieftaincies and merging others; the total number of chiefs and subchiefs was reduced from 119 and 324 to five and seventy-two, respectively. Those that remained, though, saw their positions solidified and their power expanded and "modernized": older forms of clientage for the people of Rwanda were replaced with more exploitative economic relationships. Even more, the Belgians systematically favored one group (Tutsi) over the other (Hutu), deposing Hutu chiefs and installing Tutsi chiefs in their place. By the 1930s colonial administrators asked chiefs to recruit workers for Belgian enterprises like coffee plantations and mines, and chiefs themselves became salaried officers of the colonial system. By the end of the colonial era in Rwanda, chiefs were no longer the "traditional" leaders they had once been, nor was the "traditional" politics of the colony entirely distinguishable from the colonial politics.

(Zimbabwe today), although the European population never reached majority status in the last two. In such circumstances, either initially or eventually, colonialism was based on *settler rule*, with the transplanted inhabitants exercising effective local control of the colony. Typically they at first identified with, and ruled in the interests of, the mother country, but eventually they became more locally minded, even striving (and fighting) for local independence.

4. Unlike colonies of settlement, **colonies of exploitation** never acquired large European populations, sometimes because the climate was unwelcoming, sometimes because large-scale settlement was too expensive, and sometimes because it was simply unnecessary. After all, if the purpose of the colony was to supply cheap sources of primary products like cotton or rubber or coffee, the colonizers did not need or perhaps even want a lot of settlers. But, unlike the conventional notion of colonialism as a governmental undertaking, colonies of exploitation did not require state involvement at all. Many of them were actually situations of *corporate control*. In a surprising

number of instances, the early forays into colonialism were conducted not by government and not by individuals or families but by corporations, charted companies founded to trade with other countries and societies. Some of the most famous of these are the Dutch East India Company and the British East India Company; in the Western hemisphere, the Hudson's Bay Company operated in Canada, and the Virginia Company was responsible for the settlement of Jamestown in 1607. The key thing to remember is that colonialism was about trade and profit first and foremost, and corporations then and since have been the primary mechanism of business. But profit is an effect and a cause of power, and many of these early trading companies eventually began to exert political power over non-Western territories – enforcing civil and criminal law, negotiating with local rulers, and maintaining armies and fighting battles as if they were states. In many ways, they were multinational corporate colonial states.

Even these four alternatives do not completely exhaust the diversity of colonial practices. When

CORPORATIONS AND COLONIALISM

Colonies of exploitation colonies to which few foreigners immigrate but the territory is still used for its resources, wealth, labor, markets, and/or strategic location

Sphere of influence
in European colonial practice, an area of foreign territory where the power and authority of one European state was recognized

Mercantilism
an early-modern European economic and political system in which wealth and power were determined by possession of gold and a favorable balance of trade with each other

Internal colonialism
the practice in which a society (usually a state) penetrates and occupies territory within its jurisdiction (normally, inside its borders) but that contains peoples who do not identify as and with the occupying society. In some usages, it can also refer to the condition in which colonized peoples internalize in their own minds and personalities the institutions and values of colonialism

Imperialism
the pursuit of territorial and political domination of foreign lands and peoples (building an "empire"), known since ancient history but reaching its greatest extent in the late phase of European colonialism

COLONIZING EGYPT

Western powers could not thoroughly conquer a society, **spheres of influence** often resulted. This was particularly the case in China, which was simply too large and too integrated to be controlled in its entirety or by any single foreign power. In such cases, the local society was weakened to the point at which it could not prevent foreign interference and penetration, and chunks of territory were occupied or dominated by various foreign powers. Hong Kong, which was only transferred back to China from the United Kingdom in 1997, was one such chunk; other states including France, Germany, Japan, and even the United States also had their pieces or "spheres," in which foreign law and culture was more or less formally instituted (the concept of "extraterritoriality").

Finally, **internal colonialism** was – and in some cases still is – a situation in which one group or region dominates the land, population, and resources of another region or group within "the same" state. The United States prior to the Civil War has been described as a case of internal colonialism, with the industrial North exploiting the agrarian South, and after the war the North actually militarily occupied the South. Brazil and its exploitation of the Amazonian region for the benefit of the urban eastern and southern regions could be another example, as could England with its historical domination of the Scottish, Welsh, and Irish lands and people.

Internal colonialism has also been used to refer to the process by which colonized people internalize the values and practices of the colonizer, thus participating in their own colonization. Interestingly, on many occasions non-Western societies began to adopt aspects of Western culture before they were actually colonized. Sometimes these changes came through pre-colonial cultural, financial, or military influence (as when Japan eagerly embraced many aspects of Western society after being "opened" by American warships in 1854): reformers in these societies either wanted to become "modern" like Europeans and Americans or to acquire the tools of power and prosperity to ward off colonial advances.

Diverse eras, diverse agents

The colonial experience also diverged according to the era in which it was practiced. When Europe launched its colonial adventure, just prior to 1500,

it was still a relatively weak continent in comparison to the great empires of the day – Ottoman, Chinese, Mughal (Indian), and others. Its goals and its capabilities were fairly limited. Also, its range was fairly limited: North and South America came under its sway, as did parts of the "East Indies" or the so-called Spice Islands (largely, present-day Indonesia) and a very few coastal patches of Africa and India. This phase, which has been called **mercantilism**, focused essentially on trade monopolies between states and their colonies and the accumulation of wealth, particularly gold. Colonies were often like remote farms and mines for the mother country to harvest and tap.

Many of these early mercantile colonies achieved independence from their overlords in the mid to late 1800s. Subsequently, European colonialism was reconstituted in a modern and more systematic and exploitative form, which we will call **imperialism**. Imperialism sought more than the old colonialism ever did, including territorial possession, efficient administration, and enhanced wealth production and extraction, all related to the political competitions between the "Great Powers" of Europe and their industrial and military needs and interests. In this later period, the final and complete occupation of the world was accomplished, with enormous colonial holdings, especially for England, in Africa, India, Asia, and the Middle East. For instance, following the Congress of Berlin in 1884–85, a "scramble for Africa" commenced which ended within a few years by the carving of what King Leopold of Belgium referred to as the "magnificent Africa cake," every "piece" of which was colonized except Ethiopia and Liberia – and Liberia had been founded by the American Colonization Society in 1821 in the first place.

Finally, it should be apparent by now that colonialism involved a diverse cast of characters, not merely states and their functionaries. Many "agents of colonialism" played their parts in the colonial undertaking, pursuing diverse interests that were only later coordinated and integrated into a few great national enterprises. In most locations, explorers and missionaries were the first point of contact between Europe and the non-European world. Explorers obviously were often the first foreigners to set foot on unknown lands, to map them, report information back to the home country, and claim the territories in the name of the home

BOX 12.2 A COMPARATIVE ANALYSIS OF SPANISH AND BRITISH COLONIES

The most obvious difference between colonial experiences depended on the particular cultures and practices of the specific colonizing power. Spain naturally implanted Spanish culture, the Spanish language, and Catholicism, while Britain carried along British culture, the English language, English common law, and Anglican and other Protestant Christianity. However, the fact that Spanish colonialism came relatively early and British colonialism relatively late meant that the two states practiced remarkably different styles of colonialism, according to Matthew Lange, James Mahoney, and Matthias vom Hau, basically "different *levels of colonialism*" defined as "the extent to which a colonizing power installs economic, political, and sociocultural institutions in a colonized territory" (2006: 1414). First, they argue that, because Spain's policy was more mercantile, verging on feudal, the

> Spanish generally settled and concentrated colonial institutions in those areas that were the most populous and most politically and economically developed at the beginning of the colonial epoch. In contrast, the British pursued comparatively limited settlement and institutional transformation in the more populous and more politically and economically developed precolonial areas. Hence, precolonial level of development is positively associated with level of Spanish colonialism, but negatively associated with level of British colonialism.
>
> (1414)

Not surprisingly, perhaps, they conclude that the types of societies each colonized, added to their different colonial policies, "had opposite effects on long-run socioeconomic development for the Spanish and British colonies":

> More extensive Spanish colonialism produced predatory states and dysfunctional markets, and it also left behind highly stratified societies. Less extensive Spanish colonialism did not directly lead to the creation of effective states and markets, but it did spare regions from the establishment of the most destructive institutions, giving them a chance to experience development in the aftermath of the colonial period. Conversely, more extensive British colonialism introduced a rule of law, effective administration, and competitive markets, promoting development in the postcolonial period. Yet limited forms of British colonialism distorted existing institutions in ways that greatly hindered future development. Hence, the effect of level of colonialism on development is the opposite for Spanish and British colonialism.
>
> (1414)

In summary, "the historical processes through which colonial institutions were installed and shaped subsequent development differed dramatically" (1450) under Spanish or British rule – and presumably under other colonial administrations as well – with different long-term effects for colonized societies.

country. Sometimes arriving with the explorers, and soon traveling and exploring on their own, were the missionaries. One of the most energetic missionary groups was The Society of Jesus, best known as the Jesuits, a Catholic organization formed in response to the Protestant Reformation. By the late 1500s and early 1600s, missionaries – Catholic and later Protestant – were blazing trails to the interior of the Americas, often ahead of explorers and other colonizers. While they did impose many changes on indigenous cultures, they often did important descriptive work too, in places where acculturation and cultural loss sometimes made subsequent study difficult or impossible. One of their main contributions was in the area of language, which they studied principally for the purpose of translating the Christian Bible into local languages; still, some of those linguistic analyses – dictionaries, grammars,

PLATE 12.3 Colonialism was a political and personal relationship between colonizers – like the British officer depicted here in colonial India – and colonized.

and translated documents – are the oldest or only records of native cultures.

Not far behind the explorers and the missionaries were the traders, planters, and administrators. Some traders were individual men (and occasionally women) who came to conduct economic exchanges with the native populations. They often lived relatively "native" lives, acculturating to native ways to the point of wearing native clothing, speaking native languages, and occasionally marrying native women. They thus often produced the first generation of mixed-blood children. Other traders were representatives of large formal corporations, as mentioned above. They merely wanted to make money but were forced (at least at first) to deal with local authorities and observe local customs.

Where land was good and plentiful, planters or settlers were soon to arrive, and administrators, from governors and regents to accountants and tax collectors, as well as soldiers to secure peace and compliance, were usually not far behind. While governments often did not take much interest until the colonies were functioning and profitable, it was inevitable that European law and power would eventually prevail in these colonies and that even the natives themselves would be brought under their jurisdiction. In some cases this involved military campaigns to "pacify" restless and resistant locals; in other cases, or at the same time, formal "inter-governmental" relations with the locals were often established, including actual treaties between governments and indigenous leaders. This practice was most common in English territories and the United States, where treaties still significantly shape U.S.–Indian relations today, setting the precedent of Indian tribal sovereignty.

A U.S. INDIAN TREATY

GOALS AND METHODS OF COLONIALISM

Colonialism in both its mercantile and imperialist phases had certain basic goals, as well as methods to reach those goals. At the most fundamental level, these goals were economic (the enrichment of the colonialist society and of the colonists who emigrated to the colonies) and political (the empowerment of the colonialist society through expansion of its dominion and blockage of expansion by its rivals). We can identify several more specific purposes and practices.

Wealth

Colonialist/imperialist societies sought wealth, first portable wealth that they could expropriate and carry back to their home countries. This was of course at the very heart of the mercantile system, which was based on the acquisition of precious metals – particularly gold and silver – and a favorable balance of trade that led to further accumulation of these metals. Accordingly, when Columbus set off for the "Indies," his eyes were fixed on gold (along with God, government, and glory). Later expeditions to the Americas crisscrossed the continent searching for El Dorado, the legendary city and society of gold. Where gold was found – either in use or at the source – it was theirs for the taking. The story of the gold of the Incas is only atypical in its ferocity: Spanish conquistadors, having penetrated Inca society, took the emperor Atahualpa hostage and demanded that his subjects fill an entire room with gold as his ransom. When the room was filled to the brim, the Spanish

PLATE 12.4 Colonialism typically involved the military defeat and conquest of native peoples, like these Apache women held captive by American soldiers.

christened Atahualpa with a Spanish name and garroted (strangled) him to death. Then they melted the priceless gold artifacts into bullion and shipped it to Europe. How all of this appeared to the native peoples of the Americas is best expressed in *The Indian Chronicles*: "I believe the gold makes them crazy. . . .That is truly their god. Gold is more important to them than their own people. . . .The Castilla [Spanish] worship only one God, his name is Gold" (Barreiro 1993: 191)

Access to resources and control of their source

Perhaps the main motivation was to find a path to the sources of goods including spices like cinnamon, ginger, nutmeg, and so on, which originated in the Pacific "Spice Islands." Other valued goods included unique scented woods, silks and porcelains, and products that would become staples of Western life like coffee and tea. Before 1500, some Europeans had traveled east to the sources of some of these goods, particularly China. However, for most purposes, especially for the island trade, they depended on the overland Central Asian trade system, dominated by the Muslims. This was a major problem for the Europeans, though, for two reasons, religio-political (trading with and enriching their enemies) and sheer economic (paying a middlemen for their supply). If Europeans could make their own connections to the source, they

could "cut out the middleman" and enhance their profits. So, the first tentative ventures away from Europe, starting in the mid-1400s, tended to hug the coastline of Africa, where they occasionally landed to plant a trading post; once they rounded the southern tip of Africa, they proceeded east to the islands. In many places, they found strong societies and established traders and posts; however, unlike Arab and other traders before them, Europeans soon meant to monopolize and to own. Accessing and controlling the sources of valuable goods involved finding and, where possible, taking possession of, farms, mines, forests, and any other means of production. And of course, as in the New World, nothing stood in their way. Europeans seized mines, like the great silver mines of central South America, or farmland or rivers or anything of any value to them.

Land

Colonists claimed and occupied land and then put it to whatever use they could discover or develop there. Even more, colonists needed to find a way to justify to themselves this expropriation of native land. Two concepts, "legal fictions" if you will, emerged to solve the problem – the "doctrine of discovery" and the notion of *terra nullius*. The **doctrine of discovery** stipulated that any state that could discover and claim a hitherto unknown or unclaimed land could have undisputed title to it.

Doctrine of discovery
the European colonial principle that the state that "discovered" or arrived first in a new territory had the right to occupy and administer it without interference from other states

Corvée
a colonial practice in which local people were required to provide a period of labor to the administration as a sort of "tax"

Terra nullius
the colonial doctrine of "empty land," that colonized land was empty of human inhabitants and therefore could be claimed and settled by colonists

Encomienda
in Latin American colonial history, a grant of land to a conqueror and explorer, much like medieval estates, which gave the grant-holder control over the land and inhabitants

Hacienda
the Spanish colonial practice in which land was granted as private property and in which these estates were run both for subsistence production and for the production of cash and export crops

Blackbirding
the colonial practice of abducting the populations of areas, often islands, and resettling them as a labor force in some other part of the world

See Chapter 14

The doctrine of discovery therefore gave the discovering power the first right of occupation if there were no previous inhabitants. If there were inhabitants, the discovering power had the first right to trade with them and to negotiate political relations with them, normally taking the form of subordination and/or war. This doctrine alone, though, did not justify taking away land other than by agreement or aggression. Here, the idea of **terra nullius** served well. Derived from the Latin legal principle of "no man's land," it suggested that the lands discovered and claimed by Europeans were unoccupied and therefore available to anyone who could squat on them. The only problem was that virtually no land anywhere in the world was unoccupied. If it could not be argued that the land was void of human beings, it could be argued that it was void of *completely* human beings or of *civilized* human beings. The mark of civilization was permanent settlements and cultivated farmland after the European fashion. Natives who were foragers or nomads were treated as little more than "beasts of the field," who by this logic surely did not own the lands they wandered and grazed on. So, since such people never established title to the land, original title could be claimed by the European arrivals. In other cases, title to land could be created by treaty, which extinguished native claims and invented the first "deed" for it.

Labor

There was much work to be done in the colonies, but usually there were not enough European immigrants to do it; besides, many colonists did not want to do this grueling work but rather to profit from the work of others. So the system needed more than the dispossessed property of the natives; it needed their labor too. Hence, native labor became a valuable commodity, since it produced (at little or no cost) the wealth of the colony. Indians were "employed" in the mines or farms or ports of the Americas, and in more powerful and resistant societies (like African and Indonesian ones) increasingly imbalanced and exploitative relations were established with the producers, who were converted into European employees and serfs. Europeans devised many methods to achieve the "employment" that they needed, including force and enslavement. In some cases, a system of **corvée** labor was instituted,

which required that every able-bodied person provide a certain number of days or months of labor each year. Large private farms or plantations were quick to appear. In Spanish territories, these farms were known as **encomiendas** and **haciendas** (in Portuguese Brazil, the name was *fazendas*). *Encomiendas* were essentially grants of land to conquerors and explorers, much like medieval estates; as such, control of land meant control of the people and wealth on the land. Therefore, unlucky Indians who had *encomiendas* organized under their feet found themselves changed into serfs who owed labor and tribute to their new lords. This institution was eventually replaced by a more modern but thereby more exploitative arrangement called the *hacienda*. A *hacienda* was less feudal but was truly owned by the *haciendados* who acquired workers or tenants through indebtedness and sharecropping. Mines and other interests were organized on basically the same principles: Europeans controlled or owned, and natives worked. In many cases, the natives failed to do the work satisfactorily, either because the ordeals of the work simply killed them or because they could escape and run away. This led to the introduction of a new institution, the slave trade. Slaves, mostly but not exclusively from Africa, were collected (with the cooperation of African rulers and entrepreneurs) and sold to plantation owners throughout the Americas. Of course, Europeans did not invent slavery, and long after they abolished it, other societies continued (and continue today) to practice it, but the scale of the European slave trade was truly unique. Also, Africans were not the only peoples to be enslaved. In a practice known as **blackbirding**, European sailors would often land on small Pacific islands and carry off virtually the entire populations to work on some far-off colonial project in India or Southeast Asia.

Taxation

European colonialists introduced taxation in their colonies for two reasons. One was to pay the administrative costs of the colony itself. Colonies were not always profitable ventures; colonialism was inefficient compared to some of the more "modern" means of exploitation. Rather than bearing theses costs themselves, the colonialists shifted the burden to the natives. Arguably, some improvements in the quality of life were subsidized this way, including schools and hospitals and such, but none of it was the choice of the natives. Yet another reason for taxation was to compel natives to participate in the colonial economy. The colonial administration would order that all inhabitants had to pay a cash tax on their houses, their livestock, their own heads, and so on. But natives had no cash, and the only place they could obtain it was from wage labor for European businesses. So colonialists got the natives' land and their wealth and their work and at least some of their wages.

Markets for manufactured goods

Colonialism was above all things about the economic growth of the colonizing societies. During the mercantile age, domestic European production was on the increase, first in the agricultural and then in the "light industrial" (especially textile) sectors; in England, for example, corn and wool were in abundant supply in the early 1600s, causing economic and social turmoil as prices dropped, dragging down wages of workers and profits of producers. But there was a limit to the sales that could occur within the domestic market. The colonies became a profitable new place to make these sales. Next, colonial administrations could sell the exotic products of the colonies (coffee, tea, sugar, rubber, etc.) to the home country or to each other. Colonial trading monopolies meant that colonies could only sell to the home country or to other colonies of the home country. Further, this growth in markets helped pay for the continuing and expanding growth of business and industry back home. Colonial powers could acquire raw materials cheaply, manufacture those materials into finished products, and sell those products to their own people, other Europeans, or the colonies. The wealth that was accumulated by England and France in particular was reinvested into expansion and technical innovation, ultimately financing their industrial revolutions. Of course, much of this wealth also went into military ventures and other less productive enterprises.

Geopolitics

Geopolitics means control and use of important or strategic locations of the globe. Although originally targeted principally at the Muslims, geopolitics naturally and quickly pitted European states against each other. In fact, as early as 1494, Spain and Portugal claimed, by right of a papal decree, to divide the entire New World between their two empires. Of course, England, Holland, France, and other ambitious states would not accept this arrangement for long and sought to undermine it immediately – in some cases first as pirates, then as rivals. By 1588 Spain was sufficiently tired of English interference that it sailed its armada to invade England but was summarily crushed. Dominating the sources of valuable trade goods was only the first step in the geopolitical game. Soon Europeans wanted to control territory, and for long slow intercontinental voyages, refueling and resupplying stations were necessary; therefore, claiming and occupying intermediate spots, especially Pacific island ports, was critical. Colonial competition became so fierce that, by 1756, England and France were fighting around the globe for political dominance in what American history remembers as the French and Indian War but world history calls the Seven Years War (1756–63), which England won. Yet, just at this moment, the movements for independence from this first phase of colonialism were approaching. As a result, Europeans had to find new lands to colonize (hence the "scramble for Africa"). Sometimes, the point was simply to prevent anyone else from getting a territory, even if it was not particularly valuable to the colonizers. The case of the Gambia River is one of the clearest and most absurd examples. Britain invaded and occupied a few miles of land on both banks of this northwest African waterway. France, however, occupying the surrounding territory of Senegal, suggested a land swap, offering larger and richer regions like the Ivory Coast in exchange. England refused and retained a tiny sliver of territory deep in the heart of French Africa (which went on to become a tiny sliver of an independent state). The same scenario was played out around the world, from Hong Kong and Singapore to Hawaii to Cuba.

Geopolitics
the use of geographical territory for purposes of maintenance and projection of power; the control of strategic locations in the pursuit of political goals

BOX 12.3   THE COLONIZATION OF EVERYDAY LIFE

CRIMINAL CASTES AND SALVATION SOLDIERS

While colonialism was ultimately about power and profit, those things cannot be divorced from the wider culture and the everyday habits of the people affected. John and Jean Comaroff have described how colonialism in southern Africa involved changes to and domination of the political and economic aspects of subject societies, together with religion and other cultural habits like dress, speech, marriage, gender roles, and so on – what Jean Comaroff called "the signs and structures of everyday life" (1985: 80). Therefore, the religious conversion process was designed to effect a change in these signs and structures, a "revolution in habits," "a quest to refurnish the mundane: to focus human endeavor on the humble scapes of the everyday, of the 'here-and-now' in which the narrative of Protestant redemption took on its contemporary form" (Comaroff and Comaroff 1991: 9). They have also described this struggle as "an epic of the ordinary" and "the everyday as epiphany":

> it was precisely by means of the residual, naturalized quality of habit that power takes up residence in culture, insinuating itself, apparently without agency, in the texture of a life-world. This, we believe, is why recasting mundane, routine practices has been so vital to all manner of social reformers, colonial missionaries among them.

(31)

One important site was farming techniques. Missionaries offered a model for "civilized cultivation" in the form of the "mission garden"; a major aspect of this new model was a reversal of traditional gender roles, in which women had done the bulk of horticultural work. The plow became a potent symbol of Western-style farming; fences introduced conceptions of "enclosure" and property; and inequality of output, related to intensity of labor, generated Western-style differences in wealth and status as their reward. But economic change went beyond horticulture to new institutions like markets and money. Modern labor and cash were part of a new "moral economy," stigmatizing idleness and "primitive production" and promoting "the kind of upright industry and lifestyle that would dissolve [tradition's] dirt" (189).

Yet more mundane areas like clothing and household practices were valued for their civilizing effects. Clothes not only meant covering heathen nakedness but teaching locals the proper wear and care of these articles; native clothing, it seemed to colonists, was dirty, too "natural," and lacked the necessary markers of social – especially gender – distinctions. For this purpose, old used clothes were shipped from England to clothe, and thereby transform, the pagan body, teaching them shame and pride at the same time. And as already suggested, proper (that is, Western/Christian) gender behavior was essential: women needed to be covered modestly and reassigned to the home. Home became a "domestic" sphere, which became woman's sphere, where she would literally sit, sew, and serve. But the traditional native house would not do; the house and the community had to be transformed from what the Europeans perceived as "a wild array of small, featureless huts scattered across the countryside" (282). Missionary houses and buildings again acted as the model: with right angles, specialized spaces (e.g. a room for eating, a room for sleeping, etc.), doors and locks for privacy, and modern furniture, the mission structures "became a diorama" for how people should live (292). The collection of residences that became the "town" differentiated public from private spaces, all set in a universe of square blocks and broad streets. In these and many ways, the foreigners were doing much more than bringing a new religion; they were "teaching [them] to build a world" (296), one in which civilization itself was expressed "in squares and straight lines" (127).

THE LEGACY OF COLONIALISM

Eventually, the formal colonial system came to an end, and the entities that were formerly – for the period of a few decades or a few centuries – colonies became "independent." This does not mean, of course, that everything returned to pre-colonial conditions, nor that everything had a happy ending. It certainly does not mean that external and global forces ceased to impact and indeed to be intimately enmeshed with local groups and cultures. In some ways, new intercultural realities emerged that were not all that different from the colonial relationships. The one thing that would never again be true, if it ever was, is the possibility of thinking in terms of bounded and discrete societies in isolation from each other.

While modern Western colonialism was not utterly unprecedented, its long-term effects were: it wrought changes on a scale and of types that would not be rolled back by the simple end of the system. In fact, in a variety of ways, the colonial project was not completed when it "ended." In North America, for example, British and French colonial administrations departed the scene, but local governments – American and Canadian – continued to "colonize" the territories to which they laid claim. The United States asserted possession and control of the western regions of its continent, but it still had the challenge of moving colonies of settlers into those regions and making good its assertions; the people who traveled in wagon trains along the Oregon Trail and other western routes ought rightly to be thought of as colonists too. And this process goes on

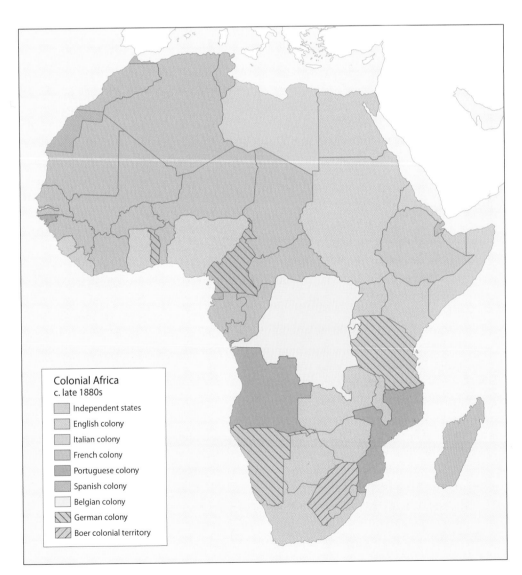

Colonial Africa
c. late 1880s

- Independent states
- English colony
- Italian colony
- French colony
- Portuguese colony
- Spanish colony
- Belgian colony
- German colony
- Boer colonial territory

MAP 12.1 Colonial Africa

TABLE 12.1   Dates of independence from colonialism, selected countries

First (mercantile) phase		Second (imperialist) phase	
United States	1776	Iraq	1932
Brazil	1815	Jordan, Syria, Lebanon	1946
Peru	1821	India, Pakistan	1947
Mexico	1821	Indonesia	1949
Argentina	1815	Ghana (Gold Coast)	1957
Bolivia	1825	Mali, Niger, Chad	1960
Venezuela	1830	Sudan	1956
Guatemala	1838	Nigeria, Cameroon, Senegal	1960
Honduras	1838	Libya	1951
El Salvador	1838	Zaire/Congo	1960
Costa Rica	1838	Malaysia	1963
Chile	1818	Algeria	1962
Ecuador	1803	Kenya	1963
Paraguay	1811	Angola, Mozambique	1975
Uruguay	1828	Zimbabwe	1980

today in many parts of the world. Some of the changes introduced by this colonial process, old and new, are environmental, some are cultural, others are demographic, and still others are "economic" and "political" in the familiar sense. All of them are of concern not only to anthropologists but to all citizens of the world.

Depopulation

In all colonial settings, there had been extensive loss of life. In some, huge numbers of native people died from diseases like smallpox, syphilis, and other plagues that were lethal to but controllable in European societies. Some estimates suggest that as much as 90 percent of the Native American population died in the early decades of contact, many before they ever saw a white person. Where disease did not ravage the local people, war often did. Many colonized people fought long and hard struggles to resist European invasion; however, in practically every case, European war technology was superior to local weapons, and where weapons alone could not suffice, economic and political pressures eventually brought the peoples to heel. In many places, there were declared wars prosecuted by professional soldiers, including the "Indian wars" in the United States. However, an untold number of native people died from unofficial and personal

violence perpetrated by settlers. In Africa, armed homesteaders often killed locals in "self-defense" when those locals attempted to defend their land.

In Australia, which was entirely inhabited by band-level foraging societies, English settlers often considered the Aboriginals little more than vermin to be exterminated, like any other native wildlife that stood in the way of farming and ranching. Massacres took place from the earliest days of Australian settlement (1788) until the early 1900s. When settlement ships arrived with the first 800 or so English convicts, it took only a year for an Aboriginal leader, Pemulwuy, to be captured and beheaded. As Euro-Australians pushed their way into central Australia, they encountered more foragers occupying land in "non-productive" activities and displaced them. The settlers who followed behind them, with the aid of the territorial police, "protected" whites against the predations of the Aboriginals, who merely saw themselves as acting in self-defense. By the mid-1800s, the era of massacres was well under way. Entire Aboriginal communities were rounded up and executed for the deaths of whites or of the cattle of whites, regardless of whether those particular Aboriginals were the culprits or not. Some of the most notorious killings came in the 1900s, such as the 1928 Coniston massacre, in which police and settlers killed fifty-one Aboriginals (most of them probably innocent of any wrongdoing); the whites were never found

PLATE 12.5 Well into the twentieth century, Australian Aboriginals were often arrested and chained.
State Library of Western Australia

guilty of any crime for these acts. In the same year, police captured another whole society of Aboriginal hunters, chained them by the neck, and killed all of them except three women. They killed and burned all of the men. Neck-chaining continued to be practiced in Australia until 1960.

Most infamously in Africa, but in other locations as well, large populations were deported into slavery. It is estimated that as many as 30 million Africans were removed, mostly bound for South America, although many fewer than that number ever arrived alive. "Blackbirding," as we noted above, also wiped out whole island societies. And where slavery as such was not practiced, people were often transferred from one area to another as labor, like the Tamils of India who were imported into highland Ceylon (Sri Lanka) as agricultural workers. Finally, many native people died from the living conditions in the colonies, including over-work, poor diet, alcoholism, internecine fighting, seizure of women and children, the difficulty of making culturally correct marriages, and the sheer hopelessness that comes with the destruction of one's traditions and culture.

Acculturation and deculturation

Native peoples were often unable to continue their pre-colonial ways of life, due to inadvertent factors or intentional policy. Indigenous societies, especially foragers and pastoralists, were often settled more or less forcibly in villages. Efforts were made to convert all locals into wage laborers

and taxpayers, and all production was integrated into the colonial and global economy, producing for export rather than local consumption. Furthermore, if people were compelled to toil on plantations or in mines, there was precious little time left for traditional social or religious activities, which were often discouraged or forbidden anyhow. When men were required to travel far away for work, traditional family structures suffered and occasionally collapsed. Kinship practices were altered, often by law, particularly when it came to matters of polygyny or child marriage. European-style marriage and sexual rules were enforced on natives, and European gender roles were imposed, often to the impoverishment of women who in some cases enjoyed better status before colonialism than afterwards. Enforced Western-style education, boarding schools, and separation of native children from their parents and societies interrupted cultural transmission and introduced competing values and institutions. Pre-colonial political systems were modified in sometimes contradictory ways: political roles and offices were often consolidated or elim-inated, even while the powers of the remaining authorities expanded, strengthened by colonial administrations and armies and given new prerog-atives like tax collecting and the right to compel labor. Simultaneously, colonial administrators and courts claimed the final right to intervene in matters of law. Religion was a particular target for change and "conversion," discrediting local spirits and gods and prohibiting or co-opting local practices and institutions. Often, key artifacts and symbols were appropriated by travelers, traders, and collectors.

Finally, particularly in colonies of settlement, indigenous societies were literally swamped by people with foreign cultures, although even a small number of settlers could radically reshape cultural relations.

Acculturation was not always a simple and direct acquisition of a foreign culture; on more than a few occasions it was a fascinating process of invention and acceptance of a novel or reinterpreted version of "tradition." Colonial authorities, some presumably well-meaning, would often try to base colonial policy on "traditional culture" – or what they thought was traditional culture. Since what was actually encountered on the ground was a messy and complicated blend of different social systems varying more or less from their own ideals, outsiders, including anthropologists, occasionally "found" more order and non-ambiguity than really

See Chapter 14

existed and fed it back to the natives, inventing a "traditional" culture that had never existed – but which might *become* tradition in persuasive and powerful ways.

Loss of economic independence

Native peoples were no longer free to make their own decisions about production or distribution; they were now working for systems over which they had no control and often little understanding. Land, resources, and other means of production had been taken into foreign hands, and this would not change with mere political "independence." Even if the colonial administration went home, this did not mean that ownership and control of land and resources suddenly – if ever – reverted back to the

---

BOX 12.4   INVENTING TRADITION IN COLONIAL FIJI

According to Clammer (1973), at the inception of colonialism the islands of Fiji were home to some 100 different language groups. In 1912 G. V. Maxwell was appointed Native Lands Commissioner of Fiji and commenced a study of native land tenure and social organization, so as to run the colony more authentically and efficiently. After six months, he arrived at a clear-cut model that featured land-right holding units called *tokatoka*, which were organized into higher-level groups called *mataqali*, which were further organized into top-level kinship groups called *yavusa* based on direct descent from a divine ancestor. Along the way, even Maxwell had noticed how contradictory Fijian social organization was, commenting that "the people are absolutely incapable of classifying themselves without assistance" (203). So Maxwell gave them a clean classification that was not only previously unknown on the islands but that was "immediately enshrined as the 'official' doctrine of native social structure" (202). Oddly enough, the locals had been complicit in its invention: when they heard he was coming to study them they would either meet in advance to iron out disagreements in their social and landowning arrangements "which could be represented to the Commission as immemorially sanctioned by tradition" (202) or just make up social units and relations that had never existed. This invention of Fijian tradition included other aspects, such as language (one dialect, Mbauan, was advanced as "traditional Fijian language," and the very social terms used by Maxwell are Mbauan) and economic/labor relations, particularly "communalism." It was determined by colonial authorities that Fijians had "traditionally" worked together communally, so land was assigned to *mataqali* groups as communal property, although land had actually previously been owned individually. Clammer concludes that "modern communalism is entirely the child of Colonial administration" (213). Almost a century later, with colonialism long abolished,

> many Fijians are "ignorant" of the *mataqali* and *yavusa* units to which they are supposed to belong. Yet, whilst in village life the system is ignored or evaded wherever possible, it is, at the national level, lauded and defended as being at the very foundation of Fijian social order.

(218)

natives. In reality, it was not governments that owned and controlled most of the wealth and property but companies and individuals, and these did not give up their power, or even leave the territory, when colonialism officially ended. Also, naturally, since they did not want the competition, most colonial administrations had discouraged the development of local industry. Colonies had few factories or other facilities to produce manufactured goods. Colonies were still suppliers of primary goods or raw materials, which were transported to Western factories for processing into finished goods and then sold back to the colonies. And since "value-added" goods (like manufactures) are almost always more expensive than primary ones, colonized peoples lost on both ends of the transaction. Finally, colonies had often been made to "specialize" in one or a few products for which each particular colony was best suited; farming colonies were often marshaled into **monoculture** agriculture, in which one single crop constituted the main if not the sole product of the colony, particularly if the crop could not be grown in Europe, such as sugar, coffee, tea, rubber, cocoa, bananas, and so on (hence the term "banana republic"). This left the colony vulnerable to food dependency, as well as to international prices and demand; a drop in prices or demand could impoverish an entire colony and its people.

Forced resettlement

Part of colonial policy was to compel local people to live according to patterns that met the economic and political needs of colonialism. In particular, colonialists (and contemporary state-level government) detested nomads and tried as aggressively as they could to settle them. Nomads like foragers and pastoralists were hard to control, hard to count, and hard to tax. They occupied large tracts of land but produced little of value to the colonial economy. Whether in America, Australia, Africa, or Amazonia, their land was a prime attraction to settlers and entrepreneurs who saw little opposition to exploiting those untapped resources. So, these societies were particular targets for "pacification" and acculturation efforts, when they were not, like many Aboriginal or many American Indian societies, simply wiped out. In addition to forced settlement of nomadic peoples, wholesale popu-

lation transfers were conducted, moving people from where they were to where colonial interests wanted them. Colonialism needed labor, if not from slavery then from other means. So colonial administrations would shift populations, either to fill jobs or to populate "underpopulated" regions. And as in other cases, this policy did not end with the colonial era; in Indonesia under its *transmigrasi* program in the 1960s and 1970s, people from high-density areas like the city of Jakarta were encouraged to relocate to less densely populated lands like Sumatra and Kalimantan. Of course, the underpopulated places were seldom if ever *unpopulated*, and such human transfers tended to create social conflicts. As long as there was a net improvement on the balance sheet of the colony or state, other considerations were secondary.

Creation of "plural societies" and mixing of cultures

One of the most enduring and significant characteristics of colonies was their *artificiality*. Before colonialism, the political entities that became colonies usually did not exist. The colonies were "artificial" in the sense that someone (a foreign power) drew lines on a map to create administrative boundaries. Suddenly there was a thing called, for example, Gambia, where there was no such thing before; there had never been a state or other polity called Gambia. However, the political aspect of this colonial artificiality is less profound than the social aspect. Not only had there never been a state called Gambia, but there had never been a society that called itself Gambian. After all, Gambia is the name for a river, not for a society. There were people living near the Gambia River, but they had various cultures and languages and religions. There was no such thing as "Gambian culture" or "Gambian language" – and in many former colonies, there still is not. So colonies like Gambia were created with little knowledge of – and quite frankly, little concern for – which people were circumscribed by their borders. The borders were administrative, not cultural. Colonial policy was sometimes explicitly to seize territory and, as much as possible, rule it as if there were no people there at all. The result was that, in virtually all colonies, diverse peoples were thrust together in unprecedented ways.

See Chapter 14

Monoculture
the specialization of production of only one crop or product for which a territory is particularly suited. This can involve food crops like corn or rice, or raw materials like lumber, coffee, rubber, tea, and so on

FIGURE 12.1
A hypothetical colonial
boundary, in relation to
societies within.

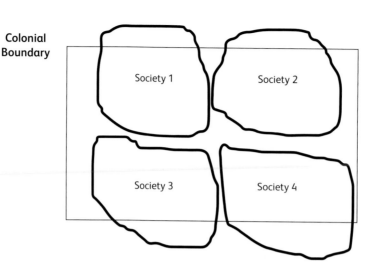

**Colonial
Boundary**

Society 1

Society 2

Society 3

Society 4

J. S. Furnivall. 1956.
*Colonial Policy and
Practice: A Comparative
Study of Burma and
Netherlands India.* New
York: New York
University Press.

See Chapter 6

Plural society

a society that contains
various cultural groups.
Such groups often occupy
"niches" in the broader
social system, such that the
groups do not interact with
each other except in limited
and often mutually
exploitive ways

This non-traditional creation and administration of multicultural social systems posed a
managerial problem. J. S. Furnivall wrote one of the
most important and influential studies on the
subject, *Colonial Policy and Practice* (1956), in which
he analyzed the social realities of two colonies,
Burma and the Dutch East Indies (Indonesia). What
he noted was that these colonies were by no means
homogeneous – made up of one kind of people –
but highly heterogeneous and "enclaved."

In other words, the groups were not fully or
even nearly integrated but rather occupied very
discrete social, and in some instances physical,
spaces in the colony. In Burma, he found, in addition to the "Burmese" (who themselves were a
diverse group), Indians, Chinese, and of course
Europeans, as well as "mixed blood" individuals of
every combination. Each group fit into the colony
in a different way, and its communal identity led to
inter-group violence in the 1920s and 1930s. To
describe this situation, Furnivall coined the term
"**plural society**," which has two characteristics. The
first or political characteristic of a plural society is
that it contains separate cultural or social sections
that "mix but do not combine." They live side by
side in the same political unit but do not form an
integrated "society" in any significant way. Social
and political life is therefore "atomized" or incomplete: the cultural sections of the society are not
coherent groups themselves but mere "aggregates of
individuals." Each "is a crowd and not a community." One prime reason for this fact is the second
or economic characteristic of plural societies, that
is, that they are purely economic arrangements, not
true societies or cultures at all. In what he calls "the

process of the survival of the cheapest," market
forces function "to eliminate all non-economic
values," leaving only economic interests and
relations with no other common social interests or
causes (299). Society is stripped of cultural significance, and only jobs and money drive the system
or unify people.

Introduction of race-concept and racism

Race, at least in the way that it is understood and
practiced in Western societies, is not a concept
shared by all societies. When colonialists began to
have prolonged contact with non-Western peoples,
their reactions to those people were not at first
entirely negative. Columbus was rather impressed
with the appearance and personality of the natives
he saw. Even Captain James Cook, one of the first
Europeans to lay eyes on Australian Aboriginals,
commented in the 1770s that they were tranquil,
non-materialistic, and happy people (Reed 1969:
136). However, as European domination of these
peoples became more widespread, it became more
common to berate them as, if not reduce them to,
abject savages worthy of no better treatment than
they were getting. The social Darwinism of the time
suggested the inferiority of some groups to others,
evidenced by the "success" of some and the "failure"
of others. However, it could be argued that Western
racism was not so much a cause as an *effect* of
colonialism. How else to justify the conduct and
policies of colonialists toward the native peoples?
If the natives were inferior – a lower race, a primitive

species, a sort of half-human/half-animal – then what better consideration did they deserve? Racism in this sense indicated the dissonant feelings of the conquerors and their attempt to assuage these feelings by rationalizing their behavior.

If racism helped the whites to legitimize colonialism, it did not do much good for the locals. It exposed them to unprecedented levels of cruelty and exploitation. But even more, it penetrated their own thinking about the identity of and relations between groups, with profound effect. In some colonies, Europeans found some peoples with whom they felt more commonality than others; the Tutsi in Rwanda, the Sikhs in northern India, and the Sinhalese in Sri Lanka are three examples. The Tutsi were the dominant segment of Rwandan society. A chiefly class or caste, they were ascribed physical traits as well – taller, thinner, and more "Caucasian" in some ways. The Hutu were seen as more "African" or Bantu. Accordingly, the European opinion of the Hutu was much lower. One colonial observer in 1925 characterized the Hutu as "generally short and thick-set with a big head, a jovial expression, a wide nose and enormous lips" whereas the Tutsi

> has nothing of the negro, apart from his color. He is usually very tall. . . .He is very thin. . . .His features are very fine: a high brow, thin nose and fine lips framing beautiful shining teeth. Batutsi women are usually lighter-skinned than their husbands, very slender and pretty in their youth, although they tend to thicken with age.
>
> (quoted in Prunier 1995: 6)

It was claimed that each had a racially specific personality too: Hutu tended to be "hardworking, not very clever, extrovert, irascible, unmannerly, obedient" – suitable to the lower class they occupied – while the Tutsi were "intelligent (in the sense of astute in political intrigues), capable of command, refined, courageous, and cruel" (Maquet 1961: 164). The 1925 observer went so far as to applaud the Tutsi for displaying "a refinement of feelings which is rare among primitive peoples." Not surprisingly, the Tutsi were preferred by the European colonialists for political service and education. This created a new dimension of animosity between them and the Hutu majority (around 85 percent), which could only make for trouble at a later date.

The same was true in colonial Ceylon (Sri Lanka), where the dominant Buddhist Sinhalese, whose history and mythology told of a northern Indian origin, absorbed the British concept of and preference for "Aryan" peoples, which they fancied themselves to be. They used this distinction against the south Indian, non-Aryan or "Dravidian" Hindu Tamils on the island to assert their own similarity to the Europeans and their superiority to the minority Tamils. Thus, the Sinhalese came to regard themselves as a race in the European sense and as a higher race than their fellow natives, creating again a new type and degree of distinction between the two local groups than ever existed in pre-colonial times. As the Sinhalese apologist Dharmapala put it:

> the Aryan race is the only race with noble customs handed down from tradition. . . [therefore] the Sinhalese [who are Aryans] should cultivate ancient codes of conduct. Aryan customs and Aryan dresses and ornaments. . . .The Sinhalese first came to this country from Bengal and the Bengalis are superior in their intelligence to other communities in India.
>
> (quoted in Dharmadasa 1992 145–46)

Racism, then, was not only a virulent force in relations between white colonizers and non-white colonized peoples but also often enough between various non-white peoples themselves. In fact, the concept of race and its inherent hierarchy helped to exacerbate inter-group differences and hostilities when such forms of distinct identities already existed or sometimes to create the very notion of disparate native "peoples" where no such distinctions had previously existed. This too would bear fruit long after colonialism was gone.

Environmental degradation and declining living conditions

In many colonial settings, the rapacious exploitation of local resources and labor left huge environmental disruption. Entire forests were cut down (and are still being cut down) to make room for farms and towns, for export of the wood, and for the production of charcoal. Erosion and pollution occurred. Squalid shantytowns rose up, often where

Maquet, Jacques. 1961. *The Premise of Inequality in Rwanda: A Study of Political Relations in a Central African Kingdom.* London: Oxford University Press.

See Chapter 2

BOX 12.5 CONTEMPORARY CULTURAL CONTROVERSIES: IS ANTHROPOLOGY COLONIALISM?

Since about 1970, anthropologists have wrestled with the historical relationship between our discipline and the practice of colonialism. As acknowledged in Chapter 2, anthropology was born during and from the colonial encounter; thus, Talal Asad argued that "the basic reality" that made early anthropology "a feasible and effective enterprise was the power relationship between dominating (European) and dominated (non-European) cultures" (1979: 91). An even angrier William Willis redefined anthropology as "the social science that studies dominated colored peoples – and their ancestors – living outside the boundaries of modern white societies" (1974: 123). This sentiment is shared by many non-Western people, including scholars like Linda Tuhiwai, a Ngati Awa/Ngait Porou (Maori of New Zealand) writer who condemned all cultural research in the strongest terms:

> From the vantage point of the colonized, a position from which I write, and choose to privilege, the term "research" is inextricably linked to European imperialism and colonialism. The word itself, "research," is probably one of the dirtiest words in the Indigenous world's vocabulary. When mentioned in many indigenous contexts, it stirs up silence, it conjures up bad memories, it raises a smile that is knowing and distrustful.

(1999: 1)

What do you think?

local people had never congregated in large numbers before. In places where indigenous people had always lived in small mobile groups, settlement only aggravated their social and physical complaints and caused despoliation of the land. Colonial officials did make certain attempts to clean up the messes they created, such as establishing hospitals and Western-style medical care. However, one unintended and undesired consequence of this humanitarianism was an enormous explosion of population. People who improved their infant mortality rates and life expectancies but did not curb their reproduction soon found themselves with up to a 10 percent annual population growth rate, resulting in doubling the population every seven years or so. In the villages, the land – already expropriated by colonial interests – simply could not support the burden of population growth.

People had no choice but to gather in burgeoning new cities, without the infrastructure or economy to handle such large inflows. Literally millions of people ended up and still end up as squatters on the fringes of cities, without adequate (or sometimes any) fresh water, sewerage, electricity, and other amenities, consuming the environment on a profligate scale. Forests were denuded for firewood, farmland was overworked to the point of exhaustion, and water and food supplies became inadequate or prohibitively expensive, as evidenced by the worldwide food riots of 2008. Meanwhile, communicable disease (like dysentery and malaria and most recently AIDS) ran rampant. Still the population grew, composed of people with lots of complaints and little to lose – a recipe for political disaster.

SUMMARY

The spread of colonies into new territories is not a uniquely modern or even human phenomenon, but modern colonialism (from the fifteenth to the twentieth centuries) escalated the process and its impact to unknown levels. It not only brought far-flung societies into prolonged contact with each other but began the centuries-long project of linking all societies into a truly global cultural network, a project that is just now reaching its fulfillment. Anthropologists who had previously looked for discrete, homogeneous, and static "traditional societies," began to understand that societies are often internally complex and even contradictory, that discrete boundaries are often lacking, and that even "traditional" societies had their histories – of which Western colonialism and even anthropology itself would now and for ever more be parts.

The goals and methods of colonialism varied by time period, colonizing power, colonized area, and other such factors, but tended to include

- Expropriation of wealth
- Access to resources at the source
- Land
- Labor
- Taxation
- Markets
- Geopolitics

These interests and the political and economic institutions that were instated to achieve them imposed extensive changes on colonized societies, many of which did not disappear when colonialism officially ended. These changes included

- Depopulation
- Acculturation and deculturation
- Loss of economic independence
- Forced settlement
- Creation of "plural societies" with artificial boundaries
- The concept of race and racism
- Environmental degradation and declining living conditions

At the most extreme, but not uncommonly, old cultures and identities were given new interpretations and valuations, or new cultures and identities were invented outright from a combination of indigenous cultural materials, colonial imperatives, and human imagination.

Q
MCQS

Q
FILL IN THE BLANKS

www

Key Terms

Blackbirding	Doctrine of discovery	Mercantilism
Colonialism	*Encomienda*	Monoculture
Colonies of exploitation	Geopolitics	Plural society
Colonies of settlement	*Hacienda*	Sphere of influence
Colony	Imperialism	*Terra nullius*
Corvée	Internal colonialism	

13 Political integration and political identity in the post-colonial world

In July 2011 the world's family of states welcomed its newest member, the Republic of South Sudan. South Sudan seceded from Sudan, creating two states where there had previously been one. The history of Sudan stretches back to ancient times, but seldom if ever as a single unified entity. The northern region, known as Kush, had important connections to ancient Egypt, but by the sixth century CE two polities had emerged in the area, one in the north and one in the south. Around the same time Christianity entered the region, followed shortly by Islam; the north gradually became more thoroughly Islamized and Arabized than the south, where numerous tribal (especially pastoral) societies lived. Sudan's history began to coalesce – but still largely as two distinct territories – in the 1800s, when Ottoman Turks conquered and unified the north. The story of the modern state of Sudan only begins, however, with European colonialism: Belgium, France, and England all invaded the region and claimed parts of the future Sudan, but England emerged as the controlling power after 1898, ruling Sudan jointly with Egypt as "Anglo-Egyptian Sudan." Even then, though, the north and south were recognized as distinct provinces. As independence approached after World War II,

Britain at first considered granting self-rule to the north, but in 1946 northern and southern Sudan were unified into a single future state, to be governed from the north. At independence in 1956, the integrated state of Sudan first appeared. However, its short life has been very troubled: civil war between the north and south from 1955 to 1972, including two political coups in 1965 and 1969, was followed by another civil war starting in 1983; more recently, the Sudan Liberation Movement Army and the Justice and Equality Movement began to struggle for rights or freedom for western Sudan, namely the Darfur region. In 2005, the north and south finally achieved an agreement that the south could hold a referendum on its political future, and that vote – held in January 2011 – resulted in almost-unanimous southern support for a separate state. However, all is not well for the fledgling state: the Republic of South Sudan has one of the lowest average incomes and literacy rates in the world, is very culturally and ethnically diverse, and has no access to the sea, while it sits on valuable oil deposits, particularly in the Abyei region which has been claimed by both Sudanese states. Understandably, many citizens of northern Sudan feel betrayed by the secession, and

MAP 13.1 The ethnic groups of northern Sudan and southern Sudan

Source Dr M. Izady/ gulf2000.columbia.edu

Legend:
- Arab (48%)
- Other/mixed

Northern Sudan
- Nubian (8%)
- Beja (6%)
- Fur (2%)
- Zaghawa (1%)

Southern Sudan
- Dinka (11%)
- Nuer (5%)
- Azande (3%)
- Bari (3%)
- Shilluk/Anwak (3%)

conflict could resume between the two Sudans at any time.

Long before modern colonialism, human groups were confronting each other, challenging each other, and dominating, absorbing, or destroying each other. Out of this constant agitation old societies have disappeared, new societies have emerged, separate societies have coalesced into mixed (and often stratified) systems, and cultural elements have been circulated, interpreted, and invented. Thus, there has always been a kind of "cultural crisis" of the sort referred to by Linton and Diamond, which was not new to modern colonialism but was greatly accelerated and globalized during that period. Group boundaries, identities, and cultures, which were forever coming into and going out of existence – but which Western observers at first took as timeless and "traditional" – became a conspicuous feature and problem of human life.

One of the key manifestations of the cultural crisis hastened by colonialism and also by the end

See Chapter 11

of colonialism was the struggle for order and control between social groups, between social groups and the states in which they live, and between states themselves. We can properly refer to this as a "political" matter in the widest possible sense – in terms of how humans in groups manage their affairs, settle their disputes, institute their laws, defend their interests, and most basically share power. And since politics is certainly a domain of culture, political matters are cultural matters. However, especially in the contemporary era, culture is especially political, as cultural differences become the basis and resource for political organization and opposition. Differences of value or interest can ignite into real competition and violence, leading to death and displacement of people.

And above all, issues of power, order, and control cannot be detached from questions of *identity*, which are further attached to questions of *authenticity* ("who we really are"), which are often integrally attached to questions of culture. In the modern world – not simply because of, but substantially related to, colonialism and the course of post-colonial events – politics and identity are inseparable, so that anthropologists can and must speak of "identity politics" or "the politics of identity" (Taylor 1994). And both identity and politics are increasingly inseparable from culture.

The notion of individual and collective identity being rooted in culture is not a new one. The German historian and philosopher Johann Herder (1744–1803) believed that every "nation" (*Volk*, as

Taylor, Charles. 1994. "The Politics of Recognition." In Amy Gutman, ed. *Multiculturalism: Examining the Politics of Recognition*. Princeton, NJ: Princeton University Press, 25–73.

PLATE 13.1 Identity politics: political action and organization have become decreasingly about class and increasingly about culture and identity.

in the English word "folk") of humanity had its own unique "spirit" (*Geist*) or "soul" (*Seele*), expressed in its language and culture. For Herder, all Germans were one nation or people, united by the essence of their common history and culture, even if they were not aware of or did not identify with their shared "German-ness." However, he vehemently insisted that the German nation – and every other nation – recognize its true identity and cultivate and preserve its special cultural genius. This interpretation of culture and identity was influential in Europe, as Germany and Italy for instance forged national states and as former multinational empires (like the Austrian and Ottoman) collapsed and fragmented into their local pieces. During and particularly after colonialism, non-Western peoples were compelled to determine how to organize and govern themselves – after significant mixing of peoples and the introduction of the Western concepts of culture, nation, and state. The result has been and continues to be a contested field of constructed identities, often if not always built on (the rubble of) culture. And too often, these struggles have made further rubble of culture, of the physical environment, and of people's lives.

POLITICS, IDENTITY, AND POST-COLONIALISM

While the relationship between politics, "traditional culture," and identity is not exclusive to the post-colonial period, it is acute in that period – in terms of the legacies that colonialism left, the path that each colony took to independence, and the choices and incidents that subsequently occurred. Especially because former colonies had been carved artificially out of indigenous territories, creating "plural" or "multicultural" polities, and because these polities had further been integrated into global imperial systems, the cultural and political situation was complicated and fraught with tension. And this political and cultural situation was certainly not a simple continuation of "traditional" forms, nor was it a straightforward absorption of Western forms. Rather, as Malinowski commented, it was an innovative amalgamation of both traditional and Western and other elements as well.

The path to independence

The immediate fate of the colonies after independence was largely shaped by the colony's path to independence. There were two main avenues: more or less gradual and orderly transition to native self-government, and more or less violent resistance and revolution, with locals fighting to dislodge Europeans and establish self-government. These "locals" could be either native peoples or the descendants of European settlers (in "colonies of settlement" where immigrants outnumbered or at least overpowered the indigenous inhabitants). It might seem on the surface that the first of these processes would lead to greater long-term stability, but such was not always the case.

Transition to native self-government

Some colonial powers were better than others about preparing their colonies for eventual independence. Britain was perhaps the best. By the end of World War II, as independence for the last colonies seemed inevitable, Britain accepted the fact and began to hand power over to native representatives who would become the first government after independence. This is not to say that it did not initially resist independence movements (often violently, as in India), but the success of the policy of transition is evidenced by the good relations between the mother country and the "children," many of whom still belong to the British Commonwealth. France did not share the British attitude about transition to independence, mainly because of the fundamentally different French view of colonies. For Britain, the colonies were part of the British Empire but not part of Britain itself; the colonized people were subjects of Britain but were not and could not be "British." For France, colonies were regarded as *overseas parts of France* (like Hawaii or Alaska to the United States), so independence was essentially unthinkable; native resistance to colonialism amounted to civil war. Other colonial powers did little or no preparation and pulled out of their colonies abruptly, leaving a power vacuum that was not easily or painlessly filled, as in the case of the Belgian Congo. Others fought bitterly into very recent history to prevent their colonies from escaping, as evidenced by Portugal's prolonged wars to stop separatist movements in Angola and Mozambique until 1975.

See Chapter 12

See Chapter 11

The peaceful-transition course had common and often ultimately troubled effects in the newly independent colonies. One of the main questions was how power would be shared and with whom. Colonies composed of multiple cultural groups – as most were – faced challenges of power-sharing and coexistence that went down to the smallest details of life: what language(s) would be spoken, what symbols (flags, etc.) would be used, what religious holidays would be celebrated, and so on. Dividing power equally between groups would alienate the majority group, but dividing it proportionally, or leaving it to the results of "democratic" elections, would disempower the minority group(s). Beyond that, the introduction of Western cultural, legal, economic, and educational institutions often created a small but influential class of acculturated native people who did not identify with any traditional groups but with either the colonial "nation" or with European culture. So even peaceful transition led to immediate and long-term competitions and conflicts.

As seen in the Ceylon/Sri Lanka case, the problem with peaceful transition was twofold. First, in a sense nothing much really changed immediately after independence. Given the choice, Western colonialists preferred to transfer power to acculturated "Westernized" natives, not the more "traditional" (and often militant) components of society. Second, the acculturated natives often did not understand the feelings and interests of the more traditional citizens of the former colony and were often soon replaced by more "nativistic" leaders and parties that played on communal identities

BOX 13.1   IDENTITY AND POWER IN COLONIAL CEYLON

England assumed complete control of Ceylon (modern-day Sri Lanka) after defeating the final independent kingdom on the island in 1815 (and wresting it from the Dutch who supplanted the earlier Portuguese). Thus Ceylon had a long and complex history of contact with the West. By the start of the twentieth century the island contained an acculturated group, referred to as "educated Ceylonese," who numbered at most 4 or 5 percent of the population and came from both of the main local groups, Sinhalese and Tamils. The Ceylon National Congress (CNC), formed in 1919, was dominated by this acculturated local elite and offered a non-ethnic alternative to culture-based politics: members regarded themselves not as Sinhalese or Tamils but as Ceylonese, and the president of the party was a (minority) Tamil, Sir Ponnambalam Arunachalam. Up to this time, ethnic Sinhalese and Tamils had been guaranteed equal representation in the Legislative Council, but reforms in 1920 replaced **communal representation** (that is, reserving seats for representatives of specific cultural groups) with the more familiar "one man, one vote" policy. As a result, ethnic Sinhalese, making up about 75 percent of the island's population, soon outnumbered Tamils in the administration thirteen to three. "Ethnic" feelings were further aggravated by the formation of a Sinhalese political party in 1935, the Sinhala Maha Sabha or Great Council of the Sinhalese; by the 1940s the Tamils responded with their own party, the Ceylon Tamil Congress, which demanded balanced (fifty/fifty) representation for Tamils and Sinhalese. It was an inclusive "national" party, the United National Party, that took power at independence in 1948, but even so, one of its first acts was the Ceylon Citizenship Act No. 18 which deprived many Tamils of their citizenship. Meanwhile, the Buddhist monks of the island had organized a Ceylon Union of Bhikkhus (monks), which was very influential among majority-Buddhist Sinhalese. Again in response, some majority-Hindu Tamils split from the Tamil Congress to form the Tamil Rule Party, presaging the separatist politics that would rend the country. When the governing Sri Lanka Freedom Party took a distinctively pro-Sinhalese turn in 1956 and took up the cause of the monks as articulated in their manifesto "The Betrayal of Buddhism," the stage was set for communal conflict. With the passage of an official language act making Sinhalese the state language, other prejudicial policies about the state flag and about educational preferences, and actual violence as early as 1958, it was clear that the idealistic days of peaceful self-government were ending.

Communal representation

the political procedure of guaranteeing that groups (ethnic groups, language groups, races, religions, etc.) will have representation in governments by setting aside offices in the government specifically for those groups and grievances. So, often enough, this first native government was truly a "transitional" one, on the way to more native – and many times, more violent – politics at a later stage.

Government by European settlers

Independence in many cases did not mean return of power to "natives" at all, if by natives we mean descendants of the originally colonized peoples. In colonies where large numbers of Europeans immigrated (like the United States), there was often a sufficient political base of local whites to constitute a white-dominated post-colonial government. The territory that would become the United States was colonized from the early 1600s. By the late 1700s, white settlers fought for independence from Britain. However, this was not a struggle by or for the "native peoples" of North America; rather, a branch of European society simply formed in a new region and carried on many of the accustomed Western policies toward the native inhabitants. Most of South and Central America followed suit. Perhaps the most extreme case was Brazil, which first claimed independence as a kingdom when members of the Portuguese royal family resettled there after the Napoleonic wars – literally transplanting Portugal to Brazil. The Brazilian indigenous people certainly were not part of the independence declaration nor included in the first (or any subsequent) government. The best-known example is South Africa, where 10 percent of the population (white) ruled 90 percent of the population (black) until about 1990. In this and similar cases, independence meant fairly little – or worse – for the colonized peoples.

Native resistance and revolution

In virtually all colonial cases, even the ones where a relatively impressive amount of preparation for independence was allowed, a degree of resistance to colonial rule occurred. Ceylon might be the case of the least struggle and violence prior to independence, which makes the extensive violence since independence all the more ironic. Elsewhere, resistance took many forms. In India, Mohandas "Mahatma" Gandhi's principle of "passive resistance" and non-violent, morality-based struggle guided the process. But it was resistance all the same

and was occasionally met with violence, nor was it the only process occurring within India at the time. In most instances, the anti-colonial resistance was more violent. Algeria in the 1950s was one of the first societies to practice modern terrorism in pursuit of anti-colonial goals, in this case against the French occupiers. In Vietnam and Angola and elsewhere "guerrilla" armies fought protracted wars against European administrations to dislodge them from native homelands. And, in Vietnam and Angola as in many other colonies, communist ideology and even soldiers from other communist states defined the course of the struggle. It must be remembered that all colonial struggles in the twentieth century took place in the context of international communist revolutions and the "Cold War." Communism was attractive to colonized peoples for two reasons – as a way to distinguish themselves from their European oppressors and as a "language" or "theory" of resistance and of the political and cultural future after victory. As a distinction, European/Western culture was equated to capitalism, which was equated to colonialism and oppression by many colonized peoples – that is, capitalism seemed naturally to lead to or include colonialism. As non-Europeans, the rebels would then naturally be non-capitalists and non-colonialists, and the opposite or antithesis of capitalism was seen to be communism.

The specific doctrines of communism also seemed to explain the global colonial system and to offer an alternative and a means to reach that alternative. Marxism explains all of history and society by class conflict. Lenin, the first leader of the Soviet Union, explicitly applied Marxian philosophy to colonialism and imperialism. Already by the turn of the twentieth century, he argued, imperialism had internationalized capitalism and transformed non-Western people into a global "lower class" or proletariat. Lenin hoped and predicted, and worked to achieve, that the awareness and understanding of this oppression would awaken their "class consciousness" and stimulate them to fight for economic and cultural freedom, that is, **self-determination**. So communism offered itself as a natural ally in the struggle against colonialism, in two senses. First, it "accounted for" colonialism, giving colonized people a way to understand it and its role in history and in the future. Second, it offered powerful allies, with the

See Chapter 6

Self-determination
the concept that groups with a distinct culture and identity have a right to choose their own political arrangements and their own collective destiny

PLATE 13.2 Colonized people often used force to end the occupation of their land as in the Algerian War where Algerians sought independence from France.

Fanon, Frantz. 1963. *The Wretched of the Earth*. Constance Farrington, trans. New York: Grove Press, Inc.

Soviet Union and the People's Republic of China (and their satellites) actively supporting such independence struggles. This is why Cuban soldiers fought alongside Angolan rebels against Portuguese colonialists into the 1970s, why China sent armies into North Korea to resist American forces in the 1950s, and why the USSR supplied North Vietnam in its war.

For many, resistance and revolution not only were but had to be violent processes. Practically speaking, the superior power of colonizing states meant that they would not leave without a fight. Theoretically or philosophically speaking, colonized peoples, especially when inspired by communist ideology, saw violent revolution as the completion of the predicted world system and also

as a kind of "cleansing" of the souls of the colonized. No one represents this position better than Frantz Fanon, author *of The Wretched of the Earth*.

In this influential book, he maintains that "decolonization is always a violent phenomenon" because colonialism itself is a violent phenomenon. The colonialists' and colonized's "first encounter was marked by violence and their existence together – that is to say the exploitation of the native by the settler – was carried on by dint of a great array of bayonets and cannons." He continues:

> The violence which has ruled over the ordering of the colonial world, which has ceaselessly drummed the rhythm for the destruction of native social forms and broken up without

reserve the systems of reference of the economy, the customs of dress and external life, that same violence will be claimed and taken over by the native at the moment when, deciding to embody history in his own person, he surges into forbidden quarters. To wreck the colonial world is henceforward a mental picture of action which is very clear, very easy to understand and which may be assumed by each one of the individuals which constitute the colonized people. To break up the colonial world does not mean that after the frontiers have been abolished lines of communication will be set up between the two zones. The destruction of the colonial world is no more and no less than the abolition of one zone, its burial in the depths of the earth or its expulsion from the country.

(Fanon 1963: 40–41)

The politics of the "new states"

Whatever the process, the formal system of colonialism eventually ended, which had to be followed by something. One conceivable possibility was a return to pre-colonial arrangements – the dissolution of the colony and its replacement with "traditional" social and political systems – but that was virtually impossible and never happened in reality. Instead, the colonial entity, regardless of its form and composition, almost always became a sovereign entity – a "state." In fact, the path to independence, as well as the entire colonial enterprise, essentially guaranteed this outcome. Where a colony had been established (artificially, even irrationally), internal institutions were established – schools, markets, transportation systems, courts, etc. – which would not disappear overnight. Furthermore, legislatures and parties were organized, especially when a peaceful transition was planned, such that the colony was intentionally groomed to become a state, with a functioning central government and the same borders, the same multicultural makeup, and usually the same name as the former colony. Little would in actuality change. In fact, Fanon quotes the president of the new state of Gabon, a former French colony in Africa, who said to officials in Paris, "Gabon is independent, but between Gabon and France

nothing has changed; everything goes on as before" (67).

The main internal problem faced by what were called the "new states," aside from the economic conditions that perpetuated its poverty and dependence, was the mixed and confused demographic situation of plural societies becoming self-governing states. A state, as we know, is merely a political system with a centralized government empowered to exercise certain authority over a specific territory. There is no particular claim made about who lives in and under the state and its government. European states had taken centuries to coalesce out of the fragments of personal kingdoms and principalities and regional tribal and village cultures, and the process had not been peaceful – nor complete, as the ongoing struggles of the Basque and Irish, to name only two, attest. In the "new states" this was a keen problem because the internal diversity was even greater and fresher and the time-scale to achieve unity shorter. By the 1960s anthropologists and others thought they were witnessing just such a unification process, an "integrative revolution," in which old "primordial" and "tribal" identities were being swapped for new "modern" and "national" ones (e.g. Geertz 1963). Some referred to this as "nation-building."

The terms state, nation, and country are often used synonymously in English, but anthropologists make some careful and useful distinctions. A **state** is a political system, whatever its constituency may be. A **nation** (from the Latin *nasci* for "to be born") is some group of humans who identify *as* a group, frequently using the idioms of birth and kinship. **Country** refers to the *territory* that a group occupies. The three concepts need not be, and routinely are not, coterminous. As explained before, a state is not an objective or natural entity but a social product, an *accomplishment*, of specific and typically modern political processes. States are "artificial" in the sense that they are human artifices. The laws and institutions of states change and evolve over time. The boundaries of states fluctuate, as land is annexed to and lost from the state, often by war. The populations of states also fluctuate, as groups are absorbed by conquest of land or by immigration or assimilation, or lost by military defeat or emigration. States rise and fall over time, disappearing where once they reigned. And states can be contested, as in the

See Chapter 14

State
a political system or level of integration in which a formal centralized government has power over a delimited territory to make and enforce laws, to establish currency and collect taxes, and to maintain an army and declare war

Nation
a corporate group that shares an identity based on such traits as history, culture, territory, etc. and that recognizes a shared political destiny. A group that is politically mobilized to achieve certain goals, usually including political recognition, rights, and sometimes an independent state

Geertz, Clifford, ed. 1963. *Old Societies and New States: The Quest for Modernity in Asia and Africa*. New York: The Free Press.

See Chapter 9

Country
commonly used as a synonym for "nation" or "state," more properly refers to the territory that a society or polity inhabits

cases of Tibet and Taiwan, or of Israel by (at least some of) its Arab neighbors.

A state is a political system, but a nation is people – or more accurately, *a people*. The "people" or social unit may or may not be politically integrated or sovereign. Anthony Smith (1991) lists the main characteristics of a nation as including a name, a historic territory or homeland, common myths and historical memory, a mass public culture, an integrated economy, and an integrated politics with common rights and duties for members. A nation, then, is first and foremost an identity group – the named unit with which an individual primarily identifies. This identity is often based on history or "tradition," but one of its key dynamics is its future orientation, its *shared sense of purpose or destiny*. The members of a nation are "in it together." They tend to think of themselves, metaphorically if not literally, as a kind of family. Benedict Anderson (1983) has noted aptly that this is an imaginary kind of

kinship, and he has accordingly called nations "imagined communities." Not everyone in the nation is actually related to nor actually knows everyone else; the point is that members feel closer to each other than to other people in the world. Fellow nation-members are "us."

There is no necessary relationship between a state and a nation. However, in the modern world, one political ideal has become the **nation-state**, which does align the political and social. A nation-state is a state that consists of all of and only one nation, or a nation that has its own state (territory and government). Many nations aspire to be or have a state. At the same time, many states aspire to be a nation. This is important because *so few states are nations*. Most states and nations find themselves in more contradictory and tortuous relationships. One such relationship is the **multinational state**, in which two or more (and sometimes many more) nations share the same state. Most modern states are

Smith, Anthony. 1991. *National Identity*. Reno, NV: University of Nevada Press.

Nation-state
a state that contains only and all of one "nation" or cultural-identity group, or a nation that has its own formal territory and government

Anderson, Benedict. 1983. *Imagined Communities: Reflections of the Origin and Spread of Nationalism.* London: Verso.

Multinational state
a state that contains some or all of two or more distinct nations or cultural groups

BOX 13.2 MUSIC AND NATION-BUILDING IN TRINIDAD

The colonial story of Trinidad began in 1498 when Christopher Columbus explored the island; originally claimed by Spain, French settlers (and their slaves) formed the major immigrant population, and England took possession of it and neighboring Tobago in 1888, importing laborers from India to work the sugar and cocoa plantations. The colony achieved independence in 1962 as the integrated islands of Trinidad and Tobago but divided internally by "social hierarchies inherited from colonialism, socio-economic differences produced by the contemporary global capitalist economy, and racial categories of Indian and African that are deployed in political and social practice in multifarious ways" (Birth 2008: 11). It is a daunting challenge to unify such a population into a single "nation," but one "political" resource of the society is its characteristic and famous music, especially calypso, and Kevin Birth finds that the new state quickly "emphasized the institutionalization of musical and cultural competitions in order to invoke and inspire national unity" (43). By sponsoring Carnival performances and "Best Village Competitions," the government sought to practice a kind of "cultural nationalism" out of music, including the distinctive calypso instrument, the steel drum or "pan." According to Birth, the steel drum even appears on some denominations of Trinidadian money. Of course it was not only music but also literature and poetry that were held up as the common patrimony of the Trinidadian "nation." So, in Trinidad and Tobago, as in many societies and states, "music is an important means for making and contesting cultural claims about identities and the nation" (12). But Birth stresses the contesting as much as the making: first, calypso is not the only music made on Trinidad, and many of the other musical styles are treated as "local" or "ethnic" rather than "national" – essentially excluding them from Trinidadian shared identity. Further, despite its best efforts, the state does not monopolize the practice or meaning of music: people still make and use music to declare local identities and relationships and sometimes even to criticize the government, including the government's attempts to co-opt and control festivities like Carnival.

multinational states, including virtually all of the states born from colonialism. Another and often enough parallel relationship is the **multi-state nation**, in which one nation is split across two or more state boundaries, with parts of the nation living in different states. This was also regularly an outcome of colonialism, in which political boundaries were drawn with little knowledge of or interest in social boundaries.

Clearly, this is a sensitive problem for new postcolonial states, but not only for them. Many if not all older states, including Western ones, find themselves in similarly complicated social positions. The Basque people in Spain comprise a distinct and often fractious minority in that state, and the various nationalities in the United Kingdom under English authority – the Welsh, Scottish, Irish, and even Breton – have at times lived uncomfortably or violently together. The United States, Canada, Australia, and most states include within their boundaries groups that maintain other sub-state or national identities, such as the various Indian or Aboriginal groups, not to mention immigrant populations.

While states are conspicuously new and artificial in most cases, there is a common impression that nations are more ancient and authentic. However, just as anthropology has become suspicious of the "reality" of concepts like "tradition" and "belief" and "culture" and "society," so we have found reasons to question the concreteness and objectivity of "nation." First, not all nations are ancient; some, like "French-Canadian," are quite modern and must be so, as there were no French in Canada – in fact, there was no Canada – in ancient times. Also, nations change throughout their history, emphasizing different parts of their culture, taking on different identities, advancing different demands. And the fact that nations do make demands transforms such entities from mere identity groups into *interest groups*, groups that have interests *as a group* and that act to achieve these interests. Among these national goals and interests are:

- Above all else, survival
- Prosperity, including rights to wealth, property, jobs, etc.
- Equality with – and sometimes superiority to – other groups within the state

- Recognition by the state and possibly the world of their existence and identity
- Cultural rights, that is, the right and freedom to practice their culture
- Self-determination, that is, the right and freedom to choose their own future
- In the most extreme case, political independence and their own state.

Thus, one of the goals of a nation may be precisely its own state, envisioned as a nation-state, a place where it can be, as the Quebecois say, *maitre chez nous*, "master of our own house." We can refer to such a cause and movement as **nationalism**. Nationalism, it would seem, is the kind of movement that is intended to promote the interests of a "real" nation; however, observers have noted that it can *create* the nation in the first place by proposing an identity and a set of interests for a group that ostensibly is, or eventually becomes, "a people." This can be what Guidieri and Pellizi (1988: 11) have called "a process of collective becoming" which involves, above all other things, a transfer of corporateness from other, perhaps older and usually smaller or more local, collectivities and identities to the new "nation." A process of collective becoming, a national genesis, is what Geertz and others meant by the "integrative revolution" – the phenomenon of integrating individuals and groups (families, villages, classes, societies) into larger "national" units by *dis-integrating* them from sectarian and often "traditional" units and identities. It can be seen, in Benedict Anderson's terms, as an exercise in "re-imagining" a community on the basis of more or less "traditional" – or sometimes outright modern or even invented – cultural materials. Nationalism is, in the final analysis, itself "a *form of culture* – an ideology, a language, mythology, symbolism, and consciousness" (Smith 1991: 91) premised on the notion that nations exist, are important, and are more "real" or "organic" or "authentic" than other means of organization and action.

FLUID, FRAGMENTED, AND FRACTIOUS CULTURES IN THE MODERN WORLD

By this point, terms like "society," "culture," and "nation" have become almost impossibly blurred,

Multi-state nation
a nation or cultural group that is divided across two or more state borders

Nationalism
a social movement to achieve recognition, rights, and sometimes an independent state for a nation

BOX 13.3   DEFINING THE NATION IN "YUGOSLAVIA"

Yugoslavia was a new state that emerged not from colonialism but from the dissolution of multinational empires after World War I. The Slavic peoples who shared it – including Serbs, Croats, Slovenes – began to migrate into southeastern Europe in the sixth or seventh centuries CE from farther east, perhaps as far as Central Asia, mixing with or displacing the previous Illyrian and Goth inhabitants. By the 900s a Croat kingdom appeared, and by the 1100s a Serb kingdom formed in the region that is Montenegro and Kosovo today. In the inland area around the Bosna River a principality arose as well. Catholicism was influential in the northwest (Slovene and Croat) regions, while the southeastern area came under Eastern Orthodox influence, and the Bosna area never effectively converted to any one religion. In the 1300s, autonomous Slav cultural development was interrupted by Ottoman invasion from the south, culminating in the Battle of Kosovo (1389) and defeat of the Slavs. Until the 1800s the Balkans region was under Ottoman authority, and many Slavs, especially in Bosnia, adopted Islam as their religion. As European states grew in power, Ottoman control of southeast Europe declined, until the northern lands of the Slavs were integrated into the Austrian Empire. However, as throughout Europe where peoples under "foreign" domination were becoming restive for "self-determination," the Balkan Slavs struggled under their Austrian and Ottoman lords. The question was what would replace them. Divergent answers were offered. In Austria, some Slavs suggested a policy of "trialism," in which Slavs would be recognized as a "third" nation in the state (in addition to Austrians and Hungarians). Others proposed "Illyrianism," harking back to the ancient (in fact, pre-Slavic) days of an independent Balkans. "Nationalists" of each constituent nation promoted the particularistic identity and interests of their group, but what made "their group" a group was unclear. Some argued that religion was the source of identity – for instance, Croats were Catholic, Serbs were Orthodox, and Bosnians were Muslim. To achieve this supposedly "authentic" identity, activists like Teofil Petranovic traveled around Orthodox villages trying to convince locals to call themselves Serbs, while Ilija Garasanin in 1844 published the *Nacertanije* or Outline calling for the unification of all Serbs in a single national state. Even more remarkable were the claims that *all* Slavs were really one nation and that "ethnic" differences were false. This too took many forms: Croat nationalists like Ante Starcevic and Josip Frank insisted that all Slavs were really Croats, while Vuk Karadzic in his 1849 document "Serbs All and Everywhere" asserted that all Slavs were Serbs. After World War I, the state of Yugoslavia was established on the basis of yet another notion, that all southern (*yugo-*) Slav peoples were related as a family of nations. This pan-Slavic state, as recent history evinces, was ultimately torn apart by rival "nationalisms" that pitted one "people" or "nation" against another and resulted in the formation of several small "nation-states" – each with more or less sizable "ethnic" minority groups within it.

Prenational people

a social group that has not yet achieved the mobilization and self-awareness that characterized a nation

Potential nation

a group that has not yet achieved national integration and self-consciousness but that is in the process of achieving them or has the characteristics necessary to achieve them

Connor, Walker. 1994. *Ethnonationalism: The Quest for Understanding.* Princeton, NJ: Princeton University Press.

since the three concepts are not synonymous or homogeneous. That is, in the twenty-first century, and possibly throughout human history, it is important to understand that

- a society does not necessarily have *a* culture, i.e., a society may embrace significant cultural diversity
- a society is not necessarily "bounded" or distinguishable from other societies in regard to culture or territory; in particular the notion that

a society or culture occupies a single unified "home area" is no longer appropriate

- a society is not necessarily politically organized as a nation or a state.

A nation is one kind of society or social organization, a kind that is *culturally self-aware* and *politically mobilized*. Walker Connor (1994) has identified a number of other forms of socio-political organization as well, including **prenational peoples** or **potential nations** that have not attained a national-political level of integration or identity but have the cultural raw materials to do so (like many indigenous societies and modern race groups); **offshoot nations** that are fragments of nations that have been separated from the main body long enough to begin to form a separate identity (such as the French-Canadians or *Quebecois* above, or the Afrikaners in southern Africa); and diasporas that have been scattered from their ancestral territories and perhaps affiliate with their host-society while still retaining some identification with their past home and group. In the twenty-first century, the most familiar and significant cultural-identity type may be the **ethnic group**, a cultural/racial group sharing a society and competing for resources (practical and symbolic) with one or more other groups. Clearly, the lines between these categories are not clear or complete either.

Diasporas

Whatever geographical isolation existed between societies ended long ago with the advent of long-distance travel and trade. In fact, the spatial boundaries between societies were never permanent and impenetrable: objects, ideas, genes, and people always flowed across social boundaries, whether in Aboriginal Australia, Native America, or pre-modern Europe. James Clifford, who has written extensively about the cultural circulation and movement, notes that there is an "unruly crowd" of concepts relating to "the contact zones of nations, cultures, and regions: terms such as *border, travel, creolization, transculturation, hybridity,* and *diaspora*" (1994: 302). In short, the old "localizing strategies" of anthropology, aimed at assigning one person or artifact or practice to one society or

Offshoot nation
a national group that emerges as a local or historical branch of an older and larger group, eventually pursuing its own cultural and political identity and interests

Clifford, James. 1994. "Diasporas." *Cultural Anthropology* 9 (3): 302–38.

Ethnic group
a corporate group based on some shared cultural traits – language, religion, history, etc. – and finds itself in competition with other groups for wealth, power, opportunity, and

MAP 13.2 African diaspora/slave routes

recognition. An ethnic group shares an identity and a destiny and therefore competes as a group

Diaspora
the dispersion of a social group from its historical homeland (often applied specifically to the Jewish community)

CULTURES IN EXILE

See Chapter 6

Barth, Fredrik, ed. 1969. *Ethnic Groups and Boundaries*. Boston, MA: Little, Brown & Co.

culture occupying one homeland is hopelessly obsolete.

One particularly common and important cultural arrangement is the **diaspora**, the dispersion of a cultural group across multiple social territories and states, potentially even globally. As coined by the ancient Greeks, diaspora (from *speiro* for "to sow" and *dia* for "over") referred to the generally voluntarily movement of Greek settlers into the islands and remote mainlands of the Mediterranean. Other and later diasporas were often involuntary. Whatever their form and motivation, Clifford regards the key characteristics of a diaspora to be "a history of dispersal, myths/memories of the homeland, alienation in the host (bad host?) country, desire for eventual return, ongoing support of the homeland, and a collective identity importantly defined by this relationship" (305).

There are obviously multiple ways for a society to find itself in a diasporic condition. One, as with the ancient Jews, is forced eviction from their land and transplantation into another land; another, as with the modern Africans, is an international trade and trafficking in humans, transporting them afar for labor. In other cases, members of a society may voluntarily migrate – permanently or cyclically – in search of work or other advantages. People may also flee their homeland to escape natural disasters (droughts, floods, etc.) or, more frequently, wars – in which case they become not only a diaspora but a refugee population (see below). They may, finally, become diasporic through the drawing of political/state borders, which divide the people without the people actually moving. Robin Cohen (1997) in particular distinguishes between *victim*, *labor*, *trade*, *imperial*, and *cultural* diasporas, with the spread of British settlers and colonists around the world an example of the imperial type.

Many, many societies exist in a diasporic condition today, including Chinese, Armenians, Asian Indians, Sikhs, Tamils, Somalis, and an endless list of others. Ultimately, it may be true that virtually all societies are to some degree diasporic, their members tossed around the world – increasingly so with expanding globalization and incessant political conflict. Indeed, as diasporas

evolve within transnational politics and are related to them, individuals within the diasporic scene are influenced by such politics.

. . .[Therefore] the "larger picture" of transnationalism and global processes affects and even transforms the informants' lives and, by implication, shapes the ethnographer's perspectives.
(Levy 2000: 146)

The diasporic condition has become increasingly relevant to anthropology and other social sciences (including a journal called *Diaspora* launched in the 1990s), partly because the phenomenon is increasingly common but also because of the light it sheds on cultural processes. First, it means that we cannot study local societies in isolation: as Paul Gilroy argues in *The Black Atlantic* (1993), the entire Atlantic region, from West Africa to the Americas, must be seen as one large cultural area when considering slavery and African culture. Accordingly, diasporic cultures are a natural candidate for multi-sited ethnography. Further, groups in diaspora may attempt to preserve their "traditional" culture and identity, or they may strive to assimilate to their host society/state, but diasporic culture and identity is never simple or given. Remembering a homeland is not the same as residing in a homeland; people in diaspora therefore stand in a problematic relation to "their culture" and "their country." As Malinowski noted decades ago, and as numerous scholars have noted since, people distanced from their homeland and home culture tend to develop an "ethnographic" perspective on both: culture or identity or origin can no longer be taken for granted but must be "worked on," constructed, intentionally practiced and perpetuated – which usually means *selectively* practiced and perpetuated. The very notion of what it means to be a Jew or an African or an Armenian, and who counts as one, becomes a cultural-political issue.

Ethnic groups

Ethnicity and ethnic groups were introduced earlier in this book, as a form, along with race, of contrasting or differentiating cultural groups from each other. DeVos defined ethnicity to highlight the distinctions between groups but also the integration of groups by so distinguishing and maintaining those differences. Ethnicity, in short, is a "boundary creating" and a "boundary maintaining" phenomenon (Barth 1969), which is only necessary or possible when multiple groups share the same social-political space – which is especially possible and common in post-colonial, globalized contexts.

Ethnic groups are "cultural" but in a highly specific and problematic way. If we think of the "ethnic groups" in Northern Ireland, for instance, it is apparent that the two groups have many cultural aspects in common: Northern Irish Catholics and Protestants are both Christian, both mostly white, and both mostly English-speaking. Yet they thought of each other as sufficiently different not only to separate but also to fight. In other words, there is no one-to-one correspondence between the number or strength of cultural similarities or differences and the degree of ethnic identity and mobilization. One small difference, despite several large similarities, can be the ground for ethnic differentiation, whereas relatively great cultural differences might make no "ethnic" difference at all. In the United States there are Catholics and Protestants, but they do not regard themselves as ethnic groups as in Northern Ireland. Thus, a cultural difference does not automatically make "ethnicity."

The key question is when a cultural difference – even a "factual" difference like ancestry – makes an *ethnic* difference. The main answer is competition. Ethnic groups by definition inhabit a "multicultural" or "multiethnic" social space, usually one in which there is a real or perceived inequity in the distribution of some valued commodity. This can include "real" commodities like land, money, jobs, political offices, and educational seats as well as "symbolic" commodities like respect, cultural rights, autonomy, and power. It is the inequalities in these "goods" that mobilize cultural groups into ethnic groups and that convert identity groups into interest groups.

So, ethnic groups are not only groups *in contrast* but groups *in competition*. Ethnicity, in the modern context, is a particularly effective way to compete in multicultural circumstances. For one thing, "cultural" identities have proven to be much more persistent and powerful than social theorists, from Marx to Geertz, thought they would; many scholars expected cultural interests to wane in favor of political/national/state or class interests, but that has not generally happened. For another, culture and ethnicity carry an aura of authenticity that is difficult to refute; if a group has a "real" and "ancient" identity and culture, that culture seems to convey certain rights. This is a perfect illustration of **identity politics**, characterized by Kauffman as "the belief that identity itself – its elaboration, expression, or affirmation – is and should be a fundamental focus of political work" (1990: 67). As such, ethnicity is cultural politics twice over: first in using culture for political purposes, and second for fomenting the political strategy that culture *can and should* be used for political purposes.

Like nationalism, ethnicity can be seen as a form of culture, one that uses culture more or less

Identity politics
the organization and mobilization of groups and parties on the basis of shared cultural characteristics, such that these groups and parties are seen to share an "identity" and to pursue economic, political, and cultural goals for and in the name of those who share that identity

PLATE 13.3 A mural in Ulster Northern Ireland depicting the "struggle" of Loyalists against Irish Catholic Nationalists.

self-consciously. The consequence is that ethnic groups do not so much compete about culture as they compete with culture. Ethnicity is certainly not about proving who is "right" or has the "better" culture, since, after all, "our" culture is "for us" and "yours" is "for you." It is about making claims to valuable resources and about legitimizing those claims. In other words, a group can say, "We demand X because we are Y." The Y, the name of the group or part(s) of the culture of the group then function(s) as the banner or flag or marker of the group – as well as a stick with which to beat the other group(s).

As a tool or weapon in contemporary political, economic, and cultural struggles, ethnicity has a complex relationship with culture or tradition. Ethnic groups typically draw their inspiration, their "sense of self," from the past in some fashion; but like tradition in general, this is not a simple past or even a past brought into the present. It is not merely "the past remembered," any more than diasporic history or culture is. Rather, in every case, ethnicity is a combination of remembering, forgetting, interpreting, and inventing "the past." The same could be said for tradition and even for culture in general. Ethnic groups tend to look backward for signs or symbols or indicators of their "true" identity or culture. They find these in stories and myths, in historic battles (both victories and losses), and customs and practices (often long lost). However, no group does or can remember all of its past; some forget spontaneously, and some forget strategically. Sinhalese in Sri Lanka "remember" that they were the first people to settle the island but forget that there were also historical Tamil kingdoms and rulers and that maybe Tamils were there before. Serbs remember that their traditional homeland was the area of Kosovo but forget that most Serbs abandoned it over 600 years ago. An important part of this memory is a history of "hurt" or grievances, as we discuss below.

Groups also cannot help but interpret their past through the lenses of the present. Things that were small then might be big today, and vice versa. French-speakers in Quebec interpret their historical claims to a francophone homeland in Canada through the lens of modern-day Quebec; they claim modern Quebec as the "traditional home" of francophones without considering that francophones never occupied all of modern Quebec, that not

all francophones live in Quebec today, and that not all of Quebec today is francophone. Serbs during the Yugoslavian conflicts of the 1990s often cast the struggle in terms of modern-day Christianity versus militant Islam, although the Bosnian Muslims were hardly militant Muslims. And, in the extreme case, the ethnic culture or past is simply made up. "Tradition" may be centuries old or days old. The classic case of "invented tradition" was Nazi Germany, which borrowed elements from pre-Christian Europe, Central Asia (the swastika), and other sources including occultism, and added purely fanciful bits and promoted this ersatz invention as "traditional German culture."

FROM CULTURE TO COMPETITION TO CONFLICT

Ethnicity is probably best known in the modern world in the form of serious, sometimes genocidal, conflict. The competitions between cultural and identity-groups over scarce and valued resources can turn deadly and have repeatedly done so, from Rwanda to Bosnia to Sri Lanka and Punjab and far beyond. The problem is only intensified by the various relationships between the ethnic group(s) and the state with its apparatus of control and coercion.

In one possible situation, the state applies pressure to groups living within its territory. The state may seek to assimilate groups to state political or economic or cultural policies, or to force them to evacuate land coveted by the state or other groups, or to annihilate the groups altogether; all of these motivations are found in the historical encounter between the United States and its indigenous populations. At the extreme, state pressures can turn into state oppression and **state terrorism**, in which the state victimizes "its own citizens" (who may not be fully participating or voluntary members of the state). Particularly when the state is associated with or dominated by one of the resident ethnic groups, this situation can be lethal.

In other cases, ethnic groups not in power or actually disempowered by the state may resist it violently. Their goals may be cultural empowerment, local cultural autonomy, or literal **separatism** from the state and the formation of their own state, sometimes in unison with their co-members on the

A CASE OF ETHNIC CONFLICT

State terrorism
the use of force and terror by a state government against its own people – either a particular group or minority within the state or the entire population

Separatism
a movement that has as its goal the cultural and/or political disengagement of two groups or societies. A separatist movement often struggles to detach its territory from a multicultural or plural state and establish its own state

other side of state boundaries. Such conditions often lead to **civil war** or **revolution**, to change, topple, or assume control over the state regime. At least it may appear like civil war from the outside, whereas the parties involved in the conflict may have never been or felt integrated into the state system in the first place. The Tamil struggle against the Sinhalese-dominated state of Sri Lanka is a good example. Finally, two or more ethnic groups, none of which holds the reins of state power, may fight against each other. Or all of these conditions may obtain simultaneously.

Two other points are worth mentioning. First, relations between groups seldom start with conflict and war; this outcome is usually the end of a long process of escalation of grievances and responses. In Sri Lanka, Tamils began with demands for inclusion and power-sharing in the new state (see above). When the Sinhalese-dominated government enacted discriminatory laws (such as an official language act) or adopted divisive political symbols (like a state flag with Buddhist imagery), tempers rose and with them demands. When those

demands went unmet or were overtly rejected, anger increased and local outbreaks of violence occurred. A heavy-handed reaction to those uprisings resulted in demands for separation and for an independent Tamil state (Tamil Eelam), and war. In a word, then, ethnic conflict is one outcome of the identity-politics process of "the recognition of a collective hurt" (Gitlin 1995: 147) allegedly delivered by the other group for which one's own group is merely seeking justice or restitution or revenge. Ironically, a hurt, even a decisive defeat, can be equally or more effective than a triumph in organizing and mobilizing a cultural/political identity group, since a defeat or humiliation is particularly "useable" in motivating people to take action and make history right.

The second point is that conflict and violence of course need not be related exclusively to ethnicity; in the twentieth century, violence was frequently related to class and "party" divisions (which were often connected with other types of cultural identities, since marginal ethnic groups tended also to be poor and "revolutionary,"

Civil war

a violent conflict within a particular state or between corporate or identity groups within the state

Revolution

a more or less sudden, complete, and often violent movement to change a political or social system

PLATE 13.4 During the 1994 genocide, Ugandan fishermen found themselves pulling dozens of bodies out of Lake Victoria. The badly decomposed bodies had traveled hundreds of miles by river from Rwanda.

especially when they embraced communist ideologies). Some of the most savage violence of the
century was committed by or against "left-wing"
movements with goals of social reform and
revolution. Cambodia under Pol Pot is a classic
example: up to one-third of the population of the
state was killed by the communist government as
part of a program of enforced social change. From
the other side, the perception of such threats often
brought violent "right-wing" forces to power, which
used all their means to suppress these movements,
even after the leftists ceased to be a threat or to exist
at all. Argentina in the 1970s is a good illustration:
from the 1960s there had been a violent leftist
guerrilla movement that killed police, soldiers,
government officials, business figures, journalists,
and scholars. The former President General

Aramburu himself was kidnapped and executed.
Rightist paramilitary groups formed to oppose these
actions, like Asociacion Anticomunista Argentina
which used virtually the same tactics in the opposite
direction. A military coup brought a right-wing
government to power in 1976 which "perpetuated
and carefully fed the myth of a subversive threat,
*even after the armed left had been virtually annihilated
in the field*" (Suarez-Orozco 1992: 232). In fact,
Suarez-Orozco argues that the regime soon developed a "paranoid ethos" that saw Argentina at
the center of an international attack on Western
civilization and that gave rise to metaphors of
"cleansing" and "curing" the society of dirty or
unhealthy influences. Among these influences were
the 10,000–30,000 citizens who were "disappeared" during the period.

BOX 13.4 TRANSITIONAL JUSTICE IN GUATEMALA

One of the crucial issues of the modern age is that when outbreaks of violence, even genocidal violence,
end, people must find ways to live together. One strategy, or set of strategies, that has been devised
and implemented is transitional justice, understood as "the process of redressing past wrongs
committed in states shifting from a violent, authoritarian past toward a more liberal, democratic future"
(Hinton 2010: 2). This noble and ambitious goal has been pursued through a number of means
including truth commissions, trials, "lustration (administrative purges of those associated with the prior
regime), memorialization, and reparation programs" (4). And, as Hinton emphasizes, transitional justice
initiatives must take into consideration the local circumstances – the local institutions and
understandings, the specific situations and players, and the particular political context – which makes
the pursuit of justice not only difficult but "often quite messy" (17). In Rwanda, for instance, transitional
justice has been sought through a combination of international tribunals, foreign courts, and a
traditional legal dispute-resolution mechanism called a *gacaca*. And despite its best intentions,
transitional justice often fails to bear results, partly because victims may be afraid to make public their
grievances or because perpetrators are beyond the reach of the proceedings. Victoria Sanford and
Martha Lincoln (2010), writing about Guatemala, call this "impunity" and find that the government
officials who were responsible for atrocities during three decades of violence have not met justice. In
1996 the Guatemalan Army made peace with the Guatemalan National Revolutionary Union, and a
Commission for Historical Clarification was established. The Commission reported in 1999 that 626
villages had been destroyed, over 200,000 people killed or "disappeared," and 1.5 million others
displaced; further, of the documented human rights violations, 93 percent were committed by the Army
and only 4 percent by the revolutionaries (Sanford and Lincoln 2010: 70). However, despite the fact
that a court ordered the arrest of numerous generals and other officials, these war criminals "continue
to make public justifications and/or deny any knowledge of human rights violations" and "none of them
have been jailed" (71). Instead, the level of violence *since the peace* has rivaled the war era, with 20,943
registered killings in five years (72). Sanford and Lincoln are particularly alarmed at what they call
"feminicide" or the killing of women – seldom if ever combatants – and, even more, "state responsibility

for these murders, whether through the commission of the actual killing, tolerance of the perpetrators' acts of violence, or omission of state responsibility to ensure the safety of its female citizens" (86). For instance, they tell the story of Claudia Isabel who was killed in August 2005 and whose killer has never been found – and is unlikely to be found, given the terrible mishandling of the crime scene and investigation.

Organizations like the Forensic Anthropology Foundation (http://www.fafg.org/Ingles/paginas/FAFG.html) help recover and identify victims to begin the justice – and the grieving – process.

Refugees

In a world of dwindling resources, escalating globalizing pressures, and seemingly continuous hostility and conflict, it is no wonder that a considerable number of people are displaced from their homelands and cultural settings. As noted above, people "leave home" for a number of reasons, from job opportunities to natural disasters to political oppression and war in their region, creating a significant international flow of refugees. In a certain sense, refugee status is one kind of, or one process in, diaspora.

The United Nations High Commissioner for Refugees, which was created by international agreement in 1951, defined a refugee in its founding document as a person who

owing to well-founded fear of being persecuted for reasons of race, religion, nationality, membership of a particular social group or political opinion, is outside the country of his nationality and is unable or, owing to such fear, is unwilling to avail himself of the protection of that country; or who, not having a nationality and being outside the country of his former habitual residence as a result of such events, is unable or, owing to such fear, is unwilling to return to it.

(2007b: 17)

While this definition focuses on political displacement, the UNHCR has added other categories of displaced persons or "persons of concern," including

www.unhcr.org

PLATE 13.5 A refugee camp in Somalia, east Africa.

- asylum-seekers – "persons who have applied for asylum or refugee status, but who have not yet received a final decision on their application" (2007a: 16)
- internally displaced persons (IDPs) – those "who have been forced or obliged to flee or to leave their homes or places of habitual residence, in particular as a result of or in order to avoid the effects of armed conflict, situations of generalized violence, violations of human rights or natural- or human-made disasters, and who have not crossed an international border" (ibid.)
- returnees – "displaced populations (mainly refugees and IDPs) who have returned to their country or place of origin," who are to be reintegrated into their former homeland (17)
- stateless persons – people who are "not considered as a national by any State under the operation of its law" (ibid.).

According to these criteria, the UNHCR reported that there were 32.9 million persons of concern to the agency at the end of 2006, including 9.9 million refugees, 744,000 asylum-seekers, 12.8 million internally displaced persons, 2.6 million returned persons, and 5.8 million stateless persons. This number, they concluded, represented a 56 percent growth over the previous year, with an 89 percent increase in Africa alone. Of the total, the single largest contingent originated from Asia (with the Middle East included in the Asian count) at 34 percent, followed by Africa (31 percent), Latin America and the Caribbean (11 percent), and Europe (5 percent). The 2006 total was especially high because of the 1.2 million Iraqis seeking refuge in neighboring states; of all states hosting refugees, Pakistan and Iran led with roughly one million each.

While the sheer scale of the refugee problem necessarily attracts scholarly attention, anthropology takes an interest in quite specific ways. First, as Harrell-Bond and Voutira suggest, refugee status – living apart from one's land and society, often in poverty and squalor, frequently unwelcome and disliked in their host country – requires that displaced persons "adapt to radically new social and material conditions. Documenting and interpreting the variety and diversity [of such responses] is the work of anthropology" (1992: 7). Further, the

international relief effort directed at refugees itself forms a social system, what they call "the machinery of humanitarian assistance." For studying the humanitarian response itself, then – that is, how aid is doled out, how refugee camps are administered, how the goals and policies of assistance are determined and implemented – "anthropologists' insights into power, and their expertise on the structure of authority, place them in an advantageous position." Anthropology can advise policy-makers, investigate the needs of refugees, and assess the impact of assistance programs on the recipients. Harrell-Bond's own study of the humanitarian system, *Imposing Aid: Emergency Assistance to Refugees* (1986), is a model for such research.

Anthropology can also examine the forces that drive people from their homes. War is one obvious cause; natural disasters are another. However, as we will discuss later, human-made but not intentionally violent conditions can force many people into refugee and exile status, including resettlement programs (explicitly to move them from one place to another) and development schemes (incidentally requiring them to move). Dam projects, for instance, in India and elsewhere have flooded vast tracts of land and with it entire villages; the current Three Gorges project in China promises to do so on an epic scale.

Finally and most significantly for anthropology, the processes that create and perpetuate refugee status also lay bare some of the most basic processes that create, perpetuate, reinterpret, and modify culture itself. As Harrell-Bond and Voutira explain, and as can be observed in diasporas and other forms of modern transnational community,

> One of the gains for anthropology in studying refugees is that it offers the chance to record the processes of social change, not merely as a process of transition within a cultural enclave, but in the dramatic context of uprootedness where a people's quest for survival becomes a model of social change.
>
> (9)

One of the most fascinating and profound aspects of this change-and-survival process is the manipulation of culture and tradition – of memory and history themselves – for specific purposes and in reaction to specific pressures for dispersed and displaced groups. Indeed, the

Harrell-Bond, Barbara E. 1986. *Imposing Aid: Emergency Assistance to Refugees.* Oxford: Oxford University Press.

See Chapter 14

ANTHROPOLOGY OF
HUMAN RIGHTS

creation of a shared history, a founding myth, is such a common phenomenon among both refugees and others forced from home that it needs probing. It has powerful creative functions, but is no sign that the uprooted have put their experience behind them and moved on to other things. . . . Resettlement does not wipe out memory, but rather provides a medium through which it is reworked, and the memory of shared experience of uprooting helps to create new forms of identity.

(Colson 2003: 9)

A number of anthropologists have accepted the challenge to study how culture and memory function in refugee and other diasporic communities, perhaps most famously Liisa Malkki (1995) in her fieldwork in a Rwandan refugee camp who found that residents engage in a kind of mythico-history intended not to remember the "facts" of the past but to select, marshal, and employ history, tradition, and culture to understand and solve problems of their current social predicament. We return to this issue in the final extended case-study at the end of this book.

Finally and most soberly, refugees, diasporas, ethnic conflicts, and other forms of modern suffering demand that anthropology take seriously and contribute something to not only the cultural roots of suffering but to the possible reduction of it. This is why J. Davis argued almost two decades ago for "an anthropology of suffering" (1992). Anthropology cannot be merely the science of "social organizations [when they are] working more or less normally" but also a solemn science of the "breakdown and repair" of societies. He called therefore for the unification of "two kinds of anthropology: the comfortable anthropology of social organization, and the painful anthropology of disruption and despair" (149). Anything less, he suggested, is not a complete or respectful account of the current human condition.

Malkki, Liisa. 1995. *Purity and Exile: Violence, Memory, and National Cosmology among Hutu Refugees in Tanzania.* Chicago, IL and London: The University of Chicago Press.

BOX 13.5   CONTEMPORARY CULTURAL CONTROVERSIES: BEDOUIN REFUGEES IN ISRAEL

One group's claim to territory or sovereignty often excludes and disadvantages another. According to the Association for Civil Rights in Israel (www.acri.org.il), "Since its establishment in 1948, Israel has ignored the Bedouin's historical presence in the region and has sought to transfer and concentrate the population into a small geographic area in the northeastern Negev – in order to confine their living space and free up the most fertile areas of the Negev for Jewish agricultural settlement. The state continues to deny recognition to the Bedouin villages and to deny the villagers their right to their own soil, which they have lived upon and worked for decades." Up to 30,000 Bedouin residents are targeted for evacuation and relocation to towns, and many others have already had their land seized and their economy undermined. Some will receive compensation, but only if they can provide documentation of ownership – something that most indigenous peoples of the world do not possess. What do you think?

SUMMARY

Politics, which concerns order, control, and power, and at the profoundest level identity, is an acute problem in the modern world, not only but especially for people in the post-colonial phase of their societies. The processes by which colonialism ended in any single colony set the tone for immediate political opportunities or challenges, whether by

- Transition to native self-government
- Transition to expatriate European government
- Native resistance and revolution.

Any of these processes might yield a temporary transitional state and a struggle for political control and cultural definition in the future. Communism was a frequent and attractive element in the battle against colonialism because it seemed to offer an explanation or theory of colonialism and anti-colonial resistance as well as a plan for the future.

The "new states" formed from independence movements faced the distinction between state, nation, and nation-state. Virtually none of them were nation-states but rather

- Multinational states and/or
- Multi-state nations.

This reality set up conditions of cultural competition and conflict between groups sharing the state. In these contests, culture itself became a useful tool for contrasting groups from each other and making and legitimizing demands. Out of "traditional" cultures came cultural movements like

- Nationalism
- Ethnicity

with their varying cultural bases and goals, including sometimes separation and sovereignty as a group. These conflicts all too often escalated into real shooting wars, with sometimes genocidal consequences. Some of the results, of anthropological significance, have been

- Ethnic conflicts
- Diasporas
- Refugees

These painful contemporary developments call for a re-examination of concepts like culture and identity – and potentially for a re-examination of the culture and identity of anthropology.

MCQS

FILL IN THE BLANKS

Key Terms

Civil war	Multi-state nation	Revolution
Communal representation	Nation	Self-determination
Country	Nation-state	Separatism
Diaspora	Nationalism	State
Ethnic group	Offshoot nation	State terrorism
Identity politics	Potential nation	
Multinational state	Prenational people	

The struggle for economic independence

Development, modernization, and globalization

The poor states of the world often do not lack resources, and they certainly do not lack hard workers. Among the answers to what they do lack is *justice*, and the "fair trade" movement aims to remedy that. In her study of Guatemalan coffee growers, Sarah Lyon defines fair trade as "a form of alternative trade that seeks to improve the position of disempowered small-scale farmers through trade as a means of development" (2011: 1), primarily by guaranteeing them higher prices and access to credit. Coffee is one of the colonial commodities par excellence, the second most-traded commodity in the world after petroleum. Coffee growing began in Guatemala in the mid-1800s, and wealthy land owners became so powerful by 1871 that they entered the government and "enacted exploitative land and labor measures intended to promote coffee cultivation and exportation" (26). Eventually, "Guatemala became one immense plantation." After a century of such exploitation, the U.S. Agency for International Development (USAID) began in 1970 to fund the formation of rural cooperatives, partly out of fear that poverty would attract the farmers to communism; by 1976 there were 510 cooperatives in highlands Guatemala with 132,000 members. Late in the twentieth century these cooperatives started to work with American companies and international agencies like the Fairtrade Labelling Organization (FLO) to get their coffee certified, labeled, and marketed to consumers as high in quality and fair in trade. While this action did result in higher prices for their coffee, Lyon warns of several less positive outcomes. First, she stresses that fair trade was about income and not about culture; it did not focus on cultural preservation and in fact imposed a number of cultural changes on local growers, both in their social organization and in their environmental practices. Second, while better paid, the growers did not necessarily feel more empowered, and cooperative programs "often serve to strengthen and entrench a small group of better-off peasants without significantly benefiting large sectors of the population" (120). Most notably, in some ways participation in fair trade networks actually *increased* the dependence of local growers, enmeshing them in global webs of governmentality that audited and certified their product, imposing outside standards of quality and methods of production that tended to intensify "the power that northern certifiers and roasters wield over coffee production and processing" (155). And of course the whole notion of fair trade depends on American

See Chapter 9

PLATE 14.1 Local farmers interact with international corporations and organizations to produce "fair trade" coffee.

See Chapter 7

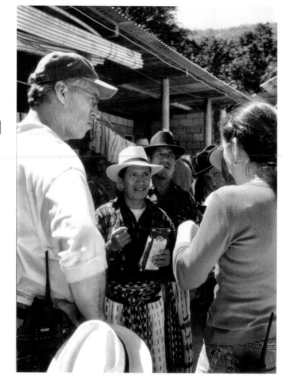

See Chapter 12

See Chapter 13

Primary production
the production of raw materials, in the form of farming, mining, foresting, etc.

and other consumers who are willing to pay more for the cause – or at least the image – of social justice.

When the formal relationship of colonialism ended, each former colony became a politically independent state. However, as we have already discussed, many negative effects of the colonial period lingered long past this independence, up to the present day. Some of these effects are primarily political. Others are more fundamentally economic – involving ownership of wealth and resources, production, distribution, and the international system of trade – although these cannot be entirely separated from politics. Ownership and control of productive resources confers political power, and political power grants influence over the economy. The upshot of the legacy of economic arrangements during and after independence highlights the point that political independence does not equal economic independence, and it certainly does not equal economic prosperity.

In this chapter we will examine the ongoing economic challenges facing the newly independent states and the societies within them as they emerged from colonialism. We will also look at some of the policies and practices which have been intended to "correct" the perceived problems, economic and

social, especially what is referred to as "development." Finally, we will see the mixed effects of contemporary development activities and globalization, not only at the state level but at the level of the small indigenous groups within those states. As we have emphasized in our earlier discussion of economics and throughout this book, societies seldom if ever operated in total economic isolation. But with the arrival of colonialism and then state and global cultural processes, it is impossible to understand the situation in any society – even the small and allegedly "traditional" ones – apart from its surrounding and interpenetrating context. At the same time, we can consider the contribution of anthropology to understanding, delivering, and critiquing these development and culture-change activities.

WHY ECONOMIC DEPENDENCE?

Political independence from colonialism only meant the departure of foreign administrators and armies and the establishment of an internal government with its own army. It did not always mean changes in the economic realities on the ground; often independence was intentionally not meant to change those realities. If a colony had a large number of landless people before independence, it still had them afterwards. If it had an economy dependent on **primary production** (producing raw materials rather than manufactured goods), like Guatemala above, it still had such an economy afterwards. And if non-local or non-indigenous individuals or corporations owned and controlled resources and wealth before independence, they still did afterwards. In fact, because political independence was a modification of relations between governments (new state and former colonizing state) and not necessarily between individuals or classes or businesses, it usually could not address those other issues, at least not at first.

There are a number of reasons why economic conditions changed more slowly, if at all, compared to political ones. In many former colonies, large or at least significant foreign populations remained after independence. The United States is a good example. When the United States became independent, power and control hardly reverted to the native peoples. Rather, expatriate Europeans and their descendants, who now identified as and called themselves "Americans," created an offshoot of Western culture, politics, and economics on new soil. Therefore, white, European-descended land-holders continued to hold land and gradually increased their holdings at the further expense of the native populations. Australia and Canada and New Zealand were the same. South Africa is the most dramatic case, where local whites, a mere 10 percent of the population, dominated the state long after independence in 1910 and actually enacted discriminatory laws (**apartheid**) to disenfranchise and restrict non-whites in many ways. When multiracial elections were held for the first time in 1994 and a black government was elected, headed by Nelson Mandela, even this did not change basic economic facts, such as the extreme poverty of many black South Africans.

In other former colonies, with or without major white segments, independence often was merely a transfer of power from one group of elites (white) to another (native). But, as in the cases of Sri Lanka and Rwanda, these native elites were commonly enculturated to Western ways and did not challenge the status quo, at least initially. In some cases, the outgoing colonizers actually set up the future government, as in Iraq, where a pro-Western king was installed in 1932 and then overthrown in 1958. These native elites sometimes continued to take inspiration, if not direction, from former colonizers, and as often as not they aimed to enrich themselves by exploiting the population no less than the colonizers had done. In fact, we might call this stage in the history of "new states" internal colonialism, as one section of the society – sometimes a regional group, sometimes an ethnic or "national" group, sometimes just an individual and his family or party – ran the state like private property. Zaire under Joseph Mobutu (later Mobutu Sese Seko) is a prime example, since Mobutu was reported to have accumulated $5 billion in personal wealth while his state slid into poverty, repression, and chaos.

Finally and most crucially, nothing did or perhaps even could change "on the ground" and in regard to the states' external relations with the global capitalist system. During colonialism, entire colonies had been turned into monoculture plantations, producing one crop (such as coffee, tea, rubber, sugar, cocoa, peanuts, etc.) for export. On the day after independence the new states did not simply plow under the coffee fields and plant food crops for local consumption – or build factories to manufacture cars and computers. For one thing, the land was usually still owned by individuals or corporations (resident in the state or not) who wanted it to continue to produce export products. Even if the resources were controlled by native elites, they too typically wanted to perpetuate the export economy and its income stream. Finally, even if the local government had wanted to alter fundamentally the economy of the state, the process would have been difficult if not impossible for financial reasons. The new states were often quite poor, as they had never been allowed to amass any wealth for their own use. Even more, they still had production contracts and other economic obligations. Many had debts to repay, and their only means of earning cash to pay their debts was exporting their existing products. Foreign banks, companies, and other agencies influenced the internal economic decisions. And finally, it cannot be overlooked that powerful forces, including the United States and European countries, pressured new states to leave their economies as they were, offering assistance or even convincing them that production-for-export was the road to economic freedom and success. The result is that the damage and injustice of colonialism were usually not reversed with the arrival of political independence but were rather perpetuated by new and less overt (and also less expensive) means.

THE PATH TO UNDERDEVELOPMENT

So colonialism left a constellation of economic legacies that would not be soon erased in most new states – even in those that made any serious effort to erase them, and not all did. The economic conditions of the new states were marked most conspicuously by poverty. In its 2000–2001 report the World Bank asserted that almost half of the world's population lived on less than $2 per day and that 20 percent lived on less than $1 per day. Of these desperately poor people, 43.5 percent lived in South Asia, 24.3 percent in sub-Saharan Africa, 23.3 percent in East Asia and the Pacific, 6.5 percent in Latin America and the Caribbean, and only 2 percent in Europe and Central Asia (World Bank 2001: 3–4). And the situation had actually

Apartheid
in twentieth-century South Africa, the official policy of separating the races within their society legally and socially

See Chapter 6

www.worldbank.org

deteriorated in South Asia and sub-Saharan Africa, which in 1987 accounted for 40.1 percent and 18.4 percent, respectively, of those living on less than $1 per day. The economic characteristics underlying this condition of poverty include:

■   Primary production (the production of raw materials, like food, lumber, metals, fuels, etc.) as the predominant element of the state economy
■   A high proportion of the population engaged in agricultural activities
■   Low incomes, individually and nationally
■   An unfavorable distribution of the national income, such that a small minority received or controlled most of the wealth and the vast majority were relatively – or sometimes absolutely – impoverished
■   Little or no industrial production
■   Dependence on foreign sources for money, skill, and manufactured goods
■   Dependence on foreign markets for their primary goods, with prices out of their control

Perhaps equally if not more significant and negative are the social consequences of these factors, affecting the quality of life in the new states:

■   A mostly rural population
■   Very high birth and death rates, combining short life expectancies and high infant mortality

with high fertility to produce a population explosion
■   Insufficient diets and poor nutrition
■   High incidence of (preventable) diseases, both infectious/parasitic and nutrition-related
■   Low education and high illiteracy
■   Poor housing and services, combined with urban overcrowding as people attempt to escape rural conditions, creating a huge urban slum-dwelling population
■   Often quite low status for women

A few numbers are necessary and sufficient to convey the scale of the problem. The wealth and economic health of a state can be measured in numerous ways, each with its distinct significance and associated advantages and limitations. One common measure is **gross national product (GNP)**, roughly defined as the total value of the goods and services produced by the state, domestically and by overseas investment. However, since it is deceptive to compare the production of a large state with that of a small state, a more meaningful statistic is **GNP per capita** or the GNP divided by the population, which suggests how much wealth is produced per inhabitant. This does not mean that every person in the state actually earns this much income per year; some have much more and many much less, making the distribution of this wealth a critical issue. Also, individuals may have access to other forms of livelihood than cash, such as subsistence

Gross national product (GNP)
the total value of goods and services produced by a society or state

Gross national product per capita
the GNP of a state divided by its population

PLATE 14.2 Many of the world's poor live in squalid conditions, like this crowded *favela* or slum in Brazil.

agriculture, but these other forms will not ordinarily allow them to participate in the cash-based economy, where they might acquire manufactured goods, medical care, and education.

From this information it is clear that the "richest" states in the world are Western or Westernized states, while the "poorest" states in the world are non-Western states. In fact, all of the lowest ten state economies are found in Africa except for Afghanistan. But average income figures do not tell the whole story, since the average may be quite high while large proportions of people live in poverty. Therefore, we must also consider income distribution. The poorest states also have some of the worst inequalities of wealth: in Malawi and Sierra Leone, the tenth and seventh poorest states

respectively by World Bank calculations, the richest 10 percent of the citizens monopolize 42.2 percent and 43.6 percent of the income, respectively. Brazil and Namibia have the greatest concentrations of wealth in the hands of the rich and the worst overall income inequalities.

We cannot measure the living conditions in a state by economic data alone; we must also consider standard-of-living indicators that measure health and education and other quality-of-life issues. Infant mortality (the rate of death of infants before one year of age) and life expectancy (the average length of life) are two telling indicators.

The next sixteen highest infant death rates are also in African states. Note that the United States is not among the ten best states for infant mortality; its

TABLE 14.1   GNP per capita 2010, in dollars

Highest 10 Countries		Lowest 10 Countries	
1. Luxembourg	63,950	1. Democratic Republic of Congo	320
2. Norway	57,850	2. Liberia	340
3. Singapore	55,380	3. Burundi	400
4. Switzerland	48,960	4. Eritrea	540
5. United States	47,120	5. Niger	720
6. Netherlands	46,610	6. Central African Republic	780
7. Denmark	40,290	7. Sierra Leone	820
8. Sweden	39,660	8. Malawi	850
9. Austria	39,390	9. Togo	890
10. Australia	38,380	10. Afghanistan	860

Source: World Bank

Note: The World Bank method calculates gross national income, based on purchasing power parity.

Note: This listing does not include states for which precise dollar amounts were unavailable, as well as extremely small polities.

TABLE 14.2   Infant mortality (per 1,000 births), 2011 estimated

Lowest 10 States		Highest 10 States	
1. Monaco	1.79	1. Angola	175.90
2. Singapore	2.32	2. Afghanistan	149.20
3. Bermuda	2.47	3. Niger	112.22
4. Sweden	2.74	4. Mali	111.35
5. Japan	2.78	5. Somalia	105.56
6. Iceland	3.20	6. South Sudan	102.00
7. France	3.29	7. Central African Republic	99.38
8. Italy	3.38	8. Guinea-Bissau	96.23
9. Spain	3.39	9. Chad	95.31
10. Finland	3.43	10. Nigeria	91.54

Source: CIA World Factbook

TABLE 14.3   Life expectancy, in years, 2011 estimated

Highest 10 States		Lowest 10 States	
1. Monaco	89.7	1. Angola	38.76
2. Japan	82.25	2. Afghanistan	45.02
3. Singapore	82.14	3. Nigeria	47.56
4. Australia	81.81	4. Chad	48.33
5. Italy	81.77	5. Swaziland	48.66
6. Canada	81.38	6. Guinea-Bissau	48.70
7. France	81.19	7. South Africa	49.33
8. Switzerland	81.07	8. Zimbabwe	49.64
9. Sweden	81.07	9. Central African Republic	50.07
10. Israel	80.96	10. Somalia	50.40

Source: CIA World Factbook

TABLE 14.4   Most and least livable states, Human Development Index 2011

Most	Least
1. Norway	1. Democratic Republic of Congo
2. Australia	2. Niger
3. New Zealand	3. Burundi
4. United States	4. Mozambique
5. Ireland	5. Chad
6. Liechtenstein	6. Liberia
7. Netherlands	7. Burkina Faso
8. Canada	8. Sierra Leone
9. Sweden	9. Central African Republic
10. Germany	10. Guinea

First World

a term not commonly used any more for the rich, powerful states in the world that dominate the international political and economic arena and consist basically of the former colonial powers

Third World

a term sometimes used to refer to the economically poor, politically and militarily weak, relatively unstable, and dependent states of the world, most of which emerged from colonialism in fairly recent history

rate is 6.06, forty-sixth in the world. The United Kingdom suffers from a rate of 4.62. The situation at the other end of life is no better for Africa, as indicated by average life expectancy.

The United States occupies fiftieth place, with 78.37 years, and the United Kingdom twenty-eighth, with 80.05, which is still about twice the life span of some African states. Indeed, the next thirty lowest life expectancies after the ones shown above are all found in Africa. While longevity is not necessarily a proof of quality of life, it can only be surmised that people who live half as long do not live very well. On measures of education, literacy, health, access to clean water, and women's rights, the picture remains consistent.

For instance, the U.N. calculates its Human Development Index as a composite score of the "livability" of various states based on life expectancy, adult literacy, school enrollment, educational attainment, and per capital national income. On this data, the most livable and least livable states in the world in 2011 are shown in Table 14.4.

As we have come to expect, all of the "best places to live" were Western or Westernized, and all of the "worst" were non-Western states – in fact, all in Africa. And eighteen of the next nineteen least-livable were African states, the one exception being Afghanistan. Incidentally, the United Kingdom ranked as the twenty-eighth most livable state.

It is easy to understand, then, why observers and scholars have divided the world's states into different levels or classes. One of the most familiar class systems is the **First World/Third World** division. The Third World refers to the set of poor states, mostly if not exclusively recent colonies, with all or most of the economic and social difficulties listed above. The term "Third World" was actually coined at a conference in Bandung, Indonesia in

1955 to describe their difference from and rejection of both the capitalist (First World) and communist (Second World) alternatives. The twenty-nine states in attendance – led by Indonesia, Burma, Ceylon (Sri Lanka), India, and Pakistan – represented more than half of the world's population and were determined to remain "non-aligned" with either of the two competing ideological systems. Instead, they intended to craft an identity and a camaraderie as a third system with its own problems and its own solutions.

This international "lower class" of states has other distinct – and unsettling – characteristics. A line drawn to separate the Third World from the rest of the world highlights two facts. The first is that there is a "north/south" aspect to the inequality, such that virtually all of the Third World states lie in the Southern Hemisphere or at least south of the rich states; in the southern half of the earth, only Australia, New Zealand, and South Africa fall outside of the Third World. Second, virtually all of these Third World states are majority non-white – Asian, African, and other non-European. It is as if the apartheid system mentioned above applies to the system of states too – as if there is a color-based stratification of states internationally, not just of races within particular states. This phenomenon has been termed **global apartheid**, which does not suggest a deliberate or formal/legal system of international racial discrimination but rather a (for the most part) unintentional and informal/situational outcome based on historical, environmental, political, and economic factors.

Another way to look at the distinction between the rich and the poor states is in terms of "development," with "developed" states and "undeveloped" or "underdeveloped" or "less developed" states. The "developed" group tends to have exactly the opposite characteristics of the dependent states list above; by contrast they tend to enjoy:

- High GNP and income
- Wealth often comparatively evenly distributed
- Agriculture as a very small (as little as 2 percent) part of the economy
- Manufacturing ("secondary sector") and services ("tertiary sector") as the bulk of the economy
- High rates of urbanization
- High life expectancy, low birth and death rates

- Adequate food supplies, mostly self-sufficient
- Generally good health-care, high education and literacy, and adequate social services and standard of living
- Relatively high women's status

Because of these traits, developed states are for the most part able to meet the needs of their populations. While there are of course poor and hungry people in the richest of states, the proportion of these people is low and the "level of poverty" is relative rather than absolute. That is, in conditions of **relative poverty**, poor people do not have as much food or as many comforts as others in their society, while in **absolute poverty** poor people do not have enough food and other resources to live reasonably if at all. Famine and starvation are common sights.

Underdevelopment as a condition and a process

It is tempting and all too easy to dismiss the less-developed states as perpetual failures – as societies that have always been unable to feed themselves or provide their own basic needs and therefore always will be unable. This has been the position taken in what has been called "modernization theory." Argued most effectively by W. W. Rostow (1965), **modernization theory** sees the fault for underdevelopment as internal, in particular "backward" values and practices. Prior to development, such societies purportedly had economies that were stagnant, even primitive, due fundamentally to a "traditional culture" consisting of values and attitudes that presented roadblocks to development. Traditional culture resulted in a kind of "cultural inertia" in which nothing changes, no one takes any risks, people simply repeat old behaviors, and there is no growth. Before development can occur, culture change must occur, including new attitudes and beliefs about progress, planning for the future, individuality and the freedom and right to accumulate private property and wealth, risk-taking and entrepreneurship, and education. Only after these cultural changes can the economy "take off." Individuals commence building the economic structures necessary for a modern economy; they will start businesses, make money, save money, and

Relative poverty
the possession of less money than others in the same society, or the inability to afford the standard of living of more comfortable individuals or that is believed to be possible or appropriate

Absolute poverty
a level of income below what is required to have a decent standard of living, sometimes measured at less than $US 1 per day

Global apartheid
the de facto division of the world's states into rich, powerful, majority-white states and poor, weak and dependent majority-non-white states

Rostow, W. W. 1965. *The Stages of Economic Growth: A Non-Communist Manifesto.* New York: Cambridge University Press.

Modernization theory
the theory that the improvement of economic and social conditions in poor states entails the creation of "modern" (generally understood as Western-like) institutions, values, and habits. Also, the specific processes or policies by which this form of social change can occur. W. W. Rostow offers one of the most complete and well-known modernization theories

invest money. The measure of successful development is economic growth, and a society and economy has reached "maturity" when it achieves "self-sustained growth": like an airplane, it can stay elevated and continue to climb, lifted by industrialization, technology, and modern culture. The ultimate goal is "high mass consumption," an economy and society that resembles the lifestyles of the Western world. This is why many supporters and critics alike have regarded modernization as basically Westernization, on the premise that Western ways of life are the best, if not the inevitable future of all human societies.

Others have seen Western/capitalist society as less the cure than the cause of global poverty. André Gunder Frank, writing primarily about the Latin American experience, insisted that the rise of the Western capitalist system, especially colonialism, had created underdevelopment in the first place. In his 1966 article "The Development of Underdevelopment" and then books such as *Dependent Accumulation and Underdevelopment* (1979) he argued that underdevelopment was not the "traditional" or pre-contact condition of most of the world. Rather, the underdevelopment in present-day states is the product of historical and persistent economic and political relationships between what he called the "metropoles" (roughly the colonizing societies like Britain, France, etc.) and the "satellites" (essentially the colonies).

In the course of "underdeveloping" or "de-developing" the dependent satellites, wealth and resources flowed from colonies, enriching the colonizing states – which Frank dubbed "**dependent accumulation**." Essentially, as the West got richer, the rest got poorer. On this model, underdevelopment then is not the "native condition" of today's poor states but is the flip side of development, both of which emerged from colonialism. As we saw, colonialism stripped traditional peoples of their wealth, dispossessed them of their land, deprived them of their own labor and the fruits of that labor, entangled them in the interests of foreign societies, bled them in the form of taxes, and rendered them dependent on foreign products to replace their lost self-sufficiency. In the cases of small, less politically integrated societies (bands, tribes, and even some chiefdoms) this was a simple process: colonizers arrived with weapons, religious convictions, economic institutions, and adequate populations to overpower natives and compel their participation in the new regime.

But of course not all pre-colonial societies were living in "tribal" arrangements. India and China had their own organized states, and they and parts of Africa had flourishing traditions of enterprise and "mass production" (although not modern industrial mass production) long before Europeans arrived. In addition to the colonial methods previously described, colonialists had to devise more muscular means to crack open and wear down these societies. Native "industries" had to be eliminated, sometimes by unfair competition (for example, dumping products onto their markets at unnaturally low prices), sometimes by creating hostile financial and business environments. The British textile industry, for instance, could not compete with the local Indian one at the outset and had to suppress and destroy it before they could underdevelop India in this regard. African native trading and financial institutions also had to be crushed.

Frank, André Gunder. 1979. *Dependent Accumulation and Underdevelopment*. New York and London: Monthly Review Press.

See Chapter 12

Dependent accumulation according to André Gunder Frank, the process by which colonialism and capitalism extracted the wealth from non-Western colonies, rendering them poor and dependent

BOX 14.1   UNDERDEVELOPING CHINA THROUGH THE DRUG TRADE

China presents probably the most interesting and shameful case of the de-development of a formerly independent society. It is well known that China had achieved a high level of literacy and prosperity while the West was still struggling through its "dark ages." Travelers like Marco Polo were dazzled by the wealth of imperial China in the 1300s and 1400s, and many Europeans could not believe the tales of a non-Christian society more advanced than their own. Chinese goods, such as silk and porcelain, were highly prized by European consumers, who traded gold to acquire them, but there was nothing that China cared to import in exchange. The Chinese emperor said it well in 1793 in a communication to the king of England: "As your Ambassador can see for himself, we possess all things. I set no value on objects strange or ingenious, and have no use for your country's manufactures." Three hundred years earlier a raja from India had expressed similar sentiments to the head of Portugal: "In my kingdom there is abundance. . . .What I seek from thy country is gold, silver, coral and scarlet" (quoted in Frank 1979: 18). European businessmen tried furiously for years to find a product that the Chinese especially would purchase or to imitate Chinese crafts for themselves in Europe. European inventors finally discovered the secrets of silk, porcelain, and other Chinese goods, but the net flow of wealth was still from Europe to China: Europe bought Chinese goods for gold but sold no goods in exchange. This "negative balance of trade" was not permanently sustainable (Americans complained bitterly about the same issue in relation to Japan in the 1990s, and increasingly again with China in the twenty-first century), until a product was discovered that Chinese would buy – opium. In the early 1800s, Western traders began to unload opium on Chinese markets, at great profit and with destructive consequences for Chinese society. The government of China, still independent at this time, outlawed the opium trade, but when England's profits and property were threatened, it fought a war (1839–42) to protect its drug trade. This first major defeat for China opened it to further exploitation, resulting in territorial loss (for example, Hong Kong was ceded away by treaty, a treaty that only expired in 1997) and more war (a second "opium war" was waged by England and France against China in 1856–60). Eventually, Beijing was occupied and the carve-up of Chinese land began, with many European states claiming their "sphere of influence" (no one state could ever hold the entire territory of China) and introducing their laws, economic practices, and people. The whole process was facilitated by being drug-pushers to the Chinese.

The source of underdevelopment, then, is not simply the "traditional" culture and institutions of most non-Western societies. It was at least partly a product or outcome of specific historical and cultural – and therefore local and diverse – processes. These practices impoverished the subordinated people, made them dependent, and then set them loose on post-independence courses that were almost certainly doomed to be economically difficult if not impossible. The political facts of the new states – that they were artificial, weak, divided, conflicted, or corrupt, not to mention in many cases too small to be economically viable – only added to the legacy of colonialism and the challenges of the future.

DEVELOPMENT: SOLUTION AND PROBLEM

From the middle of the twentieth century, the dominant answer to the "problem" of underdevelopment was, naturally, **development**. Development is understood as a form of directed change intended to correct the inadequacies and failures of the existing economic systems – their poverty, dependence on primary production, lack of industry, and low standard of living. Development then consists of planned and coordinated efforts, usually by the government of a state but sometimes by agents outside of the state, to change or improve the economy of the state – and as necessary the culture of the state – so as provide greater wealth and a higher standard of living.

Various social scientists, including historians, political scientists, and economists, have offered various definitions or understandings of the notion of development, generally recognizing that economic change cannot occur without more widespread cultural and social change. Gunnar Myrdal (1968: 1869) characterized it simply as "upward movement of the entire social system" and not just the economy (although "upward" is a vague and relative term). Wilbert Moore called it the "total transformation of a traditional or pre-modern society into the types of technology and associated social organization that characterize the 'advanced,' economically prosperous, and relatively politically stable nations of the Western world" (1963: 93). Surveying various definitions, David Apter (1968) identified some common elements: differentiation or increasing specialization of roles, stability or the

See Chapter 13

Myrdal, Gunnar. 1968. *Asian Drama: An Inquiry into the Poverty of Nations.* New York: Pantheon.

Development
a form of directed change in which a state tries to change its internal economy and society, and/or foreign states and institutions try to change it, to promote economic growth, industrialize and urbanize, and ideally achieve a higher standard of living for its inhabitants

PLATE 14.3 This Gunjari village in India was submerged because of a dam project.

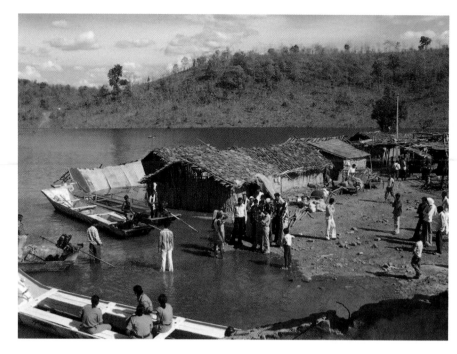

Nolan, Riall. 2002. *Development Anthropology: Encounters in the Real World*. Boulder, CO: Westview Press.

Development policy
the general priorities and decisions set by a state or by development agencies to achieve economic, political, and social goals

Import substitution
a development policy aimed at producing domestically what the state or society currently imports from other states, i.e. substituting its own local products for imported products

ability to institute changes without causing greater problems, choice or the freedom of innovation and flexibility, and emulation or the imitation of foreign/Western models.

Riall Nolan, a contemporary anthropologist involved in development issues, views development as "attempts to improve the conditions of life for people, focusing on raising standards of living, building local capacity, and encouraging local participation and decision making. Development almost always involves multiple groups, and therefore, multiple cultural perspectives" (2002: 309). This reminds us that development, like any other initiative of directed change, is ideally first and foremost about people. The 1986 U.N. General Assembly's Declaration on the Right to Development (GA Res 41/128) related development to "human rights and fundamental freedoms." Furthermore, since development is about changing how people live and work, it is also cultural to the core: it introduces new cultural ideas and practices to people and brings cultures into contact in critical ways – not only Western and non-Western cultures but various disparate cultures within the development zone. It cannot be conceived as a sheer economic or political process and takes place at multiple social levels simultaneously, including individual, household/family/kin group, community, nation/state, and international/global.

Development planning and projects

In its classic expression, development is conceived as something that a society, ordinarily a state and its government, chooses to do and thus directs at "itself." We say "itself" in quotation marks because, as we have seen and will explore again below, the state and its dominant group(s) may target areas that are within its jurisdiction but not inhabited by those groups themselves or entirely integrated into the state political/economic system. At any rate, development ordinarily exhibits the traits of large-scale, planned, and sustained decision-making and implementation.

Perhaps the first thing to understand is that development is business – big business. It starts, as all rational economic decision-making does, with the perception of a problem to solve. It then entails the formulation of a **development policy**, the broad principles or goals of the effort. Among the common development policies are "economic growth," especially as determined by rising GNP. Some states have adopted the policy of **import substitution**, in which they aim to produce domestically what they have previously had to import from abroad (i.e., substituting local production for foreign-made products). In recent decades, development policies have increasingly focused on market principles and "free trade." In fact, development policies, either internally or internationally, have turned since 1980 toward what is called **structural adjustment** (also known as "neoliberalism"), but more on this later.

A state's development policy dictates the specific **development projects** that it will undertake. Development projects are pinpointed actions that the state wishes to take to achieve its development goals, which are expected to deliver specific returns and ideally serve as the basis for additional development beyond the scope of the project itself. This means that such projects tend to emphasize "infrastructure" which provides multiple benefits, a platform for subsequent development, and ultimately self-sustaining economic growth. Therefore, some of the typical development projects include:

- energy projects, especially as hydroelectric dams if appropriate rivers are available
- transportation projects, especially roads and railroads
- agricultural projects, to increase the yield of agriculture and/or open up new land for farming

- settlement projects, to move people to less-populous or under-producing territories or to move people off of territories that are marked for "development" (e.g. flooding from a dam project)
- industrial projects, to increase (or in many cases start) the manufacturing sector of the economy and provide a new source of export income and local self-sufficiency.

In a sense, the fifth type of project is the ultimate goal of development, but it is not possible without the preceding four types. There must be power to run the factories, transportation for workers and materials to get in and manufactures to get out, adequate agriculture to feed the workers while freeing laborers from farm work to shift them to factory work, and adequate income and capital for investment which is usually skimmed off of the agricultural sector. And there must be people where the state needs them – which may or may not be where they are now and traditionally were.

Structural adjustment
a set of policies designed to reduce government control over development specifically and economic activity more generally, including "opening" or "freeing" local markets to foreign goods, eliminating economic protections like tariffs and subsidies, reducing taxes, deregulating industry, cutting government spending, and allowing the value of local currencies to "float" on international currency exchanges

Development project
a specific activity or task settled upon to achieve the economic, political, and social goals of a development policy. Such projects often include transportation, energy (especially hydro-electric), agricultural, and resettlement schemes

BOX 14.2   IRRIGATION AND AGRICULTURE IN A SENEGAL DEVELOPMENT PROJECT

Waldstein (1986) offered the SAED (Societé d'Amenagement et d'Exploitation des Terres du Delta) project in Senegal as an "archetype" of development. The agency was formed in 1965 for the purpose of "developing land for hydro-agricultural production; controlling, transforming, and marketing produce; and promoting cooperative organization among the peasants working on the land" (121). The Senegal River delta area was practically uninhabited prior to the 1960s, when SAED created five new villages there. It also constructed an irrigation system and established land-use and work-, cost-, and profit-sharing arrangements for the settlers. In the Kassak region, cooperatives were set up, with presidents and "weighers" and quartermasters to distribute supplies. SAED determined what was to be grown and the prices paid to the farmers, and all produce that was not approved for local use was handed over to the agency. Farm land was allotted to households on the basis of the number of able-bodied adult members, and households in the cooperative worked side by side. The mid-range results were less than inspiring. In 1975–76 the average household in the three villages under study lost money, and in 1976–77 the average household in two of the three villages earned less than $16 (127). A variety of problems were noted, not the least of which was that the location was not really suitable for agriculture; as he writes, "the decisions regarding where and how to develop Kassak were based on political rather than ecological considerations" (133). Also, the technical and social organization of the work involved "major departures from customary production practices in producers' home areas" (133), such as outside decision-making, powerful "internal" offices like president, and forced cooperative labor and production; together these factors "led to much intragroup conflict and factionalization. . . .In Kassak, [cooperative members] hardly knew one another; yet, they were forced by the technical design of the works to labor side by side" (125). The overall effect was a very low return on the investment in development as well as "social disorganization."

As can be seen, development entails much planning, but often not the correct kind of planning; decisions are often made for economic and political reasons but with little knowledge of or concern for the environmental or social/cultural variables and consequences of the plan. One possible remedy for this problem is **social impact analysis** or **sociocultural appraisal**, which introduces the human and cultural dimension back into the planning. Such a study examines the project and the areas and peoples affected, looking into the appropriateness of the project, its likely impact on the various groups implicated in it (including, for example, the people who will be moved, the people who will not be moved, the people already living where the new people will be moved to, extended families, women, local authorities, and state officials), and the distribution of the benefits that accrue from it (see below for a discussion of costs and benefits).

BOX 14.3   APPRAISING DEVELOPMENT: A ROLE FOR ANTHROPOLOGISTS

Hoben (1986) and Grayzel (1986) painted contrasting but mutually informing portraits of development projects and their relation to indigenous cultures, as well as the value of "applied anthropology." Hoben's research was lucky enough to come before the project, in this case to resettle 80,000 people from a heavily populated mountain region of Cameroon to a thinly populated plateau to the south. He discovered that there were as many as twenty-seven cultural or ethnic groups in the source region, in two clusters of cultures. The more northern cluster was distinguished by a denser population and higher fertility rate. They lived in scattered households with no villages but rather "sprawling hamlets" of twenty-five to fifty households, which were further aggregated into units of up to a thousand households. Worse yet, these non-Muslim mountaineers were looked down upon by the local Muslims as *kirdi* or "pagan, naked, poor, backward, and lack[ing] government" (180). In the target region, Hoben found seventy thousand already in residence, divided into ten or more groups with the Fulani comprising over 50 percent. As just noted, there were standing hostilities between the Muslims of the plateau and the incoming *kirdi*, and the relocation of the latter appeared to be not quite voluntary anyhow. Finally, the amount of quality land did not match the number of proposed settlers, almost guaranteeing environmental degradation and the gradual drifting of the settlers back to their home region. He therefore concluded that the project should not be undertaken, and the decision-makers took his advice.

Meanwhile, Grayzel investigated a land- and cattle-management project in Mali, where the Doukoloma Forest Reserve was being developed for use by Bamana (Bambara) horticulturalists and FulBe (Fulani) pastoralists. Here he found a cultural mismatch between the values of the project and those of the FulBe people. Decision-makers had assumed that the people would appreciate a plan to graze and fatten their cattle for sale to the market, but they did not understand FulBe practices. More important than owning cattle (which not all FulBe did) was a FulBe code of life called *pulaade* "which they guarded more fiercely than their animals" and which included notions of intelligence, beauty, wealth, and above all else independence. Intelligence, for instance, involved displays of cunning and calculation. The pursuit of beauty, especially female beauty, could lead a man to make certain economic choices, including selling his whole herd. And independence meant not taking orders from or being beholden to anybody. The project threatened all of these values: government planning and control deprived them of their opportunity to display intelligence and was a direct affront to independence. As far as cattle went, FulBe had never regarded them as a "fixed source of income" but rather as "convertible capital" which they could accumulate or liquidate as they saw fit, including their pursuits of beauty, intelligence, and independence. What planners had failed to consider was the "aesthetic" or "emotional" core of life for people swept into projects, for which "development projects have failed and will continue to fail" (160).

DIVERSITY OF DEVELOPMENT DISCOURSE

Development financing

Like all major business ventures, development costs money – lots of money. Often, states propose and prefer huge projects like dam or dam-system construction schemes. Poor states do not have the wealth to pay for such projects themselves, so they turn to various external sources of funding. Among these are foreign governments, **multilateral development institutions**, and private enterprise, including multinational corporations. Foreign governments, particularly rich Western ones, provide a certain amount of "foreign aid" for development purposes, in the form of either loans or outright grants. The United States, for instance, gives billions of dollars in foreign aid, although much less than previously; according to Hook (1996), in the 1950s in the heyday of development the United States accounted for 60 percent of total international aid but by the 1990s only 17 percent. In real terms, the U.S. contribution of 3 percent of its GNP to foreign aid dropped to 0.1 percent in the late 1990s, lower than any major Western state. Among the institutions through which the United States funnels assistance to poor countries is the U.S. Agency for International Development (USAID). Large corporations may elect to invest in particular places to take advantage of tax breaks, cheap labor, access to resources, or access to local markets; theirs is of course always a business decision, not a humanitarian effort.

Multilateral development institutions were mostly created around the end of World War II, originally to help rebuild Europe. Out of a meeting held at Bretton Woods, New Hampshire in 1944, two important institutions – the International Monetary Fund (IMF) and the International Bank for Reconstruction and Development (IBRD, better known as the World Bank) – emerged. The IMF was designed primarily to assist states with balance-of-payments problems, although it also offers some advisory and technical assistance. The World Bank was designed to be just that, a bank, with deposits of cash from rich states that could be loaned for particular purposes to poor states and repaid by them.

The World Bank may be the prime mover in international development financing. Underdeveloped states come to it with formal proposals for projects, which the Bank evaluates and agrees to support or not. The Bank's decision-making process, as that of all lending and aid institutions, is affected by various internal criteria, in this case:

Multilateral development institutions
organizations like the World Bank (officially the International Bank for Reconstruction and Development) and the International Monetary Fund that were established and are funded and operated by more than one government for the purpose of disbursing money, advice, and technology in the pursuit of development

PLATE 14.4 The gleaming modern headquarters of the World Bank, one of the leading institutions of global development.

Claxton, Nicholas. 1989. *The Price of Progress*. Oley PA: Bullfrog Films.

Bodley, John. 1975. *Victims of Progress*. Menlo Park, CA: Cummings.

Diseases of development the lifestyle-related diseases that are common in developed industrial societies and increasingly common in developing societies, such as high-blood pressure, heart disease, diabetes, tooth decay, and obesity

the control of the Bank, which is determined by the financial contribution made by the member state. The United States is by far the largest single contributor and therefore largest single influence on decisions. Up to 50 percent of the voting power in the World Bank is held by a half-dozen rich states;

the mission of the World Bank to lend money. It is in the business of lending, and it has annual lending targets, so it is inclined toward supporting projects rather than rejecting them;

the organization and staffing of the Bank. Kardam wrote in 1993 that "Sociological issues do not fit naturally into the goals and procedures of the World Bank" (1993: 1777), which was composed at that time of about 70 percent economists and most of the rest engineers. Only some fifty or sixty anthropologists and sociologists were employed there.

THE BENEFITS – AND COSTS – OF DEVELOPMENT

Finally, like any business venture, development involves the measuring and weighing of benefits and costs. There is no dispute that development can confer benefits, financial and otherwise. The question is what kinds of costs are incurred, who pays the costs, and how the benefits are distributed. Obvious costs include the expense of the projects themselves, for instance, the price of concrete to build a dam. As an economic exercise, development planners assign dollar values to costs and benefits and move ahead with projects that appear to have a favorable "cost/benefit ratio." However, there are other kinds of costs that are not always or easily factored into the calculations. There is the cost of cultural displacement, social disorganization, and acculturation or deculturation; these costs are paid much more dearly by the poor and "traditional" peoples whose lands are regularly targeted for development. These people often pay the cost for benefits that go to other, often distant, people, as when the aforementioned dam is constructed and electrical power is sent to remote cities or factories. The local people may find their land submerged, their previous way of life destroyed, their culture threatened. How does one put a number on that?

No one is unaware of the costs of development. In the film *The Price of Progress*, one World Bank official admits, "You can't have development without someone getting hurt" Environmentalists are particularly attuned to the environmental costs. Anthropologists are particularly attuned to the cultural costs. Many observers and critics – and observers-turned-critics – like John Bodley in his *Victims of Progress* (1975; see also 1985), have chronicled the negative and destructive consequences of development, a few of which are:

Poverty. Ironically, while development is intended and designed to raise net economic wealth, it often has the opposite effect, at least for segments of the population. Groups whose lands and livelihoods are lost end up more impoverished than they started. Wealth may be transferred from one physical or social segment of the society/state to another, so that even improved GNP numbers do not mean prosperity for all.

More difficult working conditions. Development often brings not only different work but a different work ethic that demands eight or more (sometimes ten or twelve) hour workdays away from home. This work is also often more arduous and dangerous than any traditional activity; jobs like mining and manufacturing can mean more effort for proportionately less gain. Post-development economies are frequently more exploitative than pre-development ones, not less.

Poor health. New populations in previously unpopulated or underpopulated areas, new living conditions (inadequate sanitation or clean water, overcrowding, etc.), and new practices can add up to a more unhealthy life. The gains from modern medicine are often offset by the losses to degraded health and social standards. Diet may decline; people may eat absolutely less, or they may eat less well, including overprocessed foods like sugar, flour, canned food, and junk food. "Developing" peoples regularly experience the **diseases of development** – high blood pressure, tooth decay, obesity, diabetes, and other degenerative diseases like cancer – previously unknown to them. Parasites and bacteria may flourish. People may come into contact with previously isolated pathogens like the Ebola virus, or they may spread pathogens more effectively than ever, like the HIV virus in Africa and India.

■ Loss of land and forced resettlement. States routinely look to their "least developed" regions for development schemes, which tend to be inhabited by the least efficient producers in the state – usually foragers or pastoralists – who must get out of the way of development. Lands are opened to settlers and prospectors when roads are built. Lands are submerged when dams are built. And lands are claimed by immigrating groups when poor urban people move or are moved into "lower density" areas, as in the Indonesian *transmigrasi* project in Indonesia or the Cameroon resettlement scheme above.

■ Debt. Developing states can find themselves in horrendous debt to foreign institutions. Debt restricts freedom of operation and consumes future earnings. The fallout is less money for today's and tomorrow's needs. Also, as too often occurs, if a development project fails to deliver its promises, the state still holds the obligation of repayment. Poor states struggle under significant debt burdens, as much as 4 or 5 percent of their total yearly GNP. When the burden gets too great, the state may default and refuse to repay the debt, as Argentina did in late 2002. It borrowed over $800 million from the World Bank and owed more than $77 million in interest payments alone. As a result, after sixty days of nonpayment, Argentina would become ineligible for any additional development loans.

■ Social disorder. Changes of these types and magnitude have all kinds of socially negative consequences. People under the pressures of development tend to suffer social breakdown, as their traditional orders are replaced by new orders – or sometimes what seems like no order. Crime, alcoholism, violence, suicide, juvenile delinquency, etc. appear in previously relatively well-balanced societies and sometimes destroy those societies. Ironically, Chua (2003) suggests that the much-vaunted "free market" policies underlying much contemporary development planning can actually lead to escalated violence, when these reforms interact with multicultural societies in which

there is a **market-dominant minority** which benefits disproportionately. The result can be protests and violence directed at the market reforms and the wealth of the minority, democracy and the power and rights of the majority, the minority group itself, or the majority group(s) – all of which have been witnessed in recent years.

■ Overurbanization. As people flee or are driven from rural areas, they tend to congregate in cities, which can result in **overurbanization**. In a few extreme cases, a single sprawling city may be home to 10 percent or more of the entire state's population, such as Luanda, Angola (20 percent of the state's total population), Brazzaville, Republic of Congo (30 percent), Buenos Aires, Argentina (30 percent), and Montevideo, Uruguay (over 33 percent). Cities in developing states, especially such densely populated ones, often lack the infrastructure – water, electricity, sewerage, the housing – or the jobs to support large dense populations, leaving people who were already marginalized now living on the margins of urban society, in shanty towns or squatter communities. The city of Mumbai in India houses 60 percent of its population in slums, and the United Nations has warned that one-third of the entire human population may inhabit slums by the year 2030.

■ Environmental degradation. Pollution, loss of forests, exhaustion of sometimes-fragile soils, destruction of habitat for animals, and general accumulation of the "garbage of development" can scar a state's territory almost irretrievably. Developing states often declare that they can and must "develop" their own resources, but the rate of disappearance of their and the world's valuable resources had become much more than a local problem. (Third World states sometimes complain that Western states were free to exploit their own – as well as the Third World's – resources but that now they are being denied the same freedom.)

THE PASSING OF THE CLASSIC DEVELOPMENT MODEL

The classic approach to development came under a great deal of criticism, for a number of reasons: it

Market-dominant minority

"ethnic minorities who, for widely varying reasons, tend under market conditions to dominate economically, often to a startling extent, the 'indigenous' majorities around them" (Chua 2003: 6)

Overurbanization

the growth of large cities without the infrastructure to handle the urban populations, especially when a disproportionate amount of the state's population lives in one or a few such cities

Chua, Amy. 2003. *World on Fire: How Exporting Free Market Democracy Breeds Ethnic Hatred and Global Instability*. New York: Anchor Books.

World system theory

the theory that explains the ongoing poverty and low standard of living in Third World states as the effect of external arrangements and relationships, specifically the global economic and political practices and institutions set up by the "core" of rich, powerful, industrialized states that function to their own advantage but to the disadvantage of the poor, weak, "peripheral" states

http://www.wto.org/;

http://www.imf.org/external/index.htm;

http://www.cfr.org/global-governance/group-eight-g8-industrialized-nations/p10647

Wallerstein, Immanuel. 1974. *The Modern World-System: Capitalist Agriculture and the Origins of the European World-Economy in the Sixteenth Century.* New York: Academic Press.

Core

in dependency/world system theory, the states that make up the power-center of the world system – essentially the rich industrial states and former colonialists

Periphery

in dependency or world system theory, the societies and states that have the least wealth and power and the least influence on the practices and policies in the global economy

Semi-periphery

in world system theory, those countries or states that are not completely peripheral (that is, not extremely poor and dependent) but that are not rich and powerful enough to merit inclusion in the core of the system

promoted large expensive projects that often failed to deliver results (or failed altogether), it involved government bureaucracies and public money, and it perpetuated dependencies on foreign capital, technology, and culture. Even before the 1980s, Immanuel Wallerstein, for instance, posited that poor, dependent, underdeveloped states were stuck in a "world system" that did not operate in their favor. According to his **world system theory** (1974), there really is a "world economy" or a global economic system, composed of a **core**, **periphery**, and **semi-periphery**. The core of the world system contains, naturally, rich industrial states. But it also consists of those multilateral organizations designed to shape and control the world economy, such as the World Trade Organization (WTO), the G-8, GATT (the General Agreement on Tariffs and Trade), and the World Bank and IMF. These institutions primarily involve the same few rich industrial states, whose representatives gather in diverse forums to design and manage the world economy in their own interests. Finally, the core also includes major corporations, as we will emphasize below.

The periphery of the world system is the underdeveloped states, which are not invited to sit with the G-8 and do not have much clout in the World Bank. The periphery merely feeds the core and takes orders from it. It is dependent. Meanwhile, the semi-periphery is composed of the states "in the middle" or "in transition," since it is possible (though not at all easy) to move from periphery to core. States that have been successful in their industrialization, like South Korea or Brazil or Indonesia and especially China and India, are moving from periphery to semi-periphery, while

states that were formerly core have moved out to semi-periphery, like Spain and Portugal.

In many ways, the classic development model depends on this world system – and also perpetuates it. Since around 1980, a number of alternatives to the classic development approach have appeared, frequently focusing on the small-scale or on the private sector.

Microfinance

As noted, classic development is not only business but *big* business, usually implicating governments, banks, large corporations, and huge sums of money in vast projects like dams and roads. The value of such projects to actual poor people is questionable, and often the damage outweighs the gains. An innovative and promising new direction in development is to make small loans, sometimes only a few dollars, directly to poor individuals and families which they can invest in their own products or businesses. Known as **microfinance** or microcredit, it was first attempted in Brazil in the 1970s but was more formally organized in Bangladesh by economist Muhammad Yunus (b. 1940) after he toured impoverished and war-ravaged villages. His experience suggested that credit and minimal loans offered to struggling households could yield dramatic positive results. (His first loan, $27 of his own money, went to forty-two women in the village of Jobra; interestingly, many of microfinance's borrowers are women.) Since major banks were reluctant to loan such trivial amounts to "non-credit-worthy" borrowers, Yunus eventually formed

PLATE 14.5 Indian women attending a presentation on microfinancing.

BOX 14.4 LOCAL SELF-DEVELOPMENT IN EGYPT

Large-scale development projects necessarily require rich powerful institutions to implement them. However, as in microfinance, small-scale efforts can be accomplished by local people, often representing fascinating mixtures of the traditional and the modern. For example, Sherine Hafez found an Islamic women's organization in Egypt called al-Hilal that not only offered various services to urban women in Cairo (child care, education, charity, etc.) but also operated a "modernization" project in a poor village. In their efforts to "improve" the village it is apparent "how modern liberal principles of development" and "the values of the secular modern are applied on a grassroots level" – not in place of Islam but in conjunction with Islam (2011: 128). While the women's motivation and their language is distinctly Islamic, their specific goals and "disciplinary techniques" (131) are recognizably modern. For instance, they want the village women to become more time-conscious, more tidy, and most of all more independent and productive. The methods they use to ensure these accomplishments are formal classes, inspections and detailed recordkeeping (the "audit culture"), material rewards, and verbal praise and reprimand. The traits that they desire for the poor women, and that they set out to instill in those poor women, include "punctuality, self-discipline, hygienic practices, and effective household organization and, most important, individual material production and motivation" (149). Although they were the standard fare of modernity, "'Islam' was invoked in these practices every time a new concept was introduced and even when the village women attended a lesson on astronomy. A religious rhetoric was always linked to the activities and discussions" (149).

Microfinance
an idea first promoted in the 1970s, to provide very small loans directly to poor individuals or families, for the purpose of starting or growing a small business

his own bank, the Grameen ("village/rural") Bank, in 1983. Grameen Bank has continued to make money available to individuals and families, as well as supporting irrigation, telecommunications, and other local projects. Grameen is today one of numerous microfinance institutions that interact directly with poor rural people. Some, like Kiva, allow citizens from around the world to contribute to – and even to select specific projects or individuals to receive – small-scale self-development in needy countries.

Neoliberalism

As mentioned above, "structural adjustment" became a buzzword around 1980, indicating a sea change in ideas about development. Classic development called upon governments to play a leading role in planning and implementing change; structural adjustment envisioned a diminished role for government, relying instead on practices and incentives emphasizing the market. These tended to include "opening" or "freeing" local markets to goods from other societies, eliminating economic protections like tariffs and subsidies, reducing taxes,

deregulating industry, cutting government spending, and setting the value of local currencies through international currency exchanges (thus often devaluing those currencies).

In recent years, these policies have evolved into a concept known as **neoliberalism**, which hearkens back to the earlier notion of "liberalism" or "laissez-faire" economics. The basic idea of liberalism was to "liberate" the productive energies of individuals and businesses by reducing government interference in and regulation of the economy. Neoliberalism has since become an incredibly popular way to talk about the modern world: one group of anthropologists determined that the number of anthropological articles mentioning neoliberalism quadrupled in one year, from 2004 to 2005 (Hoffman, DeHart, and Collier 2006: 9). David Harvey, in his *A Brief History of Neoliberalism*, gave this influential characterization of neoliberalism:

> Neoliberalism is in the first instance a theory of political economic practices that proposes that human well-being can best be advanced by liberating individual entrepreneurial freedoms and skills within an institutional framework characterized by strong private property rights,

www.kiva.org

Neoliberalism
according to David Harvey, a theory of political economic practices that proposes that human well-being can best be advanced by liberating individual entrepreneurial freedoms and skills within an institutional framework characterized by strong private property rights, free markets, and free trade

PLATE 14.6
Neoliberalism often exposes people to the impersonal forces of global markets. Here a woman and her daughter from the Nigerian delta stand in oily deposits resultant from a Shell oil spill.

See Chapters 12 and 13

free markets, and free trade. The role of the state is to create and preserve an institutional framework appropriate to such practices. The state has to guarantee, for example, the quality and integrity of money. It must also set up those military, defense, police, and legal structures and functions required to secure private property rights and to guarantee, by force if need be, the proper functioning of markets. Furthermore, if markets do not exist (in such areas as land, water, education, health care, social security, or environmental pollution) then they must be created, by state action if necessary. But beyond these tasks the state should not venture.

(2005: 2)

But while it claims to serve all people equally, Harvey finds that neoliberalism tends – if not intends – to transfer power and wealth to a minority of elites, providing almost colonial conditions for dependent accumulation.

With the state in a reduced capacity, and "class" largely discredited as an organizing principle, the key actors in neoliberalism become corporations. In a sense, neoliberalism is the governmentality of corporations and all of the institutions that enable global business, including states and agencies like the World Bank. As far back as 1981 June Nash stressed the significance of the multinational corporation in the global economy, which circulates goods, capital, knowledge, jobs, and even people across state borders. As we have seen, in the opening vignette to this chapter as well as in the previous two chapters, corporations can actually assume "political" and even quasi-state functions. Legally, corporations are "persons," and we often speak of corporations as "corporate citizens" participating in and contributing to society – although Thaddeus Guldbrandsen and Dorothy Holland (2001) call them *super-citizens* because of their superior power to ordinary citizens and because of their ability to portray their private interests as general social, even popular interests. Indeed, one of the features of neoliberal society is that more and more people put their faith in corporations while corporations gather ever more power and penetrate social life ever more thoroughly.

One of the messages in anthropology, of course, is diversity, and anthropologists urge that we examine the local variations in neoliberalism too. Modern industrial/market practices in the United States or the United Kingdom may not be identical to those in China or Indonesia; in the latter case,

Islam and neoliberalism have been blended in some startling ways. But as a global system, some observers and critics have likened neoliberalism to colonialism, suggesting a new kind of colonialism or **neocolonialism**. Without the armies and settlers of the past, states with the wealth and the industrial need for land, labor, resources, and markets may be recreating some of the unequal, exploitative, and dependent relationships thought to have disappeared with the end of Western colonialism. This time, though, it is a new set of neocolonial masters – not surprisingly China, but perhaps more surprisingly India and some Middle Eastern states – doing the colonizing.

For instance, the small Persian Gulf state of Abu Dhabi has begun to acquire land in Sudan as a means of ensuring food supplies for its own people. With a population of 4 million and virtually no arable land, with the price and availability of food in serious question, and with great oil wealth, the Arab state is taking advantage of Sudan's significant unexploited resources and profound weakness and poverty to establish so-called "sovereign farms," developed by the state and private companies. Other oil-rich states like Saudi Arabia and Bahrain have taken similar steps, contracting to use land in Thailand, India, Ukraine, and Brazil; Pakistan offered hundreds of thousands of acres to Saudi Arabia in exchange for oil and cash. And the director-general of the Abu Dhabi Fund for Development has assured the world that the current land acquisitions will not be the last of their neocolonial initiatives.

NEOLIBERAL ISLAM

NEOLIBERALISM OR NEOCOLONIALISM?

Neocolonialism
the reconstitution of dependent relationships between states in the post-colonial era, with poor states providing land, labor, and resources to richer industrial states; although invasion and military occupation may not be involved, the inequality of the relationship can lead to exploitation reminiscent of formal colonialism

BOX 14.5 CONTEMPORARY CULTURAL CONTROVERSIES: CHARTER CITIES FOR POOR STATES

According to Paul Romer, it is "weak or outdated rules" that create poverty in dependent states, and the world's poor would migrate to states with "better rules" if they could. His solution to global poverty, then, is to establish "charter cities" inside poor states where development could occur (http://chartercities.org/concept). A host state provides enough land to build an entire new city, a source state provides the residents/workers, and a guarantor state makes and enforces the rules. One state can actually fulfill all three roles, as China did in founding its own "special economic zones" for industrial development; it is more likely, however, that a poor government would invite a rich successful state – like the United States, Germany, or Japan – to set up and run a charter city in its territory. Some people consider this a clever idea; others regard it as another form of colonialism. What do you think?

SUMMARY

The arrival of political independence and the replacement of colonies with independent states did not necessarily or usually bring economic independence with it. The old economic relations of ownership, control, production, and export did not change substantially if at all, because economic and financial institutions were already in place, settlement was not reversed, and ownership did not change hands. The result was continued economic dependence on foreign individuals, corporations, governments, markets, and agencies.

The consequences of economic dependence add up to underdevelopment, characterized by

- Poverty
- Low standards of living, including housing, health, and education
- Mainly rural populations and agricultural or "primary" production.

These and other undesirable conditions distinguish the "Third World."

To alleviate these problems, development has been seen as the solution, with public and private development institutions created to guide and fund the process. The business of development, premised on policies and implemented in projects, seeks to build up the infrastructure and productive capacity of a poor state to the point where economic growth and improved living standards are possible. Development planning, often undertaken by politicians, economists, and business interests, has not always considered the environmental and social impact of their ideas, which is where anthropologists can contribute and have contributed.

The general approach to development has been informed by theories and models of development and underdevelopment, including

- Modernization theory
- Dependency/World System theory

each with its distinct emphasis and focus and with its pros and cons. However, one thing that all observers can agree on is that development is, from start to finish, a cultural and not purely economic or political affair and that many of its costs have offset its benefits, including such costs as

- Displacement of people
- Social disorganization
- Declining health and living standards for some
- Acculturation and deculturation
- Destruction of the environment

In recent years, new models of and approaches to alleviating global poverty have emerged, often with paradoxical results:

- Microfinance
- Neoliberalism
- Neocolonialism

However, groups "in the way" of development have begun to organize to resist or shape development, as we will consider further next.

MCQS

FILL IN THE BLANKS

WWW

See Chapter 15

Key Terms

Absolute poverty

Apartheid

Core

Dependent accumulation

Development

Development policy

Development project

Diseases of development

First World

Global apartheid

Gross National Product (GNP)

Gross National Product per capita

Import substitution

Market-dominant minority

Microfinance

Modernization theory

Multilateral development institutions

Neocolonialism

Neoliberalism

Overurbanization

Periphery

Primary production

Relative poverty

Semi-periphery

Social impact analysis

Sociocultural appraisal

Structural adjustment

Third World

World system theory

Cultural survival, revival, and revitalization in a globalized world

It is hard to imagine anything more "modern" and "Western" than hamburgers and rock music – unless it is the chain restaurant – and hamburgers, rock music, and the chain restaurant blend as one in the Hard Rock Café. However, as explained on the corporate website (http://www.hardrock.com/corporate/ownership.aspx), Hard Rock International has been owned since 2007 by the Seminole Tribe of Florida (http://www.semtribe.com/), who by the way claim to be the only Native American tribe that never signed a peace treaty with the United States. The acquisition of the Hard Rock Café corporation was not the first foray of the Seminole into modern business: in 1979 the tribe opened Hollywood Seminole Bingo, "the first tribally run high-stakes bingo hall in Native North America" (Cattelino 2011: S137), which allowed them to raise the $965 million dollars to buy Hard Rock International. While the Seminole do not run the Hard Rock Café as a "cultural" institution (there are no Seminole symbols or artifacts in the dining areas), tribal spokesman Max Osceola, Jr. did have these humorous but thought-provoking words to say about the venture:

> Our ancestors sold Manhattan for trinkets. Today, with the acquisition of the Hard Rock Café, we're going to buy Manhattan back one hamburger at a time. . . . And so to provide for the Tribe, we're looking beyond the borders, the four square borders of our reservations. We're looking not just in the United States, we're looking in the world. . . .When the British had colonies all around the world they used to say, "the sun will always shine on the union jack." Well the sun will always shine on the Seminole Hard Rock. . . . We are in 45 countries now.
>
> (quoted in Cattelino 2011: S145)

For decades or centuries, most of the world's societies have labored under dual burdens. One burden has been the system of invasion and intervention, expropriation and even extermination, that was colonialism. This system affected every part of their culture and left lasting and probably permanent legacies. The other has been a "burden of silence," in which such peoples have not been able or allowed to speak for themselves or have not been heard when they did. Early modern anthropologists, in the days of Franz Boas and Margaret Mead, felt that their duty was to "salvage" as much of "traditional" culture as possible before it all

PLATE 15.1 Hard Rock Café, owned by Seminole Tribe.

See Chapter 14

Fourth World

a collective term for the "traditional," often small-scale and indigenous non-state societies that live inside states (frequently created by colonialism) that they do not control and in which they are the minority and typically the poorest group

disappeared and was silenced forever. And many cultures did disappear forever. Others that survived, however, acquired their own voice, understood their own plight, and expressed their own perspectives on their life and culture, on the global dimension of colonialism and international culture, and even on anthropology itself.

As societies newly integrated by global processes have struggled to come to grips with them, they have responded in various important ways. At times they have retreated into or revived their "traditional" culture, while in other situations they have abandoned "tradition" and dived headlong, voluntarily or not, into "modern" culture. More likely, though, they have made modifications and interpretations – creative and complex ones – based on memory of the past, understanding of the present, and anticipation of the future. We are no longer witness to "traditional culture" (if we ever were) but to an accelerating – and acceleratingly self-conscious and intentional – dynamism of culture, in which "culture" itself becomes a resource or discourse in a cause or movement.

VOICES FROM ANOTHER WORLD

The previous chapter described the First and Third Worlds of the rich Western or Westernized states and the poorer mostly post-colonial states. The one thing that these worlds share is that they both consist of states. However, these two categories do not capture the experience of non-state peoples like the various Native American and Australian Aboriginal societies, the !Kung or Ju/hoansi, and so many of the world's other societies that have always been the primary subject of anthropology. These groups are sometimes designated as the **Fourth World** or indigenous peoples or First Peoples. Unlike the First and Third Worlds, the Fourth World consists of the mostly small-scale, "traditional," non-state or pre-state societies that dwell within states – states that they did not create and do not control and that ordinarily do not operate in their interest. Usually the original occupants of the territory held by the state, they are often the poorest and weakest citizens of the state – when they are granted citizenship at all (the United States only bestowed citizenship on Native Americans in 1924, and Australia on Aboriginals in 1967). Because they tended to be small and not highly politically

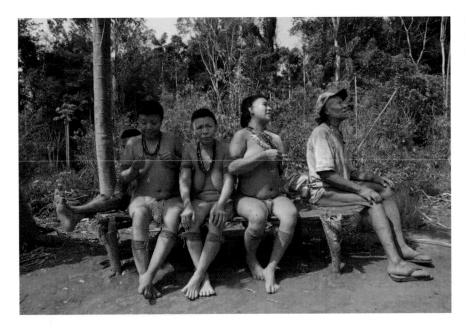

PLATE 15.2 Many indigenous societies are in danger of extinction, like the Akuntsu of South America, who are down to their last six survivors.

integrated, they often could mount limited resistance to colonialism then and to state power and globalization today.

Many of the non-state societies that existed 500 years ago have long since become extinct. Still, by some counts, there are as many as 6,000 distinct cultural or linguistic groups on earth today. Of these groups, approximately half have fewer than five thousand members. Some, on the other hand, are quite large; there may be 350 or more Fourth World societies with over a million members each. Africa alone had 104 indigenous societies of greater than one million people in 1993, and Asia 164. Papua New Guinea was the most culturally diverse area

on the planet, with over 800 identifiable language-groups, the overwhelming majority quite small.

In the early 1990s, an alarming number of indigenous societies were already considered endangered – either in danger of loss of their cultural identity or of total extinction. In Venezuela the Piaroa had declined to 500 members, in Brazil the Uru Eu Wau Wau and the Waimiri-Atroari numbered only 300 each, and in the United States the Alaskan Eyak had been reduced to one last survivor. In some cases, while the group was large, its language and culture were disappearing. The Ainu of Japan still numbered about 25,000, but fewer than 100 of them still spoke their own

TABLE 15.1 Indigenous languages and peoples

Number of languages/societies by population size and world region

Location	1–5,000	5,000–50,000	50,000–250,000	250,000–1 million	over 1 million
Africa	486	803	422	190	104
North America	303	133	17	5	0
South America	442	67	12	4	6
Asia	871	628	269	142	164
Europe	43	47	54	34	61
Pacific	1131	169	10	2	0
Papua New Guinea	685	129	6	na	na
Total	3296	1890	798	379	335

Source: Miller 1993

language (Verrengia 1993). In fact, a recent UNESCO study entitled "Atlas of the World's Languages in Danger of Disappearing" listed three thousand of the six thousand extant languages as threatened. In Australia, hundreds were already gone, in the United States fewer than 150 Indian languages have survived out of several hundred pre-Columban tongues, and in Africa about a third of today's languages (550 out of 1,400) are declining, with 250 in dire conditions. Only in the Pacific region – with more than 2,000 living languages – is linguistic and cultural diversity fairly secure.

The threats to these groups are multiple. Frequently remote, they are removed from the eye of most people within their state and the wider world. Their comparatively low population density and economic productivity makes them prime candidates for development. Their lack of modern weapons and (but not always) political integration makes armed resistance futile, and their lack of political clout makes political resistance difficult though not impossible. Their susceptibility to some of the diseases and vices of development has crippled many of them. Malaria, cholera, influenza, smallpox, AIDS, not to mention alcoholism and other social problems, have taken a great toll.

Indigenous people have lost much in the advance of colonialism, development, state integra-

tion, and globalization. These losses have involved two kinds of "property" – literal physical property or real estate (their land) and other physical or symbolical property, such as their artifacts, knowledge, and the very bodies of their ancestors. In former days, anthropologists and archaeologists would collect objects and human remains virtually at will and carry them away for study and storage. However, in both domains indigenous people have made gains in re-establishing control. For instance, in 1990 the Native American Grave Protection and Repatriation Act (NAGPRA) went into effect, requiring that all federally funded organizations (including universities and museums) in the United States catalog their holdings of Indian human remains and artifacts, inform the societies that provided the materials, and return the materials if requested. It also outlawed trafficking in illegal human or cultural materials. In Australia in 1992 a court decision called *Mabo and Others v. Queensland* declared that Eddie Mabo and his Aboriginal co-plaintiffs had property rights to their traditional homelands; instead of the presumption of *terra nullius* and state ownership, courts would have to presume native ownership unless the state could prove that there were no traditional owners or that they had voluntarily relinquished ownership (for example, through a treaty, of which there were none in Australia).

www.unesco.org

See Chapter 14

See Chapter 12

**NATIVE AMERICAN
INDEPENDENCE**

PLATE 15.3 Indigenous Aymara of Bolivia marching in support of new president Evo Morales.

Meanwhile, individually and collectively, indigenous peoples have raised their voices, in all sorts of media. A few have even been trained as anthropologists. Others have used song and writing, both fiction and nonfiction, to convey facts, feelings, and fears. Chinua Achebe's *Things Fall Apart* about the traditions and contact experiences of an African society, Mary Crow Dog's biography *Lakota Woman*, Leslie Marmon Silko's *Ceremony* about Pueblo Indian life and culture, and Sherman Alexie's *The Lone Ranger and Tonto Fistfight in Heaven* about life on the reservation are just three well-known examples. Anthropologists too have found ways to assist native peoples in telling their stories and speaking indirectly to the world, as in Griaule's (1965) conversations with Dogon elder Ogotemelli, Shostak's (1983) life of the Ju/hoansi woman Nisa, or John Neihardt's (1961) account of the life and visions of Lakota elder Black Elk.

FROM CULTURE TO CULTURAL MOVEMENT

Hopefully this book has proven that culture was never static, closed, and homogeneous; rather, it has

Griaule, Marcel. 1965. *Conversations with Ogotemelli: An Introduction to Dogon Religious Ideas.* London: Oxford University Press.

Shostak, Marjorie. 1983 [1981]. *Nisa: The Life and Words of a !Kung Woman.* New York: Vintage Books.

Neihardt, John G. 1961 *Black Elk speaks: Being the Life Story of a Holy Man of the Oglala Sioux.* Lincoln, NB: University of Nebraska Press.

Alexie, Sherman. 1994. *The Lone Ranger and Tonto Fistfight in Heaven.* New York: HarperPerennial.

BOX 15.1   SHERMAN ALEXIE ON "IMAGINING THE RESERVATION"

Imagine Crazy Horse invented the atom bomb in 1876 and detonated it over Washington, D.C. Would the urban Indians still be sprawled around the one-room apartment in the cable television reservation? Imagine a loaf of bread could feed the entire tribe. Didn't you know Jesus Christ was a Spokane Indian? Imagine Columbus landed in 1492 and some tribe or another drowned him in the ocean. Would Lester FallsApart still be shoplifting in the 7–11?

. . .Survival = Anger × Imagination. Imagination is the only weapon on the reservation.

The reservation doesn't sing anymore but the songs still hang in the air. Every molecule waits for a drumbeat; every element dreams lyrics. Today I am walking between water, two parts hydrogen, one part oxygen, and the energy expelled is named *Forgiveness*.

. . .What do you believe in? Does every Indian depend on Hollywood for a twentieth-century vision? Listen: when I was young, living on the reservation, eating potatoes every day of my life, I imagined the potatoes grew larger, filled my stomach, reversed the emptiness. My sisters saved up a few quarters and bought food coloring. For weeks we ate red potatoes, green potatoes, blue potatoes. In the dark, "The Tonight Show" on the television, my father and I telling stories about the food we wanted most. We imagined oranges, Pepsi-Cola, chocolate, deer jerky. We imagined the salt on our skin could change the world.

July 4th and all is hell. Adrian, I am waiting for someone to tell the truth. . . . But, Adrian, it's the same old story, whispered past the same false teeth. How can we imagine a new language when the language of the enemy keeps our dismembered tongues tied to his belt? How can we imagine a new alphabet when the old jumps off billboards down into our stomachs?

. . .There are so many possibilities in the reservation 7–11, so many methods of survival. Imagine every Skin on the reservation is the new lead guitarist for the Rolling Stones, on the cover of a rock-and-roll magazine. Imagine forgiveness is sold 2 for 1. Imagine every Indian is a video game with braids. Do you believe laughter can save us? All I know is that I count coyotes to help me sleep. Didn't you know? Imagination is the politics of dreams; imagination turns every word into a bottle rocket. Adrian, imagine every day is Independence Day and save us from traveling the river changed; save us from hitchhiking the long road home. Imagine an escape. Imagine that your own shadow on the wall is a perfect door. Imagine a song stronger than penicillin. Imagine a spring with water that mends broken bones. Imagine a drum which wraps itself around your heart. Imagine a story that puts wood in the fireplace.

(Alexie 1994: 149–53)

Malinowski, Bronislaw. 1961 [1945]. *The Dynamics of Culture Change: An Inquiry into Race Relations in Africa.* New Haven, CT and London: Yale University Press.

See Chapter 11

Wallace, Anthony F. C. 1956. "Revitalization Movements." *American Anthropologist* 58 (2): 264–81.

See Chapter 11

Revitalization movement according to Wallace, the deliberate, organized, and self-conscious effort of a society to create a more satisfying culture

always been (more or less, depending on the place and time) dynamic, open, and complex and heterogeneous. As a system of *adaptation*, it only stands to reason that humans would adapt ever-changing cultural forms and expressions as circumstances or simply membership changed over time. And when circumstances changed especially rapidly or unfavorably, the form of those new adaptations would be more dramatic and total.

Bronislaw Malinowski, despite his reputation as a functionalist and at a time when colonialism seemed ascendant, foresaw these profound cultural effects. The unprecedented cultural forces and experiences in the twentieth century were leading to novel cultural outcomes, which were not a mere continuation of "tradition," a passive adoption of Western styles and practices, or a simple mingling of the two. Rather, the cultural changes were eruptions of something original; commenting on the scene in Africa, he wrote, "They are all one and all entirely new products [with] no antecedents in Europe or in African tribalism" (1961: 25), although of course the same could be said about the entire world. What he observed were "new cultural realities" – but even more, cultural developments with a new attitude toward "culture." Even when culture appeared to be changing in the direction of "tradition," he noted that the "elements of the old culture [were] being revived with a secondary, almost *ethnographic* interest in racial history, customary law, and the artistic and intellectual achievements of their race" (158, emphasis added). In other words, "natives" were becoming something like anthropologists and observers of their own culture – which meant their "traditional culture" was already somewhat "foreign" to them.

In many of the circumstances in which they found themselves, people (and not just indigenous people) experienced dissatisfaction and frustration, from mild to extreme. Their land, livelihood, liberty, and very lives were under attack. Worst of all, often, was the sense that their *identity* was eroding or disappearing; hence the urge to protect or re-establish identity, on the basis of culture. But a culture or identity re-established is not quite the same as a pristine or "traditional" one. A common result was and is a "cultural movement" in which the group actively picks, preserves, and promotes part(s) of its culture. And while culture is continuously in motion, there is a major difference

between "culture in motion" and "a cultural movement." Cultural movements are much more self-conscious, even "ethnographic," as the groups engaging in them experience their cultures in new ways – particularly, as "problems" and "resources." Also, cultural movements tend to be more argumentative and mobilized than mere cultures-in-motion. They can be positively militant. "Genuine continuity of cultural identity is seldom as strident or as dramatic as artificial revivals," write Guidieri and Pellizi (1988: 29).

Cultural movements aimed at "reviving" or repairing a damaged culture or identity are sometimes called **revitalization movements**. Revitalization movements, as described by Anthony Wallace (1956: 265), are conscious, deliberate, and organized efforts on the part of some member(s) of a society to create a new, better, and more satisfying culture.

As such, they are a special type of self-directed change. Like all other instances of change, whether arising from innovation or diffusion, revitalization efforts have certain regular characteristics:

1. They appear at moments of cultural stress – when past ideas and actions no longer produce satisfactory results, especially when foreign influences or persons have disturbed the balance of the society.
2. They are usually the inspiration of one person or at most a few people. Certain individuals feel the "culture crisis" before others, and their inspiration often comes in the form of a dream, a vision, or a "near-death" experience.
3. They go through a process of acceptance, rejection, or modification. Members of the society may join or ignore the movement, and elders and traditionalists may actively oppose it. Outside forces may also oppose it as a threat to their domination.
4. They begin as unfamiliar, often "heretical" or "cultish" phenomena, but if they catch on they become "mainstream."
5. They can have unanticipated, undesired, and even undesirable consequences.
6. There may be more than one such movement occurring in the same society at the same time, sometimes with opposite goals. Differing and rival movements and movement leaders may vie for the attention and loyalty of the society, each offering a solution to the society's troubles.

7. The movement, if it survives, will become "routinized" and institutionalized – either as the new "mainstream" or as a more constricted alternative or specialty within the society.

Revitalization movements can take many forms. Very often, especially in their early manifestations, they are religious in nature (see below). Subsequently or in combination, they can take a political shape; in fact, all such movements are probably "political" in a sense, since they seek to modify the order of society, including its power arrangements and norms and rules. Groups may literally organize political parties or "congresses," like the African National Congress (South Africa), the Indian National Congress, or the Australian Aboriginal National Congress. Nationalism and ethnicity may be expressions of politicized culture and identity. Groups may generate their own media, starting newsletters or newspapers, radio and television stations, and more recently internet websites. Even more common, and sometimes equally important, are "cultural organizations" that promote and advance aspects of culture, such as language, music and dance, arts, food, or religion.

There are a few recurring components or qualities of cultural/revitalization movements. Any actual movement may exhibit one or more of these features or "types," but enough movements have been observed to distill some common patterns among them.

Syncretism

Syncretism (from the Greek *syn-* for "with" or "same") means the mixing or blending of elements from two or more cultural sources to produce a new, third, better culture or system. In a very real sense, all culture, and certainly all religion, is syncretistic; humans are forever borrowing from various sources and combining them in ways to produce whatever it is they call "their culture" or "their tradition." Of course, this borrowing and combining is not always deliberate or clearly perceived, but no culture, religion, or any other human activity is "pure" or "original" in any significant or meaningful way. All humans live in a melting pot of culture.

Among the most colorful syncretistic movements in the anthropological literature are the so-called "cargo cults" that swept through the Pacific Islands, particularly Melanesia and the southwest regions, between about 1900 and 1950 (see Worsley 1968; Lawrence 1964). During the two

Syncretism
a type of revitalization movement in which elements of two or more cultural sources are blended into a new and more satisfying cultural arrangement

See Chapter 13

Worsley, Peter. 1968. *The Trumpet Shall Sound: A Study of "Cargo Cults" in Melanesia.* New York: Shocken Books.
Lawrence, Peter. 1964. *Road Belong Cargo.* Manchester: Manchester University Press.

PLATE 15.4 Pacific Islanders adopted aspects of Western culture – including marching in formation with mock rifles – in their cargo cults.

World Wars, thousands of Western soldiers came ashore and, even more remarkably, unloaded caches of goods the likes of which no local had ever seen. Islanders could have no idea where these people and their goods came from; the one thing they knew was that the strangers had a lot of "cargo" and that they never seemed to work for any of it. They stood around, marched around, sat around, but they never produced anything – yet they had this inconceivable largesse.

Cargo cults were an indigenous attempt to make sense of this new situation and, quite literally, to get some cargo for themselves. One of the first and best-known examples is the "Vailala madness" that "broke out" in 1917 among the Elema people of Papua. The Elema first tried to incorporate the foreigners into their native economic system of reciprocity by giving them gifts, expecting that the invaders would reciprocate by sharing some of their wealth. When that failed, a man named Evara originated the notion that people needed to practice specific religious observances, including trances and jerky body movement and speech, which seemed so pathological to observers that it was dubbed "madness." More to the point was the content and expectation of the movement: if people destroyed parts of their traditional culture and replaced them with parts of the foreign culture, they could conjure cargo ships of their own. Accordingly, traditional religious and ceremonial items were discarded, gardens and animals were untended or destroyed, and imitative gestures toward Western culture were made (for instance, a pretend radio was built to talk to the phantom cargo ship). It was believed that these changes would bring forth a ship laden with cargo piloted by their dead ancestors, who would establish a better and happier culture for the Elema. Needless to say, it did not happen.

One other example of a syncretistic movement, during which 20 or 30 million people died, was the Taiping Rebellion in China (1850–64), one of a number of such movements after the Opium Wars and full-scale establishment of colonialism in China. The Taiping movement (from the Chinese *Taiping tien-quo* for Heavenly Kingdom of Great Peace) began with one man, Hung Xiuquan (also Hsiu-chuan), who had a vision of the future and his role in it. After a personal crisis and a near-death experience, he received a series of visions of an old man (supposedly God) who warned that people

had stopped worshipping Him and taken to the worship of demons. Hung was to battle these demons, as he was in fact the younger son of God and the younger brother of Jesus. In the 1840s his religious community was reorganized into a holy army, and in 1851 he announced the Taiping tien-quo, a theocratic state with himself as the Heavenly King.

His heavenly army marched against the government, capturing the city of Nanking in 1853 and from there attacking Beijing. The imperial government fought back for a decade until in June 1864 Hung died, and a conflict that claimed millions of lives in the hopes of a better day ended.

Millenarianism

Millenarianism (from the Latin *mille* for thousand) is a familiar concept to Western culture and Christianity, which think in terms of a thousand because their number system is based on ten. The point of millenarianism is not literally a thousand-year period (since not all cultures use base-ten) but the notion that the world does proceed through periods, the current one of which will end soon. Thus, **millenarianism** is a type of movement based on the conception that the present era of the world (an inferior, unhappy, or wicked one) is about to end and that a superior era is approaching. The followers of the movement must either prepare for the coming change or actively set the change in motion.

Millenarianism is common in movements among large-scale modern societies as well as small-scale traditional ones. The cargo cults and the Taiping rebellion had millenarian aspects, as did the well-known "Ghost Dance" movement among Native Americans in the late 1800s. Ghost Dancers believed that performing the special dance and wearing particular symbols and clothing would make the dancers impervious to white weapons, bring back their dead ancestors, and ultimately restore their land and independence to them. The failed armageddons of the Aum Shinrikyo and Heaven's Gate are only two of the more recent instances.

Millenarianism
a type of revitalization movement aimed at preparing for and perhaps bringing about the end of the "present era," however that era is understood, and replacing it with a new and better existence

BOX 15.2 MILLENNIUM ON THE SUBWAY: AUM SHINRIKYO

Aum Shinrikyo, a Japanese movement headed by Shoko Asahara, believed in and sought to ignite a doomsday scenario one day in 1995 when it released poison gas into the Tokyo subways. Aum Shinrikyo is a name that combines the Hindu mantra "om" with *shinri* (Japanese for "supreme truth") and *kyo* ("religious teaching"). It was a millenarian syncretistic movement, blending bits of Hindu/Buddhist, Japanese, Christian, and secular/technological cultures into one explosive system. It predicted an apocalyptic end of the world, which was referred to as Armageddon or World War III. The expected apocalypse was at least partly a function of a vast international conspiracy, which involved the Freemasons and the American government. Early in the sect's history, the goal was to prevent this event from occurring. The work of the group, then, was to intercept the negative energy in the world and transform it into positive; for this work, 30,000 members were needed, who had achieved their own enlightenment through the teachings of the guru. However, as prevention began to seem more and more unlikely, the goal shifted to survival through and after it. The only avenue to such survival was participation in Aum Shinrikyo. By 1990 the sect was talking about and constructing communes and bomb shelters where they could isolate themselves from the ignorant society and prepare for and be saved from the inevitable conflagration. These few survivors could then emerge to rebuild civilization – Aum Shinrikyo civilization. The conflagration and the forthcoming world-to-be were vague in description, but it was claimed that evil forces would attack the world with their ultimate weapons, including nuclear, biological, and chemical weapons, and gases like sarin. The group even began manufacturing, stockpiling, and testing its own supply of these weapons, releasing sarin gas on the population of Matsumoto Nagano prefecture in Japan a year before the Tokyo attack (June 1994), with almost equally deadly results – 7 fatalities, 600 injuries. The assault on the Tokyo subway in 1995 might have been an effort to jump-start Armageddon, or it might have been attempt to make their prediction appear true, perhaps as a recruiting effort. The latter interpretation seems likely in view of Asahara's claim immediately following the attack that it was actually committed by the United States, which had begun its war against Japan and already seized the Japanese government.

Irredentism

Irredentism (from the Italian *irredenta* for unredeemed) is any movement intended to reclaim and reoccupy a lost homeland. As such, irredentism is at the heart of many "ethnic conflicts" in the modern world. The Tamil struggle in Sri Lanka is a sort of irredentist movement, to (re)create and (re)occupy the homeland of Tamil Eelam. At least part of the motivation for the Yugoslavian wars of the 1990s was irredentist, Serbs reclaiming Serb territory, especially the heartland of Kosovo lost in 1389. The Zionist movement, beginning officially in the late 1800s but with much older roots, claimed as its goal the recreation of a Jewish national state in the Jewish "holy land." Zionists like Theodore Herzl, author of the *The Jewish State*, worked toward returning to their lost homeland, from which they had been dispersed for nearly 2,000 years. The subsequent establishment of the modern state of Israel in Palestine in 1948 was the end-result of this movement. Contemporary irredentists like the Jewish fundamentalist group *Gush Emunim* (The Bloc of the Faithful) not only support the recovery of their ancient homeland but seek to expand it, ideally "from the Euphrates River in Iraq to the Brook of Egypt" (Aran 1991: 268).

Modernism/vitalism

Modernism, also termed **vitalism**, includes movements to import and accept alien cultural ways, in part or in total. Some societies, when they encountered Western colonial power, determined that the best course was to imitate the foreign culture, at

Irredentism
a revitalization movement to reclaim a lost homeland

Modernism
a type of revitalization movement intended to adopt the characteristics of a foreign and "modern" society, in the process abandoning some or all of the "traditional" characteristics of the society undergoing the movement. See also *vitalism*

Vitalism
see *modernism*

MAP 15.1 Sri Lanka and "Tamil Eelam"

least in its essential aspects, to empower themselves to resist and perhaps even join the international political system. Japan presents probably the best example of a successful vitalistic movement. Japan was almost completely isolated from the external world before the mid-1800s. However, its rulers watched with interest as Europeans forced the Opium Wars and then colonialism and "spheres of influence" on the defeated Chinese. When American Commodore Matthew Perry arrived with his flotilla of gunships in Tokyo harbor in 1854, the shogun of Japan accepted trade and relations with America. Very quickly, Japan began to adapt itself to this new contact, sending observers to Europe and America to study Western culture and technology, particularly railroad and military technologies. Japanese students were sent to foreign

schools and colleges. English was widely learned, and Western-style music and dress were adopted. By 1868, a "revolution" was underway, known as the Meiji (Japanese for enlightenment) revolution. A modern-style constitution was written, the feudal system was abolished, mass state-sponsored education was established, and concentrated efforts to industrialize and to modernize the army were made. Even symbolic gestures like Western haircuts became important; instead of the long hair of the traditional samurai, barbered hair was the fashion. (A saying of the time was, "If you slap a barbered head, it rings 'civilization and enlightenment.'") This modernist/vitalist movement was so successful that, within forty years of the Meiji revolution, Japan became the first non-European state to defeat a European state in war (Russia in 1904–5). Of

---

BOX 15.3 CULTURE INCORPORATED: THE BAFOKENG OF SOUTH AFRICA AND OTHER NATIVE CORPORATIONS

One of the key modern institutions, as we have stressed throughout this book, is the corporation. Corporations played an underappreciated role in colonialism, and they play a role that cannot be underestimated in globalization and neoliberalism. Not surprisingly, then, many indigenous societies have adopted the corporate form – some buying a corporation (like the Seminole), some founding corporations or even *becoming* corporations. For example, the Bafokeng Nation is a "traditional" kingdom as well as a modern enterprise, "one of South Africa's largest community-based investment companies" (Cook 2011: S151). Not only do the Bafokeng run a complex modern political system, but Royal Bafokeng Holdings manages the society's mining interests in platinum and chrome along with a non-mining investment portfolio, totaling $4.15 billion in 2008. The Bafokeng Nation operated with a budget of $150 million in 2009, over half of which was invested in the community for infrastructure, education, and social programs (S155).

See Chapters 1, 7, 9, 12 and 14

Many indigenous peoples have embraced the corporate form, both to serve their own interests and to offer their services for sale to others. Some examples include:

1. Hawaiian Native Corporation (http://www.hnchawaii.org/)
2. Gumula Aboriginal Corporation (http://www.gumala.com.au/)
3. Juluwarlu Group Aboriginal Corporation (http://www.yindjibarndi.org.au/juluwarlu/index.php)
4. Maori Mega Mall (http://www.themaorimegamall.com/)
5. and the many Alaskan Native Regional Corporations established since 1971 (http://fairbanks-alaska.com/alaska-native-corporations.htm)

---

course, as with all vitalistic movements, there was not a wholesale replacement of local culture with foreign culture. Japan did not jettison the Japanese language, nor Japanese political, economic, or social values. Its "modernization" and industrialization pursued a distinctly Japanese path, emphasizing social duty over individualism, order over competition, and government/business cooperation over disengagement and regulation (see below).

Nativism/fundamentalism

At the opposite end of the spectrum are nativist or fundamentalist movements. **Nativism** or **fundamentalism** emphasizes local or "traditional" culture and values and resistance to or even elimination of alien culture and values. The Chinese response to colonialism was nativistic. Chinese society considered itself superior to European in every imaginable way, and they could not conceive of themselves falling prey to such backward barbarians. The emperor showed no interest in and strictly forbade European

toys like trains and clocks, and the Chinese leadership was sure that it could strengthen itself by relying on completely native resources. In other words, while in a sense the Japanese response was to become more modern, the Chinese (and many other societies') response was to become more "traditional." In the late twentieth and early twenty-first centuries, some societies and states have gone so far as to isolate themselves totally from the outside world. Burma (or Myanmar today) is a tightly closed society, North Korea cuts itself off effectively, and Cambodia under the Khmer Rouge and Pol Pot attempted to eradicate foreign and modern influences, including urbanization, education, and eyeglasses, as portrayed in the movie *The Killing Fields*. However, as these cases illustrate, extreme nativist or isolationist societies tend to end up impoverished, paranoid, and dangerous (to others and to themselves).

Fundamentalism is typically associated strongly with religion, but this need not be; a group can be "fundamentalist" about any aspect of its culture or tradition. The term merely refers to efforts

Nativism

a type of revitalization movement aimed at perpetuating, restoring, or reviving "traditional" cultural practices or characteristics, which are thought to be the source of the group's strength and to be threatened or lost

Fundamentalism

a type of cultural/revitalization movement in which members attempt to address perceived social problems or disadvantages by restoring the perceived "fundamentals" or oldest, most important, and most "genuine" elements of culture to return to the "fundamentals" of that culture, whatever they may be. Many societies and states have viewed this as returning to the rural or village culture of the society, far from the cosmopolitan and thus "mongrel" or "polluted" culture of the city. By definition, it implies an orientation to the *past*, to what the society used to do and be. In the fundamentalist vision, "we" are most crucially "who we were." But fundamentalism or nativism is not about the past, any more than ethnicity is. Rather, all of these movement types use the past to imagine and construct the future.

Nativism or fundamentalism, even more so than the other types of revitalization, is a resistance movement based on difference – the rejection of modern, foreign, or secular influences and the advancement or exaggeration of what makes the group unique or authentic. It is a way of distancing the "external" by emphasizing the "internal." Along with or because of its resistant nature, it can be distinctly militant or violent. George Marsden (1990) in fact characterizes it as traditionalism that is angry about something. What is it angry about? Different groups find different things to oppose in the current cultural condition of the world. From a non-Western perspective, often it is Western culture itself, as Hasan al-Banna, founder of the "fundamentalist" Muslim Brotherhood, said:

> Just after the First World War and during my stay in Cairo, the wave of atheism and lewdness engulfed Egypt. It started the devastation of religion and morality on the pretext of individual and intellectual freedom. Nothing could stop this storm.
>
> [Westerners introduced] their half-naked women. . ., their liquors, their theaters, their dance halls, their amusements, their stories, their newspapers, their novels, their whims, their silly games, and their vices [as well as] schools and scientific and cultural institutions in the very heart of the Islamic domain, which cast doubt and heresy into the souls of its sons and taught them how to demean themselves, disparage their religion and their fatherland, divest themselves of their traditions and beliefs, and to regard as sacred anything Western.
>
> (quoted in Voll 1991: 360–61)

One interesting and ironic fact is that nativism/fundamentalism too is culturally relative, which is entirely contrary to its claims and ideology. However, since we now know that "tradition" is culturally relative, it is necessarily true that "militant tradition" is relative too. First, any culture or cultural tradition can be fundamentalist; there are Christian fundamentalisms and Islamic fundamentalisms and Jewish fundamentalisms and Hindu fundamentalisms, etc. *Hindutva*, for instance, is a modern movement to claim India as the exclusive national homeland of Hindus and to impose Hindu religion and culture on the society. Second, each fundamentalist movement has different goals or elevates different bits of doctrine or history or culture as the defining fundamental of the group or tradition. Some, like the original "fundamentalists" in early twentieth-century America, sought only religious revival and purification, but some in the late twentieth and early twenty-first centuries add social and political goals to their change agendas. All create barriers around themselves; many scholars have characterized fundamentalism as a form of boundary-maintenance.

BOX 15.4 CHRISTIAN FUNDAMENTALISM IN THE UNITED STATES

Between 1910 and 1915 a series of publications entitled *The Fundamentals: A Testimony to the Truth* appeared in the United States, touching off the modern fundamentalist movement in favor of Biblical literalism and religious activism and against "modernizing" and "liberalizing" influences such as "Darwinism." Fundamentalists during the first fifty years of the movement saw their calling as more spiritual than political – to save souls, not change laws. Billy Graham represents this earlier approach and might better be called an "evangelical" than a "fundamentalist." However, with perceived "cultural setbacks" in the 1960s and 1970s, such as the removal of official prayers from schools and most critically the enshrinement of abortion rights, fundamentalism turned political. The 1979 formation of the Moral Majority and the increased political activity of Christian groups like Focus on the Family marked a new era in the mingling of politics and religion: since political leaders and decisions had taken America down this "wrong road," it was politics that would return it to the right path. Some, however, think that American culture is too far gone for strictly political solutions and seek a radical re-creation along Christian lines. The "Christian Reconstructionism" movement, as the name suggests, wants to reconstruct American society in absolute conformity with (its version of) Biblical principles. It would

> replace democracy with a theocratic elite that would govern by imposing their interpretation of "Biblical Law." Reconstructionism would eliminate not only democracy but many of its manifestations, such as labor unions, civil rights laws, and public schools. Women would be generally relegated to hearth and home. Insufficiently Christian men would be denied citizenship, perhaps executed. So severe is this theocracy that it would extend capital punishment beyond such crimes as kidnapping, rape, and murder to include, among other things, blasphemy, heresy, adultery, and homosexuality.
>
> (Clarkson 2005)

While that is a long-term and unlikely goal, others have set their sights on more immediate and achievable results. The "Christian Exodus" movement plans to found its own Christian-based state and society. As its own website declares, it has given up on America and intends to physically relocate members to a place where they can "reestablish constitutionally limited government founded upon Christian principles." This place – which it has been decided will be South Carolina – will be a new Christian homeland with members "electing State and local officials who will interpose on behalf of the people and refuse to enforce illegal federal acts" such as abortion rights and gay marriage. And if need be, they are prepared to secede from the Union altogether.

www.christianexodus.org

THE FUTURE OF CULTURE, AND THE CULTURE OF THE FUTURE

All cultural movements reveal in starker contrast what the study of "normal" (or non-crisis) cultural dynamics shows: if humans make their culture, if culture is in the end a social construct, not a given fact, then humans can and will remake their culture again and again. In fact humans have remade and continue to remake their cultures, with no end in sight. Whether it is colonialism or development or syncretism or fundamentalism, culture is always on the move, as humans think of new things to do, reinterpret old things to do, encounter new things from other groups, and respond to new situations and circumstances. The fiction that culture is static can no longer be believed.

"Culture" and "tradition" seem oriented to the past. However, today we can see that this is more ideology than reality. Culture and tradition refer to the past, but humans are ultimately oriented toward the future, not the past. The main question for humans is always, "Who are we today and who will we be tomorrow?" The main answer to this question, or the main resource for thinking about the answer, is the past. As humans grapple toward and construct their future, they inevitably select, examine, and assemble the bits and shards of broken and vanished pasts to create that future – partly because those pasts constitute the lenses through which they view the present and future, and partly because those pasts constitute the primary, though not only, raw materials with which to build.

Once upon a time, and still in many locations for many individuals, the construction of culture was an "invisible," spontaneous, or unselfconscious process. Increasingly in the world today, cultural construction is conspicuous, selfconscious, and even belligerent, as we have just seen. Individuals, groups, parties, classes, races, genders, etc. assert that the culture is theirs to make – that culture is not just a construction, nor even just a "negotiation," but a contest and struggle. In the process, even many non-anthropologists have achieved what Malinowski called an "ethnographic" attitude toward their own culture, seeing it "as culture" and not just as what they have always been or done unproblematically.

The culture of "modernity" and after

Much of the discussion about culture today centers on the notion of "modern" culture or "modernity." Anthropologists, historians, and other social scientists have viewed Western society as in the condition of "modernity" for at least a couple of, or as many as several, centuries. Since the European Enlightenment (1700s) and arguably as far back as the Renaissance (1400s–1500s), a certain distinct cultural complex dubbed "modern" has been in effect, with some specific qualities:

■ Rationalism – The world, including the human/social world, is rationally knowable, and rationally controllable, because it is seen as orderly, consistent, and therefore predictable.
■ Progress – The general ethos, fueled by advances in knowledge and science and by growth in economic and political power, is that things get better over time. Progress is not only desirable but inevitable, and improvement in the human condition is the natural course of things.
■ Optimism – Therefore, modernity is characterized by an overall positive outlook: what we do not know today we will know tomorrow, and what we know tomorrow will aid us in making a better world the day after. Particularly in the "social sciences" that arose in the 1700s and 1800s, the attitude was that, by manipulating culture, we could construct a better society composed of better people.
■ Integration – The early modern period leaned toward ever larger (and happier) conglomerations of humans. This involved the creation of "modern" states out of disparate polities and societies. Societies that were already "integral," like Britain for the most part, were internally connected with new systems of canals, roads, and ultimately railroads. Other societies that were not yet integral but that shared cultural

commonalities, like Germans or Italians, struggled toward integration with "culture" as their guide. Colonialism represented the largest possible integration, into a few imperial systems or even a single world system. The expectation was that small, independent, "traditional" identities and allegiances would give way to the larger, interdependent "modern" ones.
■ Bureaucratization – Instead of the subjective and "personal" leadership of kings, princes, chiefs, or headmen, society would become more "organized" and impersonal, with various departments headed by professionals making decisions relevant to their jurisdiction and expertise. All aspects of society, from law to the economy to the family, become more "rational" and less arbitrary.
■ Secularization – A final but perhaps pervasive assumption is an inherent secularization or detachment of "civil" society, especially the government and the economy, from religion. It was widely regarded that religion would lose its importance and perhaps disappear altogether.

These qualities have often been construed as the essence of modern culture, although anthropologists and others have come increasingly to regard them as distinct to modern *Western* culture (see below).

Already by the late 1800s, a few sensitive types were questioning the triumph of modernity, even in the West. Nietzsche, Freud, and others began to criticize rationalism, objectivity, mass integration, and all the other conceits of modern society. They emphasized the irrational in human life (the "will to power" or the "unconscious") as inescapable forces, and they often despaired of the homogenization that was occurring under capitalism, democracy, and mass culture. The proof of human irrationality and of the danger of modernity seemed to come in the form of World War I (1914–18), which shocked people more than we can comprehend today. Citizens who prized their rationality, their progressivism, their optimism, etc. were horrified at their behavior in the trenches, at their capacity and even thirst for destruction. When the Spanish Civil War (1936–39) and World War II (1939–45) followed, it became increasingly more difficult to believe in the rosy predictions of modernity. In fact, it was in the arts, such as painting, that much of the soul-searching occurred: artists like Picasso gave humanity disturbing irrational/emotional depictions of itself, Dali made time and space melt, and Munch captured the mood of the epoch with perhaps the best-known work of the period, *The Scream* (1893).

By the early 1900s, some critics began to feel that the "project" of modernity had failed, replaced by a condition that could only be called "postmodern." Post-modernity, or **post-modernism**, emphasizes the irrational or unconscious, the subjective, the spontaneous and non-bureaucratic, even the superficial. It doubts progress and is considerably more pessimistic, while at the same time in a sense more "playful." Since in many versions there is no "ultimate reality," no "knowable truth," no "absolute center," all things are mere representation, surface, perspective, or image. Science becomes a "culture," history becomes a "point of view," and all things become relative, so humans can mix and match fragments of this or that culture or heritage into an ersatz creation that amuses, whether or not it informs. Reality becomes something like MTV (perhaps the fulfillment of post-modernism) with rapidly changing images not meant to communicate but to evoke or merely dazzle. What *could* humans in the end communicate, since the "meaning" of the work according to the viewer may not and probably will not be the "meaning" of the author? Meaning becomes **decentered**; there is no "true" meaning, just *your* meaning or *my* meaning, and either of us can choose or create any meaning we want. The detachment gained from one's own culture creates the condition that Malinowski called "ethnographic." Or, as Walter Truett Anderson expressed it, in the pre-modern condition humans did not choose their culture; rather, "If you choose, you are at least modern. If you know you are choosing, you are postmodern" (1990: 112).

The commodification of culture

The contemporary world is a place not only where culture is chosen and created but also where it is commodified and consumed. A commodity is something that is bought and sold, to which a price can be attached. We easily think of clothes and food

and manufactured goods as commodities; culture, it might seem, is something that you *are*, not something you buy and consume. However, not only is "the consumption of culture" a more and more common occurrence, but it is a prime opportunity to observe the process of the construction of culture.

In a world in which business and "the market" increasingly define human interactions, it should be no surprise that culture becomes a business as well. In fact, a "culture industry" exists to make, distribute, and sell culture. Two of its main forms are **cultural tourism** and **popular culture**. Neither is a brand new idea, but each has become bigger, more deliberate, and more influential than ever, like all of the other intentional forms of culture we have discussed.

Cultural tourism

Cultural tourism entails seeking out a "cultural" experience as entertainment and education. Former president of the National Tourism Association, Bruce Beckham, stated that the modern American vacationer is "more into life-seeing than into sightseeing" (Brown 2000). This often means seeing someone else's life, someone exotic, someone "anthropological." The thrust of Brown's article is that cultural tourism is big business, whether it involves visiting a museum or a "heritage exhibit" like an ethnic festival or a performance of "traditional" music or dance, etc. In fact, the National Trust for Historic Preservation helped formulate the first "strategic plan" for cultural/heritage tourism, which it defined as "traveling to experience the places, artifacts, and activities that authentically represent the stories and people of the past and present" (ibid.). The key word here is "authentically."

Naturally, if someone is going to consume culture, someone else must produce and distribute it for them. This is why there are "native dance shows" and "native arts centers" and adventure/culture camps and get-aways. In Australia, one can take an "authentic" Aboriginal excursion, complete with an Aboriginal guide, during which tourists hike in the bush, eat over a campfire, and learn to throw a boomerang; never mind that most Aboriginal peoples, like the Warlpiri, never made or used returning boomerangs. Australia is one of

Post-modernism
a form of life or way of thinking, and the theory of these, of the mid- to late twentieth century, in which earlier notions of unity, progress, reason, and the increasing integration of peoples and societies breaks down and is replaced by pluralism, "irrationality" or emotion or tradition, decentering, and cultural disintegration

Cultural tourism
the practice of "consuming" culture as a form of entertainment and education. Traveling to foreign societies to observe their ways of life (not always "traditional" but sometimes designed for the tourist) in an informal manner

Popular culture
often contrasted with "high" or "official" culture, the cultural practices and creations of "the people." Often used as a pejorative term to indicate the poor quality and low intelligence of such culture, in the contemporary world it has also become an important and vibrant form of culture, although one that is not entirely "of the people," in the sense that large corporations often create and disseminate it

Anderson, Walter Truett. 1990. *Reality Isn't What It Used to Be: Theatrical Politics, Ready-to-Wear Religion, Global Myths, Primitive Chic, and Other Wonders of the Postmodern World.* New York: HarperSan Francisco.

Decentered
the absence or denial of a particular society's or culture's perspective from which to view the world, usually associated with

moving away from a Western- or Euro-centric perspective. Could potentially imply the absence of any central perspective

PLATE 15.5 Cultural tourists strolling through Aztec ruins in central Mexico.

TOURING INDIANS

BOLLYWOOD

many countries that have discovered that visitors want to consume "traditional culture": a 1993 survey of international travelers indicated that almost half wanted to see Aboriginal culture and that more than one-third actually did include such an activity in their plans. Other travelers seek out "authentic" cultural experiences on African safaris or anywhere else in the world.

The problem, of course, is that these experiences are seldom if ever "authentic." They are selected, and sometimes invented, for tourists. They perpetuate stereotypes (who would go on an Aboriginal tour without a boomerang?). Worse, they actually change the culture of the host-people; for instance, "native artists" begin producing small (portable) trinkets in styles that they know tourists will buy. And they expose the providers of these cultural experiences to the vagaries of world (mostly Western) tastes and trends.

Popular culture

If other societies produce "tradition for sale," American society produces "popular culture" in abundance. In a sense, popular culture is culture by and for the people, but then all culture is by and for people. Popular culture as a distinct phenomenon tends to mean three things: not "high culture" like opera or symphony, culture for sale and disposal, and culture mass-produced and mass-marketed. In all of these ways, it is distinct from

high or elite culture as well as from "folk culture." High/elite culture was allegedly noble (i.e., only for the upper classes) and non-commercial, whereas folk culture was supposedly crude but authentic and traditional and also non-commercial. Popular culture, a commodity for the masses, is largely seen as cheap, low-quality, even "ghastly" (Rosenberg 1957: 9). And often it is. But it is also important, if only because it is a significant part of what people make, do, and think. After all, Malinowski urged us to study "the minutiae of everyday life" and "narratives, utterances, folklore and other conventional sayings and activities" in addition to the big structural aspects of culture, and popular culture is surely conventional minutiae. More than this, though, it gives anthropologists important insights into contemporary society and the culture-making process.

Contemporary popular culture is related to other cultural forces and variables. It could not exist without mass production, disposable income to buy it, leisure time to enjoy it, and a "mass society" to sell it to. Some observers have considered this a uniformly bad thing: Ortega y Gasset famously declared that "the masses, by definition, neither should nor can direct their own personal experience, and still less rule society in general" (1932: 11) – an elitist attitude. It also has social consequences, including the "leveling" of social distinctions and the establishment of a common "language" and experience – or even the creation of new communities and institutions (as *Star Wars* and *Star Trek* have done). Popular culture can be conservative or subversive. As advertising and propaganda, it can manipulate people for the enrichment and empowerment of others. At the same time, with the machinery of cultural production in their own hands – whether the printing press, the television camera, or the internet – people can comment on and protest against social institutions and offer alternative perspectives. It is not without significance that the Warlpiri, for instance, now have their own television studio.

Finally, as trivial and banal as much popular culture seems, like all other cultural forms it communicates meaningful messages. Underneath the transitory characters and stories are the deep myths, values, and symbols of the society. Popular culture is, after all, one way that a society tells itself its stories over and over. As one brief example, Gary Engle's essay called "What Makes Superman So Darned American?" (1987) suggests that the Superman character and story embody several key American values and narratives, including immigration and the experience of being an "alien" in one's own country, the "problem" of identity, social mobility, the transformation from rural to urban life, and of course "truth, justice, and the American way." Other thinkers have conducted similar analyses of Batman, Barbie, the Simpsons, and various genres like the Western movie or the horror movie. Each is a spotlight on the society that produces it and consumes it; after all, popular culture is popular for a reason.

Popular culture can also have serious social consequences. Hip hop music was recruited conspicuously by Yoweri Musaveni in his 1986 bid to become president of Uganda; later, when people became dissatisfied with his leadership, hip hop music became a powerful tool of protest. As Ugandan musician Oz Twelve expressed it, "rappers, we are the new journalists of life. . . .We do it through the beat" (Mazurek 2009). In Brazil, Anderson Sa has used Afro-reggae music to pull youths out of a life of poverty and crime in the favelas, as well as bringing attention to police brutality.

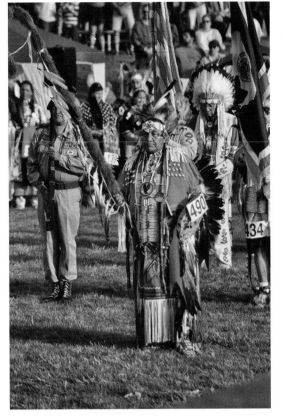

PLATE 15.6 The pow wow is a popular inter-tribal event.

Four views of the future of culture

Where does culture go from here? This is the new framing question of cultural anthropology. Long ago anthropology ceased to be the "science of the primitive," the study of the "uncontaminated Native." As Malinowski instructed, anthropology must be the study of what is, not an antiquarian (and essentially fanciful or impossible) reconstruction of the past. Anthropology not only can but must be relevant to seeing the possibilities for the future and the advantages and disadvantages of those various possibilities, as well as to constructing that future.

Various observers have offered at least four potential visions for the future.

One-world culture

Some observers foresee a future in which the human world will integrate into one vast single culture on the basis of globalization. Already in the first days of Western colonialism, events or decisions or consumption choices in one part of the world tied together other and potentially all parts. Decades ago

Barber, Benjamin. 1995. *Jihad versus McWorld*. New York: Times Books.

One-world culture
the idea that all of the peoples and cultures of the world are becoming (or should become) more similar, to the point at which all humans share a single culture. Often attributed to globalization and the universal access to technology and cultural images (like American movies), it assumes that disparate groups will continue to become more similar until all groups share the same basic values, tastes, and media

Jihad versus McWorld
Benjamin Barber's notion that two opposing but related forces operate in the modern world, one to integrate the world into a single market dominated by a few multinational corporations, and the other to disintegrate the world into exclusivist and often hostile cultural or national groups

people were speaking of the "global village" in which all humans would be citizens (although it would more likely be a "global city" with many neighborhoods and enclaves). Developments in those decades – in trade, technology, media, and the environment – have helped to hasten the dictum to "think globally." Many people herald the coming of a single global cultural system as the inevitable, if not perfectly positive, destination of integrative processes.

There are two different versions of how a **one-world culture** might evolve. The first is a hybridization of all the world's cultures, in which societies big and small contribute toward a new system that includes, affirms, and addresses all of them. Two rather obvious problems confront this view. A new syncretistic global culture that affirms local "traditional" cultures is essentially a contradiction, since it would be non-traditional – indeed, the most non-traditional culture ever devised by humans. Whether societies would be willing to embrace the new culture in place of their "old" one is a contentious question. Also, it seems patently unlikely that all societies would be able to make an equal contribution to this global culture, or that the contribution of some would be felt at all. What language would it speak? A polyglot of English, Spanish, Japanese, Warlpiri, and the 5,997 other world languages? Not likely. Rather, a few languages and cultures or even a single language and culture would be liable to dominate this new world. Therefore, the second version of a one-world culture is a "globalization" of one or a few dominant culture(s). The most likely candidates for global dominance at present are Western culture as a whole or American culture alone, as expressed in Francis Fukuyama's popular book *The End of History and the Last Man* (1992). Today, English reigns as the language of trade and diplomacy, and American popular culture (movies, music, celebrities) pervade the world. The one-world culture could be nothing more than American culture writ large. On the other hand, former dominant cultures have come and gone; French is no longer the *lingua franca*. Some see China poised to be a major international political, economic, and cultural force in the twenty-first century, which would alter the winds of cultural change and globalization yet again – and in ways not advantageous to English-speakers or the West in general.

Jihad versus McWorld

Partly out of appreciation for the obstacles to globalization, Benjamin Barber (1995) reports two opposing tendencies operating simultaneously in the contemporary world, **jihad versus McWorld**. "Jihad," the Arabic word for struggle and sometimes violent struggle, is adopted by Barber to stand for all of the "local," tradition-oriented, frequently angry and militant, "identity-based" groups and movements in the world. It represents the fragmentation of the world, the disengagement from and even hostility toward the world system and the "integrative revolution" that scholars once watched and applauded and declared victorious. It talks the talk of culture and tradition, but this is remembered tradition as well as aggravated, mobilized, and often armed tradition.

Barber's jihad is innately hostile to the "outside" world, whether that "outside" is other societies in its midst or the foreign and globalizing and modernizing influences of the world economic and cultural system. These influences come in many shapes and from many quarters, but one key aspect Barber calls "McWorld." McWorld is the culture and power of the multinational corporations and their "development" orientation. These corporations include all of the famous names that modern people know so well, like Nike, Microsoft, Pepsi-Cola, and Coca-Cola (and others that we do not know so well), although the most representative may be Disney. McWorld has two critical characteristics: it is nakedly economic in focus, and it is culturally invasive. By nakedly economic, Barber means that it has only one interest – profit. It is not concerned to any degree with social relationships or environmental issues or "tradition." All of those things can be impediments to profit and are to be minimized. Since these corporations "fly under the radar" when they can, this is not as difficult as it seems. They often come to non-Western states bearing the gift of development – jobs, income, training, "modernization," and increased GNP – but this comes with all of the costs discussed in earlier chapters, and most of the benefits accrue to the corporations themselves.

McWorld is culturally invasive in two senses – that it brings a message from another culture which is at best foreign and at worst corrosive to the host society, and that it acts, sometimes consciously, to undermine the culture of the host society. An important part of McWorld is American popular culture, embodied in Hollywood. The messages and images of the American culture and entertainment industry are seductive but also anathema to many of the values and beliefs of other societies. No wonder a few societies with the power to do so have banned satellite dishes and the internet; they consider the content of this McCulture to be decadent and disruptive. That McWorld is even intentionally "hostile" toward local cultures is evident from the fundamental requirement to "adjust" a culture so the corporations, their products, and their values can penetrate it. Before a society will drink Coke, its local tastes and preferences must be changed. Before a society will wear Nikes or Mickey Mouse T-shirts, their sense of style and their perceived needs must be altered.

Barber roughly equates jihad with tribalism (although militant tribalism) and McWorld with globalization. The one thing he does not equate either with is democracy, cultural pluralism, or cultural relativism. Both are exclusivist, in a curious way. It is easy to see the exclusivism in jihad: "our" cultural group is right and good and "yours" is wrong and bad. Groups with this mindset tend to find it undesirable if not impossible to coexist. The only option is separation, and the path to separation is often conflict. But McWorld is exclusivist too: Microsoft tolerates but hardly enjoys having Macintosh in the world, and Coke and Pepsi do not really like each other nor, even more so, local "traditional" drinks. If jihad is about separatism, McWorld is about monopoly. Neither has a taste for competition. Neither is, therefore, about choice in the end. Wherever you go in the world, the options are to be exactly the same, local variation or "flavor" eradicated. Americans already know what that looks like in "mall America"; the goal of McWorld is "mall world." In jihad, choice is also inconceivable. One is born a Basque or a Tamil or a Serb or a Christian, and these are inescapable, "natural" identities. Decisions and behaviors are "given," and individualism is not encouraged or desired.

Clash of civilizations

Samuel Huntington (1996) emphasizes a different aspect of the cultural future but one that is no more heartening and that is part of the same general

cultural dynamic – a **clash of civilizations**. Huntington suggests that the primary actors on the stage of world history and culture in the future will not be states or even societies. Prior to the modern period, he argues, history was basically the story of the struggle of powerful individuals – kings, princes, emperors, etc. – and the populations they could drag along with them. Beginning in the 1600s or 1700s, the agents in cultural history became "nations" and the states within which they could wrap themselves. However, there is something else going on today, and it was there all the time – the phenomenon of "civilization," which Huntington defines as a sort of "super-society" or "super-culture," a family of closely related cultures that share certain basic beliefs and values, often religious.

To understand his notion of civilization it is useful to think about American and British and Canadian and Australian cultures. The four are no doubt different in a number of ways; at the same time, they are also similar (for instance, English-speaking) and part of a yet larger, European, Christian, "Western" culture that Huntington would call a civilization. A civilization, then, is the largest cultural community known to humans. Within a civilization are many cultural variations, but the differences between civilizations are much more profound – and potentially insurmountable – than the differences within.

Civilizations have been there throughout the modern era; they were merely obfuscated or forgotten in the excitement of colonialism, modernization, and globalization. Western scholars believed or assumed that modern movements – communism, liberalism, progressivism, capitalism, or what have you – were or would become the true forces of cultural history, and they ignored (when they even knew about) the movements that local peoples formed for themselves or the cultural "narratives" that local peoples told to themselves. If Westerners were aware of other civilizations and their worldviews, they fully expected that Western worldviews would replace them. But as the smoke of demolished colonialism and communism clears, we see the old structures of the civilizations looming from the haze. Today and tomorrow, the world's main civilizations – Western/Christian, Islamic, Chinese, South Asian/Indian, "African," etc. – are back, although they were really never gone. And

Clash of civilizations
Huntington's notion that the key forces in the future will not be societies or states but regional cultural entities (like "Western civilization" or "Islam"); within a civilization a variety of cultural attitudes are shared, but between civilizations differences of attitude and interest will breed conflict

Huntington, Samuel. 1996. *The Clash of Civilizations and the Remaking of World Order.* New York: Simon & Schuster.

they were "back with a vengeance," as Huntington predicts that the conflicts and wars of the near-future will be between these civilizations (for instance, "the West" versus "Islam") or along the fault-lines where they meet (for instance, the Middle East and Israel or Taiwan).

Multiple modernities

Multiple modernities

the perspective that "modernity" as known in the Western tradition is not the only possible form of modern society, and that other societies can and will devise their own particular experience of and response to modern/global forces

Eisenstadt, S. N. 2000. "Multiple Modernities." *Daedalus* 129 (1): 1–29. Hefner, Robert W. 1998. "Multiple Modernities: Christianity, Islam, and Hinduism in a Globalizing Age." *Annual Review of Anthropology* 27: 83–104.

Some might find in Huntington's vision, and perhaps Barber's too, a failure of modernity, but in an important way modernity was another Western worldview and movement like colonialism and development. Accordingly, one of the most interesting, and anthropological, commentaries on the present and future of cultures – one which explicitly opposes Huntington's and Fukuyama's analysis – has recognized multiple paths to this cultural future, multiple ways to be "modern," that is, **multiple modernities** (Eisenstadt 2000; Hefner 1998).

S. N. Eisenstadt notes that all of the dominant theories and predictions regarding culture assumed

> that the cultural program of modernity as it developed in modern Europe and the basic institutional constellations that emerged there would ultimately take over in all modernizing and modern societies; with the expansion of modernity, they would prevail throughout the world.
>
> (2000: 1)

See Chapter 1

However, as he notes generally, and as Hefner notes specifically concerning religion,

> The actual developments in modernizing societies have refuted the homogenizing and hegemonic assumptions of this Western program of modernity. While a general trend toward structural differentiation developed across the wide range of institutions in most of these societies. . .the ways in which these arenas were defined and organized varied greatly, in different periods of their development, giving rise to multiple institutional and ideological patterns. Significantly, these patterns did not constitute simple continuations in the modern era of traditions of their respective societies. Such patterns were distinctively modern, though greatly influenced by specific cultural premises, traditions, and historical experiences. . . .Many of the movements that developed in non-Western societies articulate strong anti-Western or even anti-modern themes, yet all were distinctively modern.
>
> (ibid.: 1–2)

In other words, while Eisenstadt acknowledges elsewhere that Western civilization represents "the 'original' modernity" (1999: 284), the Western version of "modern culture" is neither the only possible one nor the only existing one. Rather, each society can and will find its own form of or response to the common yet unevenly distributed global processes; the future can and will hold "attempts by various groups and movements to reappropriate and redefine the discourse of modernity in their own new terms" (Eisenstadt 2000: 24), based on their particular pre-modern cultures, their particular experiences of modernization, and the particular choices of leaders and members alike. This perspective aligns well with the notion of "glocalization," in which global processes cannot help but take locally specific shapes. In the end, then, there would not be one cultural future, not two, not even several, but many diverse and continually emerging and changing ones – precisely the sort of future that cultural anthropology should expect and is uniquely poised to understand.

BOX 15.5 CONTEMPORARY CULTURAL CONTROVERSIES: WHO OWNS CULTURE?

The contemporary Western world is familiar with the concept of "intellectual property," that ideas and images can be owned. As societies, including and especially indigenous societies, become increasingly integrated into a global system and market, a new and difficult question emerges: who owns and controls "traditional culture," and which – or whose – laws will govern its production and sale? In 1997, an Aboriginal artist named Johnny Bulun Bulun sued a company called R & T Textiles for copyright infringement, claiming that the company used unauthorized images of his work on its products. As recounted by Michael Brown in his book *Who Owns Native Culture?*, Bulun Bulun was no pure traditionalist: he was an accomplished modern painter whose most famous work, "Magpie Geese and Waterlilies at the Waterhole," hung in the Museum and Art Gallery of the Northern Territory in Australia. Therefore, when R & T Textiles printed his designs on their materials, they were "stealing" his property and violating his ownership rights. However, as even Bulun Bulun would admit, images like his are not entirely private but communal, somewhere between "art" and "folklore," derived from "designs [that] belong not only to him but to his clan" (Brown 2003: 45). In a sense, then, Bulun Bulun did not exactly "own" his images; he was a sort of traditional caretaker and reproducer of them. This problem is not unique to Australia or to visual culture. In other countries, words or names or objects or other bits of culture are used commercially; think of the automobile called Dodge Cherokee, not to mention the mass production of Indian dolls, Mexican blankets, or toy bows and arrows. Many indigenous societies do not quite have concepts to deal with such uses of their cultural heritage; at the same time, modern state societies do not quite have the appropriate concepts either. In fact, note that the debate, and the litigation, is ordinarily conducted in modern/Western, not indigenous terms – about "copyright" and "property" and so on. Money is at stake, as well as cultural pride and issues of authenticity. What do you think?

Brown, Michael. 2003. *Who Owns Native Culture?* Cambridge, MA and London: Harvard University Press.

SUMMARY

While world-altering processes like colonialism, globalization, nationalism, and development have affected many peoples negatively, those peoples have not been passive victims of cultural changes. Increasingly in the contemporary world, indigenous people have raised their voices to state their demands, reclaim their cultures, and speak on their own behalf. Formerly "traditional societies" have mastered the modern tools of arts, media, politics, and organization to present formidable challenges to perceived injustices and inequalities. Along the way, anthropology has changed to reflect and study these changed cultural realities.

One of the most important aspects of culture in the twentieth and twenty-first centuries is the adaptation of culture into cultural movements intended to address some aspect of cultural frustration and dissatisfaction. A cultural movement, however, is a new kind or formation of culture itself and not merely a continuation of traditional culture or an abandonment of it. These revitalization movements have taken many shapes and are not unique to small, "traditional" societies but are an increasing part of the life of all societies. Some of the types or qualities of movements include:

- Syncretism
- Millenarianism
- Irredentism
- Modernism or vitalism
- Nativism or fundamentalism.

All of these movements are modern manifestations of the "culture-making" phenomenon. In the post-modern world, culture is perceived more or less clearly as a product and a construction, rather than as a "thing" or an "essence." People in all sorts of societies have developed a nearly

MCQS

FILL IN THE BLANKS

WWW

"ethnographic" or anthropological understanding of their own culture. At the same time, the processes of culture creation and consumption have expanded and accelerated, to include cultural tourism and popular culture. Where the culture of the future will take us, we cannot say. We can, however, appreciate that it will be a construction too – one emerging from multiple and contradictory forces and one to which anthropology has something to contribute as observer and participant.

Key Terms

Clash of civilizations

Cultural tourism

Decentered

Fourth World

Fundamentalism

Irredentism

Jihad versus McWorld

Millenarianism

Modernism

Multiple modernities

Nativism

One-world culture

Popular culture

Post-modernism

Revitalization movement

Syncretism

Vitalism

Seeing culture as a whole #3

Australian Aboriginal Islam

Australians have noted – some with much alarm – that the indigenous people (Aboriginals) of the country are increasingly converting to Islam. The Aboriginals are often described as the oldest living culture in the world, but that does not mean that they are perfectly "traditional" nor that Islam is a "new religion" for them. Islam reached Australia with or even before Western colonialism. Makassans from the Indonesian islands fished along the northern coast and introduced their Muslim religion to northern tribes; some anthropologists have argued that the north-coast Dreamtime being called *walata'walata* is a corruption of the name Allah. In the center of the continent, English colonists introduced Afghan camel-drivers in the mid-1800s to cross the harsh desert landscape; the Afghans too carried Islam and, because most of the Afghan immigrants were male and because they shared with the Aboriginals an exclusion from white colonial society, Afghan men occasionally married Aboriginal women, producing generations of "indigenous people" who were both part-Afghan and Muslim.

Thus, in many locations there were Muslim Aboriginals before there were Christian Aboriginals. In addition, Aboriginals made or found associations between their "traditional" religions and Islam; according to Peta Stephenson, the leading scholar of Aboriginal Islam, many indigenous people asserted that Islam and Aboriginal religions were compatible or even that Islam essentially *was* Aboriginal religion – either that the two shared the same beliefs or that Islamic prophets had established "traditional" Aboriginal beliefs in the first place.

Stephenson is quick to point out that for some Aboriginals, especially wives and children of Muslims, the adoption of Islam was not so much conversion as *kinversion* or "an Indigenous connection to Islam that is culturally – usually family – based" (2010: 91). Kinversion then and since provided "a powerful means of creating social cohesion, and particularly warrants recognition in a time when the rhetoric of the 'clash of civilizations' devalues ordinary sociability and the creative ways in which individuals negotiate their religious and cultural identities" (92).

In the present day, Islam has won new Aboriginal converts, catching the attention of – and raising concerns among – white Australian society. Between 2001 and 2006, the number of Aboriginal Muslims counted in the Australian census rose by 61 percent (Onnudottir, Possamai, and Turner

2010: 61). However, that dramatic growth must be seen in perspective: the actual increase was from 622 to 1,010, meaning that the reported Aboriginal Muslim population was quite small and actually a lower rate of Islam among Aboriginals (0.22 percent) than among the total Australian population (1.7 percent). The growth of Aboriginals reporting "no religion" was even greater (69 percent). Significantly, the contemporary increase in Islam among Aboriginals has occurred in urban areas rather than in remote rural areas where "tradition" is stronger: over 63 percent of Aboriginal Muslims lived in major cities, compared to only 10 percent in remote communities, and more than 68 percent of remote Aboriginals still identify with "traditional religion."

So, Islam does not appear to be making a concerted effort to convert Aboriginals. What appears to be happening is a reconstruction of modern urban Aboriginal identity. In cities, people have different experiences and are more able to choose affiliations; this is no doubt why there are also Aboriginal Buddhists, Aboriginal Hindus, and Aboriginal Baha'is in urban settings. Most contemporary Aboriginal Muslims are also male (58 percent), suggesting something about the circumstances of Aboriginal men today. Stephenson finds that Islam is mixed with the "black power" movement for urban male Aboriginals, many of whom see the American figure Malcolm X as a key inspiration. Aboriginal men, perhaps subjected to particular discrimination like black men in the United States, have been attracted to Malcolm X's brand of Islam because it "emphasized the universality of Islam 'as opposed to nationalist and racialist doctrines'" (Stephenson 2010: 251). Prominent characters like Aboriginal boxing star Anthony Mundine have become role models for Islam, and prison has emerged as a major vehicle for the transmission of Islam.

Finally, Islam serves as something of a protest identity in Australia, against historical and modern processes such as "the devaluation of their cultural and religious heritage through the processes of missionization and Christianization," as well as "industrialization, the advent of mass communication, large-scale immigration, and the shrinking of Christianity's traditional hegemony" (183). Islam then appeals as a resistance against and rejection of Western/Christian culture, which has been experienced as exclusionary, racist, and condescending to Aboriginals; at least for now, Islam seems to be more inclusive, less obsessed with race, and actually *more* tolerant of cultural diversity and *more* conducive to a moral way of life.

In short, as Onnudottir, Possamai, and Turner put it, Australian Aboriginal "conversion to Islam represents some degree of cultural continuity rather than rupture" (2010: 45). Not only is it the latest chapter in a long history of contact between Aboriginal societies and Muslim societies, but Islam is also seen by many Aboriginal individuals as a continuation of their "traditional" culture and religion. And Islam in Aboriginal Australia promises to generate new ruptures and continuities: it is a rupture from the perceived inevitable Westernization and Christianization of indigenous peoples, and it builds global connections between Aboriginal Muslims and other Muslims in the world. For instance, in the video clip "Islam in Australia (Muslim Aboriginals)" (http://www.youtube.com/watch?v=oEhcc-bAvWM), Aboriginal individuals are seen taking an active interest in international affairs like the Iraq war. One man even submits that the "real terrorists" are "the government that is occupying this [Australian] land. We were invaded 217 years ago, and they want to talk about terrorists!"

To hear a radio interview with Rocky Davis, an ex-convict and Aboriginal Muslim activist, visit http://www.abc.net.au/radionational/programs/religionreport/2006-03-22/3303462.

Glossary

Absolute poverty a level of income below what is required to have a decent standard of living, sometimes measured at less than $US 1 per day

Acheulian the stone tool technology associated with Homo erectus, which involves a more complex flaking of bifacial implements

Acculturation the process of acquiring a "second culture," usually as an effect of sustained and imbalanced contact between two societies. Members of the "weaker" society are compelled to adopt aspects of the dominant society

Achieved status a social position or role that a person acquires through some effort or accomplishment of his or her own

Adaptation changes in a system, including a species, in response to changes in its context or environment so as to make that system or species more fit to survive in the context or environment

Age grade system a non-kinship-based corporate system in which members, usually of one sex, are organized into groups or "grades" according to age and assigned roles and values as a group

Age set a division or subset of a society based on shared age characteristics, as determined by the age grade system of that society

Agents of social control individuals, groups, or institutions that play a part in instilling social norms in members and protecting and perpetuating those norms through the use of their powers and sanctions

Ambilineal a descent system in which individuals trace their membership through both "sides" or "lines" of the family, or optionally through one or the other

Ambilocal a residence practice in which individuals may live after marriage with both "sides" of the family (perhaps alternating between them), or optionally with one or the other

Ancestor spirits the spirits of dead family members who are believed to continue to reside near and interact with their living kin

Animatism a type of religious belief in which impersonal spiritual forces exist in the world and affect human life and behavior

Animism a type of religious belief in which natural objects (animals, plants, hills, lakes, moon, etc.) and forces (wind, rain, etc.) have spiritual components that interact socially with humans

Anthropological perspective the unique "angle" or point of view of anthropology, consisting of cross-cultural or comparative study, holism, and cultural relativism

Anthropometry the measurement of human bodies to determine individual and group ("racial") physical characteristics

Anti-language a speech style used by individuals or groups in the performance of roles opposing or inverting the society outside of their group

Apartheid in twentieth century South Africa, the official policy of separating the races within their society legally and socially

Archaeology the study of the diversity of human behavior in the past, based on the traces left behind by past humans or societies

Arranged marriage a practice in which family members (often parents) choose the partner for marriageable youths, sometimes with little or no input from or option for the partners themselves

Artifacts physical objects created by humans, often specifically the "portable" objects like tools, pottery, jewelry, etc. (as opposed to the non-portable ones like buildings and roads, etc.)

Ascribed status a social characteristic that is attributed to a person without any effort on their part, either innate (like sex or race) or acquired in the normal course of development (like age)

Assimilation the social process by which individuals and groups are absorbed into another, usually dominant, cultural group

Audit culture a system of power between scrutinizer and observed which depends on cultural concepts and norms – an audit "repertoire" – including "public inspection," "submission to scrutiny," "rendering visible," and "measures of performance"

Australopithecus a genus of the category Hominid, closely related to and earlier than genus Homo

Authority legitimate power or power that an individual, group, or institution is felt to rightly possess and exercise on the grounds of age, knowledge, office, and such

Avunculocal a residence practice in which a married couple lives with or near an uncle, often a mother's brother

Band a political system or "level of political integration" where small, autonomous, and typically leaderless groups constitute local segments of a decentralized society

Basic personality the psychological traits common to most or all of the members of a society (roughly synonymous with modal personality)

Berdache a "third gender" found in many Native American societies, in which biological men adopt some of the norms usually associated with women

Bilateral relating to both "sides," as in a kinship system, in which individuals regard kin related to the mother and to the father as socially equivalent

Biocultural the mutual interaction between physical/biological and behavioral/cultural factors, in which physical traits make certain behaviors possible, and behavior feeds back to influence physical traits

Bipedalism the ability and tendency to walk on two feet

Blackbirding the colonial practice of abducting the populations of areas, often islands, and resettling them as a labor force in some other part of the world

Bound morpheme a morpheme that has meaning but only when used in conjunction with a word (such as the suffix –s to indicate plural)

Bride price *see bridewealth*

Bride service the marriage wealth-exchange practice in which a man must labor for his wife's kin for some period of time before he may assume rights over his wife

Bridewealth the marriage wealth-exchange practice in which a man or his family must pay an amount of property to his wife's kin before he may assume rights over his wife

Caste a closed socio-economic status, often ascribed by birth

Cephalic index a measurement of the skull/brain volume and shape, based on a ratio of the width of the head from ear to ear relative to the depth of the head from front to back

Chiefdom a political system or "level of integration" in which a central office, often hereditary, possesses formal political power and social prestige through some degree of redistributive control over surplus and the ability to organize and manage labor

Civil war a violent conflict within a particular state or between corporate or identity groups within the state

Civilization a form of society based on cities as the centers of administration and the focus of social life, usually dependent on intensive agriculture in the surrounding countryside

Clan a kinship group, sometimes an assortment of lineages, that can trace its descent back to a common ancestor

Clash of civilizations Huntington's notion that the key forces in the future will not be societies or states but regional cultural entities (like "Western civilization" or "Islam"); within a civilization a variety of cultural attitudes are shared, but between civilizations differences of attitude and interest will breed conflict

Class an (at least ideally) open socio-economic status, which members can change through their own achievements

Coercion power based on the threat or use of force

Colonialism the more or less organized system of occupation and exploitation of foreign territories through settlement and conquest, especially as practiced by Western states since 1492

Colonies of exploitation colonies to which few foreigners immigrate but the territory is still used for its resources, wealth, labor, markets, and/or strategic location

Colonies of settlement colonies to which many foreigners immigrate, sometimes such that they and their descendants become the majority population of the territory

Colony a segment of a population (not exclusively a human population) that moves into and occupies territory not previously occupied by the population, often displacing or subduing the previous occupants

Communal representation the political procedure of guaranteeing that groups (ethnic groups, language groups, races, religions, etc.) will have representation in governments by setting aside offices in the government specifically for those groups

Competence in language, the mastery of the elements (sounds, semantics, and grammar) of a language to be able to make intelligible utterances

Contagious magic the belief and practice that objects that come in contact with each other have some supernatural connection with each other

Core in dependency/world system theory, the states that make up the power-center of the world system – essentially the rich industrial states and former colonialists

Corporate group a social group that shares some degree of practical interest, identity, residence, and destiny

Corvée a colonial practice in which local people were required to provide a period of labor to the administration as a sort of "tax"

Counterculture a group or subset within a society that more or less intentionally adopts behaviors, beliefs, or practices that are at odds with or opposed to the mainstream of society

Country commonly used as a synonym for "nation" or "state," more properly refers to the territory that a society or polity inhabits

Creole a pidgin language that has become elaborated into a multi-functional language and distributed into a first language of the community

Cross-cultural study the examination of a wide variety of societies when considering any particular cultural question, for purposes of comparison

Cultural anthropology the study of the diversity of human behavior in the present

Cultural assimilation a type of assimilation which refers specifically to the loss of distinctive cultural traits, such as language or religion

Cultural competence the skills necessary in the workplace and in life to recognize and value diversity, see one's own cultural influences, understand the dynamics and challenges of intercultural interaction, institutionalize cultural knowledge, and develop practices and policies for delivering culturally appropriate services

Cultural evolutionism the early ethnological or anthropological position or theory that Culture started at some moment in the past and evolved from its "primitive" beginnings through a series of stages to achieve its "higher" or more modern form

Cultural loss the process by which elements of a culture disappear over time, through natural/

environmental changes, social pressures, or individual choices

Cultural materialism the theory that practical/material/economic factors can explain some or all cultural phenomena

Cultural ontology a society's system of notions about what kind of things (including kinds of people) exist in the world and their characteristics and social value. A socially specific way of categorizing and valuing the physical and social world

Cultural relativism the reaction to the fact of cultural diversity in which one attempts to understand and judge the behavior of another culture in terms of its standards of good, normal, moral, legal, etc. rather than one's own

Cultural tourism the practice of "consuming" culture as a form of entertainment and education. Traveling to foreign societies to observe their ways of life (not always "traditional" but sometimes designed for the tourist) in an informal manner

Culture shock the surprise, confusion, and pain we feel when we encounter a way of life that is very foreign to our own

Decentered the absence or denial of a particular society's or culture's perspective from which to view the world, usually associated with moving away from a Western- or Euro-centric perspective. Could potentially imply the absence of any central perspective

Deculturation *see cultural loss*

Deism the form of theism or belief in god(s) that posits a creator god that does not take an active role or moral interest in human affairs

Dependent accumulation according to André Gunder Frank, the process by which colonialism and capitalism extracted the wealth from non-Western colonies, rendering them poor and dependent

Descent the kinship principle of tracing membership in a kin-based corporate group through a sequence of ancestors

Development a form of directed change in which a state tries to change its internal economy and society, and/or foreign states and institutions try to change it, to promote economic growth, industrialize and urbanize, and ideally achieve a higher standard of living for its inhabitants

Development policy the general priorities and decisions set by a state or by development agencies to achieve economic, political, and social goals

Development project a specific activity or task settled upon to achieve the economic, political, and social goals of a development policy. Such projects often include transportation, energy (especially hydro-electric), agricultural, and resettlement schemes

Diaspora the dispersion of a social group from its historical homeland (often applied specifically to the Jewish community)

Diffusion the spread of a cultural trait (object, idea, practice, institution) from one society to another

Diffusionism the early ethnological or anthropological position or theory that Culture, or specific cultural practices, objects, or institutions had appeared once or at most a few times and spread out from their original center

Diglossia the use of two varieties of a language by members of a society for distinct functions or by distinct groups or classes of people

Directed change a cultural process in which internal or external agents make more or less intentional, coordinated, and sustained modifications or reforms to a society and culture

Diseases of development the lifestyle-related diseases that are common in developed industrial societies and increasingly common in developing societies, such as high blood pressure, heart disease, diabetes, tooth decay, and obesity

Displacement the linguistic feature that allows for communication about things that are "not here" in the sense of absent or out of view, past or future, conceptual or even imaginary

Diviner a religious specialist who uses one of many techniques to "read" information from the supernatural world

Division of labor the differentiation of the economy into a set of distinct production tasks, which are assigned to different individuals, groups, or classes, usually creating economic and political inequalities

Doctrine of discovery the European colonial principle that the state that "discovered" or arrived first in a new territory had the right to occupy and administer it without interference from other states

Domestication the process of modification of plants and/or animals to establish human control over them, leading to agriculture and pastoralism

Dominance the social relationship in which certain individuals have higher prestige or power in the group, allowing them to enjoy more or better resources as well as the deference of lower-ranked members

Double descent the kinship practice of reckoning one's membership in kinship-based corporate groups through two lines of descent, ordinarily the mother's and the father's

Dowry the marriage wealth-exchange practice in which the woman's family is required to provide the husband with property (money, land, household goods, etc.) in order to make the marriage

Ecofacts the environmental remains from past human social contexts, including wood, seeds, pollen, animal bones, shells, etc.

Encomienda in Latin American colonial history, a grant of land to a conqueror and explorer, much like medieval estates, which gave the grant-holder control over the land and inhabitants

Enculturation the process by which a person learns or acquires his or her culture, usually as a child. Also known as socialization

Endogamy the marriage principle in which an individual marries someone who is in the same cultural category as himself or herself (e.g. marrying someone in your own race or religion)

Erectness the tendency to have an "upright" posture based on a spine that is vertical rather than parallel to the ground

Ethnic group a corporate group based on some shared cultural traits – language, religion, history, etc. – which finds itself in competition with other groups for wealth, power, opportunity, and recognition. An ethnic group shares an identity and a destiny and therefore competes as a group

Ethnicity the phenomenon of organizing around some aspect of shared culture to integrate an identity group, differentiate it from other groups, and compete in a multi-ethnic context for resources

Ethnocentrism the attitude or belief that one's own culture is the best or only one, and that one can understand or judge another culture in terms of one's own

Ethnocide the destruction of a group's culture, without necessarily killing any of the members of the culture

Ethnogenesis the process by which ethnic groups come into being and/or attain their cultural characteristics

Ethnography a written account or description of a particular culture, usually including its environment, economic system, kinship arrangements, political systems, and religious beliefs, and often including some discussion of culture change

Ethnopsychology the psychological "theory" or understanding used by any particularly society, including its ideas about and uses of emotions, dreams, mental illness, and personhood most generally

Ethnoscience the anthropological theory or approach that investigates the native classification systems of societies to discover the concepts, terms, and categories by which they understand their world

Eugenics the scientific practice of "improving" a population or species by selective breeding or genetic engineering, to breed out "bad" traits and breed in "good" ones

Eunuch a gender category involving non-sexual individuals (usually men), who may be castrated or merely celibate, sterile, or lacking sexual desire

Evolutionism *see cultural evolutionism*

Exogamy the marriage principle in which an individual marries someone who is not in the same cultural category as himself or herself (e.g. marrying someone of a different sex/gender)

Externalized control the source of social control that lies outside of the individual, in the form of individuals, groups, and institutions with the power to sanction behavior, such as parents, teachers, police, governments, etc.

Facial angle a concept in anthropometry that measures the shape of the face from the forehead to the bridge of the nose, on the assumption that sharper angles indicate "more primitive" kinds of humans

Features in archaeology, the large and non-portable objects or structures created and left by humans, including walls, buildings, roads, canals, and so on

Female circumcision also known as female genital mutilation, the practice of cutting off some or all of a female's external genitalia, for purposes of "beauty" or the regulation of sexual sensations

Feminist anthropology the anthropological theory or approach that focuses on how gender relations are constructed in society and how those relations subsequently shape the society. Also examines how gender concepts have affected the science of anthropology itself – the questions it asks and the issues it emphasizes

Fieldwork the anthropological method of traveling to the society one wants to study and living there for a prolonged period of time to collect data first-hand

First World a term not commonly used anymore for the rich, powerful states in the world that dominate the international political and economic arena and consist basically of the former colonial powers

Folklore the "traditional," usually oral, literature of a society, consisting of various genres such as myth, legend, folk tale, song, proverb, and many others

Foraging Also known as hunting and gathering, the production of food by collecting wild (undomesticated) animals and plants

Formal sanction a method of social control employing rewards and punishments that are explicit and well-known, often written down, and administered by special agents of control who possess the authority to administer them (such as police or courts)

Fourth World a collective term for the "traditional," often small-scale and indigenous non-state societies that live inside states (frequently created by colonialism) that they do not control and in which they are the minority and typically the poorest group

Free morpheme a morpheme that has meaning in its own right, that can stand alone as a meaningful sound (for the most part, a word)

Functionalism the method, and eventually the theory, that a cultural trait can be investigated for the contribution it makes to the survival of individual humans, the operation of other cultural items, or the culture as a whole

Fundamentalism a type of cultural/revitalization movement in which members attempt to address perceived social problems or disadvantages by restoring the perceived "fundamentals" or oldest, most important, and most "genuine" elements of culture

Garbalogy the study of contemporary trash to examine how humans make, consume, and discard material objects in the present

Gender the cultural categories and concepts relating to sexually distinct bodies, sexual preference, sexual identity, and sexual norms

Genealogy kinship or "blood" and "marriage" information about a society

Genocide the destruction of a group or society by harming, killing, or preventing the birth of its members

Geopolitics the use of geographical territory for purposes of maintenance and projection of power; the control of strategic locations in the pursuit of political goals

Ghost a religious or spiritual being, generally regarded to be the disembodied spiritual part of a deceased human

Global apartheid the de facto division of the world's states into rich, powerful, majority-white states and poor, weak and dependent majority-non-white states

Glocalization a combination of the words "globalization" and "local," suggests the unique local and situated forms and effects of widespread and even global processes

Governmentality as formulated by Michel Foucault, the assorted practices, institutions, instruments, and discourses of power by means of which a "government" (state) or any other political entity can manage a population – and manage to get that population to manage itself

Grammar *see syntax*

Gross national product (GNP) the total value of goods and services produced by a society or state

Gross national product per capita the GNP of a state divided by its population

Guided reinvention of culture the process by which individuals, ordinarily children, "acquire" ideas, concepts, and skills actively by observing the behavior of others, extracting meanings and rules, and testing those meanings and rules in social situations; fully competent members "guide" the learning by providing models of behavior and correction for inappropriate behaviors

Hacienda the Spanish colonial practice in which land was granted as private property and in which these estates were run both for subsistence production and for the production of cash and export crops

Hierarchy *see dominance*

Hijra a "third gender" in India, in which biological men renounce their sexuality (and often their sexual organs) and become socially neither male nor female

Holism the part of the "anthropological perspective" that involves consideration of every part of a culture in relation to every other part and to the whole

Hominid the category of primates that includes only modern humans and extinct human-like species that fall within the genera of Homo and Australopithecus (although other and even more ancient genera have been proposed)

Homo the genus that contains the modern human species (Homo sapiens) as well as several other extinct human species

Homo erectus an extinct human species that lived from approximately 1.8 million years ago until a few hundred thousand years ago or perhaps even more recently

Homo habilis an extinct human species that lived from over 2 million years ago until less than 2 million years ago. They are also known as the first stone tool makers

Homo sapiens the species name for modern humans

Honorifics specialized forms of speech (terms, titles, tones, grammar, etc.) that convey respect or deference

Horticulture A production system based on low-technology farming or gardening, without the use of plows, draft animals, irrigation, or fertilizers

Household all of the people who live in the same house or compound of houses and act for some or all purposes as a corporate group

Hypergamy the marriage practice of marrying "up" with a spouse in a higher status, class, or caste than oneself

Identity politics the organization and mobilization of groups and parties on the basis of shared cultural characteristics, such that these groups and parties are seen to share an "identity" and to pursue economic, political, and cultural goals for and in the name of those who share that identity

Imitative magic *see sympathetic magic*

Imperialism the pursuit of territorial and political domination of foreign lands and peoples (building an "empire"), known since ancient history but reaching its greatest extent in the late phase of European colonialism

Import substitution a development policy aimed at producing domestically what the state or society currently imports from other states, i.e. substituting its own local products for imported products

Incest taboo the nearly universal rule against marrying or having sex with "kin"

Industrialism an economic and social system based on the production of large quantities of inexpensive manufactured goods and the concentration of employment in urban factories

Informal sanction a "reward" or "punishment" that is widely understood in a society but not precisely defined, usually not written down, and for which no specialized role exists to administer the sanction

Innovation the invention or discovery of a new cultural concept, idea, behavior, or object

Intensive agriculture high-input, high-yield farming on permanent farmlands through the use of technologies like irrigation, fertilizer, pesticide, and the plow

Internal colonialism the practice in which a society (usually a state) penetrates and occupies territory within its jurisdiction (normally, inside its borders) but that contains peoples who do not identify as and with the occupying society. In some usages, it can also refer to the condition in which colonized peoples internalize in their own minds and personalities the institutions and values of colonialism

Internalized control a form or source of social control in which individuals make themselves conform to social expectations through the internalization of rules and norms; by enculturation, social rules and norms become part of the personalities of members

Irredentism a revitalization movement to reclaim a lost homeland

Jihad versus McWorld Benjamin Barber's notion that two opposing but related forces operate in the modern world, one to integrate the world into a single market dominated by a few multinational corporations, and the other to disintegrate the world into exclusivist and often hostile cultural or national groups

Kindred an ego-centered (that is, reckoned from the perspective of some particular individual) category of persons related by kinship, especially in bilateral societies, including members from "both sides" of the family in older and younger generations

Kinesics the study of how body movements are used to communicate social information, sometimes referred to as "body language"

Level of political integration the extent to which political institutions unite a group of people into a single political entity, as measured by the size of the society, the complexity of the society, the formality and centralization of political rules and roles, and the amount of coercive force available to political leaders

Leveling mechanism a practice to establish or re-establish social equality or parity, usually by "bringing down" individuals or groups that threaten to get "above" or "better than" others

Levirate a marriage practice in which the brother of a deceased man is expected to marry his brother's widow

Liminality the condition of being "in between" or "on the margins" of social roles, in particular of being in transition (as during ritual) between one social role and another

Lineage a kinship-based corporate group composed of members related by descent from a known ancestor

Linguistic anthropology the study of the diversity of human language in the past and present, and its relationship to social groups, practices, and values

Linguistic relativity hypothesis the claim that language is not only a medium for communication about experience but actually a more or less powerful constituent of that experience. Language consists of concepts, relations, and values, and speakers of different languages approach and interpret reality through different sets of concepts, relations, and values. Also known as the Sapir–Whorf hypothesis

Market exchange a form of distribution based on the use of a specialized location (the "market place") and relatively impersonal principles of supply and demand and the pursuit of profit

Market-dominant minority "ethnic minorities who, for widely varying reasons, tend under market conditions to dominate economically, often to a startling extent, the 'indigenous' majorities around them" (Chua 2003: 6)

Marriage a socially recognized relationship between two (or more) people that establishes a kin-based group and that provides norms and roles for residence, property ownership and inheritance, labor, sexual relations, and/or childrearing

Marxist/critical anthropology the theory, based on the work of Karl Marx, that emphasizes the material and economic forces that underlie society, relying on notions of power and inequality, modes of production, and class relations and conflicts

Matrilineal a descent system in which lineage relations are traced through a line of related females. Children belong to their mother's corporate group

Matrilocal the residence practice of living with or near the wife's family after marriage

Means of production the activities and tools that a society employs to satisfy its material needs. The form of "work" or "labor" that is performed in a society

Mercantilism an early-modern European economic and political system in which wealth and power were determined by possession of gold and a favorable balance of trade with each other

Microfinance an idea first promoted in the 1970s, to provide very small loans directly to poor individuals or families, for the purpose of starting or growing a small business

Millenarianism a type of revitalization movement aimed at preparing for and perhaps bringing about the end of the "present era," however that era is understood, and replacing it with a new and better existence

Miscegenation a term for the undesirable effects of the mixing of different genetic types or populations, especially race groups. Often refers to the very notion of mixing the races

Modal personality according to Du Bois, the

statistically most common personality traits in a society

Modernism a type of revitalization movement intended to adopt the characteristics of a foreign and "modern" society, in the process abandoning some or all of the "traditional" characteristics of the society undergoing the movement. Also known as *vitalism*

Modernization theory the theory that the improvement of economic and social conditions in poor states entails the creation of "modern" (generally understood as Western-like) institutions, values, and habits. Also, the specific processes or policies by which this form of social change can occur. W. W. Rostow offers one of the most complete and well-known modernization theories

Moiety one of the "halves" of a society, when kin groups are combined in such as way as to create a binary division within society

Monoculture the specialization of production of only one crop or product for which a territory is particularly suited. This can involve food crops like corn or rice, or raw materials like lumber, coffee, rubber, tea, and so on

Monogamy the marriage rule in which an individual may have only one spouse

Monotheism the form of theism that includes belief in only one god/goddess

Morpheme the smallest bit of meaningful sound in a language, usually a word but also a prefix or suffix or other meaning-conveying sound that can be used in conjunction with a word

Morphology the area of language dealing with how meaningful bits (usually but not exclusively words) are created and manipulated by the combination of language sounds

Mousterian the stone tool technology associated with Neandertals, first appearing less than 130,000 years ago

Multilateral development institutions organizations like the World Bank (officially the International Bank for Reconstruction and Development) and the International Monetary Fund that were established and are funded and operated by more than one government for the purpose of disbursing money, advice, and technology in the pursuit of development

Multinational state a state that contains some or all of two or more distinct nations or cultural groups

Multiple modernities the perspective that "modernity" as known in the Western tradition is not the only possible form of modern society, and that other societies can and will devise their own particular experience of and response to modern/global forces

Multi-state nation a nation or cultural group that is divided across two or more state borders

Myth a narrative, usually of the activities of supernatural beings, often telling of how some or all of the natural or social world was established. In addition to an "explanation" of origins, it also provides a "charter" or model for how humans should live today

Nation a corporate group that shares an identity based on such traits as history, culture, territory, etc. and that recognizes a shared political destiny. A group that is politically mobilized to achieve certain goals, usually including political recognition, rights, and sometimes an independent state

Nation-state a state that contains only and all of one "nation" or cultural-identity group, or a nation that has its own formal territory and government

National character the purported personality traits shared by an entire society or country; the term was usually applied to modern societies/ countries like the United States, China, Japan, or the Soviet Union

Nationalism a social movement to achieve recognition, rights, and sometimes an independent state for a nation

Nativism a type of revitalization movement aimed at perpetuating, restoring, or reviving "traditional" cultural practices or characteristics, which are thought to be the source of the group's strength and to be threatened or lost

Neandertal the species or subspecies of Homo that first appeared around 130,000 years ago and is associated with the cold climate of Europe. They go extinct in the last 35–40,000 years and are generally not regarded as direct human ancestors, although this interpretation is still somewhat controversial

Neocolonialism the reconstitution of dependent relationships between states in the post-colonial era, with poor states providing land, labor, and resources to richer industrial states; although invasion and military occupation may not be involved, the inequality of the relationship can lead to exploitation reminiscent of formal colonialism

Neo-evolutionism the mid-twentieth-century revival of focus on the historical development of cultures and societies, as in the work of Leslie White and Julian Steward, which generally sought to repair the failings of nineteenth-century evolutionism by proposing specific processes and a "multi-linear" path of change

Neoliberalism according to David Harvey, a theory of political economic practices that proposes that human well-being can best be advanced by liberating individual entrepreneurial freedoms and skills within an institutional framework characterized by strong private property rights, free markets, and free trade

Neolithic the "New Stone" age, beginning around ten thousand to twelve thousand years ago with the first animal and plant domestication

Neolocal the residence practice in which married people start their own household apart from their parents' or families' households

Noble savage the notion, often associated with Rousseau, that non-Western or "primitive" people are actually happier and more virtuous than Westerners. Based on the idea that humans are free and equal in "a state of nature" but that social institutions deprive them of that freedom and equality

Non-governmental organization (NGO) any non-profit, voluntary citizens' group which is organized on a local, national or international level. Task-oriented and driven by people with a common interest, NGOs perform a variety of service and humanitarian functions, bring citizen concerns to governments, advocate and monitor policies and encourage political participation through provision of information

Office a more or less formal social position with specific rights and responsibilities. One source of "political" authority and social control

Offshoot nation a national group that emerges as a local or historical branch of an older and larger group, eventually pursuing its own cultural and political identity and interests

Oldowan the earliest known stone tool technology, associated with Homo habilis and named for the location of its discovery, Olduvai Gorge in East Africa

One-world culture the idea that all of the peoples and cultures of the world are becoming (or should become) more similar, to the point at which all humans share a single culture. Often attributed to globalization and the universal access to technology and cultural images (like American movies), it assumes that disparate groups will continue to become more similar until all groups share the same basic values, tastes, and media

Oracle a religious specialist (or any religious object or process) with the power to forecast the future or answer questions through communication with or manipulation of supernatural forces

Overurbanization the growth of large cities without the infrastructure to handle the urban populations, especially when a disproportionate amount of the state's population lives in one or a few such cities

Pantheism a form of theism in which it is believed that "everything" is god, that the universe and all of the material world is the same thing as god, that god is "immanent" in and coextensive with the physical world

Paralanguage the qualities which speakers can add to language to modify the factual or social meaning of speech, such as tone of voice, volume, pitch, speed and cadence, and "non-linguistic" sounds like grunts and snickers

Participant observation the anthropological field method in which we travel to the society we want to study and spend long periods of time there, not only watching but joining in their culture as much as possible

Pastoralism a productive system based on domesticated animals as the main source of food

Patrilineal a descent system in which lineage relations are traced through a line of related males. Children belong to their father's corporate group

Patrilocal the residence practice of living with or near the husband's family after marriage

Peasant an out-of-favor term for rural and agricultural peoples who live in but are peripheral to a centralized and often urbanized society.

The peasants provide the food for the society but generally have the least power and wealth in the society

Performatives linguistics utterances that do not merely describe but actually accomplish a transformation in the social world

Periphery in dependency or world system theory, the societies and states that have the least wealth and power and the least influence on the practices and policies in the global economy

Personality the distinctive ways of thinking, feeling, perceiving, and behaving of an individual, shaped by enculturation as individuals internalize aspects of their society's culture

Persuasion a source of social and political power, based on the ability to move people to agree with or obey the persuader. Often exercised through linguistic skill (e.g. the ability to "give a good speech") and the manipulation of resources and social relationships

Phenotype the visible or physical characteristics of an individual or species, which are produced by the "genotype" or (not readily visible) genetic makeup of the individual/species

Phoneme the smallest bit of contrastive sound in a language, that is, the minimal sound-unit that serves to distinguish between word-meanings in a language

Phonology the study of how sounds are used in a language (specifically which sounds occur and the practices for how they combine and interact)

Phratry a kinship-based corporate group composed of two or more clans that recognize common ancestry

Physical anthropology the study of the diversity of human bodies in the past and present, including physical adaptation, group or "race" characteristics, and human evolution

Pidgin a simplified version of a language that is usually used for limited purposes, such as trade and economic interactions, by non-native speakers of the language (as in Melanesian pidgin versions of English). Usually an incomplete language that is not the "first" language of any group

Plural society a society that contains various cultural groups. Such groups often occupy "niches" in the broader social system, such that the groups do not interact with each other except in limited and often mutually exploitive ways

Pluralism the coexistence of multiple social/cultural groups in the same society or state

Polyandry the marriage rule in which a woman can or should marry two or more men

Polygyny the marriage rule in which a man can or should marry two or more women

Polytheism the religious belief in two or more gods

Popular culture often contrasted with "high" or "official" culture, the cultural practices and creations of "the people." Often used as a pejorative term to indicate the poor quality and low intelligence of such culture, in the contemporary world it has also become an important and vibrant form of culture, although one that is not entirely "of the people," in the sense that large corporations often create and disseminate it

Post-modernism a form of life or way of thinking, and the theory of these, of the mid- to late twentieth century, in which earlier notions of unity, progress, reason, and the increasing integration of peoples and societies breaks down and is replaced by pluralism, "irrationality" or emotion or tradition, decentering, and cultural disintegration

Potential nation a group that has not yet achieved national integration and self-consciousness but that is in the process of achieving them or has the characteristics necessary to achieve them

Pragmatics the rules or practices regarding how language is used in particular social situations to convey particular social information, such as the relative status or power of the speakers

Prayer a form of linguistic religious ritual in which humans are believed to speak and interact with supernatural beings

Preferential cousin marriage the marriage principle that a person ought to marry a "cousin," that is, a child of mother's sibling or father's sibling

Prenational people a social group that has not yet achieved the mobilization and self-awareness that characterize a nation

Priest a religious specialist, often full-time, who is trained in a religious tradition and acts as a functionary of a religious institution to lead ritual and perpetuate the religious institution

Primary innovation the invention or discovery of a totally original cultural item, as opposed to *secondary innovation*

Primary production the production of raw materials, in the form of farming, mining, foresting, etc.

Primate the term for the classification of mammals, including prosimians, monkeys, apes, and humans, that share a collection of physical characteristics including a distinct tooth pattern, five-fingered hands, a tendency toward erectness of the spine, large eyes and good vision, and a relatively large brain in relation to body weight, among others

Primatology the study of the physical and behavioral characteristics of the category of species called primates

Primitive mentality according to Lévy-Bruhl, a way of thinking characteristic of "primitive societies" in which individuals cannot understand cause and effect and do not distinguish one object from another (e.g., they believe that an animal can be a person)

Productivity the capacity of language to combine meaningless sounds to create new words or to combine words to create new utterances

Prophet a human who speaks for or receives messages from spirits

Prosimian the category with the classification Primate that includes the least derived or "most primitive" species, such as lemurs, lorises, bush babies, galagas, and so on. Most have long tails and protruding snouts, but they exhibit other basic features of primates

Proxemics the study of how cultures use personal space (or "proximity")

Psychic unity of humanity the position that all humans share a single set of mental processes, even if they think or believe different things; rejects the notion of primitive mentality

Psychological anthropology the field of anthropology that investigates the relationship between the individual and culture, or how psychological processes shape and are shaped by social experience

Racial assimilation a form of assimilation in which the physical traits of a group are lost through intermarriage

Reciprocity a form of exchange that involves giving and receiving between relative equals and as part of a larger ongoing social relationship

Redistribution a form of exchange that involves collection of surplus or wealth by a "central" individual, group, or institution that controls how the wealth is redistributed and used

Relations of production in Marxist theory, the social roles and relationships that are generated by the mode of production, including such things as class, ownership, "management," and in some lines of thinking "family"

Relative poverty the possession of less money than others in the same society, or the inability to afford the standard of living of more comfortable individuals or that is believed to be possible or appropriate

Residence the kinship principle concerning where people live, especially after marriage, and therefore what kinds of residential and corporate groups are found in the society and what tasks and values they are assigned

Revitalization movement according to Wallace, the deliberate, organized, and self-conscious effort of a society to create a more satisfying culture

Revolution a more or less sudden, complete, and often violent movement to change a political or social system

Rite of intensification a form of ritual in which members of the society are brought into greater communion, in which social bonds are intensified

Rite of passage a form of ritual intended to accompany or accomplish a change of status or role of the participants, such as initiation (change from youth to adult) or marriage

Ritual any type of formal, repetitive behavior that is felt to have significance beyond the actions themselves. In particular, religious ritual is often composed of symbols, re-enacts supernatural/mythical events, and is believed to have efficacy if performed correctly

Sacrifice a ritual behavior in which something is destroyed or killed, as a form of offering to or communication with supernatural beings, which is usually believed to affect the social or spiritual condition of the sacrificer

Sanction any type of social pressure in the form

of "reward" or "punishment" that can be imposed on people to influence and control their behavior

Secondary innovation an invention or discovery that uses or combines existing ideas, objects, or techniques in novel arrangements

Self the more or less enduring, bounded, and discrete part of an individual's identity or personality, and the reflexive awareness of this aspect of oneself

Self-determination the concept that groups with a distinct culture and identity have a right to choose their own political arrangements and their own collective destiny

Semantic range the set of meanings conveyed by a particular word, that is, the "range" of its referents or the variety of phenomena or conceptions that it names

Semantics the study of meaning in language. *See morphology*

Semi-periphery in world system theory, those countries or states that are not completely peripheral (that is, not extremely poor and dependent) but that are not rich and powerful enough to merit inclusion in the core of the system

Separatism a movement that has as its goal the cultural and/or political disengagement of two groups or societies. A separatist movement often struggles to detach its territory from a multicultural or plural state and establish its own state

Serial monogamy the marriage practice of having only one spouse at a time but perhaps having more than one spouse, at different times, during one's life

Sexual dimorphism the occurrence of two physically distinct forms of a species, based on sexual characteristics as well as non-sexual ones such as body size

Shaman a religious specialist, often part-time, who has personal power, based on unique life experiences or apprenticeship to a senior shaman, to communicate, interact, and sometimes struggle with supernatural beings or forces. Often a healer

Slash-and-burn a horticultural practice in which trees and underbrush are cut, left to dry, and then burned as preparation for planting a garden. Also known as *swidden*

Social assimilation a form of assimilation in which groups are integrated into the society (for instance, sharing the same jobs or the same neighborhoods), whether or not they share the same culture

Social control the political and general social function of getting members of a group to conform to expectations and rules and to obey authorities. Includes inculcating of social values as well as punishment of deviance from expectations

Social impact analysis a fieldwork study of the consequences that a development project or other social-change policies have on the affected peoples

Social mobility the possibility or ease with which one may change position in the social stratification system

Social reproduction the maintenance and perpetuation of society beyond mere childbearing, including enculturation and teaching of members to take their place in society and day-to-day activities to allow members of society to perform their specified tasks (including what is sometimes called "housework")

Social stratification the division of society into different and unequal groups or "layers" on the basis of wealth, power, and prestige

Socialization from an anthropological point of view, a synonym for enculturation

Society a group of humans who live in relative proximity to each other, tend to marry each other more than people outside the group, and share a set of beliefs and behaviors

Sociocultural appraisal a study examining the *appropriateness* of a development or other social-change project, its likely *impact* on the various groups affected by it, and the distribution of the benefits that accrue from it

Sociolinguistics *see pragmatics*

Sorcerer a religious specialist who uses techniques, including spells and potions, etc. to achieve supernatural effects

Sororal polygyny the marriage practice in which a man marries two or more sisters

Sororate a marriage practice in which a woman is expected to marry the husband of her sister in the event of the married sister's death

Soul a religious concept of a non-material component or components of a living human. It is widely believed that a soul survives the death of the body, at least temporarily, and continues in another form of existence

Sphere of influence in European colonial practice, an area of foreign territory where the power and authority of one European state was recognized

State a political system or level of integration in which a formal centralized government has power over a delimited territory to make and enforce laws, to establish currency and collect taxes, and to maintain an army and declare war

State terrorism the use of force and terror by a state government against its own people – either a particular group or minority within the state or the entire population

Structural adjustment a set of policies designed to reduce government control over development specifically and economic activity more generally, including "opening" or "freeing" local markets to foreign goods, eliminating economic protections like tariffs and subsidies, reducing taxes, deregulating industry, cutting government spending, and allowing the value of local currencies to "float" on international currency exchanges

Structural assimilation *see social assimilation*

Structuralism the theory (associated most closely with Claude Lévi-Strauss) that the significance of an item (word, role, practice, belief) is not so much in the particular item but in its relationship to others. In other words, the "structure" of multiple items and the location of any one in relation to others is most important

Structured interview a fieldwork method in which the anthropologist administers a prepared set of questions to an informant/consultant

Subculture a group or subset within a society that is distinguished by some unique aspects of its behavior (such as clothing styles, linguistic usages, or beliefs and values)

Swidden *see slash-and-burn*

Symbol an object, gesture, sound, or image that "stands for" some other idea or concept or object. Something that has "meaning," particularly when the meaning is arbitrary and conventional and thus culturally relative

Symbolic anthropology the school of thought (often associated with Clifford Geertz and Victor Turner) that the main goal of anthropology is to elucidate the meanings within which humans live and behave. Rather than focusing on institutions and rules, it focuses on symbols and how symbols shape our experience and are manipulated by people in social situations

Symbolic capital "resources" that humans can use to influence situations and affect other people's behavior that are not "material" or "economic." These can include knowledge, social relationships/debts, prestige, etc.

Sympathetic magic also called imitative magic, the belief and practice that objects that have something in common with each other (e.g. same shape or texture) have some supernatural connection with each other

Syncretism a type of revitalization movement in which elements of two or more cultural sources are blended into a new and more satisfying cultural arrangement

Syntax the rules in a language for how words are combined to make intelligible utterances of speech acts (for example, sentences). Also known as grammar

Terra nullius the colonial doctrine of "empty land," that colonized land was empty of human inhabitants and therefore could be claimed and settled by colonists

Theism the religious belief in one or more gods

Third World a term sometimes used to refer to the economically poor, politically and militarily weak, relatively unstable, and dependent states of the world, most of which emerged from colonialism in fairly recent history

Totemism a religious conception that human individuals or groups have a symbolic or spiritual connection with particular natural species, objects, or phenomena

Tradition some practice or idea or object that is (at least believed to be) continuous or associated with "the past." A tradition may be very ancient or very recent, but as an ideological element it is often assumed to be important, authentic, and even "superior" to non-traditional (especially foreign) practices, ideas, and objects

Travesti an alternate gender role in Brazil, in which males take on certain physical traits and sexual behaviors typically associated with females

Tribe a political system or level of integration in which multiple local communities may be organized into a single system but in which political power is still relatively informal and usually flows from institutions that are not specifically political (such as elders, lineages, age sets, religious specialists, and so on)

Unilineal descent a principle in which individuals trace their ancestry through a "line" of related kin (typically a male or a female line) such that some "blood" relatives are included in the descent group or lineage and other relatives are excluded from it

Unstructured interview a fieldwork method in which the anthropologist conducts a relatively free-flowing conversation with an informant/consultant, either without prepared questions or unconstrained by these questions

Vitalism *see modernism*

Vocalizations non-linguistic sounds that can accompany and affect the meaning of speech

Witch a religious specialist, often conceived as a human with a supernatural ability to harm others, sometimes through possession of an unnatural bodily organ or an unnatural personality. Sometimes viewed as an anti-social and even anti-human type who causes misfortune out of excessive greed or anger or jealousy

World anthropologies the perspective that anthropology as developed and practiced in the West is not the only form of anthropology, and that other societies may develop and practice other types of anthropology based on their specific experiences and interests

World system theory the theory that explains the ongoing poverty and low standard of living in Third World states as the effect of external arrangements and relationships, specifically the global economic and political practices and institutions set up by the "core" of rich, powerful, industrialized states that function to their own advantage but to the disadvantage of the poor, weak, "peripheral" states

Bibliography

Abu-Lughod, Lila. 1985. "Honor and Sentiments of Loss in a Bedouin Society." *American Ethnologist* 12 (2): 245–61.

——— 2002. "Do Muslim Women Really Need Saving? Anthropological Reflections on Cultural Relativism and Its Others." *American Anthropologist* 104 (3): 783–90.

Aldana y Villalobos, Gerardo. 2011. *The Apotheosis of Janaab' Pakal: Science, History, and Religion at Classic Maya Palenque*. Boulder, CO: University Press of Colorado.

Alexie, Sherman. 1994. *The Lone Ranger and Tonto Fistfight in Heaven*. New York: HarperPerennial.

Allison, Anne. 1997. "Japanese Mothers and *Obentos*: The Lunch-Box as Ideological State Apparatus." In Carole Counihan and Penny van Esterick, eds. *Food and Culture: A Reader*. New York and London: Routledge, 296–314.

American Anthropological Association. 1939 [1938]. "Resolution of December 1938." *Science* 89 (2298): 30.

——— 1998. "AAA Statement on Race." *American Anthropologist* 100 (3): 712–13.

Anderson, Benedict. 1983. *Imagined Communities: Reflections of the Origin and Spread of Nationalism*. London: Verso.

Anderson, Walter Truett. 1990. *Reality Isn't What It Used to Be: Theatrical Politics, Ready-to-Wear Religion, Global Myths, Primitive Chic, and Other Wonders of the Postmodern World*. New York: HarperSan Francisco.

Apter, David E. 1968. *Some Conceptual Approaches to the Study of Modernization*. Englewood Cliffs, NJ: Prentice Hall.

Aran, Gideon. 1991. "Jewish Zionist Fundamentalism: The Bloc of the Faithful in Israel (Gush Emunim)." In Martin Marty and R. Scott Appleby, eds. *Fundamentalisms Observed*. Chicago, IL: The University of Chicago Press, 265–344.

Arendt, Hannah. 1969. *On Violence*. New York: Harcourt, Brace, & World, Inc.

Arnold, Matthew. 1869. *Culture and Anarchy: An Essay in Political and Social Criticism*. Oxford: Project Gutenberg.

Asad, Talal. 1979. "Anthropology and the Colonial Encounter." In Gerrit Huizer and Bruce Mannheim, eds. *The Politics of Anthropology: From Colonialism and Sexism Toward a View from Below*. The Hague and Paris: Mouton Publishers, 85–94.

Atkinson, Jane Monnig. 1984. "'Wrapped Words': Poetry and Politics among the Wana of Central Sulawesi, Indonesia." In Donald Brenneis and Fred R. Myers, eds. *Dangerous Words: Language and Politics in the Pacific*. Prospect Heights, IL: Waveland Press, Inc., 33–68.

Atran, Scott. 2002. *In Gods We Trust: The Evolutionary Landscape of Religion*. Oxford: Oxford University Press.

Austin, J. L. 1962. *How To Do Things with Words*. Oxford: Clarendon.

Axtell, Roger E. 1991. *Gestures: The Do's and Taboos of Body Language Around the World*. New York: John Wiley & Sons, Inc.

Banton, Michael. 1987. *Racial Theories*. Cambridge: Cambridge University Press.

Barber, Benjamin. 1995. *Jihad versus McWorld*. New York: Times Books.

Barreiro, Jose. 1993. *The Indian Chronicles*. Houston, TX: Arte Publico Press.

Barth, Fredrik. 1965. *Nomads of South Persia: the Basseri Tribe of the Khamseh Confederacy*. New York: Humanities Press Inc.

Barth, Fredrik, ed. 1969. *Ethnic Groups and Boundaries*. Boston, MA: Little, Brown & Co.

Barthes, Roland. 1997. "Toward a Psychosociology of

Contemporary Food Consumption." In Carole Counihan and Penny van Esterick, eds. *Food and Culture: A Reader*. New York and London: Routledge, 20–27.

Basso, Keith H. 1970. *The Cibecue Apache*. New York: Holt, Rinehart, and Winston.

Bauman, Richard. 2001. "Verbal Art in Performance." In Alessandro Duranti, ed. *Linguistic Anthropology: A Reader*. Malden, MA and Oxford: Blackwell Publishing, 165–88.

Beals, Alan R. 1980. *Gopalpur: A South Indian Village*. New York: Holt, Rinehart, and Winston.

Beidelman, T. O. 1971. *The Kaguru: A Matrilineal People of East Africa*. New York: Holt, Rinehart, and Winston.

Bell, Diane. 1993. *Daughters of the Dreaming*, 2nd edn. Minneapolis, MN: University of Minnesota Press.

Ben-Amos, Dan. 1984. "The Seven Strands of Tradition: Varieties in its Meaning in American Folklore Studies." *Journal of Folklore Research* 21 (2/3): 97–131.

Benedict, Ruth. 1934a. "Anthropology and the Abnormal." *Journal of General Psychology* 10 (2): 59–82.

—— 1934b. *Patterns of Culture*. New York: The New American Library.

—— 1946. *The Chrysanthemum and the Sword*. Boston, MA: Houghton Mifflin.

Benet, Sula. 1974. *Abkhasians: The Long-Living People of the Caucasus*. New York: Holt, Rinehart, and Winston.

Berlin, Brent and Paul Kay. 1969. *Basic Color Terms: Their Universality and Evolution*. Berkeley, CA: University of California Press.

Beuchat, P. D. 1957. "Riddles in Bantu." *African Studies* 16: 133–49.

Birth, Kevin K. 2008. *Bacchanalian Sentiments: Musical Experiences and Political Counterpoints in Trinidad*. Durham, NC and London: Duke University Press.

Bloch, Maurice. 1983. *Marxism and Anthropology: The History of a Relationship*. Oxford: Clarendon Press.

—— 1989 [1979]. *Ritual, History, and Power: Selected Papers in Anthropology*. London: The Athlone Press.

Boas, Franz. 1896. "The Limitations of the Comparative Method of Anthropology." *Science* 4: 901–8.

—— 1928. *Anthropology and Modern Life*. New York: W. W. Norton & Company, Inc.

Bodley, John. 1975. *Victims of Progress*. Menlo Park, CA: Cummings.

—— 1985. *Anthropology and Contemporary Human Problems*, 2nd edn. Palo Alto, CA and London: Mayfield Publishing Company.

Boellstorff, Tom. 2008. *Coming of Age in Second Life: An Anthropologist Explores the Virtually Human*. Princeton, NJ: Princeton University Press.

Bogardus, Emory. 1933. "A Social Distance Scale." *Sociology and Social Research* 17: 65–71.

Boites, Salvadore Z., Pamela Geller, and Thomas C. Patterson, n.d. "The Growth and Changing Composition of Anthropology 1966–2002." www. aaanet. org/ar/changing_composition.pdf, accessed November 21, 2005.

Bonta, Bruce. 1997. "Cooperation and Competition in Peaceful Societies." *Psychological Bulletin* 121: 299–320.

Boswell, John. 1994. *Same-Sex Union in Premodern Europe*. New York: Villard Books.

Bourdieu, Pierre. 1977. *Outline of a Theory of Practice*. Cambridge: Cambridge University Press.

Bowen, John R. 2010. *Can Islam Be French? Pluralism and Pragmatism in a Secularist State*. Princeton, NJ and Oxford: Princeton University Press.

Boyer, Pascal. 2001. *Religion Explained: The Evolutionary Origins of Religious Thought*. New York: Basic Books.

Brenneis, Donald. 1984. "Straight Talk and Sweet Talk: Political Discourse in an Occasionally Egalitarian Community." In Donald Brenneis and Fred R. Myers, eds. *Dangerous Words: Language and Politics in the Pacific*. Prospect Heights, IL: Waveland Press, Inc., 69–84.

Briggs, Jean. 1970. *Never in Anger: Portrait of an Eskimo Family*. Cambridge, MA: Harvard University Press.

Brown, John Seely. 1991. "Research that Reinvents the Corporation." *Harvard Business Review* (January–February): 102–11.

Brown, Judith K. 1975. "Iroquois Women: an Ethnohistoric Note." In Rayna R. Reiter, ed. *Toward an Anthropology of Women*. New York: Monthly Review Press, 235–51.

Brown, Katherine Tandy. 2000. "Cultural or Heritage—This Tourism is Hot!" http://www.grouptraveler.com/roundups/6–00.html, accessed July 26, 2005.

Brown, Michael. 2003. *Who Owns Native Culture?* Cambridge, MA and London: Harvard University Press.

Brueggemann, Walter. 2003. *An Introduction to the Old Testament: The Canon and Christian Imagination*. Louisville, KY: Westminster John Knox Press.

Burgess, M. Elaine. 1978. "The Resurgence of Ethnicity: Myth or Reality?" *Ethnic and Racial Studies* 1: 265–85.

Cassirer, Ernst. 1954. *An Essay on Man: An Introduction to a Philosophy of Human Culture*. Garden City, NY: Doubleday & Company, Inc.

Cattelino, Jessica R. 2011. "'One Hamburger at a Time': Revisiting the State–Society Divide with the Seminole Tribe of Florida and Hard Rock International." *Current Anthropology* 52 (S3): S137–49.

Chagnon, Napoleon. 1992. *Yanomamo*, 4th edn. Fort Worth, TX: Harcourt Brace College Publishers.

Chin, Elizabeth. 1999. "Ethnically Correct Dolls: Toying with the Race Industry." *American Anthropologist* 101 (2): 305–21.

Chua, Amy. 2003. *World on Fire: How Exporting Free Market Democracy Breeds Ethnic Hatred and Global Instability*. New York: Anchor Books.

Clammer, John. 1973. "Colonialism and the Perception of Tradition in Fiji." In Talal Asad, ed. *Anthropology and the Colonial Encounter*. New York: Humanities Press, 199–220.

Clarkson, Frederick. 2005. "Christian Reconstructionism: Theocratic Dominionism Gains Influence." http://www.axisoflogic.com/artman/publish/article_18836.shtml, accessed July 26, 2005.

Claxton, Nicholas. 1989. *The Price of Progress*. Oley, PA: Bullfrog Films.

Clifford, James. 1994. "Diasporas." *Cultural Anthropology* 9 (3): 302–38.

—— 1997. *Routes: Travel and Translation in the Late Twentieth Century*. Cambridge, MA: Harvard University Press.

Clifford, James and George Marcus, eds. 1986. *Writing Culture: The Poetics and Politics of Ethnography*. Berkeley, CA: University of California Press.

Cohen, Lawrence. 2005. "The Kothi Wars: AIDS and Cosmopolitanism and the Morality of Classification." In Vincanne Adams and Stacy Leigh Pigg, eds. *Sex in Development: Science, Sexuality, and Morality in Global Perspective*. Durham, NC and London: Duke University Press, 269–303.

Cohen, Robin. 1997. *Global Diasporas: An Introduction*. Seattle, WA: University of Washington Press.

Collins, Francis S. 2004. "What We Do and Don't Know about 'Race,' 'Ethnicity,' Genetics, and Health at the Dawn of the Genome Era." *Nature Genetics* Supplement 36 (11): S13–15.

Colson, Elizabeth. 2003. "Forced Migration and the Anthropological Response." *Journal of Refugee Studies* 16 (1): 1–18.

Comaroff, Jean. 1985. *Body of Power, Spirit of Resistance: The Culture and History of a South Africa People*. Chicago, IL and London: The University of Chicago Press.

Comaroff, John L. and Jean Comaroff. 1991. *Of Revelation and Revolution: The Dialectics of Modernity on a South African Frontier*, vol. 2. Chicago, IL and London: The University of Chicago Press.

Connor, Walker. 1994. *Ethnonationalism: The Quest for Understanding*. Princeton, NJ: Princeton University Press.

Conover, Ted. 1987. *Coyotes: A Journey Through the Secret World of America's Illegal Aliens*. New York: Vintage.

—— 2000. *New Jack: Guarding Sing Sing*. New York: Random House.

Cook, Susan E. 2011. "The Business of Being Bafokeng: The Corporatization of a Tribal Authority in South Africa." *Current Anthropology* 52 (S3): S151–59.

Counihan, Carole and Penny Van Esterick, eds. 2007. *Food and Culture: A Reader*, 2nd edn. New York and London: Routledge.

Coupland, Nikolas. 2007. *Style: Language Variation and Identity*. Cambridge: Cambridge University Press.

Crapanzano, Vincent. 1992. *Hermes' Dilemma and Hamlet's Desire: On the Epistemology of Interpretation*. Cambridge, MA: Harvard University Press.

Crystal, David. 1987. *The Cambridge Encyclopedia of Language*. Cambridge and New York: Cambridge University Press.

Dahlberg, Frances, ed. 1981. *Woman the Gatherer*. New Haven, CT: Yale University Press.

Daniel, G. Reginald. 2005. "White into Black: Race and National Identity in Contemporary Brazil." In Paul Spickard, ed. *Race and Nation: Ethnic Systems in the Modern World*. New York and London: Routledge, 87–113.

Davies, Anna, Devin Fidler, and Marina Gorbis. 2011. "Future Work Skills 2020." Palo Alto, CA: Institute for the Future for the University of Phoenix Research Institute.

Davis, J. 1992. "The Anthropology of Suffering." *Journal of Refugee Studies* 5 (2): 149–61.

De Caro, F. A. 1986. "Riddles and Proverbs." In Elliott Oring, ed. *Folk Groups and Folklore Genres: An Introduction*. Logan, UT: Utah State University Press, 175–97.

Deger, Jennifer. 2006. *Shimmering Screens: Making Media in an Aboriginal Community*. Minneapolis, MN: University of Minnesota Press.

Deng, Francis Mading. 1972. *The Dinka of the Sudan*. New York: Holt, Rinehart, and Winston.

Denniston, Christine. 2003. "Couple Dancing and the Beginning of Tango." Http://www.history-of-tango.com/couple-dancing.html, accessed November 25, 2011.

Dentan, Robert Knox. 1968. *The Semai: A Non-violent People of Malaya*. New York: Holt, Rinehart, and Winston.

DeVos, George. 1975. "Ethnic Pluralism: Conflict and Accommodation." In George DeVos and Lola Romanucci-Ross, eds. *Ethnic Identity: Cultural Continuities and Change*. Palo Alto, CA: Mayfield Publishing Company, 5–41.

DeVos, George and Hiroshi Wagatsumo. 1966. *Japan's Invisible Race: Caste in Culture and Personality*. Berkeley, CA: University of California Press.

Dharmadasa, K.N.O. 1992. *Language, Religion, and Ethnic Assertiveness: The Growth of Sinhalese Nationalism in Sri Lanka*. Ann Arbor, MI: University of Michigan Press.

Diamond, Stanley. 1972 [1969]. "Anthropology in Question." In Dell Hymes, ed. *Reinventing Anthropology*. New York: Random House, Inc., 401–29.

Douglas, Mary. 1966. *Purity and Danger: An Analysis of the Concepts of Pollution and Taboo*. London: Routledge & Kegan Paul.

—— 1975. *Implicit Meanings: Essays in Anthropology*. London and Boston, MA: Routledge & Kegan Paul.

Downs, James F. 1972. *The Navajo*. New York: Holt, Rinehart, and Winston.

Du Bois, Cora. 1960 [1944]. *The People of Alor: A Social-Psychological Study of an East Indian Island*. Cambridge, MA: Harvard University Press.

Dundes, Alan. 1965. "What is Folklore?" In Alan Dundes, ed. *The Study of Folklore*. Englewood Cliffs, NJ: Prentice-Hall, Inc., 1–3.

Durkheim, Emile. 1965 [1915]. *The Elementary Forms of the Religious Life*. New York: The Free Press.

Dussart, Françoise. 2000. *The Politics of Ritual in an Aboriginal Settlement: Kinship, Gender, and the Currency of Knowledge*. Washington, DC and London: Smithsonian Institution Press.

Ehrenreich, Barbara. 2002. *Nickel and Dimed: On (Not) Getting By in America*. New York: Owl Books/Henry Holt.

Eisenstadt, S. N. 1999. "Multiple Modernities in an Age of Globalization." *Canadian Journal of Sociology* 24 (2): 283–95.

—— 2000. "Multiple Modernities." *Daedalus* 129 (1): 1–29.

Eissenstat, Howard. 2005. "Metaphors of Race and Discourse of Nation: Racial Theory and State Nationalism in the First Decades of the Turkish Republic." In Paul Spickard, ed. *Race and Nation: Ethnic Systems in the Modern World*. New York and London: Routledge, 239–56.

El-Zein, Amira. 2009. *Islam, Arabs, and the Intelligent World of the Jinn*. Syracuse, NY: Syracuse University Press.

Eller, Jack David. 1999. *From Culture to Ethnicity to Conflict: An Anthropological Perspective on International Ethnic Conflict*. Ann Arbor, MI: University of Michigan Press.

—— 2005. *Violence and Culture: A Cross-cultural and Interdisciplinary Approach*. Belmont, CA: Wadsworth Publishing.

Engle, Gary. 1987. "What Makes Superman So Darned American?" In Gary Engle and Dennis Dooley, eds. *Superman at Fifty: The Persistence of a Legend*. Cleveland, OH: Octavia Press, 79–87.

Eriksen, Thomas Hylland. 2002 [1993]. *Ethnicity and Nationalism: Anthropological Perspectives*. London: Pluto Press.

Ervin, Alexander M. 2000. *Applied Anthropology: Tools and Perspectives for Contemporary Practice*. Boston, MA: Allyn and Bacon.

Estioko-Griffin, Agnes and P. Bion Griffin. 2002. "Woman the Hunter: The Agta." In Caroline Brettell and Carolyn Sargent, eds. *Gender in Cross-Cultural Perspective*. Englewood Cliffs, NJ: Prentice-Hall, 206–15.

Evans-Pritchard, E. E. 1937. *Witchcraft, Oracles, and Magic Among the Azande*. New York: Oxford University Press.

—— 1951. *Kinship and Marriage among the Nuer*. New York: Oxford University Press.

—— 1956. *Nuer Religion*. Oxford: Oxford University Press.

—— 1962. *Social Anthropology and Other Essays*. New York: The Free Press.

Fanon, Frantz. 1963. *The Wretched of the Earth*. Constance Farrington, trans. New York: Grove Press, Inc.

Feinberg, Richard. 1996. "Spirit Encounters on a Polynesian Outlier: Anuta, Solomon Islands." In Jeannette Marie Mageo and Alan Howard, eds. *Spirits in Culture, History, and Mind*. New York and London: Routledge, 99–120.

Ferguson, James and Akhil Gupta. 2002. "Spatializing States: Toward an Ethnography of Neoliberal Governmentality." *American Ethnologist* 29 (4): 981–1002.

Finkelstein, Marni. 2005. *With No Direction Home: Homeless Youth on the Road and in the Streets*. Belmont, CA: Wadsworth Publishing.

Finnegan, Ruth. 1991. "Tradition, But What Tradition and For Whom"? *Oral Tradition* 6 (1): 104–24.

Firth, Raymond. 1975. "Speech-Making and Authority in Tikopia." In Maurice Bloch, ed. *Political Language and Oratory in Traditional Society*. London: Academic Press, 29–43.

Fischer, Johan. 2011. *The Halal Frontier: Muslim Consumers in a Globalized Market*. New York: Palgrave Macmillan.

Fiske, Shirley J. 2008. "Working for the Federal Government: Anthropology Careers." *NAPA Bulletin* 29 (1): 110–30.

Foley, William A. 1997. *Anthropological Linguistics: An Introduction*. London: Blackwell Publishers.

Fortes, Meyer and E. E. Evans-Pritchard, eds. 1940. *African Political Systems*. London: Oxford University Press.

Frake, Charles. 1962. *The Ethnographic Study of Cognitive Systems. Anthropology and Human Behavior*. Washington, DC: Society of Washington.

Frank, André Gundar. 1966. "The Development of Underdevelopment." *Monthly Review* 18: 17–31.

—— 1979. *Dependent Accumulation and Underdevelopment*. New York and London: Monthly Review Press.

Frazer, James George. 1958 [1922]. *The Golden Bough: A Study in Magic and Religion*. New York: Macmillan.

Freeman, Derek. 1983. *Margaret Mead and Samoa: The Making and Unmaking of an Anthropological Myth*. Cambridge, MA: Harvard University Press.

Freudenthal, Hans. 1973. *Mathematics as an Educational Task*. Dordrecht: Reidel.

Fried, Morton H. 1967. *The Evolution of Political Society: An Essay in Political Anthropology*. New York: Random House.

Friedl, Ernestine. 1975. *Women and Men*. New York: Holt, Rinehart, and Winston.

—— 1978. "Society and Sex Roles." *Human Nature* 1 (6): 68–75.

Friedman, John Block. 2000. *The Monstrous Races in Medieval Art and Thought*. Syracuse, NY: Syracuse University Press.

Friedman, Thomas. 2005. *The World is Flat: A Brief History of the Twenty-First Century*. New York: Farrar, Straus, & Giroux.

Fry, Douglas P. 2006. *The Human Potential for Peace: An Anthropological Challenge to Assumptions about War and Violence*. New York and Oxford: Oxford University Press.

Fujii, Lee Ann. 2009. *Killing Neighbors: Webs of Violence in Rwanda*. Ithaca, NY: Cornell University Press.

Fukuyama, Francis. 1992. *The End of History and the Last Man*. New York: The Free Press.

Furnivall, J. S. 1956. *Colonial Policy and Practice: A Comparative Study of Burma and Netherlands India*. New York: New York University Press.

Gallup, Jr., Gordon G. 1970. "Chimpanzee Self-Recognition." *Science* 167: 86–87.

Gamst, Frederick C. 1969. *The Qemant: A Pagan-Hebraic Peasantry of Ethiopia*. New York: Holt, Rinehart, and Winston.

Gans, Herbert. 1962. *The Urban Villagers: Group and Class in the Life of Italian-Americans*. New York: The Free Press.

Garfinkel, Harold. 1967. *Studies in Ethnomethodology*. Englewood Cliffs, NJ: Prentice-Hall.

Garson, John George and Charles Hercules Read, eds. 1899. *Notes and Queries on Anthropology, or A Guide to Anthropological Research for the Use of Travellers and Others*, 3rd edn. London: The Anthropological Institute.

Geertz, Clifford, ed. 1963. *Old Societies and New States: The Quest for Modernity in Asia and Africa*. New York: The Free Press.

Geertz, Clifford. 1973. *The Interpretation of Cultures*. New York: Basic Books.

—— 1976. "'From the Native's Point of View': On the Nature of Anthropological Understanding." In Keith Basso and Henry A. Selby, eds. *Meaning in Anthropology*. Albuquerque, NM: University of New Mexico Press, 221–37.

—— 1980. *Negara: The Theatre State in Nineteenth-Century Bali*. Princeton, NJ: Princeton University Press.

Gellner, Ernest. 1988. *Plough, Sword, and Book: The Structure of Human History*. Chicago, IL: University of Chicago Press.

Gershoy, Leo. 1957. *The Era of the French Revolution 1789–1799*. Princeton, NJ: D. Van Nostrand Company, Inc.

Gill, Sam D. 1981. *Sacred Words: A Study of Navajo Religion and Prayer*. Westport, CT: Greenwood Press.

Gilmore, David. 1990. *Manhood in the Making: Cultural Concepts of Masculinity*. New Haven, CT: Yale University Press.

Gilroy, Paul. 1993. *The Black Atlantic: Modernity and Double Consciousness*. Cambridge, MA: Harvard University Press.

Gitlin, Todd. 1995. *The Twilight of Common Dreams: Why America is Wracked by Culture Wars*. New York: Metropolitan.

Gittleman, Maury, and Mary Joyce. 1995. "Earnings Mobility in the United States, 1967–91." *Monthly Labor Review*, September: 3–13.

Givens, David B., Patsy Evans, and Timothy Jablonski. 2000. "1997 American Anthropological Association Summary of Anthropology Ph.D.s." www.aaanet.org/surveys/97survey.htm, accessed November 21, 2005.

Glazer, Mark et al. 2004. "Susto and Soul Loss in Mexicans and Mexican Americans." *Cross-Cultural Research* 38 (3): 270–88.

Gluckman, Max. 1956. *Custom and Conflict in Africa*. Oxford: Basil Blackwell.

Godelier, Maurice. 1978. *Perspectives in Marxist Anthropology*. Cambridge: Cambridge University Press.

Goldman, Irving. 2004. *Cubeo Hehenewa Religious Thought: Metaphysics of a Northwestern Amazonian People*. New York: Columbia University Press.

Goodall, Jane. 1986. *The Chimpanzees of Gombe: Patterns of Behavior*. Cambridge, MA: Harvard University Press.

Goodenough, Ward H. 1956. "Componential Analysis and The Study of Meaning." *Language* 32: 195–216.

Gorer, Geoffrey and John Rickman. 1950. *The People of Great Russia: A Psychological Study*. New York: Chanticleer Press.

Gould, Drusilla and Christopher Loether. 2002. *An Introduction to the Shoshoni Language*. Salt Lake City, UT: The University of Utah Press.

Gramsci, Antonio. 1971. *Selections from the Prison Notebooks of Antonio Gramsci*. Quintin Hoare and Geoffrey Nowell Smith, ed. and trans. London: Lawrence and Wishart.

Grant, Madison. 1916. *The Passing of the Great Race; or the Racial Basis of European History*. New York: Charles Scribner's Sons.

Gray, John. 1992. *Men are from Mars, Women are from Venus: A Practical Guide for Improving Communication and Getting What You Want in Your Relationships*. New York: HarperCollins Publishers.

Grayzel, John. 1986. "Libido and Development: The Importance of Emotions in Development Work." In Michael M. Horowitz and Thomas M. Painter, eds. *Anthropology and Rural Development in West Africa*. Boulder, CO: Westview Press, 147–65.

Greeley, Andrew. 1971. *Why Can't They Be Like Us? America's White Ethnic Groups*. New York: E.P. Dutton & Co.

Green, John C. 1959. *The Death of Adam: Evolution and its Impact on Western Thought*. Ames, IA: The Iowa State University Press.

Gregor, Thomas. 1981. "'Far, Far Away My Shadow Wandered. . .': The Dream Symbolism and Dream Theories of the Mehinaku Indians of Brazil." *American Ethnologist* 8 (4): 709–20.

Gregory, C. A. 1982. *Gifts and Commodities*. London: Academic Press.

Gremaux, René. 1994. "Woman Becomes Man in the Balkans." In Gilbert Herdt, ed. *Third Sex, Third Gender: Beyond Sexual Dimorphism in Culture and History*. New York: Zone Books, 241–81.

Griaule, Marcel. 1965. *Conversations with Ogotemmeli: An Introduction to Dogon Religious Ideas*. London: Oxford University Press.

Guidieri, Remo and Francesco Pellizi. 1988. "Introduction: 'Smoking Mirrors'—Modern Polity and Ethnicity." In Remo Guidieri, Francesco Pellizi, and Stanley Tambiah, eds. *Ethnicities and Nations: Processes of Interethnic Relations in Latin America, Southeast Asia, and the Pacific*. Austin, TX: University of Texas Press, 7–38.

Guldbrandsen, Thaddeus Countway and Dorothy C. Holland. 2001. "Encounters with the Super-Citizen: Neoliberalism, Environmental Activism, and the American Heritage Rivers Initiative." *Anthropological Quarterly* 74 (3): 124–34.

Guneratne, Arjun, ed. 2010. *Culture and the Environment in the Himalaya*. Abingdon UK and New York: Routledge.

Gurr, Ted Robert and Barbara Harff. 1994. *Ethnic Conflict in World Politics*. Boulder, CO: Westview Press.

Hafez, Sherine. 2011. *An Islam of Her Own: Reconsidering Religion and Secularism in Women's Islamic Movements*. New York and London: New York University Press.

Haller, John S., Jr. 1971. *Outcasts from Evolution: Scientific Attitudes of Racial Inferiority, 1859–1900*. Carbondale and Edwardsville, IL: Southern Illinois University Press.

Halliday, M. A. K. 1976. "Anti-Languages." *American Anthropologist* 78: 570–84.

Hallowell, A. Irving. 1967 [1955]. *Culture and Experience*. New York: Schocken Books.

Hannerz, Ulf. 1980. *Exploring the City: Inquiries Toward an Urban Anthropology*. New York: Columbia University Press.

Harlow, Harry. 1959. "Love in Infant Monkeys." *Scientific American* 200 (6): 68–74.

Harrell-Bond, Barbara E. 1986. *Imposing Aid: Emergency Assistance to Refugees*. Oxford: Oxford University Press.

—— and E. Voutira. 1992. "Anthropology and the Study of Refugees." *Anthropology Today* 8 (4): 6–10.

Harris, Marvin. 1968. *The Rise of Anthropological Theory*. New York: Thomas Y. Crowell.

—— 1974. *Cows, Pigs, Wars, and Witches: The Riddles of Culture*. New York: Random House.

—— 1979. *Cultural Materialism: The Struggle for a Science of Culture*. New York: Random House.

Harrison, Faye. V. 2008. *Outsider Within: Reworking Anthropology in the Global Age*. Urbana, IL: University of Illinois Press.

Hart, C. W. M. and Arnold R. Pilling. 1960. *The Tiwi of North Australia*. New York: Holt, Rinehart, and Winston.

Harvey, David. 2005. *A Brief History of Neoliberalism*. Oxford: Oxford University Press.

Heald, Suzette. 1986. "The Ritual Use of Violence: Circumcision among the Gisu of Uganda." In David Riches, ed. *The Anthropology of Violence*. Oxford: Basil Blackwell, 70–85.

Hedges, Chris. 2002. *War is a Force that Gives Us Meaning*. New York: Public Affairs.

Hefner, Robert W. 1998. "Multiple Modernities: Christianity, Islam, and Hinduism in a Globalizing Age." *Annual Review of Anthropology* 27: 83–104.

Heider, Karl. 1979. *Grand Valley Dani: Peaceful Warriors*. New York: Holt, Rinehart, and Winston.

Heitzenrater, Richard P. 2002. "Tradition and History." *Church History* 71 (3): 621–38.

Herdt, Gilbert. 1987 [1981]. *Guardians of the Flutes: Idioms of Masculinity*. New York: Columbia University Press.

—— 1994. "Introduction: Third Sexes and Third Genders." In Gilbert Herdt, ed. *Third Sex, Third Gender: Beyond Sexual Dimorphism in Culture and History*. New York: Zone Books, 21–81.

Herodotus. 1942. *The Persian Wars*. George Rawlinson, trans. New York: Modern Library.

—— 1972. *The Histories*. Aubrey de Selincourt, trans. Revised with introduction and notes by A. R. Burn. London: Penguin Books Ltd.

Herskovits, Melville J. 1958 [1941]. *The Myth of the Negro Past*. Boston, MA: Beacon Press.

Himpele, Jeff D. 2008. *Circuits of Culture: Media, Politics, and Indigenous Identity in the Andes*. Minneapolis, MN: University of Minnesota Press.

Hine, Thomas. 2003. *I Want That!: How We All Became Shoppers*. New York: Perennial.

Hinton, Alexander Laban. 2010. "Introduction: Toward an Anthropology of Transitional Justice." In Alexander Laban Hinton, ed. *Transitional Justice: Global Mechanisms and Local Realities after Genocide and Mass Violence*. New Brunswick, NJ and London: Rutgers University Press, 1–22.

Hoben, Allan. 1986. "Assessing the Social Feasibility of a Settlement Project in North Cameroon." In Michael M. Horowitz and Thomas M. Painter, eds. *Anthropology and Rural Development in West Africa*. Boulder, CO: Westview Press, 169–94.

Hobsbawm, Eric and Terence Ranger, eds. 1983. *The Invention of Tradition*. Cambridge: Cambridge University Press.

Hockett, Charles F. 1958. *A Course in Modern Linguistics*. New York: Macmillan.

—— 1977. *The View from Language: Selected Essays, 1948–1974*. Athens, GA: University of Georgia Press.

Hoebel, E. Adamson. 1960. *The Cheyennes Indians of the Great Plains*. New York: Holt, Rinehart, and Winston, Inc.

Hoffman, Lisa, Monica DeHart, and Stephen J. Collier. 2006. "Notes on the Anthropology of Neoliberalism." *Anthropology News* (September): 9–10.

Hoffman, Susanna M. and Anthony Oliver-Smith, eds. 2002. *Catastrophe and Culture: The Anthropology of Disaster*. Santa Fe, NM: School of American Research Press.

Holy, Ladislav. 1991. *Religion and Custom in a Muslim Society: The Berti of Sudan*. Cambridge: Cambridge University Press.

Hook, Stephen. 1996. "Introduction: Foreign Aid in a Transformed World." In Stephen Hook, ed. *Foreign Aid Toward the Millennium*. Boulder, CO: Lynne Rienner, 1–16.

Horowitz, David. 1985. *Ethnic Groups in Conflict*. Berkeley, CA: University of California Press.

Horton, Robin. 1960. "A Definition of Religion, and its Uses." *The Journal of the Royal Anthropological Institute of Great Britain and Ireland* 90 (2): 201–26.

Horvath, Ronald J. 1972. "A Definition of Colonialism." *Current Anthropology* 13 (1): 45–57.

Howes, David, ed. 1996. *Cross-Cultural Consumption: Global Markets, Local Realities*. London and New York: Routledge.

Hua Cai. 2001 [1997]. *A Society without Fathers or Husbands: The Na of China*. Asti Hustvedt, trans. New York: Zone Books.

Huntington, Samuel. 1996. *The Clash of Civilizations and the Remaking of World Order*. New York: Simon & Schuster.

Huxley, Julian and A. C. Haddon. 1935. *We Europeans: A Survey of "Racial" Problems*. London: Jonathan Cape.

Hymes, Dell, ed. 1972 [1969]. *Reinventing Anthropology*. New York: Random House, Inc.

Igoe, Jim. 2004. *Conservation and Globalization: A Study of National Parks and Indigenous Communities from East Africa to South Dakota*. Belmont, CA: Wadsworth Publishing.

Jordan, Ann T. 2003. *Business Anthropology*. Long Grove, IL: Waveland Press.

Kardam, Nuket. 1993. "Development Approaches and the Role of Policy Advocacy: The Case of the World Bank." *World Development* 21 (11): 1773–86.

Kardiner, Abram. 1939. *The Individual and His Society: The Psychodynamics of Primitive Social Organization*. New York: Columbia University Press.

—— 1945. *The Psychological Frontiers of Society*. New York: Columbia University Press.

Katz, Richard. 1982. *Boiling Energy: Community Healing Among the Kalahari Kung*. Cambridge, MA and London: Harvard University Press.

Kauffman, L. A. 1990. "The Anti-Politics of Identity." *Socialist Review* 90 (1): 67–80

Kawai, Masao. 1965. "Newly-acquired Pre-cultural Behavior of the Natural Troops of Japanese Monkeys on Koshima Islet." *Primates* 6: 1–30.

Kearney, M. 1995. "The Local and the Global: The Anthropology of Globalization and Transnationalism." *Annual Review of Anthropology* 24: 547–65.

Keeler, Ward. 1983. "Shame and Stage Fright in Java." *Ethos* 11 (3): 152–65.

Keen, Ian. 1994. *Knowledge and Secrecy in an Aboriginal Religion*. Melbourne and Oxford: Oxford University Press.

Kelly, Raymond. 1977. *Etoro Social Structure*. Ann Arbor, MI: University of Michigan Press.

Kertzer, David I. 1987. "Childhood and Industrialization in Italy." *Anthropological Quarterly* 60 (4): 152–59.

Kiefer, Thomas M. 1972. *The Tausug: Violence and Law in a Philippine Moslem Society*. New York: Holt, Rinehart, and Winston.

Klass, Morton. 1978. *From Field to Factory: Community Structure and Industrialization in West Bengal*. Philadelphia, PA: Institute for the Study of Human Issues.

Klima, George J. 1970. *The Barabaig: East Africa Cattle-Herders*. New York: Holt, Rinehart, and Winston.

Kosmin, Barry A., Egon Mayer, and Ariela Keysar. 2001. "American Religious Identification Survey." New York: The Graduate Center of the City University of New York.

Kulick, Don. 1997. "The Gender of Brazilian Transgendered Prostitutes." *American Anthropologist* 95: 574–85.

Kummer, Hans. 1995. *In Quest of the Sacred Baboon*. Princeton, NJ: Princeton University Press.

Kuper, Adam. 1983. *Anthropology and Anthropologists: The Modern British School*, rev. edn. London and New York: Routledge.

—— 1988. *The Invention of Primitive Society: Transformations of an Illusion*. London: Routledge.

Kuper, Hilda. 1963. *The Swazi: A South African Kingdom*. New York: Holt, Rinehart, and Winston.

Lakoff, Robin. 1975. *Language and Woman's Place*. New York: Harper.

Lambek, Michael. 1981. *Human Spirits: A Cultural Account of Trance in Mayotte*. Cambridge: Cambridge University Press.

Landmann, Michael. 1974. *Philosophical Anthropology*. David J. Parent, trans. Philadelphia, PA: The Westminster Press.

Lane, Harlan. 1977. *The Wild Boy of Aveyron*. New York: Bantam Books.

Lane, Harlan, Robert Hoffmeister, and Ben Bahan. 1996. *A Journey into Deaf-World*. San Diego, CA: Dawn Sign Press.

Lange, Matthew, James Mahoney, and Matthias vom Hau. 2006. "Colonialism and Development: A Comparative Analysis of Spanish and British Colonies." *American Journal of Sociology* 111 (5): 1412–62.

Langer, Suzanne K. 1942. *Philosophy in a New Key: A Study in the Symbolism of Reason, Rite, and Art*. New York: Mentor Books.

Laqueur, Thomas. 1990. *Making Sex: Body and Gender from the Greeks to Freud*. Cambridge, MA: Harvard University Press.

Lawrence, Peter. 1964. *Road Belong Cargo*. Manchester: Manchester University Press.

Leach, Edmund R. 1954. *Political Systems of Highland Burma*. Boston, MA: Beacon Press.

Leakey, Louis S. B. 1930. *Some Notes on the Masai of Kenya Colony*. London: Royal Anthropological Institute of Great Britain and Ireland, 60: 185–209.

Le Blanc, Steven A., with Katherine E. Register. 2003. *Constant Battles: The Myth of the Peaceful, Noble Savage*. New York: St. Martin's Press.

Lee, Dorothy. 1959. *Freedom and Culture*. Englewood Cliffs, NJ: Prentice-Hall, Inc.

Lee, Richard. 1984. *The Dobe !Kung*. New York: Holt, Rinehart, and Winston.

Lee, Richard and Irven DeVore, eds. 1968. *Man the Hunter*. Chicago, IL: Aldine Publishing Company.

Lemarchand, Rene. 1970. *Rwanda and Burundi*. New York: Praeger.

Lemke, Thomas. 2007. "An Indigestible Meal? Foucault, Governmentality, and State Theory." *Distinktion: Scandinavian Journal of Social Theory* 8 (2): 43–64.

Lenski, Gerhard and Jean Lenski. 1982. *Human Societies: An Introduction to Macrosociology*, 4th edn. New York: McGraw-Hill, Inc.

Lerner, Jimmy A. 2002. *You Got Nothing Coming: Notes from a Prison Fish*. New York: Broadway Books.

Lessa, William A. 1966. *Ulithi: A Micronesian Design for Living*. New York: Holt, Rinehart, and Winston.

Levesque, Rene. 1968. *An Option for Quebec*. London: McClelland and Stewart Ltd.

Lévi-Strauss, Claude. 1978. *The Origin of Table Manners*. New York: Harper & Row.

Levison, Iain. 2002. *A Working Stiff's Manifesto: Confessions of a Wage Slave*. New York: Soho Press.

Levy, Andre. 2000. "Diasporas through Anthropological Lenses: Contexts of Postmodernity." *Diaspora* 9 (1): 137–57.

Lewellen, Ted C. 2002. *The Anthropology of Globalization: Cultural Anthropology Enters the 21st Century*. Westport, CT: Bergin & Garvey.

Lewontin, Richard C. 1972. "The Apportionment of Human Diversity." *Evolutionary Biology* 6: 381–98.

Lie, John. 2001. *Multiethnic Japan*. Cambridge, MA and London: Harvard University Press.

Linton, Ralph. 1936. *The Study of Man*. New York: Appleton-Century.

Linton, Ralph, ed. 1945. *The Science of Man in the World Crisis*. New York: Columbia University Press.

Livingstone, Frank B. 1962. "On the Non-Existence of Human Races." *Current Anthropology* 3 (3): 279–81.

Lorenz, Konrad. 1963. *On Aggression*. Marjorie Kerr Wilson, trans. New York: Bantam Books.

Lukes, Steven. 1974. *Power: A Radical View*. Basingstoke: Palgrave Macmillan.

Lutz, Catherine A. 1998. *Unnatural Emotions: Everyday Sentiments on a Micronesian Atoll and their Challenge to Western Theory*. Chicago, IL and London: The University of Chicago Press.

Lynd, Robert S. and Helen Merrell Lynd. 1929. *Middletown: A Study in Modern American Culture*. New York: Harcourt, Brace, & World, Inc.

Lyon, Sarah. 2011. *Coffee and Community: Maya Farmers and Fair-Trade Markets*. Boulder, CO: University Press of Colorado.

Maclean, Charles. 1979. *The Wolf Children: Fact or Fantasy?* Harmondsworth, UK: Penguin Books Ltd.

Mageo, Jeannette Marie. 1991. "Ma'i Aitu: The Cultural Logic of Possession in Samoa." *Ethos* 19 (3): 352–83.

Malinowski, Bronislaw. 1927. *Sex and Repression in Savage Society*. Chicago, IL: University of Chicago Press.

—— 1948. *Magic, Science, and Religion and Other Essays*. Garden City, NY: Doubleday Anchor Books.

—— 1961 [1945]. *The Dynamics of Culture Change: An Inquiry into Race Relations in Africa*. New Haven, CT and London: Yale University Press.

—— 1964. "An Anthropological Analysis of War." In L. Bramson and G. Goethals, eds. *War: Studies from Psychology, Sociology, Anthropology*. New York: Basic Books, 245–68.

—— 1984 [1922]. *Argonauts of the Western Pacific*. Long Grove, IL: Waveland Press, Inc.

Malkki, Liisa. 1995. *Purity and Exile: Violence, Memory, and National Cosmology among Hutu Refugees in Tanzania*. Chicago, IL and London: University of Chicago Press.

Maltz, Daniel N. and Ruth A. Borker. 1996. "A Cultural Approach to Male-Female Miscommunication." In Donald Brenneis and Ronald K. S. Macaulay, eds. *The Matrix of Language: Contemporary Linguistic Anthropology*. Boulder, CO: Westview Press, 81–98.

Maquet, Jacques. 1961. *The Premise of Inequality in Rwanda: A Study of Political Relations in a Central African Kingdom*. London: Oxford University Press.

Marcus, George E. 1995. "Ethnography In/Of the World: The Emergence of Multi-Sited Ethnography." *Annual Review of Anthropology* 24: 95–117.

Marcus, George E. and Michael M. J. Fischer. 1986. *Anthropology as Cultural Critique: An Experimental Moment in the Human Sciences*. Chicago, IL: University of Chicago Press.

Marsden, George M. 1990. "Defining American Fundamentalism." In Norman J. Cohen, ed. *The Fundamentalist Phenomenon: A View from Within, A Response from Without*. Grand Rapids, MI: William B. Eerdmans Publishing Company, 22–37.

Mathers, Kathryn. 2010. *Travel, Humanitarianism, and Becoming American in Africa*. New York: Palgrave Macmillan.

Maybury-Lewis, David. 2002. *Indigenous Peoples, Ethnic Groups, and the State*, 2nd edn. Boston, MA: Allyn and Bacon.

Mazurek, Brett. 2009. "Diamonds in the Rough: A Ugandan Hip Hop Revolution." New York: Third World Newsreel.

McDowall, David. 1996. *A Modern History of the Kurds*. London: I.B. Tauris.

Mead, Margaret. 1928. *Coming of Age in Samoa: A Psychological Study of Primitive Youth for Western Civilization*. New York: W. W. Morrow.

Medina, Laurie Kroshus. 2010. "When Government Targets 'the State': Transnational NGO Government and the State in Belize." *Political and Legal Anthropology Review* 33 (2): 245–63.

Meigs, Anna. 1997. "Food as a Cultural Construction." In Carole Counihan and Penny van Esterick, eds. *Food and Culture: A Reader*. New York and London: Routledge, 95–106.

Messenger, Jr., John C. 1965. "The Role of Proverbs in a Nigerian Judicial System." In Alan Dundes, ed. *The Study of Folklore*. Englewood Cliffs, NJ: Prentice-Hall, Inc., 299–307.

Michaels, Eric. 1986. *The Aboriginal Invention of Television in Central Australia, 1982-1986*. Canberra: Australian Institute of Aboriginal Studies.

Miller, Daniel. 1998. *A Theory of Shopping*. Ithaca, NY: Cornell University Press.

Miller, Daniel and Sophie Woodward. 2007. "Manifesto for a Study of Denim." *Social Anthropology* 15 (3): 335–51.

—— eds. 2011. *Global Denim*. Oxford and New York: Berg.

Miller, Marc S., ed. 1993. *State of the Peoples: A Global Human Rights Report on Societies in Danger*. Boston, MA: Beacon Press.

Mills, C. Wright. 1959. *The Sociological Imagination*. New York: Oxford University Press.

Montagu, M. F. Ashley. 1945. *Man's Most Dangerous Myth: The Fallacy of Race*, 2nd edn. New York: Columbia University Press.

Moodie, T. Dunbar. 2005. "Race and Ethnicity in South Africa." In Paul Spickard, ed. *Race and Nation: Ethnic Systems in the Modern World*. New York and London: Routledge, 319–35.

Moore, Wilbert E. 1963. *Social Change*. Englewood Cliffs, NJ: Prentice-Hall.

Morgan, Lewis Henry. 1877. *Ancient Society, or Researches in the Lines of Human Progress from Savagery, through Barbarism to Civilization*. New York: Henry Holt and Company.

Morphy, Howard. 1991. *Ancestral Connections: Art and An Aboriginal System of Knowledge*. Chicago, IL: University of Chicago Press.

Morren, George E. B., Jr. 1984. "Warfare on the Highland

Fringe of New Guinea: The Case of the Mountain Ok." In R. Brian Ferguson, ed. *Warfare, Culture, and Environment*. Orlando, FL: Academic Press, Inc., 169–207.

Mumford, Lewis. 1962 [1922]. *The Story of Utopias*. New York: The Viking Press.

Murphy, Yolanda and Robert Murphy. 1974. *Women of the Forest*. New York: Columbia University Press.

Myrdal, Gunnar. 1968. *Asian Drama: An Inquiry into the Poverty of Nations*. New York: Pantheon.

Nagengast, Carole. 1994. "Violence, Terror, and the Crisis of the State." *Annual Review of Anthropology* 23: 109–36.

Nanda, Serena. 1999. *Neither Man nor Woman: The Hijras of India*, 2nd edn. Belmont, CA: Wadsworth Publishing Company.

Nash, June, 1981. "Ethnographic Aspects of the World Capitalist System." *Annual Review of Anthropology* 10: 393–423.

Nash, Manning. 1962. "Race and the Ideology of Race." *Current Anthropology* 3 (3): 285–88.

—— 1989. *The Cauldron of Ethnicity in the Modern World*. Chicago, IL: University of Chicago Press.

Needham, Rodney. 1972. *Belief, Language, and Experience*. Chicago, IL: University of Chicago Press.

Neihardt, John G. 1961. *Black Elk Speaks: Being the Life Story of a Holy Man of the Oglala Sioux*. Lincoln, NB: University of Nebraska Press.

Nelson, Cynthia. 1974. "Public and Private Politics: Women in the Middle Eastern World." *American Ethnologist* 1: 551–63.

Nguyen, Vinh-Kim. 2005. "Uses and Pleasures: Sexual Modernity, HIV/AIDS, and Confessional Technologies in a West African Metropolis." In Vincanne Adams and Stacy Leigh Pigg, eds. *Sex in Development: Science, Sexuality, and Morality in Global Perspective*. Durham, NC and London: Duke University Press, 245–68.

Nolan, Riall. 2002. *Development Anthropology: Encounters in the Real World*. Boulder, CO: Westview Press.

Obeyesekere, Gananath. 1981. *Medusa's Hair: An Essay on Personal Symbols and Religious Experience*. Chicago, IL: University of Chicago Press.

Ochs, Elinor Keenan. 1996. "Norm-Makers, Norm-Breakers: Uses of Speech in Men and Women in a Malagasy Community." In Donald Brenneis and Ronald K. S. Macaulay, eds. *The Matrix of Language: Contemporary Linguistic Anthropology*. Boulder, CO: Westview Press, 99–115.

O'Connor, Kaori. 2011. *Lycra: How A Fiber Shaped America*. New York: Routledge.

Ohnuki-Tierney, Emiko. 1974. *The Ainu of the Northwest Coast of Southern Sakhalin*. New York: Holt, Rinehart, and Winston.

Okello, Elialilia and Solvig Ekblad. 2006. "Lay Concepts of Depression among the Baganda of Uganda: A Pilot Study." *Transcultural Psychiatry* 43 (2): 287–312.

Ong, Aihwa. 1988. "The Production of Possession: Spirits and the Multinational Corporation in Malaysia." *American Ethnologist* 15 (1): 28–42.

Onnudottir, Helena, Adam Possamai, and Bryan S. Turner. 2010. "Islam: A New Religious Vehicle for Aboriginal Self-Empowerment in Australia?" *International Journal for the Study of New Religions* 1 (1): 49–74.

Ontario Human Rights Commission. 2003. "Paying the Price: The Human Cost of Racial Profiling." Toronto, Ontario. Http://www.ohrc.on.ca/en/ resources/discussion_consultation/RacialProfileReportEN/pdf, accessed September 16, 2001.

Ortega Y Gasset, Jose. 1932. *The Revolt of the Masses*. New York: W. W. Norton and Company.

Ortner, Sherry. 1973. "On Key Symbols." *American Anthropologist* 75: 1338–46.

—— 1974. "Is Female to Male as Nature is to Culture?" In Michelle Rosaldo and Louise Lamphere, eds. *Woman, Culture, and Society*. Stanford, CA: Stanford University Press, 68–87.

Padden, Carol A. and Tom L. Humphries. 2005. *Inside Deaf Culture*. Cambridge, MA and London: Harvard University Press.

Parks, Douglas. 1996. *Myths and Traditions of the Arikara Indians*. Lincoln, NB and London: University of Nebraska Press.

Patterson, Orlando. 1975. "Context and Choice in Ethnic Allegiance: A Theoretical Framework and Caribbean Case Study." In Nathan Glazer and Daniel Patrick Moynihan, eds. *Ethnicity: Theory and Experience*. Cambridge, MA: Harvard University Press, 305–49.

Pearce, Roy Harvey. 1965 [1953]. *Savagism and Civilization: A Study of the Indian and the American Mind*. Baltimore, MD and London: Johns Hopkins University Press.

Pedersen, Morten Axel. 2011. *Not Quite Shamans: Spirit Worlds and Political Lives in Northern Mongolia*. Ithaca, NY and London: Cornell University Press.

Pels, Peter. 1997. "The Anthropology of Colonialism: Culture, History, and the Emergence of Western Governmentality." *Annual Review of Anthropology* 26: 163–83.

Pena, Sergio D. J. and Telma de Souza Birchal. 2005–6. "The Biological Non-existence versus the Social Existence of Human Races: Can Science Instruct the Social Ethos?" Http://www.fhi.ox.ac.uk/teaching%20 and%20posters/TT08/Birchal_paper_29_04.pdf, accessed 29 October 2008.

Peterson, Richard A. and N. Anand. 2004. "The Production of Culture Perspective." *Annual Review of Sociology* 30: 311–34.

Philippine Center for Language Study. 1965. *Beginning Tagalog: A Course for Speakers of English*. Berkeley, CA: University of California Press.

Pigg, Stacy Leigh and Vincanne Adams. 2005. "Introduction: The Moral Object of Sex." In Vincanne Adams and Stacy Leigh Pigg, eds. *Sex in Development: Science, Sexuality, and Morality in Global Perspective*. Durham, NC and London: Duke University Press, 1–38.

Pinney, Christopher. 2011. *Photography and Anthropology*. London: Reaktion Books.

Polanyi, Karl. 1957. "The Economy as Instituted Process."

In Karl Polanyi, Conrad M. Arenberg, and Harry W. Pearson, eds. *Trade and Market in the Early Empires: Economies in History and Theory*. New York and London: The Free Press and Collier-Macmillan Limited, 243–70.

Pun, Ngai. 2005. *Made in China: Women Factory Workers in a Global Workplace*. Durham, NC and London: Duke University Press.

Prunier, Gerard. 1995. *The Rwandan Crisis: History of a Genocide*. New York: Columbia University Press.

Puzzo, Dante. 1964. "Racism and the Western Tradition." *Journal of the History of Ideas* 25 (4): 579–86.

Radcliffe-Brown, A. R. 1965 [1952]. *Structure and Function in Primitive Society*. New York: The Free Press.

Ramirez-Esparza, Nairan, Samuel D. Gosling, Veronica Benet-Martinez, Jeffrey P. Potter, and James W. Pennebaker. 2006. "Do Bilinguals have Two Personalities? A Special Case of Cultural Frame Switching." *Journal of Research in Personality* 40: 99–120.

Reed, A.W., ed. 1969. *Captain Cook in Australia: Extracts from the Journals of Captain James Cook*. Wellington, New Zealand: A.H. & A.W. Reed.

Reiter, Rayna. 1975a. "Men and Women in the South of France: Public and Private Domains." In Rayna Reiter, ed. *Toward an Anthropology of Women*. New York: Monthly Review Press, 252–82.

Reiter, Rayna, ed. 1975b. *Toward an Anthropology of Women*. New York and London: Monthly Review Press.

Ribeiro, Gustavo Lins and Arturo Escobar. 2006. "World Anthropologies: Disciplinary Transformations with Systems of Power." In Gustavo Lins Ribeiro and Arturo Escobar, eds. *World Anthropologies: Disciplinary Transformations within Systems of Power*. Oxford and New York: Berg, 1–25.

Ringrose, Kathryn M. 1994. "Living in the Shadows: Eunuchs and Gender in Byzantium." In Gilbert Herdt, ed. *Third Sex, Third Gender: Beyond Sexual Dimorphism in Culture and History*. New York: Zone Books, 85–109.

Ritzer, George. 2005. *Enchanting a Disenchanted World: Revolutionizing the Means of Consumption*, 2nd edn. Thousand Oaks, CA and London: Pine Forge Press.

Roheim, Geza. 1974. *The Children of the Desert: The Western Tribes of Central Australia*. New York: Basic Books.

Rosaldo, Michelle. 1974. "Woman, Culture, and Society: A Theoretical Overview." In Michelle Rosaldo and Louise Lamphere, eds. 1974. *Woman, Culture, and Society*. Stanford, CA: Stanford University Press, 17–42.

—— 1980. *Knowledge and Passion: Ilongot Notions of Self and Social Life*. Cambridge: Cambridge University Press.

—— 1984. "Words that are Moving: The Social Meanings of Ilongot Verbal Art." In Donald Brenneis and Fred R. Myers, eds. *Dangerous Words: Language and Politics in the Pacific*. Prospect Heights, IL: Waveland Press, Inc., 131–60.

Rosaldo, Michelle and Louise Lamphere, eds. 1974. *Woman, Culture, and Society*. Stanford,CA: Stanford University Press.

Roscoe, Will. 1994. "How to Become a Berdache: Toward a Unified Analysis of Gender Diversity." In Gilbert Herdt, ed. *Third Sex, Third Gender: Beyond Sexual Dimorphism in Culture and History*. New York: Zone Books, 329–72.

—— 1998. *Changing Ones: Third and Fourth Genders in Native North America*. New York: St. Martin's.

Rosenberg, Bernard. 1957. "Mass Culture in America." In Bernard Rosenberg and David Manning White, eds. *Mass Culture: The Popular Arts in America*. New York: The Free Press, 3–12.

Ross, Michael, W. Q. Elaine Xun, and Anne E. Wilson. 2002. "Language and the Bicultural Self." *Personality and Social Psychology Bulletin* 28: 1040–50.

Rostow, W. W. 1965. *The Stages of Economic Growth: A Non-Communist Manifesto*. New York: Cambridge University Press.

Sahlins, Marshall. 1976. *The Use and Abuse of Biology: An Anthropological Critique of Sociobiology*. Ann Arbor, MI: University of Michigan Press.

Sandall, Roger. 2001. *The Culture Cult: Designer Tribalism and Other Essays*. Boulder, CO: Westview Press.

Sanford, Victoria and Martha Lincoln. 2010. "Body of Evidence: Feminicide, Local Justice, and Rule of Law in 'Peacetime' Guatemala." In Alexander Laban Hinton, ed. *Transitional Justice: Global Mechanisms and Local Realities after Genocide and Mass Violence*. New Brunswick, NJ and London: Rutgers University Press, 67–91.

Sapir, Edward. 1949. *Selected Writings*. Berkeley, CA: University of California Press.

—— 2001 [1938]. "Why Cultural Anthropology Needs the Psychiatrist." *Psychiatry* 64 (1): 2–10. Original vol. 1: 7–12.

Sax, William S. 1991. *Mountain Goddess: Gender and Politics in a Himalayan Pilgrimage*. New York and Oxford: Oxford University Press.

Scheper-Hughes, Nancy. 1992. *Death without Weeping: The Violence of Everyday Life in Brazil*. Berkeley, CA: University of California Press.

—— 1995. "The Primacy of the Ethical: Propositions for a Militant Anthropology." *Current Anthropology* 36 (3): 409–40.

Scheper-Hughes, Nancy and Philippe Bourgois, eds. 2004. *Violence in War and Peace: An Anthology*. London: Blackwell Publishing.

Schieffelin, Edward L. 1983. "Anger and Shame in the Tropical Forest: On Affect as a Cultural System in Papua New Guinea." *Ethos* 11 (3): 181–91.

Schwimmer, Eric. 1984. "Male Couples in New Guinea." In Gilbert Herdt, ed. *Ritualized Homosexuality in Melanesia*. Berkeley, CA: University of California Press, 248–91.

Scott, James C. 1990. *Domination and the Arts of Resistance: Hidden Transcripts*. New Haven, CT: Yale University Press.

Sen, Amartya. 2006. *Identity and Violence: The Illusion of Destiny*. New York and London: W. W. Norton & Company.

Sen, Mala. 2001. *Death by Fire: Sati, Dowry Death, and Female Infanticide in Modern India*. New Brunswick, NJ: Rutgers University Press.

Service, Elman R. 1962. *Primitive Social Organization: An Evolutionary Perspective*. New York: Random House.

Sharp, Lauriston. 1952. "Steel Axes for Stone-Age Australians." *Human Organization* 11 (2): 17–22.

Sherzer, Joel. 1983. *Kuna Ways of Speaking*. Austin, TX: University of Texas Press.

Shore, Cris and Susan Wright. 2000. "Coercive Accountability: The Rise of Audit Culture in Higher Education." In Marilyn Strathern, ed. *Audit Cultures: Anthropological Studies in Accountability, Ethics, and the Academy*. London and New York: Routledge, 57–89.

Shorter, Aylward. 1988. *Toward a Theology of Inculturation*. Maryknoll, NY: Orbis Books.

Shostak, Marjorie. 1983 [1981]. *Nisa: The Life and Words of a !Kung Woman*. New York: Vintage Books.

Sillitoe, Paul. 1998. *An Introduction to the Anthropology of Melanesia: Culture and Tradition*. Cambridge: Cambridge University Press.

Simmons, Leo W., ed. 1942. *Sun Chief: The Autobiography of a Hopi Indian*. New Haven, CT and London: Yale University Press.

Simpson, George E. and J. Milton Yinger. 1972. *Racial and Cultural Minorities*. 4th edn. New York: Harper & Row.

Skorupski, John. 1976. *Symbol and Theory: A Philosophical Study of Theories of Religion in Social Anthropology*. Cambridge: Cambridge University Press.

Slocum, Sally. 1975. "Woman the Gatherer: Male Bias in Anthropology." In Rayna R. Reiter, ed. *Toward an Anthropology of Women*. New York and London: Monthly Review Press, 36–50.

Slotkin, J. S., ed. 1965. *Readings in Early Anthropology*. London: Methuen & Co. Ltd.

Smart, Alan and Josephine Smart. 2003. "Urbanization and the Global Perspective." *Annual Review of Anthropology* 32: 263–85.

Smedley, Audrey. 1999. *Race in North America: Origin and Evolution of a Worldview*, 2nd edn. Boulder, CO: Westview Press.

Smith, Anthony. 1991. *National Identity*. Reno, NV: University of Nevada Press.

Smith, Linda Tuhiwai. 1999. *Decolonizing Methodologies: Research and Indigenous Peoples*. London and New York: Zed Books; University of Otago Press: Dunedin.

Spindler, George and Louise Spindler. 1971. *Dreamers without Power: The Menomini Indians*. New York: Holt, Rinehart, and Winston.

Spiro, Melford. 1963 [1956]. *Kibbutz: Venture in Utopia*. New York: Schocken Books.

—— 1978 [1967]. *Burmese Supernaturalism*, expanded edition. Philadelphia, PA: Institute for the Study of Human Issues.

St. John, Graham. 2010. *The Local Scenes and Global Culture of Psytrance*. Abingdon UK and New York: Routledge.

Stack, Carol. 1974. *All Our Kin: Strategies for Survival in a Black Community*. New York: Harper & Row.

Stephenson, Peta. 2010. *Islam Dreaming: Indigenous Muslims in Australia*. Sydney: University of New South Wales Press.

Steward, Julian. 1950. *Area Research: Theory and Practice*. New York: Social Science Research Council, Bulletin 63.

—— 1953. "Evolution and Process." In Alfred Kroeber, ed. *Anthropology Today*. Chicago, IL: University of Chicago Press, 313–26.

Strathern, Marilyn, ed. 2000. *Audit Cultures: Anthropological Studies in Accountability, Ethics, and the Academy*. London and New York: Routledge.

Suarez-Orozco, Marcelo. 1992. "A Grammar of Terror: Psychocultural Responses to State Terrorism in Dirty War and Post-Dirty War Argentina." In Carolyn Nordstrom and JoAnn Martin, eds. *The Paths to Domination, Resistance, and Terror*. Berkeley, CA: University of California Press, 219–59.

Taylor, Charles. 1994. "The Politics of Recognition." In Amy Gutman, ed. *Multiculturalism: Examining the Politics of Recognition*. Princeton, NJ: Princeton University Press, 25–73.

Thompson, E. P. 1967. "Time, Work-Discipline, and Industrial Capitalism." *Past & Present* 38: 56–97.

Tilley, Virginia Q. 2005. "*Mestizaje* and the 'Ethnicization of Race in Latin America'." In Paul Spickard, ed. *Race and Nation: Ethnic Systems in the Modern World*. New York and London: Routledge, 53–68.

Tinker, George E. 1993. *Missionary Conquest: The Gospel and Native American Cultural Genocide*. Minneapolis, MN: Fortress Press.

de Tocqueville, Alexis. 1969. *Democracy in America*. J. P. Mayer, trans. Anchor City, NY: Doubleday & Company, Inc.

Trigger, Bruce G. 1969. *The Huron: Farmers of the North*. New York: Holt, Rinehart, and Winston.

Trouillot, Michel-Rolph. 1991. "Anthropology and the Savage Slot: The Poetics and Politics of Otherness." In R. Fox, ed. *Recapturing Anthropology: Working in the Present*. Santa Fe, NM: School of American Research Press, 18–44.

Tucker, Catherine M. 2010. "Private Goods and Common Property: Pottery Production in a Honduran Lenca Community." *Human Organization* 69 (1): 43–53.

Turnbull, Colin. 1962. *The Forest People*. New York: Simon & Schuster.

Turner, Victor W. 1967. *The Forest of Symbols: Aspects of Ndembu Ritual*. Ithaca, NY and London: Cornell University Press.

—— 1969. *The Ritual Process: Structure and Anti-Structure*. Chicago, IL: Aldine Publishing.

—— 1981 [1968]. *The Drums of Affliction: A Study of Religious Processes among the Ndembu of Zambia*. London: Hutchinson University Library for Africa.

Turney-High, Harry H. 1971. *Primitive War: Its Practice and Concepts*. Columbia, SC: University of South Carolina Press.

Tyler, Stephen A., ed. 1969. *Cognitive Anthropology*. New York: Holt, Rinehart, and Winston.

Tylor, E. B. 1958 [1871]. *Primitive Culture*. New York: Harper Torchbooks.

Uchendu, Victor C. 1965. *The Igbo of Southeast Nigeria*. New York: Holt, Rinehart, and Winston.

United Nations High Commissioner for Refugees. 2007a. "2006 Statistical Yearbook." Geneva: United Nations High Commissioner for Refugees.

—— 2007b. "Convention and Protocol Relating to the Status of Refugees." Geneva: United Nations High Commissioner for Refugees.

U.S. Court of Appeals for the Ninth Circuit. 2002. "Michael A. Newdow v U.S. Congress, United States of America, George W. Bush, et al." Http://www.ca9.uscourts.gov/ca9/ newopinions.nsf/ FE05EEE 79C2A97B688256BE3007FEE32/$file/0016423. pdf, accessed 27 June 2002.

Valentine, Lisa Philips. 1995. *Making It Their Own: Severn Ojibwe Communicative Practices.* Toronto: University of Toronto Press.

van den Berghe, Pierre L. 1967. *Race and Racism: A Comparative Perspective.* New York: John Wiley & Sons, Inc.

—— 1987 [1981]. *The Ethnic Phenomenon.* New York: Praeger.

van der Dennen, Johan M. G. 2002. "Nonhuman Intergroup Agonistic Behavior and 'Warfare'." Http://rint.rechten.rug.nl/rth/dennen/animwar.htm, accessed May 29, 2002.

Vasconcelos, Jose. 1979 [1925]. *The Cosmic Race.* Didier T. Jaen, trans. Baltimore, MD and London: The Johns Hopkins University Press.

Veblen, Thorstein. 1934 [1899]. *Theory of the Leisure Class: An Economic Study of Institutions.* New York: Modern Library.

Velayutham, Selvaraj, ed. 2008. *Tamil Cinema: The Cultural Politics of India's other Film Industry.* London and New York: Routledge.

Verrengia, Joseph B. 1993. "Vanishing Tribes." *Rocky Mountain News,* December 12.

Voll, John O. 1991. "Fundamentalism in the Sunni Arab World: Egypt and the Sudan." In Martin Marty and R. Scott Appleby, eds. *Fundamentalisms Observed.* Chicago, IL: University of Chicago Press, 345–402.

Von Fuerer-Haimendorf, Christoph. 1969. *The Konyak Nagas: An Indian Frontier Tribe.* New York: Holt, Rinehart, and Winston.

de Waal, Frans. 1998 [1982]. *Chimpanzee Politics: Power and Sex among Apes,* rev. edn. Baltimore, MD: Johns Hopkins University Press.

Wagner, Roy. 1975. *The Invention of Culture.* Englewood Cliffs, NJ: Prentice-Hall, Inc.

Waldstein, Alfred S. 1986. "Irrigated Agriculture as an Archetypal Development Project: Senegal." In Michael M. Horowitz and Thomas M. Painter, eds. *Anthropology and Rural Development in West Africa.* Boulder, CO: Westview Press, 119–43.

Wallace, Anthony F. C. 1956. "Revitalization Movements." *American Anthropologist* 58 (2): 264–81.

—— 1966. *Religion: An Anthropological View.* New York: Random House.

Wallerstein, Immanuel. 1974. *The Modern World-System: Capitalist Agriculture and the Origins of the European World-Economy in the Sixteenth Century.* New York: Academic Press.

Washburn, Sherwood. 1963. "The Study of Race." *American Anthropologist* 65 (3): 521–31.

Weber, Max. 1968. *Economy and Society,* vol. 1. Guenther Roth and Claus Wittich, eds. New York: Bedminster Press.

Weiner, Annette B. 1983. *Women of Value, Men of Renown: New Perspectives in Trobriand Exchange.* Austin, TX: University of Texas Press.

Wheelwright, Philip, ed. 1966. *The Presocratics.* New York: The Odyssey Press.

White, Leslie. 1940. "The Symbol: The Origin and Basis of Human Behavior." *Philosophy of Science* 7 (4): 451–63.

—— 1949. *The Science of Culture.* New York: Grove Press.

—— 1959a. "The Concept of Evolution in Cultural Anthropology." In Betty Meggers, ed. *Evolution and Anthropology: A Centennial Appraisal.* Washington, DC: The Anthropological Society of Washington, 106–25.

—— 1959b. *The Evolution of Culture.* New York: McGraw-Hill.

White, Tim et al. 2009. "*Ardipithecus ramidus* and the Paleobiology of Early Hominids." *Science* 326 (October 2): 64–86.

Whiting, Beatrice, ed. 1963. *Six Cultures: Studies of Child Rearing.* New York: John Wiley and Sons.

Whiting, John W. M. and Irvin L. Child. 1953. *Child Training and Personality.* New Haven, CT: Yale University Press.

Whorf, Benjamin Lee. 1940. "Science and Linguistics." *Technology Review* 43: 229–31, 247–48.

—— 1956. *Language, Thought, and Reality: Selected Writings of Benjamin Lee Whorf.* Cambridge, MA: Massachusetts Institute of Technology Press.

Williams, Thomas Rhys. 1965. *The Dusun: A North Borneo Society.* New York: Holt, Rinehart, and Winston.

Willis, Jr., William S. 1974 [1969]. "Skeletons in the Anthropological Closet." In Dell Hymes, ed. *Reinventing Anthropology.* New York: Vintage Books, 21–52.

Wolf, Eric. 1982. *Europe and the People without History.* Berkeley, CA: University of California Press.

—— 1994. "Perilous Ideas: Race, Culture, People." *Current Anthropology* 35 (1): 1–12.

Woodburn, James. 1968. "Stability and Flexibility in Hadza Residential Groups." In Richard Lee and Irven DeVore, eds. *Man the Hunter.* Chicago, IL: Aldine, 103–11.

World Bank. 2001. *World Development Report 2000/2001: Attacking Poverty.* Oxford: Oxford University Press.

Worsley, Peter. 1968. *The Trumpet Shall Sound: A Study of "Cargo Cults" in Melanesia.* New York: Shocken Books.

Wrangham, Richard and Dale Peterson. 1996. *Demonic Males: Apes and the Origins of Human Violence.* Boston, MA: Houghton Mifflin Company.

Wrigley, Owen. 1996. *The Politics of Deafness.* Washington, DC: Gallaudet University Press.

Yan, Hairong. 2003. "Neoliberal Governmentality and Neohumanism: Organizing Suzhi/Value Flow through Labor Recruitment Networks." *Cultural Anthropology* 18 (4): 493–523.

Yonezawa, Miyuki. 2005. "Memories of Japanese Identity and Racial Hierarchy." In Paul Spickard, ed. *Race and Nation: Ethnic Systems in the Modern World.* New York and London: Routledge, 115–32.

Index